P9-DHL-779

JBoss® 4.0

THE OFFICIAL GUIDE

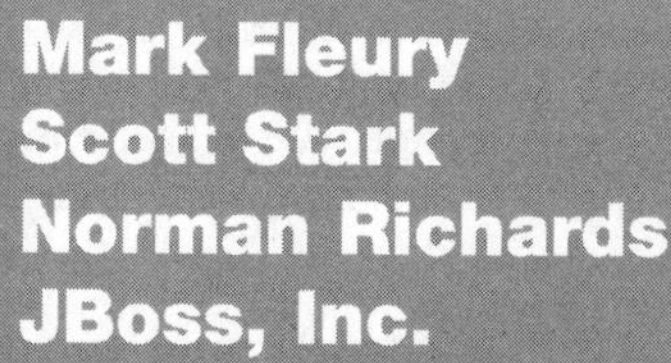

Mark Fleury
Scott Stark
Norman Richards
JBoss, Inc.

SAMS

800 East 96th Street, Indianapolis, Indiana 46240

JBoss 4.0: The Official Guide

Copyright © 2005 by Sams Publishing

All rights reserved. No part of this book shall be reproduced, stored in a retrieval system, or transmitted by any means, electronic, mechanical, photocopying, recording, or otherwise, without written permission from the publisher. No patent liability is assumed with respect to the use of the information contained herein. Although every precaution has been taken in the preparation of this book, the publisher and author assume no responsibility for errors or omissions. Nor is any liability assumed for damages resulting from the use of the information contained herein.

International Standard Book Number: 0-672-32648-5

Library of Congress Catalog Card Number: 2005900655

Printed in the United States of America

First Printing: May 2005

08 07 06 05 4 3 2 1

Trademarks

All terms mentioned in this book that are known to be trademarks or service marks have been appropriately capitalized. Sams Publishing cannot attest to the accuracy of this information. Use of a term in this book should not be regarded as affecting the validity of any trademark or service mark.

Warning and Disclaimer

Every effort has been made to make this book as complete and as accurate as possible, but no warranty or fitness is implied. The information provided is on an "as is" basis. The authors and the publisher shall have neither liability nor responsibility to any person or entity with respect to any loss or damages arising from the information contained in this book or from the use of the CD or programs accompanying it.

Bulk Sales

Sams Publishing offers excellent discounts on this book when ordered in quantity for bulk purchases or special sales. For more information, please contact

U.S. Corporate and Government Sales

1-800-382-3419

corpsales@pearsontechgroup.com

For sales outside of the U.S., please contact

International Sales

international@pearsoned.com

Associate Publisher
Michael Stephens

Acquisitions Editor
Loretta Yates

Development Editor
Mark Renfrow

Managing Editor
Charlotte Clapp

Senior Project Editor
Matthew Purcell

Copy Editor
Kitty Jarrett

Indexer
Erika Millen

Proofreader
Wendy Ostermeyer

Publishing Coordinator
Cindy Teeters

Multimedia Developer
Dan Scherf

Designer
Gary Adair

Page Layout
Michelle Mitchell

Contents at a Glance

Table of Contents

About the Authors

Scott Stark, Ph.D. started out as a chemical engineer and graduated with a B.S. from the University of Washington, and he later earned a Ph.D. from the University of Delaware. While he was at Delaware, it became apparent that computers and programming were to be his passion, so he made the study of applying massively parallel computers to difficult chemical engineering problems the subject of his Ph.D. research. It has been all about distributed programming ever since. Scott currently serves as the chief technology officer of JBoss, Inc., an elite services company based out of Atlanta.

Marc Fleury, Ph.D. started in sales at Sun Microsystems France. A graduate of the *Ecole Polytechnique*, France's top engineering school, and an ex-lieutenant in the paratroopers, he has a master's in theoretical physics from the ENS ULM and a Ph.D. in physics for work he did as a visiting scientist at MIT (working with X-ray lasers). Marc currently serves as the president of JBoss, Inc.

Norman Richards is a JBoss developer and is currently the maintainer of this guide. He graduated with a B.S. in computer science from the University of Texas at Austin, where he researched evolving neural networks to play the game of go. Norman is the co-author of *XDoclet in Action* (Manning Publications).

We Want to Hear from You!

As the reader of this book, *you* are our most important critic and commentator. We value your opinion and want to know what we're doing right, what we could do better, what areas you'd like to see us publish in, and any other words of wisdom you're willing to pass our way.

As an associate publisher for Sams Publishing, I welcome your comments. You can email or write me directly to let me know what you did or didn't like about this book—as well as what we can do to make our books better.

Please note that I cannot help you with technical problems related to the topic of this book. We do have a User Services group, however, where I will forward specific technical questions related to the book.

When you write, please be sure to include this book's title and author as well as your name, email address, and phone number. I will carefully review your comments and share them with the author and editors who worked on the book.

Email: feedback@samspublishing.com

Mail: Michael Stephens
Associate Publisher
Sams Publishing
800 East 96th Street
Indianapolis, IN 46240 USA

For more information about this book or another Sams Publishing title, visit our website at www.samspublishing.com. Type the ISBN (0672326485) or the title of a book in the Search field to find the page you're looking for.

Introduction

What This Book Covers

The primary focus of this book is the presentation of the standard JBoss 4.0 architecture components, from the perspectives of both their configuration and architecture. As a user of a standard JBoss distribution, you will gain an understanding of how to configure the standard components. Note that this book is not an introduction to J2EE or how to use J2EE in applications. It focuses on the internal details of the JBoss server architecture and how an implementation of a given J2EE container can be configured and extended.

As you read this book, you will gain a good understanding of the architecture and integration of the standard components, which should enable you to extend or replace the standard components for your infrastructure needs. This book also shows you how to obtain the JBoss source code, along with how to build and debug the JBoss server.

About JBoss

JBoss Application Server was first released in 1999. JBoss Group was founded in 2001, in order to provide expert technical support services. JBoss Group was incorporated in 2004 as JBoss Inc.:

- **Ownership**—JBoss Inc. is employee owned and is venture backed by Matrix Partners, Accel Partners, and Intel.
- **Coverage**—JBoss Inc. covers North America and Europe on a direct basis. JBoss Inc. provides coverage worldwide via its extensive authorized partner network.
- **Mission statement**—JBoss Inc. will provide middleware technology that offers the lowest cost of ownership via open-source software licenses that are backed up by expert technical support services delivered by both JBoss Inc. and our authorized service partners. Our goal is to be the safe choice for enterprises and software providers alike.
- **Company description**—JBoss Inc. is in the business of providing superior technical support to its customers. By backing up its immensely popular open-source Java products with technical support from the source, JBoss has become the new safe choice for middleware. Customers such as Apple, Best Western, Borland, Computer Associates, HP, Iona, La Quinta, MCI, Mitre, Nielsen Media Research, Siemens, Sonic, SEMA, Unisys, WebMethods, and Wells Fargo have embraced the Professional Open Source model whereby no-cost, open-source products are supported by the core development team. By providing direct access to the core developers, JBoss Inc. eliminates the runaround common with most commercial software providers.

Professional Open Source™ from JBoss Inc. offers the following:

- Standards-based and stable Java middleware technology
- No-cost, open-source product licenses
- Backing by a professional and expert support staff
- Comprehensive services, including professional support, training, and consulting
- A very large and active community of developers
- An extensive worldwide network of authorized and certified partners

Benefits of Professional Open Source from JBoss Inc. include the following:

- Lowest possible total cost of ownership
- Reliable and safe technology
- Support, accountability, and trust from a stable company
- Expedited problem resolution compared to commercial software vendors

About Open Source

The basic idea behind open source is very simple: When programmers can read, redistribute, and modify the source code for a piece of software, the software evolves: People improve it, people adapt it, people fix bugs. And this can happen at a speed that, if you are used to the slow pace of conventional software development, seems astonishing. *Open source* is an often-misunderstood term that relates to free software. The Open Source Initiative (OSI) website provides a number of resources that define the various aspects of open source, including a definition of *open source* at www.opensource.org/docs/definition.html. The following quote from the OSI home page nicely summarizes the key aspects as they relate to JBoss:

> We in the open source community have learned that this rapid evolutionary process produces better software than the traditional closed model, in which only a very few programmers can see the source and everybody else must blindly use an opaque block of bits.
>
> Open Source Initiative exists to make this case to the commercial world.
>
> Open source software is an idea whose time has finally come. For twenty years it has been building momentum in the technical cultures that built the Internet and the World Wide Web. Now it's breaking out into the commercial world, and that's changing all the rules. Are you ready?
>
> —The Open Source Initiative

About Professional Open Source

JBoss is the leader in the second generation of open source, which JBoss Inc. has termed *Professional Open Source*. The Professional Open Source methodology is based on the following:

- It hires and pays experts in the open-source community to write exceptional and innovative software full time.
- It uses only open-source licenses that are friendly to end-user IT shops, independent software vendors, and the community itself.
- Directly and through its authorized partners, JBoss Inc. delivers the best support services available, and all of them are backed up by the real product experts.
- Unlike first-generation open-source providers, JBoss Inc. controls the direction and source code for its projects. It can ensure that all bug fixes and patches are rolled into future versions of its products.
- By combining enterprise-proven technology, business-friendly open-source licenses, and world-class support services, JBoss Inc. has made Professional Open Source the safe choice for end-user enterprises and independent software vendors alike.

What's New in JBoss 4.0

The JBoss Application Server (JBoss AS) 4.0 is a production-ready Java 2 Enterprise Edition (J2EE) application server. It builds on the highly successful JBoss 3.2 line of open-source Java application servers with improved standards compliance and major feature enhancements. JBoss AS 4.0 offers the same level of quality and stability customers have grown to expect from JBoss 3.2. Key features of JBoss AS 4.0 include the following:

- It is officially certified to be fully compliant to the J2EE 1.4 specification. JBoss AS 4.0 is the first production-ready J2EE 1.4 application server in the industry.
- It provides full support for J2EE Web Services and the Service-Oriented Architecture (SOA).
- It supports the aspect-oriented programming (AOP) model for developing middleware solutions. JBoss AOP greatly improves developer productivity.
- It tightly integrates with Hibernate, the world's most popular object persistence framework, developed by JBoss, inside the application server container.
- It improves clustering and distributed caching support, with a new internal caching architecture.

J2EE Certification and Standards Compliance

JBoss AS 4.0 is the industry's first officially certified J2EE 1.4 application server. The certification guarantees that JBoss AS 4.0 conforms to the formal J2EE specification. This allows developers to safely reuse J2EE components (for example, Enterprise JavaBeans [EJBs]) across different application servers. For example, a developer could easily migrate an EJB developed for WebLogic or WebSphere to JBoss. The certification makes JBoss 4.0 a safe upgrading choice for both existing JBoss users and users of other J2EE application servers.

Compared with JBoss AS 3.2, JBoss AS 4.0 implements the following new J2EE specifications in order to be J2EE 1.4 compliant:

- JBoss AS 4.0 supports J2EE Web Services, including JAX-RPC (Java API for XML for Remote Procedure Call) and Web Services for J2EE Architecture, which leverages standard J2EE components (for example, EJBs) to provide a scalable and secure Web Services environment. It is the basis for implementing SOA in J2EE. The older JBoss.NET Web Services API in JBoss AS 3.2 is no longer supported. The new Web Services implementation is WS BasicProfile 1.0 compliant.
- JBoss AS 4.0 implements the JMS (Java Messaging Service) 1.1 specification instead of JMS 1.0 in JBoss AS 3.2. In JMS 1.0, client programming for the Point-to-Point and Pub/Sub domains was done using similar but separate class hierarchies. In JMS 1.1, there is now a domain-independent approach to programming the client application.
- JBoss AS 4.0 implements the JCA (Java Connector Architecture) 1.5 specification instead of the JCA 1.0 in JBoss AS 3.2. The JCA 1.5 specification adds support for the life cycle management of resource adapters, worker thread management, and transaction and message inflow from the resource adapter to the application server.
- JBoss AS 4.0 implements the new Java Authorization Contract for Containers (JACC) specification. JACC is a Java 2 permission-based mechanism for externalizing the authorization decision for accessing EJB methods and web resources. The new implementation is based on the JBoss AS 3.2 semantic of associating the J2EE declarative roles with the authenticated subject as a by-product of the JAAS authentication phase. JBoss AS 4.0 maintains compatibility with the JBoss AS 3.2 security configuration.
- JBoss AS 4.0 implements the EJB 2.1 specification instead of EJB 2.0 in JBoss AS 3.2. The EJB 2.1 specification extends the message-driven bean contracts to support other messaging types in addition to JMS. It supports stateless session beans as web service endpoints. It also includes a new container-managed service called the EJB timer service.

Server Configuration and Services

A big change from JBoss AS 3.2.6 to 4.0.0 is the default server configurations. On JBoss AS 4.0.0, there are four server configurations:

- **`minimal`**—The `minimal` configuration in JBoss AS 4.0.0 has the same meaning as the `minimal` configuration in JBoss AS 3.2.6. It starts the JBoss microkernel, JMX MBean server, and JNDI naming service.

- **standard**—The standard configuration in JBoss AS 4.0.0 has the same meaning as the default configuration in JBoss AS 3.2.6. It starts all J2EE services in JBoss's optimized class loader. The JBoss AS 4.0.0 standard configuration yields better performance than other configurations when the components are deployed in the same JVM. But the deployed applications are less compartmentalized in this configuration.
- **default**—The default configuration in JBoss AS 4.0.0 is new. It is the J2EE-certified configuration of the server. All J2EE services are deployed, and all components are compartmentalized. But the application performance in the JBoss AS 4.0.0 default configuration is not as optimized as that in the standard configuration.
- **all**—The all configuration in JBoss AS 4.0.0 has the same meaning as the all configuration in JBoss AS 3.2.6. It starts all services, including clustering.

From JBoss AS 4.0.1, the server configuration names switch back to the JBoss 3.2 convention. The default configuration uses the JBoss optimized class loader, and the standard configuration goes away. The J2EE 1.4 certified configuration of JBoss (that is, the default configuration in JBoss AS 4.0.0) is distributed in a separate package from JBoss AS 4.0.1.

In addition to server configuration name changes, JBoss AS 4.0 also adds support for new types of server services. SARDeployer now recognizes the *.deployer archives (both in expanded directories and in zip files) and the *-deployer.xml files as valid deployment options. The .deployer suffix is equivalent to the .sar suffix, and the -deployer.xml filename suffix is equivalent to the -service.xml descriptor filename suffix. These suffixes are sorted ahead of any other service types so that these .deployer services are started before other services. For example, the JBoss AOP services are deployed as a .deployer service archive (that is, the jboss-aop.deployer archive in the deploy directory). This makes sure that the JBoss AOP services are started early in the server startup process.

JBoss AOP Support

Aspect-oriented middleware is a key innovation in JBoss AS 4.0. It drastically simplifies middleware application development and allows developers to extend the container services. In JBoss AS 4.0, you can deploy AOP-based services and applications directly into the application server. You can find a detailed introduction to aspect-oriented programming and the JBoss AOP framework on the JBoss website, at www.jboss.org/products/aop.

In JBoss AS 4.0.0's standard and all configurations (the default and all configurations in JBoss AS 4.0.1), AOP support is provided by the jboss-aop.deployer service. It is a new .deployer-type service similar to the .sar service. The following key features are supported by the jboss-aop.deployer service:

- By default, you have to instrument the bytecode of your AOP applications offline, using the aopc utility, before you can deploy them into the application server. But you can enable load-time bytecode instrumentation via a configuration attribute in the jboss-aop.deployer/META-INF/jboss-service.xml file.

- JBoss AS 4.0 ships with several prepackaged aspects to support security transaction asynchronous threads on plain old Java objects (POJOs). There are a number of predefined annotation tags in the `baseaop.xml` file. You can use those annotations in your POJOs to take advantage of the prepackaged aspect services.
- JBoss AS 4.0 defines a new XML deployment file type with the filename `*-aop.xml`. The `*-aop.xml` file specifies the binding for user-defined aspect classes. The aspect and binding become available to applications on the server.
- JBoss AS 4.0 defines a new JAR archive file type with the `.aop` filename extension. The `.aop` file can be used to package user-defined aspects and their bindings. The `jboss-aop.xml` file must reside in the `META-INF` directory in the `.aop` archive. The `.aop` archive can be bundled inside other deployment archive files to provide aspect services to a specific application.

Hibernate Integration

Hibernate is a very popular object persistence framework developed by JBoss. It maps Java objects to tables in relational databases and vice versa. The object-relational mapping rules and datasources are specified in special Hibernate configuration files. In JBoss AS 4.0, Hibernate integration support is provided by the `jboss-hibernate.deployer` service, which is available in the `default`, `standard`, and `all` configurations. The `jboss-hibernate. deployer` service provides Hibernate framework libraries to all applications on the server.

For Hibernate applications, JBoss defines a new `.har` service archive type. You can package your Hibernate-mapped Java objects and mapping configuration files in the `.har` archive. You can also specify a datasource name and a JNDI name for this particular Hibernate configuration in the `hibernate-service.xml` file in the `.har` archive. The benefit is that, in your applications, you only need to do a JNDI lookup to retrieve the correctly configured Hibernate `SessionFactory` object. There is no need to load the mapping and datasource configuration files manually in the application via API calls. In addition, the configuration settings in the `hibernate-service.xml` file are manageable via the JBoss JMX Management Console.

The `.har` file can be bundled inside an `.ear` file or deployed on a standalone basis.

Clustering and Caching

Many of the JBoss AS 4.0 clustering and caching improvements have been backported and made available in JBoss 3.2.3 to 3.2.7. Here's an overview of those improvements:

- TreeCache, which is based on the JGroups technology, is officially adopted as the underlying distributed cache architecture for the clustering environment.
- `CacheLoader` support (store/read from secondary storage) for both shared and unshared back-end stores is added. Currently, there are `CacheLoader` implementations for the Sleepycat Berkeley DB (`BdbjeCacheLoader`), for generic JDBC datasources, and for the file system (`FileCacheLoader`).

- The `HttpSession` object is replicated across clustered servers. So if one server fails, the users are moved to a failover server without losing their sessions.
- The Single Sign-On (SSO) security context is replicated across clustered servers. This way, the user is not required to log in again when a server fails.
- The new loadbalancer service provides reverse-proxy support with silent failover.

CHAPTER 1

Installing and Building the JBoss Server

IN THIS CHAPTER

- Getting the Binary Files
- Installing the Binary Package
- Basic Installation Testing
- Booting from a Network Server
- Building the Server from Source Code

JBoss, a free J2EE 1.4–certified application server, is the most widely used open-source application server on the market. The highly flexible and easy-to-use server architecture has made JBoss the ideal choice for users just starting out with J2EE, as well as senior architects looking for a customizable middleware platform. The server binary and source code distributions are available from the SourceForge repository. (http://sourceforge.net/projects/jboss). The ready availability of the source code allows you to debug the server, learn its inner workings, and create customized versions for your personal or business use.

This chapter is a step-by-step tutorial that will show you how to install and configure JBoss 4.0. Specifically, you will learn how to do the following:

- Obtain updated binaries from the JBoss SourceForge project site
- Install the JBoss binary
- Test the installation

You will also learn about the following:

- The installation directory structure
- Key configuration files an administrator may want to use to customize the JBoss installation
- How to obtain the source code for JBoss 4.0 from the SourceForge Concurrent Versions System (CVS) repository
- How to build the server distribution

Getting the Binary Files

The most recent release of JBoss is available from the SourceForge JBoss project files page, http://sourceforge.net/projects/jboss. You will also find previous releases there, as well as beta and release candidate versions of upcoming releases.

Prerequisites

Before installing and running the server, you need to check your system to make sure you have a working JDK 1.4+ installation. The simplest way to do this is to execute the `java -version` command to ensure that the java executable is in your path and that you are using Version 1.4 or higher. For example, running the `java -version` command with a 1.4.1 JDK would produce a version number like the following:

```
[ tmp] $ java -version
java version "1.4.2_05"
Java(TM) 2 Runtime Environment, Standard Edition (build 1.4.2_05-b04)
Java HotSpot(TM) Client VM (build 1.4.2_05-b04, mixed mode)
```

It does not matter where on your system you install JBoss. Note, however, that installing JBoss into a directory that has a name that contains spaces causes problems in some situations with Sun-based VMs. This is caused by bugs with file URLs not correctly escaping the spaces in the resulting URL. There is no requirement for root access to run JBoss on Unix/Linux systems because none of the default ports are within the 0–1023 privileged port range.

Installing the Binary Package

After you have the binary archive you want to install, you use the JDK `jar` tool (or any other zip extraction tool) to extract the `jboss-4.0.1.zip` archive contents into a location of your choice. The `jboss-4.0.1.tgz` archive is a gzipped `tar` file that requires a `gnutar`-compatible `tar` that can handle the long pathnames in the archive. The default `tar` binaries on Solaris and OS X do not currently support the long pathnames. The extraction process will create a `jboss-4.0.1` directory. The following section explores the contents of this directory.

Directory Structure

As mentioned previously, installing the JBoss distribution creates a `jboss-4.0.1` directory, which contains server startup scripts, JARs, server configuration sets, and working directories. You need to know your way around the distribution layout to locate JARs for compiling code, updating configurations, deploying code, and so on. Figure 1.1 illustrates the installation directory of the JBoss server.

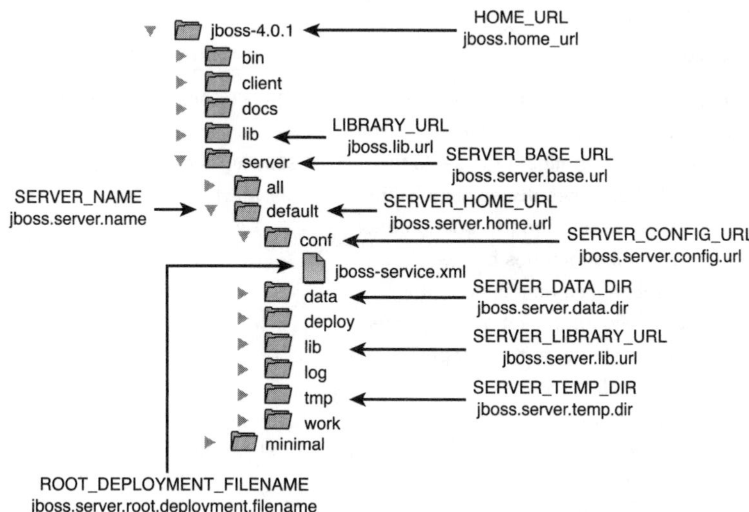

FIGURE 1.1 A view of the JBoss server installation directory structure, with the default server configuration file set expanded and overridable locations identified.

Throughout this book we refer to the top-level `jboss-4.0.1` directory as the `JBOSS_DIST` directory. In Figure 1.1, the `default` server configuration file set is shown expanded. It contains a number of subdirectories: `conf`, `data`, `deploy`, `lib`, `log`, and `tmp`. In a clean installation, only the `conf`, `deploy`, and `lib` directories will exist. The purposes of these directories are discussed in Table 1.1. In this table, the "`ServerConfig` Property" column refers to the `org.jboss.system.server. ServerConfig` interface constant and its corresponding system property string. The `ServerConfig` constant names and corresponding system property name are displayed in the blue text in Figure 1.1. The *`XXX`*`_URL` names correspond to locations that can be specified by using a URL to access remote locations—for example, HTTP URLs against a web server. You can use the properties listed in Table 1.1 to override the layout of a JBoss distribution.

TABLE 1.1 The JBoss Directory Structure

Directory	Description	`ServerConfig` Property
`bin`	All the entry-point JARs and start scripts included with the JBoss distribution are located in the `bin` directory.	
`client`	JARs required for clients are located in the `client` directory. A typical client requires `jbossall-client.jar`, `concurrent.jar`, and `log4j.jar`.	

TABLE 1.1 Continued

Directory	Description	ServerConfig Property
server	The JBoss server configuration sets are located under the server directory. The default server configuration set is the server/default set. JBoss ships with minimal, default, and all configuration sets. The subdirectories and key configuration files contained in the default configuration set are discussed in more detail later in this chapter, in the section "The Default Server Configuration File Set."	SERVER_BASE_DIR="jboss.server.base.dir" SERVER_BASE_URL="jboss.server.base.url"
lib	The lib directory contains startup JARs used by JBoss. Do not place your own libraries in this directory.	LIBRARY_URL ="jboss.lib.url"
conf	The conf directory contains the bootstrap descriptor file—jboss-service.xml by default—for a given server configuration. This defines the core services that are fixed for the lifetime of the server.	SERVER_CONFIG_URL ="jboss.server.config.url"
data	The data directory is available for use by services that want to store content in the file system.	SERVER_DATA_DIR ="jboss.server.data.dir"
deploy	The deploy directory is the default location to which the hot deployment service looks for dynamic deployment content. This may be overridden through the URLDeploymentScanner URLs attribute.	
lib	The lib directory is the default location referred to by the bootstrap descriptor. All JARs in this directory are loaded into the shared classpath.	SERVER_LIBRARY_URL ="jboss.server.lib.url"
log	The log directory is the default directory into which the bootstrap logging service places its logs. This may be overridden through the conf/log4j.xml configuration file.	
tmp	The tmp directory is the location to which deployments are copied for local use.	SERVER_TEMP_DIR="jboss.server.temp.dir"

The Default Server Configuration File Set

The `JBOSS_DIST/server` directory contains one or more configuration file sets. The `default` JBoss configuration file set is located in the `JBOSS_DIST/server/default` directory. JBoss allows you to add more than one configuration set, so a server can easily be run using alternate configurations. Creating a new configuration file set typically starts with copying the `default` file set into a directory with a new name and then modifying the configuration files as desired. Figure 1.2 shows the contents of the `default` configuration file set.

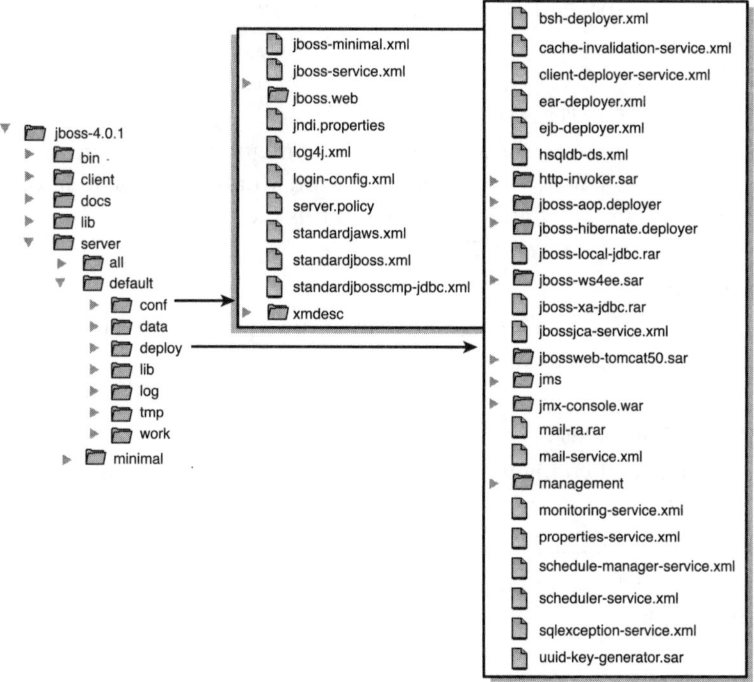

FIGURE 1.2 An expanded view of the default server configuration file set `conf` and `deploy` directories.

conf/jboss-minimal.xml

This is a minimalist example of the `jboss-service.xml` configuration file. It is the `jboss-service.xml` file that is used in the minimal configuration file set.

conf/jboss-service.xml

`jboss-service.xml` defines the core services configurations. The complete DTD and syntax of this file is described, along with the details on integrating custom services, in the next chapter.

`conf/jboss.web`

This directory is used by Tomcat.

`conf/jndi.properties`

The `jndi.properties` file specifies the JNDI `InitialContext` properties that are used within the JBoss server when an `InitialContext` is created using the no-arg constructor.

`conf/log4j.xml`

This file configures the Apache `log4j` framework category priorities and appenders used by the JBoss server code.

`conf/login-config.xml`

This file contains sample server-side authentication configurations that are applicable when using JAAS-based security. See Chapter 8, "Security on JBoss," for additional details on the JBoss security framework and the format of this file.

`conf/server.policy`

The `server.policy` file is a placeholder for Java2 security permissions. The default file simply grants all permissions to all codebases.

`conf/standardjaws.xml`

This file provides a default configuration file for the legacy EJB 1.1 JBossCMP engine.

`conf/standardjboss.xml`

This file provides the default container configurations. Use of this file is covered in Chapter 5, "EJBs on JBoss."

`conf/standardjbosscmp-jdbc.xml`

This file provides a default configuration file for the JBoss CMP engine. See Chapter 11, "The CMP Engine," for the details of this descriptor.

`conf/xmdesc/*-mbean.xml`

The `xmdesc` directory contains XMBean descriptors for several services configured in the `jboss-service.xml` file.

`deploy/bsh-deployer.xml`

This file configures the bean shell deployer, which deploys bean shell scripts as JBoss services.

`deploy/cache-invalidation-service.xml`

This is a service that allows for custom invalidation of the EJB caches via JMS notifications. It is disabled by default.

`deploy/client-deployer-service.xml`

This is a service that provides support for J2EE application clients. It manages the `java:comp/env` enterprise naming context for client applications, based on the `application-client.xml` descriptor.

`deploy/ear-deployer.xml`

The EAR deployer is the service responsible for deploying J2EE EAR files.

`deploy/ejb-deployer.xml`

The EJB deployer is the service responsible for deploying J2EE EJB JAR files.

`deploy/hsqldb-ds.xml`

`hsqldb-ds.xml` configures the Hypersonic 1.7.1 embedded database service configuration file. It sets up the embedded database and related connection factories. The format of JCA datasource files is discussed in Chapter 7, "Connectors on JBoss."

`deploy/http-invoker.sar`

`http-invoker.sar` contains the detached invoker that supports RMI/HTTP. It also sets up bindings of RMI/HTTP proxies for the JNDI naming service; these bindings allow the JBoss JNDI service to be accessed over HTTP. This is discussed in the next chapter.

`deploy/jboss-aop.deployer`

`jboss-aop.deployer` configures `AspectManagerService` and deploys JBoss AOP applications.

`deploy/jboss-hibernate.deployer`

`jboss-hibernate.deployer` deploys Hibernate archives (HAR files).

`deploy/jboss-local-jdbc.rar`

`jboss-local-jdbc.rar` is a JCA resource adaptor that implements the JCA `ManagedConnectionFactory` interface for JDBC drivers that support the `DataSource` interface but not JCA.

`deploy/jboss-ws4ee.sar`

`jboss-ws4ee.sar` provides J2EE Web Services support.

deploy/jboss-xa-jdbc.rar

`jboss-xa-jdbc.rar` is a JCA resource adaptor that implements the JCA `ManagedConnectionFactory` interface for JDBC drivers that support the `XADataSource` interface but do not provide the JCA adaptor.

deploy/jbossjca-service.sar

`jbossjca-service.sar` is the application server implementation of the JCA 1.0 specification. It provides the connection management facilities for integrating resource adaptors into the JBoss server. The JCA layer is discussed in Chapter 7.

deploy/jbossweb-tomcat50.sar

The `jbossweb-tomcat50.sar` directory is an unpacked MBean service archive for the configuration of the Tomcat 5 servlet engine. The SAR is unpacked rather than deployed as a JAR archive so that the tomcat configuration files can be easily edited. This service is discussed in Chapter 9, "Web Applications."

deploy/jms/hsqldb-jdbc2-service.xml

`hsqldb-jdbc2-service.xml` configures JMS persistence and caching by using Hypersonic. It also contains the `DestinationManager` MBean, which is the core service for the JMS implementation.

deploy/jms/jbossmq-destinations-service.xml

`jbossmq-destinations-service.xml` configures a number of JMS queues and topics used by the JMS unit tests. Configuration of JMS destinations is discussed in Chapter 6, "Messaging on JBoss."

deploy/jms/jbossmq-httpil.sar

`jbossmq-httpil.sar` provides a JMS invocation layer that allows the use of JMS over HTTP.

deploy/jms/jbossmq-service.xml

The `jbossmq-service.xml` file configures the core JBossMQ JMS service. JMS services are discussed in Chapter 6.

deploy/jms/jms-ds.xml

The `jms-ds.xml` file configures the JBossMQ JMS provider for use with the `jms-ra.rar` JCA resource adaptor.

deploy/jms/jms-ra.rar

`jms-ra.rar` is a JCA resource adaptor that implements the JCA `ManagedConnectionFactory` interface for JMS connection factories.

deploy/jms/jvm-il-service.xml

jvm-il-service.xml configures the inter-vm JMS transport invocation layer. This transport layer is described in org.jboss.mq.il.jvm.JVMServerILService.

deploy/jms/uil2-service.xml

uil2-service.xml configures the JMS version 2 unified invocation layer. It is a custom socket-based transport that is the fastest and most reliable and should be used for inter-vm messaging. This transport layer is described in org.jboss.mq.il.uil2.UILServerILService.

deploy/jmx-console.war

The jmx-console.war directory is an unpackaged web application archive that provides an HTML adaptor for the JMX MBeanServer. The WAR is unpackaged rather than deployed as a JAR archive so that the jmx-console.war/WEB-INF/*.xml descriptors can be edited to easily configure role-based security.

deploy/jmx-invoker-service.sar

jmx-invoker-service.sar is an unpacked MBean service archive that exposes a subset of the JMX MBeanServer interface methods as an RMI interface to enable remote access to the JMX core functionality. This is similar to the legacy jmx-rmi-adaptor.sar, with the difference that the transport is handled by the detached invoker architecture. This service is discussed in Chapter 2, "The JBoss JMX Microkernal."

deploy/mail-ra.rar

mail-ra.rar is a resource adaptor that provides a JavaMail connector.

deploy/mail-service.xml

The mail-service.xml file is an MBean service descriptor that provides JavaMail sessions for use inside the JBoss server.

deploy/management/console-mgr.sar **and** web-console.war

console-mgr.sar and web-console.war provide the Web Console, which is a web application/applet that provides a richer view of the JMX server management data than the JMX Console. You can view the console at http://localhost:8080/web-console/.

deploy/monitoring-service.xml

The monitoring-service.xml file configures alert monitors like the console listener and email listener used by JMX notifications.

deploy/properties-service.xml

The properties-service.xml file is an MBean service descriptor that allows for customization of the JavaBeans PropertyEditors as well as the definition of system properties. This is discussed further in Chapter 10, "MBean Services Miscellany."

deploy/scheduler-service.xml and schedule-manager-service.xml

The scheduler-service.xml and schedule-manager-service.xml files are MBean service descriptors that provide a scheduling type of service. This is discussed further in Chapter 10.

deploy/sqlexception-service.xml

The sqlexception-service.xml file is an MBean service descriptor for vendor-specific handling of java.sql.SQLExceptions. Its usage is discussed in Chapter 11.

deploy/uuid-key-generator.sar

The uuid-key-generator.sar service provides a UUID-based key-generation facility.

Basic Installation Testing

After you have installed the JBoss distribution, it is wise to perform a simple startup test to validate that there are no major problems with your Java VM/operating system combination. To test your installation, move to the JBOSS_DIST/bin directory and execute the run.bat or run.sh script, as appropriate for your operating system. Your output should be similar to the following, and it should contain no error or exception messages:

```
[bin]$ sh run.sh
=========================================================================

  JBoss Bootstrap Environment

  JBOSS_HOME: /tmp/jboss-4.0.1

  JAVA: /System/Library/Frameworks/JavaVM.framework/Home//bin/java

  JAVA_OPTS: -server -Xms128m -Xmx128m -Dprogram.name=run.sh

  CLASSPATH: /tmp/jboss-4.0.1/bin/run.jar:/System/Library/Frameworks/
➥JavaVM.framework/Home//lib/tools.jar

=========================================================================

17:29:04,702 INFO  [Server] Starting JBoss (MX MicroKernel)...
17:29:04,715 INFO  [Server] Release ID: JBoss [Zion] 4.0.1RC2 (build: CVSTag=
➥JBoss_4_0_1_RC2 date=200411302349)
```

```
17:29:04,746 INFO  [Server] Home Dir: /private/tmp/jboss-4.0.1
17:29:04,748 INFO  [Server] Home URL: file:/private/tmp/jboss-4.0.1/
17:29:04,751 INFO  [Server] Library URL: file:/private/tmp/jboss-4.0.1/lib/
17:29:04,756 INFO  [Server] Patch URL: null
17:29:04,759 INFO  [Server] Server Name: default
17:29:04,776 INFO  [Server] Server Home Dir: /private/tmp/jboss-4.0.1/
➥server/default
17:29:04,778 INFO  [Server] Server Home URL: file:/private/tmp/jboss-4.0.1/
➥server/default/
17:29:04,781 INFO  [Server] Server Data Dir: /private/tmp/jboss-4.0.1/server/
➥default/data
17:29:04,784 INFO  [Server] Server Temp Dir: /private/tmp/jboss-4.0.1/server/
➥default/tmp
17:29:04,787 INFO  [Server] Server Config URL: file:/private/tmp/jboss-4.0.1/
➥server/default/conf/
17:29:04,789 INFO  [Server] Server Library URL: file:/private/tmp/jboss-4.0.1/
➥server/default/lib/
17:29:04,791 INFO  [Server] Root Deployment Filename: jboss-service.xml
17:29:04,833 INFO  [Server] Starting General Purpose Architecture (GPA)...
17:29:06,121 INFO  [ServerInfo] Java version: 1.4.2_05,Apple Computer, Inc.
17:29:06,124 INFO  [ServerInfo] Java VM: Java HotSpot(TM) Client VM 1.4.2-38,
➥"Apple Computer, Inc."
17:29:06,127 INFO  [ServerInfo] OS-System: Mac OS X 10.3.6,ppc
17:29:07,236 INFO  [Server] Core system initialized
...
17:29:49,550 INFO  [Server] JBoss (MX MicroKernel) [4.0.1RC2 (build: CVSTag=
➥JBoss_4_0_1_RC2 date=200411302349)] Started in 44s:3ms
```

If your output is similar to this (accounting for installation directory differences), you should now be ready to use JBoss. To shut down the server, you simply issue a Ctrl+C sequence in the console in which JBoss was started. Alternatively, you can use the `shutdown.sh` command:

```
[bin]$ ./shutdown.sh

A JMX client to shutdown (exit or halt) a remote JBoss server.

usage: shutdown [options] <operation>

options:
    -h, --help                  Show this help message
    -D<name>[=<value>]          Set a system property
    --                          Stop processing options
    -s, --server=<url>          Specify the JNDI URL of the remote server
    -n, --serverName=<url>      Specify the JMX name of the ServerImpl
    -a, --adapter=<name>        Specify JNDI name of the RMI adapter to use
```

```
    -u, --user=<name>         Specify the username for authentication[not imple-
mented yet]
    -p, --password=<name>     Specify the password for authentication[not imple-
mented yet]

operations:
    -S, --shutdown            Shutdown the server (default)
    -e, --exit=<code>         Force the VM to exit with a status code
    -H, --halt=<code>         Force the VM to halt with a status code
```

Using `run.sh` without any arguments starts the server, using the default server configuration file set. To start with an alternate configuration file set, you pass in the name of the directory under `JBOSS_DIST/server` that you wish to use as the value to the `-c` command-line option. For example, to start with the minimal configuration file set, you would specify this:

```
[bin]$ ./run.sh -c minimal
...
17:40:41,092 INFO  [Server] JBoss (MX MicroKernel) [4.0.1RC2 (build: CVSTag=
➥JBoss_4_0_1_RC2 date=200411302349)] Started in 4s:920ms
```

To view all the supported command-line options for the JBoss server bootstrap class, you issue the `run-h` command, and the output looks like this:

```
usage: run.sh [options]

options:
    -h, --help                    Show this help message
    -V, --version                 Show version information
    --                            Stop processing options
    -D<name>[=<value>]            Set a system property
    -p, --patchdir=<dir>          Set the patch directory; Must be absolute
    -n, --netboot=<url>           Boot from net with the given url as base
    -c, --configuration=<name>    Set the server configuration name
    -j, --jaxp=<type>             Set the JAXP impl type (ie. crimson)
    -B, --bootlib=<filename>      Add an extra library to the front bootclasspth
    -L, --library=<filename>      Add an extra library to the loaders classpath
    -C, --classpath=<url>         Add an extra url to the loaders classpath
    -P, --properties=<url>        Load system properties from the given url
    -b, --host=<host or ip>       Bind address for all JBoss services
```

Booting from a Network Server

One very useful command-line option is the `--netboot=url` option, which causes JBoss to start up using the given URL as the base URL from which all libraries and configurations are loaded. Specifying the netboot option sets `ServerConfig.HOME_URL` to the netboot option URL argument value. In the absence of any other overrides, all the locations found in the standard JBOSS_DIST structure will be resolved relative to the HOME_URL value. This means that if you make a JBoss distribution available from a web server, you can boot JBoss using only the run scripts and run.jar file from the JBOSS_DIST/bin directory. Note that the web server must support the PROPFIND WebDAV command. JBoss includes a simple servlet filter that provides minimal support for the PROPFIND command so that JBoss itself may be used as the netboot web server.

An Ant build script example that creates a custom netboot configuration file set for booting the default configuration is available in the examples/src/main/org/jboss/chap1/build-netboot.xml file. To test the netboot feature, you run the build-netboot. xml script, specifying the location of the JBOSS_DIST you want to use as the netboot web server, as shown here:

```
[examples]$ ant -Djboss.dist=/tmp/jboss-4.0.1
➥-buildfile src/main/org/jboss/chap1/build-netboot.xml
```

You then start up the netboot server by specifying the netboot configuration, as follows:

```
[bin]$ ./run.sh -c netboot
=========================================================================

  JBoss Bootstrap Environment

  JBOSS_HOME: /tmp/jboss-4.0.1

  JAVA: /System/Library/Frameworks/JavaVM.framework/Home//bin/java

  JAVA_OPTS: -server -Xms128m -Xmx128m -Dprogram.name=run.sh

  CLASSPATH: /tmp/jboss-4.0.1/bin/run.jar:/System/Library/Frameworks/
➥JavaVM.framework/Home//lib/tools.jar

=========================================================================

17:42:52,042 INFO  [Server] Starting JBoss (MX MicroKernel)...
...
17:43:06,818 INFO  [Server] JBoss (MX MicroKernel) [4.0.1RC2 (build: CVSTag=
➥JBoss_4_0_1_RC2 date=200411302349)] Started in 13s:918ms
```

You can now start up any other instance of JBoss, using just the run script and run.jar from the JBOSS_DIST/bin directory. Here's an example:

```
[bin]$ sh run.sh --netboot=http://192.168.0.101:8080/netboot/
=========================================================================
```

```
  JBoss Bootstrap Environment

  JBOSS_HOME: /tmp/jboss-4.0.1

  JAVA: /System/Library/Frameworks/JavaVM.framework/Home//bin/java

  JAVA_OPTS: -server -Xms128m -Xmx128m -Dprogram.name=run.sh

  CLASSPATH: /tmp/jboss-4.0.1/bin/run.jar:/System/Library/Frameworks/
➥JavaVM.framework/Home//lib/tools.jar

=========================================================================

18:14:29,828 INFO  [Server] Starting JBoss (MX MicroKernel)...
18:14:29,833 INFO  [Server] Release ID: JBoss [Zion] 4.0.1RC2 (build: CVSTag=
➥JBoss_4_0_1_RC2 date=200411302349)
18:14:29,836 INFO  [Server] Home Dir: /private/tmp/jboss-4.0.1
18:14:29,838 INFO  [Server] Home URL: http://192.168.0.101:8080/netboot/
18:14:29,840 INFO  [Server] Library URL: http://192.168.0.101:8080/netboot/lib/
18:14:29,869 INFO  [Server] Patch URL: null
18:14:29,871 INFO  [Server] Server Name: default
18:14:29,874 INFO  [Server] Server Home Dir: /private/tmp/jboss-4.0.1/server/
➥default
18:14:29,879 INFO  [Server] Server Home URL: http://192.168.0.101:8080/netboot/
➥server/default/
18:14:29,881 INFO  [Server] Server Data Dir: /private/tmp/jboss-4.0.1/server/
➥default/data
18:14:29,884 INFO  [Server] Server Temp Dir: /private/tmp/jboss-4.0.1/server/
➥default/tmp
18:14:29,887 INFO  [Server] Server Config URL: http://192.168.0.101:8080/
➥netboot/server/default/conf/
18:14:29,889 INFO  [Server] Server Library URL: http://192.168.0.101:8080/
➥netboot/server/default/lib/
18:14:29,890 INFO  [Server] Root Deployment Filename: jboss-service.xml
18:14:29,900 INFO  [Server] Starting General Purpose Architecture (GPA)...
...
```

The custom netboot configuration file set consists simply of the files needed to run the `jbossweb-tomcat50.sar` web server and a `netboot.war` file whose content is the `JBOSS_DIST/lib` and `JBOSS_DIST/server/default` files.

Building the Server from Source Code

Source code is available for every JBoss module, and you can build any version of JBoss from source by downloading the appropriate version of the code from SourceForge.

Accessing the JBoss CVS Repositories at SourceForge

The JBoss source is hosted at SourceForge, a great open-source community service provided by VA Linux Systems. With more than 88,000 open-source projects and nearly 950,000 registered users, SourceForge is the largest open-source hosting service available. Many of the top open-source projects have moved their development to the SourceForge.net site. The services offered by SourceForge include hosting of project CVS repositories and a web interface for project management that includes bug tracking, release management, mailing lists, and more. Best of all, these services are free to all open-source developers. For additional details and to browse the plethora of projects, see the SourceForge home page (http://sourceforge.net).

Understanding CVS

CVS is an open-source version control system that is used pervasively throughout the open-source community. CVS is a source-control or revision-control tool that is designed to keep track of source changes made by groups of developers who are working on the same files. CVS enables developers to stay in sync with each other as each individual chooses.

Anonymous CVS Access

The JBoss project's SourceForge CVS repository can be accessed through anonymous (`pserver`) CVS. The module you want to check out must be specified as `modulename`. When prompted for a password for `anonymous`, you simply press the Enter key. The following is the general syntax of the command-line version of CVS for anonymous access to the JBoss repositories:

```
cvs -d:pserver:anonymous@cvs.sourceforge.net:/cvsroot/jboss login
cvs -z3 -d:pserver:anonymous@cvs.sourceforge.net:/cvsroot/jboss co modulename
```

The first command logs you in to the JBoss CVS repository as an anonymous user. This command needs to be performed only once for each machine on which you use CVS because the login information will be saved in your `HOME/.cvspass` file or the equivalent for your system. The second command checks out a copy of the `modulename` source code into the directory from which you run the `cvs` command. To avoid having to type the long `cvs` command line each time, you can set up a `CVSROOT` environment variable with the value `:pserver:anonymous@cvs.jboss.sourceforge.net:/cvsroot/jboss` and then use the following abbreviated versions of the previous commands:

```
cvs login
```

The name of the JBoss module alias you use depends on the version of JBoss you want. For the 4.0 branch, the module name is `jboss-4.0`, for the 3.2 branch it is `jboss-3.2`, and in general, for branch `x.y` the module name is `jboss-x.y`. To check out the `HEAD` revision of JBoss to obtain the latest code on the main branch, you would use `jboss-head` as the module name. Releases of JBoss are tagged with the pattern `JBoss_X_Y_Z`, where `X` is the major version, Y is the minor version, and Z is the patch version. Release branches of JBoss are tagged with the pattern Branch_X_Y. The following are some checkout examples:

```
cvs co -r Branch_4_0 jboss-4.0 # Checkout the current 3.0 branch code
cvs co -r JBoss_4_0_1 jboss-4.0 # Checkout the 4.0.1 release version code
cvs co -r JBoss_3_2_6 jboss-3.2 # Checkout the 3.2.6 release version code
cvs co jboss-head # Checkout the current HEAD branch code
```

Obtaining a CVS Client

The command-line version of the CVS program is freely available for nearly every platform, and it is included by default on most Linux and Unix distributions. A good port for CVS as well as numerous other Unix programs for Windows 32-bit platforms is Cygwin, at http://sources.redhat.com/cygwin/. In the next few sections, let's examine the syntax of the command-line version of CVS, which is common across all platforms.

> **Note**
>
> For complete documentation on CVS, check out the CVS home page, at www.cvshome.org.

Building the JBoss Distribution Using the Source Code

Every JBoss release includes a source archive that contains everything needed to build the release and is available from the files section of the JBoss project site, at http://sourceforge.net/projects/jboss/. The source directory structure matches that of the CVS source tree described in the following section, so once you have the source distribution, you can build the release by following the instructions given in the next section, beginning with the instructions after the step to obtain the jboss-4.0 source tree.

Building the JBoss Distribution Using the CVS Source Code

This section guides you through the task of building a JBoss distribution from the CVS source code. To start, you create a directory into which you want to download the CVS source tree, and then you move into the newly created directory. This directory is referred to as the CVS_WD directory, for *CVS working directory*. The example build in this book checks out code into a /tmp/jboss directory on a Linux system. Next, you obtain the 4.0.1 version of the source code, as shown here:

```
 [ tmp] $ mkdir jboss [ tmp] $ cd jboss
[jboss]$ export CVSROOT=:pserver:anonymous@cvs.sourceforge.net:/cvsroot/jboss
[jboss]$ cvs co -r JBoss_4_0_1 jboss-4.0
cvs checkout: Updating aop
U aop/.classpath U aop/.cvsignore
U aop/.project
U aop/RELEASE_NOTES.txt ...
```

The resulting jboss-4.0 directory structure contains all the CVS modules required to build the server. To perform the build, you cd to the jboss-all/build directory and execute the build.sh or build.bat file, as appropriate for your OS. You need to set the JAVA_HOME environment variable to the location of the JDK you wish to use for compilation, and the JDK bin directory should be on your path:

```
[jboss]$ cd jboss-4.0/build/
[ build] $ . /build. sh
Searching for build.xml ...
Buildfile: /tmp/jboss/jboss-4.0/build/build.xml ...

BUILD SUCCESSFUL
Total time: 2 minutes 41 seconds
```

Note that if you see a "Failed to launch JJTree" error, you do not have in your PATH variable the JAVA_HOME/bin directory that is required for the JavaCC JJTree Ant task.

The build process is driven by an Ant-based configuration. The main Ant build script is the build. xml file located in the jboss-4.0/build directory. This script uses a number of custom Ant tasks masked as buildmagic constructs. The purpose of the main build.xml file is to compile the various module directories under jboss-4.0 and then to integrate their output to produce the binary release. The binary release structure is found under the jboss-4.0/build/output directory. The preceding example uses the build.sh script to kick off the build process. This is just a wrapper that launches the ant binary included in the distribution. You can use Ant directly to build if your environment is configured to run it from the command line.

An Overview of the JBoss CVS Source Tree

The top-level directory structure under the jboss-4.0 source tree is illustrated in Figure 1.3, which shows the CVS source tree top-level directories. Table 1.2 describes the primary purpose of each of the top-level directories.

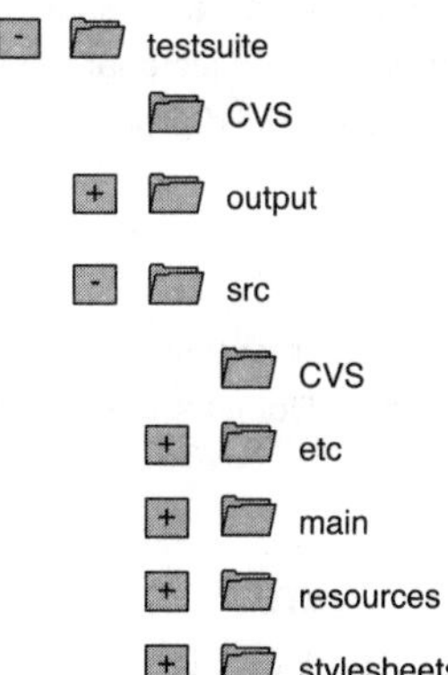

FIGURE 1.3 The testsuite CVS module directory structure.

TABLE 1.2 The Top-Level Directories of the JBoss CVS Source Tree

Directory	Description
`aop`	The JBoss AOP module
`aspects`	The JBossAOP aspect library
`build`	The main build directory from which the release builds are initiated
`cache`	The JBoss TreeCache module
`cluster`	The clustering support services source module
`common`	A source module of common utility-type code used by many of the other source modules
`connector`	The JCA support and application server integration source module
`console`	Admin apps for viewing the JMX MBeans
`deployment`	The JSR 88 J2EE application deployment module
`hibernate`	The Hibernate deployer service
`iiop`	The RMI/IIOP transport service source module
`j2ee`	The core J2EE interfaces and classes
`jaxrpc`	The J2EE Web Services module
`jboss.net`	A Web Services support source module that provides support for using SOAP to invoke operations on EJBs and MBeans
`jmx`	The JBoss JMX implementation source module
`jmx-remoting`	The JMX remoting module
`management`	The JBoss JSR-77 source module
`media`	The enterprise media beans module
`messaging`	The JBoss JMS implementation source module
`naming`	The JBoss JNDI implementation source module
`remoting`	The JBoss remoting module
`security`	The JBoss standard J2EE declarative security implementation, which is based on JAAS
`server`	The EJB container
`system`	The JMX microkernel–based bootstrap services and standard deployment services source module
`testsuite`	The JUnit unit test source module
`thirdparty`	A module that contains the third-party binary JARs used by the JBoss modules
`tomcat`	The Tomcat-5.0.x embedded service source module
`tools`	The JARs used by the JBoss build process
`transaction`	The JTA transaction manager
`varia`	Various utility services that have not been or will not be integrated into one of the higher-level modules
`webservice`	The J2EE Web Service implementation in JBoss
`xdoclet`	A directory that builds the XDoclet support library

Using the JBossTest Unit Testsuite

You can do more advanced testing of the JBoss installation and builds by using the JBoss Testsuite. The JBoss Testsuite is a collection of client-oriented unit tests of the JBoss server application. It is an Ant-based package that uses the JUnit (www.junit.org) unit test framework. The JBoss Testsuite is used as a QA benchmark by the development team to help test new functionality and prevent introduction of bugs. It is run on a nightly basis, and the results are posted to the development mailing list for all to see.

The unit tests are run using Ant, and the source for the tests are contained in the `jboss-4.0/testsuite` directory of the source tree. The structure of the testsuite CVS module is illustrated in Figure 1.3.

The two main source branches of the testsuite CVS module are `src/main` and `src/resources`. The `src/main` tree contains the Java source code for the unit tests. The `src/resources` tree contains resource files such as deployment descriptors, JAR manifest, web content, and so on. The root package of every unit test is `org.jboss.test`. The typical structure below each specific unit test subpackage (for example, `security`) consists of a test package that contains the unit test classes. The `test` subpackage is a required naming convention because this is the only directory that is searched for unit tests by the Ant build scripts. If the tests involve EJBs, then the convention is to include `interfaces` and `ejb` subpackages for these components. The unit tests themselves need to follow a naming convention for the class file. The unit test class must be named `*XXX*UnitTest.java`, where *XXX* is either the class being tested or the name of the functionality being tested.

To run the unit tests, you use the build scripts located in the `testsuite` directory. The key targets in the `build.xml` file include the following:

- **`tests`**—This target builds and runs all unit tests and generates HTML and text reports of the tests into the `testsuite/output/reports/html` and `testsuite/output/reports/text` directories, respectively.
- **`tests-standard-unit`**—This target builds all unit tests and runs a subset of the key unit tests. This is useful for quickly checking the server to test for gross problems.
- **`test`**—This target allows you to run all tests within a particular package. To run this target, you need to specify a test property and a package name, using the `-Dtest=*package*` command line. The *`package`* value is the name of the package below `org. jboss.test` that you want to run unit tests for. So, for example, to run all unit tests in the `org.jboss.test.naming` package, you would use `build.sh-Dtest=naming test`.
- **`one-test`**—This target allows you to run a single unit test. To run this target, you need to specify a test property and the classname of the unit test by using `-Dtest=*classname*` on the command line. So, for example, to run `org.jboss.test.naming.test.ENCUnitTestCase`, you would use `build.sh -Dtest=org.jboss.test.naming.test.ENCUnitTestCase one-test`.
- **`tests-report`**—This target generates HTML and text reports of the tests into the `testsuite/output/reports/html` and `testsuite/output/reports/text` directories, respectively, using the current JUnit XML results in the `testsuite/output/reports` directory. This is useful for generating nice HTML reports when you have run a subset of the tests by hand and want to generate a summary.

On completion of a test, the `testsuite/output/reports` directory will contain one or more XML files that represent the individual JUnit test runs. The `tests-report` target collates these into an HTML report located in the `html` subdirectory, along with a text report located in the text subdirectory. Figure 1.4 shows an example of the HTML report for a run of the testsuite against the JBoss 4.0.1 release.

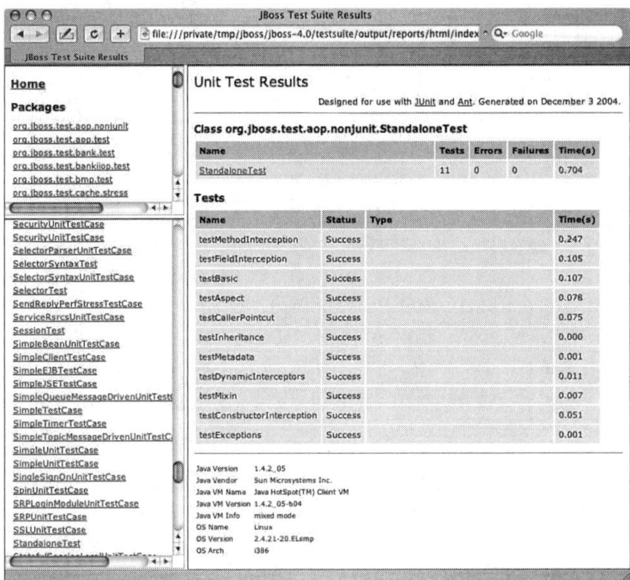

FIGURE 1.4 An example of a testsuite-run report in status HTML view, as generated by the testsuite.

You can find the results of the testsuite in the JBoss distribution under the `JBOSS_DIST/docs/tests` directory.

CHAPTER 2

The JBoss JMX Microkernel

IN THIS CHAPTER

- JMX
- The JBoss JMX Implementation Architecture
- Connecting to the JMX Server
- Using JMX as a Microkernel
- The JBoss Deployer Architecture
- Exposing MBean Events via SNMP
- Remote Access to Services, Detached Invokers

Modularly developed from the ground up, the JBoss server and container are completely implemented using component-based plug-ins. The modularization effort is supported by the use of JMX, the Java Management Extensions API. By using JMX, industry-standard interfaces help manage both JBoss server components and the applications deployed on it. Ease of use is still the number-one priority, and the JBoss Server architecture sets a new standard for modular plug-in design as well as ease of server and application management.

This high degree of modularity benefits application developers in several ways. The already tight code can be further trimmed down to support applications that must have a small footprint. For example, if EJB passivation is unnecessary in an application, you can simply take the feature out of the server. If you later decide to deploy the same application under an application service provider (ASP) model, you can simply enable the server's passivation feature for that web-based deployment. Another example is the freedom you have to drop your favorite object-to-relational database (O-R) mapping tool, such as TOPLink, directly into the container.

This chapter introduces you to JMX and its role as the JBoss server component bus. It also introduces you to the notion of JBoss MBean services, which add life cycle operations to the basic JMX management component.

JMX

The success of the full open-source J2EE stack lies with the use of JMX. JMX is the best tool for integration of software.

It provides a common spine that allows you to integrate modules, containers, and plug-ins. Figure 2.1 shows the role of JMX as an integration spine, or bus, into which components plug. Components are declared as MBean services that are then loaded into JBoss. The components may subsequently be administered by using JMX.

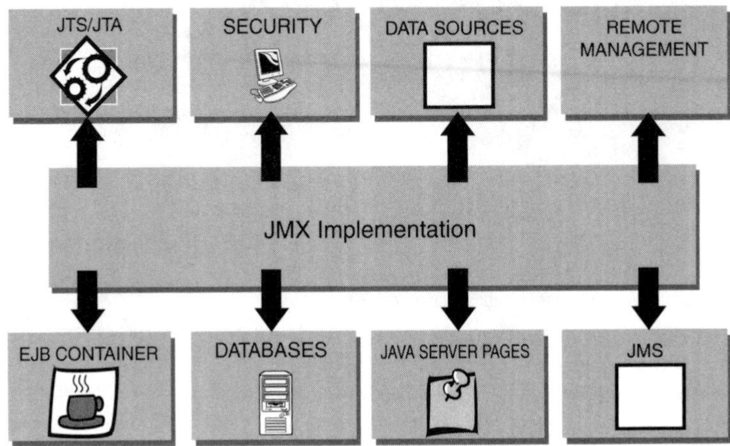

FIGURE 2.1 The JBoss JMX integration bus and the standard JBoss components.

An Introduction to JMX

Before we look at how JBoss uses JMX as its component bus, it would help to have a basic overview of what JMX is by touching on some of its key aspects.

JMX components are defined by the JMX instrumentation and agent specification, version 1.2, which is available from the JSR003 web page, at http://jcp.org/en/jsr/detail?id=3. The material in this JMX overview section is derived from the JMX instrumentation specification, with a focus on the aspects most used by JBoss. You can find a more comprehensive discussion of JMX and its application in *JMX: Managing J2EE with Java Management Extensions* (Sams Publishing).

JMX is a standard for managing and monitoring all varieties of software and hardware components from Java. Further, JMX aims to provide integration with the large number of existing management standards. Figure 2.2 shows examples of components found in a JMX environment and illustrates the relationships between them as well as how they relate to the three levels of the JMX model:

- **Instrumentation**—These are the resources to manage.
- **Agents**—These are the controllers of the instrumentation-level objects.
- **Distributed services**—These are the mechanism by which administration applications interact with agents and their managed objects.

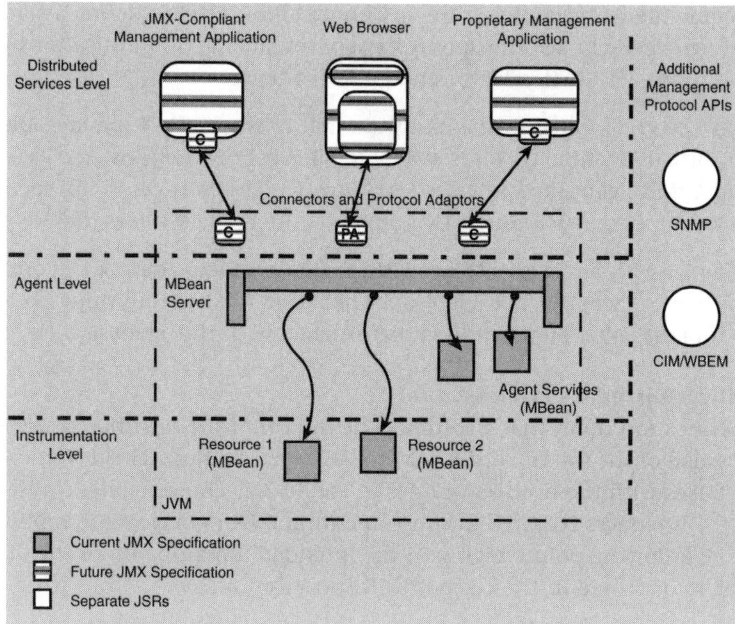

FIGURE 2.2 The relationships between the components of the JMX architecture.

The JMX Instrumentation Level

The instrumentation level defines the requirements for implementing JMX manageable resources. A JMX manageable resource can be virtually anything, including applications, service components, devices, and so on. The manageable resource exposes a Java object or wrapper that describes its manageable features, which makes the resource instrumented so that it can be managed by JMX-compliant applications.

The user provides the instrumentation of a given resource using one or more managed beans, or MBeans. There are four varieties of MBean implementations: standard, dynamic, model, and open. The differences between the various MBean types are discussed in the section "MBeans," later in this chapter.

The instrumentation level also specifies a notification mechanism. The purpose of the notification mechanism is to allow MBeans to communicate changes with their environment. This is similar to the JavaBean property change notification mechanism, and can be used for attribute change notifications, state change notifications, and so on.

The JMX Agent Level

The JMX agent level defines the requirements for implementing agents. Agents are responsible for controlling and exposing the managed resources that are registered with an agent. By default, management agents are located on the same hosts as their resources. This collocation is not a requirement.

The agent requirements make use of the instrumentation level to define a standard `MBeanServer` management agent, supporting services, and a communications connector. JBoss provides both an HTML adaptor and an RMI adaptor.

The JMX agent can be located in the hardware that hosts the JMX manageable resources when a Java Virtual Machine (JVM) is available. This is how the JBoss server uses `MBeanServer`. A JMX agent does not need to know which resources it will serve. JMX manageable resources may use any JMX agent that offers the services they require.

Managers interact with an agent's MBeans through a protocol adaptor or connector, as described in the next section. The agent does not need to know anything about the connectors or management applications that interact with the agent and its MBeans.

The JMX Distributed Services Level

The JMX specification notes that a complete definition of the distributed services level is beyond the scope of the initial version of the JMX specification. This is indicated by the component boxes with the horizontal lines in Figure 2.2. The general purpose of this level is to define the interfaces required for implementing JMX management applications or managers. The following points highlight the intended functionality of the distributed services level, as discussed in the current JMX specification:

- It provides an interface for management applications to interact transparently with an agent and its JMX manageable resources through a connector.
- It exposes a management view of a JMX agent and its MBeans by mapping their semantic meaning into the constructs of a data-rich protocol (for example, HTML, SNMP).
- It distributes management information from high-level management platforms to numerous JMX agents.
- It consolidates management information coming from numerous JMX agents into logical views that are relevant to the end user's business operations.
- It provides security.

The distributed services level components are intended to allow for cooperative management of networks of agents and their resources. These components can be expanded to provide a complete management application.

JMX Component Overview

This section offers an overview of the instrumentation- and agent-level components. The instrumentation-level components include the following:

- MBeans (standard, dynamic, open, and model MBeans)
- Notification model elements
- MBean metadata classes

The agent-level components include the following:

- The MBean server
- Agent services

MBeans An *MBean* is a Java object that implements one of the standard MBean interfaces and follows the associated design patterns. The MBean for a resource exposes all necessary information and operations that a management application needs to control the resource.

The scope of the management interface of an MBean includes the following:

- Attribute values that may be accessed by name
- Operations or functions that may be invoked
- Notifications or events that may be emitted
- The constructors for the MBean's Java class

JMX defines four types of MBeans to support different instrumentation needs:

- **Standard MBeans**—These use a simple JavaBean-style naming convention and a statically defined management interface. This is the most common type of MBean used by JBoss.
- **Dynamic MBeans**—These must implement the `javax.management.DynamicMBean` interface, and they expose their management interface at runtime, when the component is instantiated, for the greatest flexibility. JBoss makes use of Dynamic MBeans in circumstances where the components to be managed are not known until runtime.
- **Open MBeans**—These are an extension of Dynamic MBeans. Open MBeans rely on basic, self-describing, user-friendly data types for universal manageability.
- **Model MBeans**—These are also an extension of Dynamic MBeans. Model MBeans must implement the `javax.management.modelmbean.ModelMBean` interface. Model MBeans simplify the instrumentation of resources by providing default behavior. JBoss XMBeans are an implementation of Model MBeans.

Later in this chapter, you'll see an example of a Standard MBean and a Model MBean, when we discuss extending JBoss with your own custom services.

The Notification Model JMX notifications are an extension of the Java event model. Both the MBean server and MBeans can send notifications to provide information. The JMX specification defines the `javax.management` package `Notification` event object, `NotificationBroadcaster` event sender, and `NotificationListener` event receiver interfaces. The specification also defines the operations on the MBean server that allow for the registration of notification listeners.

MBean Metadata Classes A collection of metadata classes that describe the management interface of an MBean. Users can obtain a common metadata view of any of the four MBean types by querying the MBean server with which the MBeans are registered. The metadata classes cover an MBean's attributes, operations, notifications, and constructors. For each of these, the metadata includes a name, a description, and its particular characteristics. For example, one characteristic of an attribute is whether it is readable, writable, or both. The metadata for an operation contains the signature of its parameter and return types.

The different types of MBeans extend the metadata classes to be able to provide additional information, as required. This common inheritance makes the standard information available, regardless of the type of MBean. A management application that knows how to access the extended information of a particular type of MBean is able to do so.

The MBean Server A key component of the agent level is the MBean server. Its functionality is exposed through an instance of `javax.management.MBeanServer`. An MBean server is a registry for MBeans that makes the MBean management interface available for use by management applications. The MBean server never directly exposes the MBean object itself; rather, an MBean's management interface is exposed through metadata and operations available in the MBean server interface. This provides a loose coupling between management applications and the MBeans they manage.

MBeans can be instantiated and registered with the MBean server by the following:

- Another MBean
- The agent itself
- A remote management application (through the distributed services)

When you register an MBean, you must assign it a unique object name. The object name then becomes the unique handle by which management applications identify the object on which to perform management operations. The operations available on MBeans through the MBean server include the following:

- Discovering the management interfaces of MBeans
- Reading and writing attribute values
- Invoking operations defined by MBeans
- Registering for notifications events
- Querying MBeans based on their object names or their attribute values

Protocol adaptors and connectors are required to access the MBean server from outside the agent's JVM. Each adaptor provides a view via its protocol of all MBeans registered in the MBean server to which the adaptor connects. An example of an adaptor is an HTML adaptor that allows for the inspection and editing of MBeans by using a web browser. As indicated in Figure 2.2, there are no protocol adaptors defined by the current JMX specification. Later versions of the specification will address the need for remote access protocols.

A *connector* is an interface that management applications use to provide a common API for accessing the MBean server in a manner that is independent of the underlying communication protocol. Each connector type provides the same remote interface over a different protocol. This allows a remote management application to connect to an agent transparently through the network, regardless of the protocol. The specification of the remote management interface will be addressed in a future version of the JMX specification.

Adaptors and connectors make all MBean server operations available to a remote management application. For an agent to be manageable from outside its JVM, it must include at least one protocol adaptor or connector. JBoss currently includes a custom HTML adaptor implementation and a custom JBoss RMI adaptor.

Agent Services The JMX agent services are objects that support standard operations on the MBeans registered in the MBean server. The inclusion of supporting management services helps you build more powerful management solutions. Agent services are often themselves MBeans, which allow the agent and their functionality to be controlled through the MBean server. The JMX specification defines the following agent services:

- **A dynamic class-loading MLet (management applet) service**—This service allows for the retrieval and instantiation of new classes and native libraries from an arbitrary network location.
- **Monitor services**—These services observe an MBean attribute's numerical or string value and can notify other objects of several types of changes in the target.
- **Timer services**—These services provide a scheduling mechanism based on a one-time alarm-clock notification or on a repeated, periodic notification.
- **The relation service**—This service defines associations between MBeans and enforces consistency on the relationships.

Any JMX-compliant implementation will provide all these agent services. However, JBoss does not rely on any of these standard agent services.

The JBoss JMX Implementation Architecture

Let's now look at the JBoss JMX implementation.

The JBoss `ClassLoader` Architecture

JBoss employs a class-loading architecture that facilitates sharing of classes across deployment units and hot deployment of services and applications. Before we discuss the JBoss-specific class-loading model, however, you need to understand the nature of Java's type system and how class loaders fit in.

Class Loading and Types in Java

Class loading is a fundamental part of all server architectures. Arbitrary services and their supporting classes must be loaded into the server framework. This can be problematic due to the strongly typed nature of Java. Most developers know that the type of a class in Java is a function of the fully qualified name of the class. However, the type is also a function of the `java.lang.ClassLoader` that is used to define that class. This additional qualification of type is necessary to ensure that environments in which classes may be loaded from arbitrary locations may be type safe.

However, in a dynamic environment such as an application server, and especially JBoss, with its support for hot deployment, class cast exceptions, linkage errors, and illegal access errors can show up in ways not seen in more static class-loading contexts. Let's take a look at the meaning of each of these exceptions and how they can happen.

`ClassCastException`: I'm Not Your Type

A `java.lang.ClassCastException` results whenever an attempt is made to cast an instance to an incompatible type. A simple example is trying to obtain a `String` from a `List` into which a `URL` was placed:

```
ArrayList array = new ArrayList();
array.add(new URL("file:/tmp"));
String url = (String) array.get(0);

java.lang.ClassCastException: java.net.URL
at org.jboss.chap2.ex0.ExCCEa.main(Ex1CCE.java:16)
```

The `ClassCastException` tells you that the attempt to cast the array element to a `String` failed because the actual type was `URL`. This trivial case is not what we are interested in, however. Consider the case of a JAR being loaded by different class loaders. Although the classes loaded through each class loader are identical in terms of the bytecode, they are completely different types, as viewed by the Java type system. Listing 2.1 illustrates an example of this. Listing 2.2 shows the additional classes that are used.

LISTING 2.1 The `ExCCEc` Class, Used to Demonstrate `ClassCastException` Due to Duplicate Class Loaders

```
package org.jboss.chap2.ex0;

import java.io.File;
import java.net.URL;
import java.net.URLClassLoader;
import java.lang.reflect.Method;

import org.apache.log4j.Logger;
```

LISTING 2.1 Continued

```
import org.jboss.util.ChapterExRepository;
import org.jboss.util.Debug;

/**
 * An example of a ClassCastException that
 * results from classes loaded through
 * different class loaders.
 * @author Scott.Stark@jboss.org
 * @version $Revision: 1.5 $
 */
public class ExCCEc
{
    public static void main(String[] args) throws Exception
    {
        ChapterExRepository.init(ExCCEc.class);

        String chapDir = System.getProperty("chapter.dir");
        Logger ucl0Log = Logger.getLogger("UCL0");
        File jar0 = new File(chapDir+"/j0.jar");
        ucl0Log.info("jar0 path: "+jar0.toString());
        URL[] cp0 = {jar0.toURL()};
        URLClassLoader ucl0 = new URLClassLoader(cp0);
        Thread.currentThread().setContextClassLoader(ucl0);
        Class objClass = ucl0.loadClass("org.jboss.chap2.ex0.ExObj");
        StringBuffer buffer = new
            StringBuffer("ExObj Info");
        Debug.displayClassInfo(objClass, buffer, false);
        ucl0Log.info(buffer.toString());
        Object value = objClass.newInstance();

        File jar1 = new File(chapDir+"/j0.jar");
        Logger ucl1Log = Logger.getLogger("UCL1");
        ucl1Log.info("jar1 path: "+jar1.toString());
        URL[] cp1 = {jar1.toURL()};
        URLClassLoader ucl1 = new URLClassLoader(cp1);
        Thread.currentThread().setContextClassLoader(ucl1);
        Class ctxClass2 = ucl1.loadClass("org.jboss.chap2.ex0.ExCtx");
        buffer.setLength(0);
        buffer.append("ExCtx Info");
        Debug.displayClassInfo(ctxClass2, buffer, false);
        ucl1Log.info(buffer.toString());
        Object ctx2 = ctxClass2.newInstance();
```

LISTING 2.1 Continued

```
        try {
            Class[] types = {Object.class};
            Method useValue =
                ctxClass2.getMethod("useValue", types);
            Object[] margs = {value};
            useValue.invoke(ctx2, margs);
        } catch(Exception e) {
            ucl1Log.error("Failed to invoke ExCtx.useValue", e);
            throw e;
        }
    }
}
```

LISTING 2.2 The `ExCtx`, `ExObj`, and `ExObj2` Classes Used by the Examples

```
port java.io.IOException;
import org.apache.log4j.Logger;
import org.jboss.util.Debug;

/**
 * Classes used to demonstrate various class
 * loading issues
 * @author Scott.Stark@jboss.org
 * @version $Revision: 1.5 $
 */
public class ExCtx
{
    ExObj value;

    public ExCtx()
        throws IOException
    {
        value = new ExObj();
        Logger log = Logger.getLogger(ExCtx.class);
        StringBuffer buffer = new StringBuffer("ctor.ExObj");
        Debug.displayClassInfo(value.getClass(), buffer, false);
        log.info(buffer.toString());
        ExObj2 obj2 = value.ivar;
        buffer.setLength(0);
        buffer = new StringBuffer("ctor.ExObj.ivar");
        Debug.displayClassInfo(obj2.getClass(), buffer, false);
        log.info(buffer.toString());
    }
```

LISTING 2.2 Continued

```
    public Object getValue()
    {
        return value;
    }

    public void useValue(Object obj)
        throws Exception
    {
        Logger log = Logger.getLogger(ExCtx.class);
        StringBuffer buffer = new
            StringBuffer("useValue2.arg class");
        Debug.displayClassInfo(obj.getClass(), buffer, false);
        log.info(buffer.toString());
        buffer.setLength(0);
        buffer.append("useValue2.ExObj class");
        Debug.displayClassInfo(ExObj.class, buffer, false);
        log.info(buffer.toString());
        ExObj ex = (ExObj) obj;
    }

    void pkgUseValue(Object obj)
        throws Exception
    {
        Logger log = Logger.getLogger(ExCtx.class);
        log.info("In pkgUseValue");
    }
}

package org.jboss.chap2.ex0;

import java.io.Serializable;

/**
 * @author Scott.Stark@jboss.org
 * @version $Revision: 1.5 $
 */
public class ExObj
    implements Serializable
{
    public ExObj2 ivar = new ExObj2();
}

package org.jboss.chap2.ex0;
```

LISTING 2.2 Continued

```
import java.io.Serializable;

/**
 * @author Scott.Stark@jboss.org
 * @version $Revision: 1.5 $
 */
public class ExObj2
    implements Serializable
{
}
```

The `ExCCEc.main` method uses reflection to isolate the classes that are being loaded by the class loaders `ucl0` and `ucl1` from the application class loader. Both are set up to load classes from the `output/chap2/j0.jar`, the contents of which are as follows:

```
[examples]$ jar -tf output/chap2/j0.jar

org/jboss/chap2/ex0/ExCtx.class
org/jboss/chap2/ex0/ExObj.class
org/jboss/chap2/ex0/ExObj2.class
```

Let's run an example that demonstrates how a class cast exception can occur and then look at the specific issue with the example. See Appendix B, "Example Installation," for instructions on installing the examples accompanying the book, and then run the example from within the examples directory by using the following command:

```
[examples]$ ant -Dchap=chap2 -Dex=0c run-example
...
     [java] [ERROR,UCL1] Failed to invoke ExCtx.useValue
     [java] java.lang.reflect.InvocationTargetException
     [java] at sun.reflect.NativeMethodAccessorImpl.invoke0(Native Method)
     [java] at sun.reflect.NativeMethodAccessorImpl.invoke
➥(NativeMethodAccessorImpl.java:39)
     [java] at sun.reflect.DelegatingMethodAccessorImpl.invoke
➥(DelegatingMethodAccessorImpl.java:25)
     [java] at java.lang.reflect.Method.invoke(Method.java:324)
     [java] at org.jboss.chap2.ex0.ExCCEc.main(ExCCEc.java:58)
     [java] Caused by: java.lang.ClassCastException
     [java] at org.jboss.chap2.ex0.ExCtx.useValue(ExCtx.java:44)
     [java] ... 5 more
```

Only the exception is shown here. The full output can be found in the `logs/chap2-ex0c.log` file. At line 55 of `Ex-CCEc.java` you invoke `ExcCCECtx.useValue(Object)` on the instance loaded and created in lines 37–48, using `ucl1`. The `ExObj` that is passed in is the one loaded and created in lines 25–35 via ucl0. The exception results when the ExCtx.useValue code attempts to cast the argument passed in to an ExObj. To understand why this fails, consider the debugging output from the chap2-ex0c.log file shown in Listing 2.3.

LISTING 2.3 The chap2-ex0c.log Debugging Output for the ExObj Classes

```
[INFO,UCL0] ExObj Info
org.jboss.chap2.ex0.ExObj(113fe2).ClassLoader=java.net.URLClassLoader@6e3914
..java.net.URLClassLoader@6e3914
....file:/C:/Scott/JBoss/Books/AdminDevel/education/books/admin-devel/
➥examples/output/
  chap2/j0.jar
++++CodeSource:
    (file:/C:/Scott/JBoss/Books/AdminDevel/education/books/admin-devel/
➥examples/output/
  chap2/j0.jar <no certificates>)
Implemented Interfaces:
++interface java.io.Serializable(7934ad)
++++ClassLoader: null
++++Null CodeSource

[INFO,ExCtx] useValue2.ExObj class
org.jboss.chap2.ex0.ExObj(415de6).ClassLoader=java.net.URLClassLoader@30e280
..java.net.URLClassLoader@30e280
....file:/C:/Scott/JBoss/Books/AdminDevel/education/books/admin-devel/examples/
➥output/
  chap2/j0.jar
++++CodeSource:
    (file:/C:/Scott/JBoss/Books/AdminDevel/education/books/admin-devel/
➥examples/output/
  chap2/j0.jar <no certificates>)
Implemented Interfaces:
++interface java.io.Serializable(7934ad)
++++ClassLoader: null
++++Null CodeSource
```

The first output prefixed with [INFO,UCL0] shows that the ExObj class loaded at line ExCCEc.java:31 has a hash code of 113fe2 and an associated URLClassLoader instance with a hash code of 6e3914, which corresponds to ucl0. This is the class used to create the instance passed to the ExCtx.useValue method. The second output prefixed with [INFO,ExCtx] shows that the ExObj class, as seen in the context of the ExCtx.useValue method, has a hash code of 415de6 and a URLClassLoader instance with an associated hash code of 30e280, which corresponds to ucl1. So even though the ExObj classes are the same in terms of actual bytecode, since it comes from the same j0.jar, the classes are different, as shown by both the `ExObj` class hash codes and the associated `URLClassLoader` instances. Hence, attempting to cast an instance of `ExObj` from one scope to the other results in the `ClassCastException`.

This type of error is common when you're redeploying an application to which other applications are holding references to classes from the redeployed application (for example, a standalone WAR accessing an EJB). If you are redeploying an application, all dependent applications must flush their class references. Typically, this requires that the dependent applications themselves be redeployed.

An alternate means of allowing independent deployments to interact in the presence of redeployment would be to isolate the deployments by configuring the EJB layer to use the standard call-by-value semantics rather than the call-by-reference that JBoss defaults to for components collocated in the same VM. An example of how to enable call-by-value semantics is presented in Chapter 5, "EJBs on JBoss."

`IllegalAccessException`: Doing What You Should Not

A `java.lang.IllegalAccessException` is thrown when you attempt to access a method or member that visibility qualifiers do not allow. A typical example is attempting to access private or protected methods or instance variables. Another common example is accessing package-protected methods or members from a class that appears to be in the correct package but is really not, due to caller and callee classes being loaded by different class loaders. An example of this is illustrated by the code shown in Listing 2.4.

LISTING 2.4 The `ExIAEd` Class, Used to Demonstrate `IllegalAccessException` Due to Duplicate Class Loaders

```
package org.jboss.chap2.ex0;

import java.io.File;
import java.net.URL;
import java.net.URLClassLoader;
import java.lang.reflect.Method;

import org.apache.log4j.Logger;

import org.jboss.util.ChapterExRepository;
import org.jboss.util.Debug;

/**
 * An example of IllegalAccessExceptions due to
 * classes loaded by two class loaders.
 * @author Scott.Stark@jboss.org
 * @version $Revision: 1.5 $
 */
public class ExIAEd
{
```

LISTING 2.4 Continued

```
    public static void main(String[] args) throws Exception
    {
        ChapterExRepository.init(ExIAEd.class);

        String chapDir = System.getProperty("chapter.dir");
        Logger ucl0Log = Logger.getLogger("UCL0");
        File jar0 = new File(chapDir+"/j0.jar");
        ucl0Log.info("jar0 path: "+jar0.toString());
        URL[] cp0 = {jar0.toURL()};
        URLClassLoader ucl0 = new URLClassLoader(cp0);
        Thread.currentThread().setContextClassLoader(ucl0);

        StringBuffer buffer = new
            StringBuffer("ExIAEd Info");
        Debug.displayClassInfo(ExIAEd.class, buffer, false);
        ucl0Log.info(buffer.toString());

        Class ctxClass1 = ucl0.loadClass("org.jboss.chap2.ex0.ExCtx");
        buffer.setLength(0);
        buffer.append("ExCtx Info");
        Debug.displayClassInfo(ctxClass1, buffer, false);
        ucl0Log.info(buffer.toString());
        Object ctx0 = ctxClass1.newInstance();

        try {
            Class[] types = {Object.class};
            Method useValue =
                ctxClass1.getDeclaredMethod("pkgUseValue", types);
            Object[] margs = {null};
            useValue.invoke(ctx0, margs);
        } catch(Exception e) {
            ucl0Log.error("Failed to invoke ExCtx.pkgUseValue", e);
        }
    }
}
```

The `ExIAEd.main` method uses reflection to load the `ExCtx` class via the `ucl0` class loader, whereas the `ExIEAd` class is loaded by the application class loader. We will run this example to demonstrate how the `IllegalAccessException` can occur and then look at the specific issue with the example. You run the example by using the following command:

```
[examples]$ ant -Dchap=chap2 -Dex=0d run-example
Buildfile: build.xml
```

```
...
[java] [ERROR,UCL0] Failed to invoke ExCtx.pkgUseValue
[java] java.lang.IllegalAccessException: Class org.jboss.chap2.ex0.ExIAEd
  cannot access a member of class org.jboss.chap2.ex0.ExCtx with modifiers ""
[java] at sun.reflect.Reflection.ensureMemberAccess(Reflection.java:57)
[java] at java.lang.reflect.Method.invoke(Method.java:317)
[java] at org.jboss.chap2.ex0.ExIAEd.main(ExIAEd.java:48)
```

The truncated output shown here illustrates the `IllegalAccessException`. The full output can be found in the `logs/chap2-ex0d.log` file. At line 48 of `ExIAEd.java`, the `ExCtx.pkgUseValue(Object)` method is invoked via reflection. The `pkgUseValue` method has package-protected access, and even though both the invoking class `ExIAEd` and the `ExCtx` class whose method is being invoked reside in the `org.jboss.chap2.ex0` package, the invocation is seen to be invalid due to the fact that the two classes are loaded by different class loaders. You can see this by looking at the debugging output from the `chap2-ex0d.log` file:

```
[INFO,UCL0] ExIAEd Info
org.jboss.chap2.ex0.ExIAEd(65855a).ClassLoader=
➥sun.misc.Launcher$AppClassLoader@3f52a5
..sun.misc.Launcher$AppClassLoader@3f52a5
...
[INFO,UCL0] ExCtx Info
org.jboss.chap2.ex0.ExCtx(70eed6).ClassLoader=java.net.URLClassLoader@113fe2
..java.net.URLClassLoader@113fe2
...
```

The `ExIAEd` class was loaded via the default application class loader instance `sun.misc.Launcher$AppClassLoader@3f52a5`, whereas the `ExCtx` class was loaded by the `java.net.URLClassLoader@113fe2` instance. Because the classes are loaded by different class loaders, access to the package-protected method is seen to be a security violation. So, not only is the type a function of both the fully qualified classname and class loader, the package scope is as well.

An example of how this can happen in practice is including the same classes in two different SAR deployments. If classes in the deployments have a package-protected relationship, users of the SAR service may end up loading one class from SAR class that is loading at one point and then load another class from the second SAR at a later time. If the two classes in question have a protected access relationship, an `IllegalAccessError` will result. The solution is to either include the classes in a separate JAR that is referenced by the SARs or to combine the SARs into a single deployment. This can either be a single SAR or an EAR that includes both SARs.

`LinkageErrors`: Making Sure You Are Who You Say You Are

Loading constraints validate type expectations in the context of class loader scopes to ensure that a class `X` is consistently the same class when multiple class loaders are involved. This is important because Java allows for user-defined class loaders. Linkage errors are essentially an extension of the class cast exception that is enforced by the VM when classes are loaded and used.

To understand what loading constraints are and how they ensure type safety, we will first look at the nomenclature of the Liang and Bracha paper "Dynamic Class Loading in the Java Virtual Machine," along with an example from that paper. There are two types of class loaders: initiating and defining. An *initiating class loader* is one that a ClassLoader.loadClass method has been invoked on to initiate the loading of the named class. A *defining class loader* is the loader that calls one of the ClassLoader.defineClass methods to convert the class bytecode into a Class instance. The most complete expression of a class is given by <C, Ld>^{Li}, where C is the fully qualified classname, Ld is the defining class loader, and Li is the initiating class loader. In a context where the initiating class loader is not important, the type may be represented by <C, Ld>, and when the defining class loader is not important, the type may be represented by C^{Li}. In the latter case, there is still a defining class loader; it's just not important what the identity of the defining class loader is. Also, a type is completely defined by <C, Ld>. The only time the initiating loader is relevant is when a loading constraint is being validated. Now consider the classes shown in Listing 2.5.

LISTING 2.5 Classes Demonstrating the Need for Loading Constraints

```
class <C,L1> {
    void f() {
        <Spoofed, L1>L1x = <Delegated, L2>L2
        x.secret_value = 1; // Should not be allowed
    }
}
class <Delegated,L2> {
    static <Spoofed, L2>L3 g() {...}
    }
}

class <Spoofed, L1> {
    public int secret_value;
}

class <Spoofed, L2> {
    private int secret_value;
}
```

The class C is defined by L1, and so L1 is used to initiate loading of the classes Spoofed and Delegated that are referenced in the C.f() method. The Spoofed class is defined by L1, but Delegated is defined by L2 because L1 delegates to L2. Because Delegated is defined by L2, L2 will be used to initiate loading of Spoofed in the context of the Delegated.g() method. In this example, L1 and L2 define different versions of Spoofed, as indicated by the two versions shown at the end of Listing 2.5. Because `C.f()` believes `x` is an instance of `<Spoofed, L1>`, it is able to access the private field `secret_value` of `<Spoofed, L2>` that is returned by `Delegated.g()` due to the 1.1 and earlier Java VM's failure to take into account that a class type is determined by both the fully qualified name of the class and the defining class loader.

Java addresses this problem by generating loader constraints to validate type consistency when the types being used are coming from different defining class loaders. For the Listing 2.5 example, the VM generates a constraint Spoofed^{L1}=Spoofed^{L2} when the first line of method `C.f()` is verified to indicate that the type `Spoofed` must be the same, regardless of whether the load of `Spoofed` is initiated by `L1` or `L2`. It does not matter whether `L1` or `L2`—or even some other class loader—defines `Spoofed`. All that matters is that there is only one `Spoofed` class defined, regardless of whether `L1` or `L2` was used to initiate the loading. If `L1` or `L2` has already defined separate versions of `Spoofed` when this check is made, a `LinkageError` will be generated immediately. Otherwise, the constraint will be recorded, and when `Delegated.g()` is executed, any attempt to load a duplicate version of `Spoofed` will result in a `LinkageError`.

Now let's take a look at how a `LinkageError` can occur by examining a concrete example. Listing 2.6 gives the example's main class, along with the custom class loader used.

LISTING 2.6 A Concrete Example of a `LinkageError`

```
package org.jboss.chap2.ex0;
import java.io.File;
import java.net.URL;

import org.apache.log4j.Logger;
import org.jboss.util.ChapterExRepository;
import org.jboss.util.Debug;

/**
 * An example of a LinkageError due to classes being defined by more
 * than one class loader in a non-standard class loading environment.
 *
 * @author Scott.Stark@jboss.org
 * @version $Revision: 1.5 $
 */
public class ExLE
{
        public static void main(String[] args)
        throws Exception
        {
            ChapterExRepository.init(ExLE.class);

            String chapDir = System.getProperty("chapter.dir");
            Logger ucl0Log = Logger.getLogger("UCL0");
```

LISTING 2.6 Continued

```
            File jar0 = new File(chapDir+"/j0.jar");
            ucl0Log.info("jar0 path: "+jar0.toString());
            URL[] cp0 = {jar0.toURL()};
            Ex0URLClassLoader ucl0 = new Ex0URLClassLoader(cp0);
            Thread.currentThread().setContextClassLoader(ucl0);
            Class ctxClass1  = ucl0.loadClass("org.jboss.chap2.ex0.ExCtx");

                 Class obj2Class1 = ucl0.loadClass
➥("org.jboss.chap2.ex0.ExObj2");
            StringBuffer buffer = new StringBuffer("ExCtx Info");
            Debug.displayClassInfo(ctxClass1, buffer, false);
            ucl0Log.info(buffer.toString());
            buffer.setLength(0);
            buffer.append("ExObj2 Info, UCL0");
            Debug.displayClassInfo(obj2Class1, buffer, false);
            ucl0Log.info(buffer.toString());

            File jar1 = new File(chapDir+"/j1.jar");
            Logger ucl1Log = Logger.getLogger("UCL1");
            ucl1Log.info("jar1 path: "+jar1.toString());
            URL[] cp1 = {jar1.toURL()};
            Ex0URLClassLoader ucl1 = new Ex0URLClassLoader(cp1);
            Class obj2Class2 = ucl1.loadClass("org.jboss.chap2.ex0.ExObj2");
            buffer.setLength(0);
            buffer.append("ExObj2 Info, UCL1");
            Debug.displayClassInfo(obj2Class2, buffer, false);
            ucl1Log.info(buffer.toString());

            ucl0.setDelegate(ucl1);
            try {
                ucl0Log.info("Try ExCtx.newInstance()");
                Object ctx0 = ctxClass1.newInstance();
                ucl0Log.info("ExCtx.ctor succeeded, ctx0: "+ctx0);
            } catch(Throwable e) {
                ucl0Log.error("ExCtx.ctor failed", e);
            }
        }
    }
package org.jboss.chap2.ex0;

import java.net.URLClassLoader;
import java.net.URL;
```

LISTING 2.6 Continued

```
import org.apache.log4j.Logger;

/**
 * A custom class loader that overrides the standard parent delegation
 * model
 *
 * @author Scott.Stark@jboss.org
 * @version $Revision: 1.5 $
 */
public class Ex0URLClassLoader extends URLClassLoader
{
    private static Logger log = Logger.getLogger(Ex0URLClassLoader.class);
    private Ex0URLClassLoader delegate;

    public Ex0URLClassLoader(URL[] urls)
    {
        super(urls);
    }

    void setDelegate(Ex0URLClassLoader delegate)
    {
        this.delegate = delegate;
    }

    protected synchronized Class loadClass(String name, boolean resolve)
        throws ClassNotFoundException
    {
        Class clazz = null;
        if (delegate != null) {
            log.debug(Integer.toHexString(hashCode()) +
                      "; Asking delegate to loadClass: " + name);
            clazz = delegate.loadClass(name, resolve);
            log.debug(Integer.toHexString(hashCode()) +
                      "; Delegate returned: "+clazz);
        } else {
            log.debug(Integer.toHexString(hashCode()) +
                      "; Asking super to loadClass: "+name);
            clazz = super.loadClass(name, resolve);
            log.debug(Integer.toHexString(hashCode()) +
                      "; Super returned: "+clazz);
        }
        return clazz;
    }
```

LISTING 2.6 Continued

```
    protected Class findClass(String name)
        throws ClassNotFoundException
    {
        Class clazz = null;
        log.debug(Integer.toHexString(hashCode()) +
                  "; Asking super to findClass: "+name);
        clazz = super.findClass(name);
        log.debug(Integer.toHexString(hashCode()) +
                  "; Super returned: "+clazz);
        return clazz;
    }
}
```

The key component in this example is the `URLClassLoader` subclass `Ex0URLClassLoader`. This class loader implementation overrides the default parent delegation model to allow the `ucl0` and `ucl1` instances to both load the `Ex-Obj2` class and then set up a delegation relationship between `ucl0` to `ucl1`. At lines 30 and 31, the `ucl0 Ex0URLClassLoader` is used to load the `ExCtx` and `ExObj2` classes. At line 45 of `ExLE.main`, the `ucl1 Ex0URLClassLoader` is used to load the `ExObj 2` class again. At this point, both the `ucl0` and `ucl1` class loaders have defined the `ExObj2` class. A delegation relationship from `ucl0` to `ucl1` is then set up at line 51 via the `ucl0.setDelegate(ucl1)` method call. Finally, at line 54 of `ExLE.main`, an instance of `ExCtx` is created, using the class loaded via `ucl0`. The `ExCtx` class is the same as that presented in Listing 2.2, and the constructor is as follows:

```
public ExCtx()
    throws IOException
{
    value = new ExObj();
    Logger log = Logger.getLogger(ExCtx.class);
    StringBuffer buffer = new StringBuffer("ctor.ExObj");
    Debug.displayClassInfo(value.getClass(), buffer, false);
    log.info(buffer.toString());
    ExObj2 obj2 = value.ivar;
    buffer.setLength(0);
    buffer = new StringBuffer("ctor.ExObj.ivar");
    Debug.displayClassInfo(obj2.getClass(), buffer, false);
    log.info(buffer.toString());
}
```

Now, because the `ExCtx` class was defined by the `ucl0` class loader, and at the time the `ExCtx` constructor is executed, `ucl0` delegates to `ucl1`, line 24 of the `ExCtx` constructor involves the following expression, which has been rewritten in terms of the complete type expressions:

```
<ExObj2,ucl0>ucl0 obj2 = <ExObj,ucl1>ucl0 value * ivar
```

This generates a loading constraint of ExObj 2^{ucl0} = ExObj 2^{ucl1} because the ExObj 2 type must be consistent across the ucl0 and ucl1 class loader instances. Because you have loaded ExObj2 using both ucl0 and ucl1 prior to setting up the delegation relationship, the constraint will be violated and should generate a LinkageError when run. Run the example by using the following command:

```
[examples]$ ant -Dchap=chap2 -Dex=0e run-example
Buildfile: build.xml
...
[java] java.lang.LinkageError: loader constraints violated when linking org/
➥jboss/chap2/ex0/ExObj2 class
[java] at org.jboss.chap2.ex0.ExCtx.<init>(ExCtx.java:24)
[java] at sun.reflect.NativeConstructorAccessorImpl.newInstance0(Native Method)
[java] at sun.reflect.NativeConstructorAccessorImpl.newInstance
➥(NativeConstructorAccessorImpl.java:39)
[java] at sun.reflect.DelegatingConstructorAccessorImpl.newInstance
➥(DelegatingConstructorAccessorImpl.java:27)
[java] at java.lang.reflect.Constructor.newInstance(Constructor.java:274)
[java] at java.lang.Class.newInstance0(Class.java:308)
[java] at java.lang.Class.newInstance(Class.java:261)
[java] at org.jboss.chap2.ex0.ExLE.main(ExLE.java:53)
```

As expected, a LinkageError is thrown during the validation of the loader constraints required by line 24 of the ExCtx constructor.

Debugging Class-Loading Issues Debugging class-loading issues comes down to finding out where a class was loaded from. A useful tool for this is the code snippet shown in Listing 2.7, taken from the org.jboss.util.Debug class in the book examples.

LISTING 2.7 Obtaining Debugging Information for a Class

```
Class clazz =...;
StringBuffer results = new StringBuffer();

ClassLoader cl = clazz.getClassLoader();
results.append("\n" + clazz.getName() + "(" +
               Integer.toHexString(clazz.hashCode()) + ").ClassLoader=" + cl);
ClassLoader parent = cl;

while (parent != null) {
    results.append("\n.."+parent);
    URL[] urls = getClassLoaderURLs(parent);

    int length = urls != null ? urls.length : 0;
    for(int u = 0; u < length; u ++) {
        results.append("\n...."+urls[u]);
    }
```

LISTING 2.7 Continued

```
    if (showParentClassLoaders == false) {
        break;
    }
    if (parent != null) {
        parent = parent.getParent();
    }
}

CodeSource clazzCS = clazz.getProtectionDomain().getCodeSource();
if (clazzCS != null) {
    results.append("\n++++CodeSource: "+clazzCS);
} else {
    results.append("\n++++Null CodeSource");
}
```

Every `Class` object knows its defining `ClassLoader`, and this is available via the `getClassLoader()` method. This defines the scope in which the `Class` type is known, as shown in the previous sections on class cast exceptions, illegal access exceptions, and linkage errors. From the class loader you can view the hierarchy of class loaders that make up the parent delegation chain. If the class loader is a `URLClassLoader`, you can also see the URLs used for class and resource loading.

The defining class loader of a `Class` cannot tell you from what location that `Class` object was loaded. To determine that, you must obtain the `java.security.ProtectionDomain` and then the `java.security.CodeSource`. It is the `CodeSource` that has the URL location from which the class originated. Note that not every `Class` object has a `CodeSource`. If a class is loaded by the bootstrap class loader, then its `CodeSource` will be null. This is the case for all classes in the `java.*` and `javax.*` packages, for example.

Beyond that, it may be useful to view the details of classes being loaded into the JBoss server. You can enable verbose logging of the JBoss class-loading layer by using a `log4j` configuration fragment like that shown in Listing 2.8.

LISTING 2.8 An Example of a `log4j.xml` Configuration Fragment for Enabling Verbose Class-Loading Logging

```
<appender name="UCL" class="org.apache.log4j.FileAppender">
    <param name="File" value="${jboss.server.home.dir}/log/ucl.log"/>
    <param name="Append" value="false"/>
    <layout class="org.apache.log4j.PatternLayout">
        <param name="ConversionPattern" value="[%r,%c{1},%t] %m%n"/>
    </layout>
</appender>
<category name="org.jboss.mx.loading" additivity="false">
    <priority value="TRACE" class="org.jboss.logging.XLevel"/>
```

LISTING 2.8 Continued

```
    <appender-ref ref="UCL"/>
</category>
```

This places the output from the classes in the `org.jboss.mx.loading` package into the `ucl.log` file of the server configuration's log directory. Although it may not be meaningful if you have not looked at the class-loading code, it is vital information that is needed for submitting bug reports or questions regarding class-loading problems. If you have a class-loading problem that appears to be a bug, you should submit it to the JBoss project on SourceForge and include this log file as an attachment.

Inside the JBoss Class-Loading Architecture

Now that you have the role of class loaders in the Java type system defined, let's take a look at the JBoss class-loading architecture, which is shown in Figure 2.3.

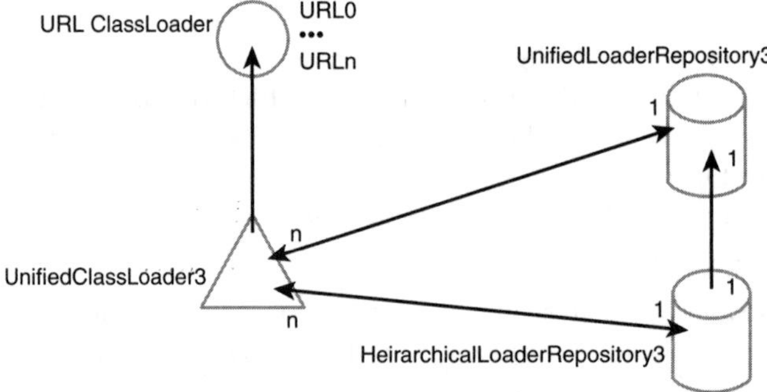

FIGURE 2.3 The core JBoss class-loading components.

The central component of the JBoss class-loading architecture is the `org.jboss.mx.loading.UnifiedClassLoader3` (UCL) class loader. This is an extension of the standard `java.net.URLClassLoader` that overrides the standard parent delegation model to use a shared repository of classes and resources. This shared repository is `org.jboss.mx.loading.UnifiedLoaderRepository3`. Every UCL is associated with a single `UnifiedLoaderRepository3`, and a `UnifiedLoaderRepository3` typically has many UCLs. A UCL may have multiple URLs associated with it for class and resource loading. Deployers use the top-level deployment's UCL as a shared class loader, and all deployment archives are assigned to this class loader. We will talk about the JBoss deployers and their interaction with the class-loading system in more detail later in this chapter, in the section "JBoss MBean Services."

When a UCL is asked to load a class, it first looks to the repository cache it is associated with to see if the class has already been loaded. The UCL loads it into the repository only if the class does not exist in the repository. By default, a single `UnifiedLoaderRepository3` is shared across all UCL instances. This means the UCLs form a single flat class loader namespace. The following is the complete sequence of steps that occur when a `UnfiedClassLoader3.loadClass(String,boolean)` method is called:

1. Check the `UnifiedLoaderRepository3` classes cache associated with the `UnifiedClassLoader3`. If the class is found in the cache, it is returned.

2. If the class is not found, ask the `UnfiedClassLoader3` if it can load the class. This is essentially a call to the superclass `URLClass-Loader.loadClass(String,boolean)` method to see if the class is among the URLs associated with the class loader or visible to the parent class loader. If the class is found, it is placed into the repository classes cache and returned.

3. If the class is not found, the repository is queried for all UCLs that are capable of providing the class based on the repository package name-to-UCL map. When a UCL is added to a repository, an association between the package names available in the URLs associated with the UCL is made, and a mapping from package names to the UCLs with classes in the package is updated. This allows for a quick determination of which UCLs are capable of loading the class. The UCLs are then queried for the requested class, in the order in which the UCLs were added to the repository. If a UCL that can load the class is found, it is returned; otherwise, a `java.lang.ClassNotFoundException` is thrown.

Viewing Classes in the Loader Repository Another useful source of information on classes is the `UnifiedLoaderRepository` itself. This is an MBean that contains operations to display class and package information. The default repository is located under the standard JMX name `JMImplementation:name=Default,service=LoaderRepository`, and you can access its MBean via the JMX Console by following its link from the front page. Figure 2.4 shows the JMX Console view of this MBean.

Two useful operations you will find here are `getPackageClassLoadersString)` and `displayClassInfo(String)`. The `getPackageClassLoaders` operation returns a set of class loaders that have been indexed to contain classes or resources for the given package name. The package name must have a trailing period. If you type in the package name `org.jboss.ejb.`, the following information is displayed:

```
[org.jboss.mx.loading.UnifiedClassLoader3@e26ae7{
  url=file:/private/tmp/jboss-4.0.1/server/default/tmp/deploy/
➥tmp11895jboss-service.xml,
  addedOrder=2}]
```

This is the string representation of the set. It shows one `UnifiedClassLoader3` instance with a primary URL pointing to the `jboss-service.xml` descriptor. This is the second class loader added to the repository (shown by `addedOrder=2`). It is the class loader that owns all the JARs in the `lib` directory of the server configuration (for example, `server/default/lib`).

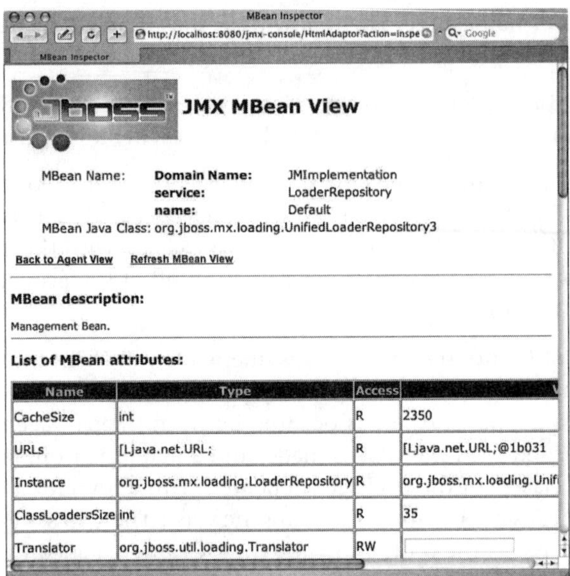

FIGURE 2.4 The default class `LoaderRepository` MBean view in the JMX Console.

To view the information for a given class, you use the `displayClassInfo` operation, passing in the fully qualified name of the class to view. For example, if you use `org.jboss.jmx.adaptor.html.HtmlAdaptorServlet`, which is from the package we just looked at, the description is displayed. The information is a dump of the information for the `Class` instance in the loader repository if one has been loaded, followed by the class loaders that are seen to have the class file available. If a class is seen to have more than one class loader associated with it, then there is the potential for class-loading–related errors.

Scoping Classes If you need to deploy multiple versions of an application, you need to use deployment-based scoping. With deployment-based scoping, each deployment creates its own class loader repository, in the form of a `HeirarchicalLoaderRepository3` that looks first to the `UnifiedClassLoader3` instances of the deployment units included in the EAR before delegating to the default `UnifiedLoaderRepository3`. To enable an EAR-specific loader repository, you need to create a `META-INF/jboss-app.xml` descriptor, as shown in Listing 2.9.

LISTING 2.9 An Example of a `jboss-app.xml` Descriptor for Enabled Scoped Class Loading at the EAR Level

```
<jboss-app>
    <loader-repository>some.dot.com:loader=webtest.ear</loader-repository>
</jboss-app>
```

The value of the loader-repository element is the JMX object name to assign to the repository created for the EAR. This must be a unique and valid JMX ObjectName, but the actual name is not important.

The Complete Class-Loading Model The previous discussion of the core class-loading components introduces the custom UnifiedClassLoader3 and UnifiedLoaderRepository3 classes that form a shared class-loading space. The complete class-loading picture must also include the parent class loader used by UnifiedClassLoader3s, as well as class loaders introduced for scoping and other specialty class-loading purposes. Figure 2.5 shows an outline of the class hierarchy that would exist for an EAR deployment containing EJBs and WARs.

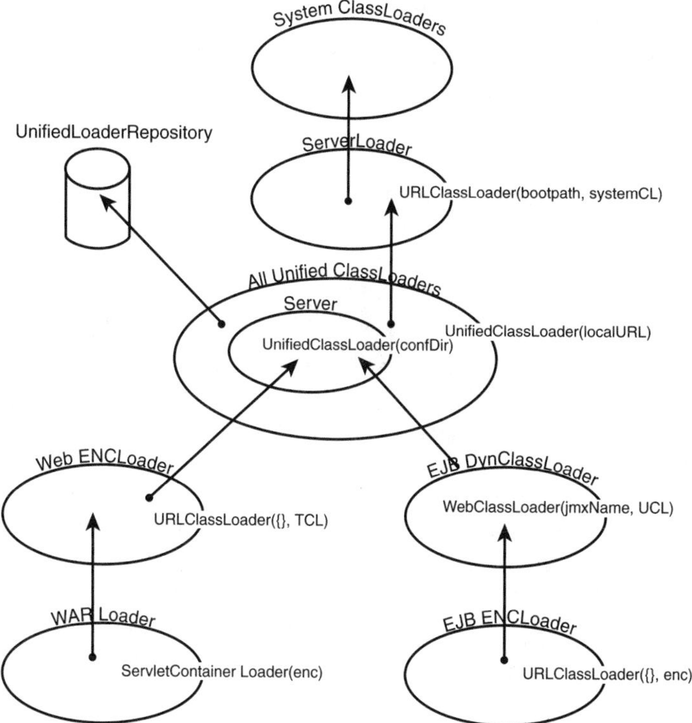

FIGURE 2.5 A complete class loader view.

The following points apply to Figure 2.5:

- **System ClassLoaders**—The System ClassLoaders node refers to either the thread context class loader (TCL) of the VM main thread or of the thread of the application that is loading the JBoss server, if it is embedded.

- **ServerLoader**—The ServerLoader node refers to a URLClassLoader that delegates to the System ClassLoaders and contains the following boot URLs:
    - All URLs referenced via the jboss.boot.library.list system property. These are path specifications relative to the libraryURL defined by the jboss.lib.url property. If there is no jboss.lib.url property specified, it defaults to jboss.home.url+/lib/. If there is no jboss.boot.library property specified, it defaults to jaxp.jar, log4j-boot.jar, jboss-common.jar, and jboss-system.jar.
    - The JAXP JAR, which is either crimson.jar or xerces.jar, depending on the -j option to the Main entry point. The default is crimson.jar.
    - The JBoss JMX JAR and GNU regex JAR, jboss-jmx.jar and gnu-regexp.jar.
    - The Oswego concurrency class's JAR, concurrent.jar.
    - Any JARs specified as libraries via -L command-line options.
    - Any other JARs or directories specified via -C command-line options.
- **Server**—The Server node represents a collection of UCLs created by the org.jboss.system.server.Server interface implementation. The default implementation creates UCLs for the patchDir entries as well as the server conf directory. The last UCL created is set as the JBoss main thread context class loader. This will be combined into a single UCL now that multiple URLs per UCL are supported.
- **All UnifiedClassLoader3s**—The All UnifiedClassLoader3 node represents the UCLs created by deployers. This covers EARs, JARs, WARs, SARs, and directories seen by the deployment scanner, as well as JARs referenced by their manifests and any nested deployment units they may contain. This is a flat namespace, and there should not be multiple instances of a class in different deployment JARs. If there are, only the first one loaded will be used, and the results may not be as expected. There is a mechanism for scoping visibility based on EAR deployment units, which is discussed earlier in this chapter, in the section "Scoping Classes." You can use this mechanism if you need to deploy multiple versions of a class in a given JBoss server.
- **EJB DynClassLoader**—The EJB DynClassLoader node is a subclass of URLClassLoader that is used to provide RMI dynamic class loading via the simple HTTP WebService. It specifies an empty URL[] and delegates to the TCL as its parent class loader. If the WebService is configured to allow system-level classes to be loaded, all classes in the UnifiedLoaderRepository3 as well as the system classpath are available via HTTP.
- **EJB ENCLoader**—The EJB ENCLoader node is a URLClassLoader that exists only to provide a unique context for an EJB deployment's java:comp JNDI context. It specifies an empty URL[] and delegates to the EJB DynClassLoader as its parent class loader.

- **`Web ENCLoader`**—The `Web ENCLoader` node is a `URLClassLoader` that exists only to provide a unique context for a web deployment's `java:comp` JNDI context. It specifies an empty `URL[]` and delegates to the TCL as its parent class loader.
- **`WAR Loader`**—The `WAR Loader` is a servlet container-specific class loader that delegates to the `Web ENCLoader` as its parent class loader. The default behavior is to load from its parent class loader and then the WAR `WEB-INF` classes and `lib` directories. If the servlet 2.3 class-loading model is enabled, it will first load from its `WEB-INF` directories and then the parent class loader.

In its current form, there are some advantages and disadvantages to the JBoss class-loading architecture. Advantages include the following:

- Classes do not need to be replicated across deployment units in order to have access to them.
- Many future possibilities including novel partitioning of the repositories into domains, dependency and conflict detection, and so on.

Disadvantages include the following:

- Existing deployments may need to be repackaged to avoid duplication of classes. Duplication of classes in a loader repository can lead to class cast exceptions and linkage errors, depending on how the classes are loaded.
- Deployments that depend on different versions of a given class need to be isolated in separate EARs, and a unique `HeirarchicalLoaderRepository3` needs to be defined, using a `jboss-app.xml` descriptor.

JBoss XMBeans

XMBeans are the JBoss JMX implementation version of the JMX model MBean. XMBeans have the richness of the dynamic MBean metadata without the tedious programming required by a direct implementation of the `DynamicMBean` interface. The JBoss model MBean implementation allows you to specify the management interface of a component through an XML descriptor, hence the X in XMBean. In addition to providing a simple mechanism for describing the metadata required for a dynamic MBean, XMBeans also allow for the specification of attribute persistence, caching behavior, and even advanced customizations such as the MBean implementation interceptors. The high-level elements of the `jboss_xmbean_1_2.dtd` for the XMBean descriptor are shown in Figure 2.6.

The `mbean` element is the root element of the document containing the required elements for describing the management interface of one MBean (constructors, attributes, operations, and notifications). It also includes an optional `description` element, which can be used to describe the purpose of the MBean, as well as an optional `descriptors` element, which allows for persistence policy specification, attribute caching, and so on.

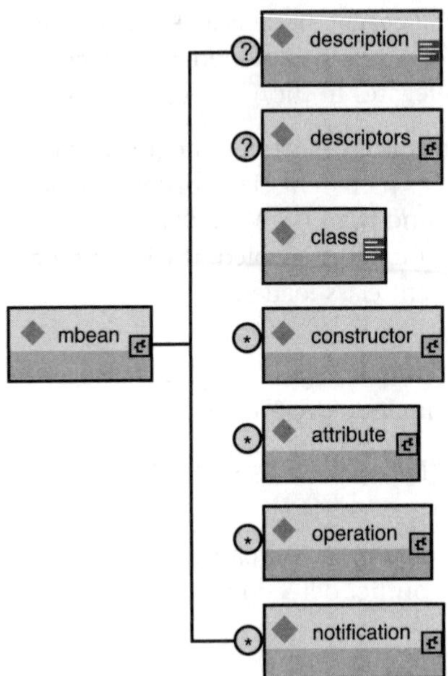

FIGURE 2.6 An overview of the JBoss 1.0 XMBean DTD (`jboss_xmbean_1_2.dtd`).

Descriptors

The `descriptors` element contains all the descriptors for a containing element, as subelements. The descriptors suggested in the JMX specification as well as those used by JBoss have predefined elements and attributes, whereas custom descriptors have a generic descriptor element with the name and value attributes shown in Figure 2.7.

The key `descriptors` child elements include the following:

- **`interceptors`**—The `interceptors` element specifies a customized stack of interceptors that will be used in place of the default stack. Currently, this is used only when specified at the MBean level, but it could define a custom attribute or operation-level interceptor stack in the future. The content of the `interceptors` element specifies a custom interceptor stack. If no `interceptors` element is specified, the standard `ModelMBean` interceptors will be used. These are the standard interceptors:
  - `org.jboss.mx.interceptor.PersistenceInterceptor`
  - `org.jboss.mx.interceptor.MBeanAttributeInterceptor`
  - `org.jboss.mx.interceptor.ObjectReferenceInterceptor`

  When specifying a custom interceptor stack, you typically include the standard interceptors, along with your own, unless you are replacing the corresponding standard interceptor.

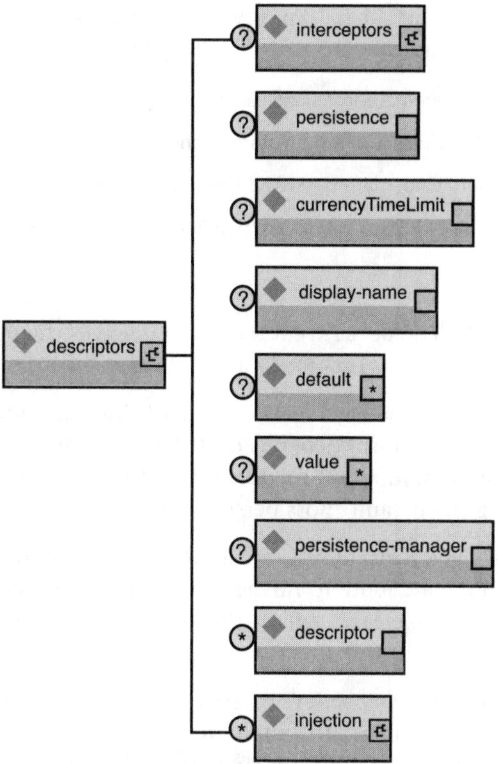

FIGURE 2.7 The `descriptors` element content model.

Each `interceptor` element content value specifies the fully qualified classname of the interceptor implementation. The class must implement the `org.jboss.mx.interceptor.Interceptor` interface. The interceptor class must also have either a `no-arg` constructor or a constructor that accepts a `javax.management.MBeanInfo`.

The `interceptor` elements may have any number of attributes that correspond to JavaBeans-style properties on the interceptor class implementation. For each `interceptor` element attribute specified, the interceptor class is queried for a matching setter method. The attribute value is converted to the true type of the interceptor class property, using the `java.beans.PropertyEditor` associated with the type. It is an error to specify an attribute for which there is no setter or `PropertyEditor`.

- **`persistence`**—The `persistence` element allows the specification of the `persistPolicy`, `persistPeriod`, `persistLocation`, and `persistName` persistence attributes suggested by the JMX specification. The following are the persistence element attributes:

  - **persistPolicy**—The persistPolicy attribute defines when attributes should be persisted, and its value must be one of the following:

    Never—Attribute values are transient values that are never persisted.

    OnUpdate—Attribute values are persisted whenever they are updated.

    OnTimer—Attribute values are persisted based on the time given by persistPeriod.

    NoMoreOftenThan—Attribute values are persisted when updated but no more often than persistPeriod.

  - **persistPeriod**—The persistPeriod attribute gives the update frequency in milliseconds if the persistPolicy attribute is NoMoreOftenThan or OnTimer.
  - **persistLocation**—The persistLocation attribute specifies the location of the persistence store. Its form depends on the JMX persistence implementation. Currently, this should refer to a directory into which the attributes will be serialized if using the default JBoss persistence manager.
  - **persistName**—The persistName attribute can be used in conjunction with the persistLocation attribute to further qualify the persistent store location. For a directory persistLocation, persistName specifies the file to which the attributes are stored within the directory.
- **currencyTimeLimit**—The currencyTimeLimit element specifies the time in seconds for which a cached value of an attribute remains valid. Its value attribute gives the time in seconds. A value of 0 indicates that an attribute value should always be retrieved from the MBean and never cached. A value of -1 indicates that a cache value is always valid.
- **display-name**—The display-name element specifies the human-friendly name of an item.
- **default**—The default element specifies a default value to use when a field has not been set. Note that this value is not written to the MBean on startup, as is the case with the jboss-service.xml attribute element content value. Rather, the default value is used only if there is no attribute accessor defined and there is no value element defined.
- **value**—The value element specifies a management attribute's current value. Unlike the default element, the value element is written through to the MBean on startup, provided that there is a setter method available.
- **persistence-manager**—The persistence-manager element gives the name of a class to use as the persistence manager. The value attribute specifies the classname that supplies the org.jboss.mx.persistence.PersistenceManager interface implementation. The only implementation currently supplied by JBoss is org.jboss.mx.persistence.ObjectStreamPersistenceManager, which serializes the ModelMBeanInfo content to a file by using Java serialization.

- **descriptor**—The descriptor element specifies an arbitrary descriptor not known to JBoss. Its name attribute specifies the type of the descriptor, and its value attribute specifies the descriptor value. The descriptor element allows for the attachment of arbitrary management metadata.
- **injection**—The injection element describes an injection point for receiving information from the microkernel. Each injection point specifies the type and the set method to use to inject the information into the resource. The injection element supports these type attributes:
    - **id**—The id attribute specifies the injection point type. These are the current injection point types:

      MBeanServerType—An MBeanServerType injection point receives a reference to the MBeanServer that the XMBean is registered with.

      MBeanInfoType—An MBeanInfoType injection point receives a reference to the XMBean ModelMBeanInfo metadata.

      ObjectNameType—The ObjectName injection point receives the ObjectName that the XMBean is registered under.
    - **setMethod**—The setMethod attribute gives the name of the method used to set the injection value on the resource. The set method should accept values of the type corresponding to the injection point type.

Note that any of the constructor, attribute, operation, or notification elements may have a descriptors element to specify the specification-defined descriptors as well as arbitrary extension descriptor settings.

The Management Class

The class element specifies the fully qualified name of the managed object whose management interface is described by the XMBean descriptor.

The Constructors

The constructor element(s) specifies the constructors available for creating an instance of the managed object. The constructor element and its content model are shown in Figure 2.8.

These are the key child elements:

- **description**—This element provides a description of the constructor.
- **name**—This element specifies the name of the constructor, which must be the same as the implementation class.
- **parameter**—The parameter element describes a constructor parameter. The parameter element has the following attributes:
    - **description**—An optional description of the parameter.
    - **name**—The required variable name of the parameter.

- **type**—The required fully qualified classname of the parameter type.

- **descriptors**—This element specifies any descriptors to associate with the constructor metadata.

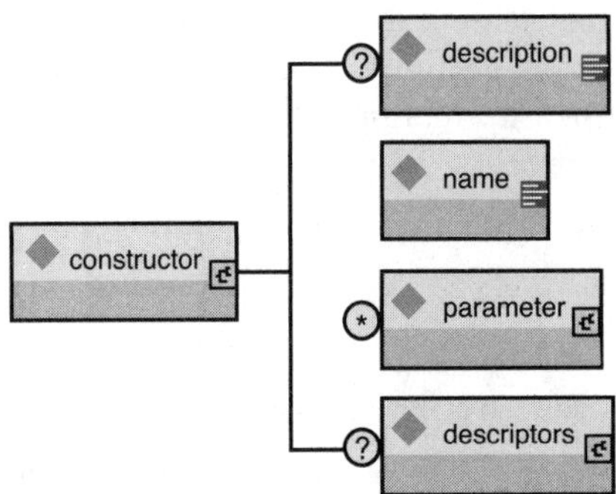

FIGURE 2.8 The XMBean `constructor` element and its content model.

The Attributes

The `attribute` element(s) specifies the management attributes exposed by the MBean. The `attribute` element and its content model are shown in Figure 2.9.

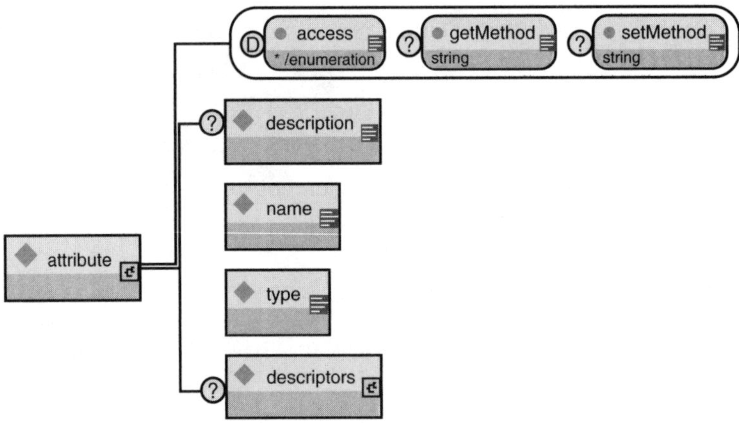

FIGURE 2.9 The XMBean `attribute` element and its content model.

The `attribute` element attributes include the following:

- **access**—The optional `access` attribute defines the read/write access modes of an attribute. It must be one of the following:
    - **read-only**—The attribute may only be read.
    - **write-only**—The attribute may only be written.

- **`read-write`**—The attribute is both readable and writable. This is the implied default.

- **`getMethod`**—The `getMethod` attribute defines the name of the method that reads the named attribute. This must be specified if the managed attribute should be obtained from the MBean instance.
- **`setMethod`**—The `setMethod` attribute defines the name of the method that writes the named attribute. This must be specified if the managed attribute should be obtained from the MBean instance. The key child elements of the `attribute` element include the following:
  - **`description`**—A description of the attribute.
  - **`name`**—The name of the attribute, as would be used in the `MBeanServer.getAttribute()` operation.
  - **`type`**—The fully qualified classname of the attribute type.
  - **`descriptors`**—Any additional descriptors that affect the attribute persistence, caching, default value, and so on.

The Operations

The management operations exposed by the XMBean are specified via one or more operation elements. The `operation` element and its content model are shown in Figure 2.10.

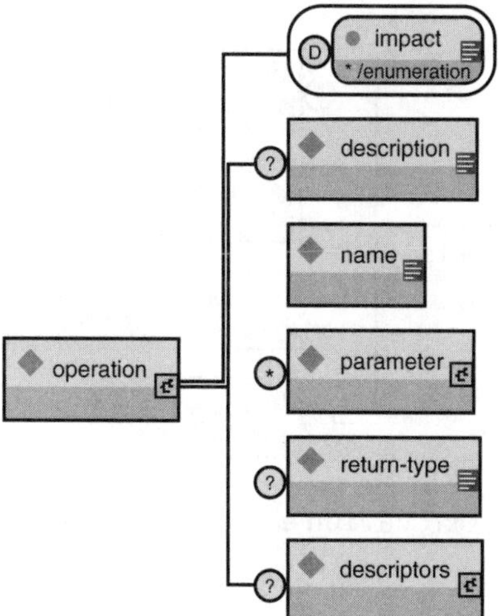

FIGURE 2.10 The XMBean `operation` element and its content model.

The `impact` attribute defines the impact of executing the operation and must be one of the following:

- **ACTION**—The operation changes the state of the MBean component (write operation).
- **INFO**—The operation should not alter the state of the MBean component (read operation).
- **ACTION_INFO**—The operation behaves like a read/write operation.

These are the child elements:

- **description**—This element specifies a human-readable description of the operation.
- **name**—This element contains the operation's name.
- **parameter**—This element describes the operation's signature.
- **return-type**—This element contains a fully qualified classname of the return type from this operation. If it is not specified, it defaults to void.
- **descriptors**—This element specifies any descriptors to associate with the operation metadata.

Notifications

The `notification` element(s) describes the management notifications that may be emitted by the XMBean. The `notification` element and its content model are shown in Figure 2.11.

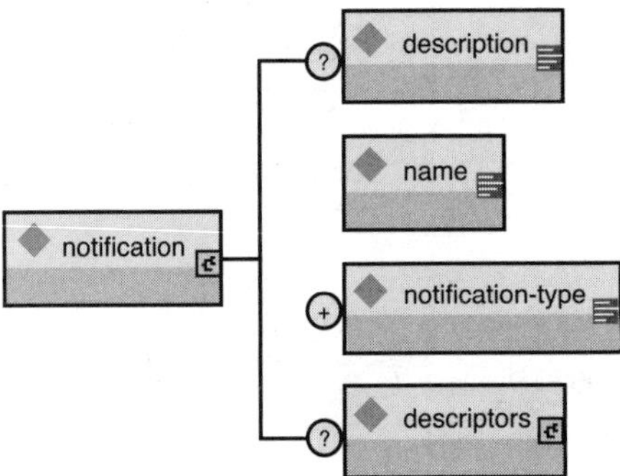

FIGURE 2.11 The XMBean `notification` element and content model.

These are the child elements:

- **description**—This element gives a human-readable description of the notification.
- **name**—This element contains the fully qualified name of the notification class.

- **`notification-type`**—This element contains the dot-separated notification type string.
- **`descriptors`**—This element specifies any descriptors to associate with the notification metadata.

Connecting to the JMX Server

JBoss includes adaptors that allow access to the JMX MBeanServer from outside the JBoss server VM. The current adaptors include HTML, an RMI interface, and an EJB.

Inspecting the Server: The JMX Console Web Application

JBoss comes with its own implementation of a JMX HTML adaptor that allows you to view the server's MBeans, using a standard web browser. The default URL for the console web application is http://localhost:8080/jmx-console/. If you browse to this location, you will see something similar to what is presented in Figure 2.12.

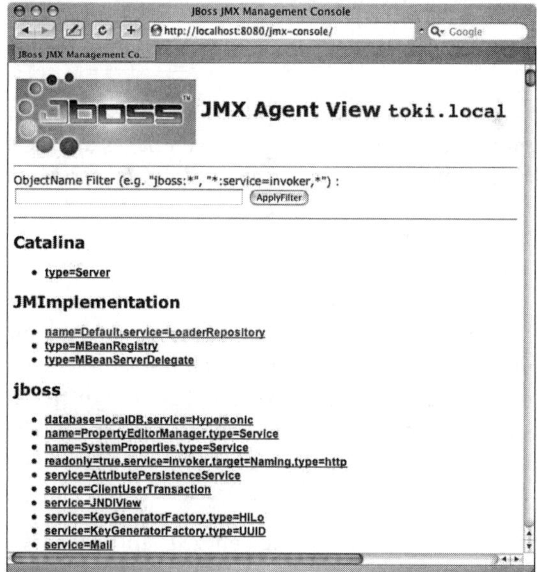

FIGURE 2.12 The JBoss JMX Console web application agent view.

The top view is called the *agent view*, and it provides a listing of all MBeans registered with the `MBeanServer`, sorted by the domain portion of the MBean's `ObjectName`. Under each domain you can see the MBeans that are in that domain. When you select one of the MBeans, you are taken to the MBean view, where you can view and edit an MBean's attributes as well as invoke operations. As an example, Figure 2.13 shows the MBean view for the `jboss.system:type=Server` MBean.

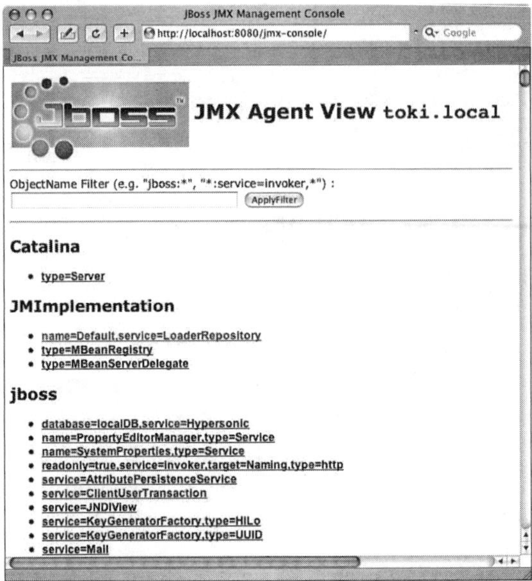

FIGURE 2.13 The MBean view for the `jboss.system:type=Server` MBean.

The source code for the JMX Console web application is located in the `varia` module, under the `src/ main/org/jboss/jmx` directory. Its web pages are located under `varia/src/resources/jmx`. The application is a simple MVC servlet with JSP views that utilize the MBeanServer.

Securing the JMX Console

Because the JMX Console web application is just a standard servlet, it can be secured using standard J2EE role-based security. The `jmx-console.war` is deployed as an unpacked WAR that includes template settings for quickly enabling simple username- and password-based access restrictions. If you look at the `jmx-console.war` in the `server/default/deploy` directory, you will find the `web.xml` and `jboss-web.xml` descriptors in the `WEB-INF` directory and `jmx-console-roles.properties` and `jmx-console-users.properties` files under `WEB-INF/classes`.

By uncommenting the security sections of the `web.xml` and `jboss-web.xml` descriptors, as shown in Listing 2.10 and Listing 2.11, you enable HTTP basic authentication that restricts access to the JMX Console application to the user `admin` with password `admin`. The username and password are determined by the `admin=admin` line in the `jmx-console-users.properties` file.

LISTING 2.10 The `jmx-console.war` `web.xml` Descriptors, with the Security Elements Uncommented

```
<?xml version="1.0"?>
<!DOCTYPE web-app PUBLIC
        "-//Sun Microsystems, Inc.//DTD Web Application 2.3//EN"
```

LISTING 2.10 Continued

```
        "http://java.sun.com/dtd/web-app_2_3.dtd">
<web-app>
    <!-- ... -->

    <!-- A security constraint that restricts access to the HTML JMX console
         to users with the role JBossAdmin. Edit the roles to what you want and
         uncomment the WEB-INF/jboss-web.xml/security-domain element to enable
         secured access to the HTML JMX console.
    -->
    <security-constraint>
        <web-resource-collection>
            <web-resource-name>HtmlAdaptor</web-resource-name>
            <description> An example security config that only allows users with
                the role JBossAdmin to access the HTML JMX console web
                application </description>
            <url-pattern>/*</url-pattern>
            <http-method>GET</http-method>
            <http-method>POST</http-method>
        </web-resource-collection>
        <auth-constraint>
            <role-name>JBossAdmin</role-name>
        </auth-constraint>
    </security-constraint>
    <login-config>
        <auth-method>BASIC</auth-method>
        <realm-name>JBoss JMX Console</realm-name>
    </login-config>
    <security-role>
        <role-name>JBossAdmin</role-name>
    </security-role>
</web-app>
```

LISTING 2.11 The `jmx-console.war` `jboss-web.xml` Descriptors, with the Security Elements Uncommented

```
<?xml version="1.0" encoding="UTF-8"?>
<!DOCTYPE jboss-web
    PUBLIC "-//JBoss//DTD Web Application 2.3//EN"
    "http://www.jboss.org/j2ee/dtd/jboss-web_3_0.dtd">
<jboss-web>
    <!--
        Uncomment the security-domain to enable security. You will
        need to edit the htmladaptor login configuration to set up the
        login modules used to authenticate users.
```

LISTING 2.11 Continued

```
    -->
    <security-domain>java:/jaas/jmx-console</security-domain>
</jboss-web>
```

Make these changes to uncomment the security code, and then when you try to access the JMX Console URL, you will see a dialog similar to the one shown in Figure 2.14.

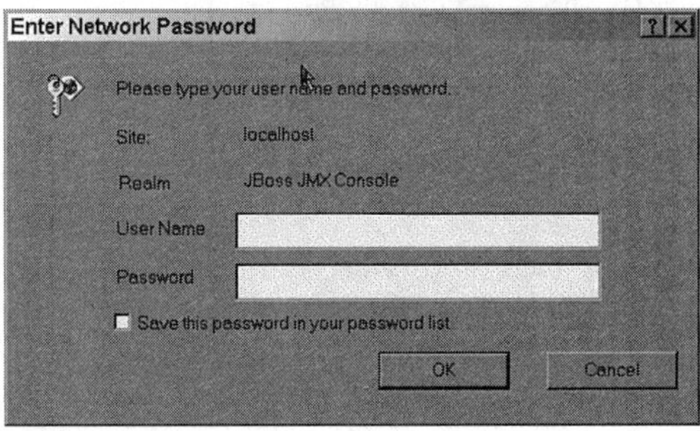

FIGURE 2.14 The JMX Console basic HTTP login dialog.

By default JBoss uses properties files for securing access to the JMX Console application. To see how to better configure the security settings of web applications, see Chapter 8, "Security on JBoss."

Connecting to JMX Using RMI

JBoss supplies an RMI interface for connecting to the JMX MBeanServer. This interface is `org.jboss.jmx.adaptor.rmi.RMIAdaptor`. The `RMIAdaptor` interface is bound into JNDI in the default location `jmx/invoker/RMIAdaptor`, as well as `jmx/rmi/RMIAdaptor` for backward compatibility with older clients.

Listing 2.12 shows a client that makes use of the `RMIAdaptor` interface to query the `MBeanInfo` for the `JNDIView` MBean. It also invokes the MBean's `list(boolean)` method and displays the result.

LISTING 2.12 A JMX Client That Uses the `RMIAdaptor` Interface

```
public class JMXBrowser
{
    /**
     * @param args the command line arguments
     */
    public static void main(String[] args) throws Exception
    {
        InitialContext ic = new InitialContext();
```

LISTING 2.12 Continued

```
        RMIAdaptor server = (RMIAdaptor) ic.lookup("jmx/invoker/RMIAdaptor");

        // Get the MBeanInfo for the JNDIView MBean
        ObjectName name = new ObjectName("jboss:service=JNDIView");
        MBeanInfo  info = server.getMBeanInfo(name);
        System.out.println("JNDIView Class: " + info.getClassName());

        MBeanOperationInfo[] opInfo = info.getOperations();
        System.out.println("JNDIView Operations: ");
        for(int o = 0; o < opInfo.length; o ++) {
            MBeanOperationInfo op = opInfo[o];

            String returnType = op.getReturnType();
            String opName     = op.getName();
            System.out.print(" + " + returnType + " " + opName + "(");

            MBeanParameterInfo[] params = op.getSignature();
            for(int p = 0; p < params.length; p++)  {
                MBeanParameterInfo paramInfo = params[p];

                String pname = paramInfo.getName();
                String type  = paramInfo.getType();

                if (pname.equals(type)) {
                    System.out.print(type);
                } else {
                    System.out.print(type + " " + name);
                }

                if (p < params.length-1) {
                    System.out.print(',');
                }
            }
            System.out.println(")");
        }

        // Invoke the list(boolean) op
        String[] sig    = {"boolean"};
        Object[] opArgs = {Boolean.TRUE};
        Object   result = server.invoke(name, "list", opArgs, sig);

        System.out.println("JNDIView.list(true) output:\n"+result);
    }
}
```

To test the client access using the RMIAdaptor, you should run the following:

```
[examples]$ ant -Dchap=chap2 -Dex=4 run-example
...

run-example4:
     [java] JNDIView Class: org.jboss.mx.modelmbean.XMBean
     [java] JNDIView Operations:
     [java]  + java.lang.String list(boolean jboss:service=JNDIView)
     [java]  + java.lang.String listXML()
     [java]  + void create()
     [java]  + void start()
     [java]  + void stop()
     [java]  + void destroy()
     [java]  + void jbossInternalLifecycle(java.lang.String jboss:service=
➥JNDIView)
     [java]  + java.lang.String getName()
     [java]  + int getState()
     [java]  + java.lang.String getStateString()
     [java] JNDIView.list(true) output:
     [java] <h1>java: Namespace</h1>
     [java] <pre>
     [java]   +- XAConnectionFactory (class: org.jboss.mq.SpyXAConnectionFactory)
     [java]   +- DefaultDS (class: javax.sql.DataSource)
     [java]   +- SecurityProxyFactory
➥(class: org.jboss.security.SubjectSecurityProxyFactory)
     [java]   +- DefaultJMSProvider
➥(class: org.jboss.jms.jndi.JNDIProviderAdapter)
     [java]   +- comp (class: javax.naming.Context)
     [java]   +- JmsXA
➥(class: org.jboss.resource.adapter.jms.JmsConnectionFactoryImpl)
     [java]   +- ConnectionFactory (class: org.jboss.mq.SpyConnectionFactory)
     [java]   +- jaas (class: javax.naming.Context)
     [java]   ¦   +- JmsXARealm
➥(class: org.jboss.security.plugins.SecurityDomainContext)
     [java]   ¦   +- jbossmq
➥(class: org.jboss.security.plugins.SecurityDomainContext)
     [java]   ¦   +- HsqlDbRealm
➥(class: org.jboss.security.plugins.SecurityDomainContext)
     [java]   +- timedCacheFactory (class: javax.naming.Context)
     [java] Failed to lookup: timedCacheFactory, errmsg=null
     [java]   +- TransactionPropagationContextExporter (class: org.jboss.tm.Trans-
actionPropagationContextFactory)
     [java]   +- StdJMSPool (class: org.jboss.jms.asf.StdServerSessionPoolFactory)
     [java]   +- Mail (class: javax.mail.Session)
```

```
     [java]   +- TransactionPropagationContextImporter (class: org.jboss.tm.Trans-
actionPropagationContextImporter)
     [java]   +- TransactionManager (class: org.jboss.tm.TxManager)
     [java] </pre>
     [java] <h1>Global JNDI Namespace</h1>
     [java] <pre>
     [java]   +- XAConnectionFactory (class: org.jboss.mq.SpyXAConnectionFactory)
     [java]   +- UIL2ConnectionFactory[link -> ConnectionFactory]
➥(class: javax.naming.LinkRef)
     [java]   +- UserTransactionSessionFactory (proxy: $Proxy11 implements
➥interface org.jboss.tm.usertx.interfaces.UserTransactionSessionFactory)
     [java]   +- HTTPConnectionFactory (class: org.jboss.mq.SpyConnectionFactory)
     [java]   +- console (class: org.jnp.interfaces.NamingContext)
     [java]   |   +- PluginManager (proxy: $Proxy36 implements interface
org.jboss.console.manager.PluginManagerMBean)
     [java]   +- UIL2XAConnectionFactory[link -> XAConnectionFactory]
➥(class: javax.naming.LinkRef)
     [java]   +- UUIDKeyGeneratorFactory (class: org.jboss.ejb.plugins.keygenera-
tor.uuid.UUIDKeyGeneratorFactory)
     [java]   +- HTTPXAConnectionFactory
➥(class: org.jboss.mq.SpyXAConnectionFactory)
     [java]   +- topic (class: org.jnp.interfaces.NamingContext)
     [java]   |   +- testDurableTopic (class: org.jboss.mq.SpyTopic)
     [java]   |   +- testTopic (class: org.jboss.mq.SpyTopic)
     [java]   |   +- securedTopic (class: org.jboss.mq.SpyTopic)
     [java]   +- queue (class: org.jnp.interfaces.NamingContext)
     [java]   |   +- A (class: org.jboss.mq.SpyQueue)
     [java]   |   +- testQueue (class: org.jboss.mq.SpyQueue)
     [java]   |   +- ex (class: org.jboss.mq.SpyQueue)
     [java]   |   +- DLQ (class: org.jboss.mq.SpyQueue)
     [java]   |   +- D (class: org.jboss.mq.SpyQueue)
     [java]   |   +- C (class: org.jboss.mq.SpyQueue)
     [java]   |   +- B (class: org.jboss.mq.SpyQueue)
     [java]   +- ConnectionFactory (class: org.jboss.mq.SpyConnectionFactory)
     [java]   +- UserTransaction
➥(class: org.jboss.tm.usertx.client.ClientUserTransaction)
     [java]   +- jmx (class: org.jnp.interfaces.NamingContext)
     [java]   |   +- invoker (class: org.jnp.interfaces.NamingContext)
     [java]   |   |   +- RMIAdaptor (proxy: $Proxy35 implements interface
➥org.jboss.jmx.adaptor.rmi.RMIAdaptor,
➥interface org.jboss.jmx.adaptor.rmi.RMIAdaptorExt)
     [java]   |   +- rmi (class: org.jnp.interfaces.NamingContext)
     [java]   |   |   +- RMIAdaptor[link -> jmx/invoker/RMIAdaptor]
➥(class: javax.naming.LinkRef)
     [java]   +- HiLoKeyGeneratorFactory (class: org.jboss.ejb.plugins.keygenera-
tor.hilo.HiLoKeyGeneratorFactory)
```

```
     [java]    +- UILXAConnectionFactory[link -> XAConnectionFactory]
➥(class: javax.naming.LinkRef)
     [java]    +- UILConnectionFactory[link -> ConnectionFactory]
➥(class: javax.naming.LinkRef)
     [java] </pre>
```

Command-Line Access to JMX

JBoss provides a simple command-line tool that allows for interaction with a remote JMX server instance. This tool is called *Twiddle* (for twiddling bits via JMX) and is located in the `bin` directory of the distribution. Twiddle is a command execution tool, not a general command shell. It is run using either the `twiddle.sh` script or the `twiddle.bat` script; and passing in a `-h(--help)` argument provides the basic syntax, and `--help-commands` shows what you can do with the tool:

```
[bin]$ ./twiddle.sh -h
A JMX client to 'twiddle' with a remote JBoss server.

usage: twiddle.sh [options] <command> [command_arguments]

options:
    -h, --help                  Show this help message
        --help-commands         Show a list of commands
    -H=<command>                Show command specific help
    -c=command.properties       Specify the command.properties file to use
    -D<name>[=<value>]          Set a system property
    --                          Stop processing options
    -s, --server=<url>          The JNDI URL of the remote server
    -a, --adapter=<name>        The JNDI name of the RMI adapter to use
    -q, --quiet                 Be somewhat more quiet
```

Connecting Twiddle to a Remote Server

By default the `twiddle` command connects to the local host at port 1099 to look up the default `jmx/rmi/RMIAdaptor` binding of the `RMIAdaptor` service as the connector for communicating with the JMX server. To connect to a different server/port combination, you can use the `-s (--server)` option:

```
[bin]$ ./twiddle.sh -s toki serverinfo -d jboss
[bin]$ ./twiddle.sh -s toki:1099 serverinfo -d jboss
```

To connect using a different `RMIAdaptor` binding, you use the `-a (--adapter)` option:

```
[bin]$ ./twiddle.sh -s toki -a jmx/rmi/RMIAdaptor serverinfo -d jboss
```

Sample Twiddle Command Usage

To access basic information about a server, you use the `serverinfo` command:

```
[bin]$ ./twiddle.sh -H serverinfo
Get information about the MBean server

usage: serverinfo [options]

options:
    -d, --domain    Get the default domain
    -c, --count     Get the MBean count
    -l, --list      List the MBeans
    --              Stop processing options
[bin]$ ./twiddle.sh --server=toki serverinfo --count
460
[bin]$ ./twiddle.sh --server=toki serverinfo --domain
jboss
```

To query the server for the name of MBeans matching a pattern, you use the `query` command:

```
[bin]$ ./twiddle.sh -H query
Query the server for a list of matching MBeans

usage: query [options] <query>
options:
    -c, --count    Display the matching MBean count
    --             Stop processing options
Examples:
 query all mbeans: query '*:*'
 query all mbeans in the jboss.j2ee domain: query 'jboss.j2ee:*'
[bin]$ ./twiddle.sh -s toki query 'jboss:service=invoker,*'
jboss:readonly=true,service=invoker,target=Naming,type=http
jboss:service=invoker,type=jrmp
jboss:service=invoker,type=local
jboss:service=invoker,type=pooled
jboss:service=invoker,type=http
jboss:service=invoker,target=Naming,type=http
```

To get the attributes of an MBean, you use the `get` command:

```
[bin]$ ./twiddle.sh -H get
Get the values of one or more MBean attributes

usage: get [options] <name> [<attr>+]
  If no attribute names are given all readable attributes are retrieved
options:
    --noprefix    Do not display attribute name prefixes
    --            Stop processing options
```

```
[bin]$ ./twiddle.sh get jboss:service=invoker,type=jrmp RMIObjectPort StateString
RMIObjectPort=4444
StateString=Started
[bin]$ ./twiddle.sh get jboss:service=invoker,type=jrmp
ServerAddress=0.0.0.0
RMIClientSocketFactoryBean=null
StateString=Started
State=3
RMIServerSocketFactoryBean=org.jboss.net.sockets.DefaultSocketFactory@ad093076
EnableClassCaching=false
SecurityDomain=null
RMIServerSocketFactory=null
Backlog=200
RMIObjectPort=4444
Name=JRMPInvoker
RMIClientSocketFactory=null
```

To query the MBeanInfo for an MBean, you use the `info` command:

```
[bin]$ ./twiddle.sh -H info
Get the metadata for an MBean

usage: info <mbean-name>
  Use '*' to query for all attributes
[bin]$ Description: Management Bean.
+++ Attributes:
 Name: ServerAddress
 Type: java.lang.String
 Access: rw
 Name: RMIClientSocketFactoryBean
 Type: java.rmi.server.RMIClientSocketFactory
 Access: rw
 Name: StateString
 Type: java.lang.String
 Access: r-
 Name: State
 Type: int
 Access: r-
 Name: RMIServerSocketFactoryBean
 Type: java.rmi.server.RMIServerSocketFactory
 Access: rw
 Name: EnableClassCaching
 Type: boolean
 Access: rw
 Name: SecurityDomain
 Type: java.lang.String
```

```
 Access: rw
 Name: RMIServerSocketFactory
 Type: java.lang.String
 Access: rw
 Name: Backlog
 Type: int
 Access: rw
 Name: RMIObjectPort
 Type: int
 Access: rw
 Name: Name
 Type: java.lang.String
 Access: r-
 Name: RMIClientSocketFactory
 Type: java.lang.String
 Access: rw
+++ Operations:
 void start()
 void jbossInternalLifecycle(java.lang.String java.lang.String)
 void create()
 void stop()
 void destroy()
```

To invoke an operation on an MBean, you use the invoker command:

```
[bin]$ ./twiddle.sh -H invoke
Invoke an operation on an MBean

usage: invoke [options] <query> <operation> (<arg>)*

options:
    -q, --query-type[=<type>]    Treat object name as a query
    --                           Stop processing options

query type:
    f[irst]    Only invoke on the first matching name [default]
    a[ll]      Invoke on all matching names
[bin]$ ./twiddle.sh invoke jboss:service=JNDIView list true
<h1>java: Namespace</h1>
<pre>
  +- XAConnectionFactory (class: org.jboss.mq.SpyXAConnectionFactory)
  +- DefaultDS (class: javax.sql.DataSource)
  +- SecurityProxyFactory (class: org.jboss.security.SubjectSecurityProxyFactory)
  +- DefaultJMSProvider (class: org.jboss.jms.jndi.JNDIProviderAdapter)
  +- comp (class: javax.naming.Context)
  +- JmsXA (class: org.jboss.resource.adapter.jms.JmsConnectionFactoryImpl)
```

```
  +- ConnectionFactory (class: org.jboss.mq.SpyConnectionFactory)
  +- jaas (class: javax.naming.Context)
  |   +- JmsXARealm (class: org.jboss.security.plugins.SecurityDomainContext)
  |   +- jbossmq (class: org.jboss.security.plugins.SecurityDomainContext)
  |   +- HsqlDbRealm (class: org.jboss.security.plugins.SecurityDomainContext)
  +- timedCacheFactory (class: javax.naming.Context)
Failed to lookup: timedCacheFactory, errmsg=null
  +- TransactionPropagationContextExporter
➥(class: org.jboss.tm.TransactionPropagationContextFactory)
  +- StdJMSPool (class: org.jboss.jms.asf.StdServerSessionPoolFactory)
  +- Mail (class: javax.mail.Session)
  +- TransactionPropagationContextImporter
➥(class: org.jboss.tm.TransactionPropagationContextImporter)
  +- TransactionManager (class: org.jboss.tm.TxManager)
</pre>
<h1>Global JNDI Namespace</h1>
<pre>
  +- XAConnectionFactory (class: org.jboss.mq.SpyXAConnectionFactory)
  +- UIL2ConnectionFactory[link -> ConnectionFactory]
➥(class: javax.naming.LinkRef)
  +- UserTransactionSessionFactory (proxy: $Proxy11 implements interface
org.jboss.tm.usertx.interfaces.UserTransactionSessionFactory)
  +- HTTPConnectionFactory (class: org.jboss.mq.SpyConnectionFactory)
  +- console (class: org.jnp.interfaces.NamingContext)
  |   +- PluginManager (proxy: $Proxy36 implements
➥interface org.jboss.console.manager.PluginManagerMBean)
  +- UIL2XAConnectionFactory[link -> XAConnectionFactory]
➥(class: javax.naming.LinkRef)
  +- UUIDKeyGeneratorFactory (class:
➥org.jboss.ejb.plugins.keygenerator.uuid.UUIDKeyGeneratorFactory)
  +- HTTPXAConnectionFactory (class: org.jboss.mq.SpyXAConnectionFactory)
  +- topic (class: org.jnp.interfaces.NamingContext)
  |   +- testDurableTopic (class: org.jboss.mq.SpyTopic)
  |   +- testTopic (class: org.jboss.mq.SpyTopic)
  |   +- securedTopic (class: org.jboss.mq.SpyTopic)
  +- queue (class: org.jnp.interfaces.NamingContext)
  |   +- A (class: org.jboss.mq.SpyQueue)
  |   +- testQueue (class: org.jboss.mq.SpyQueue)
  |   +- ex (class: org.jboss.mq.SpyQueue)
  |   +- DLQ (class: org.jboss.mq.SpyQueue)
  |   +- D (class: org.jboss.mq.SpyQueue)
  |   +- C (class: org.jboss.mq.SpyQueue)
  |   +- B (class: org.jboss.mq.SpyQueue)
  +- ConnectionFactory (class: org.jboss.mq.SpyConnectionFactory)
  +- UserTransaction (class: org.jboss.tm.usertx.client.ClientUserTransaction)
```

```
  +- jmx (class: org.jnp.interfaces.NamingContext)
  |   +- invoker (class: org.jnp.interfaces.NamingContext)
  |   |   +- RMIAdaptor (proxy: $Proxy35 implements interface
➥org.jboss.jmx.adaptor.rmi.RMIAdaptor,
➥interface org.jboss.jmx.adaptor.rmi.RMIAdaptorExt)
  |   +- rmi (class: org.jnp.interfaces.NamingContext)
  |   |   +- RMIAdaptor[link -> jmx/invoker/RMIAdaptor]
➥(class: javax.naming.LinkRef)
  +- HiLoKeyGeneratorFactory (class:
➥org.jboss.ejb.plugins.keygenerator.hilo.HiLoKeyGeneratorFactory)
  +- UILXAConnectionFactory[link -> XAConnectionFactory]
➥(class: javax.naming.LinkRef)
  +- UILConnectionFactory[link -> ConnectionFactory] (class: javax.naming.LinkRef)
</pre>
```

Connecting to JMX Using Any Protocol

With the detached invokers and a somewhat generalized proxy factory capability, you can really talk to the JMX server by using the `InvokerAdaptorService` and a proxy factory service to expose an `RMIAdaptor` or similar interface over your protocol of choice. You'll learn about the detached invoker notion, along with proxy factories, later in this chapter, in the section "Remote Access to Services, Detached Invokers." See the section "A Detached Invoker Example, the `MBeanServer` Invoker Adaptor Service," later in this chapter, for an example of an invoker service that allows you to access the MBean server by using to the `RMIAdaptor` interface over any protocol for which a proxy factory service exists.

Using JMX as a Microkernel

When JBoss starts up, one of the first steps performed is to create an MBean server instance (`javax.management.MBeanServer`). The JMX MBean server in the JBoss architecture plays the role of a microkernel. All other manageable MBean components are plugged into JBoss by registering with the MBean server. In that sense, the kernel is only a framework, and not a source of actual functionality. The functionality is provided by MBeans, and in fact all major JBoss components are manageable MBeans interconnected through the MBean server.

The Startup Process

This section describes the JBoss server startup process. The following steps occur during the JBoss server startup sequence:

1. The run startup script initiates the boot sequence, using the `org.jboss.Main.main(String[])` method entry point.

2. The `Main.main` method creates a thread group named `jboss` and then starts a thread that belongs to this thread group. This thread invokes the `Main.boot` method.

3. The `Main.boot` method processes the `Main.main` arguments and then creates an `org.jboss.system.server.ServerLoader`, using the system properties along with any additional properties specified as arguments.

4. The XML parser libraries, `jboss-jmx.jar`,`concurrent.jar`, and extra libraries and classpaths given as arguments are registered with the `ServerLoader`.

5. The JBoss server instance is created, using the `ServerLoader.load(ClassLoader)` method, with the current thread context class loader passed in as the `ClassLoader` argument. The returned server instance is an implementation of the `org.jboss.system.server.Server` interface. The creation of the server instance entails the following:

   - A `java.net.URLClassLoader` is created with the URLs of the JARs and directories registered with the `ServerLoader`. This `URLClassLoader` uses the `ClassLoader` passed in as its parent, and it is pushed as the thread context class loader.

   - The classname of the implementation of the `Server` interface to use is determined by the `jboss.server.type` property. This defaults to `org.jboss.system.server.ServerImpl`.

   - The `Server` implementation class is loaded and instantiated, using its `no-arg` constructor. The thread context class loader present on entry into the `ServerLoader.load` method is restored, and the server instance is returned.

6. The server instance is initialized with the properties passed to the `ServerLoader` constructor, using the `Server.init(Properties)` method.

7. The server instance is then started using the `Server.start()` method. The default implementation performs the following tasks:

   - Sets the thread context class loader to the class loader used to load the `ServerImpl` class.

   - Creates an `MBeanServer` under the `jboss` domain, using the `MBeanServerFactory.createMBeanServer(String)` method.

   - Registers the `ServerImpl` and `ServerConfigImpl` MBeans with the MBean server.

   - Initializes the unified class loader repository to contain all JARs in the optional patch directory, as well as the server configuration file `conf` directory (for example, `server/default/conf`). For each JAR and directory, an `org.jboss.mx.loading.UnifiedClassLoader` is created and registered with the unified repository. One of these `UnifiedClassLoaders` is then set as the thread context class loader. This effectively makes all `UnifiedClassLoaders` available through the thread context class loader.

- The org.jboss.system.ServiceController MBean is created. ServiceController manages the JBoss MBean service's life cycle. We will discuss the JBoss MBean services notion in detail later in this chapter, in the section "JBoss MBean Services."
- The org.jboss.deployment.MainDeployer is created and started. MainDeployer manages deployment dependencies and directing deployments to the correct deployer.
- The org.jboss.deployment.JARDeployer is created and started. JARDeployer handles the deployment of JARs that are simple library JARs.
- The org.jboss.deployment.SARDeployer is created and started. SARDeployer handles the deployment of JBoss MBean services.
- The MainDeployer is invoked to deploy the services defined in the conf/jboss-service.xml of the current server file set.
- Restores the thread context class loader.

The JBoss server starts out as nothing more than a container for the JMX MBean server, and then it loads its personality based on the services defined in the jboss-service.xml MBean configuration file from the named configuration set passed to the server on the command line. Because MBeans define the functionality of a JBoss server instance, it is important to understand how the core JBoss MBeans are written and how you should integrate your existing services into JBoss by using MBeans. That is the topic of the next section.

JBoss MBean Services

As you have seen, JBoss relies on JMX to load in the MBean services that make up a given server instance's personality. All the bundled functionality provided with the standard JBoss distribution is based on MBeans. The best way to add services to the JBoss server is to write your own JMX MBeans.

There are two classes of MBeans: those that are independent of JBoss services and those that are dependent on JBoss services. MBeans that are independent of JBoss services are the trivial case. You can write them per the JMX specification and add them to a JBoss server by adding an mbean tag to the deploy/user-service.xml file. Writing an MBean that relies on a JBoss service such as naming requires you to follow the JBoss service pattern. The JBoss MBean service pattern consists of a set of life cycle operations that provide state change notifications. The notifications inform an MBean service when it can create, start, stop, and destroy itself. The management of the MBean service life cycle is the responsibility of three JBoss MBeans: SARDeployer, ServiceConfigurator, and ServiceController.

The SARDeployer MBean

JBoss manages the deployment of its MBean services via a custom MBean that loads an XML variation of the standard JMX MLet configuration file. This custom MBean is implemented in the `org.jboss.deployment.SARDeployer` class. The `SARDeployer` MBean is loaded when JBoss starts up, as part of the bootstrap process. The SAR acronym stands for *service archive.*

`SARDeployer` handles services archives. A service archive can be either a JAR that ends with a `.sar` suffix and contains a `META-INF/jboss-service.xml` descriptor or a standalone XML descriptor with a naming pattern that matches `*-service.xml`. The DTD for the service descriptor is `jboss-service_4.0.dtd` and is shown in Figure 2.15.

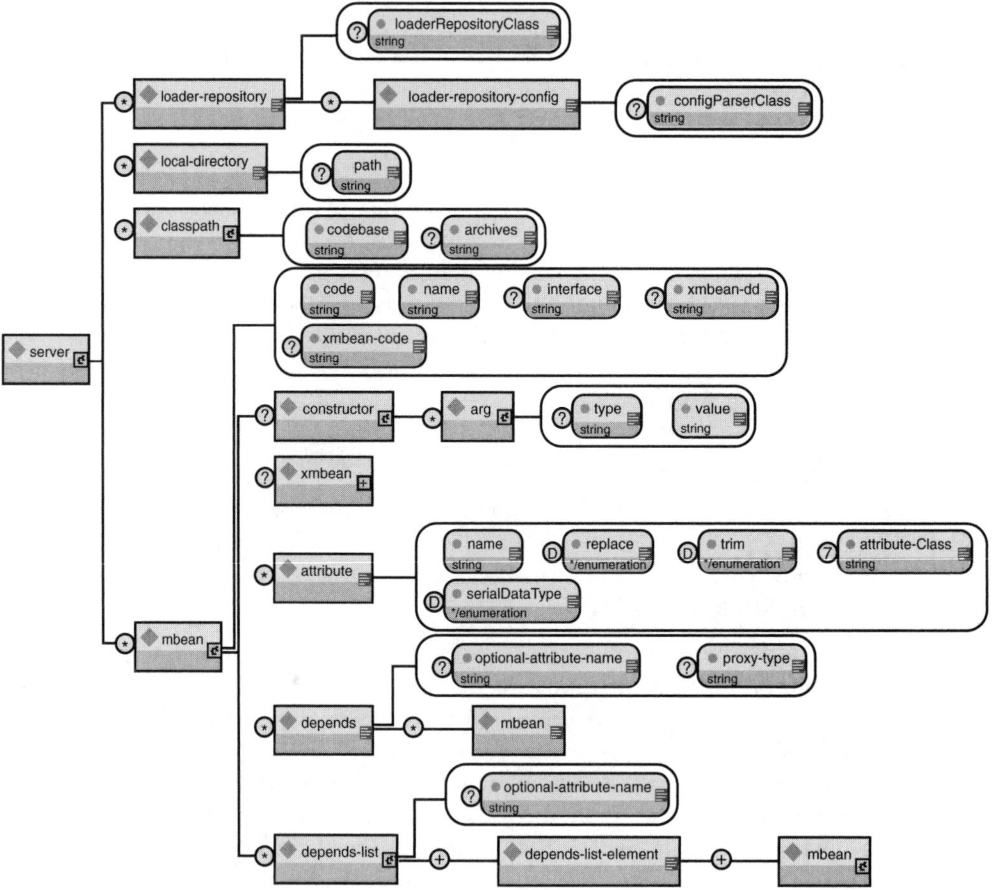

FIGURE 2.15 The DTD for the MBean service descriptor parsed by `SARDeployer`.

The following are the elements of the DTD:

- **`loader-repository`**—This element specifies the name of the `UnifiedLoaderRepository` MBean to use for the SAR to provide SAR-level scoping of classes deployed in the SAR. It is a unique JMX `ObjectName` string. It may also specify an arbitrary configuration by including a `loader-repository-config` element. The optional `loaderRepositoryClass` attribute specifies the fully qualified name of the loader repository implementation class. It defaults to `org.jboss.mx.loading.HeirachicalLoaderRepository3`.
- **`loader-repository-config`**—This optional element specifies an arbitrary configuration that may be used to configure the `loadRepositoryClass`. The optional `configParserClass` attribute gives the fully qualified name of the `org.jboss.mx.loading.LoaderRepositoryFactory.LoaderRepositoryConfigParser` implementation to use to parse the `loader-repository-config` content.
- **`local-directory`**—This element specifies a path within the deployment archive that should be copied to the `server/<config>/db` directory for use by the MBean. The `path` attribute is the name of an entry within the deployment archive.
- **`classpath`**—This element specifies one or more external JARs that should be deployed with the MBean(s). The optional `archives` attribute specifies a comma-separated list of the JAR names to load, or the `*` wildcard to signify that all JARs should be loaded. The wildcard works only with file URLs, and HTTP URLs if the web server supports the WebDAV protocol. The `codebase` attribute specifies the URL from which the JARs specified in the `archive` attribute should be loaded. If the `codebase` attribute is a path rather than a URL string, the full URL is built by treating the `codebase` value as a path relative to the JBoss distribution `server/<config>` directory. The order of JARs specified in the archives, as well as the ordering across multiple classpath elements, is used as the classpath ordering of the JARs. Therefore, if you have patches or inconsistent versions of classes that require a certain ordering, you should use this feature to ensure the correct ordering. Both the `codebase` and `archives` attribute values may reference a system property, using the pattern `${x}` to refer to replacement of the *x* system property.
- **`mbean`**—This element specifies an MBean service. The required `code` attribute gives the fully qualified name of the MBean implementation class. The required `name` attribute gives the JMX `ObjectName` of the MBean. The optional `xmbean-dd` attribute specifies the path to the XMBean resource if this MBean service uses the JBoss XMBean descriptor to define a model MBean management interface.
- **`constructor`**—The `constructor` element defines a non-default constructor to use when instantiating the MBean. The `arg` element specifies the constructor arguments in the order of the constructor signature. Each `arg` has a `type` attribute and a `value` attribute.
- **`attribute`**—Each attribute element specifies a name/value pair of the attribute of the MBean. The name of the attribute is given by the `name` attribute, and the

attribute element body gives the value. The body may be a text representation of the value or an arbitrary element and child elements, if the type of the MBean attribute is `org.w3c.dom.Element`. For text values, the text is converted to the attribute type by using the JavaBeans `java.beans.PropertyEditor` mechanism.

The text value of an attribute may reference a system property *x* by using the pattern `${x}`. In this case, the value of the attribute will be the result of `System.getProperty("x")`, or `null`, if no such property exists.

- **`server/mbean/depends` and `server/mbean/depends-list`**—These elements specify a dependency from the MBean, using the element to the MBean(s) named by the `depends` or `depends-list` element. Note that the dependency value can be another `mbean` element that defines a nested mbean.

When the `SARDeployer` is asked to deploy a service, it performs several steps. Figure 2.16 is a sequence diagram that shows the `init` through start phases of a service.

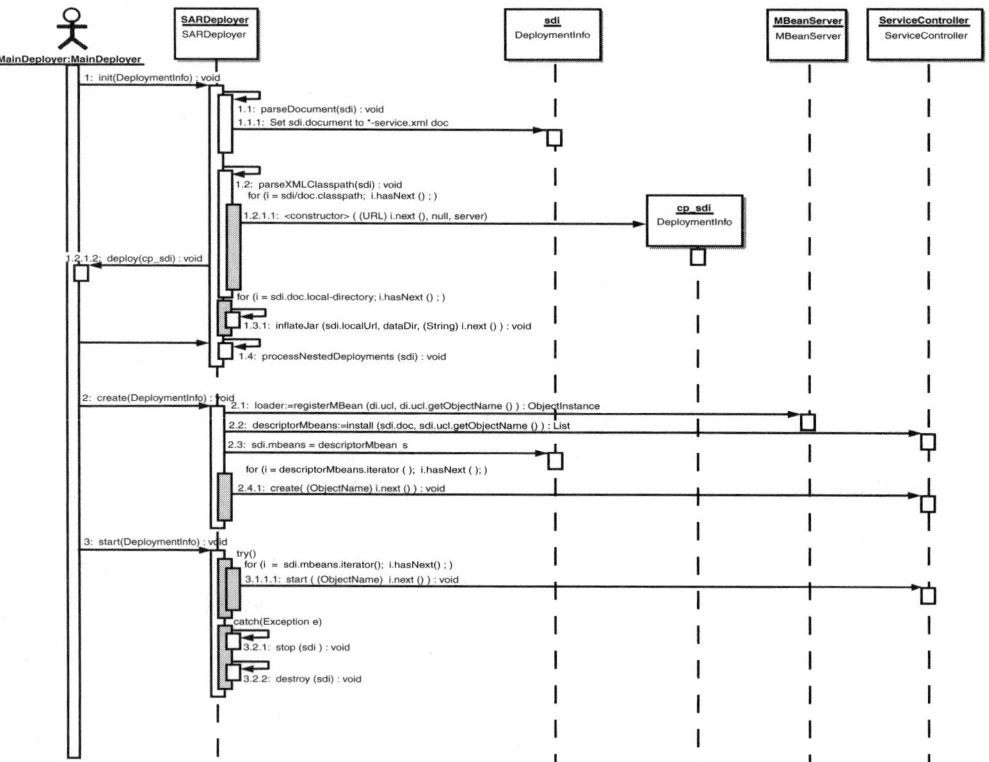

FIGURE 2.16 A sequence diagram highlighting the main activities performed by the `SARDeployer` to start a JBoss MBean service.

Figure 2.16 illustrates the following:

- **Methods prefixed with 1.1**—These methods correspond to the load and parse of the XML service descriptor.
- **Methods prefixed with 1.2**—These methods correspond to processing each classpath element in the service descriptor to create an independent deployment that makes the JAR or directory available through a `UnifiedClassLoader` registered with the unified loader repository.
- **Methods prefixed with 1.3**—These methods correspond to processing each `local-directory` element in the service descriptor. This makes a copy of the SAR elements specified in the `path` attribute to the `server/<config>/db` directory.
- **Method prefixed with 1.4**—These methods process each deployable unit nested in the service. A child deployment is created and added to the service deployment info subdeployment list.
- **Method prefixed with 2.1**—These methods mean that the `UnifiedClassLoader` of the SAR deployment unit is registered with the MBean server so that it can be used for loading the SAR MBeans.
- **Method prefixed with 2.2**—These methods mean that for each MBean element in the descriptor, create an instance and initialize its attributes with the values given in the service descriptor. This is done by calling the `ServiceController.install` method.
- **Method prefixed with 2.4.1**—These methods mean that for each MBean instance created, obtain its JMX `ObjectName` and ask the `ServiceController` to handle the creating step of the service life cycle. The `ServiceController` handles the dependencies of the MBean service. Only if the service's dependencies are satisfied is the service's create method invoked.
- **Methods prefixed with 3.1**—These methods correspond to the start of each MBean service defined in the service descriptor. For each MBean instance created, obtain its JMX `ObjectName` and ask the `ServiceController` to handle the start step of the service life cycle. The `ServiceController` handles the dependencies of the MBean service. Only if the service's dependencies are satisfied is the service start method invoked.

The Service Life Cycle Interface

The JMX specification does not define any type of life cycle or dependency management for MBeans. The JBoss `ServiceController` MBean introduces this notion. A JBoss MBean is an extension of the JMX MBean in that an MBean is expected to decouple creation from the life cycle of its service duties. This is necessary to implement any type of dependency management. For example, if you are writing an MBean that needs a JNDI naming service in order to be able to function, your MBean needs to be told when its dependencies are satisfied. This ranges from difficult to impossible to do if the only life cycle event is the MBean constructor. Therefore, JBoss introduces a service life cycle interface that describes the events a service can use to manage its behavior. The following shows the `org.jboss.system.Service` interface:

```
package org.jboss.system;
public interface Service
{
    public void create() throws Exception;
    public void start() throws Exception;
    public void stop();
    public void destroy();
}
```

The `ServiceController` MBean invokes the methods of the `Service` interface at the appropriate times of the service life cycle. The following section discusses the methods in more detail.

The `ServiceController` MBean

JBoss manages dependencies between MBeans via the `org.jboss.system.ServiceController` custom MBean.

The `SARDeployer` delegates to the `ServiceController` when initializing, creating, starting, stopping, and destroying MBean services. Figure 2.17 shows a sequence diagram that highlights interaction between the `SARDeployer` and `ServiceController`.

The `ServiceController` MBean has four key methods for the management of the service life cycle: `create`, `start`, `stop`, and `destroy`.

The create(ObjectName) Method The `create(ObjectName)` method is called whenever an event occurs that affects the named service's state. This could be triggered by an explicit invocation by the `SARDeployer`, a notification of a new class, or another service reaching its created state.

When a service's `create` method is called, all services on which the service depends have also had their create method invoked. This gives an MBean an opportunity to check that required MBeans or resources exist. A service cannot utilize other MBean services at this point, as most JBoss MBean services do not become fully functional until they have been started via their `start` method. Because of this, service implementations often do not implement `create` in favor of just the `start` method because that is the first point at which the service can be fully functional.

The start(ObjectName) Method The `start(ObjectName)` method is called whenever an event occurs that affects the named service's state. This could be triggered by an explicit invocation by the `SARDeployer`, a notification of a new class, or another service reaching its started state.

When a service's `start` method is called, all services on which the service depends have also had their `start` method invoked. Receipt of a `start` method invocation signals a service to become fully operational because all services on which the service depends have been created and started.

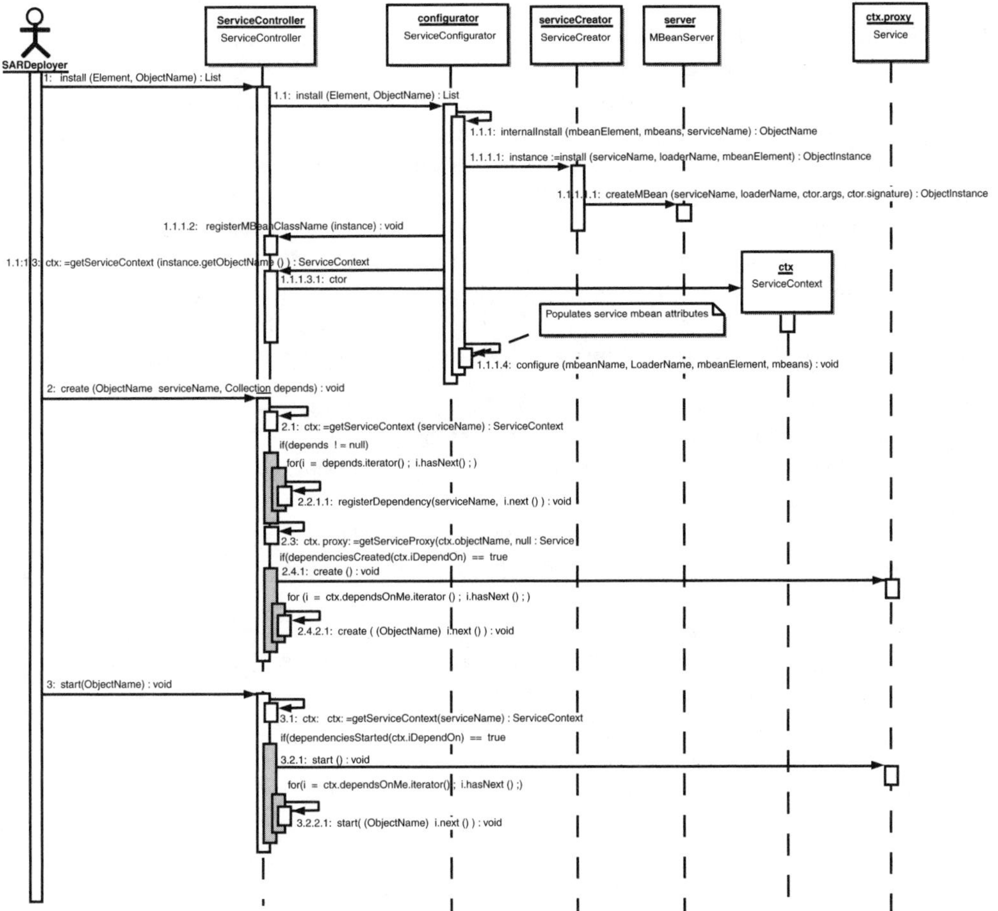

FIGURE 2.17 The interaction between the `SARDeployer` and `ServiceController` to start a service.

The stop(ObjectName) Method The `stop(ObjectName)` method is called whenever an event occurs that affects the named service's state. This could be triggered by an explicit invocation by the `SARDeployer`, notification of a class removal, or a service on which other services depend reaching its stopped state.

The destroy(ObjectName) Method The `destroy(ObjectName)` method is called whenever an event occurs that affects the named service's state. This could be triggered by an explicit invocation by the `SARDeployer`, notification of a class removal, or a service on which other services depend reaching its destroyed state.

Service implementations often do not implement `destroy` in favor of simply implementing the `stop` method—or neither `stop` nor `destroy` if the service has no state or resources that need cleanup.

Specifying Service Dependencies

To specify that an MBean service depends on other MBean services, you need to declare the dependencies in the `mbean` element of the service descriptor. This is done using the `depends` and `depends-list` elements. One difference between these two elements relates to the usage of the `optional-attribute-name` attribute. If you track the `ObjectNames` of dependencies by using single-valued attributes, you should use the `depends` element. If you track the `ObjectNames` of dependencies by using `java.util.List`-compatible attributes, you would use the `depends-list` element. If you only want to specify a dependency and don't care to have the associated service `ObjectName` bound to an attribute of your MBean, then you use whatever element is easiest. The following shows examples of service descriptor fragments that illustrate the usage of the dependency-related elements:

```
<mbean code="org.jboss.mq.server.jmx.Topic"
       name="jms.topic:service=Topic,name=testTopic">
    <!-- Declare a dependency on the "jboss.mq:service=DestinationManager" and
         bind this name to the DestinationManager attribute -->
    <depends optional-attribute-name="DestinationManager">
        jboss.mq:service=DestinationManager
    </depends>

    <!-- Declare a dependency on the "jboss.mq:service=SecurityManager" and
         bind this name to the SecurityManager attribute -->
    <depends optional-attribute-name="SecurityManager">
        jboss.mq:service=SecurityManager
    </depends>

    <!-- ... -->

    <!-- Declare a dependency on the
         "jboss.mq:service=CacheManager" without
         any binding of the name to an attribute-->
    <depends>jboss.mq:service=CacheManager</depends>
</mbean>

<mbean code="org.jboss.mq.server.jmx.TopicMgr"
       name="jboss.mq.destination:service=TopicMgr">
    <!-- Declare a dependency on the given topic destination mbeans and
         bind these names to the Topics attribute -->
    <depends-list optional-attribute-name="Topics">
        <depends-list-element>jms.topic:service=Topic,name=A
➥</depends-list-element>
```

```
        <depends-list-element>jms.topic:service=Topic,name=B
➥</depends-list-element>
        <depends-list-element>jms.topic:service=Topic,name=C
➥</depends-list-element>
    </depends-list>
</mbean>
```

Another difference between the `depends` and `depends-list` elements is that the value of the `depends` element may be a complete MBean service configuration rather than just the `ObjectName` of the service. Listing 2.13 shows an example from the `hsqldb-service.xml` descriptor. In this listing the `org.jboss.resource.connectionmanager.RARDeployment` service configuration is defined using a nested `mbean` element as the `depends` element value. This indicates that the `org.jboss.resource.connectionmanager.LocalTxConnectionManager` MBean depends on this service. The `jboss.jca:service=LocalTxDS,name=hsqldbDS ObjectName` will be bound to the `ManagedConnectionFactory-Name` attribute of the `LocalTxConnectionManager` class.

LISTING 2.13 An Example of Using the `depends` Element to Specify the Complete Configuration of a Depended-on Service

```
<mbean code="org.jboss.resource.connectionmanager.LocalTxConnectionManager"
       name="jboss.jca:service=LocalTxCM,name=hsqldbDS">
    <depends optional-attribute-name="ManagedConnectionFactoryName">
        <!--embedded mbean-->
        <mbean code="org.jboss.resource.connectionmanager.RARDeployment"
               name="jboss.jca:service=LocalTxDS,name=hsqldbDS">
            <attribute name="JndiName">DefaultDS</attribute>
            <attribute name="ManagedConnectionFactoryProperties">
                <properties>
                    <config-property name="ConnectionURL"
                                     type="java.lang.String">
                        jdbc:hsqldb:hsql://localhost:1476
                    </config-property>
                    <config-property name="DriverClass" type="java.lang.String">
                        org.hsqldb.jdbcDriver
                    </config-property>
                    <config-property name="UserName" type="java.lang.String">
                        sa
                    </config-property>
                    <config-property name="Password" type="java.lang.String"/>
                </properties>
            </attribute>
            <!-- ... -->
        </mbean>
```

LISTING 2.13 Continued

```
    </depends>
    <!-- ... -->
</mbean>
```

Identifying Unsatisfied Dependencies

The ServiceController MBean supports two operations that can help determine which MBeans are not running due to unsatisfied dependencies. The first operation is listIncompletelyDeployed. This returns a java.util.List of org.jboss.system.ServiceContext objects for the MBean services that are not in the RUNNING state.

The second operation is listWaitingMBeans. This operation returns a java.util.List of the JMX ObjectNames of MBean services that cannot be deployed because the class specified by the code attribute is not available.

Hot Deployment of Components, the URLDeploymentScanner

The URLDeploymentScanner MBean service provides the JBoss hot deployment capability. This service watches one or more URLs for deployable archives and deploys the archives as they appear or change. It also undeploys previously deployed applications if the archive from which the application was deployed is removed. The configurable attributes include the following:

- **URLs**—This property specifies a comma-separated list of URL strings for the locations that should be watched for changes. Strings that do not correspond to valid URLs are treated as file paths. Relative file paths are resolved against the server home URL (for example, JBOSS_DIST/server/default for the default config file set). If a URL represents a file, the file is deployed and watched for subsequent updates or removal. If a URL ends in /, to represent a directory, the contents of the directory are treated as a collection of deployables and scanned for content that is to be watched for updates or removal. The requirement that a URL end in a / to identify a directory follows the RFC 2518 convention and allows discrimination between collections and directories that are simply unpacked archives.

  The default value for the URLs attribute is deploy/, which means that any SARs, EARs, JARs, WARs, RARs, and so on dropped into the server/*<name>*/deploy directory will be automatically deployed and watched for updates.

  Examples of URLs attribute values include the following:

  - deploy/ scans ${ jboss.server.url} /deploy/, which is local or remote, depending on the URL used to boot the server.
  - ${jboss.server.home.dir}/deploy/ scans ${jboss.server.home.dir)/deploy, which is always local.
  - file:/var/opt/myapp.ear deploys myapp.ear from a local location.

  - `file:/var/opt/apps/` scans the specified directory.
  - `http://www.test.com/netboot/myapp.ear` deploys `myapp.ear` from a remote location.
  - `http://www.test.com/netboot/apps/` scans the specified remote location using WebDAV. This will work only if the remote HTTP server supports the WebDAV `PROPFIND` command.

- **`ScanPeriod`**—This property specifies the time, in milliseconds, between runs of the scanner thread. The default is `5000` (5 seconds).
- **`URLComparator`**—This property specifies the classname of a `java.util.Comparator` implementation used to specify a deployment ordering for deployments found in a scanned directory. The implementation must be able to compare two `java.net.URL` objects passed to its `compare` method. The default setting is the `org.jboss.deployment.DeploymentSorter` class, which orders based on the deployment URL suffix. The ordering of suffixes is `deployer`, `deployer.xml`, `sar`, `rar`, `ds.xml`, `service.xml`, `har`, `jar`, `war`, `wsr`, `ear`, `zip`, `bsh`, and `last`.

  An alternate implementation is the `org.jboss.deployment.scanner.PrefixDeploymentSorter` class. This orders the URLs based on numeric prefixes. The prefix digits are converted to an `int` (ignoring leading zeros), and smaller prefixes are ordered ahead of larger numbers. Deployments that do not start with any digits will be deployed after all numbered deployments. Deployments with the same prefix value are further sorted by the `DeploymentSorter` logic.
- **`Filter`**—This property specifies the classname of a `java.io.FileFilter` implementation that is used to filter the contents of scanned directories. Any file not accepted by this filter will not be deployed. The default is `org.jboss.deployment.scanner.DeploymentFilter`, which is an implementation that rejects the following patterns:

```
#*
%*
,*
.*
_$*
*#
*$
*%
*.BAK
*.old
*.orig
*.rej
*.bak
*.sh
*,v
```

```
*~
.make.state
.nse_de pinfo
CVS
CVS.admin
RCS
RCSLOG
SCCS
TAGS
core
tags
```

- `RecursiveSearch`—This property indicates whether deploy subdirectories are seen to be holding deployable content. If this attribute is `false`, deploy subdirectories that do not contain a dot (`.`) in their name are seen to be unpackaged JARs with nested subdeployments. If this attribute is `true`, then deploy subdirectories are just groupings of deployable content. The difference between the two views shown is related to the depth-first deployment model JBoss supports. The `false` setting, which treats directories as unpackaged JARs with nested content, triggers the deployment of the nested content as soon as the JAR directory is deployed. The `true` setting simply ignores the directory and adds its content to the list of deployable packages and calculates the order based on the previous filter logic. The default is `true`.
- **Deployer**—This property specifies the JMX `ObjectName` string of the MBean that implements the `org.jboss.deployment.Deployer` interface operations. The default setting is to use the `MainDeployer` created by the bootstrap startup process.

Writing JBoss MBean Services

Writing a custom MBean service that integrates into the JBoss server requires the use of the `org.jboss.system.Service` interface pattern if the custom service is dependent on other services. When a custom MBean depends on other MBean services, you cannot perform any service-dependent initialization in any of the `javax.management.MBeanRegistration` interface methods because JMX has no notion of dependency. Instead, you must manage dependency state by using the `Service` interface `create` and/or `start` methods. You can do this by using any one of the following approaches:

- Add any of the `Service` methods that you want called on your MBean to your MBean interface. This allows your MBean implementation to avoid dependencies on JBoss-specific interfaces.
- Have your MBean interface extend the `org.jboss.system.Service` interface.
- Have your MBean interface extend the `org.jboss.system.ServiceMBean` interface. This is a subinterface of `org.jboss.system.Service` that adds the `getName()`, `getState()`, and `getStateString()` methods.

Which approach you choose depends on whether you want your code to be coupled to JBoss-specific code. If you don't, then you should use the first approach. If you don't care about dependencies on JBoss classes, the simplest approach is to have your MBean interface extend from `org.jboss.system.ServiceMBean` and your MBean implementation class extend from the abstract `org.jboss.system.ServiceMBeanSupport` class. This class implements the `org.jboss.system.ServiceMBean` interface. `ServiceMBeanSupport` provides implementations of the `create`, `start`, `stop`, and `destroy` methods that integrate logging and JBoss service state management tracking. Each method delegates any subclass-specific work to the `createService`, `startService`, `stopService`, and `destroyService` methods, respectively. When subclassing `ServiceMBeanSupport`, you should override one or more of the `createService`, `startService`, `stopService`, and `destroyService` methods, as required.

A Standard MBean Example

This section develops a simple MBean that binds a `HashMap` into the JBoss JNDI namespace at a location determined by its `JndiName` attribute to demonstrate what is required to create a custom MBean. Because the MBean uses JNDI, it depends on the JBoss naming service MBean and must use the JBoss MBean service pattern to be notified when the naming service is available.

Version 1 of the classes, shown in Listing 2.14, is based on the service interface method pattern. This version of the interface declares the `start` and `stop` methods needed to start up correctly without using any JBoss-specific classes.

LISTING 2.14 The `JNDIMapMBean` Interface and Implementation Based on the Service Interface Method Pattern

```
package org.jboss.chap2.ex1;

// The JNDIMap MBean interface
import javax.naming.NamingException;

public interface JNDIMapMBean
{
    public String getJndiName();
    public void setJndiName(String jndiName) throws NamingException;
    public void start() throws Exception;
    public void stop() throws Exception;
}

package org.jboss.chap2.ex1;

// The JNDIMap MBean implementation
import java.util.HashMap;
import javax.naming.InitialContext;
import javax.naming.Name;
import javax.naming.NamingException;
```

```
import org.jboss.naming.NonSerializableFactory;

public class JNDIMap implements JNDIMapMBean
{
    private String jndiName;
    private HashMap contextMap = new HashMap();
    private boolean started;

    public String getJndiName()
    {
        return jndiName;
    }
    public void setJndiName(String jndiName) throws NamingException
    {
        String oldName = this.jndiName;
        this.jndiName = jndiName;
        if (started) {
            unbind(oldName);
            try {
                rebind();
            } catch(Exception e) {
                NamingException ne = new NamingException
➥("Failedto update jndiName");
                ne.setRootCause(e);
                throw ne;
            }
        }
    }

    public void start() throws Exception
    {
        started = true;
        rebind();
    }

    public void stop()
    {
        started = false;
        unbind(jndiName);
    }

    private void rebind() throws NamingException
    {
        InitialContext rootCtx = new InitialContext();
        Name fullName = rootCtx.getNameParser("").parse(jndiName);
```

```
        System.out.println("fullName="+fullName);
        NonSerializableFactory.rebind(fullName, contextMap, true);
    }

    private void unbind(String jndiName)
    {
        try {
            InitialContext rootCtx = new InitialContext();
            rootCtx.unbind(jndiName);
            NonSerializableFactory.unbind(jndiName);
        } catch(NamingException e) {
            e.printStackTrace();
        }
    }
}
```

Version 2 of the classes, shown in Listing 2.15, uses the JBoss `ServiceMBean` interface and `ServiceMBeanSupport` class. In this version, the implementation class extends the `ServiceMBeanSupport` class and overrides the `startService` and `stopService` methods. `JNDIMapMBean` also implements the abstract `getName` method to return a descriptive name for the MBean. The `JNDIMapMBean` interface extends the `org.jboss.system.ServiceMBean` interface and only declares the setter and getter methods for the `JndiName` attribute because it inherits the service life cycle methods from `ServiceMBean`. This is the third approach mentioned at the start of the section "JBoss MBean Services," earlier in this chapter.

LISTING 2.15 The `JNDIMap` MBean Interface and Implementation Based on the `ServiceMBean` Interface and `ServiceMBeanSupport` Class

```
package org.jboss.chap2.ex2;

// The JNDIMap MBean interface
import javax.naming.NamingException;

public interface JNDIMapMBean extends org.jboss.system.ServiceMBean
{
    public String getJndiName();
    public void setJndiName(String jndiName) throws NamingException;
} package org.jboss.chap2.ex2;
// The JNDIMap MBean implementation
import java.util.HashMap;
import javax.naming.InitialContext;
import javax.naming.Name;
import javax.naming.NamingException;
import org.jboss.naming.NonSerializableFactory;
```

LISTING 2.15 Continued

```
public class JNDIMap extends org.jboss.system.ServiceMBeanSupport
    implements JNDIMapMBean
{
    private String jndiName;
    private HashMap contextMap = new HashMap();

    public String getJndiName()
    {
        return jndiName;
    }

    public void setJndiName(String jndiName)
        throws NamingException
    {
        String oldName = this.jndiName;
        this.jndiName = jndiName;
        if (super.getState() == STARTED) {
            unbind(oldName);
            try {
                rebind();
            } catch(Exception e) {
                NamingException ne = new NamingException
➥("Failed to update jndiName");
                ne.setRootCause(e);
                throw ne;
            }
        }
    }

    public void startService() throws Exception
    {
        rebind();
    }

    public void stopService()
    {
        unbind(jndiName);
    }

    private void rebind() throws NamingException
    {
        InitialContext rootCtx = new InitialContext();
        Name fullName = rootCtx.getNameParser("").parse(jndiName);
        log.info("fullName="+fullName);
```

LISTING 2.15 Continued

```
        NonSerializableFactory.rebind(fullName, contextMap, true);
    }

    private void unbind(String jndiName)
    {
        try {
            InitialContext rootCtx = new InitialContext();
            rootCtx.unbind(jndiName);
            NonSerializableFactory.unbind(jndiName);
        } catch(NamingException e) {
            log.error("Failed to unbind map", e);
        }
    }
}
```

The source code for these MBeans, along with the service descriptors, is located in the `examples/src/main/org/jboss/chap2/{ex1,ex2}` directories.

The `jboss-service.xml` descriptor for Version 1 is shown here:

```
<!-- The SAR META-INF/jboss-service.xml descriptor -->
<server>
    <mbean code="org.jboss.chap2.ex1.JNDIMap"
           name="chap2.ex1:service=JNDIMap">
        <attribute name="JndiName">inmemory/maps/MapTest</attribute>
        <depends>jboss:service=Naming</depends>
    </mbean>
</server>
```

The `JNDIMap` MBean binds a `HashMap` object under the `inmemory/maps/MapTest` JNDI name, and the client code fragment demonstrates retrieving the `HashMap` object from the `inmemory/maps/MapTest` location. The corresponding client code is shown here:

```
// Sample lookup code
InitialContext ctx = new InitialContext();
HashMap map = (HashMap) ctx.lookup("inmemory/maps/MapTest");
```

XMBean Examples

This section develops a variation of the `JNDIMap` MBean introduced in the preceding section. This MBean exposes its management metadata by using the JBoss XMBean framework. The core managed component is exactly the same core code from the `JNDIMap` class, but it does not implement any specific management-related interface. This example illustrates the following capabilities that are not possible with a standard MBean:

- The ability to add rich descriptions to attributes and operations
- The ability to expose notification information
- The ability to add persistence of attributes
- The ability to add custom interceptors for security and remote access through a typed interface

Version 1: The Annotated JNDIMap XMBean Let's start with a simple XMBean variation of the standard MBean version of `JNDIMap` that adds descriptive information about the attributes and operations and their arguments. The following shows the `jboss-service.xml` descriptor and the `jndimap-xmbean1.xml` XMBean descriptor (the source can be found in the `src/main/org/jboss/chap2/xmbean` directory of the book examples):

```
<?xml version='1.0' encoding='UTF-8' ?>
<!DOCTYPE server PUBLIC
                     "-//JBoss//DTD MBean Service 3.2//EN"
                     "http://www.jboss.org/j2ee/dtd/jboss-service_3_2.dtd">
<server>
    <mbean code="org.jboss.chap2.xmbean.JNDIMap"
           name="chap2.xmbean:service=JNDIMap"
           xmbean-dd="META-INF/jndimap-xmbean.xml">
        <attribute name="JndiName">inmemory/maps/MapTest</attribute>
        <depends>jboss:service=Naming</depends>
    </mbean>
</server>
<?xml version="1.0" encoding="UTF-8"?>
<!DOCTYPE mbean PUBLIC
          "-//JBoss//DTD JBOSS XMBEAN 1.0//EN"
          "http://www.jboss.org/j2ee/dtd/jboss_xmbean_1_0.dtd">
<mbean>
    <description>The JNDIMap XMBean Example Version 1</description>
    <descriptors>
        <persistence persistPolicy="Never" persistPeriod="10"
            persistLocation="data/JNDIMap.data" persistName="JNDIMap"/>
        <currencyTimeLimit value="10"/>
        <state-action-on-update value="keep-running"/>
    </descriptors>
    <class>org.jboss.test.jmx.xmbean.JNDIMap</class>
    <constructor>
        <description>The default constructor</description>
        <name>JNDIMap</name>
    </constructor>
    <!-- Attributes -->
    <attribute access="read-write" getMethod="getJndiName" setMethod=
➥"setJndiName">
```

```
    <description>
        The location in JNDI where the Map we manage will be bound
    </description>
    <name>JndiName</name>
    <type>java.lang.String</type>
    <descriptors>
        <default value="inmemory/maps/MapTest"/>
    </descriptors>
</attribute>
<attribute access="read-write" getMethod="getInitialValues"
           setMethod="setInitialValues">
    <description>The array of initial values that will be placed into the
        map associated with the service. The array is a collection of
        key,value pairs with elements[0,2,4,...2n] being the keys and
        elements [1,3,5,...,2n+1] the associated values. The
        "[Ljava.lang.String;" type signature is the VM representation of the
        java.lang.String[] type. </description>
    <name>InitialValues</name>
    <type>[Ljava.lang.String;</type>
    <descriptors>
        <default value="key0,value0"/>
    </descriptors>
</attribute>
<!-- Operations -->
<operation>
    <description>The start lifecycle operation</description>
    <name>start</name>
</operation>
<operation>
    <description>The stop lifecycle operation</description>
    <name>stop</name>
</operation>
<operation impact="ACTION">
    <description>Put a value into the map</description>
    <name>put</name>
    <parameter>
        <description>The key the value will be store under</description>
        <name>key</name>
        <type>java.lang.Object</type>
    </parameter>
    <parameter>
        <description>The value to place into the map</description>
        <name>value</name>
        <type>java.lang.Object</type>
    </parameter>
```

```
    </operation>
    <operation impact="INFO">
        <description>Get a value from the map</description>
        <name>get</name>
        <parameter>
            <description>The key to lookup in the map</description>
            <name>get</name>
            <type>java.lang.Object</type>
        </parameter>
        <return-type>java.lang.Object</return-type>
    </operation>
    <!-- Notifications -->
    <notification>
        <description>The notification sent whenever a value has got into the map
            managed by the service</description>
        <name>javax.management.Notification</name>
        <notification-type>org.jboss.chap2.xmbean.JNDIMap.get</notification-type>
    </notification>
    <notification>
        <description>The notification sent whenever a value is put into the map
            managed by the service</description>
        <name>javax.management.Notification</name>
        <notification-type>org.jboss.chap2.xmbean.JNDIMap.put</notification-type>
    </notification>
</mbean>
```

You can build, deploy, and test the XMBean as follows:

```
[examples]$ ant -Dchap=chap2 -Dex=xmbean1  run-example
...
run-examplexmbean1:
     [copy] Copying 1 file to /tmp/jboss-4.0.1/server/default/deploy
     [java] JNDIMap Class: org.jboss.mx.modelmbean.XMBean
     [java] JNDIMap Operations:
     [java]  + void start()
     [java]  + void stop()
     [java]  + void put(java.lang.Object chap2.xmbean:service=JNDIMap,
➥java.lang.Object cha
p2.xmbean:service=JNDIMap)
     [java]  + java.lang.Object get(java.lang.Object chap2.xmbean:service=JNDIMap)
     [java]  + java.lang.String getJndiName()
     [java]  + void setJndiName(java.lang.String chap2.xmbean:service=JNDIMap)
     [java]  + [Ljava.lang.String; getInitialValues()
     [java]  + void setInitialValues([Ljava.lang.String; chap2.xmbean:
➥service=JNDIMap)
```

```
     [java] handleNotification, event: null
     [java] key=key0, value=value0
     [java] handleNotification, event: javax.management.Notification
➥[source=chap2.xmbean:s
ervice=JNDIMap,type=org.jboss.chap2.xmbean.JNDIMap.put,sequenceNumber=3,
➥timeStamp=10986315
27823,message=null,userData=null]
     [java] JNDIMap.put(key1, value1) successful
     [java] handleNotification, event: javax.management.Notification
➥[source=chap2.xmbean:s
ervice=JNDIMap,type=org.jboss.chap2.xmbean.JNDIMap.get,sequenceNumber=4,
➥timeStamp=10986315
27940,message=null,userData=null]
     [java] JNDIMap.get(key0): null
     [java] handleNotification, event: javax.management.Notification
➥[source=chap2.xmbean:s
ervice=JNDIMap,type=org.jboss.chap2.xmbean.JNDIMap.get,sequenceNumber=5,
➥timeStamp=10986315
27985,message=null,userData=null]
     [java] JNDIMap.get(key1): value1
     [java] handleNotification, event: javax.management.Notification
➥[source=chap2.xmbean:s
ervice=JNDIMap,type=org.jboss.chap2.xmbean.JNDIMap.put,sequenceNumber=6,
➥timeStamp=10986315
27999,message=null,userData=null]
```

The functionality of this code is largely the same as that of the Standard MBean, with the notable exception of the JMX notifications. A Standard MBean has no way of declaring that it will emit notifications. An XMBean may declare the notifications it emits by using notification elements, as shown in the Version 1 descriptor. We see the notifications from the get and put operations on the test client console output. Note that there is also a `jmx.attribute.change` notification emitted when the `InitialValues` attribute is changed. This is because the `ModelMBean` interface extends the `ModelMBeanNotificationBroadcaster`, which supports `AttributeChangeNotificationListeners`.

The other major difference between the Standard and XMBean versions of JNDIMap is the descriptive metadata. Look at the `chap2.xmbean:service=JNDIMap` in the JMX Console, and you will see the attributes section, as shown in Figure 2.18.

Notice that the JMX Console now displays the full attribute description, as specified in the XMBean descriptor, rather than the `MBean Attribute` text seen in standard MBean implementations. Scroll down to the operations, and you will also see that these now also have nice descriptions of their function and parameters.

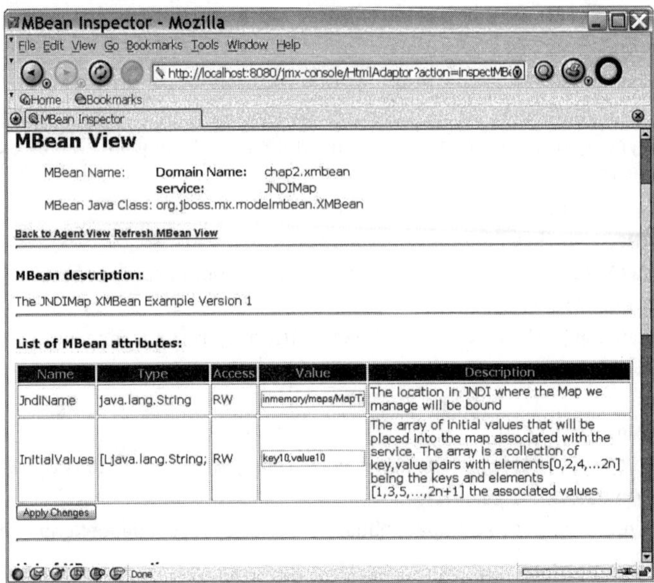

FIGURE 2.18 The Version 1 JNDIMapXMBean JMX Console view.

Version 2: Adding Persistence to the JNDIMap XMBean In Version 2 of the XMBean, you add support for persistence of the XMBean attributes. The updated XMBean deployment descriptor is shown here:

```
<?xml version="1.0" encoding="UTF-8"?>
<!DOCTYPE mbean PUBLIC
          "-//JBoss//DTD JBOSS XMBEAN 1.0//EN"
          "http://www.jboss.org/j2ee/dtd/jboss_xmbean_1_0.dtd">
<mbean>
    <description>The JNDIMap XMBean Example Version 2</description>
    <descriptors>
        <persistence persistPolicy="OnUpdate" persistPeriod="10"
            persistLocation="${jboss.server.data.dir}" persistName="JNDIMap.ser"/>
        <currencyTimeLimit value="10"/>
        <state-action-on-update value="keep-running"/>
        <persistence-manager value="org.jboss.mx.persistence.
➥ObjectStreamPersistenceManager"/>
    </descriptors>   <class>org.jboss.test.jmx.xmbean.JNDIMap</class>
    <constructor>
        <description>The default constructor</description>
        <name>JNDIMap</name>
    </constructor>
    <!-- Attributes -->
    <attribute access="read-write" getMethod="getJndiName" setMethod=
➥"setJndiName">
```

```
    <description>
        The location in JNDI where the Map we manage will be bound
    </description>
    <name>JndiName</name>
    <type>java.lang.String</type>
    <descriptors>
        <default value="inmemory/maps/MapTest"/>
    </descriptors>
</attribute>
<attribute access="read-write" getMethod="getInitialValues"
           setMethod="setInitialValues">
    <description>The array of initial values that will be placed into the
        map associated with the service. The array is a collection of
        key,value pairs with elements[0,2,4,...2n] being the keys and
        elements [1,3,5,...,2n+1] the associated values</description>
    <name>InitialValues</name>
    <type>[Ljava.lang.String;</type>
    <descriptors>
        <default value="key0,value0"/>
    </descriptors>
</attribute>
<!-- Operations -->
<operation>
    <description>The start lifecycle operation</description>
    <name>start</name>
</operation>
<operation>
    <description>The stop lifecycle operation</description>
    <name>stop</name>
</operation>
<operation impact="ACTION">
    <description>Put a value into the map</description>
    <name>put</name>
    <parameter>
        <description>The key of the value will be stored under</description>
        <name>key</name>
        <type>java.lang.Object</type>
    </parameter>
    <parameter>
        <description>The value to place into the map</description>
        <name>value</name>
        <type>java.lang.Object</type>
    </parameter>
</operation>
<operation impact="INFO">
```

```
        <description>Get a value from the map</description>
        <name>get</name>
        <parameter>
            <description>The key to lookup in the map</description>
            <name>get</name>
            <type>java.lang.Object</type>
        </parameter>
        <return-type>java.lang.Object</return-type>
    </operation>
    <!-- Notifications -->
    <notification>
        <description>The notification sent whenever a value has got into the map
            managed by the service</description>
        <name>javax.management.Notification</name>
        <notification-type>org.jboss.chap2.xmbean.JNDIMap.get</notification-type>
    </notification>
    <notification>
        <description>The notification sent whenever a value is put into the map
            managed by the service</description>
        <name>javax.management.Notification</name>
        <notification-type>org.jboss.chap2.xmbean.JNDIMap.put</notification-type>
    </notification>
</mbean>
```

You build, deploy, and test the Version 2 XMBean as follows:

```
[examples]$ ant -Dchap=chap2 -Dex=xmbean2 -Djboss.deploy.conf=rmi-adaptor
➥run-example
...
run-examplexmbean2:
     [java] JNDIMap Class: org.jboss.mx.modelmbean.XMBean
     [java] JNDIMap Operations:
     [java]  + void start()
     [java]  + void stop()
     [java]  + void put(java.lang.Object chap2.xmbean:service=JNDIMap,
➥java.lang.Object chap2.xmbean:service=JNDIMap)
     [java]  + java.lang.Object get(java.lang.Object chap2.xmbean:service=JNDIMap)
     [java]  + java.lang.String getJndiName()
     [java]  + void setJndiName(java.lang.String chap2.xmbean:service=JNDIMap)
     [java]  + [Ljava.lang.String; getInitialValues()
     [java]  + void setInitialValues([Ljava.lang.String; chap2.xmbean:
➥service=JNDIMap)
     [java] handleNotification, event: null
     [java] key=key10, value=value10
     [java] handleNotification, event: javax.management.Notification
➥[source=chap2.xmbean:s
```

```
ervice=JNDIMap,type=org.jboss.chap2.xmbean.JNDIMap.put,sequenceNumber=7,
➥timeStamp=10986326
93716,message=null,userData=null]
     [java] JNDIMap.put(key1, value1) successful
     [java] handleNotification, event: javax.management.Notification
➥[source=chap2.xmbean:s
ervice=JNDIMap,type=org.jboss.chap2.xmbean.JNDIMap.get,sequenceNumber=8,
➥timeStamp=10986326
93857,message=null,userData=null]
     [java] JNDIMap.get(key0): null
     [java] handleNotification, event: javax.management.Notification
➥[source=chap2.xmbean:s
ervice=JNDIMap,type=org.jboss.chap2.xmbean.JNDIMap.get,sequenceNumber=9,
➥timeStamp=10986326
93896,message=null,userData=null]
     [java] JNDIMap.get(key1): value1
     [java] handleNotification, event: javax.management.Notification
➥[source=chap2.xmbean:s
ervice=JNDIMap,type=org.jboss.chap2.xmbean.JNDIMap.put,sequenceNumber=10,
➥timeStamp=1098632
693925,message=null,userData=null]
```

There is nothing manifestly different about this version of the XMBean at this point because you have done nothing to test that changes to attribute value are actually persisted. You perform that test by running the example `xmbean2a` several times:

```
[examples] ant -Dchap=chap2 -Dex=xmbean2a run-example
...
     [java] InitialValues.length=2
     [java] key=key10, value=value10
[examples] ant -Dchap=chap2 -Dex=xmbean2a run-example
...
     [java] InitialValues.length=4
     [java] key=key10, value=value10
     [java] key=key2, value=value2
[examples] ant -Dchap=chap2 -Dex=xmbean2a run-example
...
     [java] InitialValues.length=6
     [java] key=key10, value=value10
     [java] key=key2, value=value2
                  [java] key=key3, value=value3
```

The `org.jboss.chap2.xmbean.TestXMBeanRestart` used in this example obtains the current `InitialValues` attribute setting and then adds another key/value pair to it. The client code is shown here:

```
package org.jboss.chap2.xmbean;

import javax.management.Attribute;
import javax.management.ObjectName;
import javax.naming.InitialContext;

import org.jboss.jmx.adaptor.rmi.RMIAdaptor;

/**
 *  A client that demonstrates the persistence of the xmbean
 *  attributes. Every time it runs it looks up the InitialValues
 *  attribute, prints it out and then adds a new key/value to the
 *  list.
 *
 *  @author Scott.Stark@jboss.org
 *  @version $Revision: 1.5 $
 */
public class TestXMBeanRestart
{
    /**
     * @param args the command line arguments
     */
    public static void main(String[] args) throws Exception
    {
        InitialContext ic = new InitialContext();
        RMIAdaptor server = (RMIAdaptor) ic.lookup("jmx/rmi/RMIAdaptor");

        // Get the InitialValues attribute
        ObjectName name = new ObjectName("chap2.xmbean:service=JNDIMap");
        String[] initialValues = (String[])
            server.getAttribute(name, "InitialValues");
        System.out.println("InitialValues.length="+initialValues.length);
        int length = initialValues.length;
        for (int n = 0; n < length; n += 2) {
            String key = initialValues[n];
            String value = initialValues[n+1];

            System.out.println("key="+key+", value="+value);
        }
        // Add a new key/value pair
        String[] newInitialValues = new String[length+2];
        System.arraycopy(initialValues, 0, newInitialValues,
                         0, length);
        newInitialValues[length] = "key"+(length/2+1);
        newInitialValues[length+1] = "value"+(length/2+1);
```

```
        Attribute ivalues = new
            Attribute("InitialValues", newInitialValues);
        server.setAttribute(name, ivalues);
    }
}
```

At this point, you might even shut down the JBoss server, restart it, and then rerun the initial example to see if the changes are persisted across server restarts:

```
[examples]$ ant -Dchap=chap2 -Dex=xmbean2 run-example
...

run-examplexmbean2:
     [java] JNDIMap Class: org.jboss.mx.modelmbean.XMBean
     [java] JNDIMap Operations:
     [java]  + void start()
     [java]  + void stop()
     [java]  + void put(java.lang.Object chap2.xmbean:service=JNDIMap,
➥java.lang.Object chap2.xmbean:service=JNDIMap)
     [java]  + java.lang.Object get(java.lang.Object chap2.xmbean:service=JNDIMap)
     [java]  + java.lang.String getJndiName()
     [java]  + void setJndiName(java.lang.String chap2.xmbean:service=JNDIMap)
     [java]  + [Ljava.lang.String; getInitialValues()
     [java]  + void setInitialValues([Ljava.lang.String; chap2.xmbean:
➥service=JNDIMap)
     [java] handleNotification, event: null
     [java] key=key10, value=value10
     [java] key=key2, value=value2
     [java] key=key3, value=value3
     [java] key=key4, value=value4
     [java] handleNotification, event: javax.management.Notification
➥[source=chap2.xmbean:service=JNDIMap,type=
➥org.jboss.chap2.xmbean.JNDIMap.put,sequenceNumber=3,timeStamp=10986336
64712,message=null,userData=null]
     [java] JNDIMap.put(key1, value1) successful
     [java] handleNotification, event: javax.management.Notification
➥[source=chap2.xmbean:service=JNDIMap,
➥type=org.jboss.chap2.xmbean.JNDIMap.get,sequenceNumber=4,
➥timeStamp=10986336
64821,message=null,userData=null]
     [java] JNDIMap.get(key0): null
     [java] handleNotification, event: javax.management.Notification
➥[source=chap2.xmbean:service=JNDIMap,type=
➥org.jboss.chap2.xmbean.JNDIMap.get,sequenceNumber=5,timeStamp=10986336
64860,message=null,userData=null]
```

```
     [java] JNDIMap.get(key1): value1
     [java] handleNotification, event: javax.management.Notification
➥[source=chap2.xmbean:service=JNDIMap,type=
➥org.jboss.chap2.xmbean.JNDIMap.put,sequenceNumber=6,timeStamp=10986336
64877,message=null,userData=null]
     [java] handleNotification, event: javax.management.Notification
➥[source=chap2.xmbean:service=JNDIMap,type=
➥org.jboss.chap2.xmbean.JNDIMap.put,sequenceNumber=7,timeStamp=10986336
64895,message=null,userData=null]
     [java] handleNotification, event: javax.management.Notification
➥[source=chap2.xmbean:service=JNDIMap,type=
➥org.jboss.chap2.xmbean.JNDIMap.put,sequenceNumber=8,timeStamp=10986336
64899,message=null,userData=null]
     [java] handleNotification, event: javax.management.Notification
➥[source=chap2.xmbean:service=JNDIMap,type=
➥org.jboss.chap2.xmbean.JNDIMap.put,sequenceNumber=9,timeStamp=10986336
65614,message=null,userData=null]
```

You can see that the last `InitialValues` attribute setting is in fact visible.

Version 3: Adding Security and Remote Access to the JNDIMap XMBean This last example version (Version 3) of the `JNDIMap` XMBean demonstrates customization of the server interceptor stack as well as the exposing of a subset of the XMBean management interface via a typed proxy to a remote client using RMI/JRMP. On the server side, you will add a simple security interceptor that allows access to attributes or operations only by a user specified in the interceptor configuration. You will also use another custom interceptor to implement the MBean detached invoker pattern described later in this chapter, in the section "Remote Access to Services, Detached Invokers." Implementing this pattern in an invoker rather than the XMBean demonstrates how to introduce a remote access aspect without having to modify the existing `JNDIMap` implementation.

You use the `JRMPProxyFactory` service to expose the `ClientInterface` to remote clients:

```
public interface ClientInterface
{
    public String[] getInitialValues();
    public void setInitialValues(String[] keyValuePairs);
    public Object get(Object key);
    public void put(Object key, Object value);
}
```

The test client will obtain the `ClientInterface` proxy from JNDI and interact with the XMBean through RMI-style calls instead of the `RMIAdaptor` and MBean `Server`-style used previously:

```
package org.jboss.chap2.xmbean;
```

```
import javax.naming.InitialContext;
import org.jboss.security.SecurityAssociation;
import org.jboss.security.SimplePrincipal;

/**
 * A client that accesses an XMBean through its RMI interface
 * @author Scott.Stark@jboss.org
 * @version $Revision: 1.5 $
 */
public class TestXMBean3
{

    /**
     * @param args the command line arguments
     */
    public static void main(String[] args) throws Exception
    {
        InitialContext ic = new InitialContext();
        ClientInterface xmbean = (ClientInterface)
            ic.lookup("secure-xmbean/ClientInterface");

        // This call should fail because we have not set a security context
        try {
            String[] tmp = xmbean.getInitialValues();
            throw new IllegalStateException("Was able to call getInitialValues");
        } catch(Exception e) {
            System.out.println("Called to getInitialValues failed as expected: "
                               + e.getMessage());
        }

        // Set a security context using the SecurityAssociation
        SecurityAssociation.setPrincipal(new SimplePrincipal("admin"));

        // Get the InitialValues attribute
        String[] initialValues = xmbean.getInitialValues();
        for(int n = 0; n < initialValues.length; n += 2) {
            String key = initialValues[n];
            String value = initialValues[n+1];

            System.out.println("key="+key+", value="+value);
        }

        // Invoke the put(Object, Object) op
        xmbean.put("key1", "value1");
        System.out.println("JNDIMap.put(key1,
```

```
                    value1) successful");
        Object result0 = xmbean.get("key0");
        System.out.println("JNDIMap.get(key0): "+result0);
        Object result1 = xmbean.get("key1");
        System.out.println("JNDIMap.get(key1): "+result1);

        // Change the InitialValues
        initialValues[0] += ".1";
        initialValues[1] += ".2";
        xmbean.setInitialValues(initialValues);

        initialValues = xmbean.getInitialValues();
        for(int n = 0; n < initialValues.length; n += 2) {
            String key = initialValues[n];
            String value = initialValues[n+1];

            System.out.println("key="+key+", value="+value);
        }
    }
}
```

The deployment descriptor is shown here:

```
<?xml version="1.0" encoding="UTF-8"?>
<!DOCTYPE mbean PUBLIC
          "-//JBoss//DTD JBOSS XMBEAN 1.0//EN"
          "http://www.jboss.org/j2ee/dtd/jboss_xmbean_1_0.dtd"
          [<!ATTLIST interceptor adminName CDATA #IMPLIED>]>
<mbean>
    <description>The JNDIMap XMBean Example Version 3</description>
    <descriptors>
        <interceptors>
            <interceptor code="org.jboss.chap2.xmbean.ServerSecurityInterceptor"
                         adminName="admin"/>
            <interceptor code="org.jboss.chap2.xmbean.InvokerInterceptor"/>
            <interceptor code="org.jboss.mx.interceptor.PersistenceInterceptor2"/>
            <interceptor code="org.jboss.mx.interceptor.ModelMBeanInterceptor"/>
            <interceptor code="org.jboss.mx.interceptor.
➥ObjectReferenceInterceptor"/>
        </interceptors>
        <persistence persistPolicy="Never"/>
        <currencyTimeLimit value="10"/>
        <state-action-on-update value="keep-running"/>
    </descriptors>
    <class>org.jboss.test.jmx.xmbean.JNDIMap</class>
    <constructor>
```

```
        <description>The default constructor</description>
        <name>JNDIMap</name>
    </constructor>
    <!-- Attributes -->
    <attribute access="read-write" getMethod="getJndiName" setMethod=
➥"setJndiName">
        <description>
            The location in JNDI where the Map we manage will be bound
        </description>
        <name>JndiName</name>
        <type>java.lang.String</type>
        <descriptors>
            <default value="inmemory/maps/MapTest"/>
        </descriptors>
    </attribute>
    <attribute access="read-write" getMethod="getInitialValues"
            setMethod="setInitialValues">
        <description>The array of initial values that will be placed into the
            map associated with the service. The array is a collection of
            key,value pairs with elements[0,2,4,...2n] being the keys and
            elements [1,3,5,...,2n+1] the associated values</description>
        <name>InitialValues</name>
        <type>[Ljava.lang.String;</type>
        <descriptors>
            <default value="key0,value0"/>
        </descriptors>
    </attribute>
    <!-- Operations -->
    <operation>
        <description>The start lifecycle operation</description>
        <name>start</name>
    </operation>
    <operation>
        <description>The stop lifecycle operation</description>
        <name>stop</name>
    </operation>
    <operation impact="ACTION">
        <description>Put a value into the map</description>
        <name>put</name>
        <parameter>
            <description>The key of the value will be stored under</description>
            <name>key</name>
            <type>java.lang.Object</type>
        </parameter>
        <parameter>
```

```
            <description>The value to place into the map</description>
            <name>value</name>
            <type>java.lang.Object</type>
        </parameter>
    </operation>
    <operation impact="INFO">
        <description>Get a value from the map</description>
        <name>get</name>
        <parameter>
            <description>The key to lookup in the map</description>
            <name>get</name>
            <type>java.lang.Object</type>
        </parameter>
        <return-type>java.lang.Object</return-type>
    </operation>
</mbean>
```

The addition over the previous versions of the `JNDIMap` XMBean is the `interceptors` element. It defines the interceptor stack through which all MBean attribute access and operations pass. The first two interceptors, `org.jboss.chap2.xmbean.ServerSecurityInterceptor` and `org.jboss.chap2.xmbean.InvokerInterceptor`, are the sample custom interceptors. The remaining three interceptors are the standard `ModelMBean` interceptors. Because you have a persistence policy of `Never`, you could in fact remove the standard `org.jboss.mx.interceptor.PersistenceInterceptor2`. The JMX interceptors are an ordered chain of filters. The standard base class of an interceptor is shown here:

```
package org.jboss.mx.interceptor;

import javax.management.MBeanInfo;
import org.jboss.mx.server.MBeanInvoker;

/**
 * Base class for all interceptors.
 *
 * @see org.jboss.mx.interceptor.StandardMBeanInterceptor
 * @see org.jboss.mx.interceptor.LogInterceptor
 *
 * @author <a href="mailto:juha@jboss.org">Juha Lindfors</a>.
 * @version $Revision: 1.5 $
 *
 */
public class AbstractInterceptor implements Interceptor
{
    // Attributes ---------------------------------------------------
    protected Interceptor next = null;
```

```
    protected String name = null;
    protected MBeanInfo info;
    protected MBeanInvoker invoker;

    // Constructors ---------------------------------------------------
    public AbstractInterceptor()
    {
        this(null);
    }
    public AbstractInterceptor(String name)
    {
        this.name = name;
    }
    public AbstractInterceptor(MBeanInfo info,
                               MBeanInvoker invoker)
    {
        this.name = getClass().getName();
        this.info = info;
        this.invoker = invoker;
    }

    // Public ---------------------------------------------------------
    public Object invoke(Invocation invocation)
        throws InvocationException
    {
        return getNext().invoke(invocation);
    }

    public Interceptor getNext()
    {
        return next;
    }

    public Interceptor setNext(Interceptor interceptor)
    {
        this.next = interceptor;
        return interceptor;
    }

}
```

The custom interceptors for the Version 3 XMBean example are `ServerSecurityInterceptor` and the `InvokerInterceptor`. The `ServerSecurityInterceptor` intercepts invoke operations and validates that the `Invocation` context includes an admin principal:

```
package org.jboss.chap2.xmbean;

import java.security.Principal;

import org.jboss.logging.Logger;
import org.jboss.mx.interceptor.AbstractInterceptor;
import org.jboss.mx.interceptor.Invocation;
import org.jboss.mx.interceptor.InvocationException;
import org.jboss.security.SimplePrincipal;


/**
 * A simple security interceptor example that restricts access to a
 * single principal
 *
 * @author Scott.Stark@jboss.org
 * @version $Revision: 1.5 $
 */

public class ServerSecurityInterceptor extends AbstractInterceptor
{
    private static Logger log = Logger.getLogger(ServerSecurityInterceptor.class);
    private SimplePrincipal admin = new SimplePrincipal("admin");

    public String getAdminName()
    {
        return admin.getName();
    }
    public void setAdminName(String name)
    {
        admin = new SimplePrincipal(name);
    }

    public Object invoke(Invocation invocation)
        throws InvocationException
    {
        String opName = invocation.getName();

        // If this is not the invoke(Invocation) op just pass it along
        if (opName.equals("invoke") == false) {
            return getNext().invoke(invocation);
        }

        Object[] args = invocation.getArgs();
        org.jboss.invocation.Invocation invokeInfo =
```

```
            (org.jboss.invocation.Invocation) args[0];
        Principal caller = invokeInfo.getPrincipal();
        log.info("invoke, opName="+opName+", caller="+caller);

        // Only the admin caller is allowed access
        if (caller == null || caller.equals(admin) == false) {
            throw new InvocationException(new SecurityException("Caller=" +
                                                                 caller +
                                                                 " is not allowed access"));
        }
        return getNext().invoke(invocation);
    }
}
```

The InvokerInterceptor implements the detached invoker pattern. (This is discussed in detail later in this chapter, in the section "Remote Access to Services, Detached Invokers.").

```
package org.jboss.chap2.xmbean;

import java.lang.reflect.Method;
import java.util.HashMap;
import javax.management.Descriptor;
import javax.management.MBeanInfo;

import org.jboss.logging.Logger;
import org.jboss.mx.interceptor.AbstractInterceptor;
import org.jboss.mx.interceptor.Invocation;
import org.jboss.mx.interceptor.InvocationException;
import org.jboss.mx.server.MBeanInvoker;
import org.jboss.invocation.MarshalledInvocation;

/** An interceptor that handles the
 *
 * @author Scott.Stark@jboss.org
 * @version $Revision: 1.5 $
 */
public class InvokerInterceptor
    extends AbstractInterceptor
{
    private static Logger log = Logger.getLogger(InvokerInterceptor.class);
    private Class exposedInterface = ClientInterface.class;
    private HashMap methodMap = new HashMap();
    private HashMap invokeMap = new HashMap();
```

```
    public InvokerInterceptor(MBeanInfo info,
                              MBeanInvoker invoker)
    {
        super(info, invoker);
        try {
            Descriptor[] descriptors = invoker.getDescriptors();
            Object resource = invoker.getResource();
            Class[] getInitialValuesSig = {};
            Method getInitialValues =
                exposedInterface.getDeclaredMethod("getInitialValues",
                                                   getInitialValuesSig);
            Long hash = new Long(MarshalledInvocation.calculateHash
➥(getInitialValues));
            InvocationInfo invokeInfo =
                new InvocationInfo("InitialValues",
                                   Invocation.ATTRIBUTE,
                                   Invocation.READ, getInitialValuesSig,
                                   descriptors, resource);
            methodMap.put(hash, getInitialValues);
            invokeMap.put(getInitialValues, invokeInfo);
            log.debug("getInitialValues hash:"+hash);

            Class[] setInitialValuesSig = {String[].class};
            Method setInitialValues =
                exposedInterface.getDeclaredMethod("setInitialValues",
                                                   setInitialValuesSig);

            hash = new Long(MarshalledInvocation.calculateHash(setInitialValues));
            invokeInfo = new InvocationInfo("InitialValues",
                                            Invocation.ATTRIBUTE,
                                            Invocation.WRITE,
                                            setInitialValuesSig,
                                            descriptors, resource);
            methodMap.put(hash, setInitialValues);
            invokeMap.put(setInitialValues, invokeInfo);
            log.debug("setInitialValues hash:"+hash);

            Class[] getSig = {Object.class};
            Method get = exposedInterface.getDeclaredMethod("get",
                                                            getSig);
            hash = new Long(MarshalledInvocation.calculateHash(get));
            invokeInfo = new InvocationInfo("get",
                                            Invocation.OPERATION,
                                            Invocation.READ, getSig,
                                            descriptors, resource);
```

```
            methodMap.put(hash, get);
            invokeMap.put(get, invokeInfo);
            log.debug("get hash:"+hash);

            Class[] putSig = {Object.class, Object.class};
            Method put = exposedInterface.getDeclaredMethod("put",
                                                            putSig);
            hash = new Long(MarshalledInvocation.calculateHash(put));
            invokeInfo = new InvocationInfo("put",
                                            Invocation.OPERATION,
                                            Invocation.WRITE, putSig,
                                            descriptors, resource);
            methodMap.put(hash, put);
            invokeMap.put(put, invokeInfo);
            log.debug("putt hash:"+hash);
        } catch(Exception e) {
            log.error("Failed to init InvokerInterceptor", e);
        }
    }

    public Object invoke(Invocation invocation)
        throws InvocationException
    {
        String opName = invocation.getName();
        Object[] args = invocation.getArgs();
        Object returnValue = null;
        if (opName.equals("invoke") == true) {
            org.jboss.invocation.Invocation invokeInfo =
                (org.jboss.invocation.Invocation) args[0];
            // Set the method hash to Method mapping
            if (invokeInfo instanceof MarshalledInvocation) {
                MarshalledInvocation mi = (MarshalledInvocation) invokeInfo;
                mi.setMethodMap(methodMap);
            }

            // Invoke the exposedInterface method via reflection if
            // this is an invoke
            Method method = invokeInfo.getMethod();
            Object[] methodArgs = invokeInfo.getArguments();
            InvocationInfo info = (InvocationInfo) invokeMap.get(method);
            Invocation methodInvocation = info.getInvocation(methodArgs);
            returnValue = getNext().invoke(methodInvocation);
        } else {
            returnValue = getNext().invoke(invocation);
        }
```

```
        return returnValue;
    }

    /**
     * A class that holds the ClientInterface method info needed to build
     * the JMX Invocation to pass down the interceptor stack.
     */
    private class InvocationInfo
    {
        private int type;
        private int impact;
        private String name;
        private String[] signature;
        private Descriptor[] descriptors;
        private Object resource;


        InvocationInfo(String name, int type, int impact,
                       Class[] signature, Descriptor[] descriptors,
                       Object resource)
        {
            this.name = name;
            this.type = type;
            this.impact = impact;
            this.descriptors = descriptors;
            this.resource = resource;
            this.signature = new String[signature.length];
            for(int s = 0; s < signature.length; s ++) {
                this.signature[s] = signature[s].getName();
            }
        }

        Invocation getInvocation(Object[] args)
        {
            return new Invocation(name, type, impact, args, signature,
                                  descriptors, resource);
        }
    }
}
```

The deployment descriptor should include the interceptor stack:

```
<?xml version='1.0' encoding='UTF-8' ?>
<server>
    <mbean code="org.jboss.chap2.xmbean.JNDIMap"
        name="chap2.xmbean:service=JNDIMap,version=3"
```

```
        xmbean-dd="META-INF/jndimap-xmbean3.xml">
        <attribute name="JndiName">inmemory/maps/MapTest</attribute>
        <depends>jboss:service=Naming</depends>
    </mbean>
    <!-- The JRMP invoker proxy configuration for
                    the naming service -->
    <mbean code="org.jboss.invocation.jrmp.server.JRMPProxyFactory"
           name="jboss.test:service=proxyFactory,type=jrmp,target=JNDIMap">
        <!-- Use the standard JRMPInvoker from
                    conf/jboss-service.xml -->
        <attribute name="InvokerName">jboss:service=invoker,type=jrmp</attribute>
        <attribute name="TargetName">chap2.xmbean:service=JNDIMap,version=3
➥</attribute>
        <attribute name="JndiName">secure-xmbean/ClientInterface</attribute>
        <attribute name="ExportedInterface">
            org.jboss.chap2.xmbean.ClientInterface
        </attribute>
        <attribute name="ClientInterceptors">
            <iterceptors>
                <interceptor>org.jboss.proxy.ClientMethodInterceptor</interceptor>
                <interceptor>org.jboss.proxy.SecurityInterceptor</interceptor>
                <interceptor>org.jboss.invocation.InvokerInterceptor</interceptor>
            </iterceptors>
        </attribute>
        <depends>jboss:service=invoker,type=jrmp</depends>
        <depends>chap2.xmbean:service=JNDIMap,version=3</depends>
    </mbean>
</server>
```

The following shows the results of running this example:

```
[examples] ant -Dchap=chap2 -Dex=xmbean3 config
...
config:
     [echo] Preparing rmi-adaptor configuration fileset
     [copy] Copying 60 files to /tmp/jboss-3.2.6/server/rmi-adaptor
   [delete] Deleting directory /tmp/jboss-3.2.6/server/rmi-adaptor/deploy/
➥jmx-invoker-adap
tor-server.sar
   [delete] Deleting directory /tmp/jboss-3.2.6/server/rmi-adaptor/deploy/
➥management
[examples]$ ant -Dchap=chap2 -Dex=xmbean3 run-example
...
run-examplexmbean3:
     [java] Called to getInitialValues failed as expected: Caller=null is
➥not allowed access
```

```
     [java] key=key0, value=value0
     [java] JNDIMap.put(key1, value1) successful
     [java] JNDIMap.get(key0): null
     [java] JNDIMap.get(key1): value1
     [java] key=key0.1, value=value0.2
[examples]$ ant -Dchap=chap2 -Dex=xmbean3 run-example
...
run-examplexmbean3:
     [java] Called to getInitialValues failed as expected: Caller=
➥null is not allowed access
     [java] key=key0.1, value=value0.2
     [java] JNDIMap.put(key1, value1) successful
     [java] JNDIMap.get(key0): null
     [java] JNDIMap.get(key1): value1
     [java] key=key0.1.1, value=value0.2.2
```

Deployment Ordering and Dependencies

You have seen how to manage dependencies by using the service descriptor `depends` and `depends-list` tags. The deployment ordering supported by the deployment scanners provides a coarse-grained dependency management in that there is an order to deployments. If dependencies are consistent with the deployment packages, then this is a simpler mechanism than having to enumerate the explicit MBean-to-MBean dependencies. By writing your own filters, you can change the coarse-grained ordering performed by the deployment scanner.

When a component archive is deployed, its nested deployment units are processed in a depth-first ordering. Structuring of components into an archive hierarchy is yet another way to manage deployment ordering. You need to explicitly state your MBean dependencies if your packaging structure does not happen to resolve the dependencies.

Let's consider an example of a component deployment that consists of an MBean that uses an EJB. Here is the structure of the sample EAR:

```
output/chap2/chap2-ex3.ear
+- META-INF/MANIFEST.MF
+- META-INF/jboss-app.xml
+- chap2-ex3.jar (archive) [EJB jar]
| +- META-INF/MANIFEST.MF
| +- META-INF/ejb-jar.xml
| +- org/jboss/chap2/ex3/EchoBean.class
| +- org/jboss/chap2/ex3/EchoLocal.class
| +- org/jboss/chap2/ex3/EchoLocalHome.class
+- chap2-ex3.sar (archive) [MBean sar]
| +- META-INF/MANIFEST.MF
| +- META-INF/jboss-service.xml
```

```
| +- org/jboss/chap2/ex3/EjbMBeanAdaptor.class
+- META-INF/application.xml
```

The EAR contains `chap2-ex3.jar` and `chap2-ex3.sar`. `chap2-ex3.jar` is the EJB archive, and `chap2-ex3.sar` is the MBean service archive. The service is implemented here as a Dynamic MBean to provide an illustration of the use of Dynamic MBeans:

```
package org.jboss.chap2.ex3;

import java.lang.reflect.Method;
import javax.ejb.CreateException;
import javax.management.Attribute;
import javax.management.AttributeList;
import javax.management.AttributeNotFoundException;
import javax.management.DynamicMBean;
import javax.management.InvalidAttributeValueException;
import javax.management.JMRuntimeException;
import javax.management.MBeanAttributeInfo;
import javax.management.MBeanConstructorInfo;
import javax.management.MBeanInfo;
import javax.management.MBeanNotificationInfo;
import javax.management.MBeanOperationInfo;
import javax.management.MBeanException;
import javax.management.MBeanServer;
import javax.management.ObjectName;
import javax.management.ReflectionException;
import javax.naming.InitialContext;
import javax.naming.NamingException;

import org.jboss.system.ServiceMBeanSupport;

/**
 *  An example of a DynamicMBean that exposes select attributes and
 *  operations of an EJB as an MBean.
 *  @author Scott.Stark@jboss.org
 *  @version $Revision: 1.5 $
 */
public class EjbMBeanAdaptor extends ServiceMBeanSupport
    implements DynamicMBean
{
    private String helloPrefix;
    private String ejbJndiName;
    private EchoLocalHome home;

    /** These are the mbean attributes we expose
     */
```

```
private MBeanAttributeInfo[] attributes = {
    new MBeanAttributeInfo("HelloPrefix", "java.lang.String",
                    "The prefix message to append to the session echo reply",
                    true, // isReadable
                    true, // isWritable
                    false), // isIs
    new MBeanAttributeInfo("EjbJndiName", "java.lang.String",
                    "The JNDI name of the session bean local home",
                    true, // isReadable
                    true, // isWritable
                    false) // isIs
};

/**
 * These are the mbean operations we expose
 */
private MBeanOperationInfo[] operations;

/**
 * We override this method to set up our echo operation info. It
 * could also be done in a ctor.
 */
public ObjectName preRegister(MBeanServer server,
                              ObjectName name)
    throws Exception
{
    log.info("preRegister notification seen");

    operations = new MBeanOperationInfo[5];

    Class thisClass = getClass();
    Class[] parameterTypes = {String.class};
    Method echoMethod =
        thisClass.getMethod("echo", parameterTypes);
    String desc = "The echo op invokes the session bean echo method and"
        + " returns its value prefixed with the helloPrefix attribute value";
    operations[0] = new MBeanOperationInfo(desc, echoMethod);

    // Add the Service interface operations from our super class
    parameterTypes = new Class[0];
    Method createMethod =
        thisClass.getMethod("create", parameterTypes);
    operations[1] = new MBeanOperationInfo("The
            JBoss Service.create", createMethod);
    Method startMethod =
```

```
        thisClass.getMethod("start", parameterTypes);
    operations[2] = new MBeanOperationInfo("The
            JBoss Service.start", startMethod);
    Method stopMethod =
        thisClass.getMethod("stop", parameterTypes);
    operations[3] = new MBeanOperationInfo("The
            JBoss Service.stop", startMethod);
    Method destroyMethod =
        thisClass.getMethod("destroy", parameterTypes);
    operations[4] = new MBeanOperationInfo("The
            JBoss Service.destroy", startMethod);
    return name;
}


// --- Begin ServiceMBeanSupport overides
protected void createService() throws Exception
{
    log.info("Notified of create state");
}

protected void startService() throws Exception
{
    log.info("Notified of start state");
    InitialContext ctx = new InitialContext();
    home = (EchoLocalHome) ctx.lookup(ejbJndiName);
}

protected void stopService()
{
    log.info("Notified of stop state");
}

// --- End ServiceMBeanSupport overides

public String getHelloPrefix()
{
    return helloPrefix;
}
public void setHelloPrefix(String helloPrefix)
{
    this.helloPrefix = helloPrefix;
}

public String getEjbJndiName()
```

```
{
    return ejbJndiName;
}
public void setEjbJndiName(String ejbJndiName)
{
    this.ejbJndiName = ejbJndiName;
}

public String echo(String arg)
    throws CreateException, NamingException
{
    log.debug("Lookup EchoLocalHome@"+ejbJndiName);
    EchoLocal bean = home.create();
    String echo = helloPrefix + bean.echo(arg);
    return echo;
}

// --- Begin DynamicMBean interface methods
/**
 *  Returns the management interface that describes this dynamic
 *  resource.  It is the responsibility of the implementation to
 *  make sure the description is accurate.
 *
 * @return the management interface descriptor.
 */
public MBeanInfo getMBeanInfo()
{
    String classname = getClass().getName();
    String description = "This is an MBean that uses a session bean in the"
        + " implementation of its echo operation.";
    MBeanInfo[] constructors = null;
    MBeanNotificationInfo[] notifications = null;
    MBeanInfo mbeanInfo = new MBeanInfo(classname,
                                        description, attributes,
                                        constructors, operations,
                                        notifications);
    // Log when this is called so we know when in the
    lifecycle this is used
        Throwable trace = new Throwable("getMBeanInfo trace");
    log.info("Don't panic, just a stack
          trace", trace);
    return mbeanInfo;
}

/**
```

```
 *  Returns the value of the attribute with the name matching the
 *  passed string.
 *
 * @param attribute the name of the attribute.
 * @return the value of the attribute.
 * @exception AttributeNotFoundException when there is no such
 * attribute.
 * @exception MBeanException wraps any error thrown by the
 * resource when
 * getting the attribute.
 * @exception ReflectionException wraps any error invoking the
 * resource.
 */
public Object getAttribute(String attribute)
    throws AttributeNotFoundException,
           MBeanException,
           ReflectionException
{
    Object value = null;
    if (attribute.equals("HelloPrefix")) {
        value = getHelloPrefix();
    } else if(attribute.equals("EjbJndiName")) {
        value = getEjbJndiName();
    } else {
        throw new AttributeNotFoundException("Unknown
            attribute("+attribute+") requested");
    }
    return value;
}

/**
 * Returns the values of the attributes with names matching the
 * passed string array.
 *
 * @param attributes the names of the attribute.
 * @return an {@link AttributeList AttributeList} of name
 * and value pairs.
 */
public AttributeList getAttributes(String[] attributes)
{
    AttributeList values = new AttributeList();
    for (int a = 0; a < attributes.length; a++) {
        String name = attributes[a];
        try {
            Object value = getAttribute(name);
```

```
                Attribute attr = new Attribute(name, value);
                values.add(attr);
            } catch(Exception e) {
                log.error("Failed to find attribute: "+name, e);
            }
        }
        return values;
    }

    /**
     *  Sets the value of an attribute. The attribute and new value
     *  are passed in the name value pair {@link Attribute
     *  Attribute}.
     *
     * @see javax.management.Attribute
     *
     * @param attribute the name and new value of the attribute.
     * @exception AttributeNotFoundException when there is no such
     * attribute.
     * @exception InvalidAttributeValueException when the new value
     * cannot be converted to the type of the attribute.
     * @exception MBeanException wraps any error thrown by the
     * resource when setting the new value.
     * @exception ReflectionException wraps any error invoking the
     * resource.
     */
    public void setAttribute(Attribute attribute)
        throws AttributeNotFoundException,
               InvalidAttributeValueException,
               MBeanException,
               ReflectionException
    {
        String name = attribute.getName();
        if (name.equals("HelloPrefix")) {
            String value = attribute.getValue().toString();
            setHelloPrefix(value);
        } else if(ename.equals("EjbJndiName")) {
            String value = attribute.getValue().toString();
            setEjbJndiName(value);
        } else {
            throw new AttributeNotFoundException
➥("Unknown attribute("+name+") requested");
        }
    }
```

```
/**
 * Sets the values of the attributes passed as an
 * {@link AttributeList AttributeList} of name and new
 * value pairs.
 *
 * @param attributes the name and new value pairs.
 * @return an {@link AttributeList AttributeList} of name and
 * value pairs that were actually set.
 */
public AttributeList setAttributes(AttributeList attributes)
{
    AttributeList setAttributes = new AttributeList();
    for(int a = 0; a < attributes.size(); a++) {
        Attribute attr = (Attribute) attributes.get(a);
        try {
            setAttribute(attr);
            setAttributes.add(attr);
        } catch(Exception ignore) {
        }
    }
    return setAttributes;
}

/**
 *  Invokes a resource operation.
 *
 *  @param actionName the name of the operation to perform.
 *  @param params the parameters to pass to the operation.
 *  @param signature the signatures of the parameters.
 *  @return the result of the operation.
 *  @exception MBeanException wraps any error thrown by the
 *  resource when performing the operation.
 *  @exception ReflectionException wraps any error invoking the
 *  resource.
 */
public Object invoke(String actionName, Object[] params,
                     String[] signature)
    throws MBeanException,
           ReflectionException
{
    Object rtnValue = null;
    log.debug("Begin invoke, actionName="+actionName);
    try {
        if (actionName.equals("echo")) {
            String arg = (String) params[0];
```

```
                rtnValue = echo(arg);
                log.debug("Result: "+rtnValue);
            } else if (actionName.equals("create")) {
                super.create();
            } else if (actionName.equals("start")) {
                super.start();
            } else if (actionName.equals("stop")) {
                super.stop();
            } else if (actionName.equals("destroy")) {
                super.destroy();
            } else {
                throw new JMRuntimeException("Invalid state,
                don't know about op="+actionName);
            }
        } catch(Exception e) {
            throw new ReflectionException(e, "echo failed");
        }


        log.debug("End invoke, actionName="+actionName);
        return rtnValue;
    }

    // --- End DynamicMBean interface methods

}
```

Believe it or not, this is a very trivial MBean. The vast majority of the code is here to provide the MBean metadata and handle the callbacks from the MBean server. This is required because a Dynamic MBean is free to expose whatever management interface it wants. A Dynamic MBean can in fact change its management interface at runtime, simply by returning different metadata from the `getMBeanInfo` method. Of course, some clients may not be happy with such a dynamic object, but the MBean server will do nothing to prevent a Dynamic MBean from changing its interface.

There are two points to this example. First, it demonstrates how an MBean can depend on an EJB for some of its functionality. Second, it shows how to create MBeans with dynamic management interfaces. If you were to write a standard MBean with a static interface for this example it would look like the following:

```
public interface EjbMBeanAdaptorMBean
{
    public String getHelloPrefix();
    public void setHelloPrefix(String prefix);
    public String getEjbJndiName();
    public void setEjbJndiName(String jndiName);
```

```
    public String echo(String arg) throws CreateException, NamingException;
    public void create() throws Exception;
    public void start() throws Exception;
    public void stop();
    public void destroy();
}
```

Lines 67–83 are where the MBean operation metadata is constructed. The `echo(String)`, `create()`, `start()`, `stop()`, and `destroy()` operations are defined by obtaining the corresponding `java.lang.reflect.Method` object and adding a description.

Let's go through the code and discuss where this interface implementation exists and how the MBean uses the EJB. Beginning with lines 40–51, the two `MBeanAttributeInfo` instances created define the attributes of the MBean. These attributes correspond to the `getHelloPrefix/setHelloPrefix` and `getEjbJndiName/setEjbJndiName` of the static interface. One thing to note in terms of why you might want to use a Dynamic MBean is that you have the ability to associate descriptive text with the attribute metadata. This is not something you can do with a static interface.

Lines 88–103 correspond to the JBoss service life cycle callbacks. Because you are subclassing the `ServiceMBeanSupport` utility class, you override the `createService`, `startService`, and `stopService` template callbacks rather than the `create`, `start`, and `stop` methods of the service interface. Note that you cannot attempt to look up the `EchoLocalHome` interface of the EJB you make use of until the `startService` method. Any attempt to access the home interface in an earlier life cycle method would result in the name not being found in JNDI because the EJB container had not gotten to the point of binding the home interfaces. Because of this dependency, you need to specify that the MBean service depends on the `EchoLocal` EJB container to ensure that the service is not started before the EJB container is started. You will see this dependency specification when we look at the service descriptor.

Lines 105–121 are the `HelloPrefix` and `EjbJndiName` attribute accessors' implementations. These are invoked in response to `getAttribute/setAttribute` invocations made through the MBean server.

Lines 123–130 correspond to the `echo(String)` operation implementation. This method invokes the `EchoLocal.echo(String)` EJB method. The local bean interface is created by using the `EchoLocalHome` that was obtained in the `startService` method.

The remainder of the class makes up the Dynamic MBean interface implementation. Lines 133–152 correspond to the MBean metadata accessor callback. This method returns a description of the MBean management interface, in the form of the `javax.management.MBeanInfo` object. This is made up of a `description`, the `MBeanAttributeInfo`, and the `MBeanOperationInfo` metadata created earlier, as well as constructor and notification information. This MBean does not need any special constructors or notifications, so this information is null.

Lines 154–258 handle the attribute access requests. This is rather tedious and error-prone code, so you should use a toolkit or an infrastructure that helps generate these methods. A model MBean framework based on XML called XBeans is currently being investigated in JBoss. Other than this, no other Dynamic MBean frameworks currently exist.

Lines 260–310 correspond to the operation invocation dispatch entry point. Here, the request operation action name is checked against those the MBean handles, and the appropriate method is invoked.

The `jboss-service.xml` descriptor for the MBean is shown next. This is the format of the EJB container MBean `ObjectName`:

```
<server>
    <mbean code="org.jboss.chap2.ex3.EjbMBeanAdaptor"
           name="jboss.book:service=EjbMBeanAdaptor">
        <attribute name="HelloPrefix">AdaptorPrefix</attribute>
        <attribute name="EjbJndiName">local/chap2.EchoBean</attribute>
        <depends>jboss.j2ee:service=EJB,jndiName=local/chap2.EchoBean</depends>
    </mbean>
</server>
```

You deploy the example EAR by running this:

```
[examples]$ ant -Dchap=chap2 -Dex=3 run-example
```

On the server console there should be messages similar to the following:

```
14:57:12,906 INFO  [EARDeployer] Init J2EE application:
➥file:/private/tmp/jboss-4.0.1/server/default/deploy/chap2-ex3.ear
14:57:13,044 INFO  [EjbMBeanAdaptor] Don't panic, just a stack trace
java.lang.Throwable: getMBeanInfo trace
        at org.jboss.chap2.ex3.EjbMBeanAdaptor.getMBeanInfo
➥(EjbMBeanAdaptor.java:153)
        at org.jboss.mx.server.RawDynamicInvoker.getMBeanInfo
➥(RawDynamicInvoker.java:172)
        at org.jboss.mx.server.RawDynamicInvoker.preRegister
➥(RawDynamicInvoker.java:187)
...
14:57:13,088 INFO  [EjbMBeanAdaptor] preRegister notification seen
14:57:13,093 INFO  [EjbMBeanAdaptor] Don't panic, just a stack trace
java.lang.Throwable: getMBeanInfo trace
        at org.jboss.chap2.ex3.EjbMBeanAdaptor.getMBeanInfo
➥(EjbMBeanAdaptor.java:153)
        at org.jboss.mx.server.RawDynamicInvoker.getMBeanInfo
➥(RawDynamicInvoker.java:172)
        at org.jboss.mx.server.registry.BasicMBeanRegistry.registerMBean
➥(BasicMBeanRegistry.java:207)
...
```

```
14:57:13,117 INFO  [EjbMBeanAdaptor] Don't panic, just a stack trace
java.lang.Throwable: getMBeanInfo trace
        at org.jboss.chap2.ex3.EjbMBeanAdaptor.getMBeanInfo
➥(EjbMBeanAdaptor.java:153)
        at org.jboss.mx.server.RawDynamicInvoker.getMBeanInfo
➥(RawDynamicInvoker.java:172)
        at org.jboss.mx.server.registry.BasicMBeanRegistry.registerMBean
➥(BasicMBeanRegistry.java:235)
...
14:57:13,140 WARN  [EjbMBeanAdaptor] Unexcepted error accessing
➥MBeanInfo for null
java.lang.NullPointerException
        at org.jboss.system.ServiceMBeanSupport.postRegister
➥(ServiceMBeanSupport.java:418)
        at org.jboss.mx.server.RawDynamicInvoker.postRegister
➥(RawDynamicInvoker.java:226)
        at org.jboss.mx.server.registry.BasicMBeanRegistry.registerMBean
➥(BasicMBeanRegistry.java:312)
...
14:57:13,203 INFO  [EjbMBeanAdaptor] Don't panic, just a stack trace
java.lang.Throwable: getMBeanInfo trace
        at org.jboss.chap2.ex3.EjbMBeanAdaptor.getMBeanInfo
➥(EjbMBeanAdaptor.java:153)
        at org.jboss.mx.server.RawDynamicInvoker.getMBeanInfo
➥(RawDynamicInvoker.java:172)
        at org.jboss.mx.server.MBeanServerImpl.getMBeanInfo
➥(MBeanServerImpl.java:481)
...
14:57:13,232 INFO  [EjbMBeanAdaptor] Don't panic, just a stack trace
java.lang.Throwable: getMBeanInfo trace
        at org.jboss.chap2.ex3.EjbMBeanAdaptor.getMBeanInfo
➥(EjbMBeanAdaptor.java:153)
        at org.jboss.mx.server.RawDynamicInvoker.getMBeanInfo
➥(RawDynamicInvoker.java:172)
        at org.jboss.mx.server.MBeanServerImpl.getMBeanInfo
➥(MBeanServerImpl.java:481)
...
14:57:13,420 INFO  [EjbModule] Deploying Chap2EchoInfoBean
14:57:13,443 INFO  [EjbModule] Deploying chap2.EchoBean
14:57:13,488 INFO  [EjbMBeanAdaptor] Don't panic, just a stack trace
java.lang.Throwable: getMBeanInfo trace
        at org.jboss.chap2.ex3.EjbMBeanAdaptor.getMBeanInfo
➥(EjbMBeanAdaptor.java:153)
        at org.jboss.mx.server.RawDynamicInvoker.getMBeanInfo
➥(RawDynamicInvoker.java:172)
```

```
        at org.jboss.mx.server.MBeanServerImpl.getMBeanInfo
➥(MBeanServerImpl.java:481)
...
14:57:13,542 INFO  [EjbMBeanAdaptor] Don't panic, just a stack trace
java.lang.Throwable: getMBeanInfo trace
        at org.jboss.chap2.ex3.EjbMBeanAdaptor.getMBeanInfo
➥(EjbMBeanAdaptor.java:153)
        at org.jboss.mx.server.RawDynamicInvoker.getMBeanInfo
➥(RawDynamicInvoker.java:172)
        at org.jboss.mx.server.MBeanServerImpl.getMBeanInfo
➥(MBeanServerImpl.java:481)
...
14:57:13,558 INFO  [EjbMBeanAdaptor] Begin invoke, actionName=create
14:57:13,560 INFO  [EjbMBeanAdaptor] Notified of create state
14:57:13,562 INFO  [EjbMBeanAdaptor] End invoke, actionName=create
14:57:13,604 INFO  [EjbMBeanAdaptor] Don't panic, just a stack trace
java.lang.Throwable: getMBeanInfo trace
        at org.jboss.chap2.ex3.EjbMBeanAdaptor.getMBeanInfo
➥(EjbMBeanAdaptor.java:153)
        at org.jboss.mx.server.RawDynamicInvoker.getMBeanInfo
➥(RawDynamicInvoker.java:172)
        at org.jboss.mx.server.MBeanServerImpl.getMBeanInfo
➥(MBeanServerImpl.java:481)
        at org.jboss.mx.server.MBeanServerImpl.isInstanceOf
➥(MBeanServerImpl.java:639)
...
14:57:13,621 INFO  [EjbMBeanAdaptor] Don't panic, just a stack trace
java.lang.Throwable: getMBeanInfo trace
        at org.jboss.chap2.ex3.EjbMBeanAdaptor.getMBeanInfo
➥(EjbMBeanAdaptor.java:153)
        at org.jboss.mx.server.RawDynamicInvoker.getMBeanInfo
➥(RawDynamicInvoker.java:172)
        at org.jboss.mx.server.MBeanServerImpl.getMBeanInfo
➥(MBeanServerImpl.java:481)
        at org.jboss.mx.util.JMXInvocationHandler.<init>
➥(JMXInvocationHandler.java:110)
        at org.jboss.mx.util.MBeanProxy.get(MBeanProxy.java:76)
        at org.jboss.mx.util.MBeanProxy.get(MBeanProxy.java:64)
14:57:13,641 INFO  [EjbMBeanAdaptor] Begin invoke, actionName=getState
14:57:13,942 INFO  [EjbMBeanAdaptor] Begin invoke, actionName=start
14:57:13,944 INFO  [EjbMBeanAdaptor] Notified of start state
14:57:13,951 INFO  [EjbMBeanAdaptor] Testing Echo
14:57:13,983 INFO  [EchoBean] echo, info=echo info, arg=, arg=startService
14:57:13,986 INFO  [EjbMBeanAdaptor] echo(startService) = startService
14:57:13,988 INFO  [EjbMBeanAdaptor] End invoke, actionName=start
```

```
14:57:13,991 INFO  [EJBDeployer] Deployed: file:/private/tmp/jboss-
4.0.1/server/default/tmp/deploy/tmp1418chap2-ex3.ear-contents/chap2-ex3.jar
14:57:14,075 INFO  [EARDeployer] Started J2EE application:
➥file:/private/tmp/jboss-4.0.1/server/default/deploy/chap2-ex3.ear
```

The stack traces are not exceptions. They are traces that come from line 150 of the `EjbMBeanAdaptor` code to demonstrate that clients ask for the MBean interface when they want to discover the MBean's capabilities. Notice that the EJB container (lines with `EjbModule`) is started before the example MBean (lines with `EjbMBeanAdaptor`).

Now, let's invoke the echo method, using the JMX Console web application. Go to the JMX Console (http://localhost:8080/jmx-console) and find `service=EjbMBeanAdaptor` in the `jboss.book` domain. Click the link and scroll down to the `echo` operation section. The view should be like that shown in Figure 2.19.

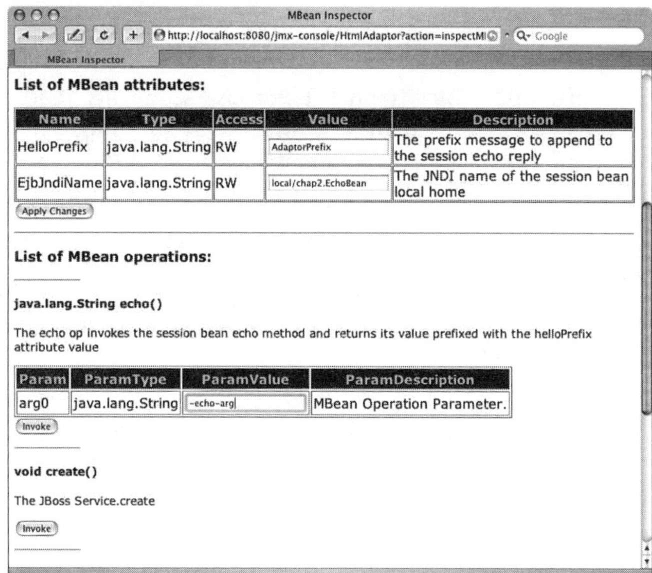

FIGURE 2.19 The `EjbMBeanAdaptor` MBean operations JMX Console view.

As shown, you have already entered an argument string of `-echo-arg` into the `ParamValue` text field. If you click the Invoke button, the result string `AdaptorPrefix-echo-arg` is displayed on the results page. The server console will show several stack traces from the various metadata queries issued by the JMX Console and the MBean invoke method debugging lines:

```
10:51:48,671 INFO [EjbMBeanAdaptor] Begin invoke, actionName=echo
10:51:48,671 INFO [EjbMBeanAdaptor] Lookup EchoLocalHome@local/chap2.EchoBean
10:51:48,687 INFO [EchoBean] echo, info=echo info, arg=, arg=-echo-arg
10:51:48,687 INFO [EjbMBeanAdaptor] Result: AdaptorPrefix-echo-arg
10:51:48,687 INFO [EjbMBeanAdaptor] End invoke, actionName=echo
```

The JBoss Deployer Architecture

JBoss has an extensible deployer architecture that allows you to incorporate components into the bare JBoss JMX microkernel. `MainDeployer` is the deployment entry point. Requests to deploy a component are sent to `MainDeployer`, which determines whether there is a subdeployer capable of handling the deployment; if there is, it delegates the deployment to the subdeployer. (You saw an example of this earlier in this chapter, when you looked at how `MainDeployer` uses the `SARDeployer` to deploy MBean services.) The following are some of the deployers provided with JBoss:

- **`AbstractWebDeployer`**—This subdeployer handles WARs. It accepts deployment archives and directories whose names end with the `.war` suffix. WARs must have a `WEB-INF/web.xml` descriptor and may have a `WEB-INF/jboss-web.xml` descriptor.
- **`EARDeployer`**—This subdeployer handles EARs. It accepts deployment archives and directories whose names end with the `.ear` suffix. EARs must have a `META-INF/application.xml` descriptor and may have a `META-INF/jboss-app.xml` descriptor.
- **`EJBDeployer`**—This subdeployer handles Enterprise Bean JARs. It accepts deployment archives and directories whose names end with the `.jar` suffix. EJB JARs must have a `META-INF/ejb-jar.xml` descriptor and may have a `META-INF/jboss.xml` descriptor.
- **`JARDeployer`**—This subdeployer handles library JAR archives. The only restriction it places on an archive is that it cannot contain a `WEB-INF` directory.
- **`RARDeployer`**—This subdeployer handles JCA RARs. It accepts deployment archives and directories whose names end with the `.rar` suffix. RARs must have a `META-INF/ra.xml` descriptor.
- **`SARDeployer`**—This subdeployer handles JBoss MBean SARs. It accepts deployment archives and directories whose names end with the `.sar` suffix, as well as standalone XML files that end with `service.xml`. SARs that are JARs must have a `META-INF/jboss-service.xml` descriptor.
- **`XSLSubDeployer`**—This subdeployer deploys arbitrary XML files. JBoss uses `XSLSubDeployer` to deploy `ds.xml` files and transform them into `service.xml` files for `SARDeployer`. However, it is not limited to just this task.
- **`HARDeployer`**—This subdeployer deploys HARs. It accepts deployment archives and directories whose names end with the `.har` suffix. HARs must have a `META-INF/hibernate-service.xml` descriptor.
- **`AspectDeployer`**—This subdeployer deploys AOP archives. It accepts deployment archives and directories whose names end with the `.aop` suffix as well as `aop.xml` files. AOP archives must have a `METAINF/jboss-aop.xml` descriptor.
- **`ClientDeployer`**—This subdeployer deploys J2EE application clients. It accepts deployment archives and directories whose names end with the `.jar` suffix. J2EE clients must have a `META-INF/application-client.xml` descriptor and may have a `META-INF/jboss-client.xml` descriptor.

- **BeanShellSubDeployer**—This subdeployer deploys bean shell scripts as MBeans. It accepts files whose names end with the .bsh suffix.

MainDeployer, JARDeployer, and SARDeployer are hard-coded deployers in the JBoss server core. All other deployers are MBean services that register themselves as deployers with the MainDeployer by using the addDeployer(SubDeployer) operation.

MainDeployer communicates information about the component to be deployed to the SubDeployer by using a DeploymentInfo object. The DeploymentInfo object is a data structure that encapsulates the complete state of a deployable component.

When MainDeployer receives a deployment request, it iterates through its registered subdeployers and invokes the accepts(DeploymentInfo) method on the subdeployer. The first subdeployer to return true is chosen. The MainDeployer will delegate the init, create, start, stop, and destroy deployment life cycle operations to the subdeployer.

Deployers and Class Loaders

Deployers are the mechanism by which components are brought into a JBoss server. Deployers are also the creators of the majority of UCL instances, and the primary creator is MainDeployer. MainDeployer creates the UCL for a deployment early on during its init method. The UCL is created by calling the DeploymentInfo.createClassLoaders() method. Only the topmost DeploymentInfo actually creates a UCL. All subdeployments add their classpaths to their parent DeploymentInfo UCL. Every deployment does have a standalone URLClassLoader that uses the deployment URL as its path. This is used to localize the loading of resources such as deployment descriptors. Figure 2.20 provides an illustration of the interaction between deployers, DeploymentInfos, and class loaders.

Figure 2.20 illustrates an EAR deployment with EJB and WAR subdeployments. The EJB deployment references the lib/util.jar utility JAR via its manifest. The WAR includes classes in its WEB-INF/classes directory as well as in WEB-INF/lib/jbosstest-web-util.jar. Each deployment has a DeploymentInfo instance that has a URLClassLoader pointing to the deployment archive. The DeploymentInfo associated with some.ear is the only one to have a UCL created. ejbs.jar and web.war DeploymentInfos add their deployment archives to the some.ear UCL classpath, and they share this UCL as their deployment UCL. The EJBDeployer also adds any manifest JARs to the EAR UCL.

The WARDeployer behaves differently than other deployers in that it only adds its WAR archive to the DeploymentInfo UCL classpath. The loading of classes from the WAR WEB-INF/classes and WEB-INF/lib locations is handled by the servlet container class loader. The servlet container class loaders delegate to the WAR DeploymentInfo UCL as their parent class loader, but the server container class loader is not part of the JBoss class loader repository. Therefore, classes inside a WAR are not visible to other components. Classes that need to be shared between web application components and other components such as EJBs and MBeans need to be loaded into the shared class loader repository either by including the classes in a SAR or EJB deployment or by referencing a JAR containing the shared classes through a manifest Class-Path entry. In the case of a SAR, the SAR classpath element in the service deployment serves the same purpose as a JAR manifest `Class-Path`.

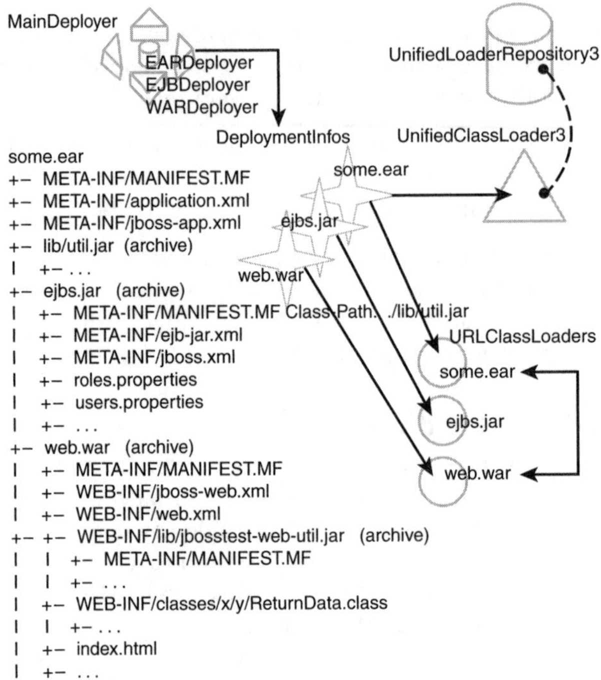

FIGURE 2.20 The class loaders involved with an EAR deployment.

Exposing MBean Events via SNMP

JBoss has an `snmp-adaptor` service that can be used to intercept JMX notifications emitted by MBeans, convert them to traps, and send them to SNMP managers. In this respect, the `snmp-adaptor` acts as an SNMP agent. Future versions may offer support for full agent get/set functionality that maps onto MBean attributes or operations.

This service can be used to integrate JBoss with higher-order system/network management platforms (HP Open-View, for example), making the MBeans visible to those systems. The MBean developer can instrument the MBeans by producing notifications for any significant event (for example, server coldstart), and the adaptor can then be configured to intercept the notification and map it onto an SNMP traps. The adaptor uses the `JoeSNMP` package from OpenNMS as the SNMP engine.

The SNMP service is configured in `snmp-adaptor.sar`. This service is available only in the `all` configuration, so you need to copy it to your configuration if you want to use it. Inside the `snmp-adaptor.sar` directory are two configuration files that that control the SNMP service:

- `managers.xml`—This file configures where to send traps. The content model for this file is shown in Figure 2.21.

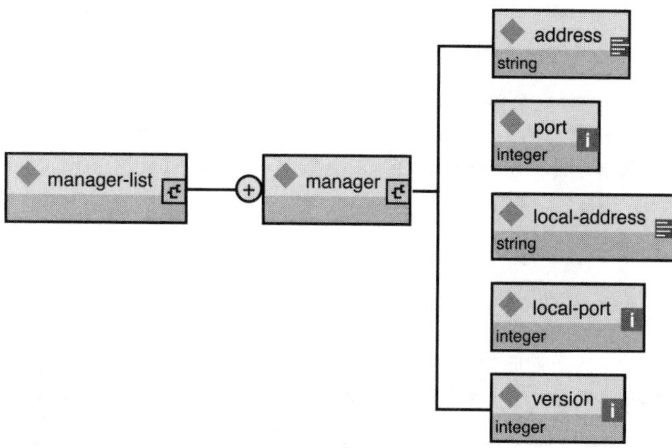

FIGURE 2.21 The schema for the SNMP managers file.

- `notifications.xml`—This file specifies the exact mapping of each notification type to a corresponding SNMP trap. The content model for this file is shown in Figure 2.22.

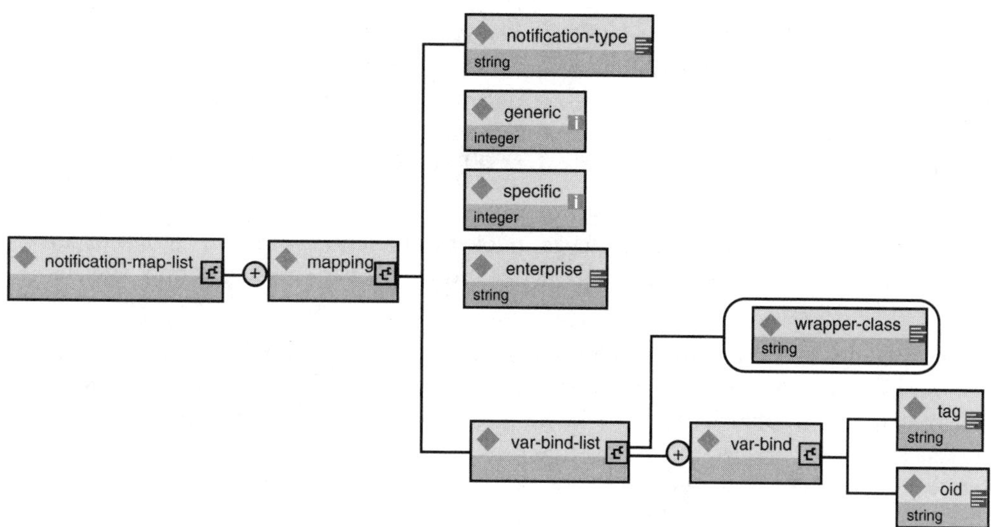

FIGURE 2.22 The schema for the notification to trap mapping file.

The `SNMPAgentService` MBean is configured in `snmp-adaptor.sar/META-INF/jboss-service.xml`. These are the configurable parameters:

- **HeartBeatPeriod**—Specifies the period, in seconds, during which heartbeat notifications are generated.
- **ManagersResName**—Specifies the resource name of the managers.xml file.
- **NotificationMapResName**—Specifies the resource name of the notications.xml file.
- **TrapFactoryClassName**—Specifies the org.jboss.jmx.adaptor.snmp.agent.TrapFactory implementation class that takes care of translation of JMX notifications into SNMP version 1 and version 2 traps.
- **TimerName**—Specifies the JMX ObjectName of the JMX timer service to use for heartbeat notifications.
- **SubscriptionList**—Specifies which MBeans and notifications to listen for.

The Event to Trap Service

TrapdService is a simple MBean that acts as an SNMP Manager. It listens to a configurable port for incoming traps and logs them as DEBUG messages, using the system logger. You can modify the log4j configuration to redirect the log output to a file. SnmpAgentService and TrapdService are not dependent on each other.

Remote Access to Services, Detached Invokers

In addition to the MBean services notion that allows for the ability to integrate arbitrary functionality, JBoss also has a detached invoker concept that allows MBean services to expose functional interfaces via arbitrary protocols for remote access by clients. The notion of a detached invoker is that remoting and the protocol by which a service is accessed is a functional aspect or service that is independent of the component. Thus, you can make a naming service available for use via RMI/JRMP, RMI/HTTP, RMI/SOAP, or any arbitrary custom transport.

Let's begin our discussion of the detached invoker architecture with an overview of the components involved. The main components in the detached invoker architecture are shown in Figure 2.23.

On the client side, a client proxy exposes the interface(s) of the MBean service. This is the same smart, compile-less dynamic proxy that you use for EJB home and remote interfaces. The only differences between the proxy for an arbitrary service and the EJB are the set of interfaces exposed and the client-side interceptors found inside the proxy. The client interceptors are represented by the rectangles inside the client proxy in Figure 2.23. An *interceptor* is an assembly-line type of pattern that allows for transformation of a method invocation and/or return values. A client obtains a proxy through some lookup mechanism, typically JNDI. Although RMI is indicated in Figure 2.23, the only real requirement on the exposed interface and its types is that they are serializable between the client server over JNDI as well as the transport layer.

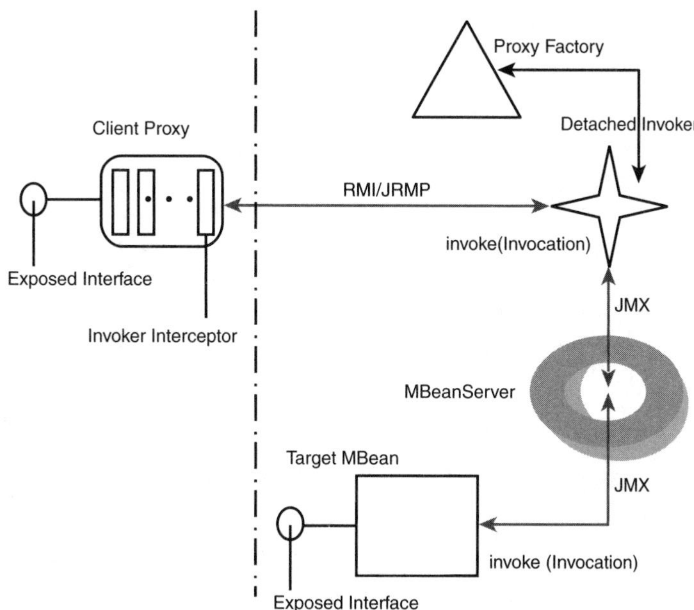

FIGURE 2.23 The main components in the detached invoker architecture.

The choice of the transport layer is determined by the last interceptor in the client proxy, which is referred to as *invoker interceptor* in Figure 2.23. The invoker interceptor contains a reference to the transport specific stub of the server-side *detached invoker* MBean service. The invoker interceptor also handles the optimization of calls that occur within the same VM as the target MBean. When the invoker interceptor detects that this is the case, the call is passed to a call-by-reference invoker that simply passes the invocation along to the target MBean.

The detached invoker service is responsible for making a generic invoke operation available via the transport that the detached invoker handles. The `Invoker` interface illustrates the generic invoke operation:

```
package org.jboss.invocation;

import java.rmi.Remote;
import org.jboss.proxy.Interceptor;
import org.jboss.util.id.GUID;


public interface Invoker
    extends Remote
{
    GUID ID = new GUID();
```

```
    String getServerHostName() throws Exception;

    Object invoke(Invocation invocation) throws Exception;
}
```

The Invoker interface extends Remote to be compatible with RMI, but this does not mean that an invoker must expose an RMI service stub. The detached invoker service simply acts as a transport gateway that accepts invocations represented as the org.jboss.invocation.Invocation object over its specific transport, unmarshals the invocation, forwards the invocation onto the destination MBean service, represented by the *target MBean* in Figure 2.23, and marshals the return value or exception resulting from the forwarded call back to the client.

The Invocation object is just a representation of a method invocation context. This includes the target MBean name, the method, the method arguments, a context of information associated with the proxy by the proxy factory, and an arbitrary map of data associated with the invocation by the client proxy interceptors.

The configuration of the client proxy is done by the server-side proxy factory MBean service, indicated by the *proxy factory* component in Figure 2.23. The proxy factory performs the following tasks:

- Creates a dynamic proxy that implements the interface the target MBean wishes to expose.
- Associates the client proxy interceptors with the dynamic proxy handler.
- Associates the invocation context with the dynamic proxy. This includes the target MBean, the detached invoker stub, and the proxy JNDI name.
- Makes the proxy available to clients by binding the proxy into JNDI.

The last component in Figure 2.23 is the *target MBean* service that wishes to expose an interface for invocations to remote clients. These steps are required for an MBean service to be accessible through a given interface:

1. Define a JMX operation that matches the signature public Object invoke(org.jboss.invocation.Invocation) throws Exception.
2. Create a HashMap<Long, Method> mapping from the exposed interface java.lang.reflect.Methods to the long hash representation, using the org.jboss.invocation.MarshalledInvocation.calculateHash method.
3. Implement the invoke(Invocation) JMX operation and use the interface method hash mapping to transform from the long hash representation of the invoked method to the java.lang.reflect.Method of the exposed interface. Reflection is used to perform the actual invocation on the object associated with the MBean service that actually implements the exposed interface.

A Detached Invoker Example: The `MBeanServer` Invoker Adaptor Service

As mentioned earlier in this chapter, there is a service that allows you to access the `javax.management.MBeanServer` via any protocol, using an invoker service. This section presents the `org.jboss.jmx.connector.invoker.InvokerAdaptorService` and its configuration for access via RMI/JRMP as an example of the steps required to provide remote access to an MBean service.

`InvokerAdaptorService` is a simple MBean service that only exists to fulfill the target MBean role in the detached invoker pattern (see Listing 2.16).

LISTING 2.16 The `InvokerAdaptorService` MBean

```
package org.jboss.jmx.connector.invoker;
public interface InvokerAdaptorServiceMBean
    extends org.jboss.system.ServiceMBean
{
    Class getExportedInterface();
    void setExportedInterface(Class exportedInterface);

    Object invoke(org.jboss.invocation.Invocation invocation)
        throws Exception;
}

package org.jboss.jmx.connector.invoker;

import java.lang.reflect.InvocationTargetException;
import java.lang.reflect.Method;
import java.lang.reflect.UndeclaredThrowableException;
import java.util.Collections;
import java.util.HashMap;
import java.util.Map;

import javax.management.MBeanServer;
import javax.management.ObjectName;

import org.jboss.invocation.Invocation;
import org.jboss.invocation.MarshalledInvocation;
import org.jboss.mx.server.ServerConstants;
import org.jboss.system.ServiceMBeanSupport;
import org.jboss.system.Registry;

public class InvokerAdaptorService
    extends ServiceMBeanSupport
    implements InvokerAdaptorServiceMBean, ServerConstants
{
```

LISTING 2.16 Continued

```
    private static ObjectName mbeanRegistry;

    static {
        try {
            mbeanRegistry = new ObjectName(MBEAN_REGISTRY);
        } catch (Exception e) {
            throw new RuntimeException(e.toString());
        }
    }

    private Map marshalledInvocationMapping = new HashMap();
    private Class exportedInterface;

    public Class getExportedInterface()
    {
        return exportedInterface;
    }

    public void setExportedInterface(Class exportedInterface)
    {
        this.exportedInterface = exportedInterface;
    }

    protected void startService()
        throws Exception
    {
        // Build the interface method map
        Method[] methods = exportedInterface.getMethods();
        HashMap tmpMap = new HashMap(methods.length);
        for (int m = 0; m < methods.length; m ++) {
            Method method = methods[m];
            Long hash = new Long(MarshalledInvocation.calculateHash(method));
            tmpMap.put(hash, method);
        }

        marshalledInvocationMapping = Collections.unmodifiableMap(tmpMap);
        // Place our ObjectName hash into the Registry so invokers can
        // resolve it
        Registry.bind(new Integer(serviceName.hashCode()), serviceName);
    }

    protected void stopService()
        throws Exception
    {
```

LISTING 2.16 Continued

```
        Registry.unbind(new Integer(serviceName.hashCode()));
    }


    public Object invoke(Invocation invocation)
        throws Exception
    {
        // Make sure we have the correct classloader before unmarshaling
        Thread thread = Thread.currentThread();
        ClassLoader oldCL = thread.getContextClassLoader();

        // Get the MBean this operation applies to
        ClassLoader newCL = null;
        ObjectName objectName = (ObjectName)
            invocation.getValue("JMX_OBJECT_NAME");
        if (objectName != null) {
            // Obtain the ClassLoader associated with the MBean deployment
            newCL = (ClassLoader)
                server.invoke(mbeanRegistry, "getValue",
                              new Object[] { objectName, CLASSLOADER },
                              new String[] { ObjectName.class.getName(),
                                             "java.lang.String" });
        }

        if (newCL != null && newCL != oldCL) {
            thread.setContextClassLoader(newCL);
        }

        try {
            // Set the method hash to Method mapping
            if (invocation instanceof MarshalledInvocation) {
                MarshalledInvocation mi = (MarshalledInvocation) invocation;
                mi.setMethodMap(marshalledInvocationMapping);
            }

            // Invoke the MBeanServer method via reflection
            Method method = invocation.getMethod();
            Object[] args = invocation.getArguments();
            Object value = null;
            try {
                String name = method.getName();
                Class[] sig = method.getParameterTypes();
                Method mbeanServerMethod =
                    MBeanServer.class.getMethod(name, sig);
```

LISTING 2.16 Continued

```
                value = mbeanServerMethod.invoke(server, args);
            } catch(InvocationTargetException e) {
                Throwable t = e.getTargetException();
                if (t instanceof Exception) {
                    throw (Exception) t;
                } else {
                    throw new UndeclaredThrowableException(t, method.toString());
                }
            }

            return value;
        } finally {
            if (newCL != null && newCL != oldCL) {
                thread.setContextClassLoader(oldCL);
            }
        }
    }
}
```

Let's go through the key details of this service. The `InvokerAdaptorServiceMBean` Standard MBean interface of the `InvokerAdaptorService` has a single `ExportedInterface` attribute and a single `invoke(Invocation)` operation. The `ExportedInterface` attribute allows customization of the type of interface the service exposes to clients. It has to be compatible with the `MBeanServer` class in terms of method name and signature. The `invoke(Invocation)` operation is the required entry point that target MBean services must expose to participate in the detached invoker pattern. This operation is invoked by the detached invoker services that have been configured to provide access to the `InvokerAdaptorService`.

Lines 54–64 of the `InvokerAdaptorService` build the `HashMap<Long,Method>` of the `ExportedInterface` class, using the `org.jboss.invocation.MarshalledInvocation.calculateHash(Method)` utility method. Because `java.lang.reflect.Method` instances are not serializable, a `MarshalledInvocation` version of the nonserializable `Invocation` class is used to marshal the invocation between the client and server. The `MarshalledInvocation` replaces the `Method` instances with their corresponding hash representation. On the server side, the `MarshalledInvocation` must be told what the hash-to-`Method` mapping is.

Line 64 creates a mapping between the `InvokerAdaptorService` service name and its hash code representation. This is used by detached invokers to determine what the target MBean `ObjectName` of an `Invocation` is. When the target MBean name is stored in the `Invocation`, it is stored by its `hashCode` because `ObjectNames` are relatively expensive objects to create. The `org.jboss.system.Registry` is a global map-like construct that invokers use to store the hash code-to-`ObjectName` mappings in.

Lines 77–93 obtain the name of the MBean on which the MBeanServer operation is being performed and look up the class loader associated with the MBean's SAR deployment. This information is available via org.jboss.mx.server.registry.BasicMBeanRegistry, a JBoss JMX implementation-specific class. It is generally necessary for an MBean to establish the correct class-loading context because the detached invoker protocol layer may not have access to the class loaders needed to unmarshal the types associated with an invocation.

Lines 101–105 install the ExposedInterface class method hash-to-Method mapping if the invocation argument is of type MarshalledInvocation. The method mapping calculated at lines 54–62 is used here.

Lines 107–114 perform a second mapping from the ExposedInterface method to the matching method of the MBeanServer class. The InvokerServiceAdaptor decouples the ExposedInterface from the MBeanServer class in that it allows an arbitrary interface. This is needed on one hand because the standard java.lang.reflect.Proxy class can only proxy interfaces. It also allows you to expose only a subset of the MBeanServer methods and add transport-specific exceptions such as java.rmi.RemoteException to the ExposedInterface method signatures.

Line 115 dispatches the MBeanServer method invocation to the MBeanServer instance to which the InvokerAdaptorService was deployed. The server instance variable is inherited from the ServiceMBeanSupport superclass.

Lines 117–124 handle any exceptions coming from the reflective invocation, including the unwrapping of any declared exception thrown by the invocation.

Line 126 is the return of the successful MBeanServer method invocation result.

Note that the InvokerAdaptorService MBean does not deal directly with any transport-specific details. There is the calculation of the method hash-to-Method mapping, but this is a transport-independent detail.

Now let's take a look at how the InvokerAdaptorService can be used to expose the same org.jboss.jmx.adaptor.rmi.RMIAdaptor interface via RMI/JRMP as seen in the section "Connecting to JMX Using RMI," earlier in this chapter. We will start by presenting the proxy factory and InvokerAdaptorService configurations found in the default setup in the jmx-invoker-adaptor-service.sar deployment. Listing 2.17 shows the jboss-service.xml descriptor for this deployment.

LISTING 2.17 The Default jmx-invoker-adaptor-server.sar jboss-service.xml Deployment Descriptor

```
<server>
    <!-- The JRMP invoker proxy configuration for the InvokerAdaptorService -->
    <mbean code="org.jboss.invocation.jrmp.server.JRMPProxyFactory"
           name="jboss.jmx:type=adaptor,name=Invoker,protocol=jrmp,
➥service=proxyFactory">
        <!-- Use the standard JRMPInvoker from conf/jboss-service.xml -->
```

LISTING 2.17 Continued

```
        <attribute name="InvokerName">jboss:service=invoker,type=jrmp</attribute>
        <!-- The target MBean is the InvokerAdaptorService configured below -->
        <attribute name="TargetName">jboss.jmx:type=adaptor,name=Invoker
➥</attribute>
        <!-- Where to bind the RMIAdaptor proxy -->
        <attribute name="JndiName">jmx/invoker/RMIAdaptor</attribute>
        <!-- The RMI compatible MBeanServer interface -->
        <attribute name="ExportedInterface">org.jboss.jmx.adaptor.rmi.RMIAdaptor
➥</attribute>
        <attribute name="ClientInterceptors">
            <interceptors>
                <interceptor>org.jboss.proxy.ClientMethodInterceptor</interceptor>
                <interceptor>
                    org.jboss.jmx.connector.invoker.client.
➥InvokerAdaptorClientInterceptor </interceptor>
                <interceptor>org.jboss.invocation.InvokerInterceptor
➥</interceptor>
            </interceptors>
        </attribute>
        <depends>jboss:service=invoker,type=jrmp</depends>
    </mbean>
    <!-- This is the service that handles the RMIAdaptor invocations by routing
         them to the MBeanServer the service is deployed under. -->
    <mbean code="org.jboss.jmx.connector.invoker.InvokerAdaptorService"
           name="jboss.jmx:type=adaptor,name=Invoker">
        <attribute name="ExportedInterface">org.jboss.jmx.adaptor.rmi.RMIAdaptor
➥</attribute>
    </mbean>
</server>
```

The first MBean, `org.jboss.invocation.jrmp.server.JRMPProxyFactory`, is the proxy factory MBean service that creates proxies for the RMI/JRMP protocol. The configuration of this service, as shown in Example 2.17, states that `JRMPInvoker` will be used as the detached invoker, `InvokerAdaptorService` is the target MBean to which requests will be forwarded, the proxy will expose the `RMIAdaptor` interface, the proxy will be bound into JNDI under the name `jmx/invoker/RMIAdaptor`, and the proxy will contain three interceptors: `ClientMethodInterceptor`, `InvokerAdaptorClientInterceptor`, and `InvokerInterceptor`. The configuration of `InvokerAdaptorService` simply sets the `RMIAdaptor` interface that the service is exposing.

The last piece of the configuration for exposing the `InvokerAdaptorService` via RMI/JRMP is the detached invoker. The detached invoker you will use is the standard RMI/JRMP invoker used by the EJB containers for home and remote invocations, and this is the `org.jboss.invocation.jrmp.server.JRMPInvoker` MBean service configured in the `conf/jboss-service.xml` descriptor. That you can use the same service instance emphasizes the detached nature of the invokers. `JRMPInvoker` simply acts as the RMI/JRMP endpoint for all RMI/JRMP proxies, regardless of the interfaces the proxies expose or the service the proxies utilize.

`JRMPInvoker`: RMI/JRMP Transport

The `org.jboss.invocation.jrmp.server.JRMPInvoker` class is an MBean service that provides the RMI/JRMP implementation of the `Invoker` interface. `JRMPInvoker` exports itself as an RMI server so that when it is used as the invoker in a remote client, the `JRMPInvoker` stub is sent to the client instead, and invocations use the RMI/JRMP protocol.

The `JRMPInvoker` MBean supports a number of attributes to configure the RMI/JRMP transport layer. The following are its configurable attributes:

- **`RMIObjectPort`**—This attribute sets the RMI server socket listening port number. This is the port RMI that clients will connect to when communicating through the proxy interface. The default setting in the `jboss-service.xml` descriptor is 4444, and if it is not specified, the attribute defaults to `0` to indicate that an anonymous port should be used.
- **`RMIClientSocketFactory`**—This attribute specifies a fully qualified classname for the `java.rmi.server.RMIClientSocketFactory` interface to use during export of the proxy interface.
- **`RMIServerSocketFactory`**—This attribute specifies a fully qualified classname for the `java.rmi.server.RMIServerSocketFactory` interface to use during export of the proxy interface.
- **`ServerAddress`**—This attribute specifies the interface address that will be used for the RMI server socket listening port. This can be either a DNS hostname or a dotted-decimal Internet address. Because `RMIServerSocketFactory` does not support a method that accepts an `InetAddress` object, this value is passed to the `RMIServerSocketFactory` implementation class, using reflection. A check for the existence of a `public void setBindAddress(java.net.InetAddress addr)` method is made, and if one exists, the `RMIServerSocketAddr` value is passed to the `RMIServerSocketFactory` implementation. If the `RMIServerSocketFactory` implementation does not support such a method, the `ServerAddress` value will be ignored.
- **`SecurityDomain`**—This attribute specifies the JNDI name of an `org.jboss.security.SecurityDomain` interface implementation to associate with the `RMIServerSocketFactory` implementation. The value will be passed to the `RMIServerSocketFactory`, using reflection, to locate a method with the signature `public void setSecurity-Domain (org.jboss.security.SecurityDomain d)`. If no such method exists, the `SecurityDomain` value will be ignored.

PooledInvoker: RMI/Socket Transport

The org.jboss.invocation.pooled.server.PooledInvoker class is an MBean service that provides RMI over a custom socket transport implementation of the Invoker interface. PooledInvoker exports itself as an RMI server so that when it is used as the Invoker in a remote client, the PooledInvoker stub is sent to the client instead, and invocations use a custom socket protocol.

The PooledInvoker MBean supports a number of attributes to configure the socket transport layer. These are its configurable attributes:

- **NumAcceptThreads**—The number of threads that exist for accepting client connections. The default is 1.
- **MaxPoolSize**—The number of server threads for processing a client. The default is 300.
- **SocketTimeout**—The socket timeout value passed to the Socket.setSoTimeout() method. The default is 60000.
- **ServerBindPort**—The port used for the server socket. A value of 0 indicates that an anonymous port should be chosen.
- **ClientConnectAddress**—The address that the client passes to the Socket(addr,port) constructor. This defaults to the server InetAddress.getLocalHost() value.
- **ClientConnectPort**—The port that the client passes to the Socket(addr,port) constructor. The default is the port of the server listening socket.
- **ClientMaxPoolSize**—The client-side maximum number of threads. The default is 300.
- **Backlog**—The backlog associated with the server accept socket. The default is 200.
- **EnableTcpNoDelay**—A Boolean flag that indicates whether client sockets will enable the TcpNoDelay flag on the socket. The default is false.
- **ServerBindAddress**—The address on which the server binds its listening socket. The default is an empty value which indicates that the server should be bound on all interfaces.
- **TransactionManagerService**—The JMX ObjectName of the JTA transaction manager service.

IIOPInvoker: RMI/IIOP Transport

The org.jboss.invocation.iiop.IIOPInvoker class is an MBean service that provides the RMI/IIOP implementation of the Invoker interface. The IIOPInvoker IIOP invoker that routes IIOP requests to CORBA servants is used by the org.jboss.proxy.ejb.IORFactory proxy factory to create RMI/IIOP proxies. However, rather than create Java proxies (as the JRMP proxy factory does), this factory creates CORBA IORs. An IORFactory is associated to a given Enterprise Bean. It registers with the IIOP invoker two CORBA servants: anEjbHomeCorbaServant for the bean's EJBHome and EjbObjectCorbaServant for the bean's EJBObjects.

The IIOPInvoker MBean has no configurable properties because all properties are configured from the conf/jacorb.properties property file used by the JacORB CORBA service.

JRMPProxyFactory: **Building Dynamic JRMP Proxies**

The org.jboss.invocation.jrmp.server.JRMPProxyFactory MBean service is a proxy factory that can expose any interface with RMI-compatible semantics for access to remote clients, using JRMP as the transport. JRMPProxyFactory supports the following attributes:

- **InvokerName**—The server-side JRMPInvoker MBean service JMX ObjectName string that will handle the RMI/JRMP transport.
- **TargetName**—The server-side MBean that exposes the invoke(Invocation) JMX operation for the exported interface. This is used as the destination service for any invocations done through the proxy.
- **JndiName**—The JNDI name under which the proxy will be bound.
- **ExportedInterface**—The fully qualified classname of the interface that the proxy implements. This is the typed view of the proxy that the client uses for invocations.
- **ClientInterceptors**—An XML fragment of interceptors/interceptor elements, with each interceptor element body specifying the fully qualified classname of an org.jboss.proxy.Interceptor implementation to include in the proxy interceptor stack. The ordering of the interceptors/interceptor elements defines the order of the interceptors.

HttpInvoker: **RMI/HTTP Transport**

The org.jboss.invocation.http.server.HttpInvoker MBean service provides support for making invocations into the JMX bus over HTTP. Unlike JRMPInvoker, HttpInvoker is not an implementation of Invoker, but it does implement the Invoker.invoke method. The HttpInvoker is accessed indirectly by issuing an HTTP POST against the org.jboss.invocation.http.servlet.InvokerServlet. The HttpInvoker exports a client-side proxy in the form of the org.jboss.invocation.http.interfaces.HttpInvokerProxy class, which is an implementation of Invoker and is serializable. HttpInvoker is a drop-in replacement for the JRMPInvoker as the target of the bean-invoker and home-invoker EJB configuration elements. The HttpInvoker and InvokerServlet are deployed in the http-invoker.sar discussed in Chapter 3, "Naming on JBoss," in the section "Accessing JNDI over HTTP."

The HttpInvoker supports the following attributes:

- **InvokerURL**—This is either the HTTP URL to the InvokerServlet mapping or the name of a system property that will be resolved inside the client VM to obtain the HTTP URL to the InvokerServlet.

- **InvokerURLPrefix**—If there is no invokerURL set, one will be constructed via the concatenation of invokerURLPrefix and the local host and invokerURLSuffix. The default prefix is http://.
- **InvokerURLSuffix**—If there is no invokerURL set, one will be constructed via the concatenation of invokerURLPrefix and the local host and invokerURLSuffix. The default suffix is :8080/invoker/JMXInvokerServlet.
- **UseHostName**—This is a Boolean flag if the InetAddress.getHostName() or getHostAddress() method should be used as the host component of the concatenation of invokerURLPrefix and host and invokerURLSuffix. If true, getHostName() is used; otherwise, getHostAddress() is used.

JRMPInvoker: Clustered RMI/JRMP Transport

The org.jboss.proxy.generic.ProxyFactoryHA service is an extension of ProxyFactoryHA, which is a cluster-aware factory. ProxyFactoryHA fully supports all the attributes of JRMPProxyFactory. This means that customized bindings of the port, interface, and socket transport are available to clustered RMI/JRMP as well. In addition, the following cluster-specific attributes are supported:

- **PartitionObjectName**—The JMX ObjectName of the cluster service to which the proxy is to be associated.
- **LoadBalancePolicy**—The classname of the org.jboss.ha.framework.interfaces.LoadBalancePolicy interface implementation to associate with the proxy.

HttpInvoker: Clustered RMI/HTTP Transport

The RMI/HTTP layer allows for software load balancing of the invocations in a clustered environment. The HA-capable extension of the HTTP invoker borrows much of its functionality from the HA-RMI/JRMP clustering. To enable HA-RMI/HTTP, you need to configure the invokers for the EJB container. This is done through either a jboss.xml descriptor or the standardjboss.xml descriptor.

HttpProxyFactory: Building Dynamic HTTP Proxies

The org.jboss.invocation.http.server.HttpProxyFactory MBean service is a proxy factory that can expose any interface with RMI-compatible semantics for access to remote clients, using HTTP as the transport. HttpProxyFactory supports the following attributes:

- **InvokerName**—The server-side MBean that exposes the invoke operation for the exported interface. The name is embedded into the HttpInvokerProxy context as the target to which the invocation should be forwarded by the HttpInvoker.
- **JndiName**—The JNDI name under which the HttpInvokerProxy will be bound. This is the name clients look up to obtain the dynamic proxy that exposes the service

interfaces and marshals invocations over HTTP. This may be specified as an empty value to indicate that the proxy should not be bound into JNDI.

- **`InvokerURL`**—This is either the HTTP URL to the `InvokerServlet` mapping or the name of a system property that will be resolved inside the client VM to obtain the HTTP URL to the `InvokerServlet`.
- **`InvokerURLPrefix`**—If there is no `invokerURL` set, one will be constructed via the concatenation of `invokerURLPrefix` and the local host and `invokerURLSuffix`. The default prefix is `http://`.
- **`InvokerURLSuffix`**—If there is no `invokerURL` set, one will be constructed via the concatenation of `invokerURLPrefix` and the local host and `invokerURLSuffix`. The default suffix is `:8080/invoker/JMXInvokerServlet`.
- **`UseHostName`**—This Boolean flag indicates whether the `InetAddress.getHostName()` or `getHostAddress()` method should be used as the host component of the concatenation of `invokerURLPrefix` and host and `invokerURLSuffix`. If `true`, `getHostName()` is used; otherwise, `getHostAddress()` is used.
- **`ExportedInterface`**—The name of the RMI-compatible interface that `HttpInvokerProxy` implements.

Steps to Expose Any RMI Interface via HTTP

By using the `HttpProxyFactory` MBean and JMX, you can expose any interface for access, using HTTP as the transport. The interface to expose does not have to be an RMI interface, but it does have to be compatible with RMI in that all method parameters and return values need to be serializable. There is also no support for converting RMI interfaces used as method parameters or return values into their stubs.

There are three steps to making an object invocable via HTTP:

1. Create a mapping of longs to the RMI interface methods, using the `MarshalledInvocation.calculateHash` method. Here, for example, is the procedure for an RMI `SRPRemoteServerInterface` interface:

```
import java.lang.reflect.Method;
import java.util.HashMap;
import org.jboss.invocation.MarshalledInvocation;

HashMap marshalledInvocationMapping = new HashMap();

// Build the Naming interface method map
Method[] methods = SRPRemoteServerInterface.class.getMethods();
for(int m = 0; m < methods.length; m ++) {
    Method method = methods[m];
    Long hash = new Long(MarshalledInvocation.calculateHash(method));
```

```
        marshalledInvocationMapping.put(hash, method);
    }
```

2. Either create or extend an existing MBean to support an invoke operation. Its signature is `Object invoke (Invocation invocation) throws Exception`, and the steps it performs are as shown here for the `SRPRemoteServerInterface` interface:

```
import org.jboss.invocation.Invocation;
import org.jboss.invocation.MarshalledInvocation;

public Object invoke(Invocation invocation)
    throws Exception
{
    SRPRemoteServerInterface theServer = <the_actual_rmi_server_object>;
    // Set the method hash to Method mapping
    if (invocation instanceof MarshalledInvocation) {
        MarshalledInvocation mi = (MarshalledInvocation) invocation;
        mi.setMethodMap(marshalledInvocationMapping);
    }

    // Invoke the Naming method via reflection
    Method method = invocation.getMethod();
    Object[] args = invocation.getArguments();
    Object value = null;
    try {
        value = method.invoke(theServer, args);
    } catch(InvocationTargetException e) {
        Throwable t = e.getTargetException();
        if (t instanceof Exception) {
            throw (Exception) e;
        } else {
            throw new UndeclaredThrowableException(t, method.toString());
        }
    }

    return value;
}
return value;
}
```

Note that this uses the `marshalledInvocationMapping` from step 1 to map from the `Long` method hashes in the `MarshalledInvocation` to the `Method` for the interface.

3. Create a configuration of the `HttpProxyFactory` MBean to make the RMI/HTTP proxy available through JNDI. Here's an example:

```
<!-- Expose the SRP service interface via HTTP -->
<mbean code="org.jboss.invocation.http.server.HttpProxyFactory"
      name="jboss.security.tests:service=SRP/HTTP">
   <attribute name="InvokerURL">http://localhost:8080/invoker/
➥JMXInvokerServlet</attribute>
   <attribute name="InvokerName">jboss.security.tests:service=SRPService
➥</attribute>
   <attribute name="ExportedInterface">org.jboss.security.srp.
➥SRPRemoteServerInterface
   </attribute><attribute name="JndiName">srp-test-http/SRPServerInterface
➥</attribute>
</mbean>
```

Any client can now look up the RMI interface from JNDI, using the name specified in the `HttpProxyFactory` (for example, `srp-test-http/SRPServerInterface`) and use the obtained proxy in exactly the same manner as the RMI/JRMP version.

CHAPTER **3**

Naming on JBoss

IN THIS CHAPTER

- An Overview of JNDI
- The JBossNS Architecture

This chapter discusses the JBoss JNDI-based naming service, JBossNS, and the role of JNDI in JBoss and J2EE. It also provides an introduction to the basic JNDI API and common usage conventions. In this chapter, you'll also learn about the JBoss-specific configuration of J2EE component-naming environments defined by the standard deployment descriptors. The final topic in this chapter is the configuration and architecture of the JBoss naming service.

The JBoss naming service plays a key role in J2EE because it provides a naming service that allows a user to map a name to an object. This is a fundamental need in any programming environment because developers and administrators want to be able to refer to objects and services by recognizable names. A good example of a pervasive naming service is the Internet's Domain Name System (DNS). DNS allows you to refer to hosts by using logical names rather than their numeric Internet addresses. JNDI serves a similar role in J2EE by enabling developers and administrators to create name-to-object bindings for use in J2EE components.

An Overview of JNDI

JNDI is a standard Java API that is bundled with JDK 1.3 and higher. JNDI provides a common interface to a variety of existing naming services: DNS, LDAP, Active Directory, RMI registry, COS registry, NIS, and file systems. The JNDI API is divided logically into a client API that is used to access naming services and a service provider interface (SPI) that allows the user to create JNDI implementations for naming services.

The SPI layer is an abstraction that naming service providers must implement to enable the core JNDI classes to expose the naming service, using the common JNDI client interface. An implementation of JNDI for a naming service is referred to as a *JNDI provider*. JBoss naming is an example of JNDI implementation, based on the SPI classes. Note that J2EE component developers do not need the JNDI SPI.

For a thorough introduction and tutorial on JNDI, which covers both the client and service provider APIs, see Sun's tutorial at http://java.sun.com/products/jndi/tutorial/.

The JNDI API

The main JNDI API package is the `javax.naming` package. It contains 5 interfaces, 10 classes, and several exceptions. There is one key class, `InitialContext`, and there are 2 key interfaces, `Context` and `Name`.

Names in JNDI

The notion of a name is of fundamental importance in JNDI. The naming system determines the syntax that the name must follow. The syntax of the naming system allows the user to parse string representations of names into its components. A name is used with a naming system to locate objects. In the simplest sense, a naming system is just a collection of objects that have unique names. To locate an object in a naming system, you provide a name to the naming system, and the naming system returns the object store under the name.

For example, consider the Unix file system's naming convention. Each file is named from its path, relative to the root of the file system, with each component in the path separated by the forward slash character (/). The file's path is ordered from left to right. The pathname `/usr/jboss/readme.txt`, for example, names the file `readme.txt` in the directory `jboss`, under the directory `usr`, located in the root of the file system. JBoss naming uses a Unix-style namespace as its naming convention.

The `javax.naming.Name` interface represents a generic name as an ordered sequence of components. It can be a composite name (one that spans multiple namespaces) or a compound name (one that is used within a single hierarchical naming system). The components of a name are numbered. The indexes of a name with *N* components range from 0 up to, but not including, *N*. The most significant component is at index 0. An empty name has no components.

A composite name is a sequence of component names that span multiple namespaces. An example of a composite name is the hostname and file combination commonly used with Unix commands such as `scp`. For example, the following command copies `localfile.txt` to the file `remotefile.txt` in the `tmp` directory on host `ahost.someorg.org`:

```
scp localfile.txt ahost.someorg.org:/tmp/remotefile.txt
```

A compound name is derived from a hierarchical namespace. Each component in a compound name is an atomic name—that is, it is a string that cannot be parsed into smaller components. A file pathname in the Unix file system is an example of a compound name. `ahost.someorg.org:/tmp/remotefile.txt` is a composite name that spans the DNS and Unix file system namespaces. The components of the composite name are `ahost.someorg.org` and `/tmp/remotefile.txt`. A *component* is a string name from the namespace of a naming system. If the component comes from a hierarchical namespace, that component can be further parsed into its atomic parts by using the `javax.naming.CompoundName` class. The JNDI API provides the `javax.naming.CompositeName` class as the implementation of the `Name` interface for composite names.

Contexts The `javax.naming.Context` interface is the primary interface for interacting with a naming service. The `Context` interface represents a set of name-to-object bindings. Every context has an associated naming convention that determines how the context parses string names into `javax.naming.Name` instances. To create a name-to-object binding, you invoke the bind method of a context and specify a name and an object as arguments. You can later retrieve the object by using its name, via the `Context` lookup method. A context typically provides operations for binding a name to an object, unbinding a name, and obtaining a listing of all name-to-object bindings. The object you bind into a context can itself be of type `Context`. The `Context` object that is bound is referred to as a *subcontext* of the context on which the bind method was invoked.

For example, consider a file directory that has a pathname `/usr` and is a context in the Unix file system. A file directory named relative to another file directory is a subcontext (commonly referred to as a *subdirectory*). A file directory with the pathname `/usr/jboss` names a `jboss` context that is a subcontext of `usr`. As another example, a DNS domain, such as `org`, is a context. A DNS domain named relative to another DNS domain is another example of a subcontext. In the DNS domain `jboss.org`, the DNS domain `jboss` is a subcontext of `org` because DNS names are parsed right to left.

Obtaining a Context by Using `InitialContext` All naming service operations are performed on some implementation of the `Context` interface. Therefore, you need a way to obtain a `Context` for the naming service you are interested in using. The `javax.naming.InitialContext` class implements the `Context` interface and provides the starting point for interacting with a naming service.

When you create an `InitialContext`, it is initialized with properties from the environment. JNDI determines each property's value by merging the values from the following two sources, in order:

- The first occurrence of the property from the constructor's environment parameter and (for appropriate properties) the applet parameters and system properties
- All `jndi.properties` resource files found on the classpath

For each property found in both of these two sources, the property's value is determined as follows. If the property is one of the standard JNDI properties that specify a list of JNDI factories, all the values are concatenated into a single colon-separated list. For other properties, only the first value found is used. The preferred method of specifying the JNDI environment properties is through a `jndi.properties` file, which allows the code to externalize the JNDI provider-specific information so that changing JNDI providers will not require changes to the code or recompilation.

The `Context` implementation used internally by the `InitialContext` class is determined at runtime. The default policy uses the environment property `java.naming.factory.initial`, which contains the classname of the `javax.naming.spi.InitialContextFactory` implementation. You obtain the name of the `InitialContextFactory` class from the naming service provider you are using.

Listing 3.1 gives a sample `jndi.properties` file that a client application would use to connect to a JBossNS service running on the local host at port 1099. The client application would need to have the `jndi.properties` file available on the application classpath. These are the properties that the JBoss JNDI implementation requires. Other JNDI providers have different properties and values.

LISTING 3.1 A Sample `jndi.properties` File

```
### JBossNS properties
java.naming.factory.initial=org.jnp.interfaces.NamingContextFactory
java.naming.provider.url=jnp://localhost:1099
➥java.naming.factory.url.pkgs=org.jboss.naming:org.jnp.interfaces
```

J2EE and JNDI: The Application Component Environment

JNDI is a fundamental aspect of the J2EE specifications. One key usage of the JNDI is to isolate J2EE component code from the environment in which the code is deployed. Use of the application component's environment allows the application component to be customized without the need to access or change the application component's source code. The application component environment is referred to as the enterprise naming context (ENC). It is the responsibility of the application component container to make an ENC available to the container components in the form of the JNDI `Context` interface. The participants involved in the life cycle of a J2EE component utilize the ENC in the following ways:

- The component provider uses the standard deployment descriptor for the component to specify the required ENC entries. The entries are declarations of the information and resources the component requires at runtime. Application component business logic should be coded to access information from its ENC.
- The container provides tools that allow a deployer of a component to map the ENC references made by the component developer to the deployment environment entity that satisfies the reference.
- The component deployer utilizes the container tools to ready a component for final deployment.
- The component container uses the deployment package information to build the complete component ENC at runtime.

The complete specification regarding the use of JNDI in the J2EE platform can be found in section 5 of the J2EE 1.4 specification, which is available at http://java.sun.com/j2ee/download.html.

An application component instance locates the ENC by using the JNDI API. An application component instance creates a `javax.naming.InitialContext` object by using the no argument constructor and then looks up the naming environment under the name `java:comp/env`. The application component's environment entries are stored directly in the ENC or in its subcontexts. Listing 3.2 illustrates the prototypical lines of code a component uses to access its ENC.

LISTING 3.2 ENC Access Sample Code

```
// Obtain the application component's ENC Context iniCtx = new InitialContext();
Context compEnv = (Context) iniCtx.lookup("java:comp/env");
```

An *application component environment* is a local environment that is accessible only by the component when the application server container thread of control is interacting with the application component. This means that an EJB `Bean1` cannot access the ENC elements of EJB `Bean2` and vice versa. Similarly, web application `Web1` cannot access the ENC elements of web application `Web2`—or `Bean1` or `Bean2`, for that matter. Also, arbitrary client code, whether it is executing inside the application server VM or externally, cannot access a component's `java:comp` JNDI context. The purpose of the ENC is to provide an isolated, read-only namespace that the application component can rely on, regardless of the type of environment in which the component is deployed. The ENC must be isolated from other components because each component defines its own ENC content. Components A and B, for example, may define the same name to refer to different objects. For example, EJB `Bean1` may define an environment entry `java:comp/env/red` to refer to the hexadecimal value for the RGB color for red, while web application `Web1` may bind the same name to the deployment environment language locale representation of red.

There are three commonly used levels of naming scope in JBoss: names under `java:comp`, names under `java:`, and any other names. As discussed, the `java:comp` context and its subcontexts are available only to the application component associated with that particular context. Subcontexts and object bindings directly under `java:` are visible only within the JBoss server virtual machine and not to remote clients. Any other context or object binding is available to remote clients, provided that the context or object supports serialization. You'll see how the isolation of these naming scopes is achieved in the next section.

An example of where restricting a binding to the `java:` context is useful is a `javax.sql.DataSource` connection factory that can be used only inside the JBoss server where the associated database pool resides. On the other hand, an EJB home interface would be bound to a globally visible name that should be accessible by remote clients.

ENC Usage Conventions

JNDI is used as the API for externalizing a great deal of information from an application component. The JNDI name that the application component uses to access the information is declared in the standard `ejb-jar.xml` deployment descriptor for EJB components and the standard `web.xml` deployment descriptor for web components. Several different types of information can be stored in and retrieved from JNDI, including the following:

- Environment entries, as declared by the `env-entry` elements
- EJB references, as declared by `ejb-ref` and `ejb-local-ref` elements
- Resource manager connection factory references, as declared by the `resource-ref` elements
- Resource environment references, as declared by the `resource-env-ref` elements

Each type of deployment descriptor element has a JNDI usage convention with regard to the name of the JNDI context under which the information is bound. Also, in addition to the standard `deploymentdescriptor` element, there is a JBoss server-specific deployment descriptor element that maps the JNDI name as used by the application component to the deployment environment JNDI name.

Environment Entries Environment entries are the simplest form of information stored in a component ENC, and they are similar to operating system environment variables, like those found on Unix or Windows. An environment entry is a name-to-value binding that allows a component to externalize a value and refer to the value by using a name.

You declare an environment entry by using an `env-entry` element in the standard deployment descriptors. The `env-entry` element contains the following child elements:

- An optional description element that provides a description of the entry
- An `env-entry-name` element that gives the name of the entry relative to `java:comp/env`
- An `env-entry-type` element that gives the Java type of the entry value, which must be one of the following:
    - `java.lang.Byte`
    - `java.lang.Boolean`
    - `java.lang.Character`
    - `java.lang.Double`
    - `java.lang.Float`
    - `java.lang.Integer`
    - `java.lang.Long`

    - `java.lang.Short`
    - `java.lang.String`
- An `env-entry-value` element that gives the value of the entry as a string

Listing 3.3 shows an example of an `env-entry` fragment from an `ejb-jar.xml` deployment descriptor. There is no JBoss-specific deployment descriptor element because an `env-entry` is a complete name and value specification. Listing 3.4 shows a sample code fragment for accessing the `maxExemptions` and `taxRate` `env-entry` values declared in the deployment descriptor.

LISTING 3.3 An Example of an `ejb-jar.xml` `env-entry` Fragment

```
<!-- ... -->
<session>
    <ejb-name>ASessionBean</ejb-name>
    <!-- ... -->
    <env-entry>
        <description>The maximum number of tax exemptions allowed </description>
        <env-entry-name>maxExemptions</env-entry-name>
        <env-entry-type>java.lang.Integer</env-entry-type>
        <env-entry-value>15</env-entry-value>
    </env-entry>
    <env-entry>
        <description>The tax rate </description>
        <env-entry-name>taxRate</env-entry-name>
        <env-entry-type>java.lang.Float</env-entry-type>
        <env-entry-value>0.23</env-entry-value>
    </env-entry>
</session>
<!-- ... -->
```

LISTING 3.4 An ENC `env-entry` Access Code Fragment

```
InitialContext iniCtx = new InitialContext();
Context envCtx = (Context) iniCtx.lookup("java:comp/env");
Integer maxExemptions = (Integer) envCtx.lookup("maxExemptions");
Float taxRate = (Float) envCtx.lookup("taxRate");
```

EJB References It is common for EJBs and web components to interact with other EJBs. Because the JNDI name under which an EJB home interface is bound is a deployment time decision, a component developer needs to have a way to declare a reference to an EJB that will be linked by the deployer. EJB references satisfy this requirement.

An *EJB reference* is a link in an application component-naming environment that points to a deployed EJB home interface. The name used by the application component is a logical link that isolates the component from the actual name of the EJB home in the deployment environment. The J2EE specification recommends that all references to Enterprise Beans be organized in the `java:comp/env/ejb` context of the application component's environment.

An EJB reference is declared using an `ejb-ref` element in the deployment descriptor. Each `ejb-ref` element describes the interface requirements that the referencing application component has for the referenced Enterprise Bean. The `ejb-ref` element contains the following child elements:

- An optional description element that provides the purpose of the reference.
- An `ejb-ref-name` element that specifies the name of the reference relative to the `java:comp/env` context. To place the reference under the recommended `java:comp/env/ejb` context, you use the form `ejb/link-name` for the `ejb-ref-name` value.
- An `ejb-ref-type` element that specifies the type of the EJB. This must be either `Entity` or `Session`.
- A `home` element that gives the fully qualified classname of the EJB home interface.
- A `remote` element that gives the fully qualified classname of the EJB remote interface.
- An optional `ejb-link` element that links the reference to another Enterprise Bean in the same EJB JAR or in the same J2EE application unit. The `ejb-link` value is the `ejb-name` of the referenced bean. If there are multiple Enterprise Beans with the same `ejb-name`, the value uses a pathname that specifies the location of the `ejb-jar` file that contains the referenced component. The pathname is relative to the referencing `ejb-jar` file. The application assembler appends the `ejb-name` of the referenced bean to the pathname, separated by #. This allows multiple beans with the same name to be uniquely identified.

An EJB reference is scoped to the application component whose declaration contains the `ejb-ref` element. This means that the EJB reference is not accessible from other application components at runtime and that other application components may define `ejb-ref` elements with the same `ejb-ref-name` without causing a naming conflict. Listing 3.5 provides an `ejb-jar.xml` fragment that illustrates the use of the `ejb-ref` element. Listing 3.6 provides a code sample that illustrates accessing the `ShoppingCartHome` reference declared in Listing 3.5.

LISTING 3.5 An Example of an `ejb-jar.xml` `ejb-ref` Descriptor Fragment

```
<description>This is a reference to the store products entity </description>
        <ejb-ref-name>ejb/ProductHome</ejb-ref-name>
        <ejb-ref-type>Entity</ejb-ref-type>
```

LISTING 3.5 Continued

```
        <home>org.jboss.store.ejb.ProductHome</home>
    </ejb-ref>
    <remote> org.jboss.store.ejb.Product</remote>
</session>

<session>
    <ejb-ref>
        <ejb-name>ShoppingCartUser</ejb-name>
        <!--.....-->
        <ejb-ref-name>ejb/ShoppingCartHome</ejb-ref-name>
        <ejb-ref-type>Session</ejb-ref-type>
        <home>org.jboss.store.ejb.ShoppingCartHome</home>
        <remote> org.jboss.store.ejb.ShoppingCart</remote>
        <ejb-link>ShoppingCartBean</ejb-link>
    </ejb-ref>
</session>

<entity>
    <description>The Product entity bean </description>
    <ejb-name>ProductBean</ejb-name>
    <!--.....-->
</entity>

<!--.....-->
```

LISTING 3.6 An ENC `ejb-ref` Access Code Fragment

```
InitialContext iniCtx = new InitialContext();
Context ejbCtx = (Context) iniCtx.lookup("java:comp/env/ejb");
➥ShoppingCartHome home = (ShoppingCartHome) ejbCtx.lookup("ShoppingCartHome");
```

EJB References with `jboss.xml` and `jboss-web.xml` The JBoss-specific `jboss.xml` EJB deployment descriptor affects EJB references in two ways. First, the `jndi-name` child element of the `session` and `entity` elements allows the user to specify the deployment JNDI name for the EJB home interface. In the absence of a `jboss.xml` specification of the `jndi-name` for an EJB, the home interface is bound under the `ejb-jar.xml` `ejb-name` value. For example, the session EJB with the `ejb-name` of `ShoppingCart-Bean` in Listing 3.5 would have its home interface bound under the JNDI name `ShoppingCartBean` in the absence of a `jboss.xml` `jndi-name` specification.

The second use of the `jboss.xml` descriptor with respect to `ejb-refs` involves the setting of the destination to which a component's ENC `ejb-ref` refers. The `ejb-link` element cannot be used to refer to EJBs in another enterprise application. If an `ejb-ref` needs to access an external EJB, you can specify the JNDI name of the deployed EJB home by using the `jboss.xml` `ejb-ref/jndi-name` element.

The `jboss-web.xml` descriptor is used only to set the destination to which a web application ENC `ejb-ref` refers. The content model for the JBoss `ejb-ref` includes the following:

- An `ejb-ref-name` element that corresponds to the `ejb-ref-name` element in the `ejb-jar.xml` or `web.xml` standard descriptor
- A `jndi-name` element that specifies the JNDI name of the EJB home interface in the deployment environment

Listing 3.7 provides an example `jboss.xml` descriptor fragment that illustrates the following usage points:

- The `ProductBeanUser` `ejb-ref` link destination is set to the deployment name `jboss/store/ProductHome`
- The deployment JNDI name of the `ProductBean` is set to `jboss/store/ProductHome`

LISTING 3.7 An Example of a `jboss.xml` `ejb-ref` Fragment

```
<!-- ... -->
<session>
    <ejb-name>ProductBeanUser</ejb-name>
    <ejb-ref>
        <ejb-ref-name>ejb/ProductHome</ejb-ref-name>
        <jndi-name>jboss/store/ProductHome</jndi-name>
    </ejb-ref>
</session>

<entity>
    <ejb-name>ProductBean</ejb-name>
    <jndi-name>jboss/store/ProductHome</jndi-name>
     <!-- ... -->
</entity>
<!-- ... -->
```

EJB Local References EJB 2.0 added local interfaces that do not use RMI call-by-value semantics. These interfaces use a call-by-reference semantic and therefore do not incur any RMI serialization overhead. An EJB local reference is a link in an application component-naming environment that points to a deployed EJB local home interface. The name used by the application component is a logical link that isolates the component from the actual name of the EJB local home in the deployment environment. The J2EE specification recommends that all references to Enterprise Beans be organized in the `java:comp/env/ejb` context of the application component's environment.

You declare an EJB local reference by using an ejb-local-ref element in the deployment descriptor. Each ejb-local-ref element describes the interface requirements that the referencing application component has for the referenced Enterprise Bean. The ejb-local-ref element contains the following child elements:

- An optional description element that provides the purpose of the reference.
- An ejb-ref-name element that specifies the name of the reference relative to the java:comp/env context. To place the reference under the recommended java:comp/env/ejb context, you use an ejb/link-name form for the ejb-ref-name value.
- An ejb-ref-type element that specifies the type of the EJB. This must be either Entity or Session.
- A local-home element that gives the fully qualified classname of the EJB local home interface.
- A local element that gives the fully qualified classname of the EJB local interface.
- An ejb-link element that links the reference to another Enterprise Bean in the ejb-jar file or in the same J2EE application unit. The ejb-link value is the ejb-name of the referenced bean. If there are multiple Enterprise Beans with the same ejb-name, the value uses the pathname that specifies the location of the ejb-jar file that contains the referenced component. The pathname is relative to the referencing ejb-jar file. The application assembler appends the ejb-name of the referenced bean to the pathname, separated by #. This allows multiple beans with the same name to be uniquely identified. An ejb-link element must be specified in JBoss to match the local reference to the corresponding EJB.

An EJB local reference is scoped to the application component whose declaration contains the ejb-local-ref element. This means that the EJB local reference is not accessible from other application components at runtime and that other application components may define ejb-local-ref elements with the same ejb-ref-name without causing a naming conflict. Listing 3.8 provides an ejb-jar.xml fragment that illustrates the use of the ejb-local-ref element. Listing 3.9 provides a code sample that illustrates accessing the ProbeLocalHome reference declared in Listing 3.8.

LISTING 3.8 An Example of an ejb-jar.xml ejb-local-ref Descriptor Fragment

```
<!-- ... -->
<session>
    <ejb-name>Probe</ejb-name>
    <home>org.jboss.test.perf.interfaces.ProbeHome</home>
    <remote>org.jboss.test.perf.interfaces.Probe</remote>
    <local-home>org.jboss.test.perf.interfaces.ProbeLocalHome</local-home>
    <local>org.jboss.test.perf.interfaces.ProbeLocal</local>
    <ejb-class>org.jboss.test.perf.ejb.ProbeBean</ejb-class>
```

LISTING 3.8 Continued

```
        <session-type>Stateless</session-type>
        <transaction-type>Bean</transaction-type>
    </session>
    <session>
        <ejb-name>PerfTestSession</ejb-name>
        <home>org.jboss.test.perf.interfaces.PerfTestSessionHome</home>
        <remote>org.jboss.test.perf.interfaces.PerfTestSession</remote>
        <ejb-class>org.jboss.test.perf.ejb.PerfTestSessionBean</ejb-class>
        <session-type>Stateless</session-type>
        <transaction-type>Container</transaction-type>
        <ejb-ref>
            <ejb-ref-name>ejb/ProbeHome</ejb-ref-name>
            <ejb-ref-type>Session</ejb-ref-type>
            <home>org.jboss.test.perf.interfaces.SessionHome</home>
            <remote>org.jboss.test.perf.interfaces.Session</remote>
            <ejb-link>Probe</ejb-link>
        </ejb-ref>
        <ejb-local-ref>
            <ejb-ref-name>ejb/ProbeLocalHome</ejb-ref-name>
            <ejb-ref-type>Session</ejb-ref-type>
            <local-home>org.jboss.test.perf.interfaces.ProbeLocalHome</local-home>
            <local>org.jboss.test.perf.interfaces.ProbeLocal</local>
            <ejb-link>Probe</ejb-link>
        </ejb-local-ref>
    </session>
    <!-- ... -->
```

LISTING 3.9 An ENC `ejb-local-ref` Access Code Fragment

```
InitialContext iniCtx = new InitialContext();
Context ejbCtx = (Context) iniCtx.lookup("java:comp/env/ejb");
➥ProbeLocalHome home = (ProbeLocalHome) ejbCtx.lookup("ProbeLocalHome");
```

Resource Manager Connection Factory References Application component code can refer to resource factories by using logical names called *resource manager connection factory references*. Resource manager connection factory references are defined by the `resource-ref` elements in the standard deployment descriptors. The deployer binds the resource manager connection factory references to the actual resource manager connection factories that exist in the target operational environment, using the `jboss.xml` and `jboss-web.xml` descriptors.

Each `resource-ref` element describes a single resource manager connection factory reference. The `resource-ref` element consists of the following child elements:

- An optional description element that provides the purpose of the reference.
- A `res-ref-name` element that specifies the name of the reference relative to the `java:comp/env` context. (The resource type–based naming convention for which subcontext to place the `res-ref-name` into is discussed shortly.)
- A `res-type` element that specifies the fully qualified classname of the resource manager connection factory.
- A `res-auth` element that indicates whether the application component code performs resource sign-on programmatically or whether the container signs on to the resource based on the principal mapping information supplied by the deployer. It must be either `Application` or `Container`.
- An optional `res-sharing-scope` element. This currently is not supported by JBoss.

The J2EE specification recommends that all resource manager connection factory references be organized in the subcontexts of the application component's environment, using a different subcontext for each resource manager type. The recommended resource manager type-to-subcontext name mapping is as follows:

- JDBC `DataSource` references should be declared in the `java:comp/env/jdbc` subcontext.
- JMS connection factories should be declared in the `java:comp/env/jms` subcontext.
- JavaMail connection factories should be declared in the `java:comp/env/mail` subcontext.
- URL connection factories should be declared in the `java:comp/env/url` subcontext.

Listing 3.10 shows an example of a `web.xml` descriptor fragment that illustrates the `resource-ref` element usage. Listing 3.11 provides a code fragment that an application component would use to access the `DefaultMail` resource declared by the `resource-ref`.

LISTING 3.10 A `web.xml` `resource-ref` Descriptor Fragment

```
<web>
    <!-- ... -->
    <servlet>
        <servlet-name>AServlet</servlet-name>
        <!-- ... -->
    </servlet>
    <!-- ... -->
    <!-- JDBC DataSources (java:comp/env/jdbc) -->
    <resource-ref>
        <description>The default DS</description>
        <res-ref-name>jdbc/DefaultDS</res-ref-name>
        <res-type>javax.sql.DataSource</res-type>
```

LISTING 3.10 Continued

```
        <res-auth>Container</res-auth>
    </resource-ref>
    <!-- JavaMail Connection Factories (java:comp/env/mail) -->
    <resource-ref>
        <description>Default Mail</description>
        <res-ref-name>mail/DefaultMail</res-ref-name>
        <res-type>javax.mail.Session</res-type>
        <res-auth>Container</res-auth>
    </resource-ref>
    <!-- JMS Connection Factories (java:comp/env/jms) -->
    <resource-ref>
        <description>Default QueueFactory</description>
        <res-ref-name>jms/QueueFactory</res-ref-name>
        <res-type>javax.jms.QueueConnectionFactory</res-type>
        <res-auth>Container</res-auth>
    </resource-ref>
</web>
```

LISTING 3.11 An ENC `resource-ref` Access Sample Code Fragment

```
Context initCtx = new InitialContext();
javax.mail.Session s = (javax.mail.Session)
initCtx.lookup("java:comp/env/mail/DefaultMail");
```

Resource Manager Connection Factory References with `jboss.xml` and `jboss-web.xml` The purpose of the JBoss `jboss.xml` EJB deployment descriptor and `jboss-web.xml` web application deployment descriptor is to provide the link from the logical name defined by the `res-ref-name` element to the JNDI name of the resource factory, as deployed in JBoss. This is accomplished by providing a `resource-ref` element in the `jboss.xml` or `jboss-web.xml` descriptor. The JBoss `resource-ref` element consists of the following child elements:

- A `res-ref-name` element that must match the `res-ref-name` of a corresponding `resource-ref` element from the `ejb-jar.xml` or `web.xml` standard descriptors
- An optional `res-type` element that specifies the fully qualified classname of the resource manager connection factory
- A `jndi-name` element that specifies the JNDI name of the resource factory, as deployed in JBoss
- A `res-url` element that specifies the URL string in the case of a `resource-ref` of type `java.net.URL`

Listing 3.12 provides a sample `jboss-web.xml` descriptor fragment that shows sample mappings of the `resource-ref` elements given in Listing 3.10.

LISTING 3.12 A Sample `jboss-web.xml` `resource-ref` Descriptor Fragment

```
<jboss-web>
    <!-- ... -->
    <resource-ref>
        <res-ref-name>jdbc/DefaultDS</res-ref-name>
        <res-type>javax.sql.DataSource</res-type>
        <jndi-name>java:/DefaultDS</jndi-name>
    </resource-ref>
    <resource-ref>
        <res-ref-name>mail/DefaultMail</res-ref-name>
        <res-type>javax.mail.Session</res-type>
        <jndi-name>java:/Mail</jndi-name>
    </resource-ref>
    <resource-ref>
        <res-ref-name>jms/QueueFactory</res-ref-name>
        <res-type>javax.jms.QueueConnectionFactory</res-type>
        <jndi-name>QueueConnectionFactory</jndi-name>
    </resource-ref>
    <!-- ... -->
</jboss-web>
```

Resource Environment References A *resource environment reference* is an element that refers to an administered object that is associated with a resource (for example, JMS destinations), using a logical name. Resource environment references are defined by the `resource-env-ref` elements in the standard deployment descriptors. The deployer binds the resource environment references to the actual administered object's location in the target operational environment by using the `jboss.xml` and `jboss-web.xml` descriptors.

Each `resource-env-ref` element describes the requirements that the referencing application component has for the referenced administered object. The `resource-env-ref` element consists of the following child elements:

- An optional description element that provides the purpose of the reference.
- A `resource-env-ref-name` element that specifies the name of the reference relative to the `java:comp/env context`. Convention places the name in a subcontext that corresponds to the associated resource factory type. For example, a JMS queue reference named `MyQueue` should have a `resource-env-ref-name` of `jms/MyQueue`.
- A `resource-env-ref-type` element that specifies the fully qualified classname of the referenced object. For example, in the case of a JMS queue, the value would be `javax.jms.Queue`.

Listing 3.13 provides an example `resource-ref-env` element declaration by a session bean. Listing 3.14 provides a code fragment that illustrates how to look up the `StockInfo` queue declared by the `resource-env-ref`.

LISTING 3.13 An Example of an `ejb -jar.xml resource-env-ref` Fragment

```
<session>
    <ejb-name>MyBean</ejb-name>

    <resource-env-ref>
        <description>This is a reference to a JMS queue used in the
            processing of Stock info
        </description>
        <resource-env-ref-name>jms/StockInfo</resource-env-ref-name>
        <resource-env-ref-type>javax.jms.Queue</resource-env-ref-type>
    </resource-env-ref>
    <!-- ... -->
</session>
```

LISTING 3.14 An ENC `resource-env-ref` Access Code Fragment

```
InitialContext iniCtx = new InitialContext();
javax.jms.Queue q = (javax.jms.Queue)
envCtx.lookup("java:comp/env/jms/StockInfo");
```

Resource Environment References with `jboss.xml` and `jboss-web.xml` The purpose of the JBoss `jboss.xml` EJB deployment descriptor and `jboss-web.xml` web application deployment descriptor is to provide the link from the logical name defined by the `resource-env-ref-name` element to the JNDI name of the administered object deployed in JBoss. This is accomplished by providing a `resource-env-ref` element in the `jboss.xml` or `jboss-web.xml` descriptor. The JBoss `resource-env-ref` element consists of the following child elements:

- A `resource-env-ref-name` element that must match the `resource-env-ref-name` of a corresponding `resource-env-ref` element from the `ejb-jar.xml` or `web.xml` standard descriptors
- A `jndi-name` element that specifies the JNDI name of the resource, as deployed in JBoss

Listing 3.15 provides a sample `jboss.xml` descriptor fragment that shows a sample mapping for the `StockInfo resource-env-ref`.

LISTING 3.15 A Sample `jboss.xml` `resource-env-ref` Descriptor Fragment

```
<session>
    <ejb-name>MyBean</ejb-name>

        <resource-env-ref>
        <resource-env-ref-name>jms/StockInfo</resource-env-ref-name>
        <jndi-name>queue/StockInfoQueue</jndi-name>
    </resource-env-ref>
    <!-- ... -->
</session>
```

The JBossNS Architecture

The JBossNS architecture is a Java socket/RMI-based implementation of the `javax.naming.Context` interface. It is a client/server implementation that can be accessed remotely. The implementation is optimized so that access from within the same VM in which the JBossNS server is running does not involve sockets. Same-VM access occurs through an object reference that is available as a global singleton. Figure 3.1 illustrates some of the key classes in the JBossNS implementation and their relationships.

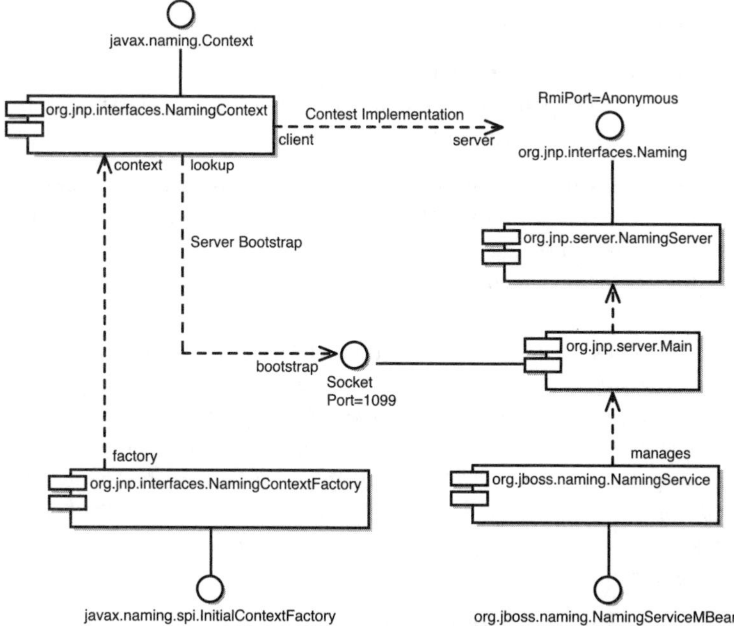

FIGURE 3.1 Key components in the JBossNS architecture.

Let's start with the NamingService MBean. The NamingService MBean provides the JNDI naming service. This is a key service that is used pervasively by the J2EE technology components. The configurable attributes for the NamingService MBean are as follows:

- **Port**—The jnp protocol listening port for the NamingService. If it is not specified, the default is 1099—the same as the RMI registry default port.
- **RmiPort**—The RMI port on which the RMI Naming implementation will be exported. If it is not specified, the default is 0, which means use any available port.
- **BindAddress**—The specific address the NamingService listens on. This can be used on a multi-homed host for a java.net.ServerSocket that will accept connect requests only on one of its addresses.
- **RmiBindAddress**—The specific address the RMI server portion of the NamingService listens on. This can be used on a multi-homed host for a java.net.ServerSocket that will accept connect requests only on one of its addresses. If this is not specified and the BindAddress is, the RmiBindAddress defaults to the BindAddress value.
- **Backlog**—The maximum queue length for incoming connection indications (a request to connect), set to the Backlog parameter. If a connection indication arrives when the queue is full, the connection is refused.
- **ClientSocketFactory**—An optional custom java.rmi.server.RMIClientSocketFactory implementation classname. If it is not specified, the default RMIClientSocketFactory is used.
- **ServerSocketFactory**—An optional custom java.rmi.server.RMIServerSocketFactory implementation classname. If it is not specified, the default RMIServerSocketFactory is used.
- **JNPServerSocketFactory**—An optional custom javax.net.ServerSocketFactory implementation classname. This is the factory for the ServerSocket that is used to bootstrap the download of the JBoss Naming interface. If it is not specified, the javax.net.ServerSocketFactory.getDefault() method value is used.

NamingService also creates the java:comp context such that access to this context is isolated based on the context class loader of the thread that accesses the java:comp context. This provides the application component private ENC that is required by the J2EE specs. This segregation is accomplished by binding a javax.naming.Reference to a context that uses org.jboss.naming.ENCFactory as its javax.naming.ObjectFactory. When a client performs a lookup of java:comp or any subcontext, the ENCFactory checks the thread context ClassLoader and performs a lookup into a map, using the ClassLoader as the key.

If a context instance does not exist for the class loader instance, one is created and associated with that class loader in the ENCFactory map. Thus, correct isolation of an application component's ENC relies on each component receiving a unique ClassLoader that is associated with the component threads of execution.

The `NamingService` delegates its functionality to an `org.jnp.server.Main` MBean. Duplicate MBeans are needed because JBossNS started out as a standalone JNDI implementation and can still be run as such. The `NamingService` MBean embeds the `Main` instance into the JBoss server so that usage of JNDI with the same VM as the JBoss server does not incur any socket overhead. The configurable attributes of the `NamingService` are really the configurable attributes of the JBossNS `Main` MBean. The setting of any attributes on the `NamingService` MBean simply sets the corresponding attributes on the `Main` MBean that the `NamingService` contains. When the `NamingService` is started, it starts the contained `Main` MBean to activate the JNDI naming service.

In addition, the `NamingService` exposes the `Naming` interface operations through a JMX detyped invoke operation. This allows the naming service to be accessed via JMX adaptors for arbitrary protocols. We will look at an example of how HTTP can be used to access the naming service using the invoke operation later in this chapter.

The details of threads and the thread context class loader are beyond the scope of this book, but the JNDI tutorial provides a concise discussion that is applicable. See http://java.sun.com/products/jndi/tutorial/beyond/misc/classloader.html for the details.

When the `Main` MBean is started, it performs the following tasks:

1. Instantiates an `org.jnp.naming.NamingService` instance and sets it as the local VM server instance. This is used by any `org.jnp.interfaces.NamingContext` instances that are created within the JBoss server VM to avoid RMI calls over TCP/IP.
2. Exports the `NamingServer` instance's `org.jnp.naming.interfaces.Naming` RMI interface, using the configured `RmiPort`, `ClientSocketFactory`, and `ServerSocketFactoryattributes`.
3. Creates a socket that listens on the interface given by the `BindAddress` and `Port` attributes.
4. Spawns a thread to accept connections on the socket.

The Naming `InitialContext` Factories

The JBoss JNDI provider currently supports several different `InitialContext` factory implementations. The most commonly used factory is the `org.jnp.interfaces.NamingContextFactory` implementation. Its properties include the following:

- **`java.naming.factory.initial`**—The name of the environment property for specifying the initial context factory to use. The value of the property should be the fully qualified classname of the factory class that will create an initial context. If it is not specified, a `javax.naming.NoInitialContextException` will be thrown when an `InitialContext` object is created.
- **`java.naming.provider.url`**—The name of the environment property for specifying the location of the JBoss JNDI service provider that the client will use. The `NamingContextFactory` class uses this information to determine which JBossNS

server to connect to. The value of the property should be a URL string. For JBossNS, the URL format is `jnp://host:port/[jndi_path]`. The `jnp:` portion of the URL is the protocol and refers to the socket/RMI-based protocol used by JBoss. The `jndi_path` portion of the URL is an optional JNDI name relative to the root context (for example, `apps` or `apps/tmp`). Everything but the host component is optional. The following examples are equivalent because the default port value is 1099:

jnp://www.jboss.org:1099/

www.jboss.org:1099

www.jboss.org

- **`java.naming.factory.url.pkgs`**—The name of the environment property for specifying the list of package prefixes to use when loading URL context factories. The value of the property should be a colon-separated list of package prefixes for the classname of the factory class that will create a URL context factory. For the JBoss JNDI provider, this must be `org.jboss.naming:org.jnp.interfaces`. This property is essential for locating the `jnp:` and `java:` URL context factories of the JBoss JNDI provider.

- **`jnp.socketFactory`**—The fully qualified classname of the `javax.net.SocketFactory` implementation to use to create the bootstrap socket. The default value is `org.jnp.interfaces.TimedSocketFactory`. `TimedSocketFactory` is a simple `SocketFactory` implementation that supports the specification of a connection and read timeout. These two properties are specified by the following:

  - **`jnp.timeout`**—The connection timeout, in milliseconds. The default value is `0`, which means the connection will block until the VM TCP/IP layer times out.

  - **`jnp.sotimeout`**—The connected socket read timeout, in milliseconds. The default value is `0`, which means reads will block. This is the value passed to `Socket.setSoTimeout` on the newly connected socket.

When a client creates an `InitialContext` with these JBossNS properties available, the `org.jnp.interfaces.NamingContextFactory` object is used to create the `Context` instance that will be used in subsequent operations. The `NamingContextFactory` is the JBossNS implementation of the `javax.naming.spi.InitialContextFactory` interface. When the `NamingContextFactory` class is asked to create a context, it creates an `org.jnp.interfaces.NamingContext` instance with the `InitialContext` environment and the name of the context in the global JNDI namespace. The `NamingContext` instance actually performs the task of connecting to the JBossNS server and implements the `Context` interface. The `Context.PROVIDER_URL` information from the environment indicates from which server to obtain a `NamingServer` RMI reference.

The association of the `NamingContext` instance to a `NamingServer` instance is done in a lazy fashion on the first `Context` operation that is performed. When a `Context` operation is performed and the `NamingContext` has no `NamingServer` associated with it, it looks to see if its environment properties define a `Context.PROVIDER_URL`. A `Context.PROVIDER_URL` defines the host and port of the JBossNS server the `Context` is to use. If there is a provider URL, the NamingContext first checks whether a Naming instance keyed by the host and port pair has already been created by checking a NamingContext class static map. It simply uses the existing Naming instance if one for the host/port pair has already been obtained. If no Naming instance has been created for the given host and port, the NamingContext connects to the host and port by using a java.net.Socket, and it retrieves a Naming RMI stub from the server by reading a java.rmi.MarshalledObject from the socket and invoking its get method. The newly obtained Naming instance is cached in the NamingContext server map under the host/port pair. If no provider URL is specified in the JNDI environment associated with the context, the NamingContext simply uses the in-VM Naming instance set by the Main MBean.

The NamingContext implementation of the Context interface delegates all operations to the Naming instance associated with the NamingContext. The NamingServer class that implements the Naming interface uses a java.util.Hashtable as the Context store. There is one unique NamingServer instance for each distinct JNDI name for a given JBossNS server. At any given moment, zero or more active transient NamingContext instances refer to a NamingServer instance. The purpose of the NamingContext is to act as a context to the Naming interface adaptor that manages translation of the JNDI names passed to the NamingContext. Because a JNDI name can be relative or a URL, it needs to be converted into an absolute name in the context of the JBossNS server to which it refers. This translation is a key function of the NamingContext.

Naming Discovery in Clustered Environments

When running in a clustered JBoss environment, you can choose not to specify a Context.PROVIDER_URL value and let the client query the network for available naming services. This only works with JBoss servers running with the all configuration or an equivalent configuration that has org.jboss.ha.framework.server.ClusterPartition and org.jboss.ha.jndi.HANamingService services deployed. The discovery process consists of sending a multicast request packet to the discovery address/port and waiting for any node to respond. The response is an HA-RMI version of the Naming interface. The following InitialContext properties affect the discovery configuration:

- **jnp.partitionName**—The name of the cluster partition that discovery should be restricted to. If you are running in an environment that has multiple clusters, you might want to restrict the naming discovery to a particular cluster. There is no default value, meaning that any cluster response will be accepted.
- **jnp.discoveryGroup**—The multicast IP/address to which the discovery query is sent. The default is 230.0.0.4.
- **jnp.discoveryPort**—The port to which the discovery query is sent. The default is 1102.
- **jnp.discoveryTimeout**—The time, in milliseconds, to wait for a discovery query response. The default value is 5000 (5 seconds).
- **jnp.disableDiscovery**—A flag that indicates whether the discovery process should be avoided. Discovery occurs when either no Context.PROVIDER_URL is specified or

no valid naming service can be located among the URLs specified. If the `jnp.disableDiscovery` flag is `true`, then discovery will not be attempted.

The HTTP `InitialContext` Factory Implementation

The JNDI naming service can be accessed over HTTP. From a JNDI client's perspective, this is a transparent change because the client continues to use the JNDI `Context` interface. Operations through the `Context` interface are translated into HTTP posts to a servlet that passes the request to the `NamingService`, using its JMX invoke operation. Advantages of using HTTP as the access protocol include better access through firewalls and proxies set up to allow HTTP, as well as the ability to secure access to the JNDI service, using standard servlet role-based security.

To access JNDI over HTTP, you use `org.jboss.naming.HttpNamingContextFactory` as the factory implementation. The following is the complete set of support `InitialContext` environment properties for this factory:

- **`java.naming.factory.initial`**—This is the name of the environment property for specifying the initial context factory, which must be `org.jboss.naming.HttpNamingContextFactory`.
- **`java.naming.provider.url`** (or **`Context.PROVIDER_URL`**)—This must be set to the HTTP URL of the JMX invoker servlet. It depends on the configuration of the `http-invoker.sar` and its contained WAR, but the default setup places the JMX invoker servlet under `/invoker/JMXInvokerServlet`. The full HTTP URL would be the public URL of the JBoss servlet container plus `/invoker/JMXInvokerServlet`. The following are some examples:

  http://www.jboss.org:8080/invoker/JMXInvokerServlet

  http://www.jboss.org/invoker/JMXInvokerServlet

  https://www.jboss.org/invoker/JMXInvokerServlet

  The first example accesses the servlet, using port 8080. The second uses the standard HTTP port 80, and the third uses an SSL-encrypted connection to the standard HTTPS port 443.
- **`java.naming.factory.url.pkgs`**—For all JBoss JNDI providers, this must be `org.jboss.naming:org.jnp.interfaces`. This property is essential for locating the `jnp:` and `java:` URL context factories of the JBoss JNDI provider.

The JNDI `Context` implementation returned by the `HttpNamingContextFactory` is a proxy that delegates invocations made on it to a bridge servlet, which forwards the invocation to the `NamingService` through the JMX bus and marshals the reply back over HTTP. The proxy needs to know what the URL of the bridge servlet is in order to operate. This value may have been bound on the server side if the JBoss web server has a well-known public interface. If the JBoss web server is sitting behind one or more firewalls or proxies, the proxy cannot know what URL is required. In this case, the proxy will be associated with a system property value that must be set in the client VM. For more information on the operation of JNDI over HTTP, see the section "Accessing JNDI over HTTP," later in this chapter.

The Login `InitialContext` Factory Implementation

JAAS is the preferred method for authenticating a remote client to JBoss. However, for simplicity and to ease the migration from other application server environments that do not use JAAS, JBoss allows the security credentials to be passed through the `InitialContext`. JAAS is still used under the covers, but there is no manifest use of the JAAS interfaces in the client application.

The factory class that provides this capability is `org.jboss.security.jndi.LoginInitialContextFactory`.

The following is the complete set of support `InitialContext` environment properties for this factory:

- **`java.naming.factory.initial`**—This is the name of the environment property for specifying the initial context factory, which must be `org.jboss.security.jndi.LoginInitialContextFactory`.
- **`java.naming.provider.url`**—This must be set to a `NamingContextFactory` provider URL. `LoginInitialContext` is really just a wrapper around `NamingContextFactory` that adds a JAAS login to the existing `NamingContextFactory` behavior.
- **`java.naming.factory.url.pkgs`**—For all JBoss JNDI providers, this must be `org.jboss.naming:org.jnp.interfaces`. This property is essential for locating the `jnp:` and `java:` URL context factories of the JBoss JNDI provider.
- **`java.naming.security.principal`** (or **`Context.SECURITY_PRINCIPAL`**)—These are the principal to authenticate. This may be either a `java.security.Principal` implementation or a string that represents the name of a principal.
- **`java.naming.security.credentials`** (or **`Context.SECURITY_CREDENTIALS`**)—These are the credentials that should be used to authenticate the principal (for example, password, session key, and so on).
- **`java.naming.security.protocol`** (or **`Context.SECURITY_PROTOCOL`**)—This gives the name of the JAAS login module to use for the authentication of the principal and credentials.

Accessing JNDI over HTTP

In addition to the legacy RMI/JRMP with a socket bootstrap protocol, JBoss provides support for accessing its JNDI naming service over HTTP. This capability is provided by `http-invoker.sar`. The following is the structure of `http-invoker.sar`:

```
http-invoker.sar
+- META-INF/jboss-service.xml
+- invoker.war
```

```
¦ +- WEB-INF/jboss-web.xml
¦ +- WEB-INF/classes/org/jboss/invocation/http/servlet/InvokerServlet.class
¦ +- WEB-INF/classes/org/jboss/invocation/http/servlet/NamingFactoryServlet.class
¦ +- WEB-INF/classes/org/jboss/invocation/http/servlet/ReadOnlyAccessFilter.class
¦ +- WEB-INF/classes/roles.properties
¦ +- WEB-INF/classes/users.properties
¦ +- WEB-INF/web.xml
¦ +- META-INF/MANIFEST.MF
+- META-INF/MANIFEST.MF
```

The `jboss-service.xml` descriptor defines the `HttpInvoker` and `HttpInvokerHA` MBeans. These services handle the routing of method invocations that are sent via HTTP to the appropriate target MBean on the JMX bus.

The `http-invoker.war` web application contains servlets that handle the details of the HTTP transport. `NamingFactoryServlet` handles creation requests for the JBoss JNDI naming service `javax.naming.Context` implementation. `InvokerServlet` handles invocations made by RMI/HTTP clients. `ReadOnlyAccessFilter` allows you to secure the JNDI naming service while making a single JNDI context available for read-only access by unauthenticated clients.

Before looking at the configurations, let's look at the operation of the `http-invoker` services. Figure 3.2 shows a logical view of the structure of a JBoss JNDI proxy and its relationship to the JBoss server-side components of the `http-invoker`. The proxy is obtained from the `NamingFactoryServlet`, using an `InitialContext` with the `Context.INITIAL_CONTEXT_FACTORY` property set to `org.jboss.naming.HttpNamingContextFactory` and the `Context.PROVIDER_URL` property set to the HTTP URL of the `NamingFactoryServlet`. The resulting proxy is embedded in an `org.jnp.interfaces.NamingContext` instance that provides the `Context` interface implementation.

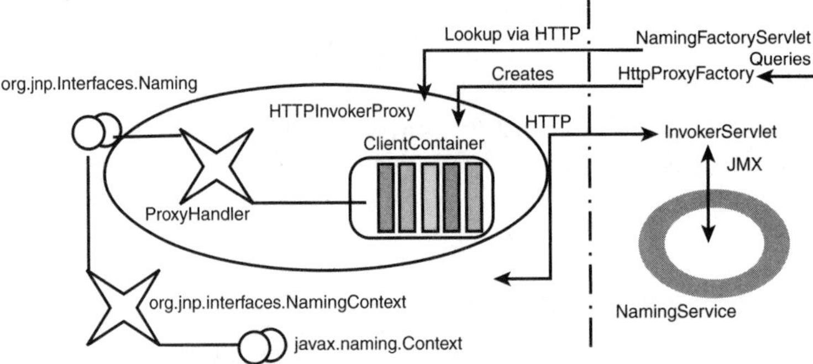

FIGURE 3.2 The HTTP invoker proxy/server structure for a JNDI context.

The proxy is an instance of `org.jboss.invocation.http.interfaces.HttpInvokerProxy`, and it implements the `org.jnp.interfaces.Naming` interface. Internally, the

HttpInvokerProxy contains an invoker that marshals the Naming interface method invocations to the InvokerServlet via HTTP posts. The InvokerServlet translates these posts into JMX invocations to the NamingService and returns the invocation response back to the proxy in the HTTP post response.

Several configuration values need to be set to tie all these components together, and Figure 3.3 illustrates the relationship between configuration files and the corresponding components.

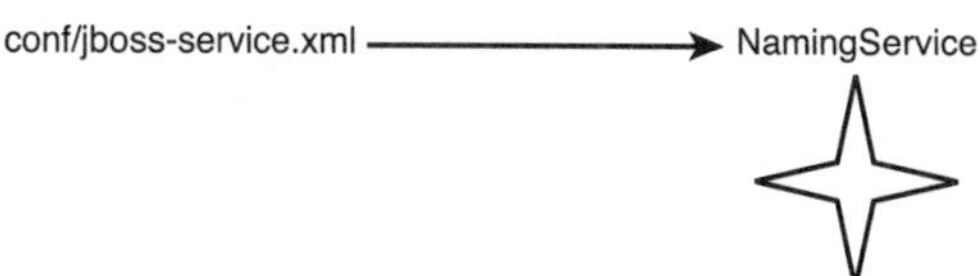

FIGURE 3.3 The relationship between configuration files and JNDI/HTTP component.

The http-invoker.sar/META-INF/jboss-service.xml descriptor defines the HttpProxyFactory that creates the HttpInvokerProxy for the NamingService. The attributes that need to be configured for the HttpProxyFactory include the following:

- **InvokerName**—The JMX ObjectName of the NamingService defined in the conf/jboss-service.xml descriptor. The standard setting used in the JBoss distributions is jboss:service=Naming.
- **InvokerURL** or **InvokerURLPrefix** + **InvokerURLSuffix** + **UseHostName**—You can specify the full HTTP URL to the InvokerServlet by using the InvokerURL attribute, or you can specify the hostname-independent parts of the URL and have the HttpProxyFactory fill them in. An example of an InvokerURL value might be http://jbosshost1.dot.com:8080/invoker/JMXInvokerServlet. This can be broken down into the following:
    - **InvokerURLPrefix**—The URL prefix prior to the hostname. Typically, this will be http:// or https://, if SSL is to be used.
    - **InvokerURLSuffix**—The URL suffix after the hostname. This will include the port number of the web server as well as the deployed path to the InvokerServlet. For the sample InvokerURL value, the InvokerURLSuffix would be :8080/invoker/JMXInvokerServlet. The port number is determined by the web container service settings. The path to the InvokerServlet is specified in the http-invoker.sar/invoker.war/WEB-INF/web.xml descriptor.
- **UseHostName**—A flag that indicates whether the hostname should be used in place of the host IP address when building the hostname portion of the full InvokerURL. If it is true, the InetAddress.getLocalHost().getHostName() method is used. Otherwise, the InetAddress.getLocalHost().getHostAddress() method is used.
- **ExportedInterface**—The org.jnp.interfaces.Naming interface the proxy will expose to clients. The actual client of this proxy is the JBoss JNDI implementation

NamingContext class, which a JNDI client obtains from InitialContext lookups when using the JBoss JNDI provider.

- **JndiName**—The name in JNDI under which the proxy is bound. This needs to be set to a blank/empty string to indicate that the interface should not be bound into JNDI. You can't use the JNDI to bootstrap itself. That is the role of the NamingFactoryServlet.

The http-invoker.sar/invoker.war/WEB-INF/web.xml descriptor defines the mappings of NamingFactoryServlet and InvokerServet along with their initialization parameters. The configuration of the NamingFactoryServlet relevant to JNDI/HTTP is the JNDIFactory entry, which defines the following:

- A namingProxyMBean initialization parameter that maps to the HttpProxyFactory MBean name. This is used by the NamingFactoryServlet to obtain the Naming proxy, which it returns in response to HTTP posts. For the default http-invoker.sar/META-INF/jboss-service.xml settings, the name is jboss:service=invoker,type=http,target=Naming.
- A proxy initialization parameter that defines the name of the namingProxyMBean attribute to query for the Naming proxy value. This defaults to the attribute name Proxy.
- The servlet mapping for the JNDIFactory configuration. The default setting for the unsecured mapping is /JNDIFactory/*. This is relative to the context root of the http-invoker.sar/invoker.war, which by default is the WAR name minus the .war suffix.

The configuration of the InvokerServlet relevant to JNDI/HTTP is the JMXInvokerServlet, which defines the servlet mapping of the InvokerServlet. The default setting for the unsecured mapping is /JMXInvokerServlet/*. This is relative to the context root of the http-invoker.sar/invoker.war, which by default is the WAR name minus the .war suffix.

Accessing JNDI over HTTPS

To be able to access JNDI over HTTP/SSL, you need to enable an SSL connector on the web container. The details of this are covered in Chapter 9, "Web Applications." This section demonstrates the use of HTTPS with a simple sample client that uses an HTTPS URL as the JNDI provider URL. This example includes an SSL connector configuration, so unless you are interested in the details of the SSL connector setup, the example is self-contained.

This example also provides a configuration of the HttpProxyFactory setup to use an HTTPS URL. The following shows the section of the http-invoker.sar jboss-service.xml descriptor that the example installs to provide this configuration:

```
<!-- Expose the Naming service interface via HTTPS -->
<mbean code="org.jboss.invocation.http.server.HttpProxyFactory"
       name="jboss:service=invoker,type=https,target=Naming">
    <!-- The Naming service we are proxying -->
    <attribute name="InvokerName">jboss:service=Naming</attribute>
    <!-- Compose the invoker URL from the cluster node address -->
    <attribute name="InvokerURLPrefix">https://</attribute>
    <attribute name="InvokerURLSuffix">:8443/invoker/JMXInvokerServlet </attribute>
    <attribute name="UseHostName">true</attribute>
    <attribute name="ExportedInterface">org.jnp.interfaces.Naming </attribute>
    <attribute name="JndiName"/>
    <attribute name="ClientInterceptors">
        <interceptors>
            <interceptor>org.jboss.proxy.ClientMethodInterceptor </interceptor>
            <interceptor>org.jboss.proxy.SecurityInterceptor</interceptor>
            <interceptor>org.jboss.naming.interceptors.ExceptionInterceptor
➥</interceptor>
            <interceptor>org.jboss.invocation.InvokerInterceptor </interceptor>
        </interceptors>
    </attribute>
</mbean>
```

All that has changed relative to the standard HTTP configuration are the `InvokerURLPrefix` and `InvokerURLSuffix` attributes, which set up an HTTPS URL by using the 8443 port.

At a minimum, for a JNDI client using HTTPS, you need to set up an HTTPS URL protocol handler. This example uses Java Secure Socket Extension (JSSE) for HTTPS. The JSSE documentation does a good job of describing what is necessary in order to use HTTPS. You need to follow these steps to configure the sample client shown in Listing 3.16:

1. You need to make available to Java a protocol handler for HTTPS URLs. The JSSE release includes an HTTPS handler in the `com.sun.net.ssl.internal.www.protocol` package. To enable the use of HTTPS URLs, you include this package in the standard URL protocol handler search property, `java.protocol.handler.pkgs`. You set the `java.protocol.handler.pkgs` property in the Ant script.

2. You install the JSSE security provider in order for SSL to work. You can do this either by installing the JSSE JARs as an extension package or programmatically. This example uses the programmatic because it is the less intrusive method.

3. The JNDI provider URL must use HTTPS as the protocol. Lines 24–25 of the `ExClient` code specify an HTTP/SSL connection to the `localhost` on port 8443. The hostname and port are defined by the web container SSL connector.

4. You disable the validation of the HHTPS URL hostname against the server certificate. By default, the JSSE HTTPS protocol handler employs a strict validation of the hostname portion of the HTTPS URL against the common name of the server certificate.

This is the same check that web browsers do when you connect to a secured website. The example in Listing 3.16 uses a self-signed server certificate that uses the common name "Chapter 8 SSL Example" rather than a particular hostname, and this is likely to be common in development environments or intranets. The JBoss `HttpInvokerProxy` will override the default hostname checking if a `org.jboss.security.ignoreHttpsHost` system property exists and has a value of `true`. You set the `org.jboss.security.ignoreHttpsHost` property to `true` in the Ant script.

LISTING 3.16 A JNDI Client That Uses HTTPS as the Transport

```
package org.jboss.chap3.ex1;

import java.security.Security;
import java.util.Properties;
import javax.naming.Context;
import javax.naming.InitialContext;

public class ExClient
{
    public static void main(String args[]) throws Exception
    {
        Properties env = new Properties();
        env.setProperty(Context.INITIAL_CONTEXT_FACTORY,
                        "org.jboss.naming.HttpNamingContextFactory");
        env.setProperty(Context.PROVIDER_URL,
                        "https://localhost:8443/invoker/JNDIFactorySSL");

        Context ctx = new InitialContext(env);
        System.out.println("Created InitialContext, env=" + env);

        Object data = ctx.lookup("jmx/invoker/RMIAdaptor");
        System.out.println("lookup(jmx/invoker/RMIAdaptor): " + data);
    }
}
```

To test the client, you first build the Chapter 3 example to create the `chap3` configuration file set:

```
[examples]$ ant -Dchap=chap3 config example
```

Next, you start the JBoss server, using the `chap3` configuration file set:

```
[bin]$ sh run.sh -c chap3
```

Finally, you run the `ExClient` by using the following:

```
[examples]$ ant -Dchap=chap3 -Dex=1 run-example
...
run-example1:
     [java] Created InitialContext,
➥env={java.naming.provider.url=https://localhost:8443/invoker/JNDIFactorySSL,
➥java.naming.factory.initial=org.jboss.naming.HttpNamingContextFactory}
     [java] lookup(jmx/invoker/RMIAdaptor):
➥org.jboss.invocation.jrmp.interfaces.JRMPInvokerProxy@cac3fa
```

Securing Access to JNDI over HTTP

One benefit to accessing JNDI over HTTP is that it is easy to secure access to the JNDI `InitialContext` factory as well as the naming operations, using standard web declarative security. This is possible because the server-side handling of the JNDI/HTTP transport is implemented with two servlets. These servlets are included in the `http-invoker.sar/invoker.war` directory found in the `default` and `all` configuration `deploy` directories, as shown previously. To enable secured access to JNDI, you need to edit the `invoker.war/WEB-INF/web.xml` descriptor and remove all unsecured servlet mappings. For example, the `web.xml` descriptor shown in Listing 3.17 allows access to the `invoker.war` servlets only if the user has been authenticated and has the role `HttpInvoker`.

LISTING 3.17 An Example of a `web.xml` Descriptor for Secured Access to the JNDI Servlets

```
<?xml version="1.0" encoding="UTF-8"?>
<!DOCTYPE web-app PUBLIC
          "-//Sun Microsystems, Inc.//DTD Web Application 2.3//EN"
          "http://java.sun.com/dtd/web-app_2_3.dtd">
<web-app>
    <!-- ### Servlets -->
    <servlet>
        <servlet-name>JMXInvokerServlet</servlet-name>
        <servlet-class>
            org.jboss.invocation.http.servlet.InvokerServlet
        </servlet-class>
        <load-on-startup>1</load-on-startup>
    </servlet>   <servlet>
        <servlet-name>JNDIFactory</servlet-name>
        <servlet-class>
            org.jboss.invocation.http.servlet.NamingFactoryServlet
        </servlet-class>
        <init-param>
            <param-name>namingProxyMBean</param-name>
            <param-value>jboss:service=invoker,type=http,target=Naming
➥</param-value>
        </init-param>
```

LISTING 3.17 Continued

```
        <init-param>
            <param-name>proxyAttribute</param-name>
            <param-value>Proxy</param-value>
        </init-param>
        <load-on-startup>2</load-on-startup>
    </servlet>
    <!-- ### Servlet Mappings -->
    <servlet-mapping>
        <servlet-name>JNDIFactory</servlet-name>
        <url-pattern>/restricted/JNDIFactory/*</url-pattern>
    </servlet-mapping>
    <servlet-mapping>
        <servlet-name>JMXInvokerServlet</servlet-name>
        <url-pattern>/restricted/JMXInvokerServlet/*</url-pattern>
    </servlet-mapping>   <security-constraint>
        <web-resource-collection>
            <web-resource-name>HttpInvokers</web-resource-name>
            <description>An example security config that only allows users with
                the role HttpInvoker to access the HTTP invoker servlets
➥</description>
            <url-pattern>/restricted/*</url-pattern>
            <http-method>GET</http-method>
            <http-method>POST</http-method>
        </web-resource-collection>
        <auth-constraint>
            <role-name>HttpInvoker</role-name>
        </auth-constraint>
    </security-constraint>
    <login-config>
        <auth-method>BASIC</auth-method>
        <realm-name>JBoss HTTP Invoker</realm-name>
    </login-config>   <security-role>
        <role-name>HttpInvoker</role-name>
    </security-role>
</web-app>
```

The `web.xml` descriptor only defines which servlets are secured and which roles are allowed to access the secured servlets. You must additionally define the security domain that will handle the authentication and authorization for the WAR. You do this through the `jboss-web.xml` descriptor. The following example uses the `http-invoker` security domain:

```
<jboss-web>
    <security-domain>java:/jaas/http-invoker</security-domain>
</jboss-web>
```

The `security-domain` element defines the name of the security domain that will be used for the JAAS login module configuration used for authentication and authorization.

See Chapter 8, "Security on JBoss," for additional details on the meaning and configuration of the security domain name.

Securing Access to JNDI with a Read-only Unsecured Context

Another feature that is available for the JNDI/HTTP naming service is the ability to define a context that can be accessed by unauthenticated users in read-only mode. This can be important for services used by the authentication layer. For example, the `SRPLoginModule` needs to look up the SRP server interface used to perform authentication. Let's now walk through how read-only JNDI works in JBoss.

First, the `ReadOnlyJNDIFactory` is declared in `invoker.sar/WEB-INF/web.xml`. It will be mapped to `/invoker/ReadOnlyJNDIFactory`:

```
<servlet>
    <servlet-name>ReadOnlyJNDIFactory</servlet-name>
    <description>A servlet that exposes the JBoss JNDI Naming service stub
          through http, but only for a single read-only context. The return content
          is serialized MarshalledValue containing the org.jnp.interfaces.Naming
          stub.
    </description>
    <servlet-class>org.jboss.invocation.http.servlet.NamingFactoryServlet
➥</servlet-class>
    <init-param>
        <param-name>namingProxyMBean</param-name>
        <param-
value>jboss:service=invoker,type=http,target=Naming,readonly=true</param-value>
    </init-param>
    <init-param>
        <param-name>proxyAttribute</param-name>
        <param-value>Proxy</param-value>
    </init-param>
    <load-on-startup>2</load-on-startup>
</servlet>

<!-- ... -->

<servlet-mapping>
    <servlet-name>ReadOnlyJNDIFactory</servlet-name>
```

```
    <url-pattern>/ReadOnlyJNDIFactory/*</url-pattern>
</servlet-mapping>
```

The factory only provides a JNDI stub which needs to be connected to an invoker. Here the invoker is `jboss:service=invoker,type=http,target=Naming,readonly=true`. This invoker is declared in the `http-invoker.sar/META-INF/jboss-service.xml` file:

```
<mbean code="org.jboss.invocation.http.server.HttpProxyFactory"
       name="jboss:service=invoker,type=http,target=Naming,readonly=true">
    <attribute name="InvokerName">jboss:service=Naming</attribute>
    <attribute name="InvokerURLPrefix">http://</attribute>
    <attribute name="InvokerURLSuffix">:8080/invoker/readonly/JMXInvokerServlet
➥</attribute>
    <attribute name="UseHostName">true</attribute>
    <attribute name="ExportedInterface">org.jnp.interfaces.Naming</attribute>
    <attribute name="JndiName"></attribute>
    <attribute name="ClientInterceptors">
        <interceptors>
            <interceptor>org.jboss.proxy.ClientMethodInterceptor</interceptor>
            <interceptor>org.jboss.proxy.SecurityInterceptor</interceptor>
            <interceptor>org.jboss.naming.interceptors.ExceptionInterceptor
➥</interceptor>
            <interceptor>org.jboss.invocation.InvokerInterceptor</interceptor>
        </interceptors>
    </attribute>
</mbean>
```

The proxy on the client side needs to talk back to a specific invoker servlet on the server side. The configuration here has the actual invocations going to `/invoker/readonly/JMXInvokerServlet`. This is actually the standard `JMXInvokerServlet` with a read-only filter attached:

```
    <filter>
        <filter-name>ReadOnlyAccessFilter</filter-name>
        <filter-class>org.jboss.invocation.http.servlet.ReadOnlyAccessFilter
➥</filter-class>
        <init-param>
            <param-name>readOnlyContext</param-name>
            <param-value>readonly</param-value>
            <description>The top level JNDI context the filter will enforce
                read-only access on. If specified only Context.lookup operations
                will be allowed on this context. Other operations or
                lookups on any other context will fail. Do not associate this
                filter with the JMXInvokerServlets if you want unrestricted
                access. </description>
        </init-param>
```

```
        <init-param>
            <param-name>invokerName</param-name>
            <param-value>jboss:service=Naming</param-value>
            <description>The JMX ObjectName of the naming service mbean
➥</description>
        </init-param>
    </filter>

    <filter-mapping>
        <filter-name>ReadOnlyAccessFilter</filter-name>
        <url-pattern>/readonly/*</url-pattern>
    </filter-mapping>

    <!-- ... -->
    <!-- A mapping for the JMXInvokerServlet that only allows invocations
            of lookups under a read-only context. This is enforced by the
            ReadOnlyAccessFilter
            -->
    <servlet-mapping>
        <servlet-name>JMXInvokerServlet</servlet-name>
        <url-pattern>/readonly/JMXInvokerServlet/*</url-pattern>
    </servlet-mapping>
```

The `readOnlyContext` parameter is set to `readonly`, which means that when you access JBoss through the `ReadOnlyJNDIFactory`, you will only be able to access data in the `readonly` context. Here is a code fragment that illustrates the usage:

```
Properties env = new Properties();
env.setProperty(Context.INITIAL_CONTEXT_FACTORY,
              "org.jboss.naming.HttpNamingContextFactory");
env.setProperty(Context.PROVIDER_URL,
              "http://localhost:8080/invoker/ReadOnlyJNDIFactory");

Context ctx2 = new InitialContext(env);
Object data = ctx2.lookup("readonly/data");
```

Attempts to look up any objects outside the `readonly` context will fail. Note that JBoss doesn't ship with any data in the `readonly` context, so the `readonly` context won't be bound usable unless you create it.

Additional Naming MBeans

In addition to the `NamingService` MBean that configures an embedded JBossNS server within JBoss, there are three other MBean services related to naming that ship with JBoss: `ExternalContext`, `NamingAlias`, and `JNDIView`.

The `org.jboss.naming.ExternalContext` MBean

The `ExternalContext` MBean allows you to federate external JNDI contexts into the JBoss server JNDI namespace. The term *external* refers to any naming service external to the JBossNS naming service running inside the JBoss server VM. You can incorporate LDAP servers, file systems, DNS servers, and so on, even if the JNDI provider root context is not serializable. The federation can be made available to remote clients if the naming service supports remote access.

To incorporate an external JNDI naming service, you have to add a configuration of the `ExternalContext` MBean service to the `jboss-service.xml` configuration file. The configurable attributes of the `ExternalContext` service are as follows:

- **`JndiName`**—The JNDI name under which the external context is to be bound.
- **`RemoteAccess`**—A Boolean flag that indicates whether the external `InitialContext` should be bound using a `Serializable` form that allows a remote client to create the external `InitialContext`. When a remote client looks up the external context via the JBoss JNDI `InitialContext`, the client effectively creates an instance of the external `InitialContext`, using the same `env` properties passed to the `ExternalContext` MBean. This works only if the client can do a new `InitialContext (env)` remotely. This requires that the `Context.PROVIDER_URL` value of `env` be resolvable in the remote VM that is accessing the context. This should work for the LDAP example. For the file system example, this most likely won't work unless the file system path refers to a common network path. If this property is not given, it defaults to `false`.
- **`CacheContext`**—The `cacheContext` flag. When it is set to `true`, the external context is created only when the MBean is started, and then it is stored as an in-memory object until the MBean is stopped. If `cacheContext` is set to `false`, the external `Context` is created on each lookup, using the MBean properties and `InitialContext` class. When a client looks up the uncached context, the client should invoke `close()` on the context to prevent resource leaks.
- **`InitialContext`**—The fully qualified classname of the `InitialContext` implementation to use. It must be one of these: `javax.naming.InitialContext`, `javax.naming.directory.InitialDirContext`, or `javax.naming.ldap.InitialLdapContext`. In the case of `InitialLdapContext`, a null `Controls` array is used. The default is `javax.naming.InitialContext`.
- **`Properties`**—The JNDI properties for the external `InitialContext`. The input should be the text equivalent of what would go into a `jndi.properties` file.
- **`PropertiesURL`**—The `jndi.properties` information for the external `InitialContext` from an external properties file. This is either a URL, a string, or a classpath resource name. The following are some examples:

  file:///config/myldap.properties

  http://config.mycompany.com/myldap.properties

/conf/myldap.properties

myldap.properties

The following MBean definition shows a binding to an external LDAP context into the JBoss JNDI namespace under the name `external/ldap/jboss`:

```
<!-- Bind a remote LDAP server -->
<mbean code="org.jboss.naming.ExternalContext"
       name="jboss.jndi:service=ExternalContext,jndiName=external/ldap/jboss">
    <attribute name="JndiName">external/ldap/jboss</attribute>
    <attribute name="Properties">
        java.naming.factory.initial=com.sun.jndi.ldap.LdapCtxFactory
        java.naming.provider.url=ldap://ldaphost.jboss.org:389/o=jboss.org
        java.naming.security.principal=cn=Directory Manager
        java.naming.security.authentication=simple
        java.naming.security.credentials=secret
    </attribute>
    <attribute name="InitialContext"> javax.naming.ldap.InitialLdapContext
</attribute>
    <attribute name="RemoteAccess">true</attribute>
</mbean>
```

With this configuration, you can access the external LDAP context located at `ldap://ldaphost.jboss.org:389/o=jboss.org` from within the JBoss VM by using the following code fragment:

```
InitialContext iniCtx = new InitialContext();
LdapContext ldapCtx = iniCtx.lookup("external/ldap/jboss");
```

Using the same code fragment outside the JBoss server VM would work in this case because the `RemoteAccess` property is set to `true`. If it were set to `false`, it would not work because the remote client would receive a `Reference` object with an `ObjectFactory` that would not be able to re-create the external `InitialContext`:

```
<!-- Bind the /usr/local file system directory  -->
<mbean code="org.jboss.naming.ExternalContext"
       name="jboss.jndi:service=ExternalContext,jndiName=external/fs/usr/local">
    <attribute name="JndiName">external/fs/usr/local</attribute>
    <attribute name="Properties">
        java.naming.factory.initial=com.sun.jndi.fscontext.RefFSContextFactory
        java.naming.provider.url=file:///usr/local
    </attribute>
    <attribute name="InitialContext">javax.naming.InitialContext</attribute>
</mbean>
```

This configuration describes binding a local file system directory `/usr/local` into the JBoss JNDI namespace under the name `external/fs/usr/local`.

With this configuration, you can access the external file system context located at the file `///usr/local` from within the JBoss VM, using the following code fragment:

```
InitialContext iniCtx = new InitialContext();
Context ldapCtx = iniCtx.lookup("external/fs/usr/local");
```

Note that this code uses one of the Sun JNDI service providers, which must be downloaded from http://java.sun.com/products/jndi/serviceproviders.html. The provider JARs should be placed in the server configuration `lib` directory.

The `org.jboss.naming.NamingAlias` MBean

The `NamingAlias` MBean is a simple utility service that allows you to create an alias in the form of a JNDI `javax.naming.LinkRef` from one JNDI name to another. This is similar to a symbolic link in the Unix file system. To an alias you add a configuration of the `NamingAlias` MBean to the `jboss-service.xml` configuration file.

The configurable attributes of the `NamingAlias` service are as follows:

- **`FromName`**—The location where the `LinkRef` is bound under JNDI.
- **`ToName`**—The to name of the alias. This is the target name to which the `LinkRef` refers. The name is a URL, or a name to be resolved relative to the `InitialContext`; or if the first character of the name is a dot (`.`), the name is relative to the context in which the link is bound.

The following example provides a mapping of the JNDI name `QueueConnectionFactory` to the name `ConnectionFactory`:

```
<mbean code="org.jboss.naming.NamingAlias"
       name="jboss.mq:service=NamingAlias,fromName=QueueConnectionFactory">
    <attribute name="ToName">ConnectionFactory</attribute>
    <attribute name="FromName">QueueConnectionFactory</attribute>
</mbean>
```

The `org.jboss.naming.JNDIView` MBean

The `JNDIView` MBean allows the user to view the JNDI namespace tree as it exists in the JBoss server, using the JMX agent view interface. To view the JBoss JNDI namespace using the `JNDIView` MBean, you connect to the JMX Agent view, using the HTTP interface. The default settings put this at http://localhost:8080/jmx-console/. On this page you see a section that lists the registered MBeans, sorted by domain. It should look something like what is shown in Figure 3.4.

Selecting the `JNDIView` link takes you to the `JNDIView` MBean view, which shows a list of the `JNDIView` MBean operations. This view should look similar to the one shown in Figure 3.5.

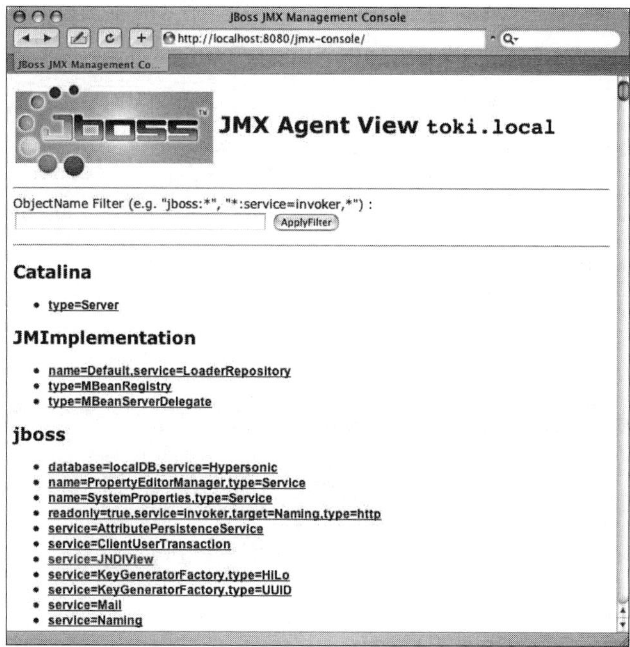

FIGURE 3.4 The JMX Console view of the configured JBoss MBeans.

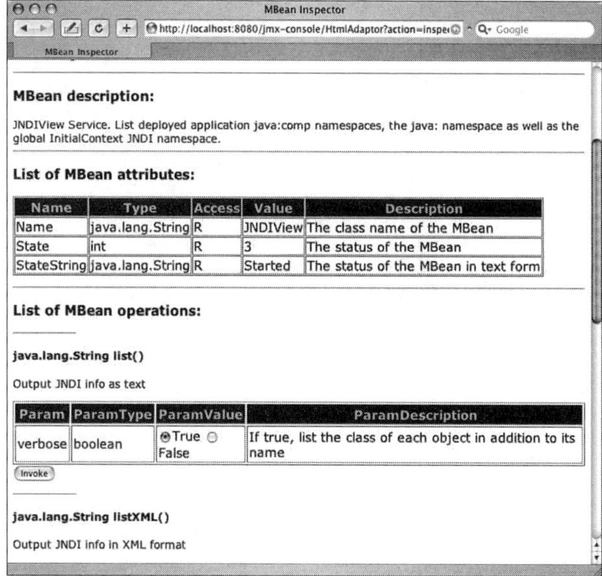

FIGURE 3.5 The JMX Console view of the `JNDIView` MBean.

The list operation dumps out the JBoss server JNDI namespace as an HTML page, using a simple text view. For example, invoking the list operation produces the view shown in Figure 3.6.

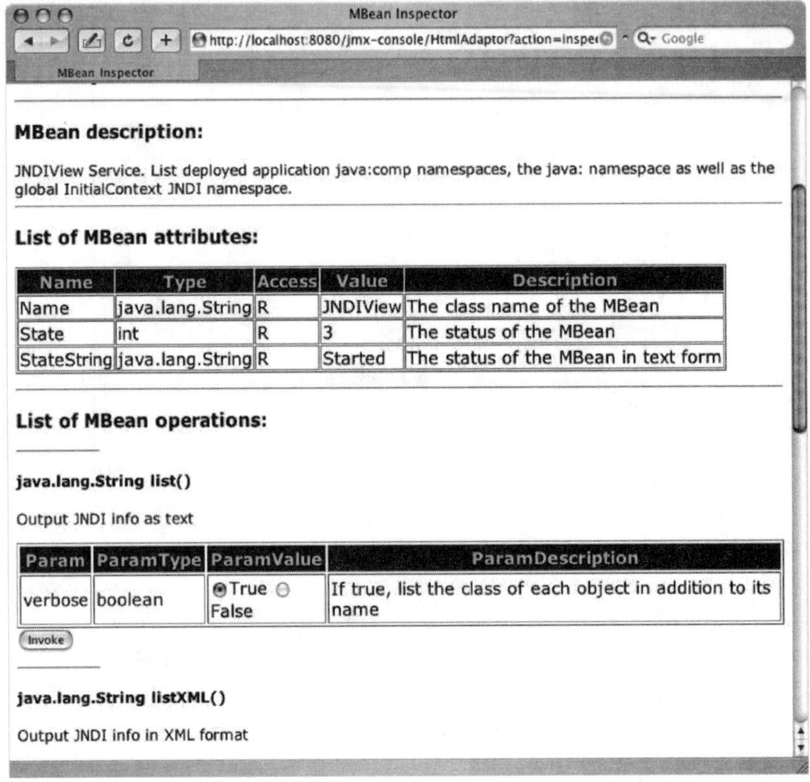

FIGURE 3.6 The JMX Console view of the JNDIView list operation output.

CHAPTER 4

Transactions on JBoss

IN THIS CHAPTER

- Transaction and JTA Overview
- JBoss Transaction Internals

This chapter discusses transaction management in JBoss and the JBossTX architecture. The JBossTX architecture allows for any Java Transaction API (JTA) transaction manager implementation to be used. JBossTX includes a fast in-VM implementation of a JTA compatible transaction manager that is used as the default transaction manager. We will first provide an overview of the key transaction concepts and notions in the JTA to provide sufficient background for the JBossTX architecture discussion. We will then discuss the interfaces that make up the JBossTX architecture and conclude with a discussion of the MBeans available for integration of alternate transaction managers.

Transaction and JTA Overview

For the purpose of this discussion, we can define a *transaction* as a unit of work containing one or more operations involving one or more shared resources having ACID properties. *ACID* is an acronym for atomicity, consistency, isolation, and durability, the four important properties of transactions. The meanings of these terms are

- **Atomicity**—A transaction must be atomic. Either all the work done in the transaction must be performed or none of it must be performed. Doing part of a transaction is not allowed.
- **Consistency**—When a transaction is completed, the system must be in a stable and consistent condition.
- **Isolation**—Different transactions must be isolated from each other. The partial work done in one transaction is not visible to other transactions until the transaction is committed, and each process in a multiuser system can be programmed as if it was the only process accessing the system.

- **Durability**—The changes made during a transaction are made persistent when it is committed. When a transaction is committed, its changes are not lost, even if the server crashes afterward.

To illustrate these concepts, consider a simple banking account application. The banking application has a database with a number of accounts. The sum of the amounts of all accounts must always be zero. An amount of money, M, is moved from account A to account B by subtracting M from account A and adding M to account B. This operation must be done in a transaction, and all four ACID properties are important.

The atomicity property means both the withdrawal and deposit are performed as an indivisible unit. If, for some reason, both cannot be done, nothing is done.

The consistency property means that after the transaction, the sum of the amounts of all accounts must still be zero.

The isolation property is important when more than one bank clerk uses the system at the same time. A withdrawal or deposit could be implemented as a three-step process: First, the amount of the account is read from the database; second, something is subtracted from or added to the amount read from the database; and, finally, the new amount is written to the database. Without transaction isolation several bad things could happen. For example, if two processes read the amount of account A at the same time, and each independently added or subtracted something before writing the new amount to the database, the first change would be incorrectly overwritten by the last.

The durability property is also important. If a money transfer transaction is committed, the bank must trust that some subsequent failure cannot undo the money transfer.

Pessimistic and Optimistic Locking

Transactional isolation is usually implemented by locking whatever is accessed in a transaction. There are two different approaches to transactional locking—pessimistic locking and optimistic locking.

The disadvantage of pessimistic locking is that a resource is locked from the time it is first accessed in a transaction until the transaction is finished, making it inaccessible to other transactions during that time. If most transactions simply look at the resource and never change it, an exclusive lock might be overkill as it can cause lock contention, and optimistic locking might be a better approach. With *pessimistic locking*, locks are applied in a fail-safe way. In the banking application example, an account is locked as soon as it is accessed in a transaction. Attempts to use the account in other transactions while it is locked either result in the other process being delayed until the account lock is released, or the process transaction being rolled back. The lock exists until the transaction has either been committed or rolled back.

With *optimistic locking*, a resource is not actually locked when it is first accessed by a transaction. Instead, the state of the resource at the time when it would have been locked with the pessimistic locking approach is saved. Other transactions are able to concurrently access the resource and the possibility of conflicting changes is higher. At commit time, when the resource is about to be updated in persistent storage, the state of the resource is read from storage again and compared to the state saved when the resource was first accessed in the transaction. If the two states differ, a conflicting update was made, and the transaction is rolled back.

In the banking application example, the amount of an account is saved when the account is first accessed in a transaction. If the transaction changes the account amount, the amount is read from the store again just before the amount is to be updated. If the amount has changed since the transaction began, the transaction fails itself; otherwise, the new amount is written to persistent storage.

The Components of a Distributed Transaction

A number of participants are in a distributed transaction. These include

- **Transaction manager**—This component is distributed across the transactional system. It manages and coordinates the work involved in the transaction. The transaction manager is exposed by the `javax.transaction.TransactionManager` interface in JTA.
- **Transaction context**—A transaction context identifies a particular transaction. In JTA the corresponding interface is `javax.transaction.Transaction`.
- **Transactional client**—A transactional client can invoke operations on one or more transactional objects in a single transaction. The transactional client that started the transaction is called the *transaction originator.* A transaction client is either an explicit or implicit user of JTA interfaces and has no interface representation in the JTA.
- **Transactional object**—A transactional object is an object whose behavior is affected by operations performed on it within a transactional context. A transactional object can also be a transactional client. Most Enterprise JavaBeans (EJB) are transactional objects.
- **Recoverable resource**—A recoverable resource is a transactional object whose state is saved to stable storage if the transaction is committed, and whose state can be reset to what it was at the beginning of the transaction if the transaction is rolled back. At commit time, the transaction manager uses the two-phase XA protocol when communicating with the recoverable resource to ensure transactional integrity when more than one recoverable resource is involved in the transaction being committed. Transactional databases and message brokers, such as JBossMQ, are examples of recoverable resources. A recoverable resource is represented using the `javax.transaction.xa.XAResource` interface in JTA.

The Two-phase XA Protocol

When a transaction is about to be committed, it is the responsibility of the transaction manager to ensure either all of it is committed or all of it is rolled back. If only a single recoverable resource is involved in the transaction, the task of the transaction manager is simple; it just has to tell the resource to commit the changes to stable storage.

When more than one recoverable resource is involved in the transaction, management of the commit gets more complicated. Simply asking each of the recoverable resources to commit changes to stable storage is not enough to maintain the atomic property of the transaction. If one recoverable resource has committed and another fails to commit, part of the transaction would be committed and the other part rolled back.

To get around this problem, the two-phase XA protocol is used. The *two-phase XA protocol* involves an extra prepare phase before the actual commit phase. Before asking any of the recoverable resources to commit the changes, the transaction manager asks all the recoverable resources to prepare to commit. When a recoverable resource indicates it is prepared to commit the transaction, it has ensured it can commit the transaction. The resource is still able to roll back the transaction if necessary.

So the first phase consists of the transaction manager asking all the recoverable resources to prepare to commit. If any of the recoverable resources fails to prepare, the transaction is rolled back. But if all recoverable resources indicate they were able to prepare to commit, the second phase of the XA protocol begins. This consists of the transaction manager asking all the recoverable resources to commit the transaction. Because all the recoverable resources have indicated they are prepared, this step cannot fail.

Heuristic Exceptions

In a distributed environment, communications' failures can happen. If communication between the transaction manager and a recoverable resource is not possible for an extended period of time, the recoverable resource might decide to unilaterally commit or roll back changes done in the context of a transaction. Such a decision is called a *heuristic decision*. It is one of the worst errors that can happen in a transaction system because it can lead to parts of the transaction being committed while other parts are rolled back, thus violating the atomicity property of the transaction and possibly leading to data integrity corruption.

Because of the dangers of heuristic exceptions, a recoverable resource that makes a heuristic decision is required to maintain all information about the decision in stable storage until the transaction manager tells it to forget about the heuristic decision. The actual data about the heuristic decision saved in stable storage depends on the type of recoverable resource and is not standardized. The idea is that a system manager can look at the data and possibly edit the resource to correct any data integrity problems.

Several different kinds of heuristic exceptions are defined by the JTA. The `javax.transaction.HeuristicCommitException` is thrown when a recoverable resource is asked to roll back to report that a heuristic decision was made and that all relevant updates have been committed. On the opposite end is the `javax.transaction.`

`HeuristicRollbackException`, which is thrown by a recoverable resource when it is asked to commit to indicate that a heuristic decision was made and that all relevant updates have been rolled back.

The `javax.transaction.HeuristicMixedException` is the worst heuristic exception. It is thrown to indicate that parts of the transaction were committed and other parts were rolled back. The transaction manager throws this exception when some recoverable resources did a heuristic commit and other recoverable resources did a heuristic rollback.

Transaction Identities and Branches

In JTA, the identity of transactions is encapsulated in objects implementing the `javax.transaction.xa.Xid` interface. The *transaction identity* is an aggregate of three parts:

- The *format identifier* indicates the transaction family and tells how the other two parts should be interpreted.
- The *global transaction ID* denotes the global transaction within the transaction family.
- The *branch qualifier* identifies a particular branch of the global transaction.

Transaction branches are used to identify different parts of the same global transaction. Whenever the transaction manager involves a new recoverable resource in a transaction, it creates a new transaction branch.

JBoss Transaction Internals

The JBoss application server is written to be independent of the actual transaction manager used. JBoss uses the JTA `javax.transaction.TransactionManager` interface as its view of the server transaction manager. Thus, JBoss may use any transaction manager which implements the JTA `TransactionManager` interface. Whenever a transaction manager is used, it is obtained from the well-known JNDI location, `java:/TransactionManager`. This is the globally available access point for the server transaction manager.

If transaction contexts are to be propagated with RMI/JRMP calls, the transaction manager must also implement two simple interfaces for the import and export of *transaction propagation contexts (TPCs)*. The interfaces are `TransactionPropagationContextImporter` and `TransactionPropagationContextFactory`, both in the `org.jboss.tm` package.

Being independent of the actual transaction manager used also means JBoss does not specify the format or type of the transaction propagation context used. In JBoss, a TPC is of type `Object`, and the only requirement is that the TPC must implement the `java.io.Serializable` interface.

When using the RMI/JRMP protocol for remote calls, the TPC is carried as a field in the `org.jboss.ejb.plugins.jrmp.client.RemoteMethodInvocation` class used to forward remote method invocation requests.

Adapting a Transaction Manager to JBoss

A transaction manager has to implement the JTA to be easily integrated with JBoss. Like almost everything in JBoss, the transaction manager is managed as an MBean. Like all JBoss services, it should implement `org.jboss.system.ServiceMBean` to ensure proper life-cycle management.

The primary requirement of the transaction manager service on startup is that it binds its implementation of the three required interfaces into JNDI. These interfaces and their JNDI locations are as follows:

- The `javax.transaction.TransactionManager` interface is used by the application server to manage transactions on behalf of the transactional objects that use container managed transactions. It must be bound under the JNDI name `java:/TransactionManager`.
- The `TransactionPropagationContextFactory` interface is called by JBoss whenever a transaction propagation context is needed for transporting a transaction with a remote method call. It must be bound under the JNDI name `java:/TransactionPropagationContextImporter`.
- The `TransactionPropagationContextImporter` interface is called by JBoss whenever a transaction propagation context from an incoming remote method invocation has to be converted to a transaction that can be used within the receiving JBoss server VM.

Establishing these JNDI bindings is all the transaction manager service needs to do to install its implementation as the JBoss server transaction manager.

The Default Transaction Manager

JBoss is by default configured to use the fast in-VM transaction manager. This transaction manager is very fast, but does have two limitations:

- It does not do transactional logging, and is thus incapable of automated recovery after a server crash.
- Although it does support propagating transaction contexts with remote calls, it does not support propagating transaction contexts to other virtual machines, so all transactional work must be done in the same virtual machine as the JBoss server.

The corresponding default transaction manager MBean service is the `org.jboss.tm.TransactionManagerService` MBean. It has four configurable attributes:

- **TransactionTimeout**—The default transaction timeout in seconds. The default value is 300 seconds (five minutes).
- **InterruptThreads**—Indicates whether the transaction manager should interrupt threads when the transaction times out. The default value is false.

- **GlobalIdsEnabled**—Indicates whether the transaction manager should use global transaction IDs. This should be set to true for transaction demarcation over IIOP. The default value is true.
- **XidFactory**—The JMX `ObjectName` of the MBean service that provides the `org.jboss.tm.XidFactoryMBean` implementation. The `XidFactoryMBean` interface is used to create `javax.transaction.xa.Xid` instances. This is a workaround for XA JDBC drivers that only work with their own Xid implementation. Examples of such drivers are the older Oracle XA drivers. The default factory is `jboss:service=XidFactory`.

`org.jboss.tm.XidFactory`

The `XidFactory` MBean is a factory for `javax.transaction.xa.Xid` instances in the form of `org.jboss.tm.XidImpl`. The `XidFactory` allows for customization of the `XidImpl` that it constructs through the following attributes:

- **BaseGlobalId**—This is used for building globally unique transaction identifiers. This must be set individually if multiple JBoss instances are running on the same machine. The default value is the hostname of the JBoss server, followed by a slash.
- **GlobalIdNumber**—A long value used as initial transaction ID. The default is zero.
- **Pad**—The pad value determines whether the byte returned by the Xid `getGlobalTransactionId` and `getBranchQualifier` methods should be equal to the maximum 64-byte length or a variable value less than or equal to 64 bytes. Some resource managers (Oracle, for example) require IDs that are the maximum length in size.

`UserTransaction` **Support**

The JTA `javax.transaction.UserTransaction` interface allows applications to explicitly control transactions. For enterprise session beans that manage transaction themselves (Bean Managed Transactions or BMT), a `UserTransaction` can be obtained by calling the `getUserTransaction` method on the bean context object, `javax.ejb.SessionContext`.

The `ClientUserTransactionService` MBean publishes a `UserTransaction` implementation under the JNDI name `UserTransaction`. When the `UserTransaction` is obtained with a JNDI lookup from an external client, a very simple `UserTransaction` suitable for thin clients is returned. This `UserTransaction` implementation only controls the transactions on the server the `UserTransaction` object was obtained from. Local transactional work done in the client is not done within the transactions started by this `UserTransaction` object.

When a `UserTransaction` object is obtained by looking up the JNDI name `UserTransaction` in the same virtual machine as JBoss, a simple interface to the JTA `TransactionManager` is returned. This is suitable for web components running in web containers embedded in JBoss. When components are deployed in an embedded web server, the deployer makes a JNDI link from the standard `java:comp/UserTransaction` Environment Naming Context (ENC) name to the global `UserTransaction` binding so the web components can look up the `UserTransaction` instance under the JNDI name as specified by the J2EE.

Note

For BMT beans, do not obtain the `UserTransaction` interface using a JNDI lookup. Doing this violates the EJB specification, and the returned `UserTransaction` object does not have the hooks the EJB container needs to make important checks.

CHAPTER 5

EJBs on JBoss

IN THIS CHAPTER

- The EJB Client-Side View
- The EJB Server-Side View
- The EJB Container
- Entity Bean Locking and Deadlock Detection

The JBoss EJB container architecture employs a modular plug-in approach. A developer can replace all key aspects of the EJB container with custom versions of a plug-in and/or an interceptor. This approach allows you to fine-tune customization of the EJB container behavior to optimally suit your needs. Most of the EJB container behavior is configurable through the EJB JAR `META-INF/jboss.xml` descriptor and the default serverwide equivalent `standardjboss.xml` descriptor. We will look at various configuration capabilities throughout this chapter, as we explore the container architecture.

The EJB Client-Side View

Let's begin our tour of the EJB container by looking at the client view of an EJB, through the home and remote proxies. It is the responsibility of the container provider to generate the `javax.ejb.EJBHome` and `javax.ejb.EJBObject` for an EJB implementation. A client never references an EJB bean instance directly; rather, it references `EJBHome`, which implements the bean home interface, and `EJBObject`, which implements the bean remote interface. Figure 5.1 shows the composition of an EJB home proxy and its relationship to the EJB deployment.

The numbered items in Figure 5.1 are as follows:

1. The `EJBDeployer` (`org.jboss.ejb.EJBDeployer`) is invoked to deploy an EJB JAR. An `EJBModule` (`org.jboss.ejb.EJBModule`) is created to encapsulate the deployment metadata.

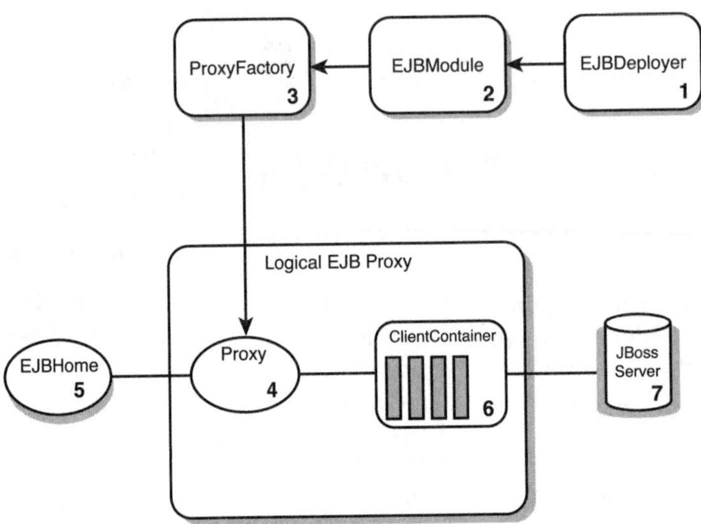

FIGURE 5.1 The composition of an EJBHome proxy in JBoss.

2. The create phase of the `EJBModule` life cycle creates an `EJBProxyFactory` (`org.jboss.ejb.EJBProxyFactory`) that manages the creation of EJB home and remote interface proxies, based on the `EJBModule` `invoker-proxy-bindings` metadata. There can be multiple proxy factories associated with an EJB, and we will look at this more closely shortly.

3. The `ProxyFactory` constructs the logical proxies and binds the homes into JNDI. A logical proxy is composed of a dynamic `Proxy` (`java.lang.reflect.Proxy`), the home interfaces of the EJB that the proxy exposes, the `ProxyHandler` (`java.lang.reflect.InvocationHandler`) implementation in the form of the `ClientContainer` (`org.jboss.proxy.ClientContainer`), and the client-side interceptors.

4. The proxy created by the `EJBProxyFactory` is a standard dynamic proxy. It is a serializable object that proxies the EJB home and remote interfaces, as defined in the `EJBModule` metadata. The proxy translates requests made through the strongly typed EJB interfaces into a detyped invocation, using the `ClientContainer` handler associated with the proxy. The dynamic proxy instance is bound into JNDI as the EJB home interface that clients look up. When a client does a lookup of an EJB home, the home proxy is transported into the client VM, along with the `ClientContainer` and its interceptors. Using dynamic proxies avoids the EJB-specific compilation step required by many other EJB containers.

5. The EJB home interface is declared in the `ejb-jar.xml` descriptor and is available from the `EJBModule` metadata. A key property of dynamic proxies is that they implement the interfaces they expose. This is true in the sense of Java's strong typing system. A proxy can be cast to any of the home interfaces, and reflection on the proxy provides the full details of the interfaces it proxies.

6. The proxy delegates calls made through any of its interfaces to the `ClientContainer` handler. The single method required of the handler is `public Object invoke(Object proxy, Method m, Object[] args) throws Throwable`. The `EJBProxyFactory` creates a `ClientContainer` and assigns this as the `ProxyHandler`. The `ClientContainer`'s state consists of an `InvocationContext` (`org.jboss.invocation.InvocationContext`) and a chain of interceptors (`org.jboss.proxy.Interceptor`). The `InvocationContext` contains the following:

   - The JMX `ObjectName` of the EJB container MBean that the `Proxy` is associated with
   - The `javax.ejb.EJBMetaData` for the EJB
   - The JNDI name of the EJB home interface
   - The transport-specific invoker (`org.jboss.invocation.Invoker`)

   The interceptor chain consists of the functional units that make up the EJB home or remote interface behavior. As discussed later in this chapter, this is a configurable aspect of an EJB, and the interceptor makeup is contained in the `EJBModule` metadata. Interceptors (`org.jboss.proxy.Interceptor`) handle the different EJB types, security, transactions, and transport. You can add your own interceptors as well.

7. The transport-specific invoker associated with the proxy has an association to the server-side detached invoker that handles the transport details of the EJB method invocation. The detached invoker is a JBoss server-side component.

You configure the client-side interceptors by using the `jboss.xml` `client-interceptors` element. When the `ClientContainer` invoke method is called, it creates an untyped `Invocation` (`org.jboss.invocation.Invocation`) to encapsulate request. This is then passed through the interceptor chain. The last interceptor in the chain is the transport handler that knows how to send the request to the server and obtain the reply, taking care of the transport-specific details.

As an example of the client interceptor configuration usage, consider the default stateless session bean configuration that is found in the `server/default/standardjboss.xml` descriptor. Listing 5.1 shows the `stateless-rmi-invoker` client interceptor configuration, referenced by the `Standard Stateless SessionBean`.

LISTING 5.1 The Client Interceptors from the `Standard Stateless SessionBean` Configuration

```
<invoker-proxy-binding>
        <name>stateless-rmi-invoker</name>
        <invoker-mbean>jboss:service=invoker,type=jrmp</invoker-mbean>
        <proxy-factory>org.jboss.proxy.ejb.ProxyFactory</proxy-factory>
        <proxy-factory-config>
```

LISTING 5.1 Continued

```
            <client-interceptors>
                <home>
                    <interceptor>org.jboss.proxy.ejb.HomeInterceptor</interceptor>
                    <interceptor>org.jboss.proxy.SecurityInterceptor</interceptor>
                    <interceptor>org.jboss.proxy.TransactionInterceptor
➥</interceptor>
                    <interceptor call-by-value="false">org.jboss.invocation.
➥InvokerInterceptor</interceptor>
                    <interceptor call-by-value="true">org.jboss.invocation.
MarshallingInvokerInterceptor</interceptor>
                </home>
                <bean>
                    <interceptor>org.jboss.proxy.ejb.StatelessSessionInterceptor
➥</interceptor>
                    <interceptor>org.jboss.proxy.SecurityInterceptor</interceptor>
                    <interceptor>org.jboss.proxy.TransactionInterceptor
➥</interceptor>
                    <interceptor call-by-value="false">
➥org.jboss.invocation.InvokerInterceptor</interceptor>
                    <interceptor call-by-value="true">org.jboss.invocation.
MarshallingInvokerInterceptor</interceptor>
                </bean>
            </client-interceptors>
        </proxy-factory-config>
    </invoker-proxy-binding>
    <container-configuration>
        <container-name>Standard Stateless SessionBean</container-name>
        <call-logging>false</call-logging>
        <invoker-proxy-binding-name>stateless-rmi-invoker
➥</invoker-proxy-binding-name>
        <!-- ... -->
    </container-configuration>
```

Listing 5.1 shows the client interceptor configuration for stateless session beans that is used in the absence of an EJB JAR `META-INF/jboss.xml` configuration that overrides these settings. The client interceptors provide the following functionality:

- **`org.jboss.proxy.ejb.HomeInterceptor`**—This interceptor handles the `getHomeHandle`, `getEJBMetaData`, and remove methods of the `EJBHome` interface locally in the client VM. Any other methods are propagated to the next interceptor.
- **`org.jboss.proxy.ejb.StatelessSessionInterceptor`**—This interceptor handles the `toString`, `equals`, `hashCode`, `getHandle`, `getEJBHome`, and `isIdentical` methods of the `EJBObject` interface locally in the client VM. Any other methods are propagated to the next interceptor.

- **org.jboss.proxy.SecurityInterceptor**—This interceptor associates the current security context with the method invocation for use by other interceptors or the server.
- **org.jboss.proxy.TransactionInterceptor**—This interceptor associates any active transaction with the invocation method invocation for use by other interceptors.
- **org.jboss.invocation.InvokerInterceptor**—This interceptor encapsulates the dispatch of the method invocation to the transport-specific invoker. It knows whether the client is executing in the same VM as the server, and it optimally routes the invocation to a by-reference invoker in this situation. When the client is external to the server VM, this interceptor delegates the invocation to the transport invoker associated with the invocation context. In the case of the configuration in Listing 5.1, this would be the invoker stub associated with the `jboss:service=invoker,type=jrmp`, which is the `JRMPInvoker` service.
- **org.jboss.invocation.MarshallingInvokerInterceptor**—This interceptor extends the `InvokerInterceptor` to not optimize in VM invocations. This is used to force `call-by-value` semantics for method calls.

Specifying the EJB Proxy Configuration

To specify the EJB invocation transport and the client proxy interceptor stack, you need to define an `invoker-proxy-binding` in either the EJB JAR `META-INF/jboss.xml` descriptor or the server `standardjboss.xml` descriptor. There are several default `invoker-proxy-binding` elements defined in the `standardjboss.xml` descriptor for the various default EJB container configurations and the standard RMI/JRMP and RMI/IIOP transport protocols. The current default proxy configurations are as follows:

- **entity-rmi-invoker**—This is an RMI/JRMP configuration for entity beans.
- **clustered-entity-rmi-invoker**—This is an RMI/JRMP configuration for clustered entity beans.
- **stateless-rmi-invoker**—This is an RMI/JRMP configuration for stateless session beans.
- **clustered-stateless-rmi-invoker**—This is an RMI/JRMP configuration for clustered stateless session beans.
- **stateful-rmi-invoker**—This is an RMI/JRMP configuration for stateful session beans.
- **clustered-stateful-rmi-invoker**—This is an RMI/JRMP configuration for clustered stateful session beans.
- **message-driven-bean**—This is a JMS invoker for message-driven beans.
- **singleton-message-driven-bean**—This is a JMS invoker for singleton message-driven beans.

- **message-inflow-driven-bean**—This is a JMS invoker for message inflow–driven beans.
- **jms-message-inflow-driven-bean**—This is a JMS inflow invoker for standard message-driven beans.
- **iiop**—This is an RMI/IIOP for use with session and entity beans.

Introducing a new protocol binding, customizing the proxy factory, or customizing the client-side interceptor stack requires defining a new `invoker-proxy-binding`. The full `invoker-proxy-binding` DTD fragment for the specification of the proxy configuration is shown in Figure 5.2.

These are the `invoker-proxy-binding` child elements:

- **name**—The `name` element gives a unique name for the `invoker-proxy-binding`. The name is used to reference the binding from the EJB container configuration when setting the default proxy binding as well as the EJB deployment level to specify additional proxy bindings. You will see how this is done later in this chapter, when we look at the `jboss.xml` elements that control the server-side EJB container configuration.
- **invoker-mbean**—The `invoker-mbean` element gives the JMX `ObjectName` string of the detached invoker MBean service that the proxy invoker will be associated with.
- **proxy-factory**—The `proxy-factory` element specifies the fully qualified classname of the proxy factory that must implement the `org.jboss.ejb.EJBProxyFactory` interface. The `EJBProxyFactory` handles the configuration of the proxy and the association of the protocol-specific invoker and context. The current JBoss implementations of the `EJBProxyFactory` interface include the following:
    - **org.jboss.proxy.ejb.ProxyFactory**—The RMI/JRMP-specific factory.
    - **org.jboss.proxy.ejb.ProxyFactoryHA**—The cluster RMI/JRMP-specific factory.
    - **org.jboss.ejb.plugins.jms.JMSContainerInvoker**—The JMS-specific factory.
    - **org.jboss.proxy.ejb.IORFactory**—The RMI/IIOP-specific factory.
- **proxy-factory-config**—The `proxy-factory-config` element specifies additional information for the `proxy-factory` implementation. Unfortunately, it is currently an unstructured collection of elements. Only a few of the elements apply to each type of proxy factory. The child elements break down into the three invocation protocols: RMI/RJMP, RMI/IIOP, and JMS.

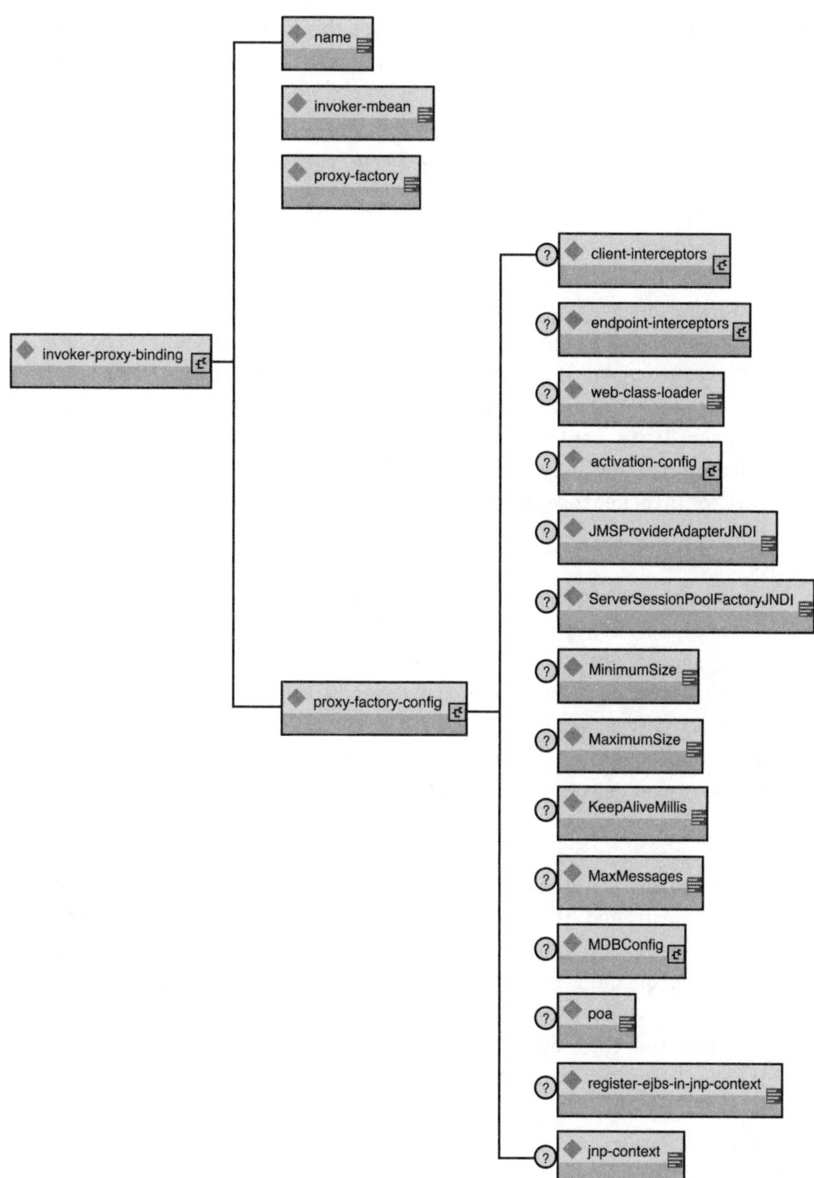

FIGURE 5.2 The `invoker-proxy-binding` schema.

For the RMI/JRMP-specific proxy factories `org.jboss.proxy.ejb.ProxyFactory` and `org.jboss.proxy.ejb.ProxyFactoryHA`, the following elements apply:

- **`client-interceptors`**—`client-interceptors` defines the home, remote, and, optionally, the multivalued proxy interceptor stacks.

- **web-class-loader**—web-class-loader defines the instance of the org.jboss.web.WebClassLoader that should be associated with the proxy for dynamic class loading.

The following proxy-factory-config is for an entity bean accessed over RMI:

```
<proxy-factory-config>
    <client-interceptors>
        <home>
            <interceptor>org.jboss.proxy.ejb.HomeInterceptor</interceptor>
            <interceptor>org.jboss.proxy.SecurityInterceptor</interceptor>
            <interceptor>org.jboss.proxy.TransactionInterceptor</interceptor>
            <interceptor call-by-value="false">org.jboss.invocation.
➥InvokerInterceptor</interceptor>
            <interceptor call-by-value="true">org.jboss.invocation.
➥MarshallingInvokerInterceptor</interceptor>
        </home>
        <bean>
            <interceptor>org.jboss.proxy.ejb.EntityInterceptor</interceptor>
            <interceptor>org.jboss.proxy.SecurityInterceptor</interceptor>
            <interceptor>org.jboss.proxy.TransactionInterceptor</interceptor>
            <interceptor call-by-value="false">org.jboss.invocation.
➥InvokerInterceptor</interceptor>
            <interceptor call-by-value="true">org.jboss.invocation.
➥MarshallingInvokerInterceptor</interceptor>
        </bean>
        <list-entity>
            <interceptor>org.jboss.proxy.ejb.ListEntityInterceptor</interceptor>
            <interceptor>org.jboss.proxy.SecurityInterceptor</interceptor>
            <interceptor>org.jboss.proxy.TransactionInterceptor</interceptor>
            <interceptor call-by-value="false">org.jboss.invocation.
➥InvokerInterceptor</interceptor>
            <interceptor call-by-value="true">org.jboss.invocation.
➥MarshallingInvokerInterceptor</interceptor>
        </list-entity>
    </client-interceptors>
</proxy-factory-config>
```

For the RMI/IIOP-specific proxy factory org.jboss.proxy.ejb.IORFactory, the following elements apply:

- **poa**—This specifies the portable object adapter usage. Valid values are per-servant and shared.

- **register-ejbs-in -jnp-context**—This specifies a flag which indicates whether the EJBs should be registered in JNDI.

- **`jnp-context`**—This specifies the JNDI context in which to register EJBs.
- **`web-class-loader`**—This defines the instance of the `org.jboss.web.WebClassLoader` that should be associated with the proxy for dynamic class loading.

The following is a `proxy-factory-config` for EJBs accessed over IIOP:

```
<proxy-factory-config>
    <web-class-loader>org.jboss.iiop.WebCL</web-class-loader>
    <poa>per-servant</poa>
    <register-ejbs-in-jnp-context>true</register-ejbs-in-jnp-context>
    <jnp-context>iiop</jnp-context>
</proxy-factory-config>
```

For the JMS-specific proxy factory `org.jboss.ejb.plugins.jms.JMSContainerInvoker`, the following elements apply:

- **`MinimumSize`**—This specifies the minimum pool size for MDB processing. The default is `1`.
- **`MaximumSize`**—This specifies the upper limit to the number of concurrent MDBs that will be allowed for the JMS destination. The default is `15`.
- **`MaxMessages`**—This specifies the `maxMessages` parameter value for the `createConnectionConsumer` method of the `javax.jms.QueueConnection` and `javax.jms.TopicConnection` interfaces, as well as the `maxMessages` parameter value for the `createDurableConnectionConsumer` method of `javax.jms.TopicConnection`. It is the maximum number of messages that can be assigned to a server session at one time. The default is `1`. You should not modify this value from the default unless your JMS provider indicates that doing so is supported.
- **`KeepAliveMillis`**—This specifies the keep-alive time interval, in milliseconds, for sessions in the session pool. The default is `30000` (30 seconds).
- **`MDBConfig`**—This specifies the configuration for the MDB JMS connection behavior. Among the elements supported are the following:
    - **`ReconnectIntervalSec`**—The time to wait (in seconds) before trying to recover the connection to the JMS server.
    - **`DeliveryActive`**—Whether the MDB is active at startup. The default is `true`.
    - **`DLQConfig`**—Configuration for an MDB's dead-letter queue, which is used when messages are redelivered too many times.
    - **`JMSProviderAdapterJNDI`**—The JNDI name of the JMS provider adapter in the `java:/` namespace. This is mandatory for an MDB and must implement `org.jboss.jms.jndi.JMSProviderAdapter`.

- **ServerSessionPoolFactoryJNDI**—The JNDI name of the session pool in the java:/ namespace of the JMS provider's session pool factory. This is mandatory for an MDB and must implement org.jboss.jms.asf.ServerSessionPoolFactory.

Listing 5.2 gives a sample proxy-factory-config fragment taken from the standardjboss.xml descriptor.

LISTING 5.2 A Sample JMSContainerInvoker proxy-factory-config

```
<proxy-factory-config>
    <JMSProviderAdapterJNDI>DefaultJMSProvider</JMSProviderAdapterJNDI>
    <ServerSessionPoolFactoryJNDI>StdJMSPool</ServerSessionPoolFactoryJNDI>
    <MinimumSize>1</MinimumSize>
    <MaximumSize>15</MaximumSize>
    <KeepAliveMillis>30000</KeepAliveMillis>
    <MaxMessages>1</MaxMessages>
    <MDBConfig>
        <ReconnectIntervalSec>10</ReconnectIntervalSec>
        <DLQConfig>
            <DestinationQueue>queue/DLQ</DestinationQueue>
            <MaxTimesRedelivered>10</MaxTimesRedelivered>
            <TimeToLive>0</TimeToLive>
        </DLQConfig>
    </MDBConfig>
</proxy-factory-config>
```

The EJB Server-Side View

Every EJB invocation must end up at a JBoss server-hosted EJB container. The following sections look at how invocations are transported to the JBoss server VM and find their way to the EJB container via the JMX bus.

Detached Invokers: The Transport Middlemen

Earlier in this chapter, we looked at the detached invoker architecture in the context of exposing RMI-compatible interfaces of MBean services. Here we will look at how detached invokers are used to expose the EJB container home and bean interfaces to clients. The generic view of the invoker architecture is presented in Figure 5.3.

For each type of home proxy, there is a binding to an invoker and its associated transport protocol. A container may have multiple invocation protocols active simultaneously. In the jboss.xml file, an invoker-proxy-binding-name maps to an invoker-proxy-binding/name element. At the container-configuration level, this specifies the default invoker that will be used for EJBs deployed to the container. At the bean level, the invoker-bindings specify one or more invokers to use with the EJB container MBean.

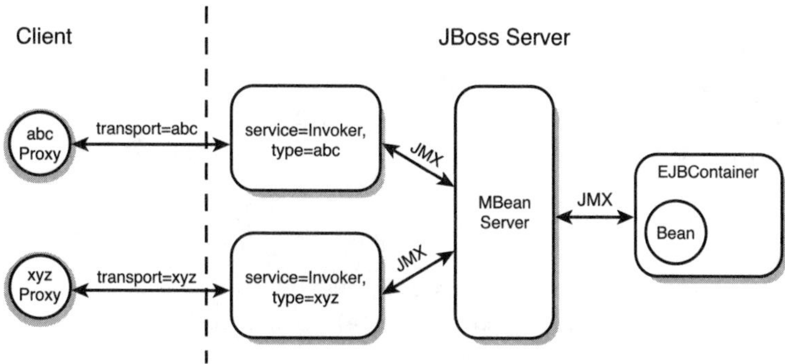

FIGURE 5.3 The transport invoker server-side architecture.

When you specify multiple invokers for a given EJB deployment, you must give the home proxy a unique JNDI binding location. You specify this in the `invoker/jndi-name` element value. Another issue when multiple invokers exist for an EJB is how to handle remote homes or interfaces obtained when the EJB calls other beans. Any such interfaces need to use the same invoker used to call the outer EJB in order for the resulting remote homes and interfaces to be compatible with the proxy through which the client has initiated the call. The `invoker/ejb-ref` elements allow you to map from a protocol-independent ENC `ejb-ref` to the home proxy binding for an `ejb-ref` target EJB home that matches the referencing invoker type.

An example of using a custom `JRMPInvoker` MBean that enables compressed sockets for session beans can be found in the `org.jboss.test.jrmp` package of the testsuite. The following example illustrates the custom `JRMPInvoker` configuration and its mapping to a stateless session bean:

```
<server>
    <mbean code="org.jboss.invocation.jrmp.server.JRMPInvoker"
          name="jboss:service=invoker,type=jrmp,socketType=
➥CompressionSocketFactory">
        <attribute name="RMIObjectPort">4445</attribute>
        <attribute name="RMIClientSocketFactory">
            org.jboss.test.jrmp.ejb.CompressionClientSocketFactory
        </attribute>
        <attribute name="RMIServerSocketFactory">
            org.jboss.test.jrmp.ejb.CompressionServerSocketFactory
        </attribute>
    </mbean>
</server>
```

Here the default `JRMPInvoker` has been customized to bind to port 4445 and to use custom socket factories that enable compression at the transport level:

```
<?xml version="1.0"?>
<!DOCTYPE jboss PUBLIC
          "-//JBoss//DTD JBOSS 3.2//EN"
          "http://www.jboss.org/j2ee/dtd/jboss_3_2.dtd">
<!-- The jboss.xml descriptor for the jrmp-comp.jar ejb unit -->
<jboss>
    <enterprise-beans>
        <session>
            <ejb-name>StatelessSession</ejb-name>
            <configuration-name>Standard Stateless SessionBean
➥</configuration-name>
            <invoker-bindings>
                <invoker>
                    <invoker-proxy-binding-name>
                        stateless-compression-invoker
                    </invoker-proxy-binding-name>
                    <jndi-name>jrmp-compressed/StatelessSession</jndi-name>
                </invoker>
            </invoker-bindings>
        </session>
    </enterprise-beans>

    <invoker-proxy-bindings>
        <invoker-proxy-binding>
            <name>stateless-compression-invoker</name>
            <invoker-mbean>
                jboss:service=invoker,type=jrmp,socketType=
➥CompressionSocketFactory
            </invoker-mbean>
            <proxy-factory>org.jboss.proxy.ejb.ProxyFactory</proxy-factory>
            <proxy-factory-config>
                <client-interceptors>
                    <home>
                        <interceptor>org.jboss.proxy.ejb.HomeInterceptor
➥</interceptor>
                        <interceptor>org.jboss.proxy.SecurityInterceptor
➥</interceptor>
                        <interceptor>org.jboss.proxy.TransactionInterceptor
➥</interceptor>
                        <interceptor>org.jboss.invocation.InvokerInterceptor
➥</interceptor>
                    </home>
                    <bean>
                        <interceptor>
                            org.jboss.proxy.ejb.StatelessSessionInterceptor
```

```
                        </interceptor>
                        <interceptor>org.jboss.proxy.SecurityInterceptor
➥</interceptor>
                        <interceptor>org.jboss.proxy.TransactionInterceptor
➥</interceptor>
                        <interceptor>org.jboss.invocation.InvokerInterceptor
➥</interceptor>
                    </bean>
                </client-interceptors>
            </proxy-factory-config>
        </invoker-proxy-binding>
    </invoker-proxy-bindings>
</jboss>
```

The `StatelessSession` EJB `invoker-bindings` settings specify that the `stateless-compression-invoker` will be used with the home interface bound under the JNDI name `j rmp-compressed/StatelessSession`. The `stateless-compression-invoker` is linked to the custom JRMP invoker we just declared.

The following example, from the `org.jboss.test.hello` testsuite package, is an example of using the `HttpInvoker` to configure a stateless session bean to use the RMI/HTTP protocol:

```
<?xml version="1.0" encoding="UTF-8"?>
<!DOCTYPE jboss PUBLIC
          "-//JBoss//DTD JBOSS 3.2//EN"
          "http://www.jboss.org/j2ee/dtd/jboss_3_2.dtd">
<jboss>
    <enterprise-beans>
        <session>
            <ejb-name>HelloWorldViaHTTP</ejb-name>
            <jndi-name>helloworld/HelloHTTP</jndi-name>
            <invoker-bindings>
                <invoker>
                    <invoker-proxy-binding-name>
                        stateless-http-invoker
                    </invoker-proxy-binding-name>
                </invoker>
            </invoker-bindings>
        </session>
    </enterprise-beans>
    <invoker-proxy-bindings>
        <!-- A custom invoker for RMI/HTTP -->
        <invoker-proxy-binding>
            <name>stateless-http-invoker</name>
            <invoker-mbean>jboss:service=invoker,type=http</invoker-mbean>
```

```
            <proxy-factory>org.jboss.proxy.ejb.ProxyFactory</proxy-factory>
            <proxy-factory-config>
                <client-interceptors>
                    <home>
                        <interceptor>org.jboss.proxy.ejb.HomeInterceptor
➥</interceptor>
                        <interceptor>org.jboss.proxy.SecurityInterceptor
➥</interceptor>
                        <interceptor>org.jboss.proxy.TransactionInterceptor
➥</interceptor>
                        <interceptor>org.jboss.invocation.InvokerInterceptor
➥</interceptor>
                    </home>
                    <bean>
                        <interceptor>
                            org.jboss.proxy.ejb.StatelessSessionInterceptor
                        </interceptor>
                        <interceptor>org.jboss.proxy.SecurityInterceptor
➥</interceptor>
                        <interceptor>org.jboss.proxy.TransactionInterceptor
➥</interceptor>
                        <interceptor>org.jboss.invocation.InvokerInterceptor
➥</interceptor>
                    </bean>
                </client-interceptors>
            </proxy-factory-config>
        </invoker-proxy-binding>
    </invoker-proxy-bindings>
</jboss>
```

Here a custom `invoker-proxy-binding` named `stateless-http-invoker` is defined. It uses the `HttpInvoker` MBean as the detached invoker. The `jboss:service=invoker,type=http` name is the default name of the `HttpInvoker` MBean, as found in the `http-invoker.sar/META-INF/jboss-service.xml` descriptor, and its service descriptor fragment is shown here:

```
<!-- The HTTP invoker service configuration -->
<mbean code="org.jboss.invocation.http.server.HttpInvoker"
       name="jboss:service=invoker,type=http">
    <!-- Use a URL of the form http://<hostname>:8080/invoker/EJBInvokerServlet
         where <hostname> is InetAddress.getHostname value on which the server
         is running. -->
    <attribute name="InvokerURLPrefix">http://</attribute>
    <attribute name="InvokerURLSuffix">:8080/invoker/EJBInvokerServlet</attribute>
    <attribute name="UseHostName">true</attribute>
</mbean>
```

The client proxy posts the EJB invocation content to the `EJBInvokerServlet` URL specified in the `HttpInvoker` service configuration.

The HA `JRMPInvoker`: Clustered RMI/JRMP Transport

The `org.jboss.invocation.jrmp.server.JRMPInvokerHA` service is an extension of the `JRMPInvoker` that is a cluster-aware invoker. The `JRMPInvokerHA` fully supports all the attributes of the `JRMPInvoker`. This means that customized bindings of the port, interface, and socket transport are available to clustered RMI/JRMP as well.

The HA `HttpInvoker`: Clustered RMI/HTTP Transport

The RMI/HTTP layer allows for software load balancing of the invocations in a clustered environment. An HA-capable extension of the HTTP invoker has been added that borrows much of its functionality from the HA-RMI/JRMP clustering.

To enable HA-RMI/HTTP, you need to configure the invokers for the EJB container. You do this through either a `jboss.xml` descriptor or the `standardjboss.xml` descriptor. Listing 5.3 shows an example of a stateless session configuration taken from the `org.jboss.test.hello` testsuite package.

LISTING 5.3 A `jboss.xml` Stateless Session Configuration for HA-RMI/HTTP

```
<jboss>
    <enterprise-beans>
        <session>
            <ejb-name>HelloWorldViaClusteredHTTP</ejb-name>
            <jndi-name>helloworld/HelloHA-HTTP</jndi-name>
            <invoker-bindings>
                <invoker>
                    <invoker-proxy-binding-name>
                        stateless-httpHA-invoker
                    </invoker-proxy-binding-name>
                </invoker>
            </invoker-bindings>
            <clustered>true</clustered>
        </session>
    </enterprise-beans>
    <invoker-proxy-bindings>
        <invoker-proxy-binding>
            <name>stateless-httpHA-invoker</name>
            <invoker-mbean>jboss:service=invoker,type=httpHA</invoker-mbean>
            <proxy-factory>org.jboss.proxy.ejb.ProxyFactoryHA</proxy-factory>
            <proxy-factory-config>
                <client-interceptors>
                    <home>
```

LISTING 5.3 Continued

```
                        <interceptor>org.jboss.proxy.ejb.HomeInterceptor
➥</interceptor>
                        <interceptor>org.jboss.proxy.SecurityInterceptor
➥</interceptor>
                        <interceptor>org.jboss.proxy.TransactionInterceptor
➥</interceptor>
                        <interceptor>org.jboss.invocation.InvokerInterceptor
➥</interceptor>
                    </home>
                    <bean>
                        <interceptor>
                            org.jboss.proxy.ejb.StatelessSessionInterceptor
                        </interceptor>
                        <interceptor>org.jboss.proxy.SecurityInterceptor
➥</interceptor>
                        <interceptor>org.jboss.proxy.TransactionInterceptor
➥</interceptor>
                        <interceptor>org.jboss.invocation.InvokerInterceptor
➥</interceptor>
                    </bean>
                </client-interceptors>
            </proxy-factory-config>
        </invoker-proxy-binding>
    </invoker-proxy-bindings>
</jboss>
```

The `stateless-httpHA-invoker` `invoker-proxy-binding` references the `jboss:service=invoker,type=httpHA` invoker service. This service would be configured as follows:

```
<mbean code="org.jboss.invocation.http.server.HttpInvokerHA"
       name="jboss:service=invoker,type=httpHA">
    <!-- Use a URL of the form
         http://<hostname>:8080/invoker/EJBInvokerHAServlet
         where <hostname> is InetAddress.getHostname value on which the server
         is running.
    -->
    <attribute name="InvokerURLPrefix">http://</attribute>
    <attribute name="InvokerURLSuffix">:8080/invoker/EJBInvokerHAServlet
➥</attribute>
    <attribute name="UseHostName">true</attribute>
</mbean>
```

The URL used by the invoker proxy is the `EJBInvokerHAServlet` mapping, as deployed on the cluster node. The `HttpInvokerHA` instances across the cluster form a collection of candidate HTTP URLs that are made available to the client-side proxy for failover and/or load balancing.

The EJB Container

An EJB container is the component that manages a particular class of EJB. In JBoss there is one instance of the `org.jboss.ejb.Container` created for each unique configuration of an EJB that is deployed. The actual object that is instantiated is a subclass of `Container`, and the creation of the container instance is managed by the `EJBDeployer` MBean.

The `EJBDeployer` MBean

The `org.jboss.ejb.EJBDeployer` MBean is responsible for the creation of EJB containers. Given an EJB JAR that is ready for deployment, the `EJBDeployer` will create and initialize the necessary EJB containers, one for each type of EJB. These are the configurable attributes of the `EJBDeployer`:

- **`VerifyDeployments`**—A Boolean flag that indicates whether the EJB verifier should be run. This validates that the EJBs in a deployment unit conform to the EJB 2.1 specification. Setting this to `true` is useful for ensuring that your deployments are valid.
- **`VerifierVerbose`**—A Boolean that controls the verbosity of any verification failures/warnings that result from the verification process.
- **`StrictVerifier`**—A Boolean that enables/disables strict verification. When strict verification is enabled, an EJB will deploy only if the verifier reports no errors.
- **`CallByValue`**—A Boolean flag which indicates that call-by-value semantics should be used by default.
- **`ValidateDTDs`**—ABoolean flag that indicates whether the `ejb-jar.xml` and `jboss.xml` descriptors should be validated against their declared DTDs. Setting this to `true` is useful for ensuring that your deployment descriptors are valid.
- **`MetricsEnabled`**—A Boolean flag that controls whether container interceptors marked with a `metricsEnabled=true` attribute should be included in the configuration. This allows you to define a container interceptor configuration that includes metric-type interceptors that can be toggled on and off.
- **`WebServiceName`**—The JMX `ObjectName` string of the web service MBean that provides support for the dynamic class loading of EJB classes.
- **`TransactionManagerServiceName`**—The JMX `ObjectName` string of the JTA transaction manager service. This must have an attribute named `TransactionManager` that returns that `javax.transaction.TransactionManager` instance.

The deployer contains two central methods: `deploy` and `undeploy`. The `deploy` method takes a URL, which either points to an EJB JAR or to a directory whose structure is the same as a valid EJB JAR (which is convenient for development purposes). After a deployment has been made, you can undeploy it by calling `undeploy` on the same URL. A call to `deploy` with an already-deployed URL will cause an undeploy followed by deployment of the URL. JBoss has support for full re-deployment of both implementation and interface classes, and it reloads any changed classes. This allows you to develop and update EJBs without ever stopping a running server.

During the deployment of the EJB JAR, the `EJBDeployer` and its associated classes perform three main functions: verify the EJBs, create a container for each unique EJB, and initialize the container with the deployment configuration information. The following sections talk about each of these functions.

Verifying EJB Deployments

When the `VerifyDeployments` attribute of `EJBDeployer` is `true`, the deployer performs a verification of EJBs in the deployment. The verification checks that an EJB meets EJB specification compliance. This entails validating that the EJB deployment unit contains the required home, remote, local home, and local interfaces. It also checks that the objects appearing in these interfaces are of the proper types and that the required methods are present in the implementation class. This is a useful behavior that is enabled by default because there are a number of steps that an EJB developer and deployer must perform correctly to construct a proper EJB JAR, and it is easy to make a mistake. The verification stage attempts to catch any errors and fail the deployment with an error that indicates what needs to be corrected.

Probably the most problematic aspect of writing EJBs is the fact that there is a disconnection between the bean implementation and its remote and home interfaces, as well as its deployment descriptor configuration. It is easy to have these separate elements get out of sync. One tool that helps eliminate this problem is XDoclet. It allows you to use custom JavaDoc-like tags in the EJB bean implementation class to generate the related bean interfaces, deployment descriptors, and related objects. See the XDoclet home page, http://sourceforge.net/projects/xdoclet, for additional details.

Deploying EJBs into Containers

The most important roles that the `EJBDeployer` performs are creating an EJB container and deploying the EJB into the container. The deployment phase consists of iterating over EJBs in an EJB JAR and extracting the bean classes and their metadata as described by the `ejb-jar.xml` and `jboss.xml` deployment descriptors. For each EJB in the EJB JAR, the following steps are performed:

1. Create a subclass of `org.jboss.ejb.Container`, depending on the type of the EJB: stateless, stateful, BMP entity, CMP entity, or message driven. The container is assigned a unique `ClassLoader` from which it can load local resources. The uniqueness of the `ClassLoader` is also used to isolate the standard `java:comp` JNDI namespace from other J2EE components.

2. Set all container-configurable attributes from a merge of the `jboss.xml` and `standardjboss.xml` descriptors.
3. Create and add the container interceptors, as configured for the container.
4. Associate the container with an application object. This application object represents a J2EE enterprise application and may contain multiple EJBs and web contexts.
5. If all EJBs are successfully deployed, the application is started, which in turn starts all containers and makes the EJBs available to clients. If any EJB fails to deploy, a deployment exception is thrown, and the deployment module is failed.

Initializing with Configuration Information

JBoss externalizes most, if not all, of the setup of the EJB containers, using an XML file that conforms to the `jboss_4_0.dtd`. The section of the DTD that relates to container configuration information is shown in Figure 5.4.

The `container-configuration` element and its subelements specify container configuration settings for a type of container, as given by the `container-name` element. Each configuration specifies information such as the default invoker type, the container interceptor makeup, instance caches/pools and their sizes, the persistence manager, security, and so on. Because this is a large amount of information that requires a detailed understanding of the JBoss container architecture, JBoss ships with a standard configuration file for the four types of EJBs. This configuration file is called `standardjboss.xml`, and it is located in the `conf` directory of any configuration file set that uses EJBs. The following is a sample of `container-configuration` from `standardjboss.xml`:

```
<container-configuration>
    <container-name>Standard CMP 2.x EntityBean</container-name>
    <call-logging>false</call-logging>
    <invoker-proxy-binding-name>entity-rmi-invoker</invoker-proxy-binding-name>
    <sync-on-commit-only>false</sync-on-commit-only>
    <insert-after-ejb-post-create>false</insert-after-ejb-post-create>
    <call-ejb-store-on-clean>true</call-ejb-store-on-clean>
    <container-interceptors>
        <interceptor>org.jboss.ejb.plugins.ProxyFactoryFinderInterceptor
➥</interceptor>
        <interceptor>org.jboss.ejb.plugins.LogInterceptor</interceptor>
        <interceptor>org.jboss.ejb.plugins.SecurityInterceptor</interceptor>
        <interceptor>org.jboss.ejb.plugins.TxInterceptorCMT</interceptor>
        <interceptor>org.jboss.ejb.plugins.CallValidationInterceptor</interceptor>
        <interceptor metricsEnabled="true">
➥org.jboss.ejb.plugins.MetricsInterceptor</interceptor>
        <interceptor>org.jboss.ejb.plugins.EntityCreationInterceptor</interceptor>
        <interceptor>org.jboss.ejb.plugins.EntityLockInterceptor</interceptor>
        <interceptor>org.jboss.ejb.plugins.EntityInstanceInterceptor</interceptor>
```

```
        <interceptor>org.jboss.ejb.plugins.EntityReentranceInterceptor
➥</interceptor>
        <interceptor>org.jboss.resource.connectionmanager.
➥CachedConnectionInterceptor</interceptor>
        <interceptor>org.jboss.ejb.plugins.EntitySynchronizationInterceptor
➥</interceptor>
        <interceptor>org.jboss.ejb.plugins.cmp.jdbc.JDBCRelationInterceptor
➥</interceptor>
    </container-interceptors>
    <instance-pool>org.jboss.ejb.plugins.EntityInstancePool</instance-pool>
    <instance-cache>org.jboss.ejb.plugins.InvalidableEntityInstanceCache
➥</instance-cache>
    <persistence-manager>org.jboss.ejb.plugins.cmp.jdbc.JDBCStoreManager
➥</persistence-manager>
    <locking-policy>org.jboss.ejb.plugins.lock.QueuedPessimisticEJBLock
➥</locking-policy>
    <container-cache-conf>
        <cache-policy>org.jboss.ejb.plugins.LRUEnterpriseContextCachePolicy
➥</cache-policy>
        <cache-policy-conf>
            <min-capacity>50</min-capacity>
            <max-capacity>1000000</max-capacity>
            <overager-period>300</overager-period>
            <max-bean-age>600</max-bean-age>
            <resizer-period>400</resizer-period>
            <max-cache-miss-period>60</max-cache-miss-period>
            <min-cache-miss-period>1</min-cache-miss-period>
            <cache-load-factor>0.75</cache-load-factor>
        </cache-policy-conf>
    </container-cache-conf>
    <container-pool-conf>
        <MaximumSize>100</MaximumSize>
    </container-pool-conf>
    <commit-option>B</commit-option>
</container-configuration>
```

The container configuration information can be specified at two levels. The first is in the `standardjboss.xml` file that is contained in the configuration file set directory. The second is at the EJB JAR level. By placing a `jboss.xml` file in the EJB JAR `META-INF` directory, you can specify either overrides for container configurations in the `standardjboss.xml` file or entirely new named container configurations. This provides great flexibility in the configuration of containers. As you have seen, all container configuration attributes have been externalized and are therefore easily modifiable. Knowledgeable developers can even implement specialized container components, such as instance pools or caches, and easily integrate them with the standard container configurations to optimize behavior for a particular application or environment.

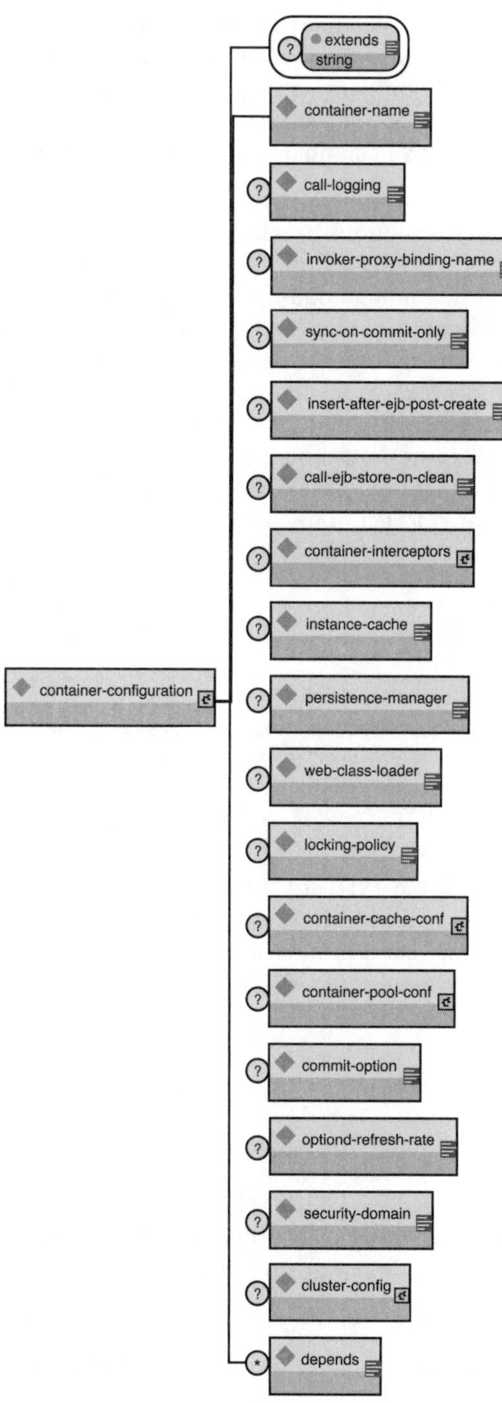

FIGURE 5.4 The `jboss_4_0` DTD elements related to container configuration.

How an EJB deployment chooses its container configuration is based on the explicit or implicit jboss/enterprise-beans/<type>/configuration-name element. The configuration-name element is a link to a container-configurations/container-configuration element in Figure 5.4. It specifies which container configuration to use for the referring EJB. The link is from a configuration-name element to a container-name element.

You can specify container configurations per class of EJB by including a container-configuration element in the EJB definition. Typically, you do not define completely new container configurations, although doing so is supported. The typical usage of a jboss.xml-level container-configuration is to override one or more aspects of a container-configuration coming from the standardjboss.xml descriptor. You do this by specifying a container-configuration that references the name of an existing standardjboss.xml container-configuration/container-name as the value for the container-configuration/extends attribute. The following example shows an example of defining a new Secured Stateless SessionBean configuration that is an extension of the Standard Stateless SessionBean configuration:

```
<?xml version="1.0"?>
<jboss>
    <enterprise-beans>
        <session>
            <ejb-name>EchoBean</ejb-name>
            <configuration-name>Secured Stateless SessionBean</configuration-name>
            <!-- ... -->
        </session>
    </enterprise-beans>
    <container-configurations>
        <container-configuration extends="Standard Stateless SessionBean">
            <container-name>Secured Stateless SessionBean</container-name>
            <!-- Override the container security domain -->
            <security-domain>java:/jaas/my-security-domain</security-domain>
        </container-configuration>
    </container-configurations>
</jboss>
```

If an EJB does not provide a container configuration specification in the deployment-unit EJB JAR, the container factory chooses a container configuration from the standardjboss.xml descriptor, based on the type of the EJB. So, in reality, there is an implicit configuration-name element for every type of EJB, and the mappings from the EJB type to default container configuration name are as follows:

- Container-managed persistence entity version 2.0 = Standard CMP 2.x EntityBean
- Container-managed persistence entity version 1.1 = Standard CMP EntityBean
- Bean-managed persistence entity = Standard BMP EntityBean

- Stateless session = `Standard Stateless SessionBean`
- Stateful session = `Standard Stateful SessionBean`
- Message driven = `Standard Message Driven Bean`

It is not necessary to indicate which container configuration an EJB is using if you want to use the default, based on the bean type. It probably provides for a more self-contained descriptor to include the `configuration-name` element, but this is purely a matter of style.

Now that you know how to specify which container configuration an EJB is using and can define a deployment unit-level override, let's look at the `container-configuration` child elements. A number of the elements specify interface class implementations whose configurations are affected by other elements, so before starting in on the configuration elements, you need to understand the `org.jboss.metadata.XmlLoadable` interface.

`XmlLoadable` is a simple interface that consists of a single method. The interface definition is as follows:

```
import org.w3c.dom.Element;
public interface XmlLoadable
{
    public void importXml(Element element) throws Exception;
}
```

Classes implement this interface to allow their configuration to be specified via an XML document fragment. The root element of the document fragment is what would be passed to the `importXml` method. You will see a few examples of this as the container configuration elements are described in the following sections.

The `container-name` Element The `container-name` element specifies a unique name for a given configuration. EJBs link to a particular container configuration by setting their `configuration-name` element to the value of the `container-name` for the container configuration.

The `call-logging` Element The `call-logging` element expects a Boolean (`true` or `false`) as its value, to indicate whether the `LogInterceptor` should log method calls to a container. This is somewhat obsolete with the change to `log4j`, which provides a fine-grained logging API.

The `invoker-proxy-binding-name` Element The `invoker-proxy-binding-name` element specifies the name of the default invoker to use. In the absence of a bean-level `invoker-bindings` specification, the `invoker-proxy-binding` whose name matches the `invoker-proxy-binding-name` element value is used to create home and remote proxies.

The `sync-on-commit-only` Element The `sync-on-commit-only` element configures a performance optimization that causes entity bean state to be synchronized with the database only at commit time. Normally, the state of all the beans in a transaction would need to be synchronized when a finder method is called or when a remove method is called, for example.

The `insert-after-ejb-post-create` Element The `insert-after-ejb-post-create` element is another entity bean optimization. It causes the database insert command for a new entity bean to be delayed until the `ejbPostCreate` method is called. This allows normal CMP fields as well as CMR fields to be set in a single insert, instead of the default insert followed by an update; this removes the requirement for relationship fields to allow null values.

The `call-ejb-store-on-clean` Element According to the EJB specification, the container is required to call `ejbStore` method on an entity bean instance when a transaction commits, even if the instance was not modified in the transaction. Setting the `call-ejb-store-on-clean` element to `false` causes JBoss to call `ejbStore` only for dirty objects.

The `container-interceptors` Element The `container-interceptors` element specifies one or more interceptor elements that are to be configured as the method interceptor chain for the container. The value of the interceptor element is a fully qualified classname of an `org.jboss.ejb.Interceptor` interface implementation. The container interceptors form a `linked-list` structure through which EJB method invocations pass. The first interceptor in the chain is invoked when the `MBeanServer` passes a method invocation to the container. The last interceptor invokes the business method on the bean. We will discuss the `Interceptor` interface later in this chapter, in the section "The Container Plug-in Framework." Generally, you need to be careful when changing an existing standard EJB interceptor configuration because the EJB contract regarding security, transactions, persistence, and thread safety derives from the interceptors.

The `instance-pool` Element The `instance-pool` element specifies the fully qualified classname of an `org.jboss.ejb.InstancePool` interface implementation to use as the container `InstancePool`. We will discuss the `InstancePool` interface in detail later in this chapter, in the section "The Container Plug-in Framework."

The `container-pool-conf` Element The `container-pool-conf` element is passed to the `InstancePool` implementation class given by the `instance-pool` element if it implements the `XmlLoadable` interface. All current JBoss `InstancePool` implementations derive from the `org.jboss.ejb.plugins.AbstractInstancePool` class, which provides support for the following elements, shown in Figure 5.5:

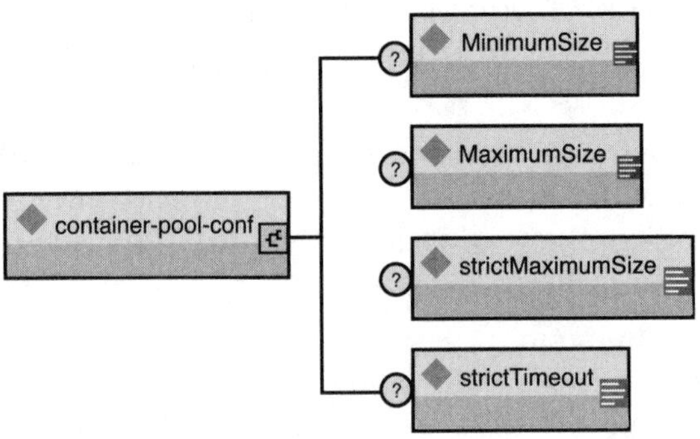

FIGURE 5.5 The `container-pool-conf` element DTD.

- **MinimumSize**—The MinimumSize element gives the minimum number of instances to keep in the pool, although JBoss does not currently seed an InstancePool to the MinimumSize value.
- **MaximumSize**—The MaximumSize element specifies the maximum number of pool instances that are allowed. The default use of MaximumSize may not be what you expect. The pool MaximumSize is the maximum number of EJB instances that are kept available, but additional instances can be created if the number of concurrent requests exceeds the MaximumSize value.
- **strictMaximumSize**—If you want to limit the maximum concurrency of an EJB to the pool MaximumSize, you need to set the strictMaximumSize element to true. When strictMaximumSize is true, only MaximumSize EJB instances can be active. When there are MaximumSize active instances, any subsequent requests will be blocked until an instance is freed back to the pool. The default value for strictMaximumSize is false.
- **strictTimeout**—How long a request blocks waiting for an instance pool object is controlled by the strict-Timeout element. strictTimeout defines the time, in milliseconds, to wait for an instance to be returned to the pool when there are MaximumSize active instances. A value less than or equal to 0 means not to wait at all. When a request times out while waiting for an instance, a java.rmi.ServerException is generated, and the call is aborted. This element is parsed as a Long, so the maximum possible wait time is 9,223,372,036,854,775,807, or about 292,471,208 years, and this is the default value.

The instance-cache Element The instance-cache element specifies the fully qualified classname of the org.jboss.ejb.InstanceCache interface implementation. This element is meaningful only for entity and stateful session beans because these are the only EJB types that have associated identities. We will discuss the InstanceCache interface in detail later in this chapter, in the section "The Container Plug-in Framework."

The container-cache-conf Element The container-cache-conf element is passed to the InstanceCache implementation if it supports the XmlLoadable interface. All current JBoss InstanceCache implementations derive from the org.jboss.ejb.plugins.AbstractInstanceCache class, which provides support for the XmlLoadable interface and uses the cache-policy child element as the fully qualified classname of an org.jboss.util.CachePolicy implementation that is used as the instance cache store. The cache-policy-conf child element is passed to the CachePolicy implementation if it supports the XmlLoadable interface. If it does not, the cache-policy-conf will silently be ignored.

Two JBoss implementations of CachePolicy that are used by the standardjboss.xml configuration support the current array of cache-policy-conf child elements: org.jboss.ejb.plugins.LRUEnterpriseContextCachePolicy and org.jboss.ejb.plugins.LRUStatefulContextCachePolicy. Entity bean containers use LRUEnterpriseContextCachePolicy, and stateful session bean containers use LRUStatefulContextCachePolicy. Both cache policies support the following cache-policy-conf child elements, which are shown in Figure 5.6:

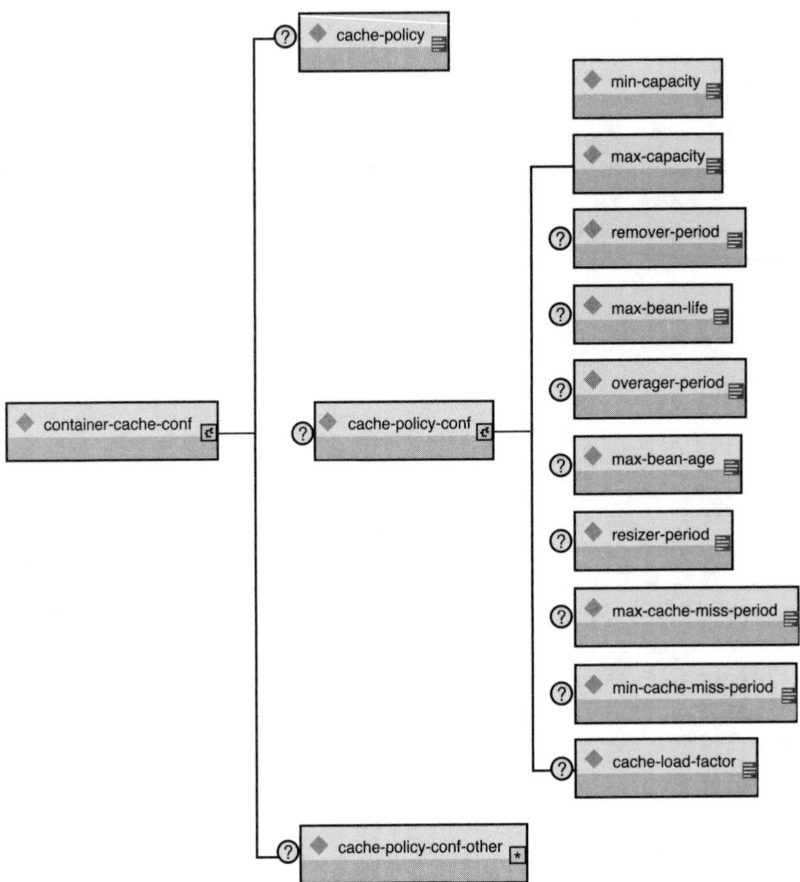

FIGURE 5.6 The `container-cache-conf` element DTD.

- **`min-capacity`**—Specifies the minimum capacity of this cache.
- **`max-capacity`**—Specifies the maximum capacity of the cache, which cannot be less than `min-capacity`.
- **`overager-period`**—Specifies the period, in seconds, between runs of the overager task. The purpose of the overager task is to see whether the cache contains beans with an age greater than the `max-bean-age` element value. Any beans that meet this criterion are passivated.
- **`max-bean-age`**—Specifies the maximum period of inactivity, in seconds, a bean can have before it will be passivated by the overager process.
- **`resizer-period`**—Specifies the period, in seconds, between runs of the resizer task. The purpose of the resizer task is to contract or expand the cache capacity, based on the remaining three element values. When the resizer task executes, it checks the current period between cache misses, and if the period is less than the

min-cache-miss-period value, the cache is expanded up to the max-capacity value, using cache-load-factor. If instead the period between cache misses is greater than the max-cache-miss-period value, the cache is contracted, using cache-load-factor.

- **max-cache-miss-period**—Specifies the time period, in seconds, in which a cache miss should signal that the cache capacity be contracted. It is equivalent to the minimum miss rate that will be tolerated before the cache is contracted.
- **min-cache-miss-period**—Specifies the time period, in seconds, in which a cache miss should signal that the cache capacity be expanded. It is equivalent to the maximum miss rate that will be tolerated before the cache is expanded.
- **cache-load-factor**—Specifies the factor by which the cache capacity is contracted and expanded. The factor should be less than 1. When the cache is contracted, the capacity is reduced so that the current ratio of beans to cache capacity is equal to the cache-load-factor value. When the cache is expanded, the new capacity is determined as current-capacity * 1/cache-load-factor. The actual expansion factor may be as high as 2, based on an internal algorithm based on the number of cache misses. The higher the cache miss rate, the closer the true expansion factor will be to 2.

LRUStatefulContextCachePolicy also supports these child elements:

- **remover-period**—Specifies the period, in seconds, between runs of the remover task. The remover task removes passivated beans that have not been accessed in more than max-bean-life seconds. This task prevents stateful session beans that were not removed by users from filling up the passivation store.
- **max-bean-life**—Specifies the maximum period of inactivity, in seconds, that a bean can exist before being removed from the passivation store.

An alternative cache policy implementation is the org.jboss.ejb.plugins.NoPassivationCachePolicy class, which simply never passivates instances. It uses an in-memory HashMap implementation that never discards instances unless they are explicitly removed. This class does not support any of the cache-policy-conf configuration elements.

The persistence-manager Element The persistence-manager element value specifies the fully qualified classname of the persistence manager implementation. The type of the implementation depends on the type of EJB. For stateful session beans, it must be an implementation of the org.jboss.ejb.StatefulSessionPersistenceManager interface. For BMP entity beans, it must be an implementation of the org.jboss.ejb.EntityPersistenceManager interface, and for CMP entity beans, it must be an implementation of the org.jboss.ejb.EntityPersistenceStore interface.

The web-class-loader Element The web-class-loader element specifies a subclass of org.jboss.web.WebClassLoader that is used in conjunction with the WebService MBean to allow dynamic loading of resources and classes from deployed EARs, EJB JARs, and WARs. A `WebClassLoader` is associated with a `Container` and must have an `org.jboss.mx.loading.UnifiedClassLoader` as its parent. It overrides the `getURLs()` method to return a different set of URLs for remote loading than what is used for local loading.

`WebClassLoader` has two methods, which are meant to be overridden by subclasses: `getKey()` and `getBytes()`. The latter is a no-op in this implementation and should be overridden by subclasses with bytecode-generation ability, such as the class loader used by the `iiop` module.

A `WebClassLoader` subclass must have a constructor with the same signature as the `WebClassLoader(ObjectNamecontainerName, UnifiedClassLoader parent)` constructor.

The `locking-policy` Element The `locking-policy` element gives the fully qualified classname of the EJB lock implementation to use. This class must implement the `org.jboss.ejb.BeanLock` interface. The current JBoss versions include the following:

- **`org.jboss.ejb.plugins.lock.QueuedPessimisticEJBLock`**—This implementation holds threads awaiting the transactional lock to be freed in a fair FIFO queue. Nontransactional threads are also put into this waiting queue as well. This class pops the next waiting transaction from the queue and notifies only those waiting threads that are associated with that transaction. `QueuedPessimisticEJBLock` is the current default used by the standard configurations.
- **`org.jboss.ejb.plugins.lock.QueuedPessimisticEJBLockNoADE`**—This behaves the same as the `QueuedPessimisticEJBLock` except that deadlock detection is disabled.
- **`org.jboss.ejb.plugins.lock.SimpleReadWriteEJBLock`**—This lock allows multiple read locks concurrently. Once a writer has requested the lock, future read-lock requests whose transactions do not already have the read lock will block until all writers are done; then all the waiting readers will concurrently go (depending on the reentrant setting/`methodLock`). A reader who promotes gets first crack at the write lock, ahead of other waiting writers. If there is already a reader that is promoting, an inconsistent read exception is thrown. Of course, writers have to wait for all read-locks to release before taking the write lock.
- **`org.jboss.ejb.plugins.lock.NoLock`**—This anti-locking policy is used with the instance-per-transaction container configurations.

Locking and deadlock detection are discussed in more detail later in this chapter, in the section "Entity Bean Locking and Deadlock Detection."

The `commit-option` and `optiond-refresh-rate` Elements The `commit-option` value specifies the EJB entity bean persistent storage commit option. It must be one of the following:

- `A`—The container caches the bean's state between transactions. This option assumes that the container is the only user accessing the persistent store. This assumption allows the container to synchronize the in-memory state from the persistent storage only when absolutely necessary. This occurs before the first business method executes on a found bean or after the bean is passivated and reactivated to serve another business method. This behavior is independent of whether the business method executes inside a transaction context.

- **B**—The container caches the bean state between transactions. However, unlike with option A, the container does not assume exclusive access to the persistent store. Therefore, the container synchronizes the in-memory state at the beginning of each transaction. Thus, business methods executing in a transaction context don't see much benefit from the container caching the bean, whereas business methods executing outside a transaction context (with transaction attributes Never, NotSupported, or Supports) access the cached (and potentially invalid) state of the bean.

- **C**—The container does not cache bean instances. The in-memory state must be synchronized on every transaction start. For business methods executing outside a transaction, the synchronization is still performed, but ejb-Load executes in the same transaction context as that of the caller.

- **D**—This is a JBoss-specific commit option that is not described in the EJB specification. It is a lazy read scheme where bean state is cached between transactions as with option A, but the state is periodically resynchronized with that of the persistent store. The default time between reloads is 30 seconds, but you can configure it by using the optiond-refresh-rate element.

The security-domain **Element** The security-domain element specifies the JNDI name of the object that implements the org.jboss.security.AuthenticationManager and org.jboss.security.RealmMapping interfaces. It is more typical to specify the security-domain under the jboss root element so that all EJBs in a given deployment are secured in the same manner. However, it is possible to configure the security domain for each bean configuration. The details of the security manager interfaces and configuring the security layer are discussed in Chapter 8, "Security on JBoss."

The cluster-config **Element** The cluster-config element allows you to specify cluster-specific settings for all EJBs that use the container configuration. You can specify the cluster configuration at the container configuration level or at the individual EJB deployment level. The cluster-config DTD fragment is shown in Figure 5.7.

The child elements are as follows:

- **partition-name**—The partition-name element indicates where to find the org.jboss.ha.framework.interfaces.HAPartition interface to be used by the container to exchange clustering information. This is not the full JNDI name under which HAPartition is bound. Rather, it should correspond to the PartitionName attribute of the ClusterPartitionMBean service that is managing the desired cluster. The actual JNDI name of the HAPartition binding will be formed by appending /HASessionState/ to the partition-name value. The default value is DefaultPartition.

- **home-load-balance-policy**—The home-load-balance-policy element indicates the Java classname to be used to load balance calls made on the home proxy. The class must implement the org.jboss.ha.framework.interface.LoadBalancePolicy interface. The default policy is org.jboss.ha.framework.interfaces.RoundRobin.
- **bean-load-balance-policy**—The bean-load-balance-policy element indicates the Java classname to be used to load balance calls in the bean proxy. The class must implement the org.jboss.ha.framework.interface.LoadBalancePolicy interface. For entity beans and stateful session beans, the default is org.jboss.ha.framework.interfaces.FirstAvailable. For stateless session beans, it is org.jboss.ha.framework.interfaces.RoundRobin.
- **session-state-manager-jndi-name**—The session-state-manager-jndi-name element indicates the name of the org.jboss.ha.framework.interfaces.HASessionState to be used by the container as a back end for state session management in the cluster. Unlike the partition-name element, this is a JNDI name under which the HASessionState implementation is bound. The default location used is /HASessionState/Default.

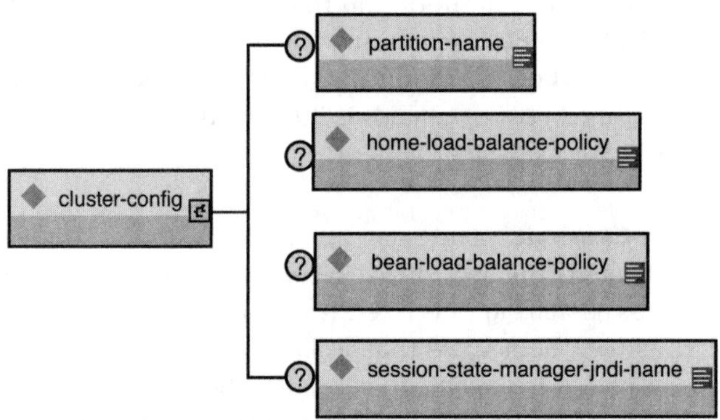

FIGURE 5.7 cluster-config and related elements.

The depends Element The depends element gives a JMX ObjectName of a service on which the container or EJB depends. Specification of explicit dependencies on other services prevents the need to worry about the natural deployment ordering of the services.

The Container Plug-in Framework

The JBoss EJB container uses a framework pattern that allows you to change implementations of various aspects of the container's behavior. The container itself does not perform any significant work other than connecting the various behavioral components together. Implementations of the behavioral components are referred to as *plug-ins* because you can plug in a new implementation by changing a container configuration. Examples of plug-in behavior you might want to change include persistence management, object pooling, object caching, container invoking, and intercepting. There are four subclasses of the `org.jboss.ejb.Container` class, each of which implements a particular bean type:

- **`org.jboss.ejb.EntityContainer`**—Handles `javax.ejb.EntityBean` types.
- **`org.jboss.ejb.StatelessSessionContainer`**—Handles stateless `javax.ejb.SessionBean` types.
- **`org.jboss.ejb.StatefulSessionContainer`**—Handles stateful `javax.ejb.SessionBean` types.
- **`org.jboss.ejb.MessageDrivenContainer`**—Handles `javax.ejb.MessageDrivenBean` types.

The EJB containers delegate much of their behavior to components known as *container plug-ins*. The interfaces that make up the container plug-in points include the following:

```
org.jboss.ejb.ContainerPlugin
org.jboss.ejb.ContainerInvoker
org.jboss.ejb.Interceptor
org.jboss.ejb.InstancePool
org.jboss.ejb.InstanceCache
org.jboss.ejb.EntityPersistanceManager
org.jboss.ejb.EntityPersistanceStore
org.jboss.ejb.StatefulSessionPersistenceManager
```

The container's main responsibility is to manage its plug-ins. This means ensuring that the plug-ins have all the information they need to implement their functionality.

The `org.jboss.ejb.ContainerPlugin` Interface

The `ContainerPlugin` interface is the parent interface of all container plug-in interfaces. It provides a callback that allows a container to give each of its plug-ins a pointer to the container the plug-in is working on behalf of. The `ContainerPlugin` interface is shown in Listing 5.4.

LISTING 5.4 The `org.jboss.ejb.ContainerPlugin` Interface

```
public interface ContainerPlugin
    extends Service, AllowedOperationsFlags
{
    /**
     * This callback is set by the container so that the plugin
     * may access its container
     *
     * @param con the container which owns the plugin
     */
    public void setContainer(Container con);
}
```

The `org.jboss.ejb.Interceptor` Interface

The `Interceptor` interface enables you to build a chain of method interceptors through which each EJB method invocation must pass. The `Interceptor` interface is shown in Listing 5.5.

LISTING 5.5 The `org.jboss.ejb.Interceptor` Interface

```
import org.jboss.invocation.Invocation;

public interface Interceptor
    extends ContainerPlugin
{
    public void setNext(Interceptor interceptor);
    public Interceptor getNext();
    public Object invokeHome(Invocation mi) throws Exception;
    public Object invoke(Invocation mi) throws Exception;
}
```

All interceptors defined in the container configuration are created and added to the container interceptor chain by `EJBDeployer`. The last interceptor is not added by the deployer but rather by the container itself because this is the interceptor that interacts with the EJB bean implementation.

The order of the interceptor in the chain is important. The idea behind ordering is that interceptors that are not tied to a particular `EnterpriseContext` instance are positioned before interceptors that interact with caches and pools.

Implementers of the `Interceptor` interface form a linked-list type of structure through which the `Invocation` object is passed. The first interceptor in the chain is invoked when an invoker passes an `Invocation` to the container via the JMX bus. The last interceptor invokes the business method on the bean. There are usually on the order of five interceptors in a chain, depending on the bean type and container configuration. `Interceptor` semantic complexity ranges from simple to complex. An example of a simple interceptor is `LoggingInterceptor`, and an example of a complex interceptor is `EntitySynchronizationInterceptor`.

One of the main advantages of an interceptor pattern is flexibility in the arrangement of interceptors. Another advantage is the clear functional distinction between different interceptors. For example, logic for transaction and security is cleanly separated between `TXInterceptor` and `SecurityInterceptor`, respectively.

If any of the interceptors fail, the call is terminated at that point. This is a fail-quickly type of semantic. For example, if a secured EJB is accessed without proper permissions, the call fails as the `SecurityInterceptor` before any transactions are started or instance caches are updated.

The `org.jboss.ejb.InstancePool` Interface

An `InstancePool` is used to manage the EJB instances that are not associated with any identity. The pools actually manage subclasses of the `org.jboss.ejb.EnterpriseContext` objects that aggregate unassociated bean instances and related data.

Listing 5.6 shows the `InstancePool` interface.

LISTING 5.6 The `org.jboss.ejb.InstancePool` Interface

```
public interface InstancePool
    extends ContainerPlugin
{
    /**
     * Get an instance without identity. Can be used
     * by finders and create-methods, or stateless beans
     *
     * @return Context /w instance
     * @exception RemoteException
     */
    public EnterpriseContext get() throws Exception;

    /** Return an anonymous instance after invocation.
     *
     * @param ctx
     */
    public void free(EnterpriseContext ctx);

    /**
     * Discard an anonymous instance after invocation.
     * This is called if the instance should not be reused,
     * perhaps due to some exception being thrown from it.
     *
     * @param ctx
     */
    public void discard(EnterpriseContext ctx);

    /**
     * Return the size of the pool.
     *
     * @return the size of the pool.
     */
    public int getCurrentSize();

    /**
     * Get the maximum size of the pool.
     *
```

LISTING 5.6 Continued

```
     * @return the size of the pool.
     */
    public int getMaxSize();
}
```

Depending on the configuration, a container may choose to have a certain size of the pool contain recycled instances, or it may choose to instantiate and initialize an instance on demand.

The `InstanceCache` implementation uses the pool to acquire free instances for activation, and interceptors use the pool to acquire instances to be used for `Home` interface methods (create and finder calls).

The `org.jboss.ebj.InstanceCache` Interface

The container `InstanceCache` implementation handles all EJB instances that are in an active state, meaning bean instances that have an identity attached to them. Only entity and stateful session beans are cached, as these are the only bean types that have state between method invocations. The cache key of an entity bean is the bean primary key. The cache key for a stateful session bean is the session ID.

Listing 5.7 shows the `InstanceCache` interface.

LISTING 5.7 The `org.jboss.ejb.InstanceCache` Interface

```
public interface InstanceCache
    extends ContainerPlugin
{
    /**
     * Gets a bean instance from this cache given the identity.
     * This method may involve activation if the instance is not
     * in the cache.
     * Implementation should have O(1) complexity.
     * This method is never called for stateless session beans.
     *
     * @param id the primary key of the bean
     * @return the EnterpriseContext related to the given id
     * @exception RemoteException in case of illegal calls
     * (concurrent / reentrant), NoSuchObjectException if
     * the bean cannot be found.
     * @see #release
     */
    public EnterpriseContext get(Object id)
        throws RemoteException, NoSuchObjectException;

    /**
```

LISTING 5.7 Continued

```
     * Inserts an active bean instance after creation or activation.
     * Implementation should guarantee proper locking and O(1) complexity.
     *
     * @param ctx the EnterpriseContext to insert in the cache
     * @see #remove
     */
    public void insert(EnterpriseContext ctx);

    /**
     * Releases the given bean instance from this cache.
     * This method may passivate the bean to get it out of the cache.
     * Implementation should return almost immediately leaving the
     * passivation to be executed by another thread.
     *
     * @param ctx the EnterpriseContext to release
     * @see #get
     */
    public void release(EnterpriseContext ctx);

    /**
     * Removes a bean instance from this cache given the identity.
     * Implementation should have O(1) complexity and guarantee
     * proper locking.
     *
     * @param id the primary key of the bean
     * @see #insert
     */
    public void remove(Object id);

    /**
     * Checks whether an instance corresponding to a particular
     * id is active
     *
     * @param id the primary key of the bean
     * @see #insert
     */
    public boolean isActive(Object id);
}
```

In addition to managing the list of active instances, the `InstanceCache` is also responsible for activating and passivating instances. If an instance with a given identity is requested, and it is not currently active, the `InstanceCache` must use the `InstancePool` to acquire a free instance, and then the persistence manager must activate the instance. Similarly, if the InstanceCache decides to passivate an active instance, it must call the persistence manager to passivate it and release the instance to the InstancePool.

The org.jboss.ejb.EntityPersistenceManager Interface

The EntityPersistenceManager interface is responsible for the persistence of entity beans. This includes the following:

- Creating an EJB instance in storage
- Loading the state of a given primary key into an EJB instance
- Storing the state of a given EJB instance
- Removing an EJB instance from storage
- Activating the state of an EJB instance
- Passivating the state of an EJB instance

Listing 5.8 shows the EntityPersistenceManager interface.

LISTING 5.8 The org.jboss.ejb.EntityPersistenceManager Interface

```
public interface EntityPersistenceManager
    extends ContainerPlugin
{
    /**
     * Returns a new instance of the bean class or a subclass of the
     * bean class.
     *
     * @return the new instance
     */
    Object createBeanClassInstance() throws Exception;

    /**
     * This method is called whenever an entity is to be created. The
     * persistence manager is responsible for calling the ejbCreate method
     * on the instance and to handle the results properly wrt the persistent
     * store.
     *
     * @param m the create method in the home interface that was
     * called
     * @param args any create parameters
     * @param instance the instance being used for this create call
     */
    void createEntity(Method m,
                      Object[] args,
                      EntityEnterpriseContext instance)
```

LISTING 5.8 Continued

```
        throws Exception;

    /**
     * This method is called whenever an entity is to be created. The
     * persistence manager is responsible for calling the ejbPostCreate method
     * on the instance and to handle the results properly wrt the persistent
     * store.
     *
     * @param m the create method in the home interface that was
     * called
     * @param args any create parameters
     * @param instance the instance being used for this create call
     */
    void postCreateEntity(Method m,
                          Object[] args,
                          EntityEnterpriseContext instance)
        throws Exception;

    /**
     * This method is called when single entities are to be found. The
     * persistence manager must find out whether the wanted instance is
     * available in the persistence store, and if so it shall use the
     * ContainerInvoker plugin to create an EJBObject to the instance, which
     * is to be returned as result.
     *
     * @param finderMethod the find method in the home interface that was
     * called
     * @param args any finder parameters
     * @param instance the instance to use for the finder call
     * @return an EJBObject representing the found entity
     */
    Object findEntity(Method finderMethod,
                      Object[] args,
                      EntityEnterpriseContext instance)
        throws Exception;

    /**
     * This method is called when collections of entities are to be
     * found. The persistence manager must find out whether the wanted
     * instances are available in the persistence store, and if so it
     * shall use the ContainerInvoker plugin to create EJBObjects to
     * the instances, which are to be returned as result.
     *
```

LISTING 5.8 Continued

```
     * @param finderMethod the find method in the home interface that was
     * called
     * @param args any finder parameters
     * @param instance the instance to use for the finder call
     * @return an EJBObject collection representing the found
     * entities
     */
    Collection findEntities(Method finderMethod,
                            Object[] args,
                            EntityEnterpriseContext instance)
                     throws Exception;

    /**
     * This method is called when an entity shall be activated. The
     * persistence manager must call the ejbActivate method on the
     * instance.
     *
     * @param instance the instance to use for the activation
     *
     * @throws RemoteException thrown if some system exception occurs
     */
    void activateEntity(EntityEnterpriseContext instance)
        throws RemoteException;

    /**
     * This method is called whenever an entity shall be loaded from the
     * underlying storage. The persistence manager must load the state
     * from the underlying storage and then call ejbLoad on the
     * supplied instance.
     *
     * @param instance the instance to synchronize
     *
     * @throws RemoteException thrown if some system exception occurs
     */
    void loadEntity(EntityEnterpriseContext instance)
        throws RemoteException;

    /**
     * This method is used to determine if an entity should be stored.
     *
     * @param instance the instance to check
     * @return true, if the entity has been modified
     * @throws Exception thrown if some system exception occurs
     */
```

LISTING 5.8 Continued

```
    boolean isModified(EntityEnterpriseContext instance) throws Exception;

    /**
     * This method is called whenever an entity shall be stored to the
     * underlying storage. The persistence manager must call ejbStore
     * on the supplied instance and then store the state to the
     * underlying storage.
     *
     * @param instance the instance to synchronize
     *
     * @throws RemoteException thrown if some system exception occurs
     */
    void storeEntity(EntityEnterpriseContext instance)
        throws RemoteException;

    /**
     * This method is called when an entity shall be passivated. The
     * persistence manager must call the ejbPassivate method on the
     * instance.
     *
     * @param instance the instance to passivate
     *
     * @throws RemoteException thrown if some system exception occurs
     */
    void passivateEntity(EntityEnterpriseContext instance)
        throws RemoteException;

    /**
     * This method is called when an entity shall be removed from the
     * underlying storage. The persistence manager must call ejbRemove
     * on the instance and then remove its state from the underlying
     * storage.
     *
     * @param instance the instance to remove
     *
     * @throws RemoteException thrown if some system exception occurs
     * @throws RemoveException thrown if the instance could not be removed
     */
    void removeEntity(EntityEnterpriseContext instance)
        throws RemoteException, RemoveException;
}
```

The `org.jboss.ejb.EntityPersistenceStore` Interface

As per the EJB 2.1 specification, JBoss supports two entity bean persistence semantics: container-managed persistence (CMP) and bean-managed persistence (BMP). The CMP implementation uses an implementation of the `org.jboss.ejb.EntityPersistenceStore` interface. By default, this is the `org.jboss.ejb.plugins.cmp.jdbc.JDBCStoreManager`, which is the entry point for the CMP2 persistence engine. The `EntityPersistenceStore` interface is shown in Listing 5.9.

LISTING 5.9 The `org.jboss.ejb.EntityPersistenceStore` Interface

```
{
    /**
     * Returns a new instance of the bean class or a subclass of the
     * bean class.
     *
     * @return the new instance
     *
     * @throws Exception
     */
    Object createBeanClassInstance()
        throws Exception;

    /**
     * Initializes the instance context.
     *
     * <p>This method is called before createEntity, and should
     * reset the value of all cmpFields to 0 or null.
     *
     * @param ctx
     *
     * @throws RemoteException
     */
    void initEntity(EntityEnterpriseContext ctx);

    /**
     * This method is called whenever an entity is to be created.  The
     * persistence manager is responsible for handling the results
     * properly wrt the persistent store.
     *
     * @param m the create method in the home interface that was
     * called
     * @param args any create parameters
     * @param instance the instance being used for this create call
     * @return The primary key computed by CMP PM or null for BMP
     *
```

LISTING 5.9 Continued

```
     * @throws Exception
     */
    Object createEntity(Method m,
                        Object[] args,
                        EntityEnterpriseContext instance)
        throws Exception;

    /**
     * This method is called when single entities are to be found. The
     * persistence manager must find out whether the wanted instance
     * is available in the persistence store, if so it returns the
     * primary key of the object.
     *
     * @param finderMethod the find method in the home interface that was
     * called
     * @param args any finder parameters
     * @param instance the instance to use for the finder call
     * @return a primary key representing the found entity
     *
     * @throws RemoteException thrown if some system exception occurs
     * @throws FinderException thrown if some heuristic problem occurs
     */
    Object findEntity(Method finderMethod,
                      Object[] args,
                      EntityEnterpriseContext instance)
        throws Exception;

    /**
     * This method is called when collections of entities are to be
     * found. The persistence manager must find out whether the wanted
     * instances are available in the persistence store, and if so it
     * must return a collection of primaryKeys.
     *
     * @param finderMethod the find method in the home interface that was
     * called
     * @param args any finder parameters
     * @param instance the instance to use for the finder call
     * @return a primary key collection representing the found
     * entities
     *
     * @throws RemoteException thrown if some system exception occurs
     * @throws FinderException thrown if some heuristic problem occurs
     */
```

LISTING 5.9 Continued

```
    Collection findEntities(Method finderMethod,
                            Object[] args,
                            EntityEnterpriseContext instance)
        throws Exception;

    /**
     * This method is called when an entity shall be activated.
     *
     * <p>With the PersistenceManager factorization most EJB
     * calls should not exist However this call permits us to
     * introduce optimizations in the persistence store. Particularly
     * the context has a "PersistenceContext" that a PersistenceStore
     * can use (JAWS does for smart updates) and this is as good a
     * callback as any other to set it up.
     * @param instance the instance to use for the activation
     *
     * @throws RemoteException thrown if some system exception occurs
     */
    void activateEntity(EntityEnterpriseContext instance)
        throws RemoteException;

    /**
     * This method is called whenever an entity shall be loaded from the
     * underlying storage. The persistence manager must load the state
     * from the underlying storage and then call ejbLoad on the
     * supplied instance.
     *
     * @param instance the instance to synchronize
     *
     * @throws RemoteException thrown if some system exception occurs
     */
    void loadEntity(EntityEnterpriseContext instance)
        throws RemoteException;

    /**
     * This method is used to determine if an entity should be stored.
     *
     * @param instance the instance to check
     * @return true, if the entity has been modified
     * @throws Exception thrown if some system exception occurs
     */
    boolean isModified(EntityEnterpriseContext instance)
        throws Exception;
```

LISTING 5.9 Continued

```
    /**
     * This method is called whenever an entity shall be stored to the
     * underlying storage. The persistence manager must call ejbStore
     * on the supplied instance and then store the state to the
     * underlying storage.
     *
     * @param instance the instance to synchronize
     *
     * @throws RemoteException thrown if some system exception occurs
     */
    void storeEntity(EntityEnterpriseContext instance)
        throws RemoteException;

    /**
     * This method is called when an entity shall be passivated. The
     * persistence manager must call the ejbPassivate method on the
     * instance.
     *
     * <p>See the activate discussion for the reason for
     * exposing EJB callback * calls to the store.
     *
     * @param instance the instance to passivate
     *
     * @throws RemoteException thrown if some system exception occurs
     */
    void passivateEntity(EntityEnterpriseContext instance)
        throws RemoteException;

    /**
     * This method is called when an entity shall be removed from the
     * underlying storage. The persistence manager must call ejbRemove
     * on the instance and then remove its state from the underlying
     * storage.
     *
     * @param instance the instance to remove
     *
     * @throws RemoteException thrown if some system exception occurs
     * @throws RemoveException thrown if the instance could not be removed
     */
    void removeEntity(EntityEnterpriseContext instance)
        throws RemoteException, RemoveException;
}
```

The default BMP implementation of the `EntityPersistenceManager` interface is `org.jboss.ejb.plugins.BMPPersistenceManager`. The BMP persistence manager is fairly simple because all persistence logic is in the entity bean itself. The only duty of the persistence manager is to perform container callbacks.

The `org.jboss.ejb.StatefulSessionPersistenceManager` Interface

The `StatefulSessionPersistenceManager` interface is responsible for the persistence of stateful session beans. This includes the following:

- Creating stateful sessions in storage
- Activating stateful sessions from storage
- Passivating stateful sessions to storage
- Removing stateful sessions from storage

The `StatefulSessionPersistenceManager` interface is shown in Listing 5.10.

LISTING 5.10 The `org.jboss.ejb.StatefulSessionPersistenceManager` Interface

```
public interface StatefulSessionPersistenceManager
    extends ContainerPlugin
{
    public void createSession(Method m, Object[] args,
                              StatefulSessionEnterpriseContext ctx)
        throws Exception;

    public void activateSession(StatefulSessionEnterpriseContext ctx)
        throws RemoteException;

    public void passivateSession(StatefulSessionEnterpriseContext ctx)
        throws RemoteException;

    public void removeSession(StatefulSessionEnterpriseContext ctx)
        throws RemoteException, RemoveException;

    public void removePassivated(Object key);
}
```

The default implementation of the `StatefulSessionPersistenceManager` interface is `org.jboss.ejb.plugins.StatefulSessionFilePersistenceManager`. As its name implies, `StatefulSessionFilePersistenceManager` utilizes the file system to persist stateful session beans. More specifically, the persistence manager serializes beans in a flat file whose name is composed of the bean name and session ID, with a `.ser` extension. The persistence manager restores a bean's state during activation and respectively stores its state during passivation from the bean's `.ser` file.

Entity Bean Locking and Deadlock Detection

The following sections provide information on what entity bean locking is and how entity beans are accessed and locked within JBoss. They also describe the problems you may encounter as you use entity beans within your system and how to combat these issues. Deadlocking is formally defined and examined. Finally, you'll learn how to fine-tune your system in terms of entity bean locking.

Why JBoss Needs Locking

Locking involves protecting the integrity of your data. Sometimes you need to be sure that only one user can update critical data at a time. Sometimes, access to sensitive objects in a system needs to be serialized so that data is not corrupted by concurrent reads and writes. Databases traditionally provide this sort of functionality with transactional scopes and table- and row-locking facilities.

Using entity beans is a great way to provide an object-oriented interface to relational data. Beyond that, entity beans can improve performance by taking the load off the database through caching and delaying updates until absolutely needed in order to maximize database efficiency. But with caching, data integrity is a problem, so some form of application server–level locking is needed for entity beans to provide the transaction isolation properties that are common with traditional databases.

The Entity Bean Life Cycle

With the default configuration of JBoss there is only one active instance of a given entity bean in memory at one time. This applies for every cache configuration and every type of commit option. The life cycle for this instance is different for every commit option, though:

- For commit option `A`, this instance is cached and used between transactions.
- For commit option `B`, this instance is cached and used between transactions, but it is marked as dirty at the end of a transaction. This means that at the start of a new transaction, `ejbLoad` must be called.
- For commit option `C`, this instance is marked as dirty, released from the cache, and marked for passivation at the end of a transaction.
- For commit option `D`, a background refresh thread periodically calls `ejbLoad` on stale beans within the cache. Otherwise, this option works in the same way as `A`.

When a bean is marked for passivation, the bean is placed in a passivation queue. Each entity bean container has a passivation thread that periodically passivates beans that have been placed in the passivation queue. A bean is pulled out of the passivation queue and reused if the application requests access to a bean with the same primary key.

On an exception or transaction rollback, the entity bean instance is thrown out of the cache entirely. It is not put into the passivation queue and is not reused by an instance pool. Except for the passivation queue, there is no entity bean instance pooling.

Default Locking Behavior

Entity bean locking is totally decoupled from the entity bean instance. The logic for locking is totally isolated and managed in a separate lock object. Because there is only one allowed instance of a given entity bean active at one time, JBoss employs two types of locks to ensure data integrity and to conform to the EJB spec:

- **Method lock**—The method lock ensures that only one thread of execution at a time can invoke on a given entity bean. This is required by the EJB spec.
- **Transaction lock**—A transaction lock ensures that only one transaction at a time has access to a given entity bean. This ensures the ACID properties of transactions at the application server level. Because, by default, there is only one active instance of any given entity bean at one time, JBoss must protect this instance from dirty reads and dirty writes. So the default entity bean locking behavior locks an entity bean within a transaction until it completes. This means that if any method at all is invoked on an entity bean within a transaction, no other transaction can have access to this bean until the holding transaction commits or is rolled back.

Pluggable Interceptors and Locking Policy

You have seen in this chapter that the basic entity bean life cycle and behavior are defined by the container configuration defined in the `standardjboss.xml` descriptor. The following is the `container-interceptors` definition for the `Standard CMP 2.x EntityBean` configuration:

```
<container-interceptors>
    <interceptor>org.jboss.ejb.plugins.ProxyFactoryFinderInterceptor</interceptor>
    <interceptor>org.jboss.ejb.plugins.LogInterceptor</interceptor>
    <interceptor>org.jboss.ejb.plugins.SecurityInterceptor</interceptor>
    <interceptor>org.jboss.ejb.plugins.TxInterceptorCMT</interceptor>
    <interceptor>org.jboss.ejb.plugins.CallValidationInterceptor</interceptor>
    <interceptor metricsEnabled="true">org.jboss.ejb.plugins.MetricsInterceptor
➥</interceptor>
    <interceptor>org.jboss.ejb.plugins.EntityCreationInterceptor</interceptor>
    <interceptor>org.jboss.ejb.plugins.EntityLockInterceptor</interceptor>
    <interceptor>org.jboss.ejb.plugins.EntityInstanceInterceptor</interceptor>
    <interceptor>org.jboss.ejb.plugins.EntityReentranceInterceptor</interceptor>
    <interceptor>org.jboss.resource.connectionmanager.CachedConnectionInterceptor
➥</interceptor>
    <interceptor>org.jboss.ejb.plugins.EntitySynchronizationInterceptor
➥</interceptor>
    <interceptor>org.jboss.ejb.plugins.cmp.jdbc.JDBCRelationInterceptor
➥</interceptor>
</container-interceptors>
```

The interceptors shown here define most of the behaviors of the entity bean. The following are the interceptors that are relevant to this section:

- **EntityLockInterceptor**—This interceptor's role is to schedule any locks that must be acquired before the invocation is allowed to proceed. This interceptor is very lightweight and delegates all locking behavior to a pluggable locking policy.
- **EntityInstanceInterceptor**—The job of this interceptor is to find the entity bean within the cache or create a new one. This interceptor also ensures that there is only one active instance of a bean in memory at one time.
- **EntitySynchronizationInterceptor**—The role of this interceptor is to synchronize the state of the cache with the underlying storage. It does this with the `ejbLoad` and `ejbStore` semantics of the EJB specification. In the presence of a transaction, this is triggered by transaction demarcation. It registers a callback with the underlying transaction monitor through the JTA interfaces. If there is no transaction, the policy is to store the state upon returning from invocation. The synchronization polices `A`, `B`, and `C` of the specification are taken care of here, as is the JBoss-specific commit option `D`.

Deadlocking

This section describes what deadlocking means, how you can detect it within an application, and how you can resolve deadlocks. A deadlock can occur when two or more threads have locks on shared resources. Figure 5.8 illustrates a simple deadlock scenario. Here, `Thread 1` has the lock for `Bean A`, and `Thread 2` has the lock for `Bean B`. At a later time, `Thread 1` tries to lock `Bean B` and blocks because `Thread 2` has it. Likewise, as `Thread 2` tries to lock `Bean A`, it also blocks because `Thread 1` has the lock. At this point, both threads are deadlocked, waiting for access to the resource already locked by the other thread.

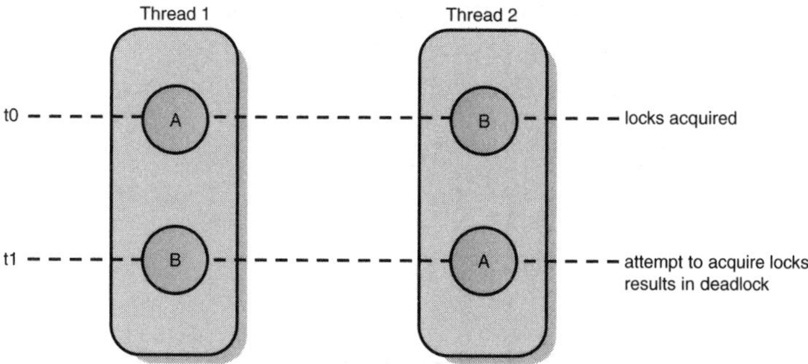

FIGURE 5.8 A deadlock definition example.

The default locking policy of JBoss is to lock an entity bean when an invocation occurs in the context of a transaction until the transaction completes. Therefore, it is very easy to encounter deadlock if you have long-running transactions that access many entity beans or if you are not careful about ordering the access to them. You can use various techniques and advanced configurations to avoid deadlocking problems. They are discussed later in this chapter.

Deadlock Detection

Fortunately, JBoss is able to perform deadlock detection. JBoss holds a global internal graph of waiting transactions and what transactions they are blocking on. Whenever a thread determines that it cannot acquire an entity bean lock, it figures out what transaction currently holds the lock on the bean and adds itself to the blocked transaction graph. Table 5.1 shows an example of what the graph might look like.

TABLE 5.1 An Example of a Blocked Transaction Graph

Blocking Transaction	Transaction That Holds Needed Lock
Tx1	Tx2
Tx3	Tx4
Tx4	Tx1

Before the thread actually blocks, it tries to detect whether there is a deadlock problem. It does this by traversing the block transaction graph. As it traverses the graph, it keeps track of what transactions are blocked. If it sees a blocked node more than once in the graph, then it knows there is deadlock and throws an `ApplicationDeadlockException`. This exception causes a transaction rollback, which in turn causes all locks that transaction holds to be released.

Catching `ApplicationDeadlockException`

Because JBoss can detect application deadlock, you should write an application so that it can retry a transaction if the invocation fails because of the `ApplicationDeadlockException`. Unfortunately, this exception can be deeply embedded within a `RemoteException`, so you have to search for it in your `catch` block. Here's an example:

```
try {
    // ...
} catch (RemoteException ex) {
    Throwable cause = null;
    RemoteException rex = ex;
    while (rex.detail != null) {
        cause = rex.detail;
        if (cause instanceof ApplicationDeadlockException) {
                // ... We have deadlock, force a retry of the transaction.
            break;
        }
        if (cause instanceof RemoteException) {
```

```
            rex = (RemoteException)cause;
        }
    }
}
```

Viewing Lock Information

The `EntityLockMonitor` MBean service allows you to view basic locking statistics as well as print out the state of the transaction locking graph. To enable this monitor, you uncomment its configuration in the `conf/jboss-service.xml` file:

```
<mbean code="org.jboss.monitor.EntityLockMonitor"
       name="jboss.monitor:name=EntityLockMonitor"/>
```

`EntityLockMonitor` has no configurable attributes. It does have the following read-only attributes:

- **`MedianWaitTime`**—The median value of all times threads had to wait to acquire a lock.
- **`AverageContenders`**—The ratio of the total number of contentions to the sum of all threads that had to wait for a lock.
- **`TotalContentions`**—The total number of threads that had to wait to acquire the transaction lock. This happens when a thread attempts to acquire a lock that is associated with another transaction
- **`MaxContenders`**—The maximum number of threads that were waiting to acquire the transaction lock.

`EntityLockMonitor` also has the following operations:

- **`clearMonitor`**—This operation resets the lock monitor state by zeroing all counters.
- **`printLockMonitor`**—This operation prints out a table of all EJB locks that lists the `ejbName` of the bean, the total time spent waiting for the lock, the count of times the lock was waited on, and the number of transactions that timed out waiting for the lock.

Advanced Configurations and Optimizations

The default locking behavior of entity beans can cause deadlock. Because access to an entity bean locks the bean into the transaction, this can also present a huge performance/throughput problem for an application. The following sections walk through various techniques and configurations that you can use to optimize performance and reduce the possibility of deadlock.

Short-Lived Transactions

You should make your transactions as short-lived and fine-grained as possible. The shorter a transaction, the less likelihood that it will have concurrent access collisions and the more the application throughput will go up.

Ordered Access

Ordering the access to entity beans can help lessen the likelihood of deadlock. This means making sure that the entity beans in a system are always accessed in exactly the same order. In most cases, user applications are just too complicated to use this approach, and more advanced configurations are needed.

Read-only Beans

Entity beans can be marked as read-only. When a bean is marked as read-only, it never takes part in a transaction. This means that it is never transactionally locked. Using commit option `D` with this option is sometimes very useful when a read-only bean's data is sometimes updated by an external source.

To mark a bean as read-only, you use the `read-only` flag in the `jboss.xml` deployment descriptor, as shown in Listing 5.11.

LISTING 5.11 Marking an Entity Bean as Read-only by Using `jboss.xml`

```
<jboss>
    <enterprise-beans>
        <entity>
            <ejb-name>MyEntityBean</ejb-name>
            <jndi-name>MyEntityHomeRemote</jndi-name>
            <read-only>True</read-only>
        </entity>
    </enterprise-beans>
</jboss>
```

Explicitly Defining Read-only Methods

Now that you understand the default locking behavior of entity beans, you're probably wondering, "Why lock the bean if it's not modifying the data?" JBoss allows you to define what methods on an entity bean are read-only so that it will not lock the bean within the transaction if only these types of methods are called. You can define these read-only methods within a `jboss.xml` deployment descriptor. Wildcards are allowed for method names. Listing 5.12 shows an example of declaring all getter methods and the `anotherReadOnlyMethod` as read-only.

LISTING 5.12 Defining Entity Bean Methods as Read-only

```
<jboss>
    <enterprise-beans>
        <entity>
```

LISTING 5.12 Continued

```
            <ejb-name>nextgen.EnterpriseEntity</ejb-name>
            <jndi-name>nextgen.EnterpriseEntity</jndi-name>
            <method-attributes>
                <method>
                    <method-name>get*</method-name>
                    <read-only>true</read-only>
                </method>
                <method>
                    <method-name>anotherReadOnlyMethod</method-name>
                    <read-only>true</read-only>
                </method>
            </method-attributes>
        </entity>
    </enterprise-beans>
</jboss>
```

The Instance per Transaction Policy

The Instance per Transaction policy is an advanced configuration that can totally wipe away deadlock and throughput problems caused by JBoss's default locking policy. The default entity bean locking policy is to allow only one active instance of a bean. The Instance per Transaction policy breaks this requirement by allocating a new instance of a bean per transaction and dropping that instance at the end of the transaction. Because each transaction has its own copy of the bean, there is no need for transaction-based locking.

This option does sound great, but it has some drawbacks right now. First, the transactional isolation behavior of this option is equivalent to `READ_COMMITTED`. This can create repeatable reads when they are not desired. In other words, a transaction could have a copy of a stale bean. Second, this configuration option currently requires commit option `B` or `C`, which can be a performance drain because an `ejbLoad` must happen at the beginning of the transaction. But, if an application currently requires commit option `B` or `C` anyway, then this is the way to go. The JBoss developers are currently exploring ways to allow commit option `A` as well (which would allow the use of caching for this option).

JBoss has container configurations named `Instance Per Transaction CMP 2.x EntityBean` and `Instance Per Transaction BMP EntityBean` defined in the `standardjboss.xml` file that implements this locking policy. To use this configuration, you just have to reference the name of the container configuration to use with your bean in the `jboss.xml` deployment descriptor, as shown in Listing 5.13.

LISTING 5.13 An Example of Using the Instance per Transaction Policy

```
<jboss>
    <enterprise-beans>
        <entity>
```

LISTING 5.13 Continued

```
            <ejb-name>MyCMP2Bean</ejb-name>
            <jndi-name>MyCMP2</jndi-name>
            <configuration-name>
                Instance Per Transaction CMP 2.x EntityBean
            </configuration-name>
        </entity>
        <entity>
            <ejb-name>MyBMPBean</ejb-name>
            <jndi-name>MyBMP</jndi-name>
            <configuration-name>
                Instance Per Transaction BMP EntityBean
            </configuration-name>
        </entity>
    </enterprise-beans>
</jboss>
```

Running Within a Cluster

Currently, there is no distributed locking capability for entity beans within a cluster. This functionality has been delegated to the database and must be supported by the application developer. For clustered entity beans, it is suggested to use commit option `B` or `C` in combination with a row-locking mechanism. For CMP, there is a row-locking configuration option. This option uses a SQL `select for update` when the bean is loaded from the database. With commit option `B` or `C`, this implements a transactional lock that can be used across the cluster. For BMP, you must explicitly implement the `select for update` invocation within the BMP's `ejbLoad` method.

Troubleshooting

The following sections describe some common locking problems and their solutions.

Locking Behavior Not Working

Many JBoss users observe that locking does not seem to be working and see concurrent access to their beans—and thus dirty reads. Here are some common solutions for this:

- If you have custom `container-configurations`, make sure you have updated these configurations.
- Make absolutely sure that you have implemented `equals` and `hashCode` correctly from custom/complex primary key classes.
- Make absolutely sure that your custom/complex primary key classes serialize correctly. One common mistake is to assume that member variable initializations will be executed when a primary key is unmarshaled.

`IllegalStateException`

An `IllegalStateException` with the message "removing bean lock and it has tx set!" usually means that you have not implemented `equals` and/or `hashCode` correctly for your custom/complex primary key class; it may also mean that your primary key class is not implemented correctly for serialization.

Hangs and Transaction Timeouts

One long outstanding bug of JBoss is that on a transaction timeout, that transaction is only marked for a rollback and not actually rolled back. This responsibility is delegated to the invocation thread. This can cause major problems if the invocation thread hangs indefinitely because things like entity bean locks will never be released. The solution to this problem is not a good one: You really just need to avoid doing anything within a transaction that could hang indefinitely. Common mistakes are making connections across the Internet and running a web crawler within a transaction.

CHAPTER **6**

Messaging on JBoss

IN THIS CHAPTER

- JMS Examples
- JBossMQ Overview
- JBossMQ Configuration and MBeans
- Specifying the MDB JMS Provider

Applications use the *Java Message Service Application Programming Interface (JMS API)* to send asynchronous *business-quality* messages to other applications. In the messaging world, messages are not sent directly to other applications. Instead, messages are sent to destinations known as *queues* or *topics*. Applications that send messages do not need to worry if the receiving applications are up and running; conversely, receiving applications do not need to worry about the sending application's status. Both senders and receivers only interact with the destinations.

The JMS API is the standardized interface to a JMS provider, sometimes called a Message-Oriented Middleware (MOM) system. JBoss comes with a JMS 1.1–compliant JMS provider called JBoss Messaging (JBossMQ). When you use the JMS API with JBoss, you are using the engine transparently. JBossMQ fully implements the JMS specification; therefore, the best JBossMQ user guide is the JMS specification.

This chapter focuses on the JBoss-specific aspects of using JMS and message-driven beans as well as the JBossMQ configuration and MBeans.

JMS Examples

The following sections discuss the basics needed to use the JBoss JMS implementation. JMS leaves the details of accessing JMS connection factories and destinations as provider-specific details. You need to know the following to use the JBossMQ layer:

- **The location of the queue and topic connect factories**—In JBoss both connection factory implementations are located under the JNDI name `ConnectionFactory`.

- **How to look up JMS destinations (queues and topics)**—Destinations are configured via MBeans, as you will see later in this chapter. JBoss comes with a few queues and topics preconfigured. You can find them under the `jboss.mq.destination` domain in the JMX Console.
- **Which JARS JMS requires**—These include `concurrent.jar`, `jbossmq-client.jar`, `jboss-common-client.jar`, `jboss-system-client.jar`, `jnp-client.jar`, and `log4j.jar`.

The following sections look at examples of the various JMS messaging models and message-driven beans. You can find the source for this chapter's examples under the `src/main/org/jboss/chap6` directory of the book examples.

A Point-to-Point Example

Let's start out with a point-to-point (P2P) example. In the P2P model, a sender delivers messages to a queue, and a single receiver pulls the message off the queue. The receiver does not need to be listening to the queue at the time the message is sent. Listing 6.1 shows a complete P2P example that sends a `javax.jms.TextMessage` to the queue `queue/testQueue` and asynchronously receives the message from the same queue.

LISTING 6.1 A P2P JMS Client Example

```
package org.jboss.chap6.ex1;

import javax.jms.JMSException;
import javax.jms.Message;
import javax.jms.MessageListener;
import javax.jms.Queue;
import javax.jms.QueueConnection;
import javax.jms.QueueConnectionFactory;
import javax.jms.QueueReceiver;
import javax.jms.QueueSender;
import javax.jms.QueueSession;
import javax.jms.TextMessage;
import javax.naming.InitialContext;
import javax.naming.NamingException;

import EDU.oswego.cs.dl.util.concurrent.CountDown;
import org.apache.log4j.Logger;
import org.jboss.util.ChapterExRepository;

/**
 * A complete JMS client example program that sends a
 * TextMessage to a Queue and asynchronously receives the
 * message from the same Queue.
 *
```

LISTING 6.1 Continued

```
 * @author  Scott.Stark@jboss.org
 * @version $Revision: 1.4 $
 */
public class SendRecvClient
{
    static Logger log;
    static CountDown done = new CountDown(1);

    QueueConnection conn;
    QueueSession session;
    Queue que;

    public static class ExListener
        implements MessageListener
    {
        public void onMessage(Message msg)
        {
            done.release();
            TextMessage tm = (TextMessage) msg;
            try {
                log.info("onMessage, recv text=" + tm.getText());
            } catch(Throwable t) {
                t.printStackTrace();
            }
        }
    }

    public void setupPTP()
        throws JMSException,
               NamingException
    {
        InitialContext iniCtx = new InitialContext();
        Object tmp = iniCtx.lookup("ConnectionFactory");
        QueueConnectionFactory qcf = (QueueConnectionFactory) tmp;
        conn = qcf.createQueueConnection();
        que = (Queue) iniCtx.lookup("queue/testQueue");
        session = conn.createQueueSession(false,
                                          QueueSession.AUTO_ACKNOWLEDGE);
        conn.start();
    }

    public void sendRecvAsync(String text)
        throws JMSException,
               NamingException
```

LISTING 6.1 Continued

```
    {
        log.info("Begin sendRecvAsync");
        // Set up the PTP connection, session
        setupPTP();

        // Set the async listener
        QueueReceiver recv = session.createReceiver(que);
        recv.setMessageListener(new ExListener());

        // Send a text msg
        QueueSender send = session.createSender(que);
        TextMessage tm = session.createTextMessage(text);
        send.send(tm);
        log.info("sendRecvAsync, sent text=" + tm.getText());
        send.close();
        log.info("End sendRecvAsync");
    }

    public void stop()
        throws JMSException
    {
        conn.stop();
        session.close();
        conn.close();
    }

    public static void main(String args[])
        throws Exception
    {
        ChapterExRepository.init(SendRecvClient.class);
        log = Logger.getLogger("SendRecvClient");

        log.info("Begin SendRecvClient, now=" + System.currentTimeMillis());
        SendRecvClient client = new SendRecvClient();
        client.sendRecvAsync("A text msg");
        client.done.acquire();
        client.stop();
        log.info("End SendRecvClient");
        System.exit(0);
    }
}
```

You can run the client by using the following command line:

```
[examples]$ ant -Dchap=chap6 -Dex=1p2p run-example
...
run-example1p2p:
     [java] [INFO,SendRecvClient] Begin SendRecvClient, now=1102808673386
     [java] [INFO,SendRecvClient] Begin sendRecvAsync
     [java] [INFO,SendRecvClient] onMessage, recv text=A text msg
     [java] [INFO,SendRecvClient] sendRecvAsync, sent text=A text msg
     [java] [INFO,SendRecvClient] End sendRecvAsync
     [java] [INFO,SendRecvClient] End SendRecvClient
```

A Pub-Sub Example

The JMS publish/subscribe (pub-sub) message model is a one-to-many model. A publisher sends a message to a topic, and all active subscribers of the topic receive the message. Subscribers that are not actively listening to the topic will miss the published message. Listing 6.2 shows a complete JMS client that sends `javax.jms.TextMessage` to a topic and asynchronously receives the message from the same topic.

LISTING 6.2 A Pub-Sub JMS Client Example

```
package org.jboss.chap6.ex1;

import javax.jms.JMSException;
import javax.jms.Message;
import javax.jms.MessageListener;
import javax.jms.Topic;
import javax.jms.TopicConnection;
import javax.jms.TopicConnectionFactory;
import javax.jms.TopicPublisher;
import javax.jms.TopicSubscriber;
import javax.jms.TopicSession;
import javax.jms.TextMessage;
import javax.naming.InitialContext;
import javax.naming.NamingException;

import EDU.oswego.cs.dl.util.concurrent.CountDown;

/**
 *  A complete JMS client example program that sends a TextMessage to
 *  a Topic and asynchronously receives the message from the same
 *  Topic.
 *
 *  @author Scott.Stark@jboss.org
 *  @version $Revision: 1.4 $
 */
```

LISTING 6.2 Continued

```
public class TopicSendRecvClient
{
    static CountDown done = new CountDown(1);
    TopicConnection conn = null;
    TopicSession session = null;
    Topic topic = null;

    public static class ExListener implements MessageListener
    {
        public void onMessage(Message msg)
        {
            done.release();
            TextMessage tm = (TextMessage) msg;
            try {
                System.out.println("onMessage, recv text=" + tm.getText());
            } catch(Throwable t) {
                t.printStackTrace();
            }
        }
    }

    public void setupPubSub()
        throws JMSException, NamingException
    {
        InitialContext iniCtx = new InitialContext();
        Object tmp = iniCtx.lookup("ConnectionFactory");
        TopicConnectionFactory tcf = (TopicConnectionFactory) tmp;
        conn = tcf.createTopicConnection();
        topic = (Topic) iniCtx.lookup("topic/testTopic");
        session = conn.createTopicSession(false,
                                          TopicSession.AUTO_ACKNOWLEDGE);
        conn.start();
    }

    public void sendRecvAsync(String text)
        throws JMSException, NamingException
    {
        System.out.println("Begin sendRecvAsync");
        // Setup the PubSub connection, session
        setupPubSub();
        // Set the async listener

        TopicSubscriber recv = session.createSubscriber(topic);
        recv.setMessageListener(new ExListener());
```

LISTING 6.2 Continued

```
        // Send a text msg
        TopicPublisher send = session.createPublisher(topic);
        TextMessage tm = session.createTextMessage(text);
        send.publish(tm);
        System.out.println("sendRecvAsync, sent text=" + tm.getText());
        send.close();
        System.out.println("End sendRecvAsync");
    }

    public void stop() throws JMSException
    {
        conn.stop();
        session.close();
        conn.close();
    }

    public static void main(String args[]) throws Exception
    {
        System.out.println("Begin TopicSendRecvClient, now=" +
                           System.currentTimeMillis());
        TopicSendRecvClient client = new TopicSendRecvClient();
        client.sendRecvAsync("A text msg, now="+System.currentTimeMillis());
        client.done.acquire();
        client.stop();
        System.out.println("End TopicSendRecvClient");
        System.exit(0);
    }

}
```

You can run the client by using the following command line:

```
[examples]$ ant -Dchap=chap6 -Dex=1ps run-example
...
run-example1ps:
     [java] Begin TopicSendRecvClient, now=1102809427043
     [java] Begin sendRecvAsync
     [java] onMessage, recv text=A text msg, now=1102809427071
     [java] sendRecvAsync, sent text=A text msg, now=1102809427071
     [java] End sendRecvAsync
     [java] End TopicSendRecvClient
```

Now let's break the publisher and subscribers into separate programs to demonstrate that subscribers only receive messages while they are listening to a topic. Listing 6.3 shows a variation of the pub-sub client from Listing 6.2 that only publishes messages to the `topic/testTopic` topic. The subscriber client is shown in Listing 6.4.

LISTING 6.3 A JMS Publisher Client

```
package org.jboss.chap6.ex1;

import javax.jms.JMSException;
import javax.jms.Message;
import javax.jms.MessageListener;
import javax.jms.Topic;
import javax.jms.TopicConnection;
import javax.jms.TopicConnectionFactory;
import javax.jms.TopicPublisher;
import javax.jms.TopicSubscriber;
import javax.jms.TopicSession;
import javax.jms.TextMessage;
import javax.naming.InitialContext;
import javax.naming.NamingException;

/**
 *  A JMS client example program that sends a TextMessage to a Topic
 *
 *  @author Scott.Stark@jboss.org
 *  @version $Revision: 1.4 $
 */
public class TopicSendClient
{
    TopicConnection conn = null;
    TopicSession session = null;
    Topic topic = null;

    public void setupPubSub()
        throws JMSException, NamingException
    {
        InitialContext iniCtx = new InitialContext();
        Object tmp = iniCtx.lookup("ConnectionFactory");
        TopicConnectionFactory tcf = (TopicConnectionFactory) tmp;
        conn = tcf.createTopicConnection();
        topic = (Topic) iniCtx.lookup("topic/testTopic");
        session = conn.createTopicSession(false,
                                          TopicSession.AUTO_ACKNOWLEDGE);
        conn.start();
    }

    public void sendAsync(String text)
```

LISTING 6.3 Continued

```
        throws JMSException, NamingException
    {
        System.out.println("Begin sendAsync");
        // Set up the pub/sub connection, session
        setupPubSub();
        // Send a text msg
        TopicPublisher send = session.createPublisher(topic);
        TextMessage tm = session.createTextMessage(text);
        send.publish(tm);
        System.out.println("sendAsync, sent text=" +  tm.getText());
        send.close();
        System.out.println("End sendAsync");
    }

    public void stop()
        throws JMSException
    {
        conn.stop();
        session.close();
        conn.close();
    }

    public static void main(String args[])
        throws Exception
    {
        System.out.println("Begin TopicSendClient, now=" +
                           System.currentTimeMillis());
        TopicSendClient client = new TopicSendClient();
            client.sendAsync("A text msg, now="+System.currentTimeMillis());
        client.stop();
        System.out.println("End TopicSendClient");
        System.exit(0);
    }

}
```

LISTING 6.4 A JMS Subscriber Client

```
package org.jboss.chap6.ex1;

import javax.jms.JMSException;
import javax.jms.Message;
import javax.jms.MessageListener;
import javax.jms.Topic;
```

LISTING 6.4 Continued

```
import javax.jms.TopicConnection;
import javax.jms.TopicConnectionFactory;
import javax.jms.TopicPublisher;
import javax.jms.TopicSubscriber;
import javax.jms.TopicSession;
import javax.jms.TextMessage;
import javax.naming.InitialContext;
import javax.naming.NamingException;

/**
 * A JMS client example program that synchronously receives a message a Topic
 *
 * @author Scott.Stark@jboss.org
 * @version $Revision: 1.4 $
 */
public class TopicRecvClient
{
    TopicConnection conn = null;
    TopicSession session = null;
    Topic topic = null;

    public void setupPubSub()
        throws JMSException, NamingException
    {
        InitialContext iniCtx = new InitialContext();
        Object tmp = iniCtx.lookup("ConnectionFactory");
        TopicConnectionFactory tcf = (TopicConnectionFactory) tmp;
        conn = tcf.createTopicConnection();
        topic = (Topic) iniCtx.lookup("topic/testTopic");
        session = conn.createTopicSession(false,
                                          TopicSession.AUTO_ACKNOWLEDGE);
        conn.start();
    }

    public void recvSync()
        throws JMSException, NamingException
    {
        System.out.println("Begin recvSync");
        // Set up the pub/sub connection, session
        setupPubSub();

        // Wait up to 5 seconds for the message
        TopicSubscriber recv = session.createSubscriber(topic);
        Message msg = recv.receive(5000);
```

LISTING 6.4 Continued

```
        if (msg == null) {
            System.out.println("Timed out waiting for msg");
        } else {
            System.out.println("TopicSubscriber.recv, msgt="+msg);
        }
    }

    public void stop()
        throws JMSException
    {
        conn.stop();
        session.close();
        conn.close();
    }

    public static void main(String args[])
        throws Exception
    {
        System.out.println("Begin TopicRecvClient, now=" +
                           System.currentTimeMillis());
        TopicRecvClient client = new TopicRecvClient();
        client.recvSync();
        client.stop();
        System.out.println("End TopicRecvClient");
        System.exit(0);
    }

}
```

You run TopicSendClient followed by TopicRecvClient as follows:

```
[examples]$ ant -Dchap=chap6 -Dex=1ps2 run-example
...
run-example1ps2:
     [java] Begin TopicSendClient, now=1102810007899
     [java] Begin sendAsync
     [java] sendAsync, sent text=A text msg, now=1102810007909
     [java] End sendAsync
     [java] End TopicSendClient
     [java] Begin TopicRecvClient, now=1102810011524
     [java] Begin recvSync
     [java] Timed out waiting for msg
     [java] End TopicRecvClient
```

The output shows that the topic subscriber client (`TopicRecvClient`) fails to receive the message sent by the publisher due to a timeout.

An Example of a Pub-Sub with a Durable Topic

JMS supports a messaging model that is a cross between the P2P and pub-sub models. When a pub-sub client wants to receive all messages posted to the topic it subscribes to, even when it is not actively listening to the topic, it may achieve this behavior by using a durable topic. Let's look at a variation of the Listing 6.4 subscriber client that uses a durable topic to ensure that it receives all messages, including those published when the client is not listening to the topic. Listing 6.5 shows the durable topic client.

LISTING 6.5 A Durable Topic JMS Client Example

```
package org.jboss.chap6.ex1;

import javax.jms.JMSException;
import javax.jms.Message;
import javax.jms.MessageListener;
import javax.jms.Topic;
import javax.jms.TopicConnection;
import javax.jms.TopicConnectionFactory;
import javax.jms.TopicPublisher;
import javax.jms.TopicSubscriber;
import javax.jms.TopicSession;
import javax.jms.TextMessage;
import javax.naming.InitialContext;
import javax.naming.NamingException;

/**
 * A JMS client example program that synchronously receives a message a Topic
 *
 * @author Scott.Stark@jboss.org
 * @version $Revision: 1.4 $
 */
public class DurableTopicRecvClient
{
    TopicConnection conn = null;
    TopicSession session = null;
    Topic topic = null;

    public void setupPubSub()
        throws JMSException, NamingException
    {
        InitialContext iniCtx = new InitialContext();
        Object tmp = iniCtx.lookup("ConnectionFactory");
```

LISTING 6.5 Continued

```
        TopicConnectionFactory tcf = (TopicConnectionFactory) tmp;
        conn = tcf.createTopicConnection("john", "needle");
        topic = (Topic) iniCtx.lookup("topic/testTopic");

        session = conn.createTopicSession(false,
                                          TopicSession.AUTO_ACKNOWLEDGE);
        conn.start();
    }

    public void recvSync()
        throws JMSException, NamingException
    {
        System.out.println("Begin recvSync");
        // Set up the pub/sub connection, session
        setupPubSub();
        // Wait up to 5 seconds for the message
        TopicSubscriber recv = session.createDurableSubscriber
➥(topic, "chap6-ex1dtps");
        Message msg = recv.receive(5000);
        if (msg == null) {
            System.out.println("Timed out waiting for msg");
        } else {
            System.out.println("DurableTopicRecvClient.recv, msgt=" + msg);
        }
    }

    public void stop()
        throws JMSException
    {
        conn.stop();
        session.close();
        conn.close();
    }

    public static void main(String args[])
        throws Exception
    {
        System.out.println("Begin DurableTopicRecvClient, now=" +
                           System.currentTimeMillis());
        DurableTopicRecvClient client = new DurableTopicRecvClient();
        client.recvSync();
        client.stop();
        System.out.println("End DurableTopicRecvClient");
```

LISTING 6.5 Continued

```
        System.exit(0);
    }

}
```

Now you can run the previous topic publisher with the durable topic subscriber, as follows:

```
[examples]$ ant -Dchap=chap6 -Dex=1psdt run-example
...
run-example1psdt:
     [java] Begin DurableTopicSetup
     [java] End DurableTopicSetup
     [java] Begin TopicSendClient, now=1102899834273
     [java] Begin sendAsync
     [java] sendAsync, sent text=A text msg, now=1102899834345
     [java] End sendAsync
     [java] End TopicSendClient
     [java] Begin DurableTopicRecvClient, now=1102899840043
     [java] Begin recvSync
     [java] DurableTopicRecvClient.recv, msgt=SpyTextMessage {
     [java] Header {
     [java]    jmsDestination  : TOPIC.testTopic.DurableSubscription
➥[clientId=DurableSubscriberExample name=chap6-ex1dtps selector=null]
     [java]    jmsDeliveryMode : 2
     [java]    jmsExpiration   : 0
     [java]    jmsPriority     : 4
     [java]    jmsMessageID    : ID:3-11028998375501
     [java]    jmsTimeStamp    : 1102899837550
     [java]    jmsCorrelationID: null
     [java]    jmsReplyTo      : null
     [java]    jmsType         : null
     [java]    jmsRedelivered  : false
     [java]    jmsProperties   : {}
     [java]    jmsPropReadWrite: false
     [java]    msgReadOnly     : true
     [java]    producerClientId: ID:3
     [java] }
     [java] Body {
     [java]    text            :A text msg, now=1102899834345
     [java] }
     [java] }
     [java] End DurableTopicRecvClient
```

Items of note for the durable topic example include the following:

- The TopicConnectionFactory creation in the durable topic client uses a username and password, and the TopicSubscriber creation is done via the createDurableSubscriber(Topic,String) method. This is a requirement of durable topic subscribers: The messaging server needs to know what client is requesting the durable topic and what the name of the durable topic subscription is. We will discuss the details of durable topic setup later in this chapter.
- An org.jboss.chap6.DurableTopicSetup client is run prior to the TopicSendClient. The reason for this is that a durable topic subscriber must have registered a subscription at some point in the past in order for the messaging server to save messages. JBoss supports dynamic durable topic subscribers, and the DurableTopicSetup client simply creates a durable subscription receiver and then exits. This leaves an active durable topic subscriber on the topic/testTopic, and the messaging server knows that any messages posted to this topic must be saved for latter delivery.
- The TopicSendClient does not change for the durable topic. The notion of a durable topic is a subscriber-only notion.
- The DurableTopicRecvClient sees the message published to the topic/testTopic even though it was not listening to the topic at the time the message was published.

An Example of P2P with MDB

Listing 6.6 shows a message-driven bean (MDB) that transforms the TextMessages it receives and sends the transformed messages to the queue found in the incoming message JMSReplyTo header.

LISTING 6.6 A TextMessage-Processing MDB

```
package org.jboss.chap6.ex2;

import javax.ejb.MessageDrivenBean;
import javax.ejb.MessageDrivenContext;
import javax.ejb.EJBException;
import javax.jms.JMSException;
import javax.jms.Message;
import javax.jms.MessageListener;
import javax.jms.Queue;
import javax.jms.QueueConnection;
import javax.jms.QueueConnectionFactory;
import javax.jms.QueueSender;
import javax.jms.QueueSession;
import javax.jms.TextMessage;
import javax.naming.InitialContext;
import javax.naming.NamingException;
```

LISTING 6.6 Continued

```
/**
 * An MDB that transforms the TextMessages it receives and sends the
 * transformed messages to the Queue found in the incoming message
 * JMSReplyTo header.
 *
 * @author Scott.Stark@jboss.org
 * @version $Revision: 1.4 $
 */
public class TextMDB
    implements MessageDrivenBean, MessageListener
{
    private MessageDrivenContext ctx = null;
    private QueueConnection conn;
    private QueueSession session;

    public TextMDB()
    {
        System.out.println("TextMDB.ctor, this="+hashCode());
    }

    public void setMessageDrivenContext(MessageDrivenContext ctx)
    {
        this.ctx = ctx;
        System.out.println("TextMDB.setMessageDrivenContext, this=" +
                           hashCode());
    }

    public void ejbCreate()
    {
        System.out.println("TextMDB.ejbCreate, this="+hashCode());
        try {
            setupPTP();
        } catch (Exception e) {
            throw new EJBException("Failed to init TextMDB", e);
        }
    }

    public void ejbRemove()
    {
        System.out.println("TextMDB.ejbRemove, this="+hashCode());
        ctx = null;
        try {
            if (session != null) {
```

LISTING 6.6 Continued

```
                session.close();
            }
            if (conn != null) {
                conn.close();
            }
        } catch(JMSException e) {
            e.printStackTrace();
        }
    }

    public void onMessage(Message msg)
    {
        System.out.println("TextMDB.onMessage, this="+hashCode());
        try {
            TextMessage tm = (TextMessage) msg;
            String text = tm.getText() + "processed by: "+hashCode();
            Queue dest = (Queue) msg.getJMSReplyTo();
            sendReply(text, dest);
        } catch(Throwable t) {
            t.printStackTrace();
        }
    }

    private void setupPTP()
        throws JMSException, NamingException
    {
        InitialContext iniCtx = new InitialContext();
        Object tmp = iniCtx.lookup("java:comp/env/jms/QCF");
        QueueConnectionFactory qcf = (QueueConnectionFactory) tmp;
        conn = qcf.createQueueConnection();
        session = conn.createQueueSession(false,
                                          QueueSession.AUTO_ACKNOWLEDGE);
        conn.start();
    }

    private void sendReply(String text, Queue dest)
        throws JMSException
    {
        System.out.println("TextMDB.sendReply, this=" +
                           hashCode() + ", dest="+dest);
        QueueSender sender = session.createSender(dest);
        TextMessage tm = session.createTextMessage(text);
        sender.send(tm);
```

LISTING 6.6 Continued

```
        sender.close();
    }
}
```

The MDB `ejb-jar.xml` and `jboss.xml` deployment descriptors are shown in Listings 6.7 and 6.8, respectively.

LISTING 6.7 The MDB `ejb-jar.xml` Descriptor

```
<?xml version="1.0"?>
<!DOCTYPE ejb-jar PUBLIC
          "-//Sun Microsystems, Inc.//DTD Enterprise JavaBeans 2.0//EN"
          "http://java.sun.com/dtd/ejb-jar_2_0.dtd">
<ejb-jar>
    <enterprise-beans>
        <message-driven>
            <ejb-name>TextMDB</ejb-name>
            <ejb-class>org.jboss.chap6.ex2.TextMDB</ejb-class>
            <transaction-type>Container</transaction-type>
            <acknowledge-mode>AUTO_ACKNOWLEDGE</acknowledge-mode>
            <message-driven-destination>
                <destination-type>javax.jms.Queue</destination-type>
            </message-driven-destination>
            <res-ref-name>jms/QCF</res-ref-name>
            <resource-ref>
                <res-type>javax.jms.QueueConnectionFactory</res-type>
                <res-auth>Container</res-auth>
            </resource-ref>
        </message-driven>
    </enterprise-beans>
</ejb-jar>
```

LISTING 6.8 The MDB `jboss.xml` Descriptor

```
<?xml version="1.0"?>
<jboss>
    <enterprise-beans>
        <message-driven>
            <ejb-name>TextMDB</ejb-name>
            <destination-jndi-name>queue/B</destination-jndi-name>
            <resource-ref>
                <res-ref-name>jms/QCF</res-ref-name>
                <jndi-name>ConnectionFactory</jndi-name>
            </resource-ref>
```

LISTING 6.8 Continued

```
        </message-driven>
    </enterprise-beans>
</jboss>
```

Listing 6.9 shows a variation of the P2P client that sends several messages to the `queue/B` destination and asynchronously receives the messages as modified by `TextMDB` from Queue A.

LISTING 6.9 A JMS Client That Interacts with `TextMDB`

```
package org.jboss.chap6.ex2;

import javax.jms.JMSException;
import javax.jms.Message;
import javax.jms.MessageListener;
import javax.jms.Queue;
import javax.jms.QueueConnection;
import javax.jms.QueueConnectionFactory;
import javax.jms.QueueReceiver;
import javax.jms.QueueSender;
import javax.jms.QueueSession;
import javax.jms.TextMessage;
import javax.naming.InitialContext;
import javax.naming.NamingException;

import EDU.oswego.cs.dl.util.concurrent.CountDown;

/**
 *  A complete JMS client example program that sends N TextMessages to
 *  a Queue B and asynchronously receives the messages as modified by
 *  TextMDB from Queue A.
 *
 *  @author Scott.Stark@jboss.org
 *  @version $Revision: 1.4 $
 */
public class SendRecvClient
{
    static final int N = 10;
    static CountDown done = new CountDown(N);

    QueueConnection conn;
    QueueSession session;
    Queue queA;
    Queue queB;
```

LISTING 6.9 Continued

```
    public static class ExListener
        implements MessageListener
    {
        public void onMessage(Message msg)
        {
            done.release();
            TextMessage tm = (TextMessage) msg;
            try {
                System.out.println("onMessage, recv text="+tm.getText());
            } catch(Throwable t) {
                t.printStackTrace();
            }
        }
    }

    public void setupPTP()
        throws JMSException, NamingException
    {
        InitialContext iniCtx = new InitialContext();
        Object tmp = iniCtx.lookup("ConnectionFactory");
        QueueConnectionFactory qcf = (QueueConnectionFactory) tmp;
        conn = qcf.createQueueConnection();
        queA = (Queue) iniCtx.lookup("queue/A");
        queB = (Queue) iniCtx.lookup("queue/B");
        session = conn.createQueueSession(false,
                                          QueueSession.AUTO_ACKNOWLEDGE);
        conn.start();
    }

    public void sendRecvAsync(String textBase)
        throws JMSException, NamingException, InterruptedException
    {
        System.out.println("Begin sendRecvAsync");

        // Set up the PTP connection, session
        setupPTP();

        // Set the async listener for queA
        QueueReceiver recv = session.createReceiver(queA);
        recv.setMessageListener(new ExListener());
```

LISTING 6.9 Continued

```
        // Send a few text msgs to queB
        QueueSender send = session.createSender(queB);

        for(int m = 0; m < 10; m ++) {
            TextMessage tm = session.createTextMessage(textBase+"#"+m);
            tm.setJMSReplyTo(queA);
            send.send(tm);
            System.out.println("sendRecvAsync, sent text=" + tm.getText());
        }
        System.out.println("End sendRecvAsync");
    }

    public void stop()
        throws JMSException
    {
        conn.stop();
        session.close();
        conn.close();
    }

    public static void main(String args[])
        throws Exception
    {
        System.out.println("Begin SendRecvClient,now=" +
                           System.currentTimeMillis());
        SendRecvClient client = new SendRecvClient();
        client.sendRecvAsync("A text msg");
        client.done.acquire();
        client.stop();
        System.exit(0);
        System.out.println("End SendRecvClient");
    }
}
```

You can run the client as follows:

```
[examples]$ ant -Dchap=chap6 -Dex=2 run-example
...
run-example2:
     [copy] Copying 1 file to /tmp/jboss-4.0.1/server/default/deploy
     [echo] Waiting 5 seconds for deploy...
     [java] Begin SendRecvClient, now=1102900541558
     [java] Begin sendRecvAsync
     [java] sendRecvAsync, sent text=A text msg#0
```

```
[java] sendRecvAsync, sent text=A text msg#1
[java] sendRecvAsync, sent text=A text msg#2
[java] sendRecvAsync, sent text=A text msg#3
[java] sendRecvAsync, sent text=A text msg#4
[java] sendRecvAsync, sent text=A text msg#5
[java] sendRecvAsync, sent text=A text msg#6
[java] sendRecvAsync, sent text=A text msg#7
[java] sendRecvAsync, sent text=A text msg#8
[java] sendRecvAsync, sent text=A text msg#9
[java] End sendRecvAsync
[java] onMessage, recv text=A text msg#0processed by: 12855623
[java] onMessage, recv text=A text msg#5processed by: 9399816
[java] onMessage, recv text=A text msg#9processed by: 6598158
[java] onMessage, recv text=A text msg#3processed by: 8153998
[java] onMessage, recv text=A text msg#4processed by: 10118602
[java] onMessage, recv text=A text msg#2processed by: 1792333
[java] onMessage, recv text=A text msg#7processed by: 14251014
[java] onMessage, recv text=A text msg#1processed by: 10775981
[java] onMessage, recv text=A text msg#8processed by: 6056676
[java] onMessage, recv text=A text msg#6processed by: 15679078
```

The corresponding JBoss server console output looks like this:

```
19:15:40,232 INFO  [EjbModule] Deploying TextMDB
19:15:41,498 INFO  [EJBDeployer] Deployed:
➥file:/private/tmp/jboss-4.0.1/server/default/deploy/chap6-ex2.jar
19:15:45,606 INFO  [TextMDB] TextMDB.ctor, this=10775981
19:15:45,620 INFO  [TextMDB] TextMDB.ctor, this=1792333
19:15:45,627 INFO  [TextMDB] TextMDB.setMessageDrivenContext, this=10775981
19:15:45,638 INFO  [TextMDB] TextMDB.ejbCreate, this=10775981
19:15:45,640 INFO  [TextMDB] TextMDB.setMessageDrivenContext, this=1792333
19:15:45,640 INFO  [TextMDB] TextMDB.ejbCreate, this=1792333
19:15:45,649 INFO  [TextMDB] TextMDB.ctor, this=12855623
19:15:45,658 INFO  [TextMDB] TextMDB.setMessageDrivenContext, this=12855623
19:15:45,661 INFO  [TextMDB] TextMDB.ejbCreate, this=12855623
19:15:45,742 INFO  [TextMDB] TextMDB.ctor, this=8153998
19:15:45,744 INFO  [TextMDB] TextMDB.setMessageDrivenContext, this=8153998
19:15:45,744 INFO  [TextMDB] TextMDB.ejbCreate, this=8153998
19:15:45,763 INFO  [TextMDB] TextMDB.ctor, this=10118602
19:15:45,764 INFO  [TextMDB] TextMDB.setMessageDrivenContext, this=10118602
19:15:45,764 INFO  [TextMDB] TextMDB.ejbCreate, this=10118602
19:15:45,777 INFO  [TextMDB] TextMDB.ctor, this=9399816
19:15:45,779 INFO  [TextMDB] TextMDB.setMessageDrivenContext, this=9399816
19:15:45,779 INFO  [TextMDB] TextMDB.ejbCreate, this=9399816
19:15:45,792 INFO  [TextMDB] TextMDB.ctor, this=15679078
19:15:45,798 INFO  [TextMDB] TextMDB.setMessageDrivenContext, this=15679078
```

```
19:15:45,799 INFO  [TextMDB] TextMDB.ejbCreate, this=15679078
19:15:45,815 INFO  [TextMDB] TextMDB.ctor, this=14251014
19:15:45,816 INFO  [TextMDB] TextMDB.setMessageDrivenContext, this=14251014
19:15:45,817 INFO  [TextMDB] TextMDB.ejbCreate, this=14251014
19:15:45,829 INFO  [TextMDB] TextMDB.ctor, this=6056676
19:15:45,831 INFO  [TextMDB] TextMDB.setMessageDrivenContext, this=6056676
19:15:45,864 INFO  [TextMDB] TextMDB.ctor, this=6598158
19:15:45,903 INFO  [TextMDB] TextMDB.ejbCreate, this=6056676
19:15:45,906 INFO  [TextMDB] TextMDB.setMessageDrivenContext, this=6598158
19:15:45,906 INFO  [TextMDB] TextMDB.ejbCreate, this=6598158
19:15:46,236 INFO  [TextMDB] TextMDB.onMessage, this=12855623
19:15:46,238 INFO  [TextMDB] TextMDB.sendReply, this=12855623, dest=QUEUE.A
19:15:46,734 INFO  [TextMDB] TextMDB.onMessage, this=9399816
19:15:46,736 INFO  [TextMDB] TextMDB.onMessage, this=8153998
19:15:46,737 INFO  [TextMDB] TextMDB.onMessage, this=6598158
19:15:46,768 INFO  [TextMDB] TextMDB.sendReply, this=9399816, dest=QUEUE.A
19:15:46,768 INFO  [TextMDB] TextMDB.sendReply, this=6598158, dest=QUEUE.A
19:15:46,774 INFO  [TextMDB] TextMDB.sendReply, this=8153998, dest=QUEUE.A
19:15:46,903 INFO  [TextMDB] TextMDB.onMessage, this=10118602
19:15:46,904 INFO  [TextMDB] TextMDB.sendReply, this=10118602, dest=QUEUE.A
19:15:46,927 INFO  [TextMDB] TextMDB.onMessage, this=1792333
19:15:46,928 INFO  [TextMDB] TextMDB.sendReply, this=1792333, dest=QUEUE.A
19:15:47,002 INFO  [TextMDB] TextMDB.onMessage, this=14251014
19:15:47,007 INFO  [TextMDB] TextMDB.sendReply, this=14251014, dest=QUEUE.A
19:15:47,051 INFO  [TextMDB] TextMDB.onMessage, this=10775981
19:15:47,051 INFO  [TextMDB] TextMDB.sendReply, this=10775981, dest=QUEUE.A
19:15:47,060 INFO  [TextMDB] TextMDB.onMessage, this=6056676
19:15:47,061 INFO  [TextMDB] TextMDB.sendReply, this=6056676, dest=QUEUE.A
19:15:47,064 INFO  [TextMDB] TextMDB.onMessage, this=15679078
19:15:47,065 INFO  [TextMDB] TextMDB.sendReply, this=15679078, dest=QUEUE.A
```

Items of note in this example include the following:

- The JMS client has no explicit knowledge that it is dealing with an MDB. The client simply uses the standard JMS APIs to send messages to a queue and receive messages from another queue.
- The MDB declares whether it will listen to a queue or topic in the `ejb-jar.xml` descriptor. The name of the queue or topic must be specified using a `jboss.xml` descriptor. In this example, the MDB also sends messages to a JMS queue. MDBs may act as queue senders or topic publishers within their `onMessage` callback.
- The messages received by the client include a "processed by: *NNN*" suffix, where *NNN* is the `hashCode` value of the MDB instance that processed the message. This shows that many MDBs may actively process messages posted to a destination. Concurrent processing is one of the benefits of MDBs.

JBossMQ Overview

JBossMQ is composed of several services that work together to provide JMS API–level services to client applications. The services that make up the JBossMQ JMS implementation are introduced in the following sections.

The Invocation Layer Services

The invocation layer (IL) services are responsible for handling the communication protocols that clients use to send and receive messages. JBossMQ can support running different types of ILs concurrently. All ILs support bidirectional communication, which allows clients to send and receive messages concurrently. ILs only handle the transport details of messaging. They delegate messages to the JMS server JMX gateway service known as the *invoker*. This is similar to how the detached invokers expose the EJB container via different transports.

Each IL service binds a JMS connection factory to a specific location in the JNDI tree. Clients choose the protocol they wish to use by the JNDI location used to obtain the JMS connection factory. JBossMQ currently has several different ILs:

- **UIL2 IL**—The Unified IL, version 2 (UIL2) is the preferred IL for remote messaging. A multiplexing layer is used to provide bidirectional communication. The multiplexing layer creates two virtual sockets over one physical socket. This allows communication with clients that cannot have a connection created from the server back to the client due to firewall or other restrictions. Unlike the older UIL invocation layer, which uses a blocking round-trip message at the socket level, the UIL2 protocol uses true asynchronous send and receive messaging at the transport level, providing for improved throughput and utilization.
- **JVM IL**—The Java Virtual Machine (JVM) IL was developed to cut out the TCP/IP overhead when the JMS client is running in the same JVM as the server. This IL uses direct method calls for the server to service the client requests. This increases efficiency because no sockets are created and there is no need for the associated worker threads. This is the IL that should be used by MDBs or any other component that runs in the same VM as the server, such as servlets, MBeans, or EJBs.
- **HTTP IL**—The HTTP IL allows for accessing the JBossMQ service over the HTTP or HTTPS protocols. This IL relies on the servlet deployed in the `deploy/jms/jbossmq-httpil.sar` to handle the HTTP traffic. This IL is useful for access to JMS through a firewall when the only port allowed requires HTTP.

The `SecurityManager` Service

The JBossMQ `SecurityManager` service enforces an access control list to guard access to your destinations. This subsystem works closely with the `StateManager` service.

The `DestinationManager` Service

You can think of the `DestinationManager` service as being the central service in JBossMQ. It keeps track of all the destinations that have been created on the server. It also keeps track of the other key services, such as `MessageCache`, `StateManager`, and `PersistenceManager`.

The `MessageCache` Service

Messages created in the server are passed to the `MessageCache` service for memory management. JVM memory usage goes up as messages are added to a destination that does not have any receivers. These messages are held in the main memory until the receiver picks them up. If the `MessageCache` service notices that the JVM memory usage starts passing the defined limits, `MessageCache` starts moving those messages from memory to persistent storage on disk. The `MessageCache` uses a least recently used (LRU) algorithm to determine which messages should go to disk.

The `StateManager` Service

The `StateManager` (SM) service is in charge of keeping track of who is allowed to log in to the server and what their durable subscriptions are.

The `PersistenceManager` Service

A destination uses the `PersistenceManager` service to store messages marked as being persistent. JBossMQ has several different implementations of the persistence manager (PM), but only one can be enabled per server instance. You should enable the PM that best matches your requirements:

- **The JDBC2 PM**—The JDBC2 PM allows you to store persistent messages to a relational database by using JDBC. The performance of this PM is directly related to the performance that can be obtained from the database. This PM has a very low memory overhead compared to the other PMs. Furthermore, it is highly integrated with the `MessageCache` to provide efficient persistence on a system that has a very active `MessageCache`.
- **The null PM**—This wrapper PM can delegate to a real PM.

Configurations on the destinations decide whether persistence and caching are actually performed. You can find an example of a configuration in `docs/examples/jms`. To use the null PM backed by a real PM, you need to change the `ObjectName` of the real PM and link the new name to the null PM.

Destinations

A *destination* is the object on the JBossMQ server that clients use to send and receive messages. There are two types of destination objects: queues and topics. References to the destinations created by JBossMQ are stored in JNDI.

Queues

Clients that are in the P2P paradigm typically use queues. They expect that messages sent to a queue will be received by only one other client, only once. If multiple clients are receiving messages from a single queue, the messages will be load balanced across the receivers. Queue objects, by default, are stored under the JNDI `queue/` subcontext.

Topics

Topics are used in the pub-sub paradigm. When a client publishes a message to a topic, he or she expects that a copy of the message will be delivered to each client that has subscribed to the topic. Topic messages are delivered in a manner similar to how a television show is delivered: Unless you have the TV on and are watching the show, you will miss it. Similarly, if the client is not up, running, and receiving messages from the topics, it will miss messages published to the topic. To get around this problem of missing messages, clients can start a durable subscription. This is like having a VCR or DVR record a show you cannot watch at its scheduled time so that you can see what you missed when you turn your TV back on.

JBossMQ Configuration and MBeans

The following sections define the MBean services that correspond to the components introduced in the previous section, along with their MBean attributes. The configuration and service files that make up the JBossMQ system include the following:

- **`deploy/hsqldb-jdbc-state-service.xml`**—This service descriptor configures the JDBC state service for storing state in the embedded Hypersonic database.
- **`deploy/jms/hsqldb-jdbc2-service.xml`**—This service descriptor configures the `DestinationManager`, `MessageCache`, and JDBC2 `PersistenceManager` services for the embedded Hypersonic database.
- **`deploy/jms/jbossmq-destinations-service.xml`**—This service defines the default JMS queue and topic destination configurations used by the testsuite unit tests. You can add destinations to this file, remove destinations from this file, or deploy another `*-service.xml` descriptor with the destination configurations.
- **`jbossmq-httpil.sar`**—This SAR file configures the HTTP IL.
- **`deploy/jms/jbossmq-service.xml`**—This service descriptor configures the core JBossMQ MBeans, such as the `Invoker`, `SecurityManager`, `DynamicStateManager`, and core interceptor stack. It also defines the MDB default dead-letter queue, `DLQ`.
- **`deploy/jms/jms-ds.xml`**—This is a JCA connection factory and JMS provider MDB integration services configuration that sets JBossMQ as the JMS provider.
- **`deploy/jms/jms-ra.rar`**—This is a JCA resource adaptor for JMS providers.
- **`deploy/jms/jvm-il-service.xml`**—This service descriptor configures the `JVMServerILService`, which provides the JVM IL transport.

- **`deploy/jms/rmi-il-service.xml`**—This service descriptor configures the `RMIServerILService`, which provides the RMI IL. The queue and topic connection factory for this IL is bound under the name `RMIConnectionFactory`.
- **`deploy/jms/uil2-service.xml`**—This service descriptor configures the `UILServerILService`, which provides the UIL2 transport. The queue and topic connection factory for this IL is bound under the name `UIL2ConnectionFactory` as well as `UILConnectionFactory`, to replace the deprecated version 1 UIL service.

The following sections discuss the associated MBeans.

The `org.jboss.mq.il.jvm.JVMServerILService` MBean

You use the `org.jboss.mq.il.jvm.JVMServerILService` MBean to configure the JVM IL. The configurable attributes are as follows:

- **`Invoker`**—This attribute specifies the JMX `ObjectName` of the JMS entry point service that is used to pass incoming requests to the JMS server. This is not something you would typically change from the `jboss.mq:service=Invoker` setting unless you change the entry point service.
- **`ConnectionFactoryJNDIRef`**—This is the JNDI location that this IL will bind a `ConnectionFactory` setup to in order to use this IL.
- **`XAConnectionFactoryJNDIRef`**—This is the JNDI location that this IL will bind a `XAConnectionFactory` setup to in order to use this IL.
- **`PingPeriod`**—This attribute specifies how often, in milliseconds, the client should send a `ping` message to the server to validate that the connection is still valid. If this is set to `0`, no `ping` message will be sent. Because it is impossible for a JVM IL connection to go bad, it is recommended that you keep this set to `0`.

The `org.jboss.mq.il.uil2.UILServerILService` MBean

You use the `org.jboss.mq.il.uil2.UILServerILService` MBean to configure the UIL2 IL. Its configurable attributes are as follows:

- **`Invoker`**—This attribute specifies the JMX `ObjectName` of the JMS entry point service that is used to pass incoming requests to the JMS server. This is not something you would typically change from the `jboss.mq:service=Invoker` setting unless you change the entry point service.
- **`ConnectionFactoryJNDIRef`**—This is the JNDI location that this IL will bind a `ConnectionFactory` setup to in order to use this IL.
- **`XAConnectionFactoryJNDIRef`**—This is the JNDI location that this IL will bind a `XAConnectionFactory` setup to in order to use this IL.

- **PingPeriod**—This attribute specifies how often, in milliseconds, the client should send a ping message to the server to validate that the connection is still valid. If this is set to 0, no ping message will be sent.
- **ReadTimeout**—This is the period, in milliseconds, of the SoTimeout value of the UIL2 socket. This allows detection of dead sockets that are not responsive and are not capable of receiving ping messages. Note that this setting should be longer in duration than the PingPeriod setting.
- **BufferSize**—This is the size, in bytes, used as the buffer over the basic socket streams. This corresponds to the java.io.BufferedOutputStream buffer size.
- **ChunkSize**—This is the size, in bytes, between stream listener notifications. UIL2 uses the org.jboss.util.stream.NotifyingBufferedOutputStream and NotifyingBufferedInputStream implementations that support the notion of a heartbeat that is triggered based on data read/written to the stream. This serves as a ping or keep-alive notification when large reads or writes require a duration greater than the PingPeriod.
- **ServerBindPort**—This is the protocol listening port for this IL. If it is not specified, the default is 0, which means that a random port will be chosen.
- **BindAddress**—This is the specific address on which this IL listens. This can be used on a multi-homed host for a java.net.ServerSocket that will only accept connection requests on one of its addresses.
- **EnableTcpNoDelay**—TcpNoDelay causes TCP/IP packets to be sent as soon as the request is flushed. This may improve request response times. Otherwise, the operating system may buffer request packets to create larger IP packets.
- **ServerSocketFactory**—This is the javax.net.ServerSocketFactory implementation classname to use to create the service java.net.ServerSocket. If it is not specified, the default factory will be obtained from javax.net.ServerSocketFactory.getDefault().
- **ClientAddress**—This is the address passed to the client as the address that should be used to connect to the server.
- **ClientSocketFactory**—This is the javax.net.SocketFactory implementation classname to use on the client. If it is not specified, the default factory will be obtained from javax.net.SocketFactory.getDefault().
- **SecurityDomain**—This attribute specifies the security domain name to use with JBoss SSL-aware socket factories. This is the JNDI name of the security manager implementation, as described for the security-domain element of the jboss.xml and jboss-web.xml descriptors in Chapter 8, "Security on JBoss."

Configuring UIL2 for SSL

The UIL2 service support the use of SSL through custom socket factories that integrate JSSE, using the security domain associated with the IL service. An example of a UIL2 service descriptor fragment that illustrates the use of the custom JBoss SSL socket factories is shown in Listing 6.10.

LISTING 6.10 An Example of a UIL2 Config Fragment for Using SSL

```
<mbean code="org.jboss.mq.il.uil2.UILServerILService"
    name="jboss.mq:service=InvocationLayer,type=HTTPSUIL2">
    <depends optional-attribute-name="Invoker">jboss.mq:service=Invoker</depends>
    <attribute name="ConnectionFactoryJNDIRef">SSLConnectionFactory</attribute>
    <attribute name="XAConnectionFactoryJNDIRef">SSLXAConnectionFactory
➥</attribute>

    <!-- ... -->

    <!-- SSL Socket Factories -->
    <attribute name="ClientSocketFactory">
        org.jboss.security.ssl.ClientSocketFactory
    </attribute>
    <attribute name="ServerSocketFactory">
        org.jboss.security.ssl.DomainServerSocketFactory
    </attribute>
    <!-- Security domain - see below -->
    <attribute name="SecurityDomain">java:/jaas/SSL</attribute>
</mbean>

<!-- Configures the keystore on the "SSL" security domain
     This mbean is better placed in conf/jboss-service.xml where it
     can be used by other services, but it will work from anywhere.
     Use keytool from the sdk to create the keystore. -->

<mbean code="org.jboss.security.plugins.JaasSecurityDomain"
      name="jboss.security:service=JaasSecurityDomain,domain=SSL">
    <!-- This must correlate with the java:/jaas/SSL above -->
    <constructor>
        <arg type="java.lang.String" value="SSL"/>
    </constructor>
    <!-- The location of the keystore resource: loads from the
         classpath and the server conf dir is a good default -->
    <attribute name="KeyStoreURL">resource:uil2.keystore</attribute>
    <attribute name="KeyStorePass">changeme</attribute>
</mbean>
```

JMS Client Properties for the UIL2 Transport

A JMS client using the UIL2 transport can set several system properties to control the client connection back to the server:

- **org.jboss.mq.il.uil2.useServerHost**—This system property allows a client to connect to the server InetAddress.getHostName rather than the InetAddress.getHostAddress value. This makes a difference only if name resolution differs between the server and client environments.
- **org.jboss.mq.il.uil2.localAddr**—This system property allows a client to define the local interface to which its sockets should be bound.
- **org.jboss.mq.il.uil2.localPort**—This system property allows a client to define the local port to which its sockets should be bound.
- **org.jboss.mq.il.uil2.serverAddr**—This system property allows a client to override the address to which it attempts to connect. This is useful for networks where NAT is occurring between the client and the JMS server.
- **org.jboss.mq.il.uil2.serverPort**—This system property allows a client to override the port to which it attempts to connect. This is useful for networks where port forwarding is occurring between the client and the JMS server.
- **org.jboss.mq.il.uil2.retryCount**—Thissystem property controls the number of attempts to retry connecting to the JMS server. Retries are made only for java.net.ConnectException failures. A value that is less than or equal to zero means no retry attempts will be made.
- **org.jboss.mq.il.uil2.retryDelay**—This system property controls the delay, in milliseconds, between retries due to ConnectException failures.

The org.jboss.mq.il.http.HTTPServerILService MBean

You use org.jboss.mq.il.http.HTTPServerILService to manage the HTTP/HTTPS IL. This IL allows for the use of the JMS service over HTTP or HTTPS connections. It relies on the servlet deployed in the deploy/jms/jbossmq-httpil.sar to handle the HTTP traffic. The configurable attributes are as follows:

- **TimeOut**—The default timeout, in seconds, that the client HTTP requests will wait for messages. You can override this on the client by setting the system property org.jboss.mq.il.http.timeout to the number of seconds.
- **RestInterval**—The number of seconds the client will sleep after each request. The default is 0, but you can set this value in conjunction with the TimeOut value to implement a purely time-based polling mechanism. For example, you could simply do a short-lived request by setting the TimeOut value to 0 and then setting RestInterval to 60. This would cause the client to send a single nonblocking request to the server, return any messages, if available, and sleep for 60 seconds before issuing another request. As with the TimeOut value, you can override this value explicitly on a given client by specifying the org.jboss.mq.il.http.restinterval with the number of seconds to wait between requests.

- **URL**—The servlet URL. This value takes precedence over any individual values set (for example, `URLPrefix`, `URLSuffix`, `URLPort`). It may be an actual URL or a property name that will be used on the client side to resolve the proper URL by calling `System.getProperty(`*`propertyname`*`)`. If it is not specified, the URL will be formed from `URLPrefix+URLHostName+":"+URLPort+"/"+URLSuffix`.
- **URLPrefix**—The prefix portion of the servlet URL.
- **URLHostName**—The hostname portion of the servlet URL.
- **URLPort**—The port portion of the URL.
- **URLSuffix**—The trailing path portion of the URL.
- **UseHostName**—A flag that, if set to `true`, means the default setting for the `URLHostName` attribute will be taken from `InetAddress.getLocalHost().getHostName()`. If it is `false`, the default setting for the `URLHostName` attribute will be taken from `InetAddress.getLocalHost().getHostAddress()`.

The `org.jboss.mq.server.jmx.Invoker` MBean

You use `org.jboss.mq.server.jmx.Invoker` to pass IL requests down to the `DestinationManager` service through an interceptor stack. There is one configurable attribute:

- **NextInterceptor**—The JMX `ObjectName` of the next request interceptor. All the interceptors use this attribute to create the interceptor stack. The last interceptor in the chain should be the `DestinationManager`.

The `org.jboss.mq.server.jmx.InterceptorLoader` MBean

You use `org.jboss.mq.server.jmx.InterceptorLoader` to load a generic interceptor and make it part of the interceptor stack. You typically use this MBean to load custom interceptors such as `org.jboss.mq.server.TracingInterceptor`, which you can use to efficiently log all client requests via trace-level log messages. The configurable attributes are as follows:

- **NextInterceptor**—The JMX `ObjectName` of the next request interceptor. All the interceptors use this attribute to create the interceptor stack. The last interceptor in the chain should be the `DestinationManager`. This attribute should be set up via a `<depends optional-attribute-name="NextInterceptor">` XML tag.
- **InterceptorClass**—The classname of the interceptor that will be loaded and made part of the interceptor stack. The class specified here must extend the `org.jboss.mq.server.JMSServerInterceptor` class.

The `org.jboss.mq.sm.jdbc.JDBCStateManager` MBean

You use the `JDBCStateManager` MBean as the default state manager assigned to the `DestinationManager` service. It stores user and durable subscriber information in the database. The configurable attributes are as follows:

- **`ConnectionManager`**—This is the `ObjectName` of the datasource that the JDBC state manager will write to. For Hypersonic, it is `jboss.jca:service=DataSourceBinding,name=DefaultDS`.
- **`SqlProperties`**—This defines the SQL statements to be used to persist JMS state data. If the underlying database is changed, the SQL statements used may need to change.

The `org.jboss.mq.security.SecurityManager` MBean

If `org.jboss.mq.security.SecurityManager` is part of the interceptor stack, it will enforce the access control lists assigned to the destinations. `SecurityManager` uses JAAS, and it therefore requires that an application policy be set up in the JBoss `login-config.xml` file. The default configuration is as follows:

```
<application-policy name="jbossmq">
    <authentication>
        <login-module code="org.jboss.security.auth.spi.DatabaseServerLoginModule"
➥flag="required">
            <module-option name="unauthenticatedIdentity">guest</module-option>
            <module-option name="dsJndiName">java:/DefaultDS</module-option>
            <module-option name="principalsQuery">SELECT PASSWD FROM JMS_USERS
                WHERE USERID=?</module-option>
            <module-option name="rolesQuery">SELECT ROLEID, 'Roles' FROM
                JMS_ROLES WHERE USERID=?</module-option>
        </login-module>
    </authentication>
</application-policy>
```

The configurable attributes of the `SecurityManager` MBean are as follows:

- **`NextInterceptor`**—The JMX `ObjectName` of the next request interceptor. This attribute is used by all the interceptors to create the interceptor stack. The last interceptor in the chain should be `DestinationManager`.
- **`SecurityDomain`**—The security domain name to use for authentication and role-based authorization. This is the JNDI name of the JAAS domain against which to perform authentication and authorization.
- **`DefaultSecurityConfig`**—The default security configuration settings for destinations. This applies to temporary queues and topics as well as queues and topics that do not specify a security configuration. `DefaultSecurityConfig` should declare some

number of `role` elements, which represent each role that is allowed access to a destination. Each `role` should have the following attributes:

- **`name`**—The `name` attribute defines the name of the role.
- **`create`**—The `create` attribute is a `true/false` value that indicates whether the role has the ability to create durable subscriptions on the topic.
- **`read`**—The `read` attribute is a `true/false` value that indicates whether the role can receive messages from the destination.
- **`write`**—The `write` attribute is a `true/false` value that indicates whether the role can send messages to the destination.

The `org.jboss.mq.server.jmx.DestinationManager` MBean

`org.jboss.mq.server.jmx.DestinationManager` must be the last interceptor in the interceptor stack. The configurable attributes are as follows:

- **`PersistenceManager`**—The JMX `ObjectName` of the PM service the server should use.
- **`StateManager`**—The JMX `ObjectName` of the SM service the server should use.
- **`MessageCache`**—The JMX `ObjectName` of the message cache service the server should use.

Additional read-only attributes and operations that support monitoring include the following:

- **`ClientCount`**—The number of clients connected to the server.
- **`Clients`**—The `java.util.Map<org.jboss.mq.ConnectionToken,org.jboss.mq.server.ClientConsumer>` instances for the clients connected to the server.
- **`MessageCounter`**—An array of `org.jboss.mq.server.MessageCounter` instances that provide statistics for a JMS destination.
- **`listMessageCounter()`**—An operation that generates an HTML table that contains the following:
    - **`Type`**—Either `Queue` or `Topic`, indicating the destination type.
    - **`Name`**—The name of the destination.
    - **`Subscription`**—The subscription ID for a topic.
    - **`Durable`**—A Boolean that indicates whether the topic subscription is durable.
    - **`Count`**—The number of messages delivered to the destination.
    - **`CountDelta`**—The change in message count since the previous access of `Count`.
    - **`Depth`**—The number of messages in the destination.

- **DepthDelta**—The change in the number of messages in the destination since the previous access of Depth.
- **Last Add**—The date/time string, in DateFormat.SHORT/DateFormat.MEDIUM format, of the last time a message was added to the destination.

- **resetMessageCounter()**—A method that zeros all destination counts and last added times.

You can create and destroy queues and topics at runtime through the DestinationManager MBean. DestinationManager provides createQueue and createTopic operations for this. Each of these methods has a one-argument version that takes the destination name and a two-argument version that takes the destination and the JNDI name of the destination. You can remove queues and topics by using the destroyQueue and destroyTopic operations, both of which take a destination name as input.

The org.jboss.mq.server.MessageCache MBean

The server determines when to move messages to secondary storage by using the org.jboss.mq.server.MessageCache MBean. The configurable attributes are as follows:

- **CacheStore**—The JMX ObjectName of the service that will act as the cache store. MessageCache uses the cache store to move messages to persistent storage. The value you set here typically depends on the type of PM you are using.
- **HighMemoryMark**—The amount of JVM heap memory, in megabytes, that must be reached before the MessageCache starts to move messages to secondary storage.
- **MaxMemoryMark**—The maximum amount of JVM heap memory, in megabytes, that the MessageCache considers to be the maximum memory mark. As memory usage approaches the maximum memory mark, MessageCache will move messages to persistent storage so that the number of messages kept in memory approaches zero.
- **MakeSoftReferences**—Whether the message cache will keep soft references to messages that need to be removed. The default is true.
- **MinimumHard**—The minimum number of the in-memory cache. JBoss won't try to go below this number of messages in the cache. The default value is 1.
- **MaximumHard**—The upper bound on the number of hard references to messages in the cache. JBoss will soften messages to reduce the number of hard references to this level. A value of 0 means that there is no size-based upper bound. The default is 0.
- **SoftenWaitMillis**—The maximum wait time before checking whether messages need softening. The default is 1000 milliseconds (1 second).
- **SoftenNoMoreOftenThanMillis**—The minimum amount of time between checks to soften messages. A value of 0 means that this check should be skipped. The default is 0 milliseconds.

- **SoftenAtLeastEveryMillis**—The maximum amount of time between checks to soften messages. A value of 0 means that this check should be skipped. The default is 0.

Additional read-only cache attributes that provide statistics include the following:

- **CacheHits**—The number of times a hard referenced message was accessed.
- **CacheMisses**—The number of times a softened message was accessed.
- **HardRefCacheSize**—The number of messages in the cache that are not softened.
- **SoftRefCacheSize**—The number of messages that are currently softened.
- **SoftenedSize**—The total number of messages softened since the last boot.
- **TotalCacheSize**—The total number of messages that are being managed by the cache.

The `org.jboss.mq.pm.jdbc2.PersistenceManager` MBean

You should use `org.jboss.mq.pm.jdbc.PersistenceManager` as the PM assigned to the `DestinationManager` service if you want to store messages in a database. This PM has been tested against the HypersonSQL, Microsoft SQL, Oracle, MySQL, and PostgreSQL databases. The configurable attributes are as follows

- **MessageCache**—The JMX `ObjectName` of the `MessageCache` that has been assigned to the `DestinationManager`.
- **ConnectionManager**—The JMX `ObjectName` of the JCA data source that will be used to obtain JDBC connections.
- **ConnectionRetryAttempts**—An integer count used to allow the PM to retry attempts at getting a connection to the JDBC store. There is a 1500-millisecond delay between each failed connection attempt and the next attempt. This value must be greater than or equal to `1` and defaults to `5`.
- **SqlProperties**—A property list that is used to define the SQL queries and other JDBC2 PM options. You need to adjust these properties if you want to run against a database other than Hypersonic. Listing 6.11 shows the default setting for this attribute for the Hypersonic database.

LISTING 6.11 The Default JDBC2 `PeristenceManager` `SqlProperties` Attribute Setting for Hypersonic

```
<attribute name="SqlProperties">
      CREATE_TABLES_ON_STARTUP = TRUE
      CREATE_USER_TABLE = CREATE TABLE JMS_USERS (USERID VARCHAR(32) NOT NULL,
➥PASSWD VARCHAR(32) NOT NULL, \
```

LISTING 6.11 Continued

```
                                                CLIENTID VARCHAR(128), PRIMARY
➥ KEY(USERID))
    CREATE_ROLE_TABLE = CREATE TABLE JMS_ROLES (ROLEID VARCHAR(32) NOT NULL,
➥USERID VARCHAR(32) NOT NULL, \
                                                PRIMARY KEY(USERID, ROLEID))
    CREATE_SUBSCRIPTION_TABLE = CREATE TABLE JMS_SUBSCRIPTIONS (CLIENTID
➥ VARCHAR(128) NOT NULL, \
                                                SUBNAME VARCHAR(128)
➥NOT NULL, TOPIC VARCHAR(255) NOT NULL, \
                                                SELECTOR VARCHAR(255),
➥PRIMARY KEY(CLIENTID, SUBNAME))
    GET_SUBSCRIPTION = SELECT TOPIC, SELECTOR FROM JMS_SUBSCRIPTIONS
➥WHERE CLIENTID=? AND SUBNAME=?
    LOCK_SUBSCRIPTION = SELECT TOPIC, SELECTOR FROM JMS_SUBSCRIPTIONS
➥WHERE CLIENTID=? AND SUBNAME=?
    GET_SUBSCRIPTIONS_FOR_TOPIC = SELECT CLIENTID, SUBNAME, SELECTOR
➥FROM JMS_SUBSCRIPTIONS WHERE TOPIC=?
    INSERT_SUBSCRIPTION = INSERT INTO JMS_SUBSCRIPTIONS
➥(CLIENTID, SUBNAME, TOPIC, SELECTOR) VALUES(?,?,?,?)
    UPDATE_SUBSCRIPTION = UPDATE JMS_SUBSCRIPTIONS SET TOPIC=?,
➥SELECTOR=? WHERE CLIENTID=? AND SUBNAME=?
    REMOVE_SUBSCRIPTION = DELETE FROM JMS_SUBSCRIPTIONS
➥WHERE CLIENTID=? AND SUBNAME=?
    GET_USER_BY_CLIENTID = SELECT USERID, PASSWD, CLIENTID
➥FROM JMS_USERS WHERE CLIENTID=?
    GET_USER = SELECT PASSWD, CLIENTID FROM JMS_USERS WHERE USERID=?
    POPULATE.TABLES.01 = INSERT INTO JMS_USERS (USERID, PASSWD)
➥VALUES ('guest', 'guest')
    POPULATE.TABLES.02 = INSERT INTO JMS_USERS (USERID, PASSWD)
➥VALUES ('j2ee', 'j2ee')
    POPULATE.TABLES.03 = INSERT INTO JMS_USERS (USERID, PASSWD, CLIENTID)
➥VALUES ('john', 'needle', 'DurableSubscriberExample')
    POPULATE.TABLES.04 = INSERT INTO JMS_USERS (USERID, PASSWD) VALUES
➥ ('nobody', 'nobody')
    POPULATE.TABLES.05 = INSERT INTO JMS_USERS (USERID, PASSWD) VALUES
➥ ('dynsub', 'dynsub')
    POPULATE.TABLES.06 = INSERT INTO JMS_ROLES (ROLEID, USERID) VALUES
➥ ('guest','guest')
    POPULATE.TABLES.07 = INSERT INTO JMS_ROLES (ROLEID, USERID) VALUES
➥ ('j2ee','guest')
    POPULATE.TABLES.08 = INSERT INTO JMS_ROLES (ROLEID, USERID) VALUES
➥ ('john','guest')
    POPULATE.TABLES.09 = INSERT INTO JMS_ROLES (ROLEID, USERID) VALUES
➥ ('subscriber','john')
```

LISTING 6.11 Continued

```
      POPULATE.TABLES.10 = INSERT INTO JMS_ROLES (ROLEID, USERID) VALUES
➥ ('publisher','john')
      POPULATE.TABLES.11 = INSERT INTO JMS_ROLES (ROLEID, USERID) VALUES
➥ ('publisher','dynsub')
      POPULATE.TABLES.12 = INSERT INTO JMS_ROLES (ROLEID, USERID) VALUES
➥ ('durpublisher','john')
      POPULATE.TABLES.13 = INSERT INTO JMS_ROLES (ROLEID, USERID) VALUES
➥ ('durpublisher','dynsub')
      POPULATE.TABLES.14 = INSERT INTO JMS_ROLES (ROLEID, USERID) VALUES
➥ ('noacc','nobody')
</attribute>
```

Listing 6.12 shows an alternate setting for Oracle.

LISTING 6.12 A Sample JDBC2 `PeristenceManager` `SqlProperties` Attribute Setting for Oracle

```
<attribute name="SqlProperties">
      BLOB_TYPE=BINARYSTREAM_BLOB
      INSERT_TX = INSERT INTO JMS_TRANSACTIONS (TXID) values(?)
      INSERT_MESSAGE = INSERT INTO JMS_MESSAGES (MESSAGEID, DESTINATION,
➥MESSAGEBLOB, TXID, TXOP) VALUES(?,?,?,?,?)
      SELECT_ALL_UNCOMMITED_TXS = SELECT TXID FROM JMS_TRANSACTIONS
      SELECT_MAX_TX = SELECT MAX(TXID) FROM JMS_MESSAGES
      SELECT_MESSAGES_IN_DEST = SELECT MESSAGEID, MESSAGEBLOB FROM JMS_MESSAGES
➥ WHERE DESTINATION=?
      SELECT_MESSAGE = SELECT MESSAGEID, MESSAGEBLOB FROM JMS_MESSAGES WHERE
➥ MESSAGEID=? AND DESTINATION=?
      MARK_MESSAGE = UPDATE JMS_MESSAGES SET TXID=?, TXOP=? WHERE MESSAGEID=?
➥ AND DESTINATION=?
      UPDATE_MESSAGE = UPDATE JMS_MESSAGES SET MESSAGEBLOB=? WHERE MESSAGEID=?
➥ AND DESTINATION=?
      UPDATE_MARKED_MESSAGES = UPDATE JMS_MESSAGES SET TXID=?, TXOP=?
➥ WHERE TXOP=?
      UPDATE_MARKED_MESSAGES_WITH_TX = UPDATE JMS_MESSAGES SET TXID=?,
➥TXOP=? WHERE TXOP=? AND TXID=?
      DELETE_MARKED_MESSAGES_WITH_TX = DELETE FROM JMS_MESSAGES MESS WHERE
➥ TXOP=:1 AND EXISTS (SELECT TXID FROM JMS_TRANSACTIONS TX
➥WHERE TX.TXID = MESS.TXID)
      DELETE_TX = DELETE FROM JMS_TRANSACTIONS WHERE TXID = ?
      DELETE_MARKED_MESSAGES = DELETE FROM JMS_MESSAGES WHERE TXID=? AND TXOP=?
      DELETE_TEMPORARY_MESSAGES = DELETE FROM JMS_MESSAGES WHERE TXOP='T'
      DELETE_MESSAGE = DELETE FROM JMS_MESSAGES WHERE MESSAGEID=? AND DESTINATION=?
      CREATE_MESSAGE_TABLE = CREATE TABLE JMS_MESSAGES
➥( MESSAGEID INTEGER NOT NULL, \
```

LISTING 6.12 Continued

```
        DESTINATION VARCHAR(255) NOT NULL, TXID INTEGER, TXOP CHAR(1), \
        MESSAGEBLOB BLOB, PRIMARY KEY (MESSAGEID, DESTINATION) )
    CREATE_IDX_MESSAGE_TXOP_TXID = CREATE INDEX JMS_MESSAGES_TXOP_TXID ON
➥JMS_MESSAGES (TXOP, TXID)
    CREATE_IDX_MESSAGE_DESTINATION = CREATE INDEX JMS_MESSAGES_DESTINATION ON
➥JMS_MESSAGES (DESTINATION)
    CREATE_TX_TABLE = CREATE TABLE JMS_TRANSACTIONS ( TXID INTEGER, PRIMARY KEY
➥(TXID) )
    CREATE_TABLES_ON_STARTUP = TRUE
</attribute>
```

You can find additional examples in the `docs/examples/jms` directory of the distribution.

Destination MBeans

The following sections describe the destination MBeans used in the `jbossmq-destinations-service.xml` and `jbossmq-service.xml` descriptors.

The `org.jboss.mq.server.jmx.Queue` MBean

You use the `Queue` MBean to define a queue destination in JBoss. The following shows the configuration of one of the default JBoss queues:

```
<mbean code="org.jboss.mq.server.jmx.Queue"
       name="jboss.mq.destination:service=Queue,name=testQueue">
    <depends optional-attribute-name="DestinationManager">
        jboss.mq:service=DestinationManager
    </depends>
    <depends optional-attribute-name="SecurityManager">
        jboss.mq:service=SecurityManager
    </depends>
    <attribute name="MessageCounterHistoryDayLimit">-1</attribute>
    <attribute name="SecurityConf">
        <security>
            <role name="guest"     read="true"  write="true"/>
            <role name="publisher" read="true"  write="true" create="false"/>
            <role name="noacc"     read="false" write="false" create="false"/>
        </security>
    </attribute>
</mbean>
```

You use the `name` attribute of the JMX `ObjectName` of this MBean to determine the destination name. For example, the name of the queue we just looked at is `testQueue`. The configurable attributes are as follows:

- **DestinationManager**—The JMX ObjectName of the destination manager service for the server. This attribute should be set via a <depends optional-attribute-name="DestinationManager"> XML tag.
- **SecurityManager**—The JMX ObjectName of the security manager service that is being used to validate client requests.
- **SecurityConf**—An XML fragment that describes the access control list to be used by the SecurityManager to authorize client operations against the destination. The content model is the same as for the SecurityConf attribute on the SecurityManager.
- **JNDIName**—The location in JNDI to which the queue object will be bound. If this is not set, it will be bound under the queue context, using the name of the queue. For the testQueue shown earlier, the JNDI name would be queue/testQueue.
- **MaxDepth**—An upper limit to the backlog of messages that can exist for a destination. If this value is exceeded, attempts to add new messages will result in an org.jboss.mq.DestinationFullException. The MaxDepth can still be exceeded in a number of situations, such as when a message is placed back into the queue. Also, transactions performing read-committed processing look at the current size of queue, ignoring any messages that may be added as a result of the current transaction or other transactions. This is because you don't want the transaction to fail during the commit phase, when the message is physically added to the queue.
- **MessageCounterHistoryDayLimit**—The destination message counter history day limit, which has a value less than 0 to indicate unlimited history, a 0 value to disable the history, and a value greater than 0 to give the history days count.

Additional read-only attributes that provide statistics information include the following:

- **MessageCounter**—An array of org.jboss.mq.server.MessageCounter instances that provide statistics for this destination.
- **QueueDepth**—The current backlog of waiting messages.
- **ReceiversCount**—The number of receivers currently associated with the queue.
- **ScheduledMessageCount**—The number of messages waiting in the queue for their scheduled delivery time to arrive.
- **listMessageCounter()**—An operation that generates an HTML table that contains the same data as the listMessageCounter operation on the DestinationManager, but only for this one queue.
- **resetMessageCounter()**—A method that zeros all destination counts and last added times.

- **listMessageCounterHistory()**—An operation that displays an HTML table showing the hourly message counts per hour for each day in the history.
- **resetMessageCounterHistory()**—An operation that resets the day history message counts.

The `org.jboss.mq.server.jmx.Topic` MBean

You use `org.jboss.mq.server.jmx.Topic` to define a topic destination in JBoss. The following shows the configuration of one of the default JBoss topics:

```
<mbean code="org.jboss.mq.server.jmx.Topic"
       name="jboss.mq.destination:service=Topic,name=testTopic">
    <depends optional-attribute-name="DestinationManager">
        jboss.mq:service=DestinationManager
    </depends>
    <depends optional-attribute-name="SecurityManager">
        jboss.mq:service=SecurityManager
    </depends>
    <attribute name="SecurityConf">
        <security>
            <role name="guest"        read="true" write="true" />
            <role name="publisher"    read="true" write="true" create="false" />
            <role name="durpublisher" read="true" write="true" create="true" />
        </security>
    </attribute>
</mbean>
```

The `name` attribute of the JMX object name of this MBean is used to determine the destination name. For example, the name of the topic we just looked at is `testTopic`. The configurable attributes are as follows:

- **DestinationManager**—The JMX object name of the destination manager configured for the server.
- **SecurityManager**—The JMX object name of the security manager that is being used to validate client requests.
- **SecurityConf**—An element that specifies an XML fragment that describes the access control list that `SecurityManager` should use to authorize client operations against the destination. The content model is the same as that for the `SecurityManager` `SecurityConf` attribute.
- **JNDIName**—The location in JNDI to which the topic object will be bound. If this is not set, it will be bound under the `topic` context, using the name of the queue. For the `testTopic` shown earlier, the JNDI name would be `topic/testTopic`.
- **MaxDepth**—An upper limit to the backlog of messages that can exist for a destination. If this value is exceeded, attempts to add new messages will result in a `org.jboss.mq.DestinationFullException`. The `MaxDepth` can still be exceeded in a

number of situations, such as when a message is placed back into the queue. Also, transactions that perform read-committed processing look at the current size of the queue, ignoring any messages that may be added as a result of the current transaction or other transactions. This is because you don't want the transaction to fail during the commit phase, when the message is physically added to the topic.

- **`MessageCounterHistoryDayLimit`**—The destination message counter history day limit, which is set with a value less than `0` to indicate unlimited history, a `0` value to disable history, and a value greater than `0` to give the history days count.

Additional read-only attributes that provide statistics information include the following:

- **`AllMessageCount`**—The message count across all queue types associated with the topic.
- **`AllSubscriptionsCount`**—The count of durable and non-durable subscriptions.
- **`DurableMessageCount`**—The count of messages in durable subscription queues.
- **`DurableSubscriptionsCount`**—The count of durable subscribers.
- **`MessageCounter`**—An array of `org.jboss.mq.server.MessageCounter` instances that provide statistics for this destination.
- **`NonDurableMessageCount`**—The count of messages in non-durable subscription queues.
- **`NonDurableSubscriptionsCount`**—The count of non-durable subscribers.
- **`listMessageCounter()`**—An operation that generates an HTML table that contains the same data as the `listMessageCounter` operation on the `DestinationManager`, but only for this one topic.
- **`resetMessageCounter()`**—An operation that zeros all destination counts and last added times.
- **`listMessageCounterHistory()`**—An operation that displays an HTML table showing the hourly message counts per hour for each day of history.
- **`resetMessageCounterHistory()`**—An operation that resets the day history message counts.

Specifying the MDB JMS Provider

Up to this point we have looked at the standard JMS client/server architecture. The JMS specification defines an advanced set of interfaces that allow for concurrent processing of a destination's messages, and collectively this functionality is referred to as *application server facilities (ASF)*. Two of the interfaces that support concurrent message processing, `javax.jms.ServerSessionPool` and `javax.jms.ServerSession`, must be provided by the application server in which the processing will occur. Thus, the set of components that make up the JBossMQ ASF involves both JBossMQ components and JBoss server components. The JBoss server MDB container utilizes the JMS service's ASF to concurrently process messages sent to MDBs.

The responsibilities of the ASF domains are well defined by the JMS specification, so we won't go into a discussion of how the ASF components are implemented. Rather, we'll discuss how ASF components used by the JBoss MDB layer are integrated, using MBeans that allow either the application server interfaces or the JMS provider interfaces to be replaced with alternate implementations.

Let's start with the `org.jboss.jms.jndi.JMSProviderLoader` MBean. This MBean is responsible for loading an instance of the `org.jboss.jms.jndi.JMSProviderAdaptor` interface into the JBoss server and binding it into JNDI. The `JMSProviderAdaptor` interface is an abstraction that defines how to get the root JNDI context for the JMS provider, and an interface for getting and setting the JNDI names for the `Context.PROVIDER_URL` for the root `InitialContext`, and the `QueueConnectionFactory` and `TopicConnectionFactory` locations in the root context.

This is all that is really necessary to bootstrap use of a JMS provider. By abstracting this information into an interface, you can use alternate JMS ASF provider implementations with the JBoss MDB container. `org.jboss.jms.jndi.JBossMQProvider` is the default implementation of the `JMSProviderAdaptor` interface, and it provides the adaptor for the JBossMQ JMS provider. To replace the JBossMQ provider with an alternate JMS ASF implementation, you simply create an implementation of the `JMSProviderAdaptor` interface and configure the `JMSProviderLoader` with the classname of the implementation. You'll see an example of this later in this chapter.

In addition to being able to replace the JMS provider used for MDBs, you can also replace the `javax.jms.ServerSessionPool` interface implementation. This is possible by configuring the classname of the `org.jboss.jms.asf.ServerSessionPoolFactory` implementation, using the `org.jboss.jms.asf.ServerSessionPoolLoader` MBean `PoolFactoryClass` attribute. The default `ServerSessionPoolFactory` factory implementation is the JBoss `org.jboss.jms.asf.StdServerSessionPoolFactory` class.

The `org.jboss.jms.jndi.JMSProviderLoader` MBean

The `JMSProviderLoader` MBean service creates a JMS provider adaptor and binds it into JNDI. A *JMS provider adaptor* is a class that implements the `org.jboss.jms.jndi.JMSProviderAdaptor` interface. It is used by the MDB container to access a JMS service provider in a provider-independent manner. The configurable attributes of the `JMSProviderLoader` service are as follows:

- **`ProviderName`**—A unique name for the JMS provider. This will be used to bind the `JMSProviderAdaptor` instance into JNDI under `java :/`*`<ProviderName>`* unless it is overridden by the `AdapterJNDIName` attribute.
- **`ProviderAdapterClass`**—The fully qualified classname of the `org.jboss.jms.jndi.JMSProviderAdaptor` interface to create an instance of. To use an alternate JMS provider, such as SonicMQ, you create an implementation of the

JMSProviderAdaptor interface that allows the administration of the InitialContext provider URL, and the locations of the QueueConnectionFactory and TopicConnectionFactory in JNDI.

- **AdapterJNDIName**—The exact JNDI name under which the JMSProviderAdaptor instance will be bound.
- **ProviderURL**—The JNDI Context.PROVIDER_URL value to use when creating the JMS provider root InitialContext.
- **QueueFactoryRef**—The JNDI name under which the provider javax.jms.QueueConnectionFactory will be bound.
- **TopicFactoryRef**—The JNDI name under which the javax.jms.TopicConnectionFactory will be bound.

Listing 6.13 shows a JMSProviderLoader for accessing a remote JBossMQ server.

LISTING 6.13 A JMSProviderLoader for Accessing a Remote JBossMQ Server

```
<mbean code="org.jboss.jms.jndi.JMSProviderLoader"
       name="jboss.mq:service=JMSProviderLoader,name=RemoteJBossMQProvider">
    <attribute name="ProviderName">RemoteJMSProvider</attribute>
    <attribute name="ProviderUrl">jnp://remotehost:1099</attribute>
    <attribute name="ProviderAdapterClass">
        org.jboss.jms.jndi.JBossMQProvider
    </attribute>
    <attribute name="QueueFactoryRef">XAConnectionFactory</attribute>
    <attribute name="TopicFactoryRef">XAConnectionFactory</attribute>
</mbean>
```

The RemoteJMSProvider can be referenced on the MDB invoker config, as shown in the jboss.xml fragment in Listing 6.14.

LISTING 6.14 A jboss.xml Fragment for Specifying the MDB JMSProviderAdapter

```
<proxy-factory-config>
    <JMSProviderAdaptorJNDI>RemoteJMSProvider</JMSProviderAdaptorJNDI>
    <ServerSessionPoolFactoryJNDI>StdJMSPool</ServerSessionPoolFactoryJNDI>
    <MaximumSize>15</MaximumSize>
    <MaxMessages>1</MaxMessages>
    <MDBConfig>
        <ReconnectIntervalSec>10</ReconnectIntervalSec>
        <DLQConfig>
            <DestinationQueue>queue/DLQ</DestinationQueue>
            <MaxTimesRedelivered>10</MaxTimesRedelivered>
            <TimeToLive>0</TimeToLive>
        </DLQConfig>
```

LISTING 6.14 Continued

```
    </MDBConfig>
</proxy-factory-config>
```

Incidentally, being able to specify multiple `invoker-proxy-binding` elements allows an MDB to listen to the same queue/topic on multiple servers because you can configure multiple bindings with different `JMSProviderAdaptorJNDI` settings. Alternatively, you can integrate the JMS provider by using a JCA configuration like the one shown in Listing 6.15.

LISTING 6.15 A `jms-ds.xml` Descriptor for Integrating a `JMSProviderAdapter` via JCA

```
<tx-connection-factory>
    <jndi-name>RemoteJmsXA</jndi-name>
    <xa-transaction/>
    <adapter-display-name>JMS Adapter</adapter-display-name>
    <config-property name="JMSProviderAdaptorJNDI"
                     type="java.lang.String">RemoteJMSProvider</config-property>
    <config-property name="SessionDefaultType"
                     type="java.lang.String">javax.jms.Topic</config-property>

    <security-domain-and-application>JmsXARealm</security-domain-and-application>
</tx-connection-factory>
```

The `org.jboss.jms.asf.ServerSessionPoolLoader` MBean

The `ServerSessionPoolLoader` MBean manages a factory for `javax.jms.ServerSessionPool` objects used by the MDB container. The configurable attributes of the `ServerSessionPoolLoader` service are as follows:

- **`PoolName`**—A unique name for the session pool. This will be used to bind the `ServerSessionPoolFactory` instance into JNDI under `java:/PoolName`.
- **`PoolFactoryClass`**—The fully qualified classname of the `org.jboss.jms.asf.ServerSessionPoolFactory` interface to create an instance of.
- **`XidFactory`**—The JMX `ObjectName` of the service to use for generating `javax.transaction.xa.Xid` values for local transactions when a two-phase commit is not required. The `XidFactory` MBean must provide an `Instance` operation that returns a `org.jboss.tm.XidFactoryMBean` instance.

Integrating Non-JBoss JMS Providers

As mentioned previously in this chapter, you can replace the JBossMQ JMS implementation with a foreign implementation. You can take a variety of approaches to doing the replacement:

- Change the `JMSProviderLoader` from the `JBossMQProvider` class to one that instantiates the correct JNDI context for communicating with the foreign JMS provider's managed objects.
- Use the `ExternalContext` MBean to federate the foreign JMS provider's managed objects into the JBoss JNDI tree.
- Use MBeans to instantiate the foreign JMS objects into the JBoss JNDI tree. An example of this approach can be found for Websphere MQ at http://sourceforge.net/tracker/index.php?func=detail&aid=753022&group_id=22866&atid=376687.

CHAPTER 7

Connectors on JBoss

IN THIS CHAPTER

- JCA Overview
- An Overview of the JBossCX Architecture
- Configuring JDBC Datasources
- Configuring Generic JCA Adaptors

This chapter discusses the JBoss server implementation of the J2EE Connector Architecture (JCA). JCA is a resource manager integration API whose goal is to standardize access to non-relational resources in the same way the JDBC API standardizes access to relational data. This chapter introduces the utility of the JCA APIs and then describes the architecture of JCA in JBoss

JCA Overview

J2EE 1.4 contains a connector architecture specification called JCA that allows for the integration of transacted and secure resource adaptors into a J2EE application server environment. The JCA specification describes the notion of such resource managers as enterprise information systems (EISs). Examples of EISs include enterprise resource planning packages, mainframe transaction processing, and non-Java legacy applications.

The reason for focusing on EIS is primarily because the notions of transactions, security, and scalability are requirements in enterprise software systems. However, the JCA is applicable to any resource that needs to integrate into JBoss in a secure, scalable, and transacted manner. This section focuses on resource adapters as a generic notion rather than something specific to the EIS environment.

The JCA defines a standard service provider interface (SPI) for integrating the transaction, security, and connection-management facilities of an application server with those of a resource manager. The SPI defines the system-level contract between the resource adaptor and the application server.

The JCA also defines a common client interface (CCI) for accessing resources. The CCI is targeted at EIS development tools and other sophisticated users of integrated resources. The CCI provides a way to minimize the EIS-specific code required by such tools. Typically, J2EE developers access a resource by using such a tool or a resource-specific interface rather than using CCI directly. The reason is that the CCI is not a type-specific API. To be used effectively, CCI must be used in conjunction with metadata that describes how to map from the generic CCI API to the resource manager–specific data types used internally by the resource manager.

The purpose of the JCA is to enable a resource vendor to provide a standard adaptor for its product. A *resource adaptor* is a system-level software driver that a Java application uses to connect to a resource. The resource adaptor plugs into an application server and provides connectivity between the resource manager, the application server, and the enterprise application. A resource vendor need only implement a JCA-compliant adaptor once to allow use of the resource manager in any JCA-capable application server.

An application server vendor extends its architecture once to support the JCA and is then assured of seamless connectivity to multiple resource managers. Likewise, a resource manager vendor provides one standard resource adaptor, and it has the capability to plug in to any application server that supports the JCA.

Figure 7.1 illustrates that the application server is extended to provide support for the JCA SPI to allow a resource adaptor to integrate with the server connection pooling, transaction management, and security management facilities. This integration API defines a three-part system contract:

- **Connection management**—This contract allows the application server to pool resource connections. The purpose of this pool management is to allow for scalability. Resource connections are typically expense objects to create, and pooling them allows for more effective reuse and management.
- **Transaction management**—This contract allows the application server transaction manager to manage transactions that engage resource managers.
- **Security management**—This contract enables secured access to resource managers.

The resource adaptor implements the resource manager side of the system contract. This entails using the application server connection pooling, providing transaction resource information, and using the security integration information. The resource adaptor also exposes the resource manager to the application server components. This can be done using the CCI and/or a resource adaptor–specific API.

The application component integrates into the application server by using a standard J2EE container-to-component contract. For an EJB component, this contract is defined by the EJB specification. The application component interacts with the resource adaptor in the same way it would with any other standard resource factory, such as a `javax.sql.DataSource` JDBC resource factory. The only difference with a JCA resource adaptor is that the client has the option of using the resource adaptor–independent CCI API if the resource adaptor supports this.

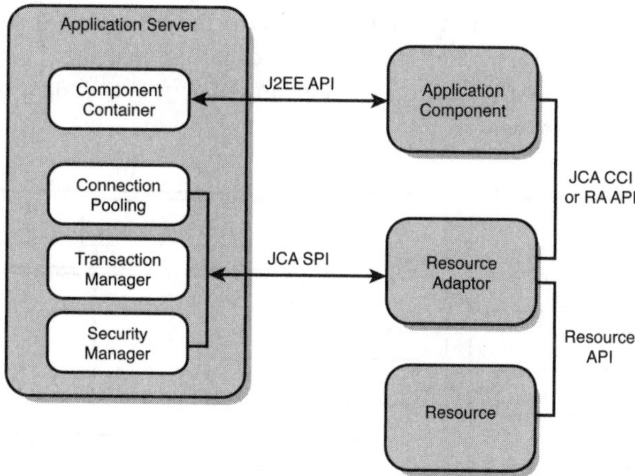

FIGURE 7.1 The relationship between a J2EE application server and a JCA resource adaptor.

Figure 7.2 (from the JCA 1.5 specification) illustrates the relationship between the JCA architecture participants in terms of how they relate to the JCA SPI, CCI, and JTA packages.

The JBossCX architecture provides the implementation of the application server–specific classes. Figure 7.2 shows that this comes down to the implementation of the `javax.resource.spi.ConnectionManager` and `javax.resource.spi.ConnectionEventListener` interfaces. The key aspects of this implementation are discussed in the following section.

An Overview of the JBossCX Architecture

The JBossCX framework provides the application server architecture extension required for the use of JCA resource adaptors. This is primarily a connection-pooling and management extension, and it includes a number of MBeans for loading resource adaptors into the JBoss server. Figure 7.3 expands the generic view given by Figure 7.2 to illustrate how the JBoss JCA layer implements the application server–specific extension, along with an example of a file system resource adaptor that is discussed later in this chapter.

Three coupled MBeans make up a RAR deployment: `org.jboss.resource.RARDeployment`, `org.jboss.resource.connectionmanager.RARDeployment`, and `org.jboss.resource.connectionmanager.BaseConnectionManager2`. `org.jboss.resource.RARDeployment` is simply an encapsulation of the metadata of a RAR `META-INF/ra.xml` descriptor. It exposes this information as a `DynamicMBean` simply to make it available to the `org.jboss.resource.connectionmanager.RARDeployment` MBean.

The `RARDeployer` service handles the deployment of archive files that contain resource adaptors (RARs). It creates the `org.jboss.resource.RARDeployment` MBean when a RAR file is deployed. Deploying the RAR file is the first step in making the resource adaptor available to application components. For each deployed RAR, one or more connection factories must be configured and bound into JNDI. You perform this task by using a JBoss service descriptor that sets up an `org.jboss.resource.connectionmanager.BaseConnectionManager2` MBean implementation with an `org.jboss.resource.connectionmgr.RARDeployment`.

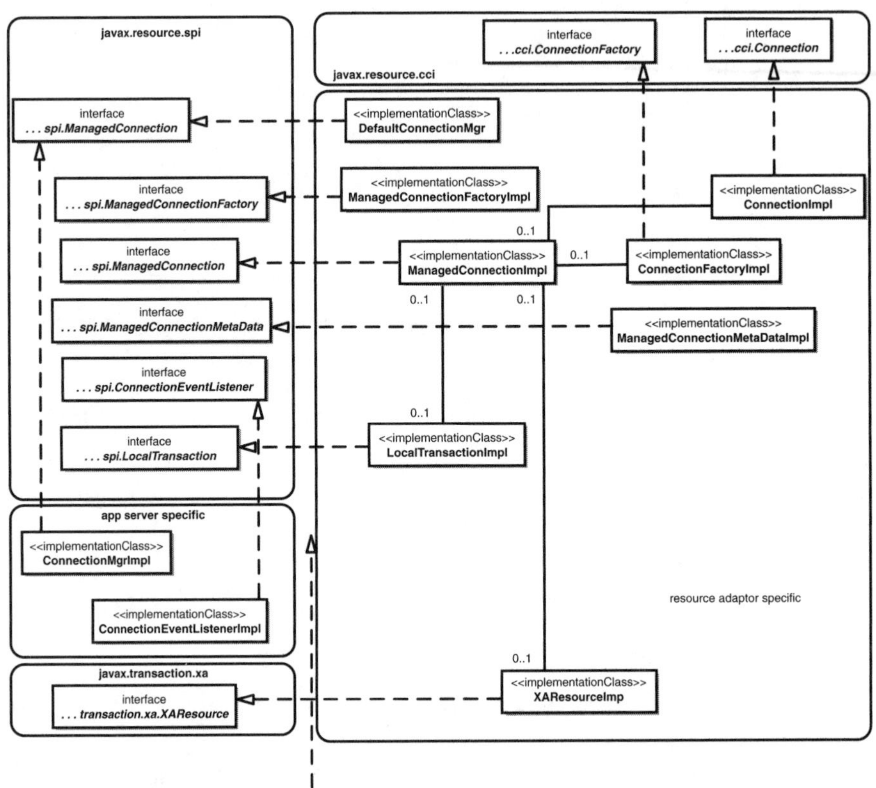

FIGURE 7.2 The JCA 1.5 specification class diagram for the connection management architecture.

The `BaseConnectionManager2` MBean

The `org.jboss.resource.connectionmanager.BaseConnectionManager2` MBean is a base class for the various types of connection managers required by the JCA specification. Subclasses include `NoTxConnectionManager`, `LocalTx-ConnectionManager`, and `XATxConnectionManager`. These correspond to resource adaptors that support no transactions, local transactions, and XA transactions, respectively. You choose which subclass to use based on the type of transaction semantics you want, provided that the JCA resource adaptor supports the corresponding transaction capability.

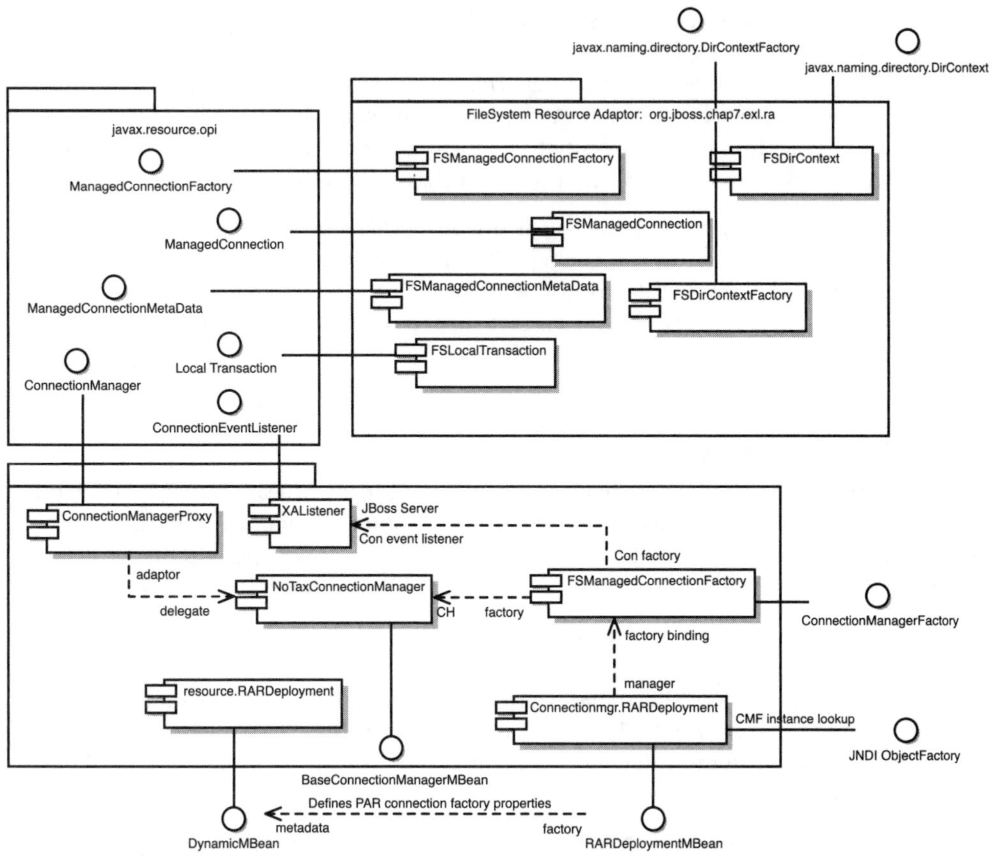

FIGURE 7.3 The JBoss JCA implementation components.

The `BaseConnectionManager2` MBean supports the following common attributes:

- **`ManagedConnectionPool`**—This specifies the `ObjectName` of the MBean that represents the pool for this connection manager. The MBean must have a `ManagedConnectionPool` attribute that is an implementation of the `org.jboss.resource.connectionmanager.ManagedConnectionPool` interface. Normally, it will be an embedded MBean in a `depends` tag rather than an `ObjectName` reference to an existing MBean. The default MBean for use is the `org.jboss.resource.connectionmanager.JBossManagedConnectionPool`. Its configurable attributes are discussed later in this chapter.

- **`CachedConnectionManager`**—This specifies the `ObjectName` of the `CachedConnectionManager` MBean implementation used by the connection manager. Normally, this will be specified using a `depends` tag with the `ObjectName` of the unique `CachedConnectionManager` for the server. The name `jboss.jca:service=CachedConnectionManager` is the standard setting to use.

- **SecurityDomainJndiName**—This specifies the JNDI name of the security domain to use for authentication and authorization of resource connections. This is typically in the form java:/jaas/*<domain>*, where the *<domain>* value is the name of an entry in the conf/login-config.xml JAAS login module configuration file. This defines which JAAS login modules execute to perform authentication. Chapter 8, "Security on JBoss," provides more information on the security settings.
- **JaasSecurityManagerService**—This is the ObjectName of the security manager service. You should set this to the security manager MBean name, as defined in the conf/jboss-service.xml descriptor, which currently is jboss.security:service=JaasSecurityManager. This attribute will likely be removed in the future.

The RARDeployment MBean

The org.jboss.resource.connectionmanager.RARDeployment MBean manages configuration and instantiation ManagedConnectionFactory instances. It does this by using the resource adaptor metadata settings from the RAR META-INF/ra.xml descriptor, along with the RARDeployment attributes. These are the configurable attributes:

- **OldRarDeployment**—This is the ObjectName of the org.jboss.resource.RarDeployment MBean that contains the resource adaptor metadata. The form of this name is jboss.jca:service=RARDeployment,name=*<ra-display-name>*, where the *<ra-display-name>* is the ra.xml descriptor display-name attribute value. RARDeployer creates this when it deploys a RAR file. This attribute will likely be removed in the future.
- **ManagedConenctionFactoryProperties**—This is a collection of (name, type, value) triples that define attributes of the ManagedConnectionFactory instance. Therefore, the names of the attributes depend on the resource adaptor ManagedConnectionFactory instance. The following example shows the structure of the content of this attribute:

```
<properties>
    <config-property>
        <config-property-name>Attr0Name</config-property-name>
        <config-property-type>Attr0Type</config-property-type>
        <config-property-value>Attr0Value</config-property-value>
    </config-property>
    <config-property>
        <config-property-name>Attr1Name</config-property-name>
        <config-property-type>Attr2Type</config-property-type>
        <config-property-value>Attr2Value</config-property-value>
    </config-property>
    ...
</properties>
```

AttrXName is the Xth attribute name, AttrXType is the fully qualified Java type of the attribute, and AttrXValue is the string representation of the value. The conversion from string to AttrXType is done using the java.beans.PropertyEditor class for the AttrXType.

- **JndiName**—This is the JNDI name under which the resource will be made available. Clients of the resource adaptor use this name to obtain either the javax.resource.cci.ConnectionFactory or resource adaptor–specific connection factory. The full JNDI name will be java:/*<JndiName>*, meaning that the JndiName attribute value will be prefixed with java:/. This prevents use of the connection factory outside the JBoss server VM. In the future this restriction may be configurable.

The JBossManagedConnectionPool MBean

The org.jboss.resource.connectionmanager.JBossManagedConnectionPool MBean is a connection-pooling MBean. It is typically used as the embedded MBean value of the BaseConnectionManager2 ManagedConnectionPool attribute. When you set up a connection manager MBean, you typically embed the pool configuration in the connection manager descriptor. The following are the configurable attributes of JBossManagedConnectionPool:

- **ManagedConnectionFactoryName**—This specifies the ObjectName of the MBean that creates javax.resource.spi.ManagedConnectionFactory instances. Normally, you configure this as an embedded MBean in a depends element rather than as a separate MBean reference, using the RARDeployment MBean. The MBean must provide an appropriate startManagedConnectionFactory operation.
- **MinSize**—This attribute indicates the minimum number of connections this pool should hold. These connections are not created until a Subject is known from a request for a connection. MinSize connections will be created for each sub-pool.
- **MaxSize**—This attribute indicates the maximum number of connections for a pool. No more than MaxSize connections will be created in each sub-pool.
- **BlockingTimeoutMillis**—This attribute indicates the maximum time to block while waiting for a connection before throwing an exception. Note that this blocks only while waiting for a permit for a connection, and it will never throw an exception if creating a new connection takes an inordinately long time.
- **IdleTimeoutMinutes**—This attribute indicates the maximum time a connection may be idle before being closed. The actual maximum time also depends on the idle remover thread scan time, which is half the smallest idle timeout of any pool.
- **NoTxSeparatePools**—Setting this to true doubles the available pools. One pool is for connections used outside a transaction, and the other is for connections inside a transaction. The actual pools are lazily constructed on first use. This is relevant only when setting the pool parameters associated with the LocalTxConnectionManager and XATxConnectionManager. Its use case is for Oracle (and possibly other vendors)

XA implementations that don't like using an XA connection with and without a JTA transaction.

- **`Criteria`**—This attribute indicates whether the JAAS `javax.security.auth.Subject` from the security domain associated with the connection or application-supplied parameters (such as from `getConnection(user,pw)`) are used to distinguish connections in the pool. These are the allowed values:
    - **`ByContainer`**—Use `Subject`.
    - **`ByApplication`**—Use application-supplied parameters only.
    - **`ByContainerAndApplication`**—Use both.
    - **`ByNothing`**—All connections are equivalent, which is usually the case if an adapter supports re-authentication.

The `CachedConnectionManager` MBean

The `org.jboss.resource.connectionmanager.CachedConnectionManager` MBean manages associations between meta-aware objects (those accessed through interceptor chains) and connection handles, as well as between user transactions and connection handles. Normally there should be only one such MBean, and this is configured in the core `jboss-service.xml` descriptor. It is used by `CachedConnectionInterceptor`, the JTA `UserTransaction` implementation, and all `BaseConnectionManager2` instances. These are the configurable attributes of the `CachedConnectionManager` MBean:

- **`SpecCompliant`**—You enable this Boolean attribute for reconnect processing of specification-compliant non-shareable connections. This allows a connection to be opened in one call and used in another. Note that specifying this behavior disables connection close processing.
- **`Debug`**—You enable this Boolean property for connection close processing. At the completion of an EJB method invocation, unclosed connections are registered with a transaction synchronization. If the transaction ends without the connection being closed, an error is reported, and JBoss closes the connection. This is a development feature that should be turned off in production for optimal performance.
- **`TransactionManagerServiceName`**—This attribute specifies the JMX `ObjectName` of the JTA transaction manager service. Connection close processing is now synchronized with the transaction manager, and this attribute specifies the transaction manager to use.

A Sample Skeleton of a JCA Resource Adaptor

To conclude our discussion of the JBoss JCA framework, let's create and deploy a single non-transacted resource adaptor that simply provides a skeleton implementation that stubs out the required interfaces and logs all method calls. This section does not discuss the details of the requirements of a resource adaptor provider because they are discussed in detail in the JCA specification. The purposes of the adaptor are to demonstrate the steps required to create and deploy a RAR in JBoss and to show how JBoss interacts with the adaptor.

The adaptor described in this section could be used as the starting point for a non-transacted file system adaptor. You can find the source for the example adaptor in the `src/main/org/jboss/chap7/ex1` directory of the book examples. Figure 7.4 shows a class diagram of the mapping from the required `javax.resource.spi` interfaces to the resource adaptor implementation.

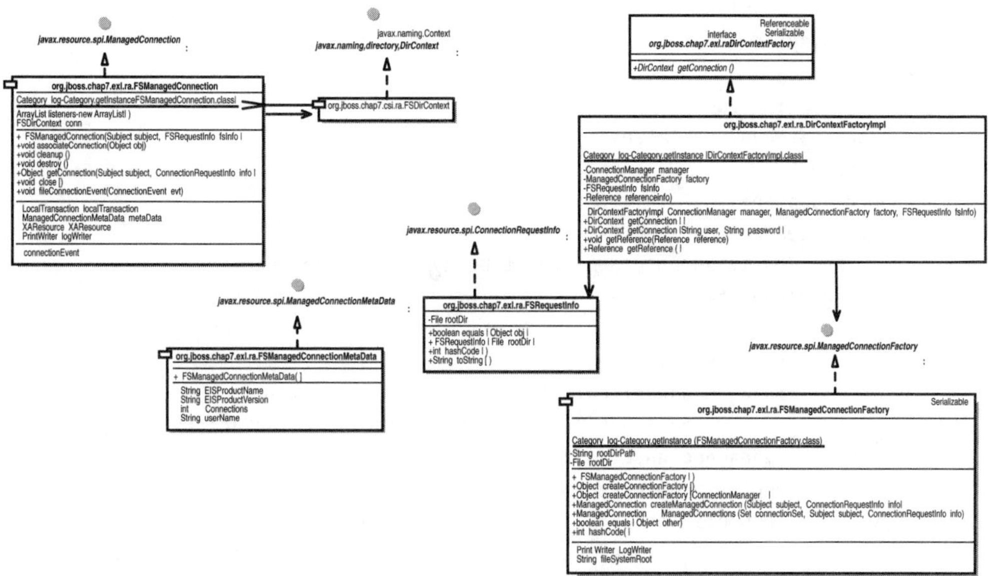

FIGURE 7.4 The file system RAR class diagram.

In this section you will build the adaptor, deploy it to the JBoss server, and then run an example of the client against an EJB that uses the resource adaptor to demonstrate the basic steps in a complete context. You'll then take a look at the JBoss server log to see how the JBoss JCA framework interacts with the resource adaptor to help you better understand the components in the JCA system-level contract.

To build the example and deploy the RAR to the JBoss server `deploy/lib` directory, you need to execute the following Ant command in the book examples directory:

```
[examples]$ ant -Dchap=chap7 build-chap
```

The deployed files include a `chap7-ex1.sar` file and a `notxfs-service.xml` service descriptor. Listing 7.1 shows an example of the resource adaptor deployment descriptor.

LISTING 7.1 A Non-transactional File System Resource Adaptor Deployment Descriptor

```
<?xml version="1.0" encoding="UTF-8"?>
<connector xmlns="http://java.sun.com/xml/ns/j2ee"
    xmlns:xsi="http://www.w3.org/2001/XMLSchema-instance"
    xsi:schemaLocation="http://java.sun.com/xml/ns/j2ee
                        http://java.sun.com/xml/ns/j2ee/
➥connector_1_5.xsd" version="1.5">
    <display-name>File System Adapter</display-name>
    <vendor-name>JBoss</vendor-name>
    <eis-type>FileSystem</eis-type>
    <resourceadapter-version>1.0</resourceadapter-version>
    <license>
        <description>LGPL</description>
        <license-required>false</license-required>
    </license>
    <resourceadapter>
        <resourceadapter-class>
            org.jboss.resource.deployment.DummyResourceAdapter
        </resourceadapter-class>
        <outbound-resourceadapter>
            <connection-definition>
                <managedconnectionfactory-class>
                    org.jboss.chap7.ex1.ra.FSManagedConnectionFactory
                </managedconnectionfactory-class>
                <config-property>
                   <config-property-name>FileSystemRootDir</config-property-name>
                   <config-property-type>java.lang.String</config-property-type>
                   <config-property-value>/tmp/db/fs_store</config-property-value>
                </config-property>
                <config-property>
                   <config-property-name>UserName</config-property-name>
                   <config-property-type>java.lang.String</config-property-type>
                   <config-property-value/>
                </config-property>
                <config-property>
                   <config-property-name>Password</config-property-name>
                   <config-property-type>java.lang.String</config-property-type>
                   <config-property-value/>
                </config-property>
                <connectionfactory-interface>
                    org.jboss.chap7.ex1.ra.DirContextFactory
➥</connectionfactory-interface>
                <connectionfactory-impl-class>
                    org.jboss.chap7.ex1.ra.DirContextFactoryImpl
➥</connectionfactory-impl-class>
```

LISTING 7.1 Continued

```
                <connection-interface>
                    javax.naming.directory.DirContext
                </connection-interface>
                <connection-impl-class>
                    org.jboss.chap7.ex1.ra.FSDirContext
                </connection-impl-class>
            </connection-definition>
            <transaction-support>NoTransaction</transaction-support>
            <authentication-mechanism>
                <authentication-mechanism-type>BasicPassword
➥</authentication-mechanism-type>
                <credential-interface>
                    javax.resource.spi.security.PasswordCredential
                </credential-interface>
            </authentication-mechanism>
            <reauthentication-support>true</reauthentication-support>
        </outbound-resourceadapter>
        <security-permission>
            <description> Read/Write access is required to the contents of the
                FileSystemRootDir </description>
            <security-permission-spec> permission java.io.FilePermission
                "/tmp/db/fs_store/*", "read,write"; </security-permission-spec>
        </security-permission>
    </resourceadapter>
</connector>
```

The key items in the resource adaptor deployment descriptor are highlighted in bold. These items define the classes of the resource adaptor, and the elements are as follows:

- **managedconnectionfactory-class**—This is the implementation of the ManagedConnectionFactory interface, org.jboss.chap7.ex1.ra.FSManagedConnectionFactory.
- **connectionfactory-interface**—This is the interface that clients will obtain when they look up the connection factory instance from JNDI, which in this case is a proprietary resource adaptor value, org.jboss.chap7.ex1.ra.DirContextFactory. This value will be needed when you create the JBoss ds.xml to use the resource.
- **connectionfactory-impl-class**—This is the class that provides the implementation of connectionfactory-interface,org.jboss.chap7.ex1.ra.DirContextFactoryImpl.
- **connection-interface**—This is the interface for the connections returned by the resource adaptor connection factory, which in this case is the JNDI javax.naming.directory.DirContext interface.

- **connection-impl-class**—This is the class that provides the connection-interface implementation, org.jboss.chap7.ex1.ra.FSDirContext.
- **transaction-support**—This is the level of transaction support, which in this case is defined as NoTransaction, meaning the file system resource adaptor does not do transactional work.

The RAR classes and deployment descriptor define only a resource adaptor. Before you can use the resource adaptor, it must be integrated into the JBoss application server, using a ds.xml descriptor file. An example of this file for the file system adaptor is shown in Listing 7.2.

LISTING 7.2 The notxfs-ds.xml Resource Adaptor MBeans Service Descriptor

```
<!DOCTYPE connection-factories PUBLIC
          "-//JBoss//DTD JBOSS JCA Config 1.5//EN"
          "http://www.jboss.org/j2ee/dtd/jboss-ds_1_5.dtd">
<!--
       The non-transaction FileSystem resource adaptor service configuration
-->
<connection-factories>
    <no-tx-connection-factory>
        <jndi-name>NoTransFS</jndi-name>
        <rar-name>chap7-ex1.rar</rar-name>
        <connection-definition>
             org.jboss.chap7.ex1.ra.DirContextFactory
        </connection-definition>
        <config-property name="FileSystemRootDir"
                         type="java.lang.String">/tmp/db/fs_store
➥</config-property>
    </no-tx-connection-factory>
</connection-factories>
```

The main attributes are as follows:

- **jndi-name**—This specifies where the connection factory will be bound into JNDI. For this deployment, that binding will be java:/NoTransFS.
- **rar-name**—This is the name of the RAR file that contains the definition for the resource you want to provide. For nested RAR files, the name would look like *myapplication.ear*#my.rar. In this example, it is simply chap7-ex1.rar.
- **connection-definition**—This is the connection factory interface class. It should match the connectionfactory-interface in the ra.xml file. In this case, the connection factory interface is org.jboss.chap7.ex1.ra.DirContextFactory.

- **config-property**—This can be used to provide non-default settings to the resource adaptor connection factory. In this case, the `FileSystemRootDir` is being set to `/tmp/db/fs_store`. This overrides the default value in the `ra.xml` file.

To deploy the RAR and connection manager configuration to the JBoss server, you run the following:

```
[examples]$ ant -Dchap=chap7 config
```

The server console will display some logging output, indicating that the resource adaptor has been deployed.

Now you need to test access of the resource adaptor by a J2EE component. To do this, you can create a trivial stateless session bean that has a single method called `echo`. Inside the `echo` method, the EJB accesses the resource adaptor connection factory, creates a connection, and then immediately closes the connection. The `echo` method code is shown in Listing 7.3.

LISTING 7.3 The Stateless Session Bean `echo` Method Code That Shows the Access of the Resource Adaptor Connection Factory

```
public String echo(String arg)
{
    log.info("echo, arg="+arg);
    try {
        InitialContext ctx = new InitialContext();
        Object         ref = ctx.lookup("java:comp/env/ra/DirContextFactory");
        log.info("echo, ra/DirContextFactory=" + ref);

        DirContextFactory dcf = (DirContextFactory) ref;
        log.info("echo, found dcf=" + dcf);

        DirContext dc = dcf.getConnection();
        log.info("echo, lookup dc=" + dc);

        dc.close();
    } catch(NamingException e) {
        log.error("Failed during JNDI access", e);
    }
    return arg;
}
```

The EJB is not using the CCI interface to access the resource adaptor. Rather, it is using the resource adaptor–specific API based on the proprietary `DirContextFactory` interface that returns a JNDI `DirContext` object as the connection object. The EJB in the example is simply exercising the system contract layer by looking up the resource adaptor connection factory, creating a connection to the resource, and closing the connection. The EJB does not actually do anything with the connection, as that would only exercise the resource adaptor implementation because this is a non-transactional resource.

You run the test client, which calls the `EchoBean.echo` method, by running Ant as follows from the examples directory:

```
[examples]$ ant -Dchap=chap7 -Dex=1 run-example
```

You'll see some output from the bean in the system console, but you can find much more detailed logging output in the `server/default/log/server.log` file. Don't worry if you see exceptions. They are just stack traces to highlight the call path into parts of the adaptor.

To help understand the interaction between the adaptor and the JBoss JCA layer, the sequence diagram shown in Figure 7.5 summarizes the events that occur when the `EchoBean` accesses the resource adaptor connection factory from JNDI and creates a connection.

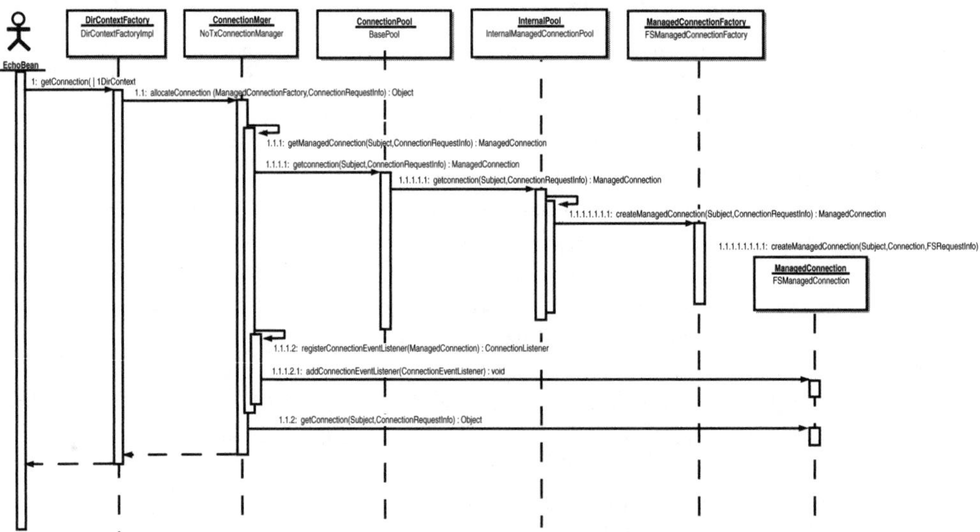

FIGURE 7.5 A sequence diagram that illustrates how `EchoBean` accesses the resource adaptor connection factory.

The starting point is the client's invocation of the `EchoBean.echo` method. For the sake of conciseness of the diagram, the client is shown directly invoking the `EchoBean.echo` method, when in reality the JBoss EJB container handles the invocation. There are three distinct interactions between the `EchoBean` and the resource adaptor: the lookup of the connection factory, the creation of a connection, and the close of the connection.

The lookup of the resource adaptor connection factory is illustrated by the 1.1 sequences of events, which are as follows.:

1. The echo method invokes the `getConnection` method on the resource adaptor connection factory obtained from the JNDI lookup on the `java:comp/env/ra/DirContextFactory` name, which is a link to the `java:/NoTransFS` location.

1.1. The `DirContextFactoryImpl` class asks its associated `ConnectionManager` to allocate a connection. It passes in the `ManagedConnectionFactory` and `FSRequestInfo` that were associated with the `DirContextFactoryImpl` during its construction.

1.1.1. The `ConnectionManager` invokes its `getManagedConnection` method with the current `Subject` and `FSRequestInfo`.

1.1.1.1. The `ConnectionManager` asks its object pool for a connection object. The `JBossManagedConnection-Pool$BasePool` gets the key for the connection and then asks the matching `InternalPool` for a connection.

1.1.1.1.1. Because no connections have been created, the pool must create a new connection. This is done by requesting a new managed connection from the `ManagedConnectionFactory`. The `Subject` associated with the pool as well as the `FSRequestInfo` data are passed as arguments to the `createManagedConnection` method invocation.

1.1.1.1.1.1. The `ConnectionFactory` creates a new `FSManagedConnection` instance and passes in the `Subject` and `FSRequestInfo` data.

1.1.1.2. A `javax.resource.spi.ConnectionListener` instance is created. The type of listener created is based on the type of `ConnectionManager`. In this case, it is an `org.jboss.resource.connectionmgr.BaseConnectionManager2$NoTransactionListener` instance.

1.1.1.2.1. The listener registers as a `javax.resource.spi.ConnectionEventListener` with the `ManagedConnection` instance created in 1.2.1.1.

1.1.2. The `ManagedConnection` is asked for the underlying resource manager connection. The `Subject` and `FSRequestInfo` data are passed as arguments to the `getConnection` method invocation.

The resulting connection object is cast to a `javax.naming.directory.DirContext` instance because that is the public interface defined by the resource adaptor.

After the `EchoBean` has obtained the `DirContext` for the resource adaptor, it simply closes the connection to indicate that its interaction with the resource manager is complete.

This concludes the resource adaptor example. This investigation into the interaction between the JBossCX layer and a trivial resource adaptor should give you sufficient understanding of the steps required to configure any resource adaptor. The adaptor in this example can also serve as a starting point for the creation of your own custom resource adaptors if you need to integrate non-JDBC resources into the JBoss server environment.

Configuring JDBC Datasources

Rather than configure the connection manager factory-related MBeans discussed in the previous section via an MBean services deployment descriptor, you can use the simplified datasource-centric descriptor that JBoss provides. This is transformed into the standard `jboss-service.xml` MBean services deployment descriptor by using a XSL transform applied by the `org.jboss.deployment.XSLSubDeployer` included in the `jboss-jca.sar` deployment. The simplified configuration descriptor is deployed the same as other deployable components. The descriptor must be named by using a `*-ds.xml` pattern in order to be recognized by the `XSLSubDeployer`.

Figure 7.6 shows the schema for the top-level datasource elements of the `*-ds.xml` configuration deployment file.

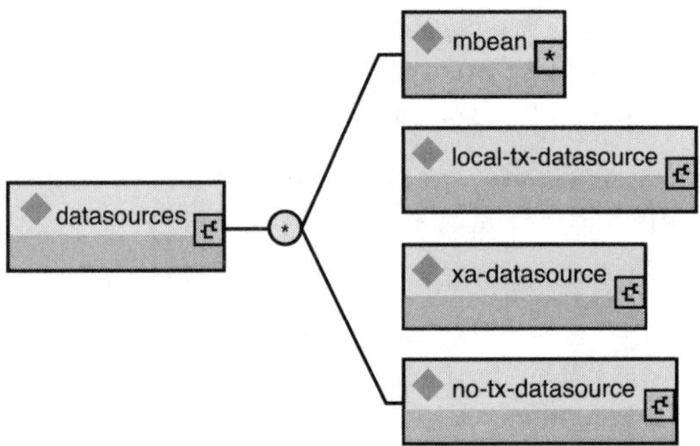

FIGURE 7.6 The simplified JCA datasource configuration descriptor top-level schema elements.

You can specify multiple datasource configurations in a configuration deployment file. These are the child elements of the datasources root element:

- **`mbean`**—You can specify any number of `mbean` elements to define MBean services that should be included in the `jboss-service.xml` descriptor that results from the transformation. You can use this element to configure services used by the datasources.
- **`no-tx-datasource`**—You use this element to specify the `(org.jboss.resource.connectionmanager) NoTxConnectionManager` service configuration. `NoTxConnectionManager` is a JCA connection manager with no transaction support. The `no-tx-datasource` child element schema is shown in Figure 7.7.

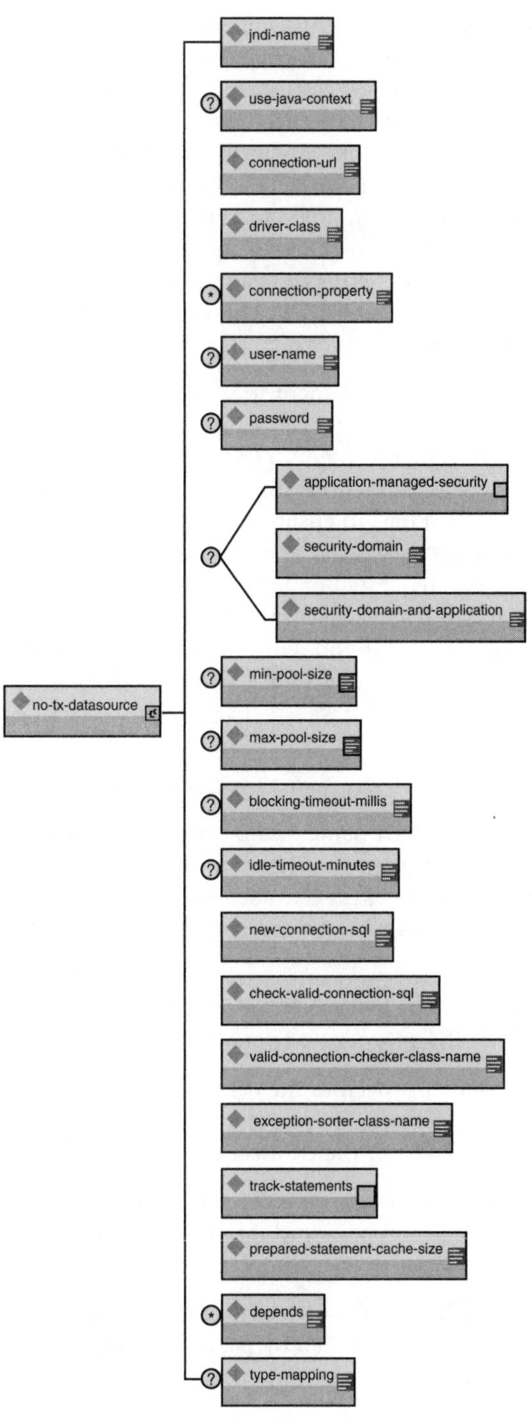

FIGURE 7.7 The non-transactional `DataSource` configuration schema.

- **`local-tx-datasource`**—You use this element to specify the (`org.jboss.resource.connectionmanager`) `LocalTx-ConnectionManager` service configuration. `LocalTxConnectionManager` implements a `ConnectionEventListener` that implements `XAResource` to manage transactions through the transaction manager. To ensure that all work in a local transaction occurs over the same `ManagedConnection`, it includes an XID-to-`ManagedConnection` map. When a connection is requested or a transaction is started with a connection handle in use, it checks to see if a `ManagedConnection` already exists, enrolled in the global transaction, and it uses it if found. Otherwise, a free `ManagedConnection` has its `LocalTransaction` started and is used. The `local-tx-datasource` child element schema is shown in Figure 7.8.
- **`xa-datasource`**—You use this element to specify the (`org.jboss.resource.connectionmanager`) `XATxConnectionManager` service configuration. `XATxConnectionManager` implements a `ConnectionEventListener` that obtains the `XAResource` to manage transactions through the transaction manager from the adaptor `ManagedConnection`. To ensure that all work in a local transaction occurs over the same `ManagedConnection`, it includes an XID-to-`ManagedConnection` map. When a connection is requested or a transaction is started with a connection handle in use, it checks to see if a `ManagedConnection` already exists, enrolled in the global transaction, and it uses it if found. Otherwise, a free `ManagedConnection` has its `LocalTransaction` started and is used. The `XADataSource` child element schema is shown in Figure 7.9.

Elements that are common to all datasources include the following:

- **`jndi-name`**—This is the JNDI name under which the `DataSource` wrapper will be bound. Note that this name is relative to the `java:/` context, unless `use-java-context` is set to `false`. `DataSource` wrappers are not usable outside the server VM, so they are normally bound under `java:/`, which isn't shared outside the local VM.
- **`use-java-context`**—If this is set to `false`, the datasource will be bound in the global JNDI context rather than the `java:` context.
- **`user-name`**—This element specifies the default username that is used when creating a new connection. The actual username may be overridden by the application code `getConnection` parameters or the connection creation context JAAS `Subject`.
- **`password`**—This element specifies the default password that is used when creating a new connection. The actual password may be overridden by the application code `getConnection` parameters or the connection creation context JAAS `Subject`.
- **`application-managed-security`**—Specifying this element indicates that connections in the pool should be distinguished by parameters supplied by application code, such as from `getConnection(user,pw)`.

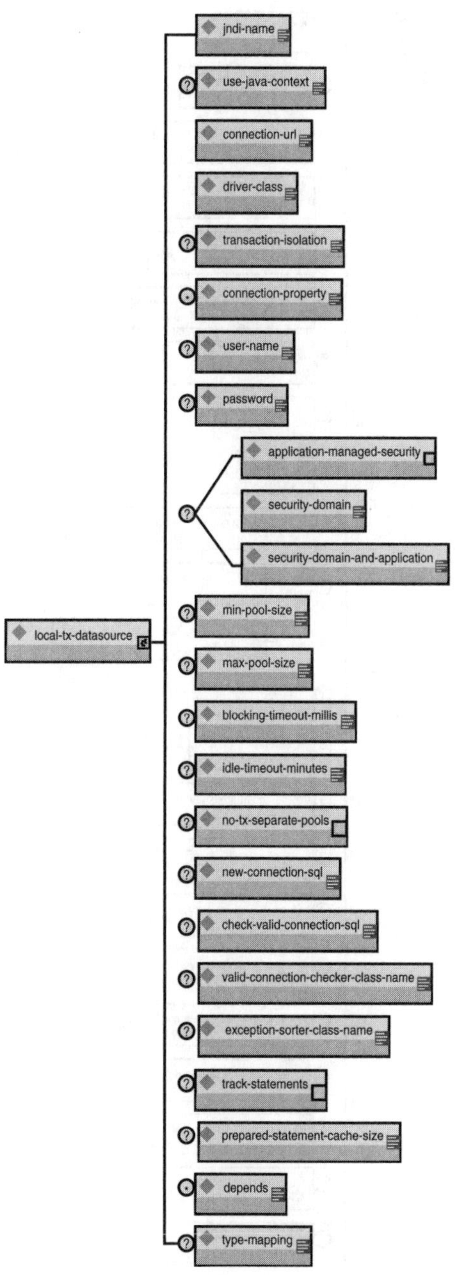

FIGURE 7.8 The non-XA `DataSource` configuration schema.

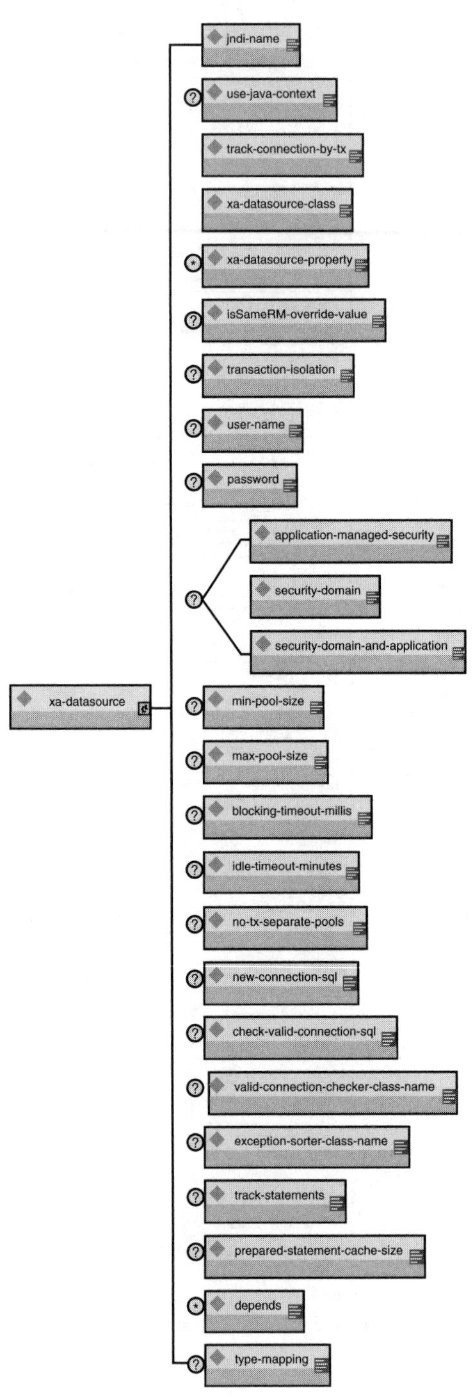

FIGURE 7.9 The `XADataSource` configuration schema.

- **`security-domain`**—Specifying this element indicates that connections in the pool should be distinguished by JAAS `Subject`-based information. The content of the `security-domain` is the name of the JAAS security manager that will handle authentication. This name correlates to the JAAS `login-config.xml` descriptor `application-policy/name` attribute.
- **`security-domain-and-application`**—Specifying this element indicates that connections in the pool should be distinguished both by application code–supplied parameters and JAAS `Subject`-based information. The content of the `security-domain` is the name of the JAAS security manager that will handle authentication. This name correlates to the JAAS `login-config.xml` descriptor `application-policy/name` attribute.
- **`min-pool-size`**—This element specifies the minimum number of connections a pool should hold. These pool instances are not created until an initial request for a connection is made. The default is `0`.
- **`max-pool-size`**—This element specifies the maximum number of connections for a pool. No more than the `max-pool-size` number of connections will be created in a pool. The default is `20`.
- **`blocking-timeout-millis`**—This element specifies the maximum time, in milliseconds, to block while waiting for a connection before throwing an exception. Note that this blocks only while waiting for a permit for a connection, and it will never throw an exception if creating a new connection takes an inordinately long time. The default is `5000`.
- **`idle-timeout-minutes`**—This element specifies the maximum time, in minutes, a connection may be idle before being closed. The actual maximum time also depends on the `IdleRemover` scan time, which is half the smallest `idle-timeout-minutes` of any pool.
- **`new-connection-sql`**—This SQL statement should be executed when a new connection is created. You can use this element to configure a connection with database-specific settings that are not configurable via connection properties.
- **`check-valid-connection-sql`**—This SQL statement should be run on a connection before it is returned from the pool to test its validity to test for stale pool connections. An example of a statement is `selectcount(*)fromx`.
- **`exception-sorter-class-name`**—This specifies a class that implements the `org.jboss.resource.adapter.jdbc.ExceptionSorter` interface to filter `SQLExceptions` to determine whether a connection error event should be generated. Current implementations include the following:

  ```
  org.jboss.resource.adapter .jdbc.vendor.OracleExceptionSorter
  org.jboss.resource.adapter .jdbc.vendor.SybaseExceptionSorter
  ```

- **`valid-connection-checker-class-name`**—This specifies a class that implements the `org.jboss.resource.adapter.jdbc.ValidConnectionChecker` interface to provide a `SQLExceptionisValidConnection(Connection e)` method that is called with a connection that is to be returned from the pool to test its validity. This overrides `check-valid-connection-sql` when present. Current implementations include the following:

  `org.jboss.resource.adapter.jdbc.vendor.OracleValidConnectionChecker`

- **`track-statements`**—This Boolean element specifies whether to check for unclosed statements when a connection is returned to the pool. If it is `true`, a warning message is issued for each unclosed statement. If the `log4j` category `org.jboss.resource.adapter.jdbc.WrappedConnection` has trace level enabled, a stack trace of the connection close call is logged as well. This is a debug feature that can be turned off in production.
- **`prepared-statement-cache-size`**—This element specifies the number of prepared statements per connection in an LRU cache, which is keyed by the SQL query. Setting this to `0` disables the cache.
- **`depends`**—The `depends` element specifies the JMX `ObjectName` string of a service that the connection manager services depend on. The connection manager service will not be started until the dependent services have been started.
- **`type-mapping`**—This element declares a default type mapping for this datasource. The type mapping should match a `type-mapping/name` element from `standardjbosscmp-jdbc.xml`.

Additional common child elements for both `no-tx-datasource` and `local-tx-datasource` include the following:

- **`connection-url`**—This is the JDBC driver connection URL string (for example, `jdbc:hsqldb:hsql://localhost:1701`).
- **`driver-class`**—This is the fully qualified name of the JDBC driver class (for example, `org.hsqldb.jdbcDriver`).
- **`connection-property`**—This element allows you to pass arbitrary connection properties to the `java.sql.Driver.connect(url,props)` method. Each `connection-property` specifies a string name/value pair with the property name coming from the `name` attribute and the value coming from the element content.

The `local-tx-datasource` and `xa-datasource` have the following elements in common:

- **`transaction-isolation`**—This element specifies the `java.sql.Connection` transaction isolation level to use. The constants defined in the `Connection` interface are the possible element content values and include the following:

```
TRANSACTION_READ_UNCOMMITTED
TRANSACTION_READ_COMMITTED
TRANSACTION_REPEATABLE_READ
TRANSACTION_SERIALIZABLE
TRANSACTION_NONE
```

- **no-tx-separate-pools**—The presence of this element indicates that two connection pools are required to isolate connections used with a JTA transaction from those used without a JTA transaction. The pools are lazily constructed on first use. The use case for this element is for Oracle (and possibly other vendors) XA implementations that don't like using an XA connection with and without a JTA transaction.

The following are the unique xa-datasource child elements:

- **track-connection-by-tx**—Specifying a true value for this element makes the connection manager keep an XID-to-connection map and put the connection back in the pool only when the transaction completes and all the connection handles are closed or disassociated (by the method calls returning). As a side effect, you never suspend and resume the XID on the connection's XAResource. This is the same connection tracking behavior used for local transactions.

  The XA specification implies that any connection may be enrolled in any transaction, using any XID for that transaction at any time from any thread (suspending other transactions, if necessary). The original JCA implementation assumed this and aggressively delisted connections and put them back in the pool as soon as control left the EJB they were used in or handles were closed. Because some other transaction can be using the connection the next time work needs to be done on the original transaction, there is no way to get the original connection back. It turns out that most XADataSource driver vendors do not support this, and require that all work done under a particular XID go through the same connection.

- **xa-datasource-class**—This is the fully qualified name of the javax.sql.XADataSource implementation class (for example, com.informix.jdbcx.IfxXADataSource).
- **xa-datasource-property**—The xa-datasource-property element allows for specification of the properties to assign to the XADataSource implementation class. Each property is identified by the name attribute, and the property value is given by the xa-datasource-property element content. The property is mapped onto the XADataSource implementation by looking for a JavaBeans-style getter method for the property name. If one is found, the value of the property is set by using the JavaBeans setter, with the element text translated to the true property type, using the java.beans.PropertyEditor for the type.
- **isSameRM-override-value**—This Boolean flag allows you to override the behavior of the javax.transaction.xa.XAResource.isSameRM(XAResource xaRes) method behavior on the XA managed connection. If specified, this value is used unconditionally as the isSameRM(xaRes) return value, regardless of the xaRes parameter.

Examples of configurations for many third-party JDBC drivers are included in the `JBOSS_DIST/docs/examples/jca` directory. Current example configurations include the following:

```
asapxcess -jb3.2-ds.xml
cicsr9s-service.xml
db2-ds.xml
db2-xa-ds.xml
facets-ds.xml
fast-objects-jboss32-ds.xml
firebird-ds.xml
```

Connectors on JBoss include the following:

```
firstsql-ds.xml
firstsql-xa-ds.xml
generic-ds.xml
hsqldb-ds.xml
informix-ds.xml
informix-xa-ds.xml
jdatastore-ds.xml
jms-ds.xml
j sql-ds.xml
lido-versant-service.xml
mimer-ds.xml
mimer-xa-ds.xml
msaccess-ds.xml
mssql-ds.xml
mssql-xa-ds.xml
mysql-ds.xml
oracle-ds.xml
oracle-xa-ds.xml
postgres-ds.xml
sapdb-ds.xml
sapr3-ds.xml
solid-ds.xml
sybase-ds.xml
```

Configuring Generic JCA Adaptors

`XSLSubDeployer` also supports the deployment of arbitrary non-JDBC JCA resource adaptors. Figure 7.10 shows the schema for the top-level connection factory elements of the `*-ds.xml` configuration deployment file.

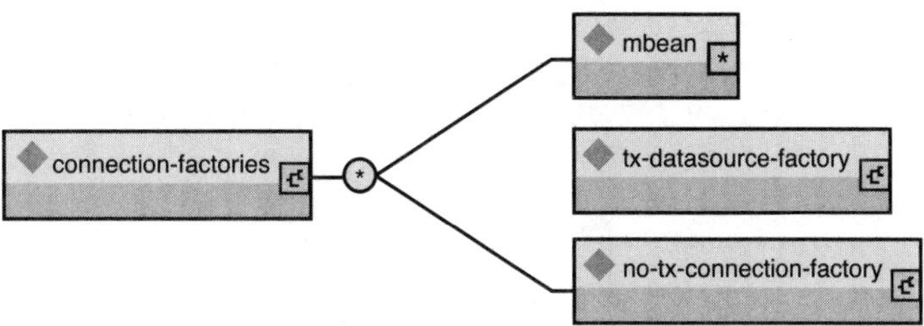

FIGURE 7.10 The simplified JCA adaptor connection factory configuration descriptor top-level schema elements.

You can specify multiple connection factory configurations in a configuration deployment file. These are the child elements of the `connection-factories` root element:

- **`mbean`**—You can specify any number of `mbean` elements to define MBean services that should be included in the `jboss-service.xml` descriptor that results from the transformation. You can use this element to configure additional services used by the adaptor.
- **`no-tx-connection-factory`**—You use this element to specify the (`org.jboss.resource.connectionmanager`)`NoTxConnectionManager` service configuration. `NoTxConnectionManager` is a JCA connection manager with no transaction support. The `no-tx-connection-factory` child element schema is shown in Figure 7.11.

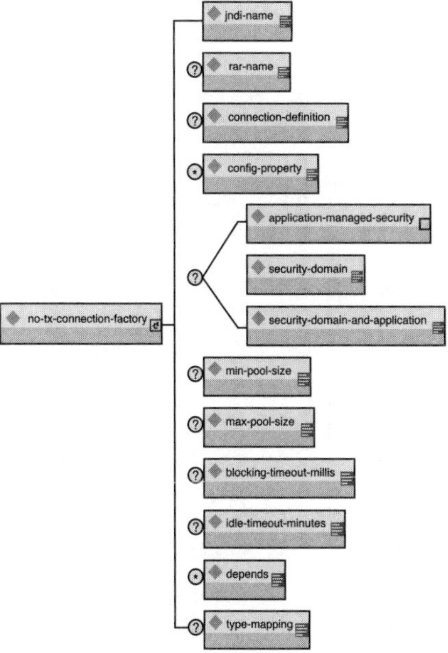

FIGURE 7.11 The `no-tx-connection-factory` element schema.

- **`tx-connection-factory`**—You use this element to specify the (`org.jboss.resource.connectionmanager)TxConnectionManager` service configuration. The `tx-connection-factory` child element schema is shown in Figure 7.12.

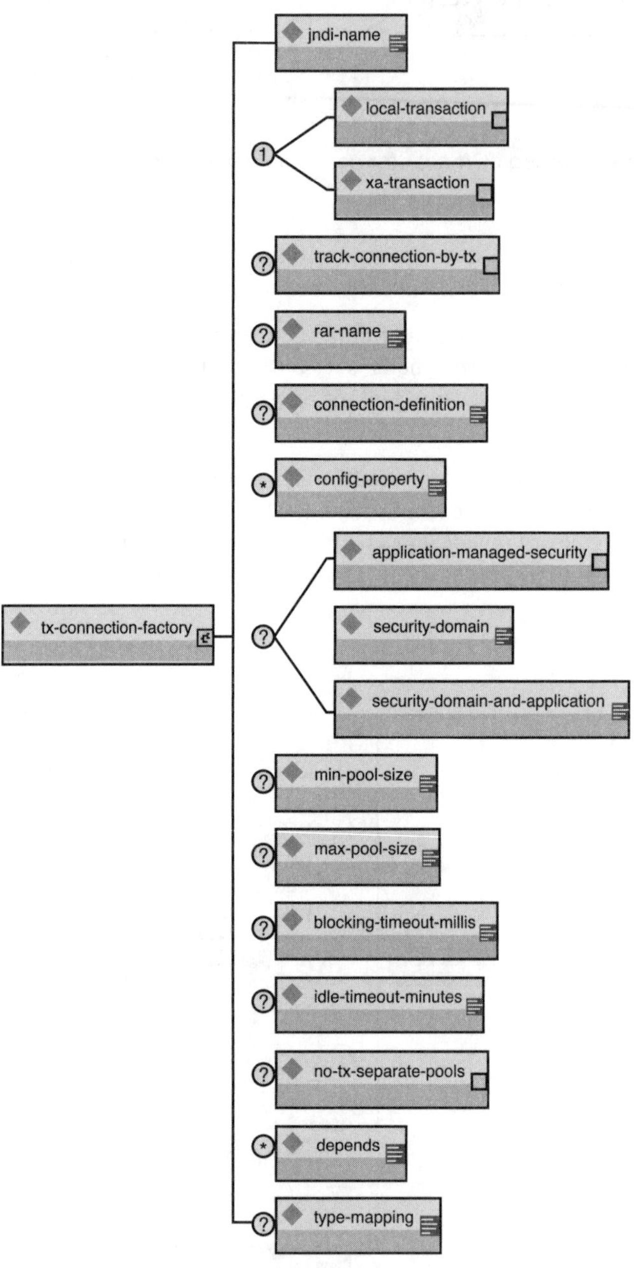

FIGURE 7.12 The `tx-connection-factory` element schema.

The majority of the elements here are the same as those of the datasource configuration. The elements that are unique to the connection factory configuration include the following:

- **`adaptor-display-name`**—This is a human-readable display name to assign to the connection manager MBean.
- **`local-transaction`**—This element specifies that the `tx-connection-factory` supports local transactions.
- **`xa-transaction`**—This element specifies that the `tx-connection-factory` supports XA transactions.
- **`track-connection-by-tx`**—This element specifies that a connection should be used only on a single transaction and that a transaction should be associated with only one connection.
- **`rar-name`**—This is the name of the RAR file that contains the definition for the resource you want to provide. For nested RAR files, the name would look like *`myapplication.ear`*`#my.rar`.
- **`connection-definition`**—This is the connection factory interface class. It should match the `connectionfactory-interface` in the `ra.xml` file.
- **`config-property`**—You can specify any number of properties to supply to the `ManagedConnectionFactory` MBean service configuration. Each `config-property` element specifies the value of a `ManagedConnectionFactory` property. The `config-property` element has two required attributes:
  - **`name`**—The name of the property.
  - **`type`**—The fully qualified type of the property.

The content of the `config-property` element provides the string representation of the property value. This is converted to the true property type by using the associated type `PropertyEditor`.

CHAPTER **8**

Security on JBoss

IN THIS CHAPTER

- J2EE Declarative Security Overview
- An Introduction to JAAS
- The JBoss Security Model
- The JBossSX Architecture
- The Secure Remote Password (SRP) Protocol
- Running JBoss with a Java 2 Security Manager
- Using SSL with JBoss Using JSSE
- Configuring JBoss for Use Behind a Firewall
- Securing the JBoss Server

Security is a fundamental part of any enterprise application. You need to be able to restrict who is allowed to access your applications and control what operations application users may perform. The J2EE specifications define a simple role-based security model for EJBs and web components. The JBoss component framework that handles security is the JBossSX extension framework. The JBossSX security extension provides support for both the role-based declarative J2EE security model and integration of custom security via a security proxy layer. The default implementation of the declarative security model is based on Java Authentication and Authorization Service (JAAS) login modules and subjects. The security proxy layer allows custom security that cannot be described using the declarative model to be added to an EJB in a way that is independent of the EJB business object. Before getting into the JBoss security implementation details, we will review EJB and servlet specification security models, as well as JAAS, to establish the foundation for these details.

J2EE Declarative Security Overview

The security model that the J2EE specification advocates is a declarative model. It is declarative in that you describe the security roles and permissions by using a standard XML descriptor rather than embedding security into your business component. This isolates security from business-level code because security tends to be more a function of where the component is deployed than an inherent aspect of the component's business logic. For example, consider an ATM component that is to be used to access a bank account. The security requirements, roles, and permissions will vary, independently of how you access the bank account, based on what bank is managing the account, where the ATM is deployed, and so on.

Securing a J2EE application is based on the specification of the application security requirements via the standard J2EE deployment descriptors. You secure access to EJBs and web components in an enterprise application by using the `ejb-jar.xml` and `web.xml` deployment descriptors. The following sections look at the purpose and usage of the various security elements.

Security References

Both EJBs and servlets can declare one or more `security-role-ref` elements (see Figure 8.1). You use this element to declare that a component is using the `role-name` value as an argument to the `isCallerInRole(String)` method. By using the `isCallerInRole` method, a component can verify whether the caller is in a role that has been declared with a `security-role-ref/role-name` element. The `role-name` element value must link to a `security-role` element through the `role-link` element. The typical use of `isCallerInRole` is to perform a security check that cannot be defined by using the role-based `method-permissions` elements.

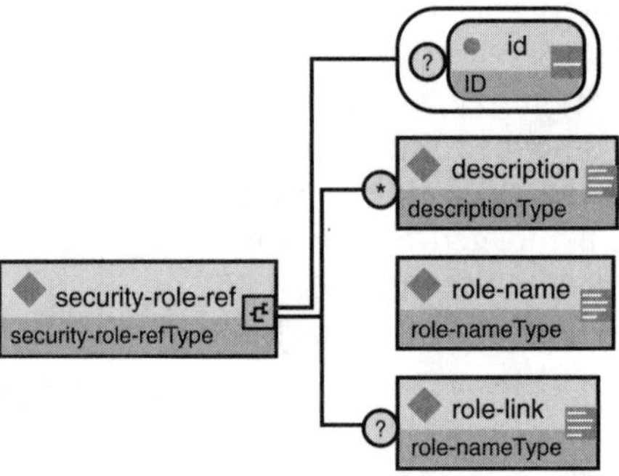

FIGURE 8.1 The `security-role-ref` element.

Listing 8.1 shows the use of `security-role-ref` in an `ejb-jar.xml` file.

LISTING 8.1 An Example of an `ejb-jar.xml` Descriptor Fragment That Illustrates `security-role-ref` Element Usage

```
<!-- A sample ejb-jar.xml fragment -->
<ejb-jar>
  <enterprise-beans>
    <session>
      <ejb-name>ASessionBean</ejb-name>
      ...
      <security-role-ref>
          <role-name>TheRoleICheck</role-name>
          <role-link>TheApplicationRole</role-link>
```

LISTING 8.1 Continued

```
      </security-role-ref>
    </session>
  </enterprise-beans>
  ...
</ejb-jar>
```

Listing 8.2 shows the use of `security-role-ref` in a `web.xml` file.

LISTING 8.2 An Example of a `web.xml` Descriptor Fragment That Illustrates `security-role-ref` Element Usage

```
<web-app>
    <servlet>
        <servlet-name>AServlet</servlet-name>
        ...
        <security-role-ref>
            <role-name>TheServletRole</role-name>
            <role-link>TheApplicationRole</role-link>
        </security-role-ref>
    </servlet>
    ...
</web-app>
```

Security Identity

An EJB has the capability to specify what identity an EJB should use when it invokes methods on other components, using the `security-identity` element (see Figure 8.2).

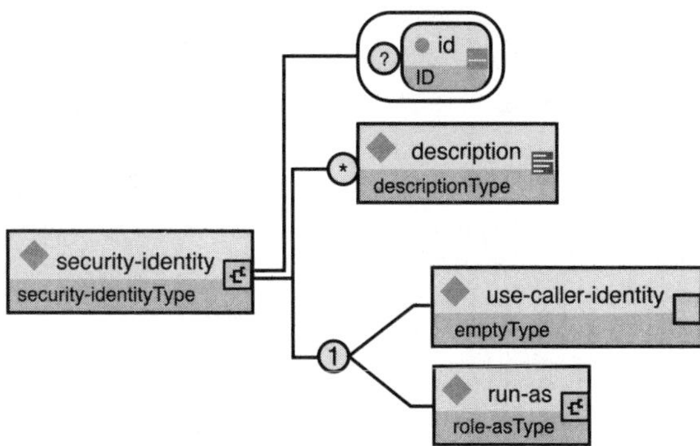

FIGURE 8.2 The `security-identity` element.

The invocation identity can be that of the current caller, or it can be a specific role. The application assembler uses the `security-identity` element with a `use-caller-identity` child element to indicate that the current caller's identity should be propagated as the security identity for method invocations made by the EJB. Propagation of the caller's identity is the default used in the absence of an explicit `security-identity` element declaration.

Alternatively, the application assembler can use the `run-as/role-name` child element to specify that a specific security role given by the `role-name` value should be used as the security identity for method invocations made by the EJB. Note that this does not change the caller's identity, as shown by `EJBContext.getCallerPrincipal()`. Rather, the caller's security roles are set to the single role specified by the `run-as/role-name` element value. One use case for the `run-as` element is to prevent external clients from accessing internal EJBs. You accomplish this by assigning the internal EJB `method-permission` elements that restrict access to a role never assigned to an external client. EJBs that need to use internal EJBs are then configured with a `run-as/role-name` equal to the restricted role. Listing 8.3 shows an example of a descriptor fragment that illustrates `security-identity` element usage.

LISTING 8.3 An Example of an `ejb-jar.xml` Descriptor Fragment That Illustrates `security-identity` Element Usage

```
<!-- A sample ejb-jar.xml fragment -->
<ejb-jar>
    <enterprise-beans>
        <session>
            <ejb-name>ASessionBean</ejb-name>
            <!-- ... -->
            <security-identity>
                <use-caller-identity/>
            </security-identity>
        </session>
        <session>
            <ejb-name>RunAsBean</ejb-name>
            <!-- ... -->
            <security-identity>
                <run-as>
                    <description>A private internal role</description>
                    <role-name>InternalRole</role-name>
                </run-as>
            </security-identity>
        </session>
    </enterprise-beans>
    <!-- ... -->
</ejb-jar>
```

Security Roles

The security role name referenced by either the security-role-ref or security-identity element needs to map to one of the application's declared roles. An application assembler defines logical security roles by declaring security-role elements (see Figure 8.3). The role-name value is a logical application role name, such as Administrator, Architect, or SalesManager.

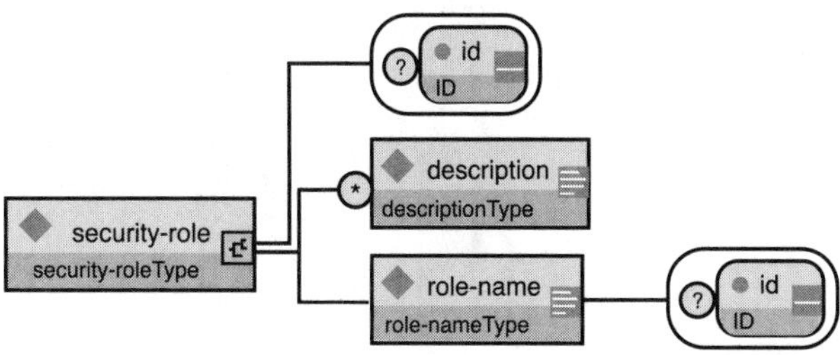

FIGURE 8.3 The security-role element.

The J2EE specifications note that it is important to keep in mind that the security roles in the deployment descriptor are used to define the logical security view of an application. Roles defined in the J2EE deployment descriptors should not be confused with the user groups, users, principals, and other concepts that exist in the target enterprise's operational environment. The deployment descriptor roles are application constructs with application-domain–specific names. For example, a banking application might use role names such as BankManager, Teller, and Customer.

In JBoss, a security-role element is only used to map security-role-ref/role-name values to the logical role that the component role references. The user's assigned roles are a dynamic function of the application's security manager, as you will see when we discuss the JBossSX implementation details. JBoss does not require the definition of security-role elements in order to declare method permissions. However, the specification of security-role elements is still a recommended practice, to ensure portability across application servers and for deployment descriptor maintenance. Listing 8.4 shows the usage of the security-role element in an ejb-jar.xml file.

LISTING 8.4 An Example of an ejb-jar.xml Descriptor Fragment That Illustrates security-role Element Usage

```
<!-- A sample ejb-jar.xml fragment -->
<ejb-jar>
    <!-- ... -->
    <assembly-descriptor>
        <security-role>
            <description>The single application role</description>
            <role-name>TheApplicationRole</role-name>
        </security-role>
```

LISTING 8.4 Continued

```
    </assembly-descriptor>
</ejb-jar>
```

Listing 8.5 shows the usage of the `security-role` element in a `web.xml` file.

LISTING 8.5 An Example of a `web.xml` Descriptor Fragment That Illustrates `security-role` Element Usage

```
<!-- A sample web.xml fragment -->
<web-app>
    <!-- ... -->
    <security-role>
        <description>The single application role</description>
        <role-name>TheApplicationRole</role-name>
    </security-role>
</web-app>
```

EJB Method Permissions

An application assembler can set the roles that are allowed to invoke an EJB's home and remote interface methods through `method-permission` element declarations (see Figure 8.4).

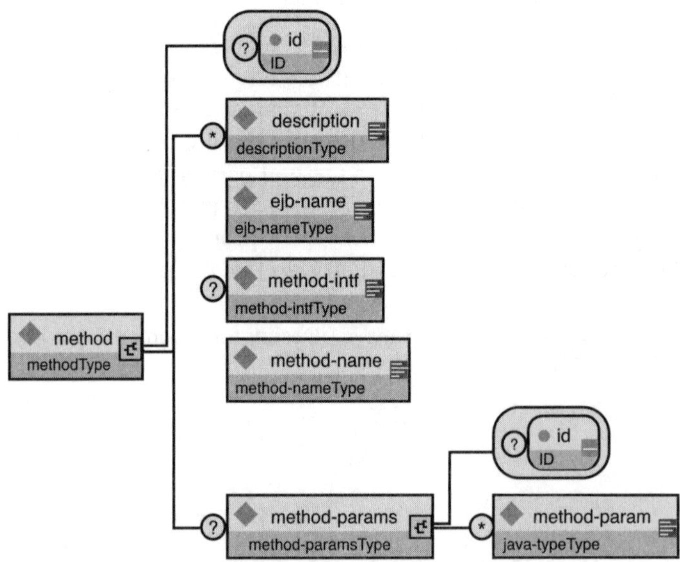

FIGURE 8.4 The `method-permission` element.

Each `method-permission` element contains one or more `role-name` child elements that define the logical roles that are allowed to access the EJB methods as identified by `method` child elements (see Figure 8.5). You can also specify an `unchecked` element instead of the `role-name` element to declare that any authenticated user can access the methods identified by `method` child elements. In addition, you can declare that no one should have access to a method that has the `exclude-list` element. If an EJB has methods that have not been declared as accessible by a role using a `method-permission` element, the EJB methods default to being excluded from use. This is equivalent to defaulting the methods into the `exclude-list`.

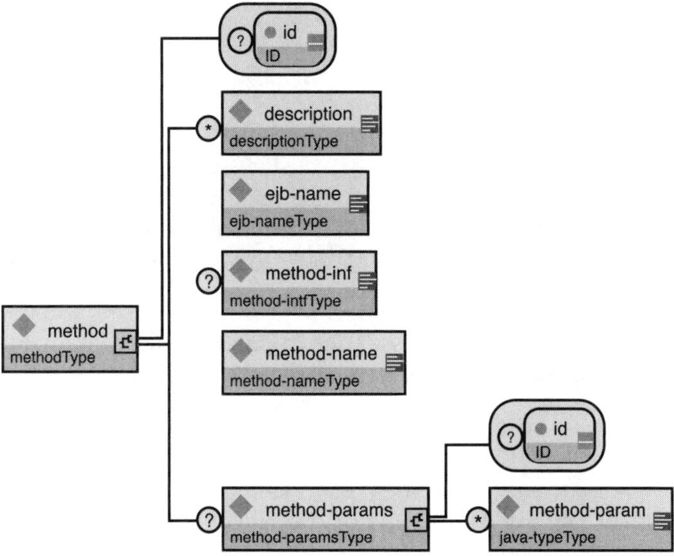

FIGURE 8.5 The `method` element.

There are three supported styles of `method` element declarations:

- The first style is used for referring to all the home and component interface methods of the named enterprise bean:

```
<method>
    <ejb-name>EJBNAME</ejb-name>
    <method-name>*</method-name>
</method>
```

- The second style is used for referring to a specified method of the home or component interface of the named enterprise bean:

```
<method>
    <ejb-name>EJBNAME</ejb-name>
    <method-name>METHOD</method-name>
</method>
```

If there are multiple methods with the same overloaded name, this style refers to all the overloaded methods.

- The third style is used to refer to a specified method within a set of methods with an overloaded name:

```
<method>
    <ejb-name>EJBNAME</ejb-name>
    <method-name>METHOD</method-name>
    <method-params>
        <method-param>PARAMETER_1</method-param>
        <!-- ... -->
        <method-param>PARAMETER_N</method-param>
    </method-params>
</method>
```

  The method must be defined in the specified enterprise bean's home or remote interface. The `method-param` element values are the fully qualified name of the corresponding method parameter type. If there are multiple methods with the same overloaded signature, the permission applies to all the matching overloaded methods.

The optional `method-intf` element can be used to differentiate methods with the same name and signature that are defined in both the home and remote interfaces of an enterprise bean.

Listing 8.6 provides complete examples of the usage of the `method-permission` element.

LISTING 8.6 An Example of an `ejb-jar.xml` Descriptor Fragment That Illustrates `method-permission` Element Usage

```
<ejb-jar>
    <assembly-descriptor>
        <method-permission>
            <description>The employee and temp-employee roles may access any
                method of the EmployeeService bean </description>
            <role-name>employee</role-name>
            <role-name>temp-employee</role-name>
            <method>
                <ejb-name>EmployeeService</ejb-name>
                <method-name>*</method-name>
            </method>
        </method-permission>
        <method-permission>
            <description>The employee role may access the findByPrimaryKey,
                getEmployeeInfo, and the updateEmployeeInfo(String) method of
                the AardvarkPayroll bean </description>
            <role-name>employee</role-name>
```

LISTING 8.6 Continued

```
            <method>
                <ejb-name>AardvarkPayroll</ejb-name>
                <method-name>findByPrimaryKey</method-name>
            </method>
            <method>
                <ejb-name>AardvarkPayroll</ejb-name>
                <method-name>getEmployeeInfo</method-name>
            </method>
            <method>
                <ejb-name>AardvarkPayroll</ejb-name>
                <method-name>updateEmployeeInfo</method-name>
                <method-params>
                    <method-param>java.lang.String</method-param>
                </method-params>
            </method>
        </method-permission>
        <method-permission>
            <description>The admin role may access any method of the
                EmployeeServiceAdmin bean </description>
            <role-name>admin</role-name>
            <method>
                <ejb-name>EmployeeServiceAdmin</ejb-name>
                <method-name>*</method-name>
            </method>
        </method-permission>
        <method-permission>
            <description>Any authenticated user may access any method of the
                EmployeeServiceHelp bean</description>
            <unchecked/>
            <method>
                <ejb-name>EmployeeServiceHelp</ejb-name>
                <method-name>*</method-name>
            </method>
        </method-permission>
        <exclude-list>
            <description>No fireTheCTO methods of the EmployeeFiring bean may be
                used in this deployment</description>
            <method>
                <ejb-name>EmployeeFiring</ejb-name>
                <method-name>fireTheCTO</method-name>
            </method>
        </exclude-list>
    </assembly-descriptor>
</ejb-jar>
```

Web Content Security Constraints

In a web application, security is defined by the roles that are allowed access to content by a URL pattern that identifies the protected content. This set of information is declared by using the `web.xml` `security-constraint` element (see Figure 8.6).

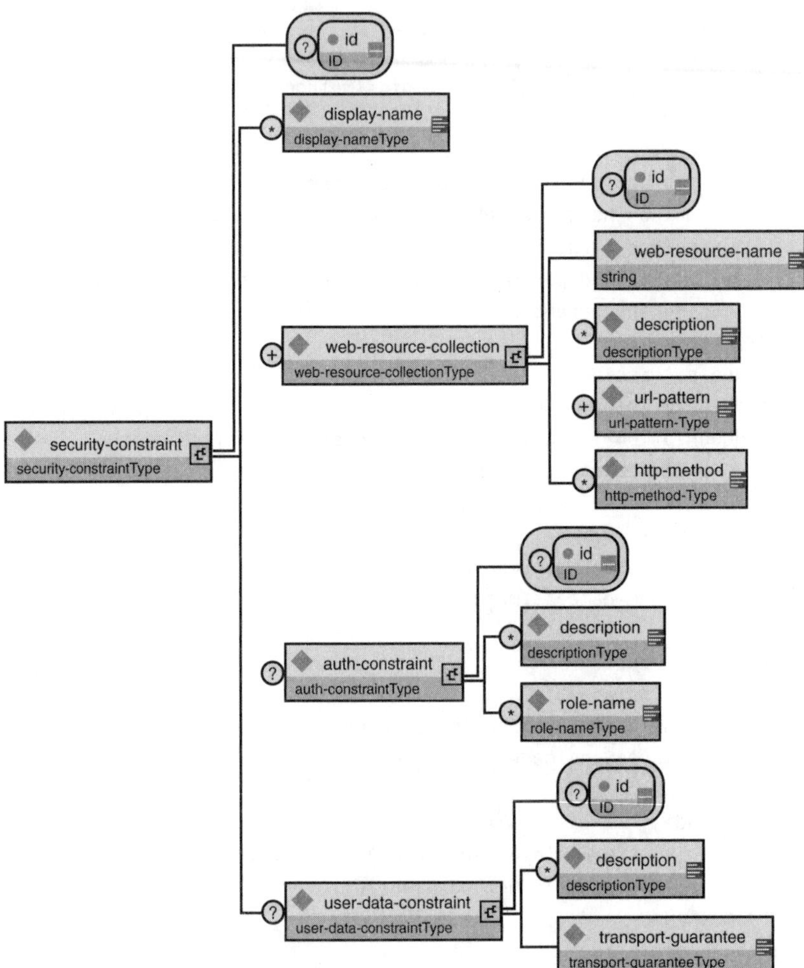

FIGURE 8.6 The `security-constraint` element.

The content to be secured is declared by using one or more `web-resource-collection` elements. Each `web-resource-collection` element contains an optional series of `url-pattern` elements, followed by an optional series of `http-method` elements. The `url-pattern` element value specifies a URL pattern against which a request URL must match for the request to correspond to an attempt to access secured content. The `http-method` element value specifies a type of HTTP request to allow.

The optional user-data-constraint element specifies the requirements for the transport layer of the client-to-server connection. The requirement may be for content integrity (preventing data tampering in the communication process) or for confidentiality (preventing reading while in transit). The transport-guarantee element value specifies the degree to which communication between the client and server should be protected. Its values are NONE, INTEGRAL, and CONFIDENTIAL. A value of NONE means that the application does not require any transport guarantees. A value of INTEGRAL means that the application requires the data sent between the client and server to be sent in such a way that it can't be changed in transit. A value of CONFIDENTIAL means that the application requires the data to be transmitted in a fashion that prevents other entities from observing the contents of the transmission. In most cases, the presence of the INTEGRAL or CONFIDENTIAL flag indicates that the use of SSL is required.

The optional login-config element is used to configure the authentication method that should be used, the realm name that should be used for the application, and the attributes that are needed by the form login mechanism (see Figure 8.7).

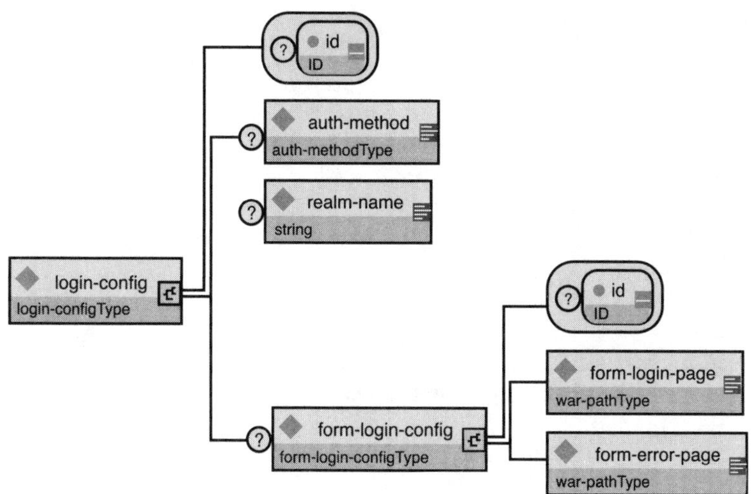

FIGURE 8.7 The login-config element.

The auth-method child element specifies the authentication mechanism for the web application. As a prerequisite to gaining access to any web resources that are protected by an authorization constraint, a user must have authenticated using the configured mechanism. Legal values for auth-method element are BASIC, DIGEST, FORM, and CLIENT-CERT. The realm-name child element specifies the realm name to use in HTTP basic and digest authorization. The form-login-config child element specifies the login as well as error pages that should be used in form-based login. If the auth-method value is not FORM, then form-login-config and its child elements are ignored. For example, the web.xml descriptor fragment given in Listing 8.7 indicates that any URL lying under the web application's

/restricted path requires an AuthorizedUser role. There is no required transport guarantee, and the authentication method used for obtaining the user identity is basic HTTP authentication.

LISTING 8.7 A web.xml Descriptor Fragment That Illustrates the Use of security-constraint and Related Elements

```
<web-app>
    <!-- ... -->
    <security-constraint>
        <web-resource-collection>
            <web-resource-name>Secure Content</web-resource-name>
            <url-pattern>/restricted/*</url-pattern>
        </web-resource-collection>
        <auth-constraint>
            <role-name>AuthorizedUser</role-name>
        </auth-constraint>
        <user-data-constraint>
            <transport-guarantee>NONE</transport-guarantee>
        </user-data-constraint>
    </security-constraint>
    <!-- ... -->
    <login-config>
        <auth-method>BASIC</auth-method>
        <realm-name>The Restricted Zone</realm-name>
    </login-config>
    <!-- ... -->
    <security-role>
        <description>The role required to access restricted content </description>
        <role-name>AuthorizedUser</role-name>
    </security-role>
</web-app>
```

Enabling Declarative Security in JBoss

The J2EE security elements that have been covered so far describe the security requirements only from the application's perspective. Because J2EE security elements declare logical roles, the application deployer maps the roles from the application domain onto the deployment environment. The J2EE specifications omit these application-server specific details. In JBoss, mapping the application roles onto the deployment environment entails specifying a security manager that implements the J2EE security model, using JBoss server-specific deployment descriptors. The details behind the security configuration are discussed later in this chapter, in the section "The JBoss Security Model."

An Introduction to JAAS

The JBossSX framework is based on the JAAS API. It is important that you understand the basic elements of the JAAS API to understand the implementation details of JBossSX. The following sections provide an introduction to JAAS to prepare you for the JBossSX architecture discussion later in this chapter.

What Is JAAS?

The JAAS 1.0 API consists of a set of Java packages that are designed for user authentication and authorization. It implements a Java version of the standard Pluggable Authentication Module (PAM) framework and compatibly extends the Java 2 platform's access control architecture to support user-based authorization. JAAS was first released as an extension package for JDK 1.3 and is bundled with JDK 1.4+. Because the JBossSX framework uses only the authentication capabilities of JAAS to implement the declarative role-based J2EE security model, this introduction focuses on only that topic.

JAAS authentication is performed in a pluggable fashion. This permits Java applications to remain independent from underlying authentication technologies and allows the JBossSX security manager to work in different security infrastructures. Integration with a security infrastructure can be achieved without changing the JBossSX security manager implementation. All that needs to change is the configuration of the authentication stack that JAAS uses.

The JAAS Core Classes

The JAAS core classes can be broken down into three categories: common, authentication, and authorization. The following list presents only the common and authentication classes because these are the specific classes used to implement the functionality of JBossSX that is covered in this chapter.

These are the common classes:

- `Subject (javax.security.auth.Subject)`
- `Principal (java.security.Principal)`

These are the authentication classes:

- `Callback (javax.security.auth.callback.Callback)`
- `CallbackHandler (javax.security.auth.callback.CallbackHandler)`
- `Configuration (javax.security.auth.login.Configuration)`
- `LoginContext (javax.security.auth.login.LoginContext)`
- `LoginModule (javax.security.auth.spi.LoginModule)`

The Subject and Principal Classes To authorize access to resources, applications first need to authenticate the request's source. The JAAS framework defines the term *subject* to represent a request's source. The `Subject` class is the central class in JAAS. A `Subject` represents information for a single entity, such as a person or service. It encompasses the entity's principals, public credentials, and private credentials. The JAAS APIs use the existing Java 2 `java.security.Principal` interface to represent a principal, which is essentially just a typed name.

During the authentication process, a subject is populated with associated identities, or principals. A subject may have many principals. For example, a person may have a name principal (John Doe), a Social Security number principal (123-45-6789), and a username principal (johnd), all of which help distinguish the subject from other subjects. To retrieve the principals associated with a subject, two methods are available:

```
public Set getPrincipals() {...}
public Set getPrincipals(Class c) {...}
```

The first method returns all principals contained in the `Subject`. The second method returns only those principals that are instances of class `c` or one of its subclasses. An empty set is returned if the `Subject` has no matching principals. Note that the `java.security.acl.Group` interface is a subinterface of `java.security.Principal`, so an instance in the principals set may represent a logical grouping of other principals or groups of principals.

Authentication of a Subject Authentication of a subject requires JAAS login. The login procedure consists of the following steps:

1. An application instantiates a `LoginContext` and passes in the name of the login configuration and a `Callback-Handler` to populate the `Callback` objects, as required by the configuration `LoginModules`.
2. The `LoginContext` consults a `Configuration` to load all the `LoginModules` included in the named login configuration. If no such named configuration exists, the `other` configuration is used as a default.
3. The application invokes the `LoginContext.login` method.
4. The login method invokes all the loaded `LoginModules`. As each `LoginModule` attempts to authenticate the subject, it invokes the handle method on the associated `CallbackHandler` to obtain the information required for the authentication process. The required information is passed to the handle method in the form of an array of `Callback` objects. Upon success, the `LoginModules` associate relevant principals and credentials with the subject.
5. The `LoginContext` returns the authentication status to the application. Success is represented by a return from the login method. Failure is represented through a `LoginException` being thrown by the login method.
6. If authentication succeeds, the application retrieves the authenticated subject by using the `LoginContext.getSubject` method.

7. After the scope of the subject authentication is complete, you can remove all principals and related information associated with the subject by the login method by invoking the `LoginContext.logout` method.

The `LoginContext` class provides the basic methods for authenticating subjects and offers a way to develop an application, independently of the underlying authentication technology. The `LoginContext` consults a `Configuration` to determine the authentication services configured for a particular application. `LoginModule` classes represent the authentication services. Therefore, you can plug different login modules into an application without changing the application itself. The following code shows the steps required by an application to authenticate a `Subject`:

```
CallbackHandler handler = new MyHandler();
LoginContext lc = new LoginContext("some-config", handler);

try {
    lc.login();
    Subject subject = lc.getSubject();
} catch(LoginException e) {
    System.out.println("authentication failed");
    e.printStackTrace();
}

// Perform work as authenticated Subject
// ...

// Scope of work complete, logout to remove authentication info
try {
    lc.logout();
} catch(LoginException e) {
    System.out.println("logout failed");
    e.printStackTrace();
}

// A sample MyHandler class
class MyHandler
    implements CallbackHandler
{
    public void handle(Callback[] callbacks) throws
        IOException, UnsupportedCallbackException
    {
        for (int i = 0; i < callbacks.length; i++) {
            if (callbacks[i] instanceof NameCallback) {
                NameCallback nc = (NameCallback)callbacks[i];
                nc.setName(username);
```

```
            } else if (callbacks[i] instanceof PasswordCallback) {
                PasswordCallback pc = (PasswordCallback)callbacks[i];
                pc.setPassword(password);
            } else {
                throw new UnsupportedCallbackException(callbacks[i],
                                                        "Unrecognized Callback");
            }
        }
    }
}
```

To integrate, you can use an authentication technology by creating an implementation of the `LoginModule` interface. This allows an administrator to plug different authentication technologies into an application. You can chain together multiple `LoginModules` to allow for more than one authentication technology to participate in the authentication process. For example, one `LoginModule` may perform username/password-based authentication, while another may interface to hardware devices such as smart card readers or biometric authenticators.

The life cycle of a `LoginModule` is driven by the `LoginContext` object against which the client creates and issues the login method. The two-phase process consists of the following steps:

1. The `LoginContext` creates each configured `LoginModule` by using its public `no-arg` constructor.
2. Each `LoginModule` is initialized with a call to its initialize method. The `Subject` argument is guaranteed to be non-null. The signature of the initialize method is `public void initialize(Subject subject, CallbackHandler callbackHandler, Map sharedState, Map options)`.
3. The `login` method is called to start the authentication process. For example, a method implementation might prompt the user for a username and password and then verify the information against data stored in a naming service such as NIS or LDAP. Alternative implementations might interface to smart cards and biometric devices, or they might simply extract user information from the underlying operating system. The validation of user identity by each `LoginModule` is considered Phase 1 of JAAS authentication. The signature of the `login` method is `boolean login()throws LoginException`. A `LoginException` being thrown indicates failure. A return of `true` indicates that the method succeeded, whereas a return of `false` indicates that the login module should be ignored.
4. If the `LoginContext`'s overall authentication succeeds, `commit` is invoked on each `LoginModule`. If Phase 1 succeeds for a `LoginModule`, then the commit method continues with Phase 2: associating relevant principals, public credentials, and/or private credentials with the subject. If Phase 1 fails for a `LoginModule`, then `commit` removes any previously stored authentication state, such as usernames or passwords. The signature of the `commit` method is `boolean commit() throws LoginException`.

A `LoginException` being thrown indicates failure to complete the commit phase. A return of `true` indicates that the method succeeded, whereas a return of `false` indicates that the login module should be ignored.

5. If the `LoginContext`'s overall authentication fails, then the `abort` method is invoked on each `LoginModule`. The `abort` method removes or destroys any authentication state created by the login or initialize methods. The signature of the `abort` method is `boolean abort() throws LoginException`. A `LoginException` being thrown indicates failure to complete the `abort` phase. A return of `true` indicates that the method succeeded, whereas a return of `false` indicates that the login module should be ignored.

6. When the application invokes `logout` on the `LoginContext`, the authentication state is removed after a successful login. This in turn results in a `logout` method invocation on each `LoginModule`. The `logout` method removes the principals and credentials originally associated with the subject during the `commit` operation. Credentials should be destroyed upon removal. The signature of the `logout` method is `boolean logout() throws LoginException`. A `LoginException` being thrown indicates failure to complete the logout process. A return of `true` indicates that the method succeeded, whereas a return of `false` indicates that the login module should be ignored.

When a `LoginModule` must communicate with the user to obtain authentication information, it uses a `CallbackHandler` object. Applications implement the `CallbackHandler` interface and pass it to the `LoginContext`, which forwards it directly to the underlying login modules. Login modules use the `CallbackHandler` both to gather input from users, such as a password or smart card PIN, and to supply information to users, such as status information. By allowing the application to specify the `CallbackHandler`, underlying `LoginModules` remain independent from the different ways applications interact with users. For example, a `CallbackHandler`'s implementation for a GUI application might display a window to solicit user input. On the other hand, a `callbackhandler`'s implementation for a non-GUI environment, such as an application server, might simply obtain credential information by using an application server API. The `callbackhandler` interface has one method to implement:

```
void handle(Callback[] callbacks)
    throws java.io.IOException,
             UnsupportedCallbackException;
```

Finally, the last authentication class we need to cover is the `Callback` interface. This is a tagging interface for which several default implementations are provided, including the `NameCallback` and `PasswordCallback` used in an earlier example. A `LoginModule` uses a `Callback` to request information required by the authentication mechanism. `LoginModules` pass an array of `Callbacks` directly to the `CallbackHandler.handle` method during the authentication's login phase. If a `callbackhandler` does not understand how to use a `Callback` object passed into the `handle` method, it throws an `UnsupportedCallbackException` to abort the login call.

The JBoss Security Model

Similar to the rest of the JBoss architecture, security at the lowest level is defined as a set of interfaces for which alternate implementations may be provided. Three basic interfaces define the JBoss server security layer: `org.jboss.security.AuthenticationManager`, `org.jboss.security.RealmMapping`, and `org.jboss.security.SecurityProxy`. Figure 8.8 shows a class diagram of the security interfaces and their relationship to the EJB container architecture.

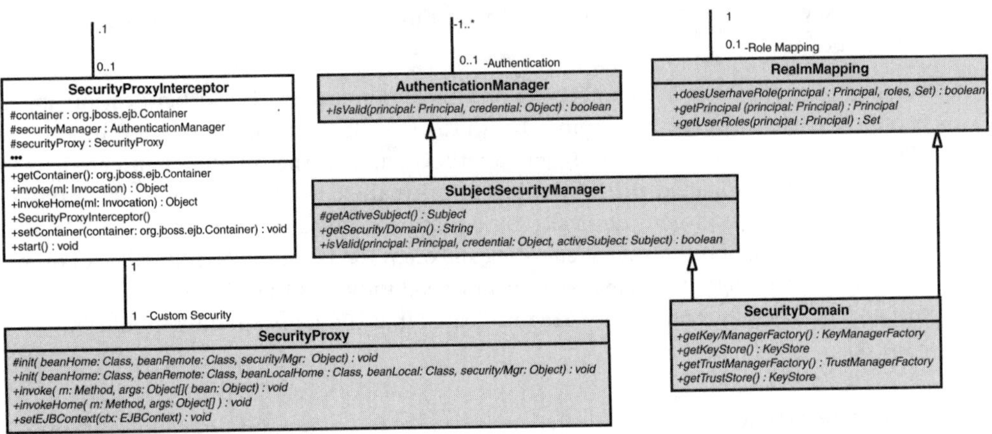

FIGURE 8.8 The key security model interfaces and their relationship to the JBoss server EJB container elements.

The shaded classes in Figure 8.8 represent the security interfaces, whereas the nonshaded classes represent the EJB container layer. The two interfaces required for the implementation of the J2EE security model are `org.jboss.security.AuthenticationManager` and `org.jboss.security.RealmMapping`. The roles of the security interfaces presented in Figure 8.8 are summarized in the following list:

- **`AuthenticationManager`**—This is an interface that is responsible for validating credentials associated with principals. Principals are identities; examples of principals include usernames, employee numbers, and Social Security numbers. Credentials are proof of the identity; examples of credentials include passwords, session keys, and digital signatures. You invoke the `isValid` method to determine whether a user identity and associated credentials, as known in the operational environment, are valid proof of the user's identity.

- **`RealmMapping`**—This is an interface that is responsible for principal mapping and role mapping. The `getPrincipal` method takes a user identity, as known in the operational environment, and returns the application domain identity. The `doesUserHaveRole` method validates that the user identity in the operational environment has been assigned the indicated role from the application domain.

- **SecurityProxy**—This is an interface that describes the requirements for a custom SecurityProxyInterceptor plug-in. A SecurityProxy allows for the externalization of custom security checks on a per-method basis for both the EJB home and remote interface methods.
- **SubjectSecurityManager**—This is a subinterface of AuthenticationManager that simply adds accessor methods for obtaining the security domain name of the security manager and the current thread's authenticated Subject.
- **SecurityDomain**—This is an extension of the AuthenticationManager, RealmMapping, and SubjectSecurityManager interfaces. It is a move to a comprehensive security interface based on the JAAS Subject, a java.security.KeyStore, and the JSSE com.sun.net.ssl.KeyManagerFactory and com.sun.net.ssl.TrustManagerFactory interfaces. This interface is a work in progress that will be the basis of a multi-domain security architecture that will better support ASP-style deployments of applications and resources.

Note that the AuthenticationManager, RealmMapping, and SecurityProxy interfaces have no association to JAAS-related classes. Although the JBossSX framework is heavily dependent on JAAS, the basic security interfaces required for implementation of the J2EE security model are not. The JBossSX framework is simply an implementation of the basic security plug-in interfaces that are based on JAAS. The component diagram presented in Figure 8.9 illustrates this fact. The implication of this plug-in architecture is that you are free to replace the JAAS-based JBossSX implementation classes with your own custom security manager implementation that does not make use of JAAS, if you so desire. You'll see how to do this when you look at the JBossSX MBeans available for the configuration of JBossSX in Figure 8.9.

Enabling Declarative Security in JBoss, Revisited

Earlier in this chapter, the discussion of the J2EE standard security model ends with a requirement for the use of JBoss server-specific deployment descriptor to enable security. The details of this configuration are presented here because they are part of the generic JBoss security model. Figure 8.10 shows the JBoss-specific EJB and web application deployment descriptor's security-related elements.

The value of a security-domain element specifies the JNDI name of the security manager interface implementation that JBoss uses for the EJB and web containers. This is an object that implements both the AuthenticationManager and RealmMapping interfaces. When specified as a top-level element, it defines what security domain is in effect for all EJBs in the deployment unit. This is the typical usage because mixing security managers within a deployment unit complicates inter-component operation and administration.

To specify the security domain for an individual EJB, you specify the security-domain at the container configuration level. This overrides any top-level security-domain element.

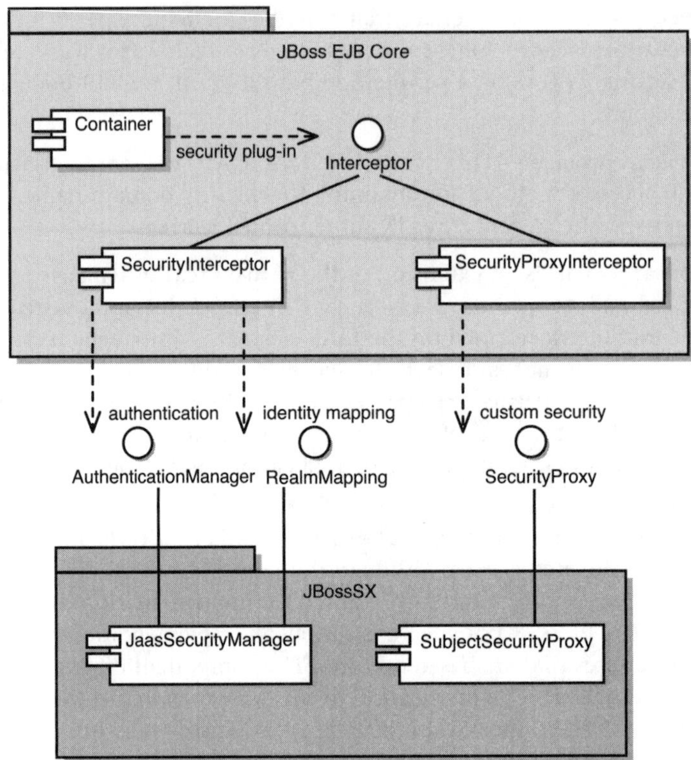

FIGURE 8.9 The relationship between the JBossSX framework implementation classes and the JBoss server EJB container layer.

The `unauthenticated-principal` element specifies the name to use for the `Principal` object returned by the `EJBContext.getUserPrincipal` method when an unauthenticated user invokes an EJB. Note that this conveys no special permissions to an unauthenticated caller. Its primary purpose is to allow unsecured servlets and JSP pages to invoke unsecured EJBs and allow the target EJB to obtain a non-null `Principal` for the caller, using the `getUserPrincipal` method. This is a J2EE specification requirement.

The `security-proxy` element identifies a custom security proxy implementation that allows per-request security checks outside the scope of the EJB declarative security model, without requiring you to embed security logic into the EJB implementation. This may be an implementation of the `org.jboss.security.SecurityProxy` interface or just an object that implements methods in the home, remote, local home, or local interfaces of the EJB to secure without implementing any common interface. If the given class does not implement the `SecurityProxy` interface, the instance must be wrapped in a `SecurityProxy` implementation that delegates the method invocations to the object. The `org.jboss.security.SubjectSecurityProxy` is an example of a `SecurityProxy` implementation that is used by the default JBossSX installation.

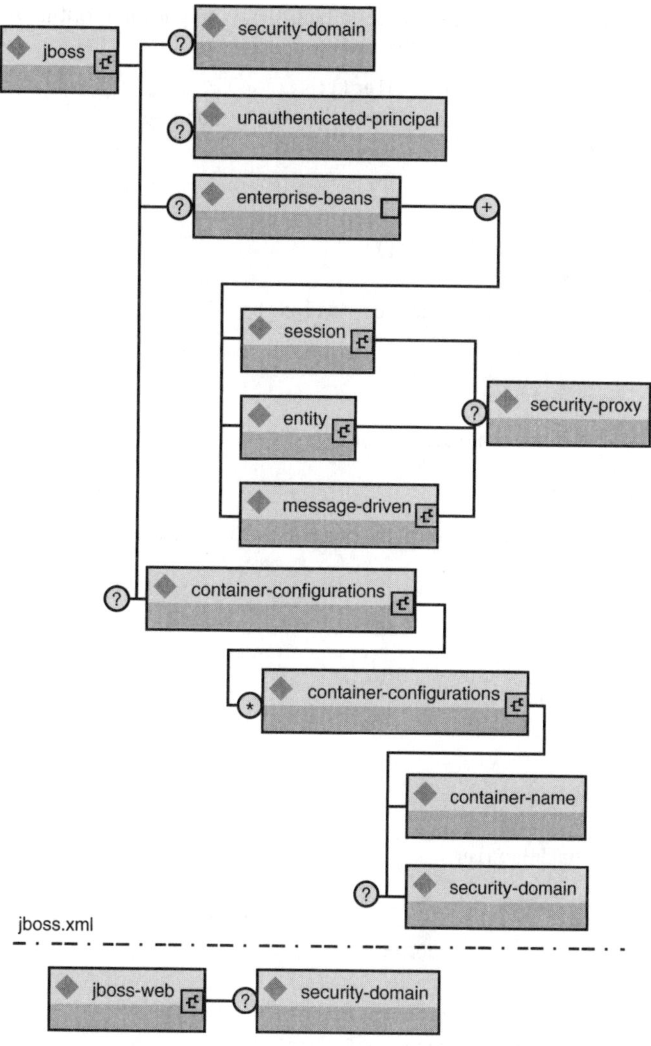

FIGURE 8.10 The security element subsets of the JBoss server `jboss.xml` and `jboss-web.xml` deployment descriptors.

Let's take a look at a simple example of a custom `SecurityProxy` in the context of a trivial stateless session bean. The custom `SecurityProxy` validates that no one invokes the bean's `echo` method with a four-letter word as its argument. This is a check that is not possible with role-based security; you cannot define a `FourLetterEchoInvoker` role because the security context is the method argument, not a property of the caller. The code for the custom `SecurityProxy` is given in Listing 8.8, and the full source code is available in the `src/main/org/jboss/chap8/ex1` directory of the book examples.

LISTING 8.8 The Example 1 Custom `EchoSecurityProxy` Implementation That Enforces the `echo` Argument-Based Security Constraint

```
CallbackHandler handler = new MyHandler();
LoginContext lc = new LoginContext("some-config", handler);

try {
    lc.login();
    Subject subject = lc.getSubject();
} catch(LoginException e) {
    System.out.println("authentication failed");
    e.printStackTrace();
}

// Perform work as authenticated Subject
// ...

// Scope of work complete, log out to remove authentication info
try {
    lc.logout();
} catch(LoginException e) {
    System.out.println("logout failed");
    e.printStackTrace();
}

// A sample MyHandler class
class MyHandler
    implements CallbackHandler
{
    public void handle(Callback[] callbacks) throws
        IOException, UnsupportedCallbackException
    {
        for (int i = 0; i < callbacks.length; i++) {
            if (callbacks[i] instanceof NameCallback) {
                NameCallback nc = (NameCallback)callbacks[i];
                nc.setName(username);
            } else if (callbacks[i] instanceof PasswordCallback) {
                PasswordCallback pc = (PasswordCallback)callbacks[i];
                pc.setPassword(password);
            } else {
                throw new UnsupportedCallbackException(callbacks[i],
                                                       "Unrecognized Callback");
            }
        }
    }
}
```

`EchoSecurityProxy` checks that the method to be invoked on the bean instance corresponds to the `echo(String)` method that was looked up in the init method. If there is a match, the method argument is obtained, and its length is compared against `4` or null. Either case results in a `SecurityException` being thrown. Certainly, this is a contrived example, but only in its application. It is a common requirement that applications must perform security checks based on the value of method arguments. The point of the example is to demonstrate how you can introduce custom security beyond the scope of the standard declarative security model, independently of the bean implementation. This allows the specification and coding of the security requirements to be delegated to security experts. Because the security proxy layer can be done independently of the bean implementation, security can be changed to match the deployment environment requirements.

Listing 8.9 shows the associated `jboss.xml` descriptor that installs `EchoSecurityProxy` as the custom proxy for `EchoBean`.

LISTING 8.9 The `jboss.xml` Descriptor, Which Configures `EchoSecurityProxy` as the Custom Security Proxy for `EchoBean`

```
<jboss>
    <security-domain>java:/jaas/other</security-domain>

    <enterprise-beans>
        <session>
            <ejb-name>EchoBean</ejb-name>
            <security-proxy>org.jboss.chap8.ex1.EchoSecurityProxy</security-proxy>
        </session>
    </enterprise-beans>
</jboss>
```

Now you can test the custom proxy by running a client that attempts to invoke the `EchoBean.echo` method with the arguments `Hello` and `Four`, as illustrated in this fragment:

```
public class ExClient
{
    public static void main(String args[])
        throws Exception
    {
        Logger log = Logger.getLogger("ExClient");
        log.info("Looking up EchoBean");

        InitialContext iniCtx = new InitialContext();
        Object ref = iniCtx.lookup("EchoBean");
        EchoHome home = (EchoHome) ref;
        Echo echo = home.create();
```

```
        log.info("Created Echo");
        log.info("Echo.echo('Hello') = "+echo.echo("Hello"));
        log.info("Echo.echo('Four') = "+echo.echo("Four"));
    }
}
```

The first call should succeed, and the second should fail due to the fact that `Four` is a four-letter word. You can run the client as follows, using Ant from the examples directory:

```
[examples]$ ant -Dchap=chap8 -Dex=1 run-example
run-example1:
     [copy] Copying 1 file to /tmp/jboss-4.0.1/server/default/deploy
     [echo] Waiting for 5 seconds for deploy...
     [java] [INFO,ExClient] Looking up EchoBean
     [java] [INFO,ExClient] Created Echo
     [java] [INFO,ExClient] Echo.echo('Hello') = Hello
     [java] Exception in thread "main" java.rmi.ServerException:
➥RemoteException occurred in server thread; nested exception is:
     [java]     java.rmi.AccessException: SecurityException; nested exception is:
     [java]     java.lang.SecurityException: No 4 letter words
...
     [java]     at org.jboss.chap8.ex1.ExClient.main(ExClient.java:25)
     [java] Caused by: java.rmi.AccessException: SecurityException;
➥nested exception is:
     [java]     java.lang.SecurityException: No 4 letter words
...
```

The result is that the `echo('Hello')` method call succeeds, as expected, and the `echo('Four')` method call results in a rather messy-looking exception, which is also expected. (The preceding output has been truncated to fit in the book.)

The key part to the exception is that the `SecurityException("No 4 letter words")` generated by the `EchoSecurityProxy` was thrown to abort the attempted method invocation, as desired.

The JBossSX Architecture

The preceding discussion of the general JBoss security layer states that the JBossSX security extension framework is an implementation of the security layer interfaces. This is the primary purpose of the JBossSX framework. The details of the implementation are interesting in that the implementation offers a great deal of customization for integration into existing security infrastructures. A security infrastructure can be anything from a database or an LDAP server to a sophisticated security software suite. The integration flexibility is achieved by using the pluggable authentication model that is available in the JAAS framework.

The heart of the JBossSX framework is `org.jboss.security.plugins.JaasSecurityManager`. This is the default implementation of the `AuthenticationManager` and `RealmMapping` interfaces. Figure 8.11 shows how `JaasSecurityManager` integrates into the EJB and web container layers, based on the `security-domain` element of the corresponding component deployment descriptor.

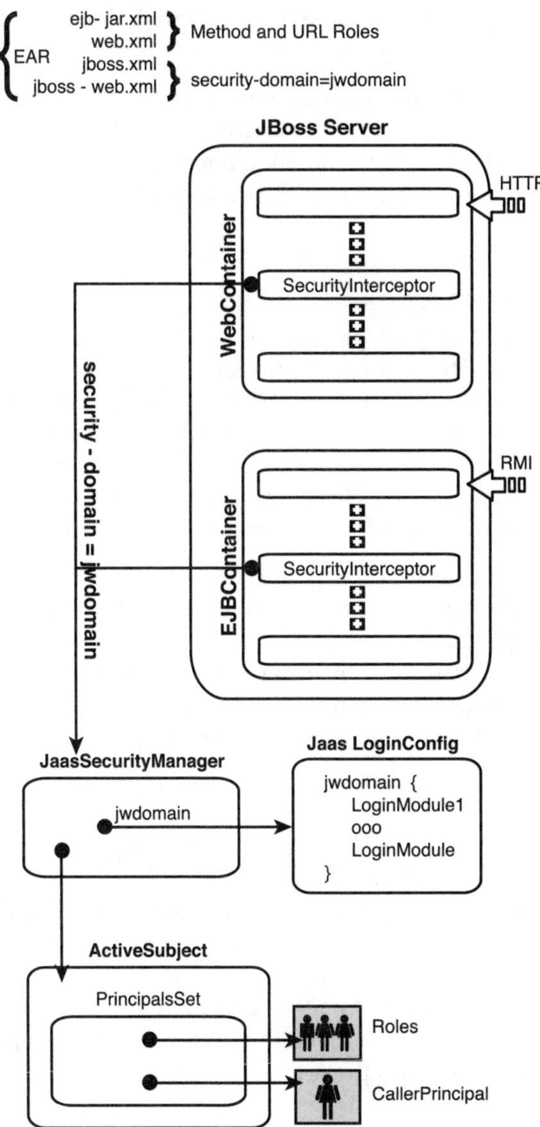

FIGURE 8.11 The relationship between the `security-domain` component deployment descriptor value, the component container, and `JaasSecurityManager`.

Figure 8.11 depicts an enterprise application that contains both EJBs and web content, secured under the security domain `jwdomain`. The EJB and web containers have a request interceptor architecture that includes a security interceptor, which enforces the container security model. At deployment time, the `security-domain` element value in the `jboss.xml` and `jboss-web.xml` descriptors is used to obtain the security manager instance associated with the container. The security interceptor then uses the security manager to perform its role. When a secured component is requested, the security interceptor delegates security checks to the security manager instance associated with the container.

The JBossSX `JaasSecurityManager` implementation performs security checks based on the information associated with the `Subject` instance that results from executing the JAAS login modules configured under the name that matches the `security-domain` element value. The following section drills into the `JaasSecurityManager` implementation and its use of JAAS.

How `JaasSecurityManager` Uses JAAS

`JaasSecurityManager` uses the JAAS packages to implement the `AuthenticationManager` and `RealmMapping` interface behavior. In particular, its behavior derives from the execution of the login module instances that are configured under the name that matches the security domain to which `JaasSecurityManager` has been assigned. The login modules implement the security domain's principal authentication and role-mapping behavior. Thus, you can use the `JaasSecurityManager` across different security domains simply by plugging in different login module configurations for the domains.

To illustrate the details of `JaasSecurityManager`'s usage of the JAAS authentication process, you will walk through a client invocation of an EJB home method invocation. The prerequisite setting is that the EJB has been deployed in the JBoss server, its home interface methods have been secured by using `method-permission` elements in the `ejb-jar.xml` descriptor, and it has been assigned a security domain named `jwdomain`, using the `jboss.xml` descriptor `security-domain` element.

Figure 8.12 provides a view of the client-to-server communication discussed in this section.

The following are the numbered steps shown in Figure 8.12:

1. The client performs a JAAS login to establish the principal and credentials for authentication. This is how clients establish their login identities in JBoss. Support for presenting the login information via JNDI `InitialContext` properties is provided via an alternate configuration. A JAAS login entails creating a `LoginContext` instance and passing the name of the configuration to use. The configuration name is `other`. This one-time login associates the login principal and credentials with all subsequent EJB method invocations. Note that the process might not authenticate the user. The nature of the client-side login depends on the login module configuration that the client uses. In this example, the `other` client-side login configuration entry is set up to use the `ClientLoginModule` module (an `org.jboss.security.ClientLoginModule`). This is the default client-side module, and it simply binds the

username and password to the JBoss EJB invocation layer for later authentication on the server. The identity of the client is not authenticated on the client.

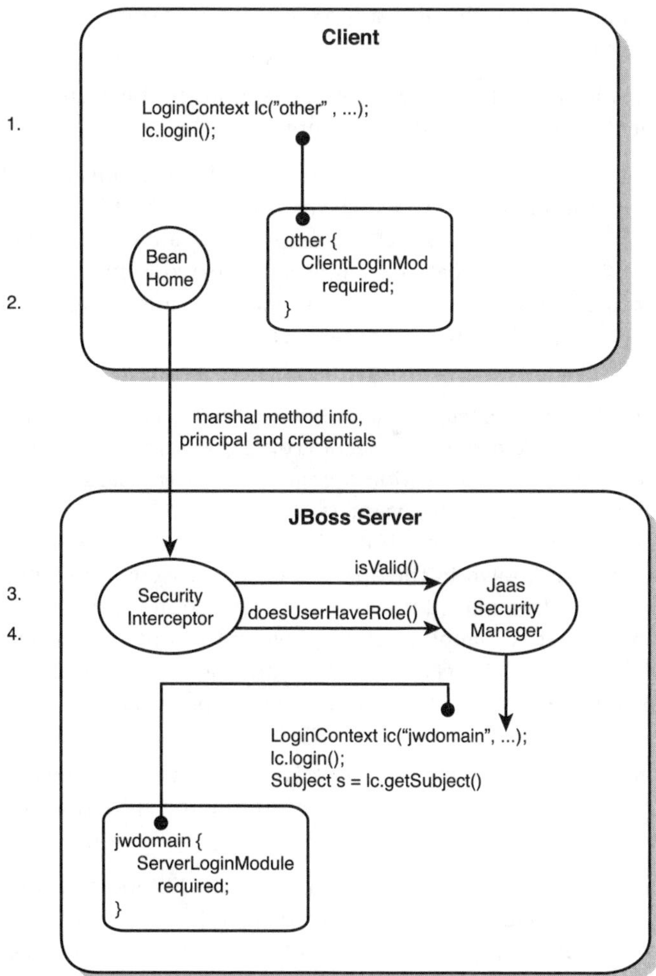

FIGURE 8.12 The steps involved in the authentication and authorization of a secured EJB home method invocation.

2. The client obtains the EJB home interface and attempts to create a bean. This results in a home interface method invocation being sent to the JBoss server. The invocation includes the method arguments passed by the client, along with the user identity and credentials from the client-side JAAS login performed in step 1.

3. On the server side, the security interceptor first requires authentication of the user invoking the call. As on the client side, this involves a JAAS login.

4. The security domain under which the EJB is secured determines the choice of login modules. The security domain name is used as the login configuration entry name passed to the LoginContext constructor. The EJB security domain is jwdomain. If the JAAS login authenticates the user, a JAAS Subject is created, and it contains the following in its PrincipalsSet:

    - A java.security.Principal that corresponds to the client identity, as known in the deployment security environment.
    - A java.security.acl.Group named Roles that contains the role names from the application domain to which the user is assigned. org.jboss.security.SimplePrincipal objects are used to represent the role names; SimplePrincipal is a simple string-based implementation of Principal. These roles are used to validate the roles assigned to methods in ejb-jar.xml and in the EJBContext.isCallerInRole(String) method implementation.
    - An optional java.security.acl.Group named CallerPrincipal, which contains a single org.jboss.security.SimplePrincipal that corresponds to the identity of the application domain's caller. The CallerPrincipal sole group member will be the value returned by the EJBContext.getCallerPrincipal() method. The purpose of this mapping is to allow a Principal, as known in the operational security environment, to map to a Principal with a name known to the application. In the absence of a CallerPrincipal mapping, the deployment security environment principal is used as the get-CallerPrincipal method value. That is, the operational principal is the same as the application domain principal.

The final step of the security interceptor check is to verify that the authenticated user has permission to invoke the requested method. Performing the authorization entails the following processes:

- Obtain the names of the roles allowed to access the EJB method from the EJB container. The role names are determined by ejb-jar.xml descriptor role-name elements of all method-permission elements that contain the invoked method.
- If no roles have been assigned, or if the method is specified in an exclude-list element, access to the method is denied. Otherwise, the doesUserHaveRole method is invoked on the security manager by the security interceptor to see if the caller has one of the assigned role names. This method iterates through the role names and checks whether the authenticated user's Subject Roles group contains a SimplePrincipal with the assigned role name. Access is allowed if any role name is a member of the Roles group. Access is denied if none of the role names are members.
- If the EJB was configured with a custom security proxy, the method invocation is delegated to it. If the security proxy wants to deny access to the caller, it throws a java.lang.SecurityException. If no SecurityException is thrown, access to the

EJB method is allowed, and the method invocation passes to the next container interceptor. Note that the SecurityProxyInterceptor handles this check, and this interceptor is not shown in Figure 8.12.

Every secured EJB method invocation or secured web content access requires the authentication and authorization of the caller because security information is handled as a stateless attribute of the request that must be presented and validated on each request. This can be an expensive operation if the JAAS login involves client-to-server communication. Therefore, JaasSecurityManager supports the notion of an authentication cache that is used to store principal and credential information from previous successful logins. You can specify the authentication cache instance to use as part of the JaasSecurityManager configuration, as you will see in the following section. In the absence of any user-defined cache, a default cache that maintains credential information for a configurable period of time is used.

The JaasSecurityManagerService MBean

The JaasSecurityManagerService MBean service manages security managers. Although its name begins with Jaas, the security managers it handles need not use JAAS in their implementation. The name arose from the fact that the default security manager implementation is JaasSecurityManager. The primary role of JaasSecurityManagerService is to externalize the security manager implementation. You can change the security manager implementation by providing an alternate implementation of the AuthenticationManager and RealmMapping interfaces.

The second fundamental role of JaasSecurityManagerService is to provide a JNDI javax.naming.spi.ObjectFactory implementation to allow for simple code-free management of the JNDI name-to-security manager implementation mapping. As mentioned previously, you enable security by specifying the JNDI name of the security manager implementation via the security-domain deployment descriptor element. When you specify a JNDI name, there has to be an object-binding to use. To simplify the setup of the JNDI name-to-security manager bindings, JaasSecurityManagerService manages the association of security manager instances to names by binding the next naming system reference with itself as the JNDI ObjectFactory under the name java:/jaas. This allows you to use a naming convention in the form java:/jaas/XYZ as the value for the security-domain element, and the security manager instance for the XYZ security domain will be created as needed for you. The security manager for the domain XYZ is created on the first lookup against the java:/jaas/XYZ binding by creating an instance of the class specified by the SecurityManagerClassName attribute, using a constructor that takes the name of the security domain. For example, consider the following container security configuration snippet:

```
<jboss>
    <!-- Configure all containers to be secured under the
➥"hades" security domain -->
```

```
    <security-domain>java:/jaas/hades</security-domain>
    <!-- ... -->
</jboss>
```

Any lookup of the name `java:/jaas/hades` will return a security manager instance that has been associated with the security domain named `hades`. This security manager will implement the `AuthenticationManager` and `RealmMapping` security interfaces and will be of the type specified by the `JaasSecurityManagerService` `SecurityManagerClassName` attribute.

The `JaasSecurityManagerService` MBean is configured by default for use in the standard JBoss distribution, and you can often use the default configuration as is. The configurable attributes of the `JaasSecurityManagerService` include the following:

- **`SecurityManagerClassName`**—The name of the class that provides the security manager implementation. The implementation must support both the `org.jboss.security.AuthenticationManager` and `org.jboss.security.RealmMapping` interfaces. If not specified, this defaults to the JAAS-based `org.jboss.security.plugins.JaasSecurityManager`.
- **`CallbackHandlerClassName`**—The name of the class that provides the `javax.security.auth.callback.CallbackHandler` implementation used by `JaasSecurityManager`. You can override the handler used by `JaasSecurityManager` if the default implementation (`org.jboss.security.auth.callback.SecurityAssociationHandler`) does not meet your needs. This is a rather deep configuration that you generally should not set unless you know what you are doing.
- **`SecurityProxyFactoryClassName`**—The name of the class that provides the `org.jboss.security.SecurityProxyFactory` implementation. If not specified, this defaults to `org.jboss.security.SubjectSecurityProxyFactory`.
- **`AuthenticationCacheJndiName`**—The location of the security credential cache policy. This is first treated as an `ObjectFactory` location that is capable of returning `CachePolicy` instances on a per-security-domain basis. This is done by appending the name of the security domain to this name when looking up the `CachePolicy` for a domain. If that fails, the location is treated as a single `CachePolicy` for all security domains. As a default, a timed cache policy is used.
- **`DefaultCacheTimeout`**—The default timed cache policy timeout, in seconds. The default value is `1800` (30 minutes). The value you use for the timeout is a tradeoff between frequent authentication operations and how long credential information may be out of sync with respect to the security information store. If you want to disable caching of security credentials, you can set this to `0` to force authentication to occur every time. This has no effect if `AuthenticationCacheJndiName` has been changed from the default value.
- **`DefaultCacheResolution`**—The default timed cache policy resolution, in seconds. This controls the interval at which the cache current timestamp is updated and

should be less than `DefaultCacheTimeout` in order for the timeout to be meaningful. The default resolution is `60` (1 minute). This has no effect if `AuthenticationCacheJndiName` has been changed from the default value.

- **`DefaultUnauthenticatedPrincipal`**—The principal to use for unauthenticated users. This setting makes it possible to set default permissions for users who have not been authenticated.

`JaasSecurityManagerService` also supports a number of useful operations. These include flushing any security domain authentication cache at runtime, getting the list of active users in a security domain authentication cache, and using any of the security manager interface methods.

You can flush a security domain authentication cache in order to drop all cached credentials when the underlying store has been updated and you want the store state to be used immediately. The MBean operation signature is `public void flushAuthenticationCache(String securityDomain)`. The following code invokes this operation:

```
MBeanServer server = ...;
String jaasMgrName = "jboss.security:service=JaasSecurityManager";
ObjectName jaasMgr = new ObjectName(jaasMgrName);
Object[] params = {domainName};
String[] signature = {"java.lang.String"};
server.invoke(jaasMgr, "flushAuthenticationCache", params, signature);
```

Getting the list of active users provides a snapshot of the unexpired `Principals` keys in a security domain authentication cache. The MBean operation signature is `public List getAuthenticationCachePrincipals(String securityDomain)`. The following code invokes this operation:

```
MBeanServer server = ...;
String jaasMgrName = "jboss.security:service=JaasSecurityManager";
ObjectName jaasMgr = new ObjectName(jaasMgrName);
Object[] params = {domainName};
String[] signature = {"java.lang.String"};
server.invoke(jaasMgr, "flushAuthenticationCache", params, signature);
```

The security manager has a few additional access methods:

```
public boolean isValid(String securityDomain, Principal principal,
➥Object credential);
public Principal getPrincipal(String securityDomain, Principal principal);
public boolean doesUserHaveRole(String securityDomain, Principal principal,
                                Object credential, Set roles);
public Set getUserRoles(String securityDomain, Principal principal,
➥Object credential);
```

These access methods provide access to the corresponding `AuthenticationManager` and `RealmMapping` interface method of the associated security domain named by the `securityDomain` argument.

The `JaasSecurityDomain` MBean

`org.jboss.security.plugins.JaasSecurityDomain` is an extension of `JaasSecurityManager` that adds the notion of a `KeyStore`, a JSSE `KeyManagerFactory`, and a `TrustManagerFactory` for supporting SSL and other cryptographic use cases. The additional configurable attributes of the `JaasSecurityDomain` include the following:

- **`KeyStoreType`**—The type of the `KeyStore` implementation. This is the type argument that is passed to the `java.security.KeyStore.getInstance(String type)` factory method.The default is `JKS`.
- **`KeyStoreURL`**—A URL to the location of the `KeyStore` database. This is used to obtain an `InputStream` to initialize the `KeyStore`. If the string is not a value URL, it is treated as a file.
- **`KeyStorePass`**—The password associated with the `KeyStore` database contents. The `KeyStorePass` is also used in combination with the `Salt` and `IterationCount` attributes to create a PBE secret key that is used with the encode/decode operations. The `KeyStorePass` attribute value format is one of the following:
    - **The plaintext password for the `KeyStore`**—The `toCharArray()` value of the string is used without any manipulation.
    - **A command to execute to obtain the plaintext password**—The format is `{EXT}...` where the `...` is the exact command line that will be passed to the `Runtime.exec(String)` method to execute a platform-specific command. The first line of the command output is used as the password.
    - **A class to create to obtain the plaintext password**—The format is `{CLASS}classname[:ctorarg]` where `[:ctorarg]` is an optional string that will be passed to the constructor when instantiating *`classname`*. The password is obtained from *`classname`* by invoking a `toCharArray()` method, if found; otherwise, the `toString()` method is used.
- **`Salt`**—The `PBEParameterSpec` salt value.
- **`IterationCount`**—The `PBEParameterSpec` iteration count value.
- **`TrustStoreType`**—The type of the `TrustStore` implementation. This is the type argument that is passed to the `java.security.KeyStore.getInstance(String type)` factory method. The default is `JKS`.
- **`TrustStoreURL`**—A URL to the location of the `TrustStore` database. This is used to obtain an `InputStream` to initialize the `KeyStore`. If the string is not a value `URL`, it is treated as a file.

- **TrustStorePass**—The password associated with the trust store database contents. TrustStorePass is a simple password and doesn't have the same configuration options as KeyStorePass.
- **ManagerServiceName**—The JMX object name string of the security manager service MBean. This is used to register the defaults to register the JaasSecurityDomain as the security manager under java:/jaas/*<domain>*, where *<domain>* is the name that is passed to the MBean constructor. The name defaults to jboss.security:service=JaasSecurityManager.

An XML JAAS Login Configuration MBean

XMLLoginConfig is a service that loads standard JAAS application configurations from a local configuration file. This MBean supports the following attributes:

- **ConfigURL**—This attribute specifies the URL of the XML login configuration file that this MBean should load on startup. This must be a valid URL string representation.
- **ConfigResource**—This attribute specifies the resource name of the XML login configuration file that this MBean should load on startup. The name is treated as a classpath resource for which a URL is located, using the thread context class loader.
- **ValidateDTD**—This flag indicates whether the XML configuration should be validated against its DTD. This defaults to true.

The XML configuration file conforms to the DTD shown in Figure 8.13. This DTD can be found in docs/dtd/security_config.dtd.

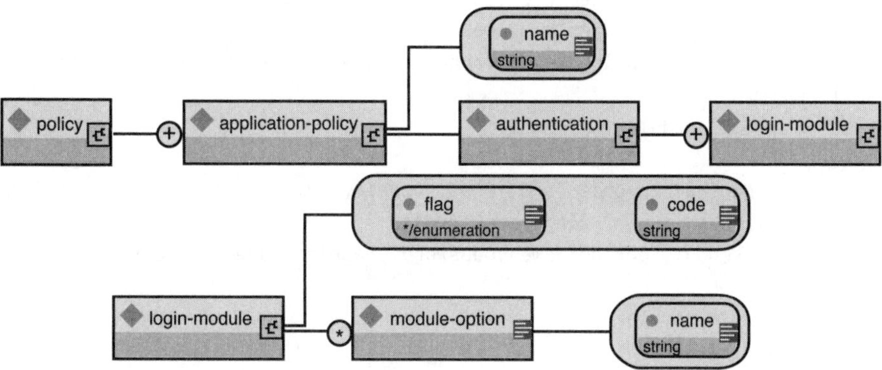

FIGURE 8.13 The XMLLoginConfig DTD.

The name attribute of application-policy is the login configuration name. This corresponds to the portion of the jboss.xml and jboss-web.xml security-domain element value after the java:/jaas/ prefix. The code attribute of the login-module element specifies the classname of the login module implementation. The flag attribute controls the overall behavior of the authentication stack. The allowed values and meanings are as follows:

- **required**—The LoginModule is required to succeed. If it succeeds or fails, authentication still continues to proceed down the LoginModule list.
- **requisite**—The LoginModule is required to succeed. If it succeeds, authentication continues down the LoginModule list. If it fails, control immediately returns to the application (authentication does not proceed down the LoginModule list).
- **sufficient**—The LoginModule is not required to succeed. If it does succeed, control immediately returns to the application (authentication does not proceed down the LoginModule list). If it fails, authentication continues down the LoginModule list.
- **optional**—The LoginModule is not required to succeed. If it succeeds or fails, authentication still continues to proceed down the LoginModule list.

Zero or more module-option elements may be specified as child elements of a login-module. These define name/value string pairs that are made available to the login module during initialization. The name attribute specifies the option name, and the module-option body provides the value. An example of a login configuration is shown in Listing 8.10.

LISTING 8.10 A Sample Login Module Configuration Suitable for Use with XMLLoginConfig

```
<policy>
    <application-policy name="srp-test">
        <authentication>
            <login-module code="org.jboss.security.srp.jaas.SRPCacheLoginModule"
                          flag="required">
                <module-option name="cacheJndiName">srp-test/AuthenticationCache
➥</module-option>
            </login-module>

            <login-module code="org.jboss.security.auth.spi.UsersRolesLoginModule"
                             flag="required">
                <module-option name="password-stacking">useFirstPass
➥</module-option>
            </login-module>
        </authentication>
    </application-policy>
</policy>
```

The MBean also supports the following operations that allow you to dynamically extend the login configurations at runtime. Note that any operation that attempts to alter the login configuration requires a javax.security.auth.AuthPermission ("refreshLoginConfiguration") when running with a security manager. The `org.jboss.chap8.service.SecurityConfig` service demonstrates how you can use this to add/remove a deployment-specific security configuration dynamically:

- **`void addAppConfig(String appName,AppConfigurationEntry[] entries)`**—This adds the given login module configuration stack to the current configuration, under the given `appName`. This replaces any existing entry under that name.
- **`void removeAppConfig(String appName)`**—This removes the login module configuration registered under the given `appName`.
- **`String[] loadConfig(URL configURL) throws Exception`**—This loads one or more login configurations from a URL that represents either an XML or a legacy Sun login configuration file. Note that all login configurations must be added, or none will be added. It returns the names of the login configurations that were added.
- **`void removeConfigs(String[] appNames)`**—This removes the login configuration's specified `appNames` array.
- **`String displayAppConfig(String appName)`**—This operation displays a simple string format of the named configuration, if it exists.

The JAAS Login Configuration Management MBean

The installation of the custom `javax.security.auth.login.Configuration` is managed by the `org.jboss.security.plugins.SecurityConfig` MBean. There is one configurable attribute:

- **`LoginConfig`**—This attribute specifies the JMX `ObjectName` string of the MBean that provides the default JAAS login configuration. When the `SecurityConfig` is started, you query this MBean for its `javax.security.auth.login.Configuration` by calling its `getConfiguration(Configuration currentConfig)` operation. If the `LoginConfig` attribute is not specified, the default Sun `Configuration` implementation that is described in the `Configuration` class JavaDocs is used.

In addition to allowing for a custom JAAS login configuration implementation, this service allows configurations to be chained together in a stack at runtime. This enables you to push a login configuration onto the stack and later pop it. The security unit tests use this feature to install custom login configurations into a default JBoss installation. Pushing a new configuration is done using the following:

```
public void pushLoginConfig(String objectName)
     throws JMException,
            MalformedObjectNameException;
```

The `objectName` parameter specifies an MBean similar to the `LoginConfig` attribute. You can remove the current login configuration by using the following:

```
public void popLoginConfig()
    throws JMException;
```

Using and Writing JBossSX Login Modules

The `JaasSecurityManager` implementation allows complete customization of the authentication mechanism, using JAAS login module configurations. By defining the login module configuration entry that corresponds to the security domain name you have used to secure access to your J2EE components, you define the authentication mechanism and integration implementation.

The JBossSX framework includes a number of bundled login modules that are suitable for integration with standard security infrastructure store protocols, such as LDAP and JDBC. It also includes standard base class implementations that help enforce the expected `LoginModule-to-Subject` usage pattern that is described later in this chapter, in the section "Writing Custom Login Modules." These implementations allow for easy integration of your own authentication protocol if none of the bundled login modules prove suitable. The following sections first describe the useful bundled login modules and their configuration, and then discuss how to create your own custom `LoginModule` implementations for use with JBoss.

org.jboss.security.auth.spi.IdentityLoginModule

`IdentityLoginModule` is a simple login module that associates the principal specified in the module options with any subject authenticated against the module. It creates a `SimplePrincipal` instance, using the name specified by the `principal` option. Although this is certainly not an appropriate login module for production-strength authentication, it can be of use in development environments when you want to test the security associated with a given principal and associated roles.

The supported login module configuration options include the following:

- **`principal`**—This is the name to use for the `SimplePrincipal` that all users are authenticated as. The principal name defaults to `guest` if no principal option is specified.
- **`roles`**—This is the names of the roles that will be assigned to the user principal. The value is a comma-delimited list of role names.
- **`password-stacking`**—When the `password-stacking` option is set to `useFirstPass`, this module first looks for a shared username under the property name `javax.security.auth.login.name` in the login module's shared state map. If that is found, this is used as the principal name. If it is not found, the principal name set by this login module is stored under the property name `javax.security.auth.login.name`.

The following is a sample `XMLLoginConfig` configuration entry that would authenticate all users as the principal named `jduke` and assign the role names `TheDuke` and `AnimatedCharacter`:

```
<policy>
    <application-policy name="testIdentity">
        <authentication>
            <login-module code="org.jboss.security.auth.spi.IdentityLoginModule"
```

```
                        flag="required">
                <module-option name="principal">jduke</module-option>
                <module-option name="roles">TheDuke,AnimatedCharater
➥</module-option>
            </login-module>
        </authentication>
    </application-policy>
</policy>
```

`org.jboss.security.auth.spi.UsersRolesLoginModule`

`UsersRolesLoginModule` is a simple login module that supports multiple users and user roles loaded from Java properties files. The username-to-password mapping file is called `users.properties`, and the username-to-roles mapping file is called `roles.properties`. The properties files are loaded during initialization, using the `initialize` method thread context class loader. This means that these files can be placed into the J2EE deployment JAR, the JBoss configuration directory, or any directory on the JBoss server or system classpath. The primary purpose of this login module is to easily test the security settings of multiple users and roles, using properties files deployed with the application.

The `users.properties` file uses a `username=password` format with each user entry on a separate line, as shown here:

```
username1=password1
username2=password2
...
```

The `roles.properties` file uses the `username=role1,role2,...` format, with an optional group name value. Here's an example:

```
username1=role1,role2,...
username1.RoleGroup1=role3,role4,...
username2=role1,role3,...
```

The `username.XXX` form of property name is used to assign the username roles to a particular named group of roles, where the `XXX` portion of the property name is the group name. The `username=...` form is an abbreviation for `username.Roles=...`, where the `Roles` group name is the standard name the `JaasSecurityManager` expects to contain the roles that define the user's permissions.

The following would be equivalent definitions for the `jduke` username:

```
jduke=TheDuke,AnimatedCharacter
jduke.Roles=TheDuke,AnimatedCharacter
```

The supported login module configuration options include the following:

- **`unauthenticatedIdentity`**—This option defines the principal name that should be assigned to requests that contain no authentication information. You can use this option to allow unprotected servlets to invoke methods on EJBs that do not require a specific role. Such a principal has no associated roles and so can only access either unsecured EJBs or EJB methods that are associated with the unchecked permission constraint.

- **password-stacking**—When this option is set to useFirstPass, this module first looks for a shared username and password under the property names javax.security.auth.login.name and javax.security.auth.login.password, respectively, in the login module shared state map. If these are found, they are used as the principal name and password. If they are not found, the principal name and password are set by this login module and stored under the property names javax.security.auth.login.name and javax.security.auth.login.password, respectively.
- **hashAlgorithm**—This option specifies the name of the java.security.MessageDigest algorithm to use to hash the password. There is no default, so this option must be specified to enable hashing. When hashAlgorithm is specified, the clear-text password obtained from callbackhandler is hashed before it is passed to UsernamePasswordLoginModule.validatePassword as the inputPassword argument. The expectedPassword, as stored in the users.properties file, must be comparably hashed.
- **hashEncoding**—The string format for the hashed pass and must be either base64 or hex. base64 is the default.
- **hashCharset**—This option specifies the encoding used to convert the clear-text password to a byte array. The platform default encoding is the default.
- **usersProperties**—This option specifies the name of the properties resource that contains the username-to-password mappings. The default is users.properties.
- **rolesProperties**—This option specifies the name of the properties resource that contains the username-to-roles mappings. The default is roles.properties.

The following is a sample legacy XMLLoginConfig configuration entry that assigns unauthenticated users the principal name nobody and contains Base 64–encoded MD5 hashes of the passwords in a usersb64.properties file:

```
<policy>
    <application-policy name="testUsersRoles">
        <authentication>
            <login-module code="org.jboss.security.auth.spi.UsersRolesLoginModule"
                          flag="required">
                <module-option name="usersProperties">usersb64.properties
➥</module-option>
                <module-option name="hashAlgorithm">MD5</module-option>
                <module-option name="hashEncoding">base64</module-option>
                <module-option name="unauthenticatedIdentity">nobody
➥</module-option>
```

```
            </login-module>
        </authentication>
    </application-policy>
</policy>
```

`org.jboss.security.auth.spi.LdapLoginModule`

`LdapLoginModule` is a `LoginModule` implementation that authenticates against an LDAP server, using JNDI login, using the login module configuration options. You would use `LdapLoginModule` if your username and credential information are stored in an LDAP server that is accessible via a JNDI LDAP provider.

The LDAP connectivity information is provided as configuration options that are passed through to the environment object used to create the JNDI initial context. The standard LDAP JNDI properties used include the following:

- **`java.naming.factory.initial`**—The classname of the `InitialContextFactory` implementation. This defaults to the Sun LDAP provider implementation `com.sun.jndi.ldap.LdapCtxFactory`.
- **`java.naming.provider.url`**—The LDAP URL for the LDAP server.
- **`java.naming.security.authentication`**—The security level to use. This defaults to `simple`.
- **`java.naming.security.protocol`**—The transport protocol to use for secure access, such as `ssl`.
- **`java.naming.security.principal`**—The principal for authenticating the caller to the service. This is built from other properties, as described later in this section.
- **`java.naming.security.credentials`**—The value of the property, which depends on the authentication scheme. For example, it could be a hashed password, clear-text password, key, certificate, and so on.

The supported login module configuration options include the following:

- **`principalDNPrefix`**—This option specifies a prefix to add to the username to form the user-distinguished name. See the following bullet for more information.
- **`principalDNSuffix`**—This option specifies a suffix to add to the username when forming the user-distinguished name. This is useful if you prompt a user for a username and you don't want the user to have to enter the fully distinguished name. By using this property and `principalDNSuffix`, the `userDN` will be formed as `principalDNPrefix` + username + `principalDNSuffix`.
- **`useObjectCredential`**—This option specifies a `true`/`false` value which indicates that the credential should be obtained as an opaque `Object`, using the `org.jboss.security.auth.callback.ObjectCallback` type of `Callback` rather than as a `char[]` password, using a JAAS `PasswordCallback`. This allows for passing non-`char[]` credential information to the LDAP server.

- **rolesCtxDN**—This option specifies the fixed distinguished name to the context to search for user roles.
- **userRolesCtxDNAttributeName**—This option specifies the name of an attribute in the user object that contains the distinguished name of the context to search for user roles. This differs from rolesCtxDN in that the context to search for a user's roles can be unique for each user.
- **roleAttributeID**—This option specifies the name of the attribute that contains the user roles. If not specified, this defaults to roles.
- **roleAttributeIsDN**—This option specifies a flag that indicates whether roleAttributeID contains the fully distinguished name of a role object, or the role name. If false, the role name is taken from the value of roleAttributeID. If true, the role attribute represents the distinguished name of a role object. The role name is taken from the value of the roleNameAttributeId attribute of the context name specified by the roleattributeId distinguished name. In certain directory schemas (for example, Microsoft Active Directory), role attributes in the user object are stored as DNs to role objects instead of as simple names, and in such a case, this property should be set to true. The default is false.
- **roleNameAttributeID**—This option specifies the name of the attribute of the context pointed to by the roleCtxDN distinguished name value, which contains the role name. If the roleAttributeIsDN property is set to true, this property is used to find the role object's name attribute. The default is group.
- **uidAttributeID**—This option specifies the name of the attribute in the object that contains the user roles that correspond to the user ID. This is used to locate the user roles. If not specified, it defaults to uid.
- **matchOnUserDN**—This option specifies a true/false flag that indicates whether the search for user roles should match the user's fully distinguished name. If false, just the username is used as the match value against the uidAttributeName attribute. If true, the full userDN is used as the match value.
- **unauthenticatedIdentity**—This option specifies the principal name that should be assigned to requests that contain no authentication information. This behavior is inherited from the UsernamePasswordLoginModule superclass.
- **password-stacking**—When the password-stacking option is set to useFirstPass, this module first looks for a shared username and password under the property names javax.security.auth.login.name and javax.security.auth.login.password, respectively, in the login module shared state map. If found, these are used as the principal name and password. If not found, the principal name and password are set by this login module and stored under the property names javax.security.auth.login.name and javax.security.auth.login.password, respectively.

- **allowEmptyPasswords**—This option specifies a flag that indicates whether if empty (length 0) passwords should be passed to the LDAP server. Some LDAP servers treat an empty password as an anonymous login, and this may not be a desirable feature. You set this to false to reject empty passwords or true to have the LDAP server validate the empty password. The default is true.

The authentication of a user is performed by connecting to the LDAP server, based on the login module configuration options. Connecting to the LDAP server is done by creating an InitialLdapContext with an environment composed of the LDAP JNDI properties described previously in this section. The Context.SECURITY_PRINCIPAL is set to the distinguished name of the user, as obtained by the callback handler in combination with the principalDNPrefix and principalDNSuffix option values, and the Context.SECURITY_CREDENTIALS property is either set to the String password or the Object credential, depending on the useObjectCredential option.

When authentication has succeeded by virtue of being able to create an InitialLdapContext instance, the user's roles are queried by performing a search on the rolesCtxDN location with search attributes set to the roleAttributeName and uidAttributeName option values. The role names are obtained by invoking the toString method on the role attributes in the search result set.

The following is a sample login-config.xml entry:

```
<policy>
    <application-policy name="testLDAP">
        <authentication>
            <login-module code="org.jboss.security.auth.spi.LdapLoginModule"
                          flag="required">
                <module-option name="java.naming.factory.initial">
                    com.sun.jndi.ldap.LdapCtxFactory
                    </module-option>
                <module-option name="java.naming.provider.url">
                    ldap://ldaphost.jboss.org:1389/
                </module-option>
                <module-option name="java.naming.security.authentication">
                    simple
                </module-option>
                <module-option name="principalDNPrefix">uid=</module-option>
                <module-option name="principalDNSuffix">
                    ,ou=People,dc=jboss,dc=org
                </module-option>

                <module-option name="rolesCtxDN">
                    ou=Roles,dc=jboss,dc=org
                </module-option>
                <module-option name="uidAttributeID">member</module-option>
                <module-option name="matchOnUserDN">true</module-option>
```

```
                <module-option name="roleAttributeID">cn</module-option>
                <module-option name="roleAttributeIsDN">false </module-option>
            </login-module>
        </authentication>
    </application-policy>
</policy>
```

An LDIF file representing the structure of the directory this data operates against is shown here:

```
dn: dc=jboss,dc=org
objectclass: top
objectclass: dcObject
objectclass: organization
dc: jboss
o: JBoss

dn: ou=People,dc=jboss,dc=org
objectclass: top
objectclass: organizationalUnit
ou: People

dn: uid=jduke,ou=People,dc=jboss,dc=org
objectclass: top
objectclass: uidObject
objectclass: person
uid: jduke
cn: Java Duke
sn: Duke
userPassword: theduke

dn: ou=Roles,dc=jboss,dc=org
objectclass: top
objectclass: organizationalUnit
ou: Roles

dn: cn=JBossAdmin,ou=Roles,dc=jboss,dc=org
objectclass: top
objectclass: groupOfNames
cn: JBossAdmin
member: uid=jduke,ou=People,dc=jboss,dc=org
description: the JBossAdmin group
```

If you look back at the `testLDAP` login module configuration, you see that the `java.naming.factory.initial`, `java.naming.factory.url`, and `java.naming.security` options indicate that the Sun LDAP JNDI provider implementation will be used, the LDAP server is located on host `ldaphost.jboss.org` on port 1389, and the LDAP simple authentication method will be use to connect to the LDAP server.

The login module attempts to connect to the LDAP server by using a DN that represents the user it is trying to authenticate. This DN is constructed from the `principalDNPrefix`, passed in the username of the user, and the `principalDNSuffix`, as described earlier in this chapter. In this example, the username `jduke` would map to `uid=jduke, ou=People,dc=jboss,dc=org`. Here we assume that the LDAP server authenticates users by using the `user-Password` attribute of the user's entry (`theduke`, in this example). This is the way most LDAP servers work; however, if your LDAP server handles authentication differently, you need to set the authentication credentials in a way that makes sense for your server.

When authentication succeeds, you retrieve the roles on which authorization will be based by performing a subtree search of the `rolesCtxDN` for entries whose `uidAttributeID` matches the user. If `matchOnUserDN` is `true`, the search is based on the full DN of the user. Otherwise, the search is based on the actual username entered. In this example, the search is under `ou=Roles,dc=jboss,dc=org` for any entries that have a `member` attribute equal to `uid=jduke,ou=People,dc=jboss,dc=org`. The search would locate `cn=JBossAdmin` under the `roles` entry.

The search returns the attribute specified in the `roleAttributeID` option. In this example, the attribute is `cn`. The value returned would be `JBossAdmin`, so the `jduke` user is assigned to the `JBossAdmin` role.

It's often the case that a local LDAP server provides identity and authentication services but is unable to use the authorization services. This is because application roles don't always map well to LDAP groups, and LDAP administrators are often hesitant to allow external application-specific data in central LDAP servers. For this reason, the LDAP authentication module is often paired with another login module, such as the database login module, that can provide roles more suitable to the application being developed.

`org.jboss.security.auth.spi.DatabaseServerLoginModule`

`DatabaseServerLoginModule` is a JDBC-based login module that supports authentication and role mapping. You would use this login module if you have your username, password, and role information in a relational database. `DatabaseServerLoginModule` is based on two logical tables:

```
Table Principals(PrincipalID text, Password text)
Table Roles(PrincipalID text, Role text, RoleGroup text)
```

The `Principals` table associates the user `PrincipalID` with the valid password, and the `Roles` table associates the user `PrincipalID` with its role sets. The roles used for user permissions must be contained in rows, with a `RoleGroup` column value of `Roles`. The tables are logical in that you can specify the SQL query that the login module uses. All that is required is that the `java.sql.ResultSet` has the same logical structure as the `Principals` and `Roles` tables described previously. The actual names of the tables and columns are not relevant because the results are accessed based on the column index. To clarify this notion, consider a database with two tables, `Principals` and `Roles`, as already declared. The following statements build the tables to contain a `PrincipalID java` with the `Password` of `echoman` in the `Principals` table, a `PrincipalID java` with a role named `Echo` in the `Roles RoleGroup` in the `Roles` table, and a `PrincipalID java` with a role named `caller_java` in the `CallerPrincipal RoleGroup` in the `Roles` table:

```
INSERT INTO Principals VALUES('java', 'echoman')
INSERT INTO Roles VALUES('java', 'Echo', 'Roles')
INSERT INTO Roles VALUES('java', 'caller_java', 'CallerPrincipal')
```

The supported login module configuration options include the following:

- **`dsJndiName`**—This option specifies the JNDI name for the `DataSource` of the database that contains the logical `Principals` and `Roles` tables. If not specified, this defaults to `java:/DefaultDS`.
- **`principalsQuery`**—This option specifies the prepared statement query equivalent to `select Password from Principals where PrincipalID=?`. If not specified, this is exactly the prepared statement that will be used.
- **`rolesQuery`**—This option specifies the prepared statement query equivalent to `select Role, RoleGroup from Roles where PrincipalID=?`. If not specified, this is exactly the prepared statement that will be used.
- **`unauthenticatedIdentity`**—This option specifies the principal name that should be assigned to requests that contain no authentication information.
- **`password-stacking`**—When this option is set to `useFirstPass`, this module first looks for a shared username and password under the property names `javax.security.auth.login.name` and `javax.security.auth.login.password`, respectively, in the login module shared state map. If found, these are used as the principal name and password. If not found, the principal name and password are set by this login module and stored under the property names `javax.security.auth.login.name` and `javax.security.auth.login.password`, respectively.
- **`hashAlgorithm`**—This option specifies the name of the `java.security.MessageDigest` algorithm to use to hash the password. There is no default, so this option must be specified to enable hashing. When `hashAlgorithm` is specified, the clear-text password obtained from `callbackhandler` is hashed before it is passed to `UsernamePasswordLoginModule.validatePassword` as the `inputPassword` argument. The `expectedPassword`, as obtained from the database, must be comparably hashed.
- **`hashEncoding`**—This option specifies the string format for the hashed pass and must be either `base64` or `hex`. `base64` is the default.
- **`hashCharset`**—This option specifies the encoding used to convert the clear-text password to a byte array. The platform default encoding is the default.

- **ignorePasswordCase**—This option specifies a Boolean flag that indicates whether the password comparison should ignore case. This can be useful for hashed password encoding where the case of the hashed password is not significant.
- **principalClass**—This option specifies a `Principal` implementation class. This must support a constructor that takes a string argument for the principal name.

As an example of a `DatabaseServerLoginModule` configuration, consider a custom table schema like the following:

```
CREATE TABLE Users(username VARCHAR(64) PRIMARY KEY, passwd VARCHAR(64))
CREATE TABLE UserRoles(username VARCHAR(64), userRoles VARCHAR(32))
```

A corresponding `login-config.xml` entry would look like this:

```
<policy>
    <application-policy name="testDB">
        <authentication>
            <login-module code="org.jboss.security.auth.spi.
➥DatabaseServerLoginModule"
                             flag="required">
                <module-option name="dsJndiName">java:/MyDatabaseDS
➥</module-option>
                <module-option name="principalsQuery">
                    select passwd from Users username where username=?
➥</module-option>
                <module-option name="rolesQuery">
                    select userRoles, 'Roles' from UserRoles where username=?
➥</module-option>
            </login-module>
        </authentication>
    </application-policy>
</policy>
```

BaseCertLoginModule

`BaseCertLoginModule` is a login module that authenticates users based on X509 certificates. A typical use case for this login module is `CLIENT-CERT` authentication in the web tier. This login module only performs authentication. You need to combine it with another login module that is capable of acquiring the authorization roles to completely define access to a secured web or EJB component. Two subclasses of this login module, `CertRolesLoginModule` and `Database-CertLoginModule`, extend its behavior to obtain the authorization roles from either a properties file or database.

`BaseCertLoginModule` needs a `KeyStore` to perform user validation. This is obtained through an `org.jboss.security.SecurityDomain` implementation. Typically, the `SecurityDomain` implementation is configured using the `org.jboss.security.plugins.JaasSecurityDomain` MBean, as shown in this `jboss-service.xml` configuration fragment:

```
<mbean code="org.jboss.security.plugins.JaasSecurityDomain"
       name="jboss.web:service=SecurityDomain">
    <constructor>
        <arg type="java.lang.String" value="jmx-console"/>
    </constructor>
    <attribute name="KeyStoreURL">resource:localhost.keystore</attribute>
    <attribute name="KeyStorePass">unit-tests-server</attribute>
</mbean>
```

This creates a security domain with the name `jmx-console` whose `SecurityDomain` implementation is available via JNDI under the name `java:/jaas/jmx-console`, following the JBossSX security domain naming pattern. To secure a web application such as the `jmx-console.war` by using client certificates and role-based authorization, you would first modify `web.xml` to declare the resources to be secured, along with the allowed roles and security domain to be used for authentication and authorization, as shown here:

```
<?xml version="1.0"?>
<!DOCTYPE web-app PUBLIC
                 "-//Sun Microsystems, Inc.//DTD Web Application 2.3//EN"
                 "http://java.sun.com/dtd/web-app_2_3.dtd">
<web-app>
    ...
    <security-constraint>
        <web-resource-collection>
            <web-resource-name>HtmlAdaptor</web-resource-name>
            <description>An example security config that only allows users with
               the role JBossAdmin to access the HTML JMX console web
               application </description>
            <url-pattern>/*</url-pattern>
            <http-method>GET</http-method>
            <http-method>POST</http-method>
        </web-resource-collection>
        <auth-constraint>
            <role-name>JBossAdmin</role-name>
        </auth-constraint>
    </security-constraint>
    <login-config>
        <auth-method>CLIENT-CERT</auth-method>
        <realm-name>JBoss JMX Console</realm-name>
    </login-config>
    <security-role>
        <role-name>JBossAdmin</role-name>
    </security-role>
</web-app>
```

Next, you need to specify the JBoss security domain in `jboss-web.xml`:

```
<jboss-web>
    <security-domain>java:/jaas/jmx-console</security-domain>
</jboss-web>
```

Finally, you need to define the login module configuration for the `jmx-console` security domain you just specified. You do this in the `conf/login-config.xml` file:

```
<application-policy name="jmx-console">
    <authentication>
        <login-module code="org.jboss.security.auth.spi.BaseCertLoginModule"
                      flag="required">
            <module-option name="password-stacking">useFirstPass</module-option>
            <module-option name="securityDomain">java:/jaas/jmx-console
➥</module-option>
        </login-module>
        <login-module code="org.jboss.security.auth.spi.UsersRolesLoginModule"
                      flag="required">
            <module-option name="password-stacking">useFirstPass</module-option>
            <module-option name="usersProperties">jmx-console-users.properties
➥</module-option>
            <module-option name="rolesProperties">jmx-console-roles.properties
➥</module-option>
        </login-module>
    </authentication>
</application-policy>
```

Here `BaseCertLoginModule` is used for authentication of the client certificate, and `UsersRolesLoginModule` is only used for authorization due to the `password-stacking=useFirstPass` option. Both `localhost.keystore` and `jmx-console-roles.properties` need an entry that maps to the principal associated with the client certificate. By default, the principal is created using the client certificate distinguished name. Consider the following certificate:

```
[starksm@banshee9100 conf]$ keytool -printcert -file unit-tests-client.export
Owner: CN=unit-tests-client, OU=JBoss Inc., O=JBoss Inc., ST=Washington, C=US
Issuer: CN=jboss.com, C=US, ST=Washington, L=Snoqualmie Pass, EMAILADDRESS=admin
@jboss.com, OU=QA, O=JBoss Inc.
Serial number: 100103
Valid from: Wed May 26 07:34:34 PDT 2004 until: Thu May 26 07:34:34 PDT 2005
Certificate fingerprints:
         MD5:  4A:9C:2B:CD:1B:50:AA:85:DD:89:F6:1D:F5:AF:9E:AB
         SHA1: DE:DE:86:59:05:6C:00:E8:CC:C0:16:D3:C2:68:BF:95:B8:83:E9:58
```

localhost.keystore would need this certificate to be stored with an alias of CN=unit-tests-client,OU=JBoss Inc.,O=JBoss Inc.,ST=Washington,C=US, and jmx-console-roles.properties would also need an entry for the same entry. Because the DN contains many characters that are normally treated as delimiters, you need to escape the problem characters with a backslash (\), as shown here:

```
# A sample roles.properties file for use with the UsersRolesLoginModule
CN\=unit-tests-client,\ OU\=JBoss\ Inc.,\ O\=JBoss\ Inc.,\ ST\=Washington,
➥\ C\=US=JBossAdmin
admin=JBossAdmin
```

org.jboss.security.auth.spi.RunAsLoginModule

JBoss has a helper login module called RunAsLoginModule that pushes a run-as role for the duration of the login phase of authentication, and it pops the run-as role in either the commit or abort phase. The purpose of this login module is to provide a role for other login modules that need to access secured resources in order to perform their authentication. An example is a login module that accesses a secured EJB; this login module must be configured ahead of the login module(s) that needs a run-as role established.

The only login module configuration option is roleName, which is the name of the role to use as the run-as role during the login phase. If not specified, the default of nobody is used.

org.jboss.security.ClientLoginModule

ClientLoginModule is an implementation of LoginModule for use by JBoss clients for the establishment of the caller identity and credentials. This simply sets org.jboss.security.SecurityAssociation.principal to the value of the NameCallback filled in by the callbackhandler, and it sets org.jboss.security.SecurityAssociation.credential to the value of the PasswordCallback filled in by the callbackhandler. This is the only supported mechanism for a client to establish the current thread's caller. Both standalone client applications and server environments, acting as JBoss EJB clients where the security environment has not been configured to use JBossSX transparently, need to use ClientLoginModule. Of course, you could always set the org.jboss.security.SecurityAssociation information directly, but this is considered an internal API that is subject to change without notice.

Note that this login module does not perform any authentication. It merely copies the login information provided to it into the JBoss server EJB invocation layer for subsequent authentication on the server. If you need to perform client-side authentication of users, you need to configure another login module in addition to ClientLoginModule.

The supported login module configuration options include the following:

- **multi-threaded**—When this option is set to true, each login thread has its own principal and credential storage. This is useful in client environments where multiple user identities are active in separate threads. When it is true, each separate thread must perform its own login. When it is set to false, the login identity and credentials are global variables that apply to all threads in the VM. The default for this option is `false`.

- **`password-stacking`**—When this option is set to `useFirstPass`, this module first looks for a shared username and password, using `javax.security.auth.login.name` and `javax.security.auth.login.password`, respectively, in the login module shared state map. This allows a module configured prior to this one to establish a valid username and password that should be passed to JBoss. You use this option if you want to perform client-side authentication of clients by using some other login module, such as `LdapLoginModule`.
- **`restore-login-identity`**—When this option is `true`, the `SecurityAssociation` principal and credential seen on entry to the `login()` method are saved and restored on either abort or logout. When it is `false` (the default), the abort and logout simply clear the `SecurityAssociation`. A `restore-login-identity` of `true` is needed if you need to change identities and then restore the original caller identity.

A sample login configuration for `ClientLoginModule` is the default configuration entry found in the JBoss distribution `client/auth.conf` file, which is as follows:

```
other {
    // Put your login modules that work without jBoss here

    // jBoss LoginModule
    org.jboss.security.ClientLoginModule required;

    // Put your login modules that need jBoss here
};
```

Writing Custom Login Modules

If the login modules bundled with the JBossSX framework do not work with your security environment, you can write your own custom login module implementation that does.

Recall from the section "The JBossSX Architecture," earlier in this chapter, that the `JaasSecurityManager` expects a particular usage pattern of the `Subject` principals set. You need to understand the JAAS `Subject` class's information storage features and the expected usage of these features to be able to write a login module that works with the `JaasSecurityManager`. This section examines this requirement and introduces two abstract base `LoginModule` implementations that can help you implement your own custom login modules.

You can obtain security information associated with a `Subject` in six ways in JBoss, using the following methods:

```
java.util.Set getPrincipals()
java.util.Set getPrincipals(java.lang.Class c)
java.util.Set getPrivateCredentials()
```

```
java.util.Set getPrivateCredentials(java.lang.Class c)
java.util.Set getPublicCredentials()
java.util.Set getPublicCredentials(java.lang.Class c)
```

For `Subject` identities and roles, JBossSX has selected the most natural choice: the principals' sets obtained via `getPrincipals()` and `getPrincipals(java.lang.Class)`. The usage pattern is as follows:

- User identities (username, Social Security number, employee ID, and so on) are stored as `java.security.Principal` objects in the `Subject Principals` set. The `Principal` implementation that represents the user identity must base comparisons and equality on the name of the principal. A suitable implementation is available as the `org.jboss.security.SimplePrincipal` class. You can add other `Principal` instances to the `Subject Principals` set as needed.
- The assigned user roles are also stored in the `Principals` set, but they are grouped in named role sets, using `java.security.acl.Group` instances. The `Group` interface defines a collection of `Principals` and/or `Groups`, and it is a subinterface of `java.security.Principal`. Any number of role sets can be assigned to a `Subject`. Currently, the JBossSX framework uses two well-known role sets with the names `Roles` and `CallerPrincipal`. The `Roles` group is the collection of `Principals` for the named roles, as known in the application domain under which the `Subject` has been authenticated. This role set is used by methods such as `EJBContext.isCallerInRole (String)`, which EJBs can use to see whether the current caller belongs to the named application domain role. The security interceptor logic that performs method permission checks also uses this role set. The `CallerPrincipal Group` consists of the single `Principal` identity assigned to the user in the application domain. The `EJBContext.getCallerPrincipal()` method uses the `CallerPrincipal` to allow the application domain to map from the operation environment identity to a user identity suitable for the application. If a `Subject` does not have a `CallerPrincipal Group`, the application identity is the same as the operational environment identity.

Support for the `Subject` Usage Pattern

To simplify correct implementation of the `Subject` usage patterns described in the preceding section, JBossSX includes two abstract login modules that handle the population of the authenticated `Subject` with a template pattern that enforces correct `Subject` usage. The most generic of the two is the `org.jboss.security.auth.spi.AbstractServerLoginModule` class. It provides a concrete implementation of the `javax.security.auth.spi.LoginModule` interface and offers abstract methods for the key tasks that are specific to an operation environment security infrastructure. The key details of the class are shown in the following class fragment, and the JavaDoc comments detail the responsibilities of subclasses:

```
package org.jboss.security.auth.spi;
/**
```

```
 * This class implements the common functionality required for a JAAS
 * server-side LoginModule and implements the JBossSX standard
 * Subject usage pattern of storing identities and roles. Subclass
 * this module to create your own custom LoginModule and override the
 * login(), getRoleSets(), and getIdentity() methods.
 */
public abstract class AbstractServerLoginModule
    implements javax.security.auth.spi.LoginModule
{
    protected Subject subject;
    protected CallbackHandler callbackHandler;
    protected Map sharedState;
    protected Map options;
    protected Logger log;

    /** Flag indicating if the shared credential should be used */
    protected boolean useFirstPass;
    /**
     * Flag indicating if the login phase succeeded. Subclasses that
     * override the login method must set this to true on successful
     * completion of login
     */
    protected boolean loginOk;

    // ...
    /**
     * Initialize the login module. This stores the subject,
     * callbackHandler and sharedState and options for the login
     * session. Subclasses should override if they need to process
     * their own options. A call to super.initialize(...)  must be
     * made in the case of an override.
     *
     * <p>
     * The options are checked for the  <em>password-stacking</em> parameter.
     * If this is set to "useFirstPass", the login identity will be taken from the
     * <code>javax.security.auth.login.name</code> value of the sharedState map,
     * and the proof of identity from the
     * <code>javax.security.auth.login.password</code> value of the
➥sharedState map.
     *
     * @param subject the Subject to update after a successful login.
     * @param callbackHandler the CallbackHandler that will be used to obtain
     * the user identity and credentials.
     * @param sharedState a Map shared between all configured login
➥module instances
```

```
     * @param options the parameters passed to the login module.
     */
    public void initialize(Subject subject,
                           CallbackHandler callbackHandler,
                           Map sharedState,
                           Map options)
    {
        // ...
    }


    /**
     *  Looks for javax.security.auth.login.name and
     *  javax.security.auth.login.password values in the sharedState
     *  map if the useFirstPass option was true and returns true if
     *  they exist. If they do not or are null this method returns
     *  false.
     *  Note that subclasses that override the login method
     *  must set the loginOk ivar to true if the login succeeds in
     *  order for the commit phase to populate the Subject. This
     *  implementation sets loginOk to true if the login() method
     *  returns true, otherwise, it sets loginOk to false.
     */
    public boolean login()
        throws LoginException
    {
        // ...
    }

    /**
     *  Overridden by subclasses to return the Principal that
     *  corresponds to the user primary identity.
     */
    abstract protected Principal getIdentity();

    /**
     *  Overridden by subclasses to return the Groups that correspond
     *  to the role sets assigned to the user. Subclasses should
     *  create at least a Group named "Roles" that contains the roles
     *  assigned to the user.  A second common group is
     *  "CallerPrincipal," which provides the application identity of
     *  the user rather than the security domain identity.
     *
     *  @return Group[] containing the sets of roles
```

```
     */
    abstract protected Group[] getRoleSets() throws LoginException;
}
```

You need to pay attention to the `loginOk` instance variable. Any subclasses that override the login method must set this to `true` if the login succeeds and `false` otherwise. Failure to set this variable correctly results in the commit method either not updating the subject when it should or updating the subject when it should not. Tracking the outcome of the login phase was added to allow login modules to be chained together with control flags that do not require that the login module succeed in order for the overall login to succeed.

The second abstract base login module suitable for custom login modules is `org.jboss.security.auth.spi.UsernamePasswordLoginModule`. This login module further simplifies custom login module implementation by enforcing a string-based username as the user identity and a `char[]` password as the authentication credentials. It also supports the mapping of anonymous users (indicated by null username and password) to a principal with no roles. The key details of the class are shown in the following class fragment, and the JavaDoc comments detail the responsibilities of subclasses:

```
package org.jboss.security.auth.spi;

/**
 *  An abstract subclass of AbstractServerLoginModule that imposes a
 *  an identity == String username, credentials == String password
 *  view on the login process. Subclasses override the
 *  getUsersPassword() and getUsersRoles() methods to return the
 *  expected password and roles for the user.
 */
public abstract class UsernamePasswordLoginModule
    extends AbstractServerLoginModule
{
    /** The login identity */
    private Principal identity;
    /** The proof of login identity */
    private char[] credential;
    /** The principal to use when a null username and password are seen */
    private Principal unauthenticatedIdentity;

    /**
     * The message digest algorithm used to hash passwords. If null then
     * plain passwords will be used. */
    private String hashAlgorithm = null;

    /**
     *  The name of the charset/encoding to use when converting the
     * password String to a byte array. Default is the platform's
```

```
     * default encoding.
     */
    private String hashCharset = null;

    /** The string encoding format to use. Defaults to base64. */
    private String hashEncoding = null;

    // ...

    /**
     * Override the superclass method to look for an
     * unauthenticatedIdentity property. This method first invokes
     * the super version.
     *
     * @param options,
     * @option unauthenticatedIdentity: the name of the principal to
     * assign and authenticate when a null username and password are
     * seen.
     */
    public void initialize(Subject subject,
                           CallbackHandler callbackHandler,
                           Map sharedState,
                           Map options)
    {
        super.initialize(subject, callbackHandler, sharedState,
                         options);
        // Check for unauthenticatedIdentity option.
        Object option = options.get("unauthenticatedIdentity");
        String name = (String) option;
        if (name != null) {
            unauthenticatedIdentity = new SimplePrincipal(name);
        }
    }

    // ...

    /**
     * A hook that allows subclasses to change the validation of the
     * input password against the expected password. This version
     * checks that neither inputPassword or expectedPassword are null
     * and that inputPassword.equals(expectedPassword) is true;
     *
     * @return true if the inputPassword is valid, false otherwise.
     */
```

```
    protected boolean validatePassword(String inputPassword,
                                       String expectedPassword)
    {
        if (inputPassword == null || expectedPassword == null) {
            return false;
        }
        return inputPassword.equals(expectedPassword);
    }

    /**
     *  Get the expected password for the current username available
     * via the getUsername() method. This is called from within the
     * login() method after the CallbackHandler has returned the
     * username and candidate password.
     *
     * @return the valid password String
     */
    abstract protected String getUsersPassword()
        throws LoginException;
}
```

The choice of subclassing the `AbstractServerLoginModule` versus `UsernamePasswordLoginModule` is simply based on whether a string-based username and credentials are usable for the authentication technology you are writing the login module for. If the string-based semantic is valid, then you should subclass `UsernamePasswordLoginModule`; otherwise, you should subclass `AbstractServerLoginModule`.

The steps you are required to perform when writing a custom login module depend on which base login module class you choose. When writing a custom login module that integrates with your security infrastructure, you should start by subclassing `AbstractServerLoginModule` or `UsernamePassword-LoginModule` to ensure that your login module provides the authenticated `Principal` information in the form that the JBossSX security manager expects.

When subclassing `AbstractServerLoginModule`, you need to override the following:

- **`void initialize(Subject,CallbackHandler,Map,Map)`**—You override this if you have custom options to parse.
- **`boolean login()`**—You override this to perform the authentication activity. You need to be sure to set the `loginOk` instance variable to `true` if login succeeds and `false` if it fails.
- **`Principal getIdentity()`**—You override this to return the `Principal` object for the user authenticated by the `log()` step.

- **Group[]getRoleSets()**—You override this to return at least one Group named Roles that contains the roles assigned to the Principal authenticated during login(). A second common Group is named CallerPrincipal and provides the user's application identity rather than the security domain identity.

When subclassing the UsernamePasswordLoginModule, you need to override the following:

- **void initialize (Subject,CallbackHandler,Map,Map)**—You override this if you have custom options to parse.
- **Group[] getRoleSets()**—You override this to return at least one Group named Roles that contains the roles assigned to the Principal authenticated during login(). A second common Group is named CallerPrincipal and provides the user's application identity rather than the security domain identity.
- **String getUsersPassword()**—You override this to return the expected password for the current username available via the getUsername() method. The getUsersPassword() method is called from within login() after the callbackhandler returns the username and candidate password.

A Custom LoginModule Example

In this section, you will develop a custom login module example that extends the UsernamePasswordLoginModule and obtains a user's password and role names from a JNDI lookup. The idea is that there is a JNDI context that returns a user's password if you perform a lookup on the context by using a name in the form password/*<username>*, where *<username>* is the current user being authenticated. Similarly, a lookup in the form roles/*<username>* returns the requested user's roles.

The source code for the example is located in the src/main/org/jboss/chap8/ex2 directory of the book examples. Listing 8.11 shows the source code for the JndiUserAndPass custom login module. Note that because this extends the JBoss UsernamePasswordLoginModule, all the JndiUserAndPass does is obtain the user's password and roles from the JNDI store. The JndiUserAndPass does not concern itself with the JAAS LoginModule operations.

LISTING 8.11 A JndiUserAndPass Custom Login Module

```
package org.jboss.chap8.ex2;

import java.security.acl.Group;
import java.util.Map;
import javax.naming.InitialContext;
import javax.naming.NamingException;
import javax.security.auth.Subject;
import javax.security.auth.callback.CallbackHandler;
import javax.security.auth.login.LoginException;
```

LISTING 8.11 Continued

```
import org.jboss.security.SimpleGroup;
import org.jboss.security.SimplePrincipal;
import org.jboss.security.auth.spi.UsernamePasswordLoginModule;

/**
 *  An example custom login module that obtains passwords and roles
 *  for a user from a JNDI lookup.
 *
 *  @author Scott.Stark@jboss.org
 *  @version $Revision: 1.5 $
*/
public class JndiUserAndPass
    extends UsernamePasswordLoginModule
{
    /** The JNDI name to the context that handles the password/username lookup */
    private String userPathPrefix;
    /** The JNDI name to the context that handles the roles/ username lookup */
    private String rolesPathPrefix;

    /**
     * Override to obtain the userPathPrefix and rolesPathPrefix options.
     */
    public void initialize(Subject subject, CallbackHandler callbackHandler,
                           Map sharedState, Map options)
    {
        super.initialize(subject, callbackHandler, sharedState, options);
        userPathPrefix = (String) options.get("userPathPrefix");
        rolesPathPrefix = (String) options.get("rolesPathPrefix");
    }

    /**
     *  Get the roles the current user belongs to by querying the
     * rolesPathPrefix + '/' + super.getUsername() JNDI location.
     */
    protected Group[] getRoleSets() throws LoginException
    {
        try {
            InitialContext ctx = new InitialContext();
            String rolesPath = rolesPathPrefix + '/' + super.getUsername();

            String[] roles = (String[]) ctx.lookup(rolesPath);
            Group[] groups = {new SimpleGroup("Roles")};
            log.info("Getting roles for user="+super.getUsername());
            for(int r = 0; r < roles.length; r ++) {
```

LISTING 8.11 Continued

```
                SimplePrincipal role = new SimplePrincipal(roles[r]);
                log.info("Found role="+roles[r]);
                groups[0].addMember(role);
            }
            return groups;
        } catch(NamingException e) {
            log.error("Failed to obtain groups for
                        user="+super.getUsername(), e);
            throw new LoginException(e.toString(true));
        }
    }

    /**
     * Get the password of the current user by querying the
     * userPathPrefix + '/' + super.getUsername() JNDI location.
     */
    protected String getUsersPassword()
        throws LoginException
    {
        try {
            InitialContext ctx = new InitialContext();
            String userPath = userPathPrefix + '/' + super.getUsername();
            log.info("Getting password for user="+super.getUsername());
            String passwd = (String) ctx.lookup(userPath);
            log.info("Found password="+passwd);
            return passwd;
        } catch(NamingException e) {
            log.error("Failed to obtain password for
                        user="+super.getUsername(), e);
            throw new LoginException(e.toString(true));
        }
    }
}
```

You can find the details of the JNDI store in the `org.jboss.chap8.ex2.service.JndiStore` MBean. This service binds an `ObjectFactory` that returns a `javax.naming.Context` proxy into JNDI. The proxy handles lookup by checking the prefix of the lookup name against `password` and `roles`. When the name begins with `password`, a user's password is being requested. When the name begins with `roles`, the user's roles are being requested. The sample implementation always returns the password `theduke` and an array of role names equal to `{"TheDuke","Echo"}`, regardless of the username. You can experiment with other implementations as you wish.

The example's code includes a simple session bean for testing the custom login module. To build, deploy, and run the example, you execute the following command in the examples directory:

```
[examples]$ ant -Dchap=chap8 -Dex=2 run-example
...
run-example2:
     [copy] Copying 1 file to /tmp/jboss-4.0.1/server/default/deploy
     [echo] Waiting for 5 seconds for deploy...
     [java] [INFO,ExClient] Login with username=jduke, password=theduke
     [java] [INFO,ExClient] Looking up EchoBean2
     [java] [INFO,ExClient] Created Echo
     [java] [INFO,ExClient] Echo.echo('Hello') = Hello
19:06:13,266 INFO  [EjbModule] Deploying EchoBean2
19:06:13,482 INFO  [JndiStore] Start, bound security/store
19:06:13,486 INFO  [SecurityConfig] Using JAAS AuthConfig: jar:file:
➥/private/tmp/jboss-4.0.1/server/default/tmp/deploy/
➥tmp23012chap8-ex2.jar-contents/chap8-ex2.sar!/META-INF/login-config.xml
19:06:13,654 INFO  [EJBDeployer] Deployed: file:/private/tmp/jboss-4.0.1/
➥server/default/deploy/chap8-ex2.jar
```

Whether to use the `JndiUserAndPass` custom login module for the server-side authentication of the user is determined based on the login configuration for the sample security domain. The EJB JAR `META-INF/jboss.xml` descriptor sets the security domain as follows:

```
<?xml version="1.0"?>
<jboss>
    <security-domain>java:/jaas/chap8-ex2</security-domain>
</jboss>
```

The SAR `META-INF/login-config.xml` descriptor defines the login module configuration as follows:

```
<application-policy name = "chap8-ex2">
    <authentication>
        <login-module code="org.jboss.chap8.ex2.JndiUserAndPass"
                      flag="required">
            <module-option name = "userPathPrefix">/security/store/password
➥</module-option>
            <module-option name = "rolesPathPrefix">/security/store/roles
➥</module-option>
        </login-module>
    </authentication>
</application-policy>
```

The DynamicLoginConfig Service

Security domains defined in the login-config.xml file are essentially static. They are read when JBoss starts up, but there is no easy way to add a new security domain or change the definition for an existing one. The DynamicLoginConfig service allows you to dynamically deploy security domains. This allows you to specify JAAS login configuration as part of a deployment (or just as a standalone service) rather than having to edit the static login-config.xml file.

The service supports the following attributes:

- **AuthConfig**—The resource path to the JAAS login configuration file to use. This defaults to login-config.xml.
- **LoginConfigService**—The XMLLoginConfig service name to use for loading. This service must support a String loadConfig(URL) operation to load the configurations.
- **SecurityManagerService**—The SecurityManagerService name used to flush the registered security domains. This service must support a flushAuthenticationCache(String) operation to flush the case for the argument security domain. Setting this triggers the flush of the authentication caches when the service is stopped.

Here is an example of an MBean definition that uses the DynamicLoginConfig service:

```
<server>
    <mbean code="org.jboss.security.auth.login.DynamicLoginConfig" name="...">
        <attribute name="AuthConfig">login-config.xml</attribute>

        <!-- The service which supports dynamic processing of login-config.xml
         configurations.
        -->
        <depends optional-attribute-name="LoginConfigService">
            jboss.security:service=XMLLoginConfig </depends>

        <!-- Optionally specify the security mgr service to use when
         this service is stopped to flush the auth caches of the domains
         registered by this service.
        -->
        <depends optional-attribute-name="SecurityManagerService">
            jboss.security:service=JaasSecurityManager </depends>
    </mbean>
</server>
```

This loads the specified AuthConfig resource, using the specified LoginConfigService MBean by invoking loadConfig with the appropriate resource URL. When the service is stopped, the configurations are removed. The resource that is specified may be either an XML file or a Sun JAAS login configuration.

The Secure Remote Password (SRP) Protocol

The SRP protocol is an implementation of a public key exchange handshake described in the Internet Standards Working Group RFC 2945. The RFC 2945 abstract states the following:

> This document describes a cryptographically strong network authentication mechanism known as the Secure Remote Password (SRP) protocol. This mechanism is suitable for negotiating secure connections using a user-supplied password, while eliminating the security problems traditionally associated with reusable passwords. This system also performs a secure key exchange in the process of authentication, allowing security layers (privacy and/or integrity protection) to be enabled during the session. Trusted key servers and certificate infrastructures are not required, and clients are not required to store or manage any long-term keys. SRP offers both security and deployment advantages over existing challenge-response techniques, making it an ideal drop-in replacement where secure password authentication is needed.

Note

You can obtain the complete RFC 2945 specification from www.rfc-editor.org/rfc.html. Additional information on the SRP algorithm and its history can be found at http://srp.stanford.edu/.

SRP is similar in concept and security to other public key exchange algorithms, such as Diffie-Hellman and RSA. SRP is based on simple string passwords in a way that does not require a clear-text password to exist on the server. This is in contrast to other public key–based algorithms that require client certificates and the corresponding certificate management infrastructure.

Algorithms such as Diffie-Hellman and RSA are known as *public key exchange algorithms*. The concept of public key algorithms is that there are two keys: one that is public and is available to everyone and one that is private and known only to you. When someone wants to send encrypted information to you, that person encrypts the information using your public key. Only you are able to decrypt the information using your private key. This contrasts with the more traditional shared password–based encryption schemes that require the sender and receiver to know the shared password. Public key algorithms eliminate the need to share passwords.

The JBossSX framework includes an implementation of SRP that consists of the following elements:

- An implementation of the SRP handshake protocol that is independent of any particular client/server protocol

- An RMI implementation of the handshake protocol as the default client/server SRP implementation
- A client-side JAAS `LoginModule` implementation that uses the RMI implementation for use in authenticating clients in a secure fashion
- A JMX MBean for managing the RMI server implementation. The MBean allows the RMI server implementation to be plugged into a JMX framework and externalizes the configuration of the verification information store. It also establishes an authentication cache that is bound into the JBoss server JNDI namespace.
- A server-side JAAS `LoginModule` implementation that uses the authentication cache managed by the SRP JMX MBean.

Figure 8.14 shows a diagram of the key components involved in the JBossSX implementation of the SRP client/server framework.

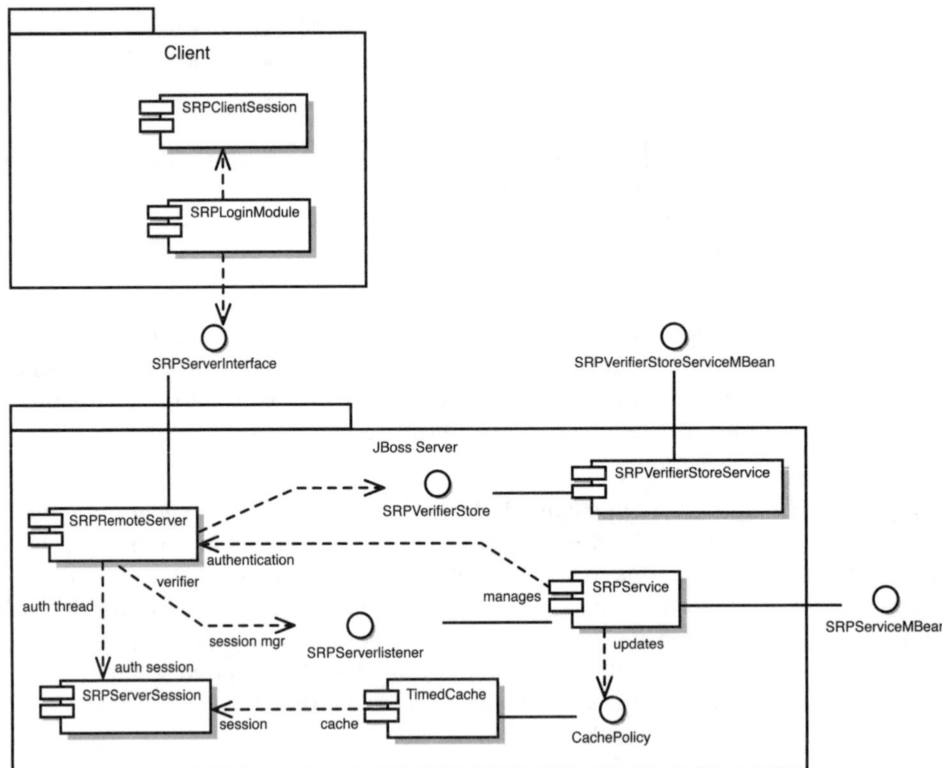

FIGURE 8.14 The JBossSX components of the SRP client/server framework.

On the client side, SRP shows up as a custom JAAS `LoginModule` implementation that communicates to the authentication server through an `org.jboss.security.srp.SRPServerInterface` proxy. A client enables authentication using SRP by creating a login configuration entry that includes the `org.jboss.security.srp.jaas.SRPLoginModule`. This module supports the following configuration options:

- **`principalClassName`**—This option is no longer supported. The principal class is now always `org.jboss.security.srp.jaas.SRPPrincipal`.
- **`srpServerJndiName`**—This option specifies the JNDI name of the `SRPServerInterface` object to use for communicating with the SRP authentication server. If both `srpServerJndiName` and `srpServerRmiUrl` options are specified, the `srpServerJndiName` is tried before `srpServerRmiUrl`.
- **`srpServerRmiUrl`**—This option specifies the RMI protocol URL string for the location of the `SRPServerInterface` proxy to use for communicating with the SRP authentication server.
- **`externalRandomA`**—This option is a `true/false` flag that indicates whether the random component of client public key A should come from the user callback. This can be used to input a strong cryptographic random number that comes from a hardware token, for example.
- **`hasAuxChallenge`**—This option is a `true/false` flag that indicates whether a string will be sent to the server as an additional challenge for the server to validate. If the client session supports an encryption cipher, then a temporary cipher is created, using the session private key and the challenge object, sent as a `javax.crypto.SealedObject`.
- **`multipleSessions`**—This option is a `true/false` flag that indicates whether a given client may have multiple SRP login sessions active simultaneously.

Any other options that are passed in and do not match one of the previously named options is treated as a JNDI property to use for the environment passed to the `InitialContext` constructor. This is useful if the SRP server interface is not available from the default `InitialContext`.

The `SRPLoginModule` needs to be configured along with the standard `ClientLoginModule` to allow the SRP authentication credentials to be used for validation of access to security J2EE components. The following is an example of a login configuration entry that demonstrates such a setup:

```
srp {
    org.jboss.security.srp.jaas.SRPLoginModule required
    srpServerJndiName="SRPServerInterface"
    ;

    org.jboss.security.ClientLoginModule required
    password-stacking="useFirstPass"
    ;
};
```

On the JBoss server side, two MBeans manage the objects that collectively make up the SRP server: `org.jboss.security.srp.SRPService` and `org.jboss.security.srpSRPVerifierStoreService`. The primary service is the `org.jboss.security.srp.SRPService` MBean, and it is responsible for exposing an RMI-accessible version of the `SRPServerInterface` as well as updating the SRP authentication session cache. The configurable `SRPService` MBean attributes include the following:

- **`JndiName`**—The JNDI name from which the `SRPServerInterface` proxy should be available. This is the location where the `SRPService` binds the serializable dynamic proxy to the `SRPServerInterface`. If not specified, it defaults to `srp/SRPServerInterface`.
- **`VerifierSourceJndiName`**—The JNDI name of the `SRPVerifierSource` implementation that should be used by the `SRPService`. If not set, it defaults to `srp/DefaultVerifierSource`.
- **`AuthenticationCacheJndiName`**—The JNDI name under which the authentication `org.jboss.util.CachePolicy` implementation to be used for caching authentication information is bound. The SRP session cache is made available for use through this binding. If not specified, it defaults to `srp/AuthenticationCache`.
- **`ServerPort`**—The RMI port for the `SRPRemoteServerInterface`. If not specified, it defaults to `10099`.
- **`ClientSocketFactory`**—An optional custom `java.rmi.server.RMIClientSocketFactory` implementation classname that is used during the export of the `SRPServerInterface`. If not specified, the default `RMIClientSocketFactory` is used.
- **`ServerSocketFactory`**—An optional custom `java.rmi.server.RMIServerSocketFactory` implementation classname that is used during the export of the `SRPServerInterface`. If not specified, the default `RMIServerSocketFactory` is used.
- **`AuthenticationCacheTimeout`**—The timed cache policy timeout, in seconds. If not specified, this defaults to `1800` (30 minutes).
- **`AuthenticationCacheResolution`**—The timed cache policy resolution, in seconds. This controls the interval between checks for timeouts. If not specified, this defaults to `60` (1 minute).
- **`RequireAuxChallenge`**—An option that, when set, causes the client to supply an auxiliary challenge as part of the verify phase. This gives control over whether the `SRPLoginModule` configuration used by the client must have the `useAuxChallenge` option enabled.
- **`OverwriteSessions`**—A flag that indicates whether a successful user authentication for an existing session should overwrite the current session. This controls the behavior of the server SRP session cache when clients have not enabled the multiple-sessions-per-user mode. The default is `false`, which means that the second attempt

by a user to authentication will succeed but the resulting SRP session will not overwrite the previous SRP session state.

The one input setting is the `VerifierSourceJndiName` attribute. This is the location of the SRP password information store implementation that must be provided and made available through JNDI. The `org.jboss.security.srpSRPVerifierStoreService` is an example of an MBean service that binds an implementation of the `SRPVerifierStore` interface that uses a file of serialized objects as the persistent store. Although this MBean is not realistic for a production environment, it does allow for testing of the SRP protocol and provides an example of the requirements for an `SRPVerifierStore` service. The configurable `SRPVerifierStoreService` MBean attributes include the following:

- **`JndiName`**—The JNDI name from which the `SRPVerifierStore` implementation should be available. If not specified, it defaults to `srp/DefaultVerifierSource`.
- **`StoreFile`**—The location of the user password verifier serialized object store file. This can be either a URL or a resource name to be found in the classpath. If not specified, it defaults to `SRPVerifierStore.ser`.

The `SRPVerifierStoreService` MBean also supports `addUser` and `delUser` operations for addition and deletion of users. These are the signatures:

```
public void addUser(String username, String password)
     throws IOException;
public void delUser(String username) \
     throws IOException;
```

Providing Password Information for SRP

The default implementation of the `SRPVerifierStore` interface is not likely to be suitable for your production security environment because it requires all password hash information to be available as a file of serialized objects. You need to provide an MBean service that provides an implementation of the `SRPVerifierStore` interface that integrates with your existing security information stores. The `SRPVerifierStore` interface is shown in Listing 8.12.

LISTING 8.12 The `SRPVerifierStore` Interface

```
package org.jboss.security.srp;

import java.io.IOException;
import java.io.Serializable;
import java.security.KeyException;

public interface SRPVerifierStore
{
```

LISTING 8.12 Continued

```
    public static class VerifierInfo implements Serializable
    {
        /**
         * The username the information applies to. Perhaps redundant
         * but it makes the object self contained.
         */
        public String username;

        /** The SRP password verifier hash */
        public byte[] verifier;
        /** The random password salt originally used to verify the password */
        public byte[] salt;
        /** The SRP algorithm primitive generator */
        public byte[] g;
        /** The algorithm safe-prime modulus */
        public byte[] N;
    }

    /**
     *  Get the indicated user's password verifier information.
     */
    public VerifierInfo getUserVerifier(String username)
        throws KeyException, IOException;
    /**
     *  Set the indicated users' password verifier information. This
     *  is equivalent to changing a user's password and should
     *  generally invalidate any existing SRP sessions and caches.
     */
    public void setUserVerifier(String username, VerifierInfo info)
        throws IOException;

    /**
     * Verify an optional auxiliary challenge sent from the client to
     * the server.  The auxChallenge object will have been decrypted
     * if it was sent encrypted from the client. An example of an
     * auxiliary challenge would be the validation of a hardware token
     * (SafeWord, SecureID, iButton) that the server validates to
     * further strengthen the SRP password exchange.
     */
     public void verifyUserChallenge(String username, Object auxChallenge)
         throws SecurityException;
}
```

The primary function of a `SRPVerifierStore` implementation is to provide access to the `SRPVerifier-Store.VerifierInfo` object for a given username. `SRPService` calls the `getUserVerifier(String)` method at that start of a user SRP session to obtain the parameters needed by the SRP algorithm. The elements of the `VerifierInfo` objects are as follows:

- **`username`**—The user's name or ID that is used to log in.
- **`verifier`**—The one-way hash of the password or PIN the user enters as proof of his or her identity. The `org.jboss.security.Util` class has a `calculateVerifier` method that performs that password-hashing algorithm. The output password is `H(salt | H(username | ':' | password))`, as defined in RFC 2945. Here `H` is the SHA secure hash function. The username is converted from a string to a `byte[]`, using UTF-8 encoding.
- **`salt`**—A random number that is used to increase the difficulty of a brute-force dictionary attack on the verifier password database in the event that the database is compromised. It is a value that should be generated from a cryptographically strong random number algorithm when the user's existing clear-text password is hashed.
- **`g`**—The SRP algorithm primitive generator. In general, this can be a well-known fixed parameter rather than a per-user setting. The `org.jboss.security.srp.SRPConf` utility class provides several settings for `g`, including a good default that you can obtain via `SRPConf.getDefaultParams().g()`.
- **`N`**—The SRP algorithm safe-prime modulus. In general, this can be a well-known fixed parameter rather than a per-user setting. The `org.jboss.security.srp.SRPConf` utility class provides several settings for `N`, including a good default that you can obtain via `SRPConf.getDefaultParams().N()`.

These are the steps in integrating your existing password store:

1. Create a hashed version of the password information. If your passwords are already stored in an irreversible hashed form, then you can do this step only on a per-user basis (as part of an upgrade procedure, for example). Note that the `setUserVerifier (String, VerifierInfo)` method is not used by the current `SRPService` and may be implemented as a no-op method or even as one that throws an exception stating that the store is read-only.
2. Create the custom `SRPVerifierStore` interface implementation that knows how to obtain the `VerifierInfo` from the store you created in step 1. The `verifyUserChallenge(String, Object)` method of the interface is called only if the client `SRPLoginModule` configuration specifies the `hasAuxChallenge` option. This can be used to integrate existing hardware token-based schemes such as SafeWord or Radius into the SRP algorithm.
3. Create an MBean that makes the step 2 implementation of the `SRPVerifierStore` interface available via JNDI and exposes any configurable parameters you need. In

addition to the default `org.jboss.security.srp.SRPVerifierStoreService` example, the SRP example presented later in this chapter provides a Java properties file–based `SRPVerifierStore` implementation. Between the two examples, you should have enough to integrate your security store.

Inside the SRP Algorithm

The appeal of the SRP algorithm is that is allows for mutual authentication of the client and server, using simple text passwords without a secure communication channel. You might be wondering how this is done. If you want the complete details and theory behind the algorithm, refer to http://srp.stanford.edu. Six steps are performed to complete authentication:

1. The client-side `SRPLoginModule` retrieves the `SRPServerInterface` instance for the remote authentication server from the naming service.

2. The client-side `SRPLoginModule` requests the SRP parameters associated with the username that is attempting the login. You must choose a number of parameters that are involved in the SRP algorithm when the user password is first transformed into the verifier form used by the SRP algorithm. Rather than hard-coding the parameters (which you could do with minimal security risk), the JBossSX implementation allows you to retrieve this information as part of the exchange protocol, by using the `getSRPParameters(username)` call.

3. The client-side `SRPLoginModule` begins an SRP session by creating an `SRPClientSession` object, using the login username, clear-text password, and SRP parameters obtained in step 2. The client then creates a random number `A` that will be used to build the private SRP session key. The client then initializes the server side of the SRP session by invoking the `SRPServerInterface.init` method and passes in the username and client-generated random number `A`. The server returns its own random number `B`. This step corresponds to the exchange of public keys.

4. The client-side `SRPLoginModule` obtains the private SRP session key that has been generated as a result of the previous message exchanges. This is saved as a private credential in the login `Subject`. The server challenge response `M2` from step 4 is verified by invoking the `SRPClientSession.verify` method. If it succeeds, mutual authentication of the client to the server and of the server to the client have been completed. The client-side `SRPLogin-Module` next creates a challenge `M1` to the server by invoking `SRPClientSession.response` method, passing the server random number `B` as an argument. This challenge is sent to the server via the `SRPServerInterface.verify` method, and the server's response is saved as `M2`. This step corresponds to an exchange of challenges. At this point, the server has verified that the user is who he or she claims to be.

5. The client-side `SRPLoginModule` saves the login username and `M1` challenge into the `LoginModule` `sharedState` map. The standard JBoss `ClientLoginModule` uses this as the `Principal` name and credentials. The `M1` challenge is used in place of the password as proof of identity on any method invocations on J2EE components. The `M1` challenge is a cryptographically strong hash associated with the SRP session. Its interception via a third party cannot be used to obtain the user's password.
6. At the end of this authentication protocol, the `SRPServerSession` is placed into the `SRPService` authentication cache for subsequent use by the `SRPCacheLoginModule`.

Although SRP has many interesting properties, it is still an evolving component in the JBossSX framework and has some limitations of which you should be aware. Issues of note include the following:

- Because of how JBoss detaches the method transport protocol from the component container where authentication is performed, an unauthorized user could snoop the SRP `M1` challenge and effectively use the challenge to make requests under the associated username. You can use custom interceptors that encrypt the challenge via the SRP session key to prevent this issue.
- The `SRPService` maintains a cache of SRP sessions that time out after a configurable period. After they time out, any subsequent J2EE component access will fail because at the time, there is no mechanism for transparently renegotiating the SRP authentication credentials. You must either set the authentication cache timeout very long (up to 2,147,483,647 seconds, or approximately 68 years) or handle re-authentication in your code on failure.
- By default, there can be only one SRP session for a given username. Because the negotiated SRP session produces a private session key that can be used for encryption/decryption between the client and server, the session is effectively a stateful one. JBoss supports multiple SRP sessions per user, but you cannot encrypt data with one session key and then decrypt it with another.

To use end-to-end SRP authentication for J2EE component calls, you need to configure the security domain under which the components are secured to use the `org.jboss.security.srp.jaas.SRPCacheLoginModule`. The `SRPCacheLoginModule` has a single configuration option named `cacheJndiName` that sets the JNDI location of the SRP authentication `CachePolicy` instance. This must correspond to the `AuthenticationCacheJndiName` attribute value of the `SRPService` MBean. The `SRPCacheLoginModule` authenticates user credentials by obtaining the client challenge from the `SRPServerSession` object in the authentication cache and comparing this to the challenge passed as the user credentials. Figure 8.15 illustrates the operation of the `SRPCacheLoginModule.login` method implementation.

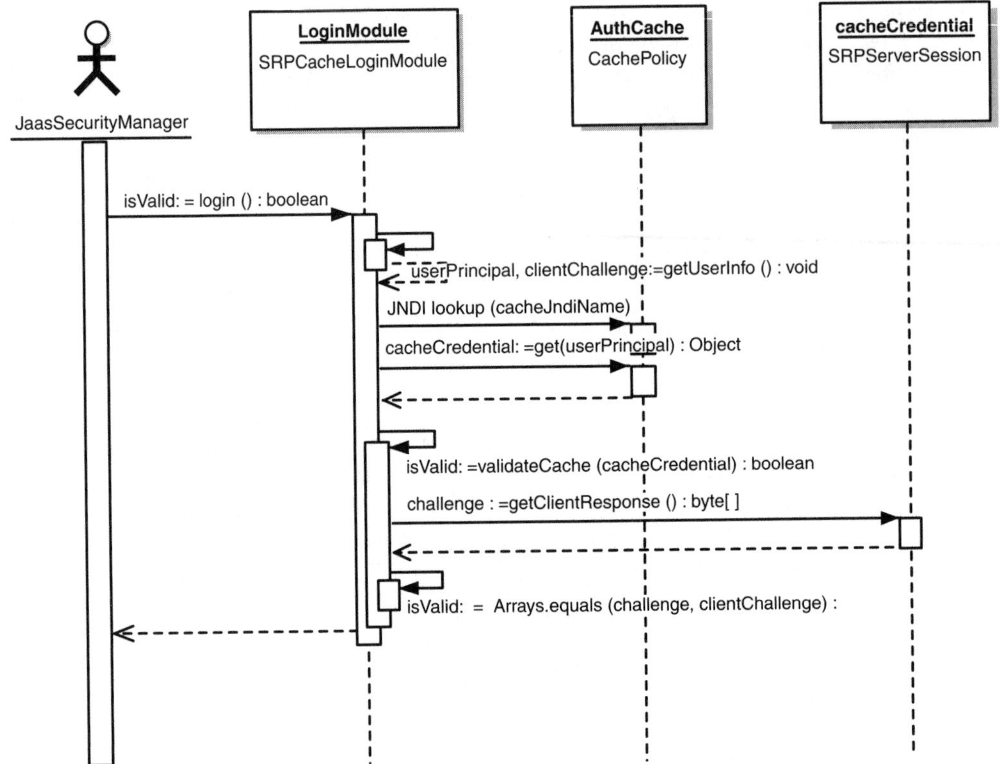

FIGURE 8.15 A sequence diagram that illustrates the interaction of the `SRPCacheLoginModule` with the SRP session cache.

An SRP Example

This chapter has covered quite a bit of material on SRP, and now it is time to demonstrate SRP in practice with an example. This example demonstrates client-side authentication of the user via SRP as well as subsequent secured access to a simple EJB, using the SRP session challenge as the user credential. The test code deploys an EJB JAR that includes a SAR for the configuration of the server-side login module configuration and SRP services. As in the previous examples, in this example you will dynamically install the server-side login module configuration by using the `SecurityConfig` MBean. This example also uses a custom implementation of the `SRPVerifierStore` interface that uses an in-memory store that is seeded from a Java properties file rather than a serialized object store, as used by the `SRPVerifierStoreService`. This custom service is `org.jboss.chap8.ex3.service.PropertiesVerifierStore`. The following shows the contents of the JAR that contains the sample EJB and SRP services:

```
[examples]$ java -cp output/classes ListJar output/chap8/chap8-ex3.jar
output/chap8/chap8-ex3.jar
+- META-INF/MANIFEST.MF
+- META-INF/ejb-jar.xml
```

```
+- META-INF/jboss.xml
+- org/jboss/chap8/ex3/Echo.class
+- org/jboss/chap8/ex3/EchoBean.class
+- org/jboss/chap8/ex3/EchoHome.class
+- roles.properties
+- users.properties
+- chap8-ex3.sar (archive)
| +- META-INF/MANIFEST.MF
| +- META-INF/jboss-service.xml
| +- META-INF/login-config.xml
| +- org/jboss/chap8/ex3/service/PropertiesVerifierStore$1.class
| +- org/jboss/chap8/ex3/service/PropertiesVerifierStore.class
| +- org/jboss/chap8/ex3/service/PropertiesVerifierStoreMBean.class
| +- org/jboss/chap8/service/SecurityConfig.class
| +- org/jboss/chap8/service/SecurityConfigMBean.class
```

The key SRP-related items in this example are the SRP MBean services configuration and the SRP login module configurations. The `jboss-service.xml` descriptor of `chap8-ex3.sar` is shown in Listing 8.13, and Listing 8.14 and Listing 8.15 show the sample client-side and server-side login module configurations.

LISTING 8.13 The `chap8-ex3.sar` `jboss-service.xml` Descriptor for the SRP Services

```
<server>
    <!-- The custom JAAS login configuration that installs
         a Configuration capable of dynamically updating the
         config settings -->

    <mbean code="org.jboss.chap8.service.SecurityConfig"
           name="jboss.docs.chap8:service=LoginConfig-EX3">
        <attribute name="AuthConfig">META-INF/login-config.xml</attribute>
        <attribute name="SecurityConfigName">jboss.security:name=SecurityConfig
➥</attribute>
    </mbean>

    <!-- The SRP service that provides the SRP RMI server and server side
         authentication cache -->
    <mbean code="org.jboss.security.srp.SRPService"
           name="jboss.docs.chap8:service=SRPService">
        <attribute name="VerifierSourceJndiName">srp-test/chap8-ex3</attribute>
        <attribute name="JndiName">srp-test/SRPServerInterface</attribute>
        <attribute name="AuthenticationCacheJndiName">srp-test/AuthenticationCache
➥</attribute>
        <attribute name="ServerPort">0</attribute>
```

LISTING 8.13 Continued

```
        <depends>jboss.docs.chap8:service=PropertiesVerifierStore</depends>
    </mbean>

    <!-- The SRP store handler service that provides the user password verifier
         information -->
    <mbean code="org.jboss.chap8.ex3.service.PropertiesVerifierStore"
           name="jboss.docs.chap8:service=PropertiesVerifierStore">
        <attribute name="JndiName">srp-test/chap8-ex3</attribute>
    </mbean>
</server>
```

LISTING 8.14 The Client-Side Standard JAAS Configuration

```
srp {
    org.jboss.security.srp.jaas.SRPLoginModule required
    srpServerJndiName="srp-test/SRPServerInterface"
    ;

    org.jboss.security.ClientLoginModule required
    password-stacking="useFirstPass"
    ;
};
```

LISTING 8.15 The Server-Side `XMLLoginConfig` Configuration

```
<application-policy name="chap8-ex3">
    <authentication>
        <login-module code="org.jboss.security.srp.jaas.SRPCacheLoginModule"
                      flag = "required">
            <module-option name="cacheJndiName">srp-test/AuthenticationCache
➥</module-option>
        </login-module>
        <login-module code="org.jboss.security.auth.spi.UsersRolesLoginModule"
                      flag = "required">
            <module-option name="password-stacking">useFirstPass</module-option>
        </login-module>
    </authentication>
</application-policy>
```

The sample services are `ServiceConfig` and the `PropertiesVerifierStore` and `SRPService` MBeans. Note that the `JndiName` attribute of `PropertiesVerifierStore` is equal to the `VerifierSourceJndiName` attribute of `SRPService` and that `SRPService` depends on `PropertiesVerifierStore`. This is required because `SRPService` needs an implementation of the SRPVerifierStore interface for accessing user password verification information.

The client-side login module configuration makes use of SRPLoginModule with a srpServerJndiName option value that corresponds to the JBoss server component SRPService JndiName attribute value (srptest/SRPServerInterface). Also needed is ClientLoginModule, configured with the password-stacking="useFirstPass" value to propagate the user authentication credentials generated by the SRPLoginModule to the EJB invocation layer.

There are two issues to note about the server-side login module configuration. First, note that the cacheJndiName=srp-test/AuthenticationCache configuration option tells SRPCacheLoginModule the location of the CachePolicy that contains the SRPServerSession for users who have authenticated against the SRPService. This value corresponds to the SRPService AuthenticationCacheJndiName attribute value. Second, the configuration includes a UsersRolesLoginModule with the password-stacking=useFirstPass configuration option. You need to use a second login module with the SRPCacheLoginModule because SRP is only an authentication technology. You need to configure a second login module that accepts the authentication credentials validated by the SRPCacheLoginModule to set the principal's roles to determine the principal's permissions. The UsersRolesLoginModule augments the SRP authentication with properties file–based authorization. The user's roles are coming from the roles.properties file included in the EJB JAR.

Now, you can run the client by executing the following command from the book examples directory:

```
 [examples]$ ant -Dchap=chap8 -Dex=3 run-example
...
run-example3:
     [copy] Copying 1 file to /tmp/jboss-4.0.1/server/default/deploy
     [echo] Waiting for 5 seconds for deploy...
     [java] Logging in using the 'srp' configuration
     [java] Created Echo
     [java] Echo.echo()#1 = This is call 1
     [java] Echo.echo()#2 = This is call 2
```

In the examples/logs directory is a file called ex3-trace.log. This is a detailed trace of the client side of the SRP algorithm. Such traces show step-by-step the construction of the public keys, challenges, session key, and verification.

Note that the client in this example takes a long time to run relative to the other simple examples. The reason for this is the construction of the client's public key, which involves the creation of a cryptographically strong random number; this process takes quite a bit of time the first time it occurs. If you were to log out and log in again within the same VM, the process would be much faster. Also note that Echo.echo()#2 fails with an authentication exception. The client code sleeps for 15 seconds after making the first call to demonstrate the behavior of the SRPService cache expiration. The SRPService cache policy timeout is set to a mere 10 seconds to force this issue. As stated earlier, you need to make the cache timeout very long or handle re-authentication on failure.

Running JBoss with a Java 2 Security Manager

By default, the JBoss server does not start with a Java 2 security manager. If you want to use Java 2 permissions to restrict code privileges, you need to configure the JBoss server to run under a security manager. You do this by configuring the Java VM options in the `run.bat` or `run.sh` scripts in the JBoss server distribution `bin` directory. There are two required VM options:

- **`java.security.manager`**—You use this option without any value to specify that the default security manager should be used. This is the preferred security manager. You can also pass a value to the `java.security.manager` option to specify a custom security manager implementation. The value must be the fully qualified classname of a subclass of `java.lang.SecurityManager`. This form specifies that the policy file should augment the default security policy, as configured by the VM installation.
- **`java.security.policy`**—You use this option to specify the policy file that will augment the default security policy information for the VM. This option takes two forms: `java.security.policy=policyFileURL` and `java.security.policy==policyFileURL`. The first form specifies that the policy file should augment the default security policy, as configured by the VM installation. The second form specifies that only the indicated policy file should be used. The `policyFileURL` value can be any URL for which a protocol handler exists, or it can be a file path specification.

Both the `run.bat` and `run.sh` start scripts reference a `JAVA_OPTS` variable that you can use to set the security manager properties.

Enabling Java 2 security is the easy part. The difficult part of Java 2 security is establishing the allowed permissions. If you look at the `server.policy` file that is contained in the default configuration file set, you'll see that it contains the following permission grant statement:

```
grant {
    // Allow everything for now
    permission java.security.AllPermission;
};
```

This effectively disables security permission checking for all code because it says any code can do anything, which is not a reasonable default. What is a reasonable set of permissions is entirely up to you.

Table 8.1 lists the current set of JBoss-specific `java.lang.RuntimePermissions` that are required.

TABLE 8.1 Required JBoss-Specific `java.lang.RuntimePermissions`

TargetName	What the Permission Allows	Risks
`org.jboss.security.SecurityAssociation.getPrincipalInfo`	Access to the `org.jboss.security.SecurityAssociation` `getPrincipal()` and `getCredentials()` methods.	The ability to see the current thread caller and credentials.
`org.jboss.security.SecurityAssociation.setPrincipalInfo`	Access to the `org.jboss.security.SecurityAssociation` `setPrincipal()` and `setCredentials()` methods.	The ability to set the current thread caller and credentials.
`org.jboss.security.SecurityAssociation.setServer`	Access to the `org.jboss.security.SecurityAssociation` `setServer` method.	The ability to enable or disable multithread storage of the caller principal and credential.
`org.jboss.security.SecurityAssociation.setRunAsRole`	Access to the `org.jboss.security.SecurityAssociation` `pushRunAsRole` and `popRunAsRole` methods.	The ability to change the current caller run-as role principal.

To conclude this discussion, here is a little-known tidbit on debugging security policy settings: You can set various debugging flags to determine how the security manager is using your security policy file as well as what policy files are contributing permissions. Running the VM as follows shows the possible debugging flag settings:

```
[bin]$ java -Djava.security.debug=help

all           turn on all debugging
access        print all checkPermission results
combiner      SubjectDomainCombiner debugging
jar           jar verification
logincontext  login context results
policy        loading and granting
provider      security provider debugging
scl           permissions SecureClassLoader assigns

The following can be used with access:

stack     include stack trace
domain    dumps all domains in context
failure   before throwing exception, dump stack
          and domain that didn't have permission

Note: Separate multiple options with a comma
```

Running with `-Djava.security.debug=all` provides the most output, but the output volume is torrential. This might be a good place to start if you don't understand a given security failure at all. A less verbose setting that helps debug permission failures is `-Djava.security.debug=access,failure`. This is still relatively verbose, but it's not nearly as bad as the `all` mode because the security domain information is displayed only on access failures.

Using SSL with JBoss and JSSE

JBoss uses Java Secure Socket Extension (JSSE) for SSL. JSSE is bundled with JDK 1.4. To get started with JSSE, you need a public key/private key pair in the form of an X509 certificate for use by the SSL server sockets. For the purpose of this example, we have created a self-signed certificate by using the JDK `keytool` and included the resulting keystore file in the `chap8` source directory as `chap8.keystore`. We created it by using the following command and input:

```
keytool -genkey -keystore chap8.keystore -storepass rmi+ssl -keypass rmi+ssl
➥-keyalg RSA -alias chapter8 -validity 3650 -dname "cn=chapter8
➥example,ou=admin book,dc=jboss,dc=org"
```

This produces a keystore file called `chap8.keystore`. (A *keystore* is a database of security keys.) There are two different types of entries in a keystore:

- **Key entries**—Each entry holds very sensitive cryptographic key information, which is stored in a protected format to prevent unauthorized access. Typically, a key stored in this type of entry is a secret key or a private key accompanied by the certificate chain for the corresponding public key. The `keytool` and `jarsigner` tools only handle the latter type of entry—that is, private keys and their associated certificate chains.
- **Trusted certificate entries**—Each entry contains a single public key certificate that belongs to another party. It is called a *trusted certificate* because the keystore owner trusts that the public key in the certificate indeed belongs to the identity identified by the subject (owner) of the certificate. The issuer of the certificate vouches for this by signing the certificate.

Listing the `src/main/org/jboss/chap8/chap8.keystore` examples file contents by using `keytool` shows one self-signed certificate:

```
[examples]$ keytool -list -v -keystore src/main/org/jboss/chap8/chap8.keystore
Enter keystore password:  rmi+ssl

Keystore type: jks
Keystore provider: SUN

Your keystore contains 1 entry
```

```
Alias name: chapter8
Creation date: Dec 16, 2004
Entry type: keyEntry
Certificate chain length: 1
Certificate[1]:
Owner: CN=chapter8 example, OU=admin book, DC=jboss, DC=org
Issuer: CN=chapter8 example, OU=admin book, DC=jboss, DC=org
Serial number: 41c23d6c
Valid from: Thu Dec 16 19:59:08 CST 2004 until: Sun Dec 14 19:59:08 CST 2014
Certificate fingerprints:
         MD5:  36:29:FD:1C:78:44:14:5E:5A:C7:EB:E5:E8:ED:06:86
         SHA1: 37:FE:BB:8A:A5:CF:D9:3D:B9:61:8C:53:CE:19:1E:4D:BC:C9:18:F2


*******************************************
*******************************************
```

With JSSE working and a keystore with the certificate you will use for the JBoss server, you are ready to configure JBoss to use SSL for EJB access. You do this by configuring the EJB invoker RMI socket factories. The JBossSX framework includes implementations of the `java.rmi.server.RMIServerSocketFactory` and `java.rmi.server.RMIClientSocketFactory` interfaces that enable the use of RMI over SSL-encrypted sockets. The implementation classes are `org.jboss.security.ssl.RMISSLServerSocketFactory` and `org.jboss.security.ssl.RMISSLClientSocketFactory`, respectively. There are two steps to enable the use of SSL for RMI access to EJBs. The first is to enable the use of a keystore as the database for the SSL server certificate, which you do by configuring an `org.jboss.security.plugins.JaasSecurityDomain` MBean. The `jboss-service.xml` descriptor in the `chap8/ex4` directory includes the `JaasSecurityDomain` definition shown in Listing 8.16.

LISTING 8.16 A Sample `JaasSecurityDomain` Configuration for RMI/SSL

```
<!-- The SSL domain setup -->
<mbean code="org.jboss.security.plugins.JaasSecurityDomain"
       name="jboss.security:service=JaasSecurityDomain,domain=RMI+SSL">
    <constructor>
        <arg type="java.lang.String" value="RMI+SSL"/>
    </constructor>
    <attribute name="KeyStoreURL">chap8.keystore</attribute>
    <attribute name="KeyStorePass">rmi+ssl</attribute>
</mbean>
```

The `JaasSecurityDomain` is a subclass of the standard `JaasSecurityManager` class that adds the notions of a keystore as well JSSE `KeyManagerFactory` and `TrustManagerFactory` access. It extends the basic security manager to allow support for SSL and other cryptographic operations that require security keys. This configuration simply loads the `chap8.keystore` from the Example 4 MBean SAR, using the indicated password.

The second step is to define an EJB invoker configuration that uses the JBossSX RMI socket factories that support SSL. To do this, you need to define a custom configuration for the `JRMPInvoker` shown in Chapter 5, "EJBs on JBoss," as well as an EJB setup that makes use of this invoker. The following code shows the `jboss-service.xml` descriptor that defines the custom `JRMPInovker`:

```
<mbean code="org.jboss.invocation.jrmp.server.JRMPInvoker"
       name="jboss:service=invoker,type=jrmp,socketType=SSL">
    <attribute name="RMIObjectPort">14445</attribute>
    <attribute name="RMIClientSocketFactory">
        org.jboss.security.ssl.RMISSLClientSocketFactory
    </attribute>
    <attribute name="RMIServerSocketFactory">
        org.jboss.security.ssl.RMISSLServerSocketFactory
    </attribute>
    <attribute name="SecurityDomain">java:/jaas/RMI+SSL</attribute>
    <depends>jboss.security:service=JaasSecurityDomain,domain=RMI+SSL</depends>
</mbean>
```

To set up an SSL invoker, you can create an invoker binding named `stateless-ssl-invoker` that uses the custom `JRMPInvoker`. You can declare the invoker binding and connect it to `EchoBean4`, as shown in the following `jboss.xml` file:

```
<?xml version="1.0"?>
<jboss>
    <enterprise-beans>
        <session>
            <ejb-name>EchoBean4</ejb-name>
            <configuration-name>Standard Stateless SessionBean
➥</configuration-name>
            <invoker-bindings>
                <invoker>
                    <invoker-proxy-binding-name>stateless-ssl-invoker
➥</invoker-proxy-binding-name>
                </invoker>
            </invoker-bindings>
        </session>
    </enterprise-beans>

    <invoker-proxy-bindings>
        <invoker-proxy-binding>
            <name>stateless-ssl-invoker</name>
```

```
            <invoker-mbean>jboss:service=invoker,type=jrmp,socketType=SSL
➥</invoker-mbean>
            <proxy-factory>org.jboss.proxy.ejb.ProxyFactory</proxy-factory>
            <proxy-factory-config>
            <client-interceptors>
                <home>
                    <interceptor>org.jboss.proxy.ejb.HomeInterceptor</interceptor>
                    <interceptor>org.jboss.proxy.SecurityInterceptor</interceptor>
                    <interceptor>org.jboss.proxy.TransactionInterceptor
➥</interceptor>
                    <interceptor>org.jboss.invocation.InvokerInterceptor
➥</interceptor>
                </home>
                <bean>
                    <interceptor>org.jboss.proxy.ejb.StatelessSessionInterceptor
➥</interceptor>
                    <interceptor>org.jboss.proxy.SecurityInterceptor</interceptor>
                    <interceptor>org.jboss.proxy.TransactionInterceptor
➥</interceptor>
                    <interceptor>org.jboss.invocation.InvokerInterceptor
➥</interceptor>
                </bean>
            </client-interceptors>
            </proxy-factory-config>
        </invoker-proxy-binding>
    </invoker-proxy-bindings>
</jboss>
```

The Example 4 code is located under the `src/main/org/jboss/chap8/ex4` directory of the book examples. This is another simple stateless session bean with an echo method that returns its input argument. It is hard to tell when SSL is in use unless it fails, so you can run the Example 4 client in two different ways to demonstrate that the EJB deployment is in fact using SSL. You need to start the JBoss server, using the default configuration, and then run Example 4b as follows:

```
[examples]$ ant -Dchap=chap8 -Dex=4b run-example
...
run-example4b:
     [copy] Copying 1 file to /tmp/jboss-4.0.1/server/default/deploy
     [echo] Waiting for 15 seconds for deploy...
...
     [java] Exception in thread "main" java.rmi.ConnectIOException:
➥error during JRMP connection establishment; nested exception is:
     [java]      javax.net.ssl.SSLHandshakeException: sun.security.validator.
➥ValidatorException: No trusted certificate found
...
```

The resulting exception is expected, and it is the purpose of the 4b version of the example. Note that the exception stack trace has been edited to fit into the book format, so you can expect some differences. The key item to notice about the exception is that it clearly shows that you are using the Sun JSSE classes to communicate with the JBoss EJB container. The exception is saying that the self-signed certificate you are using as the JBoss server certificate cannot be validated as signed by any of the default certificate authorities. This is expected because the default certificate authority keystore that ships with the JSSE package includes only well-known certificate authorities such as VeriSign, Thawte, and RSA Data Security. To get the EJB client to accept your self-signed certificate as valid, you need to tell the JSSE classes to use your `chap8.keystore` as its truststore. (A *truststore* is a keystore that contains public key certificates used to sign other certificates.) To do this, you run Example 4, using `-Dex=4` rather than `-Dex=4b` to pass the location of the correct truststore, using the `javax.net.ssl.trustStore` system property:

```
[examples]$ ant -Dchap=chap8 -Dex=4 run-example
...
run-example4:
     [copy] Copying 1 file to /tmp/jboss-4.0.1/server/default/deploy
     [echo] Waiting for 5 seconds for deploy...
...
     [java] Created Echo
     [java] Echo.echo()#1 = This is call 1
```

This time the only indication that an SSL socket is involved is the `SSL handshakeCompleted` message. This comes from the `RMISSLClientSocketFactory` class as a debug-level log message. If you did not have the client configured to print out `log4j` debug-level messages, there would be no direct indication that SSL was involved. If you note the runtimes and the load on your system CPU, you see that there definitely is a difference. SSL, like SRP, involves the use of cryptographically strong random numbers that take time to seed the first time they are used. This shows up as high CPU utilization and startup times.

One consequence of this is that if you are running on a system that is slower than the one used to run the examples for this book, such as when running example 4b, you might see an exception similar to the following:

```
javax.naming.NameNotFoundException: EchoBean4 not bound
   at sun.rmi.transport.StreamRemoteCall.exceptionReceivedFromServer
...
```

The problem is that the JBoss server has not finished deploying the sample EJB in the time the client allowed. This is due to the initial setup time of the secure random number generator used by the SSL server socket. If you see this problem, you can simply rerun the example or increase the deployment wait time in the Chapter 8 `build.xml` Ant script.

Configuring JBoss for Use Behind a Firewall

JBoss comes with many socket-based services that open listening ports. This section lists the services that open ports that you might need to configure to work when accessing JBoss behind a firewall. Table 8.2 shows the ports, socket types, and associated services for the services in the default configuration file set. Table 8.3 shows the same information for the additional ports that exist in the `all` configuration file set.

TABLE 8.2 The Ports in the Default Configuration

Port	Type	Service
1099	TCP	`org.jboss.naming.NamingService`
1098	TCP	`org.jboss.naming.NamingService`
4444	TCP	`org.jboss.invocation.jrmp.server.JRMPInvoker`
4445	TCP	`org.jboss.invocation.pooled.server.PooledInvoker`
8009	TCP	`org.jboss.web.tomcat.tc4.EmbeddedTomcatService`
8080	TCP	`org.jboss.web.tomcat.tc4.EmbeddedTomcatService`
8083	TCP	`org.jboss.web.WebService`
8093	TCP	`org.jboss.mq.il.uil2.UILServerILService`

TABLE 8.3 Additional Ports in the `all` Configuration

Port	Type	Service
1100	TCP	`org.jboss.ha.jndi.HANamingService`
0[a]	TCP	`org.jboss.ha.jndi.HANamingService`
1102	UDP	`org.jboss.ha.jndi.HANamingService`
1161	UDP	`org.jboss.jmx.adaptor.snmp.agent.SnmpAgentService`
1162	UDP	`org.jboss.jmx.adaptor.snmp.trapd.TrapdService`
3528	TCP	`org.jboss.invocation.iiop.IIOPInvoker`
45566[b]	UDP	`org.jboss.ha.framework.server.ClusterPartition`

aThis is currently anonymous but can be set via the RmiPort attribute.

bThere are two additional anonymous UDP ports: one can be set by using rcv_port, and the other cannot be set.

Securing the JBoss Server

JBoss comes with several admin access points that need to be secured or removed to prevent unauthorized access to admin functions in a deployment. The following sections describe the various admin services and how to secure them.

The `jmx-console.war` Service

The `jmx-console.war` found in the deploy directory provides an HTML view into the JMX microkernel. Therefore, it provides access to arbitrary admin-type access, such as shutting down the server, stopping services, deploying new services, and so on. It should either be secured like any other web application or removed.

The `web-console.war` Service

The `web-console.war` found in the `deploy/management` directory is another web application view into the JMX microkernel. This uses a combination of an applet and an HTML view and provides the same level of access to admin functionality as the `jmx-console.war`. Therefore, it should either be secured or removed. The `web-console.war` contains commented-out templates for basic security in its `WEB-INF/web.xml` as well as commented-out setup for a security domain in `WEB-INF/jboss-web.xml`.

The `http-invoker.sar` Service

The `http-invoker.sar` found in the deploy directory is a service that provides RMI/HTTP access for EJBs and the JNDI `Naming` service. This includes a servlet that processes posts of marshaled `org.jboss.invocation.Invocation` objects that represent invocations that should be dispatched onto the `MBeanServer`. This effectively allows access to MBeans that support the detached invoker operation via HTTP because someone could figure out how to format an appropriate HTTP post. To secure this access point, you would need to secure the `JMXInvokerServlet` servlet found in the `http-invoker.sar/invoker.war/WEB-INF/web.xml` descriptor. A secure mapping is defined for the `/restricted/JMXInvokerServlet` path by default; to use it, you would simply have to remove the other paths and configure the `http-invoker` security domain setup in the `http-invoker.sar/invoker.war/WEB-INF/jboss-web.xml` descriptor.

The `jmx-invoker-adaptor-server.sar` Service

The `jmx-invoker-adaptor-server.sar` is a service that exposes the JMX `MBeanServer` interface via an RMI-compatible interface, using the RMI/JRMP detached invoker service. Currently, the only way for this service to be secured would be to switch the protocol to RMI/HTTP and secure the `http-invoker.sar` as described in the previous section. In the future, this service will be deployed as an XMBean with a security interceptor that supports role-based access checks. If you are so inclined, you can set up this configuration today, following the procedure demonstrated in the section "Version 3: Adding Security and Remote Access to the `JNDIMap` XMBean" in Chapter 2, "The JBoss JMX Microkernel."

CHAPTER 9

Web Applications

IN THIS CHAPTER

- The Tomcat Service
- The Tomcat `server.xml` File
- The `Engine` Element
- The `Host` Element
- Using SSL with the JBoss/Tomcat Bundle
- Setting the Context Root of a Web Application
- Setting Up Virtual Hosts
- Serving Static Content
- Using Apache with Tomcat
- Using Clustering
- Integrating Third-Party Servlet Containers

This chapter discusses configuration of web applications in JBoss. It looks at general issues that are specific to the JBoss/Tomcat 5 integration bundle.

The Tomcat Service

Tomcat 5, the latest release of the Apache Java servlet container, supports the Servlet 2.4 and JSP 2.0 specifications. Tomcat is distributed as a deployable service in `jbossweb-tomcat-5.0.sar` in the `deploy` directory. It is shipped in exploded directory form, so it's easy to inspect and update the configuration of an embedded Tomcat instance.

The main service file is `META-INF/jboss-service.xml`. It configures the `org.jboss.web.tomcat.tc5.Tomcat5` MBean, which controls Tomcat. Its configurable attributes include the following:

- **`DefaultSecurityDomain`**—This specifies the JAAS security domain to use in the absence of an explicit `security-domain` specification in the `jboss-web.xml` of a WAR file.
- **`Java2ClassLoadingCompliance`**—This enables the standard Java 2 parent delegation class-loading model rather than the servlet model, which loads from the WAR first. It is `true` by default because loading from WARs that include client JARs with classes used by EJBs causes class-loading conflicts. If you enable the servlet class-loading model by setting this flag to `false`, you need to organize your deployment package to avoid having duplicate classes in the deployment.

- **UseJBossWebLoader**—This flag indicates that Tomcat should use a JBoss unified class loader as the web application class loader. The default is `true`, which means that the classes inside the `WEB-INF/classes` and `WEBINF/lib` directories of the WAR file are incorporated into the default shared class loader repository described in Chapter 2, "The JBoss JMX Microkernel." This may not be what you want because it is contrary to the default servlet class-loading model and can result in sharing of classes/resources between web applications. You can disable this by setting this attribute to `false`.
- **LenientEjbLink**—This flag indicates that `ejb-link` errors should be ignored in favor of trying the `jndi-name` in the `jboss-web.xml`. The default is `true`.
- **ManagerClass**—This is the class to use as the session manager for replicating the state of web applications marked as distributable. The only provided implementation session manager is `org.jboss.web.tomcat.tc5.session.JBossCacheManager`, which uses `JBossCache` to track the distributed state.
- **SubjectAttributeName**—If set, this represents the request attribute name under which the JAAS subject will be stored. There is no default value, meaning that the subject is not set in the request.
- **SessionIdAlphabet**—This is the set of characters used to create a session's ID. It must be made up of exactly 65 unique characters.
- **SnapshotMode**—This sets the snapshot mode in a clustered environment. It must be either `instant` or `interval`. In instant mode, changes to a clustered session are instantly propagated whenever a modification is made. In interval mode, all modifications are periodically propagated according to the `SnapshotInterval`.
- **SnapshotInterval**—This sets the snapshot interval, in milliseconds, for the interval snapshot mode. The default is `1000ms`, which is 1 second.
- **UseLocalCache**—This flag indicates whether the local HTTP session value should be used if it exists. When it is `true`, the existing local HTTP session values are used, and updates are replicated, but updates to the same session on other nodes do not update the local session value. This mode is useful only for failover. When it is `false`, the session value is obtained from the distributed cache. This mode can be used with load balancing. The default is `true`.
- **UseJK**—This specifies that you are using `MOD_JK(2)` for load balancing with sticky session combined with `JvmRoute`. If set to `true`, it will insert a `JvmRouteFilter` to intercept every request and replace the `JvmRoute` if it detects a failover. This additionally requires the `JvmRoute` to be set inside the engine definition in the Tomcat `server.xml` file. The default is `false`.
- **Domain**—This is the JMX domain under which Tomcat will register additional MBeans. The default is `jboss.web`.
- **SecurityManagerService**—This is a reference to the JAAS security manager for Tomcat to use. It defaults to `jboss.security:service=JaasSecurityManager`.

- **CacheName**—This is a reference to the JBossCache to be used for HTTP session replication, if session replication is being used. The default is jboss.cache:service=TomcatClusteringCache.

The Tomcat server.xml File

While the jboss-service.xml file controls the JBoss/Tomcat integration, Tomcat has its own configuration file, which guides its operation. This is the server.xml descriptor that you will find in the jbossweb-tomcat50.sar directory. Although this file doesn't have a formal DTD or schema definition, Figure 9.1 shows the general structure of the file.

We'll now look at some of the configuration options that are available in the server.xml file. The top-level element is the Server element; it is the root element, and it should contain a Service element that represents the entire web subsystem. The only supported attribute is name, which is a unique name by which the service is known.

The Connector Element

The Connector element configures a transport mechanism that allows clients to send requests and receive responses from the Service it is associated with. Connectors forward requests to the engine and return the results to the requesting client. The Connector element supports these attributes:

- **enableLookups**—This is a flag that enables DNS resolution of the client hostname, as accessed via the ServletRequest.getRemoteHost method. This flag defaults to false.
- **redirectPort**—This is the port to which non-SSL requests will be redirected when a request for content secured under a transport confidentiality or integrity constraint is received. This defaults to the standard HTTPS port of 443.
- **secure**—This attribute sets the ServletRequest.isSecure method value flag to indicate whether the transport channel is secure. This flag defaults to false.
- **scheme**—This attribute sets the protocol name as accessed by the ServletRequest.getScheme method. The scheme defaults to http.
- **acceptCount**—This is the maximum queue length for incoming connection requests when all possible request processing threads are in use. Any requests received when the queue is full will be refused. The default value is 10.
- **address**—For servers with more than one IP address, this attribute specifies which address will be used for listening on the specified port. By default, this port will be used on all IP addresses associated with the server.
- **bufferSize**—This is the size (in bytes) of the buffer to be provided for input streams created by this connector. By default, buffers of 2048 bytes are provided.

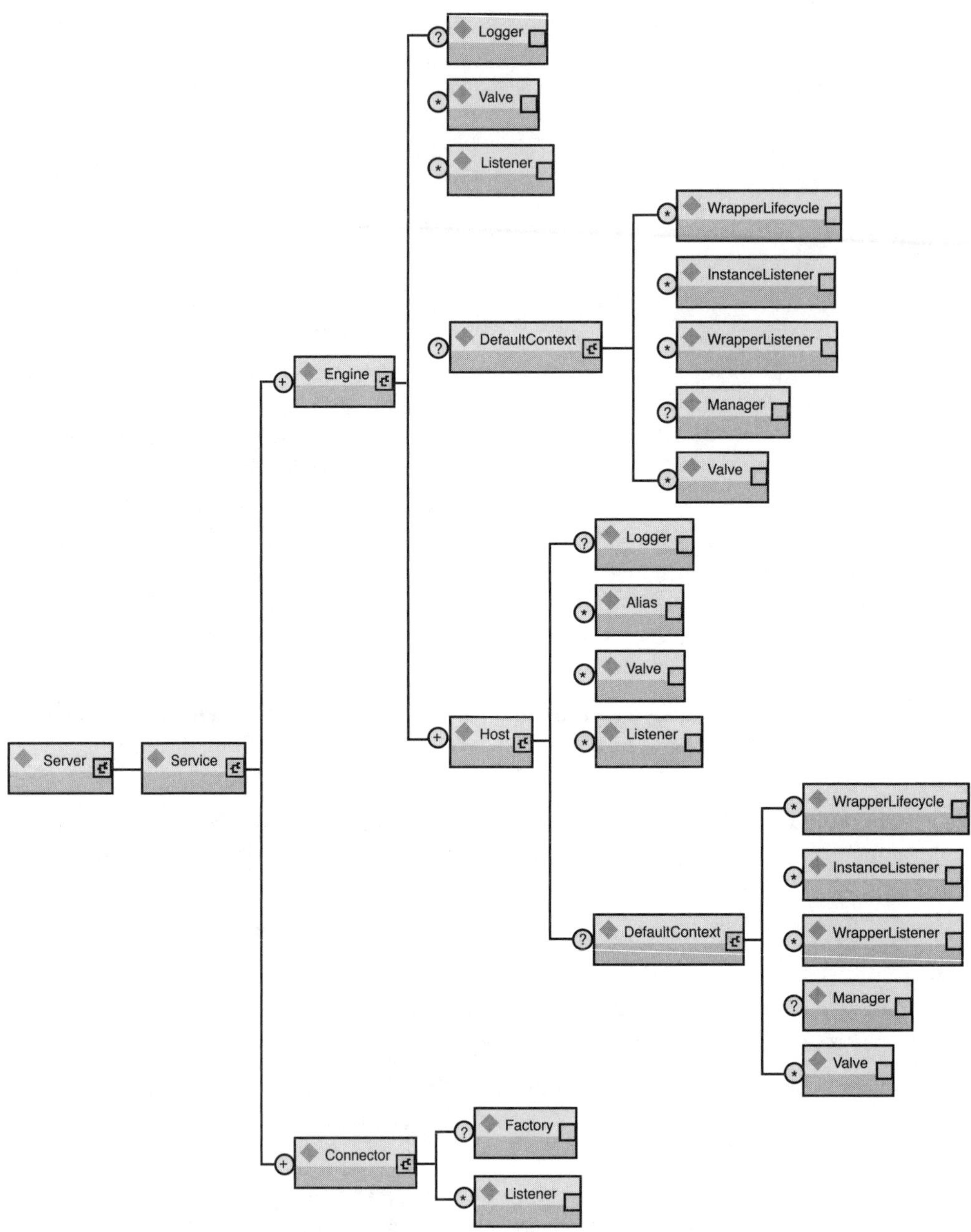

FIGURE 9.1 An overview of the Tomcat `server.xml` file.

- **connectionTimeout**—This is the number of milliseconds this connector will wait, after accepting a connection, for the request URI line to be presented. The default value is 60000 (that is, 60 seconds).
- **debug**—This attribute specifies the debugging detail level of log messages generated by this component, with higher numbers creating more detailed output. If not specified, this attribute is set to zero (0). Whether or not this shows up in the log further depends on the log4j category org.jboss.web.tomcat.tc5.Tomcat5 threshold.
- **maxThreads**—This attribute specifies the maximum number of request-processing threads to be created by this connector, which therefore determines the maximum number of simultaneous requests that can be handled. If not specified, this attribute is set to 200.
- **maxSpareThreads**—This attribute specifies the maximum number of unused request-processing threads that will be allowed to exist until the thread pool starts stopping the unnecessary threads. The default value is 50.
- **minSpareThreads**—This attribute specifies the number of request-processing threads that will be created when this connector is first started. The connector will also make sure it has the specified number of idle processing threads available. This attribute should be set to a value smaller than that set for maxThreads. The default value is 4.
- **port**—This attribute specifies the TCP port number on which this connector will create a server socket and await incoming connections. The operating system allows only one server application to listen to a particular port number on a particular IP address.
- **proxyName**—If this connector is being used in a proxy configuration, you configure this attribute to specify the server name to be returned for calls to request.getServerName().
- **proxyPort**—If this connector is being used in a proxy configuration, you configure this attribute to specify the server port to be returned for calls to request.getServerPort().
- **tcpNoDelay**—If set to true, the TCP_NO_DELAY option will be set on the server socket, which improves performance under most circumstances. This is set to true by default.

You can find additional attribute descriptions in the Tomcat documentation at http://jakarta.apache.org/tomcat/tomcat-5.0-doc/config/http.html.

The Engine Element

Each Service element must have a single Engine configuration. An engine handles the requests submitted to a service via the configured connectors. The child elements supported by the embedded service include Host, Logger, Default-Context, Valve, and Listener. The supported attributes include the following:

- **className**—This is the fully qualified classname of the org.apache.catalina.Engine interface implementation to use. If not specified, it defaults to org.apache.catalina.core.StandardEngine.
- **defaultHost**—This is the name of a Host configured under the Engine that will handle requests with hostnames that do not match a Host configuration.
- **name**—This is a logical name to assign to the Engine element. It will be used in log messages produced by the Engine element.

You can find additional information on the Engine element in the Tomcat documentation at http://jakarta.apache.org/tomcat/tomcat-5.0-doc/config/engine.html.

The Host Element

A Host element represents a virtual host configuration. It is a container for web applications with a specified DNS hostname. The child elements supported by the embedded service include Alias, Logger, DefaultContext, Valve, and Listener. The supported attributes include the following:

- **className**—This is the fully qualified classname of the org.apache.catalina.Host interface implementation to use. If not specified, it defaults to org.apache.catalina.core.StandardHost.
- **name**—This is the DNS name of the virtual host. At least one Host element must be configured with a name that corresponds to the defaultHost value of the containing Engine element.

The Alias element is an optional child element of the Host element. Each Alias element's content specifies an alternate DNS name for the enclosing Host.

You can find additional information on the Host element in the Tomcat documentation at http://jakarta.apache.org/tomcat/tomcat-5.0-doc/config/host.html.

The DefaultContext Element

The DefaultContext element is a configuration template for web application contexts. It can be defined at the Engine or Host level. The child elements supported by the embedded service include WrapperLifecycle, InstanceListener, WrapperListener, and Manager. The supported attributes include the following:

- **className**—This is the fully qualified classname of the org.apache.catalina.core.DefaultContext implementation. It defaults to org.apache.catalina.core.DefaultContext, and if it is overridden, it must be a subclass of DefaultContext.

- **`cookies`**—This flag indicates whether sessions will be tracked by using cookies. The default is `true`.
- **`crossContext`**—This flag indicates whether the `ServletContext.getContext(String path)` method should return contexts for other web applications deployed in the calling web application's virtual host. The default is `false`.

The `Logger` Element

The `Logger` element specifies a logging configuration for the Tomcat instance. The supported attributes include the following:

- **`className`**—This is the fully qualified classname of the `org.apache.catalina.Logger` interface implementation. For integration with JBoss logging, this should be set to `org.jboss.web.tomcat.Log4jLogger`.
- **`verbosity`**—This is the default log level.
- **`category`**—This is the default log category.

The `Valve` Element

The `Valve` element configures a hook into the request-processing pipeline for the web container. The `Valve` element must implement the `org.apache.catalina.Valve` interface. There is only one required configuration attribute, `className`, which is the fully qualified classname of the `org.apache.catalina.Valve` interface implementation. The most commonly used `Valve` element is `AccessLogValve`, which keeps a standard HTTP access log of incoming requests. The `className` for the access log value is `org.jboss.web.catalina.valves.AccessLogValue`. The additional `Valve` attributes that it supports include the following:

- **`directory`**—This is the directory path into which the access log files will be created.
- **`pattern`**—This pattern specifier defines the format of the log messages. It defaults to `common`.
- **`prefix`**—This is the prefix to add to each log file name. It defaults to `access_log`.
- **`suffix`**—This is the suffix to add to each log file name. It defaults to an empty string, meaning that no suffix will be added.

You can find additional information on the `Valve` element and the available valve implementations in the Tomcat documentation at http://jakarta.apache.org/tomcat/tomcat-5.0-doc/config/valve.html.

Using SSL with the JBoss/Tomcat Bundle

There are a few ways you can configure HTTP over SSL for the embedded Tomcat servlet container. The main difference between them is whether you use the JBoss-specific connector socket factory, which allows you to obtain the JSSE server certificate information from a JBossSX SecurityDomain. This requires establishing a SecurityDomain by using the org.jboss.security.plugins.JaasSecurityDomain MBean. These two steps are similar to the procedure used in Chapter 8, "Security on JBoss," to enable RMI with SSL encryption. The following is a server.xml configuration file that illustrates the setup of only an SSL connector via this approach:

```
<Server>
   <Service name="jboss.web" className=
➥"org.jboss.web.tomcat.tc5.StandardService">

      <Connector port="8080" address="${jboss.bind.address}" maxThreads="150"
         minSpareThreads="25" maxSpareThreads="75" enableLookups="false"
         redirectPort="443" acceptCount="100" connectionTimeout="20000"
         disableUploadTimeout="true"/>

      <Connector port="443" address="${jboss.bind.address}" maxThreads="100"
         minSpareThreads="5" maxSpareThreads="15" scheme="https"
         secure="true" clientAuth="false"
         keystoreFile="${jboss.server.home.dir}/conf/chap8.keystore"
         keystorePass="rmi+ssl" sslProtocol="TLS"/>

      <Engine name="jboss.web" defaultHost="localhost">
         <Realm
            className="org.jboss.web.tomcat.security.JBossSecurityMgrRealm"
            certificatePrincipal="org.jboss.securia.Log4jLogger"
            verbosityLevel="WARNING" category=
➥"org.jboss.web.localhost.Engine"/>
         <Host name="localhost" autoDeploy="false" deployOnStartup="false"
              deployXML="false">
            <DefaultContext cookies="true" crossContext="true"
➥override="true"/>
         </Host>
      </Engine>
   </Service>
</Server>
```

This configuration includes the same JaasSecurityDomain setup as in Chapter 8, but because the descriptor is not being deployed as part of a SAR that includes chap8.keystore, you need to copy chap8.keystore to the server/default/conf directory.

You can do a quick test of this configuration by accessing the JMX Console web application, using the URL https://localhost/jmx-console/index.jsp.

Note

If you're running on a Unix system (Linux, Solaris, or OS X) that allows only root to open ports below 1024, you need to change the port number in the preceding code to something like 8443.

The following are the factory configuration attributes:

- **`algorithm`**—This is the certificate encoding algorithm to be used. If it is not specified, the default value is `SunX509`.
- **`className`**—This is the fully qualified classname of the SSL server socket factory implementation class. You must specify `org.apache.coyote.tomcat4.CoyoteServerSocketFactory` here. Using any other socket factory will not cause an error, but the server socket will not be using SSL.
- **`clientAuth`**—You set this attribute to `true` if you want the SSL stack to require a valid certificate chain from the client before accepting a connection. A `false` value (which is the default) does not require a certificate chain unless the client requests a resource protected by a security constraint that uses `CLIENT-CERT` authentication.
- **`keystoreFile`**—This is the pathname of the `keystore` file where you have stored the server certificate to be loaded. By default, the pathname is the `file.keystore` in the operating system home directory of the user who is running Tomcat.
- **`keystorePass`**—This is the password used to access the server certificate from the specified `keystore` file. The default value is `changeit`.
- **`keystoreType`**—This is the type of `keystore` file to be used for the server certificate. If not specified, the default value is `JKS`.
- **`protocol`**—This is the version of the SSL protocol to use. If not specified, the default is `TLS`.

Note that if you try to test this configuration by using the self-signed certificate from the Chapter 8 `chap8.keystore` and attempt to access content over an HTTPS connection, your browser should display a warning dialog indicating that it does not trust the certificate authority that signed the certificate of the server you are connecting to. For example, when we tested the first configuration example, Internet Explorer 5.5 showed the initial security alert dialog listed in Figure 9.2. Figure 9.3 shows the server certificate details. This warning is important because anyone can generate a self-signed certificate with any information desired. Your only way to verify that the system on the other side really represents the party it claims to is by verifying that it is signed by a trusted third party.

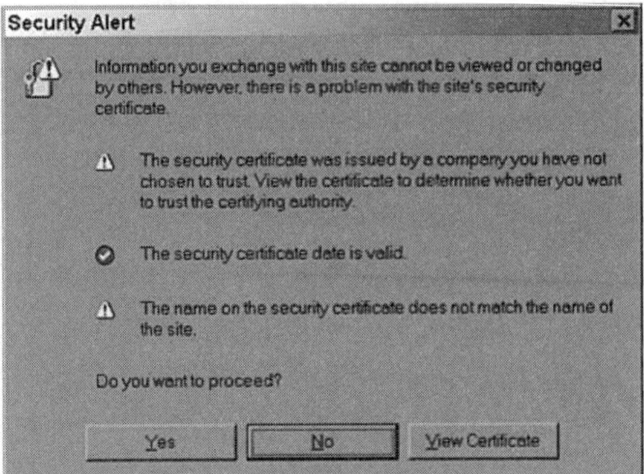

FIGURE 9.2 The Internet Explorer 5.5 security alert dialog.

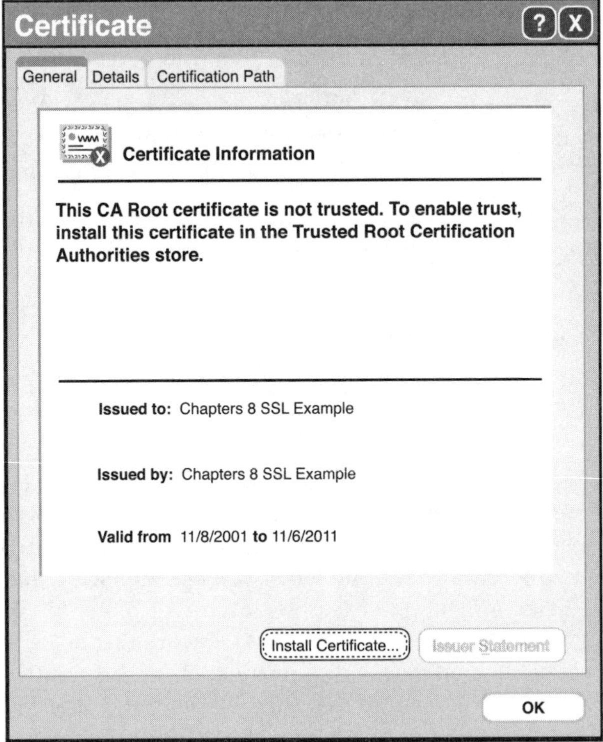

FIGURE 9.3 The Internet Explorer 5.5 SSL certificate details dialog.

Setting the Context Root of a Web Application

The context root of a web application determines which URLs Tomcat will delegate to your web application. If your application's context root is myapp, then any request for /myapp or /myapp/* will be handled by your application unless a more specific context root exists. If a second web application were assigned the context root myapp/help, a request for /myapp/help/help.jsp would be handled by the second web application, not the first.

This relationship also holds when the context root is set to /, which is known as the *root context*. When an application is assigned to the root context, it will respond to all requests not handled by a more specific context root.

The context root for an application is determined by how the application is deployed. When a web application is deployed inside an EAR file, the context root is specified in the application.xml file of the EAR, using a context-root element inside a web module. In the following example, the context root of the web-client.war application is set to bank:

```
<application xmlns="http://java.sun.com/xml/ns/j2ee" version="1.4"
    xmlns:xsi="http://www.w3.org/2001/XMLSchema-instance"
    xsi:schemaLocation="http://java.sun.com /xml/ns/j2ee
➥http://java.sun.com/xml/ns/j2ee/application_1_4.xsd">
    <display-name>JBossDukesBank</display-name>

    <module>
        <ejb>bank-ejb.jar</ejb>
    </module>
    <module>
        <web>
            <web-uri>web-client.war</web-uri>
            <context-root>bank</context-root>
        </web>
    </module>

</application>
```

For web applications that are deployed outside an EAR file, the context root can be specified in two ways. First, the context root can be specified inside the WEB-INF/jboss-web.xml file. The following example shows what the jboss-web.xml file would look like for the same web-client.war file shown previously if it weren't bundled inside an EAR file:

```
<jboss-web>
    <context-root>bank</context-root>
</jboss-web>
```

Finally, if no context root specification exists, the context root will be the base name of the WAR file. For `web-client.war`, the context root would default to `web-client`. The only special case to this naming is the special name `ROOT`. To deploy an application under the root context, you simply name it `ROOT.war`. JBoss already contains a `ROOT.war` web application in the `jbossweb-tomcat50.sar` directory. So you need to remove or rename that one to create your own root application.

Naming your WAR file after the context root it is intended to handle is a very good practice. Not only does it reduce the number of configuration settings to manage, but it improves the maintainability of the application by making clear the intended function of the web application.

Setting Up Virtual Hosts

Virtual hosts allow you to group web applications according to the various DNS names by which the machine running JBoss is known. For example, consider the `server.xml` configuration file given in Listing 9.1. This configuration defines a default host named `vhost1.mydot.com` and a second host named `vhost2.mydot.com`, which also has the alias `www.mydot.com` associated with it.

LISTING 9.1 An Example of a Virtual Host Configuration

```
<Server>
   <Service name="jboss.web"
      className="org.jboss.web.tomcat.tc5.StandardService">

      <!-- A HTTP/1.1 Connector on port 8080 -->
      <Connector port="8080" address="${jboss.bind.address}"
                 maxThreads="150" minSpareThreads="25" maxSpareThreads="75"
                 enableLookups="false" redirectPort="8443" acceptCount="100"
                 connectionTimeout="20000" disableUploadTimeout="true"/>

      <Engine name="jboss.web" defaultHost="vhost1">
         <Realm className="org.jboss.web.tomcat.security.JBossSecurityMgrRealm"
               certificatePrincipal=
➥"org.jboss.security.auth.certs.SubjectDNMapping"
            />
         <Logger className="org.jboss.web.tomcat.Log4jLogger"
                 verbosityLevel="WARNING"
                 category="org.jboss.web.localhost.Engine"/>

            <Host name="vhost1" autoDeploy="false"
                  deployOnStartup="false" deployXML="false">
                <Alias>vhost1.mydot.com</Alias>
                <Valve className="org.apache.catalina.valves.AccessLogValve"
```

LISTING 9.1 Continued

```
                        prefix="vhost1" suffix=".log" pattern="common"
                        directory="${jboss.server.home.dir}/log"/>


                <DefaultContext cookies="true" crossContext="true" override=
➥"true"/>
            </Host>
            <Host name="vhost2" autoDeploy="false"
                  deployOnStartup="false" deployXML="false">
                <Alias>vhost2.mydot.com</Alias>
                <Alias>www.mydot.com</Alias>

                <Valve className="org.apache.catalina.valves.AccessLogValve"
                        prefix="vhost2" suffix=".log" pattern="common"
                        directory="${jboss.server.home.dir}/log"/>

                <DefaultContext cookies="true" crossContext="true" override=
➥"true"/>
            </Host>
        </Engine>
    </Service>
</Server>
```

When a WAR file is deployed, it is by default associated with the virtual host whose name matches the `defaultHost` attribute of the containing `Engine`. To deploy a WAR to a specific virtual host, you need to specify an appropriate `virtual-host` definition in your `jboss-web.xml` descriptor. The following `jboss-web.xml` descriptor demonstrates how to deploy a WAR to the virtual host `www.mydot.com`. Note that you can use either the virtual hostname in the config file or the actual hostname:

```
<jboss-web>
    <context-root>/</context-root>
    <virtual-host>www.mydot.com</virtual-host>
</jboss-web>
```

Serving Static Content

JBoss provides a default application that serves content for the root application context. This default context is the `ROOT.war` application in the `jbossweb-tomcat50.sar` directory. You can serve static files not associated with any other application by adding that content to the `ROOT.war` directory. For example, if you want to have a shared image directory, you can create an image subdirectory inside `ROOT.war` and place the images there. You can then access an image named `myimage.jpg` at http://localhost:8080/images/myimage.jpg.

Using Apache with Tomcat

In some architectures, it is useful to put an Apache web server in front of the JBoss server. External web clients talk to an Apache instance, which in turn speaks to the Tomcat instance on behalf of the clients. Apache needs to be configured to use the `mod_jk` module, which speaks the AJP protocol to an AJP connector running in Tomcat. The provided `server.xml` file comes with this AJP connector enabled:

```
<Connector port="8009" address="${jboss.bind.address}"
           enableLookups="false" redirectPort="8443" debug="0"
           protocol="AJP/1.3" />
```

You need to consult the Apache and `mod_jk` documentation for complete installation instructions. Assuming that you have a properly configured Apache instance, the following configuration fragment shows an example of how to connect with a WAR deployed with a context root of `/jbosstest`:

```
...
LoadModule jk_module libexec/mod_jk.so
AddModule mod_jk.c

<IfModule mod_jk.c>
    JkWorkersFile /tmp/workers.properties
    JkLogFile /tmp/mod_jk.log
    JkLogLevel debug
    JkMount /jbosstest/* ajp13
</IfModule>
```

The `workers.properties` file contains the details of how to contact the JBoss instance.

Using Clustering

JBoss supports clustering in the embedded Tomcat service. The steps to set up clustering of Tomcat embedded containers are as follows:

1. If you are using a load balancer, make sure that your setup uses sticky sessions. This means that if a user starts a session on node `A`, all subsequent requests are forwarded to node `A`, as long node `A` is up and running. For details on configuration of Apache sticky sessions, see www.ubeans.com/tomcat.
2. If you aren't using the `all` configuration, make sure that `cluster-service.xml` is in your `deploy` directory. If it isn't there, copy `cluster-service.xml` from `server/all/deploy` into your `deploy` directory. You also need the `jgroups.jar` in your `lib` directory. You can find it in the `server/all/lib` directory.
3. Start JBoss to check whether your setup works. Look at the JMX management console (http://localhost:8080/jmx-console/). Find the `jboss.cache:service=TomcatClusteringCache` MBean. `StateString` must be `Started`. If it is `Stopped`, look in the server's log file.

4. To enable clustering of web applications, you must mark them as distributable in the `web.xml` descriptor. Here's an example:

```
<?xml version="1.0"?>
<!DOCTYPE web-app PUBLIC
    "-//Sun Microsystems, Inc.//DTD Web Application 2.3//EN"
    "http://java.sun.com/dtd/web-app_2_3.dtd ">
<web-app>
    <distributable/>
    <!-- ... -->
</web-app>
```

5. Deploy your WAR as usual, and it should now be clustered.

If you have deployed and accessed your application, go back to the `jboss.cache:service=TomcatClusteringCache` MBean and invoke the `printDetails` operation. You should see output resembling the following:

```
/JSESSION

/n6HywRwITbY-xvzaZ0LS5Q**
n6HywRwITbY-xvzaZ0LS5Q**: org.jboss.invocation.MarshalledValue@9c1dddab

/R1T4Dapn7c8T-+Ynd9v9MA**
R1T4Dapn7c8T-+Ynd9v9MA**: org.jboss.invocation.MarshalledValue@8c0f60b6
```

This output shows two separate web sessions that are being shared via `JBossCache`. If you don't see any output, either the application was not correctly marked as `distributable` or you haven't accessed the part of application that places values in the HTTP session.

Integrating Third-Party Servlet Containers

This section describes the steps for integrating a third-party web container into the JBoss application server framework. A *web container* is a J2EE server component that enables access to servlets and JSP pages. The most widely used servlet container is Tomcat, which is the default web container used by JBoss.

Integrating a servlet container into JBoss consists of mapping `web.xml` JNDI information into the JBoss JNDI namespace, using an optional `jboss-web.xml` descriptor as well as delegating authentication and authorization to the JBoss security layer. The `org.jboss.web.AbstractWebContainer` class exists to simplify these tasks.

The `AbstractWebContainer` Class

The `org.jboss.web.AbstractWebContainer` class is an implementation of a template pattern for web container integration in JBoss. Web container providers wishing to integrate a container into a JBoss server should create a subclass of `AbstractWebContainer` and provide the web container–specific setup and WAR deployment steps. The AbstractWebContainer provides support for parsing the standard J2EE web.xml web application deployment descriptor JNDI and security elements, as well as support for parsing the JBoss-specific jboss-web.xml descriptor. Parsing of these deployment descriptors is done to generate an integrated JNDI environment and security context.

The AbstractWebContainer Contract

AbstractWebContainer is an abstract class that implements the org.jboss.web.AbstractWebContainerMBean interface used by the JBoss J2EE deployer to delegate the task of installing WAR files that need to be deployed. We'll look at some of the key methods of the AbstractWebContainer next.

Here's the accepts method:

```
public boolean accepts(DeploymentInfo sdi)
{
    String warFile = sdi.url.getFile();
    return warFile.endsWith("war") || warFile.endsWith("war/");
}
```

JBoss deployers implement the accepts method to indicate which type of deployments they accept. AbstractWebContainer handles the deployments of WARs as JARs or unpacked directories.

The following section is the start method:

```
public synchronized void start(DeploymentInfo di) throws DeploymentException
{
    Thread thread = Thread.currentThread();
    ClassLoader appClassLoader = thread.getContextClassLoader();

    try {
        // Create a classloader for the war to ensure a unique ENC
        URL[] empty = {};
        URLClassLoader warLoader = URLClassLoader.newInstance(empty, di.ucl);
        thread.setContextClassLoader(warLoader);
        WebDescriptorParser webAppParser = new DescriptorParser(di);

        String webContext = di.webContext;
        if (webContext != null) {
            if (webContext.length() > 0 && webContext.charAt(0) !=
                '/') {
                webContext = "/" + webContext;
            }
        }

        // Get the war URL
```

```
        URL warURL = di.localUrl != null ? di.localUrl : di.url;
        if (log.isDebugEnabled()) {
            log.debug("webContext: " + webContext);
            log.debug("warURL: " + warURL);
            log.debug("webAppParser: " + webAppParser);
        }

        // Parse the web.xml and jboss-web.xml descriptors
        WebMetaData metaData = (WebMetaData) di.metaData;
        parseMetaData(webContext, warURL, di.shortName, metaData);

        WebApplication warInfo = new WebApplication(metaData);
        warInfo.setDeploymentInfo(di);
        performDeploy(warInfo, warURL.toString(), webAppParser);
        deploymentMap.put(warURL.toString(), warInfo);

        // Generate an event for the startup
        super.start(di);
    } catch(DeploymentException e) {
        throw e;
    } catch(Exception e) {
        throw new DeploymentException("Error during deploy", e);
    } finally {
        thread.setContextClassLoader(appClassLoader);
    }
}
```

The start method is a template pattern method implementation. The argument to the deploy method is the WAR deployment info object. This contains the URL to the WAR, the UnifiedClassLoader for the WAR, the parent archive (such as an EAR), and the J2EE application.xml context-root if the WAR is part of an EAR.

The first step of the start method is to save the current thread context class loader and then create another URLClassCloader (warLoader) by using the WAR UnifiedClassLoader as its parent. This warLoader is used to ensure that a unique JNDI enterprise naming context (ENC) for the WAR will be created. Chapter 3, "Naming on JBoss," mentions that the java:comp context's uniqueness is determined by the class loader that creates the java:comp context. The war-Loader ClassLoader is set as the current thread context class loader before the performDeploy call is made. Next, the web.xml and jboss-web.xml descriptors are parsed by calling parseMetaData. Next, the web container–specific subclass is asked to perform the actual deployment of the WAR through the performDeploy call. The WebApplication object for this deployment is stored in the deployed application map, using warUrl as the key. The final step is to restore the thread context class loader to the one that existed at the start of the method.

The following is the signature for the abstract performDeploy method:

```
protected abstract void performDeploy(WebApplication webApp, String warUrl,
                                      WebDescriptorParser webAppParser)
    throws Exception;
```

The performDeploy method is called by the start method and must be overridden by subclasses to perform the web container–specific deployment steps. WebApplication is provided as an argument, and this contains the metadata from the web.xml descriptor, and the jboss-web.xml descriptor. The metadata contains the context-root value for the web module from the J2EE application.xml descriptor, or, if this is a standalone deployment, from the jboss-web.xml descriptor. The metadata also contains any jboss-web.xml descriptor virtual-host value. On return from performDeploy, the WebApplication must be populated with the class loader of the servlet context for the deployment. The warUrl argument is the string for the URL of the web application WAR to deploy. The webAppParser argument is a callback handle the subclass must use to invoke the parseWebAppDescriptors method to set up the web application JNDI environment. This callback provides a hook for the subclass to establish the web application JNDI environment before any servlets are created that are to be loaded on startup of the WAR. A subclass's performDeploy method implementation needs to be arranged so that it can call parseWebAppDescriptors before starting any servlets that need to access JNDI for JBoss resources such as EJBs, resource factories, and so on. One important setup detail that needs to be handled by a subclass implementation is to use the current thread context class loader as the parent class loader for any web container–specific class loader created. Failure to do this results in problems for web applications that attempt to access EJBs or JBoss resources through the JNDI ENC.

This is the stop method:

```
public synchronized void stop(DeploymentInfo di)
    throws DeploymentException
{
    URL warURL = di.localUrl != null ? di.localUrl : di.url;
    String warUrl = warURL.toString();
    try {
        performUndeploy(warUrl);
        // Remove the web application ENC...
        deploymentMap.remove(warUrl);
        // Generate an event for the stop
        super.stop(di);
    } catch(DeploymentException e) {
        throw e;
    } catch(Exception e) {
        throw new DeploymentException("Error during deploy", e);
    }
}
```

The stop method calls the subclass performUndeploy method to perform the container-specific undeployment steps. After undeploying the application, the warUrl is unregistered from the deployment map. The warUrl argument is the string URL of the WAR, as originally passed to the performDeploy method.

This is the signature of the abstract performUndeploy method, which is called from the stop method:

```
protected abstract void performUndeploy(String warUrl) throws Exception;
```

A call to performUndeploy asks the subclass to perform the web container–specific undeployment steps.

The setConfig method is a stub method that subclasses can override if they want to support an arbitrary extended configuration beyond that which is possible through MBean attributes:

```
public void setConfig(Element config)
{
}
```

The config argument is the parent DOM element for an arbitrary hierarchy given by the child element of the Config attribute in the mbean element specification of the jboss-service.xml descriptor of the web container service. You'll see an example use of this method and config value when you look at the MBean that supports embedding Tomcat into JBoss.

The parseWebAppDescriptors method is invoked from within the subclass performDeploy method when it invokes the webAppParser.parseWebAppDescriptors callback to set up the web application ENC (java:comp/env) env-entry, resource-env-ref, resource-ref, local-ejb-ref, and ejb-ref values declared in the web.xml descriptor:

```
protected void parseWebAppDescriptors(DeploymentInfo di,
                                      ClassLoader loader,
                                      WebMetaData metaData)
    throws Exception
{
    log.debug("AbstractWebContainer.parseWebAppDescriptors, Begin");
    InitialContext iniCtx = new InitialContext();
    Context envCtx = null;
    Thread currentThread = Thread.currentThread();
    ClassLoader currentLoader = currentThread.getContextClassLoader();
    try {
        // Create a java:comp/env environment unique for the web application
        log.debug("Creating ENC using ClassLoader: "+loader);
        ClassLoader parent = loader.getParent();
        while (parent != null ) {
            log.debug(".."+parent);
```

```
            parent = parent.getParent();
        }
        currentThread.setContextClassLoader(loader);
        metaData.setENCLoader(loader);
        envCtx = (Context) iniCtx.lookup("java:comp");
        // Add a link to the global transaction manager
        envCtx.bind("UserTransaction", new LinkRef("UserTransaction"));
        log.debug("Linked java:comp/UserTransaction to JNDI name:
➥UserTransaction");
        envCtx = envCtx.createSubcontext("env");
    } finally {
        currentThread.setContextClassLoader(currentLoader);
    }

    Iterator envEntries = metaData.getEnvironmentEntries();
    log.debug("addEnvEntries");
    addEnvEntries(envEntries, envCtx);

    Iterator resourceEnvRefs = metaData.getResourceEnvReferences();
    log.debug("linkResourceEnvRefs");
    linkResourceEnvRefs(resourceEnvRefs, envCtx);

    Iterator resourceRefs = metaData.getResourceReferences();
    log.debug("linkResourceRefs");
    linkResourceRefs(resourceRefs, envCtx);

    Iterator ejbRefs = metaData.getEjbReferences();
    log.debug("linkEjbRefs");
    linkEjbRefs(ejbRefs, envCtx, di);

    Iterator ejbLocalRefs = metaData.getEjbLocalReferences();
    log.debug("linkEjbLocalRefs");
    linkEjbLocalRefs(ejbLocalRefs, envCtx, di);

    String securityDomain = metaData.getSecurityDomain();
    log.debug("linkSecurityDomain");
    linkSecurityDomain(securityDomain, envCtx);

    log.debug("AbstractWebContainer.parseWebAppDescriptors, End");
}
```

The creation of the `env-entry` values does not require a `jboss-web.xml` descriptor. The creation of the `resource-env-ref`, `resource-ref`, and `ejb-ref` elements does require a `jboss-web.xml` descriptor for the JNDI name of the deployed resources/EJBs. Because the ENC context is private to the web application, the web application class loader is used to identify the ENC. The `loader` argument is the class loader for the web application, and it may not be null. The `metaData` argument is the `WebMetaData` argument passed to the subclass `performDeploy` method. The implementation of `parseWebAppDescriptors` uses the metadata information from the WAR deployment descriptors and then creates the JNDI ENC bindings.

The `addEnvEntries` method creates the `java:comp/env` web application `env-entry` bindings specified in the `web.xml` descriptor:

```
protected void addEnvEntries(Iterator envEntries, Context envCtx)
    throws ClassNotFoundException, NamingException
{
}
```

The `linkResourceEnvRefs` method maps the `java:comp/env/xxx` web application JNDI ENC `resource-env-ref web.xml` descriptor elements onto the deployed JNDI names, using the mappings specified in the `jboss-web.xml` descriptor:

```
protected void linkResourceEnvRefs(Iterator resourceEnvRefs, Context envCtx)
    throws NamingException
{
}
```

The `linkResourceRefs` method maps the `java:comp/env/xxx` web application JNDI ENC `resource-ref` `web.xml` descriptor elements onto the deployed JNDI names, using the mappings specified in the `jboss-web.xml` descriptor:

```
protected void linkResourceRefs(Iterator resourceRefs, Context envCtx)
    throws NamingException
{
}
```

The `linkEjbRefs` method maps the `java:comp/env/ejb` web application JNDI ENC `ejb-ref` `web.xml` descriptor elements onto the deployed JNDI names, using the mappings specified in the `jboss-web.xml` descriptor:

```
protected void linkEjbRefs(Iterator ejbRefs, Context envCtx, DeploymentInfo di)
    throws NamingException
{
}
```

The `linkEjbLocalRefs` method maps the `java:comp/env/ejb` Web application JNDI ENC `ejb-local-ref` `web.xml` descriptor elements onto the deployed JNDI names, using the `ejb-link` mappings specified in the `web.xml` descriptor:

```
protected void linkEjbLocalRefs(Iterator ejbRefs, Context envCtx,
                                DeploymentInfo di)
    throws NamingException
```

```
{
}
```

The `linkSecurityDomain` method creates a `java: comp/env/security` context that contains a `securityMgr` binding that points to the `AuthenticationManager` implementation and a `realmMapping` binding that points to the `RealmMapping` implementation that is associated with the security domain for the web application:

```
protected void linkSecurityDomain(String securityDomain, Context envCtx)
    throws NamingException
{
}
```

The `linkSecurityDomain` method also creates is a subject binding that provides dynamic access to the authenticated `Subject` associated with the request thread. If the `jboss-web.xml` descriptor contains a `security-domain` element, the bindings are `javax.naming.LinkRefs` to the JNDI name specified by the `security-domain` element, or they are subcontexts of this name. If there is no `security-domain` element, the bindings are to an `org.jboss.security.plugins.NullSecurityManager` instance that simply allows all authentication and authorization checks.

The `getCompileClasspath` method is a utility method that is available for web containers to generate a classpath that walks up the class loader chain, starting at the given loader, and queries each class loader for the URLs it serves to build a complete classpath of URL strings:

```
public String[] getCompileClasspath(ClassLoader loader)
{
}
```

This is needed by some JSP compiler implementations (Jasper, for one) that expect to be given a complete classpath for compilation.

Creating an `AbstractWebContainer` Subclass

To integrate a web container into JBoss, you need to create a subclass of `AbstractWebContainer` and implement the required `performDeploy(WebApplication, String, WebDescriptorParser)` and `performUndeploy(String)` methods, as described in the preceding section. The additional integration points described in the following sections should be considered as well.

Using the Thread Context Class Loader Although this issue is noted in the `performDeploy` method description earlier in this chapter, we repeat it here because it is such a critical detail. During the setup of a WAR container, the current thread context class loader must be used as the parent class loader for any web container–specific class loader that is created. Failure to do this will result in problems for web applications that attempt to access EJBs or JBoss resources through the JNDI ENC.

Integrating Logging by Using `log4j` JBoss uses the Apache `log4j` logging API as its internal logging API. For a web container to integrate well with JBoss, it needs to provide a mapping between the web container logging abstraction and the `log4j` API. As a subclass of `AbstractWebContainer`, your integration class has access to the `log4j` interface via the `super.log` instance variable or, equivalently, the superclass `getLog()` method. This is an instance of the `org.jboss.logging.Logger` class that wraps the `log4j` category. The name of the `log4j` category is the name of the container subclass.

Delegating Web Container Authentication and Authorization to JBossSX Ideally, both web application and EJB authentication and authorization are handled by the same security manager. To enable this for a web container, you must hook into the JBoss security layer. This typically requires a request interceptor that maps from the web container security callouts to the JBoss security API. Integration with the JBossSX security framework is based on the establishment of a `java:comp/env/security` context, as described in the `linkSecurityDomain` method comments earlier in this chapter. The security context provides access to the JBossSX security manager interface implementations associated with the web application for use by subclass request interceptors. An outline of the steps for authenticating a user using the security context is presented in Listing 9.2 in quasi pseudo-code. Listing 9.3 provides the equivalent process for the authorization of a user.

LISTING 9.2 A Pseudo-code Description of Authenticating a User via the JBossSX API and the `java:comp/env/security` JNDI Context

```
// Get the username and password from the request context...
HttpServletRequest request = ...;
String username = getUsername(request);
String password = getPassword(request);

// Get the JBoss security manager from the ENC context
InitialContext iniCtx = new InitialContext();
AuthenticationManager securityMgr = (AuthenticationManager)
    iniCtx.lookup("java:comp/env/security/securityMgr");

SimplePrincipal principal = new SimplePrincipal(username);
if (securityMgr.isValid(principal, password)) {
    // Indicate the user is allowed access to the web content...
    // Propagate the user info to JBoss for any calls made by the servlet
    SecurityAssociation.setPrincipal(principal);
    SecurityAssociation.setCredential(password.toCharArray());
} else {
    // Deny access...
}
```

LISTING 9.3 A Pseudo-code Description of Authorizing a User via the JBossSX API and the `java:comp/env/security` JNDI Context

```
// Get the username & required roles from the request context...
HttpServletRequest request = ...;
String username = getUsername(request);
String[] roles = getContentRoles(request);

// Get the JBoss security manager from the ENC context
InitialContext iniCtx = new InitialContext();
RealmMapping securityMgr = (RealmMapping)
    iniCtx.lookup("java:comp/env/security/realmMapping");

SimplePrincipal principal = new SimplePrincipal(username);
Set requiredRoles = new HashSet(java.util.Arrays.asList(roles));

if (securityMgr.doesUserHaveRole(principal, requiredRoles)) {
    // Indicate user has the required roles for the web content...
} else {
    // Deny access...
}
```

CHAPTER 10

MBean Services Miscellany

IN THIS CHAPTER

- System Properties Management
- Property Editor Management
- Services Binding Management
- Scheduling Tasks
- The `Log4j Service` MBean
- RMI Dynamic Class Loading

This chapter discusses useful MBean services that are not discussed elsewhere in this book, either because they are utility services not necessary for running JBoss or they don't fit into a section of the book.

System Properties Management

The management of system properties can be done using the system properties service. This service supports setting of the VM global property values just as the `java.lang.System.setProperty` method and the VM command line arguments do.

The configurable attributes of the system properties service include the following:

- **`Properties`**—This is a specification of multiple property `name=value` pairs, using the `java.util.Properites.load(java.io.InputStream)` method format. Each `property=value` statement is given on a separate line within the body of the `Properties` attribute element.
- **`URLList`**—This is a comma-separated list of URL strings from which to load properties file-formatted content. If a component in the list is a relative path rather than a URL, it will be treated as a file path relative to the `<jboss-dist>/server/<config>` directory. For example, a component of `conf/local.properties` would be treated as a file URL that points to the `<jboss-dist>/server/default/conf/local.properties` file when running with the `default` configuration file set.

The following example illustrates the usage of the system properties service with an external properties file:

```
<mbean code="org.jboss.varia.property.SystemPropertiesService"
        name="jboss.util:type=Service,name=SystemProperties">

    <!-- Load properties from each of the given comma separated URLs -->
    <attribute name="URLList">
        http://somehost/some-location.properties,
        ./conf/somelocal.properties
    </attribute>
</mbean>
```

The following example illustrates the usage of the system properties service with an embedded properties list:

```
<mbean code="org.jboss.varia.property.SystemPropertiesService"
        name="jboss.util:type=Service,name=SystemProperties">
    <!-- Set properties using the properties file style. -->
    <attribute name="Properties">
       property1=This is the value of my property
       property2=This is the value of my other property
    </attribute>
</mbean>
```

Property Editor Management

JavaBeans property editors are used in JBoss to read data types from service files and for editing values in the JMX Console. The `java.bean.PropertyEditorManager` class controls the `java.bean. PropertyEditor` instances in the system. The property editor manager can be managed in JBoss by using the `org.jboss.varia.property. PropertyEditorManagerService` MBean. The property editor manager service is configured in `deploy/properties-service.xml` and supports the following attributes:

- **`BootstrapEditors`**—This is a listing of `property_editor_class=editor_value_type_class` pairs that define the property editor–to–type mappings that should be preloaded into the property editor manager. The value type of this attribute is a string so that it may be set from a string without requiring a custom property editor.
- **`Editors`**—This serves the same function as the `BootstrapEditors` attribute, but its type is `java.util. Properties`. Setting it from a string value in a service file requires a custom property editor for properties' objects to be loaded. JBoss provides a suitable property editor.

- **`EditorSearchPath`**—This attribute allows you to set the editor package's search path on the `PropertyEditorManager`. Because there can be only one search path, setting this value overrides the default search path established by JBoss. If you set this attribute, make sure to add the JBoss search path, including `org.jboss.util.propertyeditor` and `org.jboss.mx.util.propertyeditor`, to the front of the new search path.

Services Binding Management

With all the independently deployed services available in JBoss, running multiple instances on a given machine can be a tedious exercise in configuration file editing to resolve port conflicts. The binding service allows you to centrally configure the ports for multiple JBoss instances. After the service is normally loaded by JBoss, `ServiceConfigurator` queries the service binding manager to apply any overrides that may exist for the service. The service binding manager is configured in `conf/jboss-service.xml`. The configurable attributes it supports include the following:

- **`ServerName`**—This is the name of the server configuration with which this JBoss instance is associated. The binding manager will apply the overrides defined for the named configuration.
- **`StoreFactoryClassName`**—This is the name of the class that implements the `ServicesStoreFactory` interface. You may provide your own implementation or use the default XML based store, `org.jboss.services.binding.XMLServicesStoreFactory`. The factory provides a `ServicesStore` instance that is responsible for providing the named configuration sets.
- **`StoreURL`**—This is the URL of the configuration store contents, which is passed to the `ServicesStore` instance to load the server configuration sets from. For the XML store, this is a simple service binding file.

The following is a sample service binding manager configuration that uses the `ports-01` configuration from the `sample-bindings.xml` file provided in the JBoss examples directory:

```
<mbean code="org.jboss.services.binding.ServiceBindingManager"
       name="jboss.system:service=ServiceBindingManager">
    <attribute name="ServerName">ports-01</attribute>
    <attribute name="StoreURL">
        ../docs/examples/binding-manager/sample-bindings.xml
    </attribute>
    <attribute name="StoreFactoryClassName">
        org.jboss.services.binding.XMLServicesStoreFactory
    </attribute>
</mbean>
```

The structure of the binding file is shown in Figure 10.1.

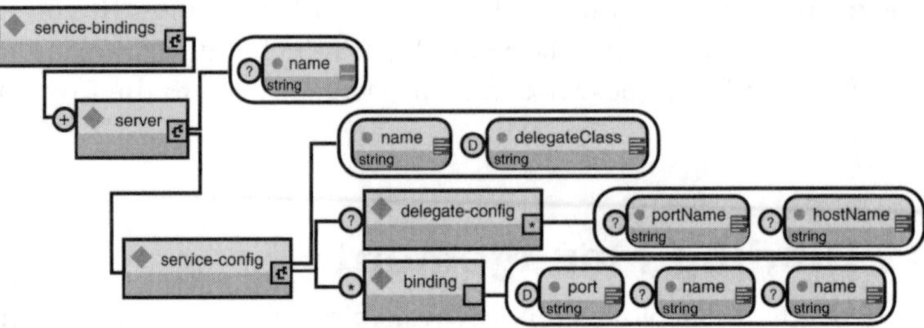

FIGURE 10.1 The binding service file structure.

The elements of this configuration are as follows:

- **service-bindings**—This is the root element of the configuration file. It contains one or more server elements.
- **server**—This is the base of a JBoss server instance configuration. It has a required name attribute that defines the JBoss instance name to which it applies. This is the name that correlates with the ServiceBindingManager ServerName attribute value. The server element content consists of one or more service-config elements.
- **service-config**—This element represents a configuration override for an MBean service. It has a required name attribute that is the JMX ObjectName string of the MBean service the configuration applies to. It also has a required delegateClass name attribute that specifies the classname of the ServicesConfigDelegate implementation that knows how to handle bindings for the target service. Its contents consist of an optional delegate-config element and one or more binding elements.
- **binding**—A binding element specifies a named port and address pair. It has an optional name attribute that can be used to provide multiple bindings for a service. An example would be multiple virtual hosts for a web container. The port and address are specified via the optional port and host attributes, respectively. If the port is not specified, it defaults to 0, meaning choose an anonymous port. If the host is not specified, it defaults to null, meaning any address.
- **delegate-config**—The delegate-config element is an arbitrary XML fragment for use by the ServicesConfigDelegate implementation. The hostName and portName attributes apply only to the AttributeMappingDelegate of the example and are there to prevent DTD-aware editors from complaining about their existence in the AttributeMappingDelegate configurations. Generally, both the attributes and content of the delegate-config are arbitrary, but there is no way to specify, and an element can have any number of attributes with a DTD.

The two ServicesConfigDelegate implementations are AttributeMappingDelegate and XSLTConfigDelegate. The AttributeMappingDelegate class is an implementation of the ServicesConfigDelegate that expects a delegate-config element in this form:

```
<delegate-config portName="portAttrName" hostName="hostAttrName">
    <attribute name="someAttrName">someHostPortExpr</attribute>
    <!-- ... -->
</delegate-config>
```

portAttrName is the attribute name of the MBean service to which the binding port value should be applied, and hostAttrName is the attribute name of the MBean service to which the binding host value should be applied. If the portName attribute is not specified, the binding port is not applied. Likewise, if the hostName attribute is not specified, the binding host is not applied. The optional attribute elements specify arbitrary MBean attribute names whose values are a function of the host and/or port settings. Any reference to ${host} in the attribute content is replaced with the host binding, and any ${port} reference is replaced with the port binding. The portName and hostName attribute values and attribute element content may reference system properties, using the ${ x} syntax that is supported by the JBoss services descriptor.

The following example illustrates the usage of AttributeMappingDelegate:

```
<service-config name="jboss:service=Naming"
       delegateClass="org.jboss.services.binding.AttributeMappingDelegate">
    <delegate-config portName="Port"/>
    <binding port="1099" />
</service-config>
```

Here the jboss:service=Naming MBean service has its Port attribute value overridden to 1099. The corresponding setting from the jboss1 server configuration overrides the port to 1199.

The XSLTConfigDelegate class is an implementation of ServicesConfigDelegate that expects a delegate-config element in this form:

```
<delegate-config>
    <xslt-config configName="ConfigurationElement"><![CDATA[
        Any XSL document contents...
        ]]>
     </xslt-config>
     <xslt-param name="param-name">param-value</xslt-param>
     <!-- ... -->
</delegate-config>
```

The xslt-config child element content specifies an arbitrary XSL script fragment that is to be applied to the MBean service attribute named by the configName attribute. The named attribute must be of type org.w3c .dom.Element. The optional xslt-param elements specify XSL script parameter values for parameters used in the script. There are two XSL parameters defined by default—called host and port—and their values are set to the configuration host and port bindings.

XSLTConfigDelegate is used to transform services whose port/interface configuration is specified by using a nested XML fragment. The following example maps the Tomcat servlet container listening port to 8180 and maps the AJP listening port to 8109:

```
<!-- jbossweb-tomcat50.sar -->
      <service-config name="jboss.web:service=WebServer"
         delegateClass="org.jboss.services.binding.XSLTFileDelegate">
         <delegate-config>
            <xslt-config configName="ConfigFile"><![CDATA[
   <xsl:stylesheet
         xmlns:xsl='http://www.w3.org/1999/XSL/Transform' version='1.0'>

     <xsl:output method="xml" />
     <xsl:param name="port"/>

     <xsl:variable name="portAJP" select="$port - 71"/>
     <xsl:variable name="portHttps" select="$port + 363"/>

     <xsl:template match="/">
       <xsl:apply-templates/>
     </xsl:template>

      <xsl:template match = "Connector">
         <Connector>
            <xsl:for-each select="@*">
            <xsl:choose>
               <xsl:when test="(name() = 'port' and . = '8080')">
                  <xsl:attribute name="port"><xsl:value-of select="$port" />
                  </xsl:attribute>
               </xsl:when>
               <xsl:when test="(name() = 'port' and . = '8009')">
                  <xsl:attribute name="port"><xsl:value-of select="$portAJP" />
                  </xsl:attribute>
               </xsl:when>
               <xsl:when test="(name() = 'redirectPort')">
                  <xsl:attribute name="redirectPort"><xsl:value-of
➥select="$portHttps" />
                  </xsl:attribute>
               </xsl:when>
               <xsl:when test="(name() = 'port' and . = '8443')">
                  <xsl:attribute name="port"><xsl:value-of select="$portHttps" />
                  </xsl:attribute>
               </xsl:when>
               <xsl:otherwise>
                  <xsl:attribute name="{name()}"><xsl:value-of select="." />
                  </xsl:attribute>
```

```
                </xsl:otherwise>
            </xsl:choose>
            </xsl:for-each>
            <xsl:apply-templates/>
        </Connector>
    </xsl:template>

    <xsl:template match="*|@*">
      <xsl:copy>
        <xsl:apply-templates select="@*|node()"/>
      </xsl:copy>
    </xsl:template>
  </xsl:stylesheet>
  ]]>
            </xslt-config>
        </delegate-config>
        <binding port="8180"/>
            </service-config>
```

JBoss ships with a service binding configuration file for starting up to three separate JBoss instances on one host.

Next, let's walk through the steps to bring up the two instances and look at the sample configuration.

You start by making two server configuration file sets called `j boss0` and `jboss1` by running the following command from this book's examples directory:

```
[examples]$ ant -Dchap=chap10 -Dex=1 run-example
```

This creates duplicates of the `server/default` configuration file sets as `server/jboss0` and `server/jboss1`, and then it replaces the `conf/jboss-service.xml` descriptor with one that has the `ServiceBindingManager` configuration enabled, as follows:

```
<mbean code="org.jboss.services.binding.ServiceBindingManager"
       name="jboss.system:service=ServiceBindingManager">
    <attribute name="ServerName">${jboss.server.name}</attribute>
    <attribute name="StoreURL">${jboss.server.base.dir}/chap10ex1-
➥bindings.xml</attribute>
    <attribute name="StoreFactoryClassName">
        org.jboss.services.binding.XMLServicesStoreFactory
    </attribute>
</mbean>
```

Here the configuration name is `${jboss.server.name}`. JBoss replaces this with the name of the actual JBoss server configuration that you pass to the run script by using the `-c` option. That will be either `jboss0` or `jboss1`, depending on which configuration is being run. The binding manager will find the corresponding server configuration section from `chap10ex1-bindings.xml` and apply the configured overrides. The `jboss0` configuration uses the default settings for the ports, and the `jboss1` configuration adds 100 to each port number.

To test the sample configuration, you can start two JBoss instances, using the `jboss0` and `jboss1` configuration file sets created previously. You can observe that the port numbers in the console log are different for the `jboss1` server. To test whether both instances work correctly, you can try to access the web server of the first JBoss on port 8080 and then try the second JBoss instance on port 8180.

Scheduling Tasks

Java includes a simple timer-based capability through the `java.util.Timer` and `java.util.TimerTask` utility classes. JMX also includes a mechanism for scheduling JMX notifications at a given time with an optional repeat interval as the `javax.management.timer.TimerMBean` agent service.

JBoss includes two variations of the JMX timer service in the `org.jboss.varia.scheduler.Scheduler` and `org.jboss.varia. scheduler.ScheduleManager` MBeans. Both of these MBeans rely on the JMX timer service for the basic scheduling. They extend the behavior of the timer service as described in the following sections.

The `org.jboss.varia.scheduler.Scheduler` MBean

The `Scheduler` MBean differs from `TimerMBean` in that `Scheduler` directly invokes a callback on an instance of a user-defined class or an operation of a user-specified MBean.

The following are the configurable attributes of Scheduler MBean:

- **`InitialStartDate`**—The date when the initial call is scheduled. It can be one of the following:
    - `NOW`, in which case the date will be the current time plus 1 second.
    - A number representing the milliseconds since 1/1/1970.
    - The date as a string that is able to be parsed by `SimpleDateFormat`, with the default format pattern `"M/d/yy h:mm a"`. If the date is in the past, the `Scheduler` MBean will search a start date in the future with respect to the initial repetitions and the period between calls. This means that when you restart the MBean (that is, restart JBoss and so on), it will start at the next scheduled time. When no start date is available in the future, `Scheduler` will not start.

  For example, if you start your `Schedulable` class every day at noon and you restart your JBoss server, it will start at the next noon.

- **InitialRepetitions**—The number of times the scheduler will invoke the target's callback. If `-1`, then the callback will be repeated until the server is stopped.
- **StartAtStartup**—A flag that determines whether `Scheduler` will start when it receives its `startService` life cycle notification. If `true`, the `Scheduler` MBean starts on its startup. If `false`, an explicit `startSchedule` operation must be invoked on the `Scheduler` to begin.
- **SchedulePeriod**—The interval between scheduled calls, in milliseconds. This value must be bigger than `0`.
- **SchedulableClass**—The fully qualified classname of the `org.jboss.varia.scheduler.Schedulable` interface implementation that is to be used by the `Scheduler Mbean. SchedulableArguments` and `SchedulableArgumentTypes` must be populated to correspond to the constructor of the `Schedulable` implementation.
- **SchedulableArguments**—A comma-separated list of arguments for the `Schedulable` implementation class constructor. Only primitive data types, `String`, and classes with a constructor that accepts a `String` as its sole argument are supported.
- **SchedulableArgumentTypes**—A comma-separated list of argument types for the `Schedulable` implementation class constructor. This will be used to find the correct constructor via reflection. Only primitive data types, `String`, and classes with a constructor that accepts a `String` as its sole argument are supported.
- **SchedulableMBean**—The fully qualified JMX `ObjectName` name of the schedulable MBean to be called. If the MBean is not available, it will not be called, but the remaining repetitions will be decremented. When you're using `SchedulableMBean`, `SchedulableMBeanMethod` must also be specified.
- **SchedulableMBeanMethod**—The operation name to be called on the schedulable MBean. It can optionally be followed by an opening bracket, a comma-separated list of parameter keywords, and a closing bracket. The supported parameter keywords include the following:
    - `NOTIFICATION`, which will be replaced by the timer's notification instance (`javax.management.Notification`)
    - `DATE`, which will be replaced by the date of the notification call (`java.util.Date`)
    - `REPETITIONS`, which will be replaced by the number of remaining repetitions (`long`)
    - `SCHEDULER_NAME`, which will be replaced by the `ObjectName` of the `Scheduler`
    - Any fully qualified classname, which the `Scheduler` will set to null. A given `Scheduler` instance supports only a single schedulable instance. If you need to configure multiple scheduled events, you use multiple `Scheduler` instances, each with a unique `ObjectName`. The following is an example of configuring a

Scheduler MBean to call a Schedulable implementation as well as a configuration for calling an MBean:

```
<server>
    <mbean code="org.jboss.varia.scheduler.Scheduler"
           name="jboss.docs.chap10:service=Scheduler">
        <attribute name="StartAtStartup">true</attribute>
        <attribute name="SchedulableClass">org.jboss.chap10.ex2.
➥ExSchedulable</attribute>
        <attribute name="SchedulableArguments">TheName,123456789
➥</attribute>
        <attribute name="SchedulableArgumentTypes">java.lang.String,long
➥</attribute>

        <attribute name="InitialStartDate">NOW</attribute>
        <attribute name="SchedulePeriod">60000</attribute>
        <attribute name="InitialRepetitions">-1</attribute>
    </mbean>
</server>
```

The SchedulableClass org.jboss.chap10.ex2.ExSchedulable example class is shown here:

```
package org.jboss.chap10.ex2;

import java.util.Date;
import org.jboss.varia.scheduler.Schedulable;

import org.apache.log4j.Logger;

/**
 * A simple Schedulable example.
 * @author Scott.Stark@jboss.org
 * @version $Revision: 1.5 $
 */
public class ExSchedulable implements Schedulable
{
    private static final Logger log = Logger.getLogger(ExSchedulable.class);

    private String name;
    private long value;

    public ExSchedulable(String name, long value)
    {
        this.name = name;
        this.value = value;
```

```
        log.info("ctor, name: " + name + ", value: " + value);
    }

    public void perform(Date now, long remainingRepetitions)
    {
        log.info("perform, now: " + now +
                 ", remainingRepetitions: " + remainingRepetitions +
                 ", name: " + name + ", value: " + value);
    }
}
```

You deploy the timer SAR by running this command:

```
[examples]$ ant -Dchap=chap10 -Dex=2 run-example
```

The server console shows the following, which includes the first two timer invocations, separated by 60 seconds:

```
21:09:27,716 INFO [ExSchedulable] ctor, name: TheName, value: 123456789
21:09:28,925 INFO [ExSchedulable] perform, now: Mon Dec 20 21:09:28 CST 2004,
➥remainingRepetitions: -1,
21:10:28,899 INFO [ExSchedulable] perform, now: Mon Dec 20 21:10:28 CST 2004,
➥remainingRepetitions: -1,
21:11:28,897 INFO [ExSchedulable] perform, now: Mon Dec 20 21:11:28 CST 2004,
➥remainingRepetitions: -1,
```

The Log4j Service MBean

The Log4j Service MBean configures the Apache log4j system. JBoss uses the log4j framework as its internal logging API.

The Log4j Service MBean supports the following attributes:

- **ConfigurationURL**—This is the URL for the log4j configuration file. It can refer to either an XML document parsed by org.apache.log4j.xml.DOMConfigurator or a Java properties file parsed by org.apache.log4j. PropertyConfigurator. The type of the file is determined by the URL content type, or if that is null, by the file extension. The default setting of resource:log4j.xml refers to the conf/log4j.xml file of the active server configuration file set.
- **RefreshPeriod**—This is the time in seconds between checks for changes in the log4j configuration specified by the ConfigurationURL attribute. The default value is 60 seconds.
- **CatchSystemErr**—This Boolean flag, if true, indicates whether the System. err stream should be redirected onto a log4j category called STDERR. The default is true.
- **CatchSystemOut**—This Boolean flag, if true, indicates whether the System.out stream should be redirected onto a log4j category called STDOUT. The default is true.

- **`Log4jQuietMode`**—This Boolean flag, if `true`, sets `org.apache.log4j.helpers.LogLog.setQuiteMode`. As of log4j 1.2.8, this needs to be set to avoid a possible deadlock on exception at the appender level. See bug #696819.

RMI Dynamic Class Loading

The `WebService` MBean provides dynamic class loading for RMI access to the server EJBs. The configurable attributes for the service are as follows:

- **`Port`**—The `WebService` listening port number. A port of `0` will use any available port.
- **`Host`**—The name of the public interface to use for the host portion of the RMI codebase URL.
- **`BindAddress`**—The specific address the `WebService` listens on. This can be used on a multi-homed host for `java.net.ServerSocket` that will only accept connect requests to one of its addresses.
- **`Backlog`**—The maximum queue length for incoming connection indications (a request to connect), set to the `backlog` parameter. If a connection indication arrives when the queue is full, the connection is refused.
- **`DownloadServerClasses`**—A flag that indicates whether the server should attempt to download classes from the thread context class loader when a request arrives that does not have a class loader key prefix.

CHAPTER **11**

The CMP Engine

IN THIS CHAPTER

- Example Code
- The `jbosscmp-jdbc` Structure
- Entity Beans
- CMP Fields
- Container-Managed Relationships
- Declaring Queries
- Optimized Loading
- The Loading Process
- Transactions
- Optimistic Locking
- Entity Commands and Primary Key Generation
- JBoss Global Defaults
- Datasource Customization

This chapter explores the use of container-managed persistence (CMP) in JBoss. It assumes that you have a basic familiarity with the EJB CMP model and focuses on the operation of the JBoss CMP engine. Specifically, this chapter looks at how to configure and optimize CMP applications on JBoss. For more introductory coverage of basic CMP concepts, see *Enterprise Java Beans* (O'Reilly Publishing).

Example Code

This chapter is example driven. In it, you will work with a crime portal application that stores information about imaginary criminal organizations. The data model you will work with is shown in Figure 11.1.

The source code for the crime portal is available in the `src/main/org/jboss/cmp2` directory of the example code. To build the example code, you run Ant, as shown here:

```
[examples]$ ant -Dchap=cmp2 config
```

This command builds and deploys the application to the JBoss server. When you start your JBoss server, or if it is already running, you should see the following deployment messages:

```
15:46:36,704 INFO  [OrganizationBean$Proxy] Creating
organization Yakuza, Japanese
➥ Gangsters
15:46:36,790 INFO  [OrganizationBean$Proxy] Creating
organization Mafia, Italian
➥Bad Guys
15:46:36,797 INFO  [OrganizationBean$Proxy] Creating
organization Triads, Kung Fu
➥ Movie Extras
```

```
15:46:36,877 INFO  [GangsterBean$Proxy] Creating Gangster 0 'Bodyguard' Yojimbo
15:46:37,003 INFO  [GangsterBean$Proxy] Creating Gangster 1 'Master' Takeshi
15:46:37,021 INFO  [GangsterBean$Proxy] Creating Gangster 2 'Four finger' Yuriko
15:46:37,040 INFO  [GangsterBean$Proxy] Creating Gangster 3 'Killer' Chow
15:46:37,106 INFO  [GangsterBean$Proxy] Creating Gangster 4 'Lightning' Shogi
15:46:37,118 INFO  [GangsterBean$Proxy] Creating Gangster 5 'Pizza-Face' Valentino
15:46:37,133 INFO  [GangsterBean$Proxy] Creating Gangster 6 'Toothless' Toni
15:46:37,208 INFO  [GangsterBean$Proxy] Creating Gangster 7 'Godfather' Corleone
15:46:37,238 INFO  [JobBean$Proxy] Creating Job 10th Street Jeweler Heist
15:46:37,247 INFO  [JobBean$Proxy] Creating Job The Great Train Robbery
15:46:37,257 INFO [JobBean$Proxy] Creating Job Cheap Liquor Snatch and Grab
```

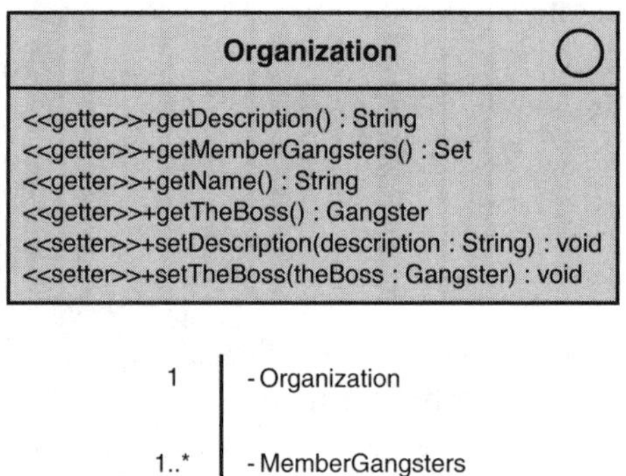

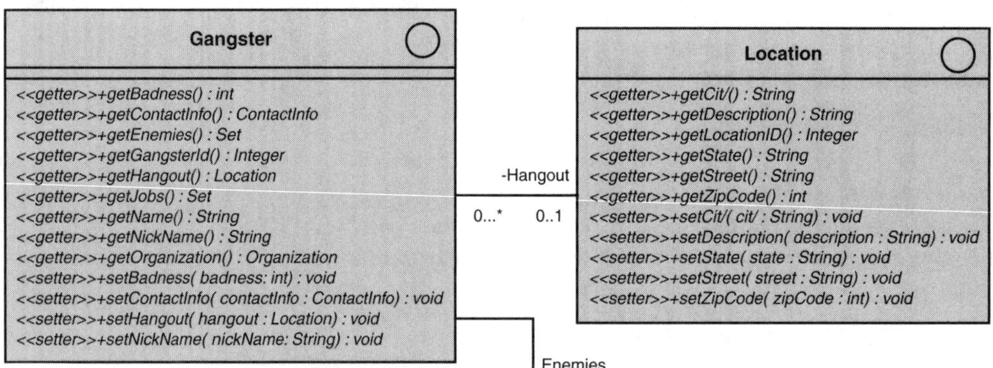

FIGURE 11.1 The crime portal example classes.

Because the beans in the examples are configured to have their tables removed on undeployment, any time you restart the JBoss server, you need to rerun the config target to reload the example data and redeploy the application.

Enabling CMP Debug Logging

To get meaningful feedback from the example code, you will want to increase the log level of the CMP subsystem before running the test. To enable debug logging, you need to add the following category to your log4j.xml file:

```
<category name="org.jboss.ejb.plugins.cmp">
    <priority value="DEBUG"/>
</category>
```

In addition, you need to decrease the threshold on the CONSOLE appender to allow debug-level messages to be logged to the console. You also need to apply the following changes to the log4j.xml file:

```
<appender name="CONSOLE" class="org.apache.log4j.ConsoleAppender">
    <errorHandler class="org.jboss.logging.util.OnlyOnceErrorHandler"/>
    <param name="Target"    value="System.out"/>
    <param name="Threshold" value="DEBUG" />

    <layout class="org.apache.log4j.PatternLayout">
        <!-- The default pattern: Date Priority [Category] Message\n -->
        <param name="ConversionPattern" value="%d{ABSOLUTE} %-5p [%c{1}] %m%n"/>
    </layout>
</appender>
```

To see the full workings of the CMP engine, you need to enable the custom TRACE level priority on the org.jboss.ejb.plugins.cmp category, as shown here:

```
<category name="org.jboss.ejb.plugins.cmp">
    <priority value="TRACE" class="org.jboss.logging.XLevel"/>
</category>
```

Running the Examples

The first test target illustrates a number of the customization features that are discussed in this chapter. To run these tests, you execute the following Ant target:

```
[examples]$ ant -Dchap=cmp2 -Dex=test run-example
```

The output log will show the following output:

```
22:30:09,862 DEBUG [OrganizationEJB#findByPrimaryKey] Executing SQL: SELECT t0_
➥ OrganizationEJB.name FROM ORGANIZATION t0_OrganizationEJB WHERE
➥t0_OrganizationEJB.name=?
22:30:09,927 DEBUG [OrganizationEJB] Executing SQL: SELECT desc, the_boss
➥FROM ORGANIZATION WHERE (name=?)
22:30:09,931 DEBUG [OrganizationEJB] load relation SQL: SELECT id
➥FROM GANGSTER WHERE (organization=?)
```

```
22:30:09,947 DEBUG [StatelessSessionContainer] Useless invocation of remove()
➥for stateless session bean
22:30:10,086 DEBUG [GangsterEJB#findBadDudes_ejbql] Executing SQL: SELECT
➥t0_g.id FROM GANGSTER t0_g WHERE (t0_g.badness > ?)
22:30:10,097 DEBUG [GangsterEJB#findByPrimaryKey] Executing SQL: SELECT
➥t0_GangsterEJB.id FROM GANGSTER t0_GangsterEJB WHERE t0_GangsterEJB.id=?
22:30:10,102 DEBUG [GangsterEJB#findByPrimaryKey] Executing SQL: SELECT
➥t0_GangsterEJB.id FROM GANGSTER t0_GangsterEJB WHERE t0_GangsterEJB.id=?
```

These tests, which are mentioned throughout this chapter, exercise various finders, selectors, and object-to-table mapping issues.

The other main target runs a set of tests to demonstrate the optimized loading configurations presented in the section "Optimized Loading," later in this chapter. When the logging is set up correctly, the read-ahead tests will display useful information about the queries performed. Note that you do not have to restart the JBoss server for it to recognize the changes to the `log4j.xml` file, but it may take a minute or so. Running the following shows the actual execution of the read-ahead client:

```
[examples]$ ant -Dchap=cmp2 -Dex=readahead run-example
```

When the read-ahead client is executed, all the SQL queries executed during the test are displayed in the JBoss server console. The important items of note when analyzing the output are the number of queries executed, the columns selected, and the number of rows loaded. The following shows the `read-ahead none` portion of the JBoss server console output from read-ahead:

```
22:44:31,570 INFO  [ReadAheadTest]
#######################################################
### read-ahead none
###
22:44:31,582 DEBUG [GangsterEJB#findAll_none] Executing SQL: SELECT t0_g.id
➥FROM GANGSTER t0_g ORDER BY t0_g.id ASC
22:44:31,604 DEBUG [GangsterEJB] Executing SQL: SELECT name, nick_name, badness,
➥  organization, hangout FROM GANGSTER WHERE (id=?)
22:44:31,615 DEBUG [GangsterEJB] Executing SQL: SELECT name, nick_name, badness,
➥  organization, hangout FROM GANGSTER WHERE (id=?)
22:44:31,622 DEBUG [GangsterEJB] Executing SQL: SELECT name, nick_name, badness,
➥ organization, hangout FROM GANGSTER WHERE (id=?)
22:44:31,628 DEBUG [GangsterEJB] Executing SQL: SELECT name, nick_name, badness,
➥  organization, hangout FROM GANGSTER WHERE (id=?)
22:44:31,635 DEBUG [GangsterEJB] Executing SQL: SELECT name, nick_name, badness,
➥ organization, hangout FROM GANGSTER WHERE (id=?)
22:44:31,644 DEBUG [GangsterEJB] Executing SQL: SELECT name, nick_name, badness,
➥ organization, hangout FROM GANGSTER WHERE (id=?)
22:44:31,649 DEBUG [GangsterEJB] Executing SQL: SELECT name, nick_name, badness,
➥  organization, hangout FROM GANGSTER WHERE (id=?)
```

```
22:44:31,658 DEBUG [GangsterEJB] Executing SQL: SELECT name, nick_name, badness,
➥ organization, hangout FROM GANGSTER WHERE (id=?)
22:44:31,670 INFO  [ReadAheadTest]
###
##########################################################
...
```

We will revisit this example and explore the output when we discuss the settings for optimized loading later in this chapter.

The `jbosscmp-jdbc` Structure

You use the `jbosscmp-jdbc.xml` descriptor to control the behavior of the JBoss engine. You can do this globally through the `conf/standardjbosscmp-jdbc.xml` descriptor found in the server configuration file set or by using EJB JAR deployment via a `META-INF/jbosscmp-jdbc.xml` descriptor.

You can find the DTD for the `jbosscmp-jdbc.xml` descriptor in `JBOSS_DIST/docs/dtd/jbosscmp-jdbc_4_0.dtd`. The public doctype for this DTD is as follows:

```
<!DOCTYPE jbosscmp-jdbc PUBLIC
      "-//JBoss//DTD JBOSSCMP-JDBC 4.0//EN"
      "http://www.jboss.org/j2ee/dtd/jbosscmp-jdbc_4_0.dtd">
```

The top-level child elements of the `jbosscmp-jdbc` element are shown in Figure 11.2.

The public doctype for this DTD is as follows:

- **`defaults`**—The `defaults` section allows for the specification of default behavior/settings for behavior that controls entity beans. Use of this section simplifies the amount of information needed for the common behaviors found in the entity beans section. See the "JBoss Global Defaults" section, later in this chapter, for the details of the `defaults` section content.
- **`enterprise-beans`**—The `enterprise-beans` element allows for customization of entity beans defined in the `ejb-jar.xml enterprise-beans` descriptor. This is described in detail in the "Entity Beans" section, later in this chapter.
- **`relationships`**—The `relationships` element allows for the customization of tables and the loading behavior of entity relationships. This is described in detail later in this chapter, in the section "Container-Managed Relationships."
- **`dependent-value-classes`**—The `dependent-value-classes` element allows for the customization of the mapping of dependent value classes (DVCs) to tables. DVCs are described in detail later in this chapter, in the "Dependent Value Classes " section.

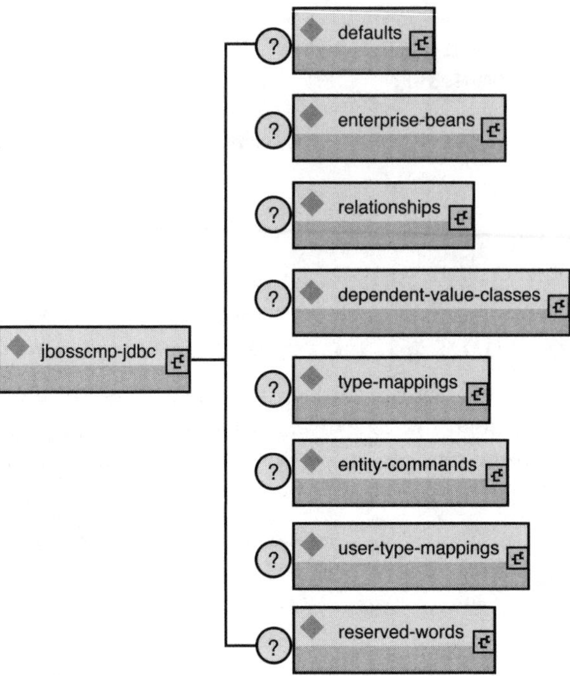

FIGURE 11.2 The `jbosscmp-jdbc` content model.

- **`type-mappings`**—The `type-mappings` element defines the Java-to-SQL type mappings for a database, along with SQL templates and function mappings. This is described in detail in the "Datasource Customization" section, later in this chapter.
- **`entity-commands`**—The `entity-commands` element allows for the definition of entity creation command instances that know how to create an entity instance in a persistent store. This is described in detail in the "Entity Commands and Primary Key Generation" section, later in this chapter.
- **`user-type-mappings`**—The `user-type-mappings` element defines a mapping of user types to a column, using a `mapper` class. A `mapper` is like a mediator. When storing, it takes an instance of the user type and translates it to a column value. When loading, it translates a column value to an instance of the user type. Details of the user type mappings are described in the "User Type Mappings" section, later in this chapter.
- **`reserved-words`**—The `reserved-words` element defines one or more reserved words that should be escaped when generating tables. Each reserved word is specified as the content of a `word` element.

Entity Beans

Let's start our look at entity beans in JBoss by examining one of the CMP entity beans in the crime portal. Let's look at the gangster bean, which is implemented as a local CMP entity bean. Although JBoss can provide remote entity beans with pass-by-reference semantics for calls in the same VM to get the performance benefit as from local entity beans, the use of local entity beans is strongly encouraged.

Let's start with the required home interface. Because you're only concerned with the CMP fields at this point, the following code shows only the methods that deal with the CMP fields:

```
// Gangster Local Home Interface
public interface GangsterHome
    extends EJBLocalHome
{
    Gangster create(Integer id, String name, String nickName)
        throws CreateException;
    Gangster findByPrimaryKey(Integer id)
        throws FinderException;
}
```

The local interface is what clients use to talk. Again, it contains only the CMP field accessors:

```
// Gangster Local Interface
public interface Gangster
    extends EJBLocalObject
{
    Integer getGangsterId();

    String getName();

    String getNickName();
    void setNickName(String nickName);

    int getBadness();
    void setBadness(int badness);
}
```

Finally, the following is the actual gangster bean:

```
// Gangster Implementation Class
public abstract class GangsterBean
    implements EntityBean
{
     private EntityContext ctx;
```

```
    private Category log = Category.getInstance(getClass());
    public Integer ejbCreate(Integer id, String name, String nickName)
        throws CreateException
    {
        log.info("Creating Gangster " + id + " '" + nickName + "' "+ name);
        setGangsterId(id);
        setName(name);
        setNickName(nickName);
        return null;
    }

    public void ejbPostCreate(Integer id, String name, String nickName) {
    }

    // CMP field accessors -----------------------------------------
    public abstract Integer getGangsterId();
    public abstract void setGangsterId(Integer gangsterId);
    public abstract String getName();
    public abstract void setName(String name);
    public abstract String getNickName();
    public abstract void setNickName(String nickName);
    public abstract int getBadness();
    public abstract void setBadness(int badness);
    public abstract ContactInfo getContactInfo();
    public abstract void setContactInfo(ContactInfo contactInfo);
    //...

    // EJB callbacks -----------------------------------------------
    public void setEntityContext(EntityContext context) { ctx = context; }
    public void unsetEntityContext() { ctx = null; }
    public void ejbActivate() { }
    public void ejbPassivate() { }
    public void ejbRemove() { log.info("Removing " + getName()); }
    public void ejbStore() { }
    public void ejbLoad() { }
}
```

Despite the size if this bean, very little code is actually required. The bulk of the class is the `create` method.

The only thing missing now is the `ejb-jar.xml` deployment descriptor. Although the actual bean class is named `GangsterBean`, the entity is called `GangsterEJB`:

```
<?xml version="1.0" encoding="UTF-8"?>
<ejb-jar xmlns="http://java.sun.com/xml/ns/j2ee" version="2.1"
```

```
    xmlns:xsi="http://www.w3.org/2001/XMLSchema-instance"
    xsi:schemaLocation="http://java.sun.com/xml/ns/j2ee http://java.sun.com
➥ /xml/ns/j2ee/ejb-jar_\2_1.xsd">
   <display-name>Crime Portal</display-name>

    <enterprise-beans>
        <entity>
            <display-name>Gangster Entity Bean</display-name>
            <ejb-name>GangsterEJB</ejb-name>
            <local-home>org.jboss.cmp2.crimeportal.GangsterHome</local-home>
            <local>org.jboss.cmp2.crimeportal.Gangster</local>

            <ejb-class>org.jboss.cmp2.crimeportal.GangsterBean</ejb-class>
            <persistence-type>Container</persistence-type>
            <prim-key-class>java.lang.Integer</prim-key-class>
            <reentrant>False</reentrant>
            <cmp-version>2.x</cmp-version>
            <abstract-schema-name>gangster</abstract-schema-name>

            <cmp-field>
                <field-name>gangsterId</field-name>
            </cmp-field>
            <cmp-field>
                <field-name>name</field-name>
            </cmp-field>
            <cmp-field>
                <field-name>nickName</field-name>
            </cmp-field>
            <cmp-field>
                <field-name>badness</field-name>
            </cmp-field>
            <cmp-field>
                <field-name>contactInfo</field-name>
            </cmp-field>
            <primkey-field>gangsterId</primkey-field>

            <!-- ... -->
        </entity>
    </enterprise-beans>
</ejb-jar>
```

Note that the CMP version of 2.x indicates that this is the EJB 2.x CMP entity bean. The abstract schema name is set to `gangster`. This will be important when you look at EJB-QL queries in the “Declaring Queries” section, later in this chapter.

Entity Mapping

The JBoss configuration for the entity is declared with an `entity` element in the `jbosscmp-jdbc.xml` file. This file is located in the `META-INF` directory of the EJB JAR and contains all the optional configuration information for configuring the CMP mapping. The entity elements for each entity bean are grouped together in the `enterprise-beans` element, under the top-level `jbosscmp-jdbc` element. A stubbed-out entity configuration is shown here:

```
<?xml version="1.0" encoding="UTF-8"?>
<!DOCTYPE jbosscmp-jdbc PUBLIC
     "-//JBoss//DTD JBOSSCMP-JDBC 3.2//EN"
     "http://www.jboss.org/j2ee/dtd/jbosscmp-jdbc_3_2.dtd">
<jbosscmp-jdbc>
    <defaults>
        <!-- application-wide CMP defaults -->
    </defaults>
    <enterprise-beans>
        <entity>
            <ejb-name>GangsterEJB</ejb-name>
            <!-- overrides to defaults section -->
            <table-name>gangster</table-name>
            <!-- CMP Fields (see CMP-Fields) -->
            <!-- Load Groups (see Load Groups)-->
            <!-- Queries (see Queries) -->
        </entity>
    </enterprise-beans>
</jbosscmp-jdbc>
```

The `ejb-name` element is required to match the entity specification here with the one in the `ejb-jar.xml` file. The remainder of the elements specify either overrides of the global or application-wide CMP defaults or CMP mapping details specific to the bean. The application defaults come from the `defaults` section of the `jbosscmp-jdbc.xml` file, and the global defaults come from the `defaults` section of the `standardjbosscmp-jdbc.xml` file in the `conf` directory for the current server configuration file set. The `defaults` section is discussed later in this chapter, in the "JBoss Global Defaults" section. Figure 11.3 shows the full entity content model.

Detailed descriptions of the elements follow:

- **`ejb-name`**—This required element is the name of the EJB to which this configuration applies. This element must match an `ejb-name` of an entity in the `ejb-jar.xml` file.
- **`datasource`**—This optional element is the `jndi-name` used to look up the datasource. All database connections used by an entity or relation-table are obtained from the datasource. Having different datasources for entities is not recommended because it vastly constrains the domain over which finders and `ejbSelects` can query. The default is `java:/DefaultDS`, unless that is overridden in the `defaults` section.

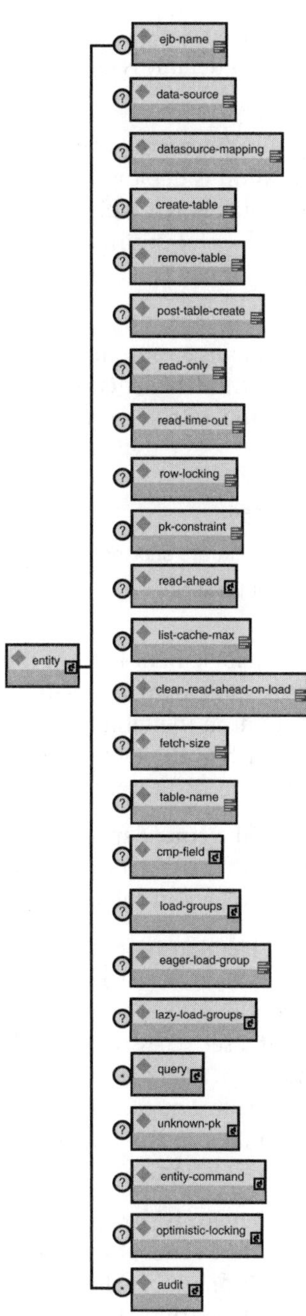

FIGURE 11.3 The entity element content model.

- **datasource-mapping**—This optional element specifies the name of the type-mapping, which determines how Java types are mapped to SQL types and how

EJB-QL functions are mapped to database-specific functions. (Type mappings are discussed later in this chapter.) The default is `Hypersonic SQL`, unless that is overridden in the `defaults` section.

- **`create-table`**—When this optional element is `true`, JBoss attempts to create a table for the entity. When the application is deployed, JBoss checks whether a table already exists before creating the table. If a table is found, it is logged, and the table is not created. This option is very useful during the early stages of development, when the table structure changes often. The default is `false` unless that is overridden in the `defaults` section.
- **`alter-table`**—If `create-table` is used to automatically create the schema, `alter-table` can be used to keep the schema current with changes to the entity bean. `alter-table` performs the following specific tasks:

  It creates new fields.

  It removes fields that are no longer used.

  It increases the length of string fields that are shorter than the declared length to the declared length. (This is not supported by all databases.)

- **`remove-table`**—When this optional element is `true`, JBoss attempts to drop the table for each entity and each relation-table mapped relationship. When the application is undeployed, JBoss attempts to drop the table. This option is very useful during the early stages of development, when the table structure changes often. The default is `false`, unless that is overridden in the `defaults` section.
- **`post-table-create`**—This optional element specifies an arbitrary SQL statement that should be executed immediately after the database table is created. This command is executed only if `create-table` is `true` and the table did not previously exist.
- **`read-only`**—When this optional element is `true`, the bean provider is not allowed to change the values of any fields. A field that is read-only will not be stored in, or inserted into, the database. If a primary key field is read-only, the `create` method will throw a `CreateException`. If a set accessor is called on a read-only field, it throws an `EJBException`. Read-only fields are useful for fields that are filled in by database triggers, such as last update. The read-only option can be overridden on a per-`cmp-field` basis, as discussed later in this chapter. The default is `false`, unless that is overridden in the `defaults` section.
- **`read-time-out`**—This optional element is the amount of time, in milliseconds, that a read on a read-only field is valid. A value of `0` means that the value is always reloaded at the start of a transaction, and a value of `-1` means that the value never times out. This option can also be overridden on a per-`cmp-field` basis. If read-only is `false`, this value is ignored. The default is `-1`, unless that is overridden in the `defaults` section.
- **`row-locking`**—If this optional element is `true`, JBoss locks all rows loaded in a transaction. Most databases implement this by using the `SELECT FOR UPDATE` syntax

when loading the entity, but the actual syntax is determined by the `row-locking-template` in the `datasource-mapping` used by this entity. The default is `false`, unless that is overridden in the `defaults` section.

- **`pk-constraint`**—This optional element, if `true`, specifies that JBoss will add a primary key constraint when creating tables. The default is `true`, unless that is overridden in the `defaults` section.
- **`read-ahead`**—This optional element controls caching of query results and `cmr-fields` for the entity. This option is discussed later in this chapter.
- **`fetch-size`**—This optional element specifies the number of entities to read in one round-trip to the underlying datastore. The default is `0`, unless that is overridden in the `defaults` section.
- **`list-cache-max`**—This optional element specifies the number of `read-lists` that can be tracked by this entity. This option is discussed in `on-load`. The default is `1000`, unless that is overridden in the `defaults` section.
- **`clean-read-ahead-on-load`**—When an entity is loaded from the read-ahead cache, JBoss can remove the data used from the read-ahead cache. The default is `false`.
- **`table-name`**—This optional element is the name of the table that will hold data for this entity. Each entity instance will be stored in one row of this table. The default is the `ejb-name`.
- **`cmp-field`**—The optional element allows you to define how the `ejb-jar.xml` `cmp-field` is mapped onto the persistence store. This is discussed later in this chapter.
- **`load-groups`**—This optional element specifies one or more groupings of CMP fields to declare load groupings of fields.
- **`eager-load-groups`**—This optional element defines one or more load groupings as eager load groups.
- **`lazy-load-groups`**—This optional element defines one or more load groupings as lazy load groups.
- **`query`**—This optional element specifies the definition of finders and selectors. This is discussed later in this chapter.
- **`unknown-pk`**—This optional element allows you to define how an unknown primary key type of `java.lang.Object` maps to the persistent store.
- **`entity-command`**—This optional element allows you to define the entity creation command instance. Typically, this is used to define a custom command instance to allow for primary key generation.
- **`optimistic-locking`**—This optional element defines the strategy to use for optimistic locking.
- **`audit`**—This optional element defines the CMP fields that will be audited.

CMP Fields

CMP fields are declared on the bean class as abstract getter and setter methods that follow the JavaBean property accessor conventions. The gangster bean, for example, has a getName() method and a setName() method for accessing the name CMP field. The following sections look at how to configure these declared CMP fields and control the persistence and behavior.

CMP Field Declaration

The declaration of a CMP field starts in the ejb-jar.xml file. On the gangster bean, for example, the gangsterId, name, nickName, and badness are declared in the ejb-jar.xml file as follows:

```
<ejb-jar>
  <enterprise-beans>
    <entity>
        <ejb-name>GangsterEJB</ejb-name>
        <cmp-field><field-name>gangsterId</field-name></cmp-field>
        <cmp-field><field-name>name</field-name></cmp-field>
        <cmp-field><field-name>nickName</field-name></cmp-field>
        <cmp-field><field-name>badness</field-name></cmp-field>
    </entity>
  </enterprise-beans>
</ejb-jar>
```

Note that the J2EE deployment descriptor doesn't declare any object-relational mapping details or other configuration. It is nothing more than a simple declaration of the CMP fields.

CMP Field Column Mapping

You do the relational mapping configuration of a CMP field in the jbosscmp-jdbc.xml file. The structure is similar to that of the ejb-jar.xml file, with an entity element that has cmp-field elements under it, with the additional configuration details.

The following shows the basic column name and data type mappings for the gangster bean:

```
<jbosscmp-jdbc>
  <enterprise-beans>
    <entity>
      <ejb-name>GangsterEJB</ejb-name>
      <table-name>gangster</table-name>

      <cmp-field>
        <field-name>gangsterId</field-name>
        <column-name>id</column-name>
```

```
    </cmp-field>
    <cmp-field>
      <field-name>name</field-name>
      <column-name>name</column-name>
      <not-null/>
    </cmp-field>
    <cmp-field>
      <field-name>nickName</field-name>
      <column-name>nick_name</column-name>
      <jdbc-type>VARCHAR</jdbc-type>
      <sql-type>VARCHAR(64)</sql-type>
    </cmp-field>
    <cmp-field>
      <field-name>badness</field-name>
      <column-name>badness</column-name>
    </cmp-field>
  </entity>
 </enterprise-beans>
</jbosscmp-jdbc>
```

The full content model of the `cmp-field` element of the `jbosscmp-jdbc.xml` is shown in Figure 11.4.

Detailed descriptions of the `entity` elements follow:

- **`field-name`**—This required element is the name of the `cmp-field` that is being configured. It must match the `field-name` element of a `cmp-field` declared for this entity in the `ejb-jar.xml` file.
- **`read-only`**—This element declares that the field in question is read-only. This field will not be written to the database by JBoss. Read-only fields are discussed later in this chapter.
- **`read-only-timeout`**—This is the time, in milliseconds, that a read-only field value will be considered valid.
- **`column-name`**—This optional element is the name of the column to which the `cmp-field` is mapped. The default is the `field-name` value.
- **`not-null`**—This optional element indicates that JBoss should add a `NOT NULL` to the end of the column declaration when automatically creating the table for this entity. The default for primary key fields and primitives is `not null`.
- **`jdbc-type`**—This is the JDBC type that is used when setting parameters in a JDBC prepared statement or loading data from a JDBC result set. The valid types are defined in `java.sql.Types`. This is required only if `sql-type` is specified. The default JDBC type is based on the database type in the `datasource-mapping`.

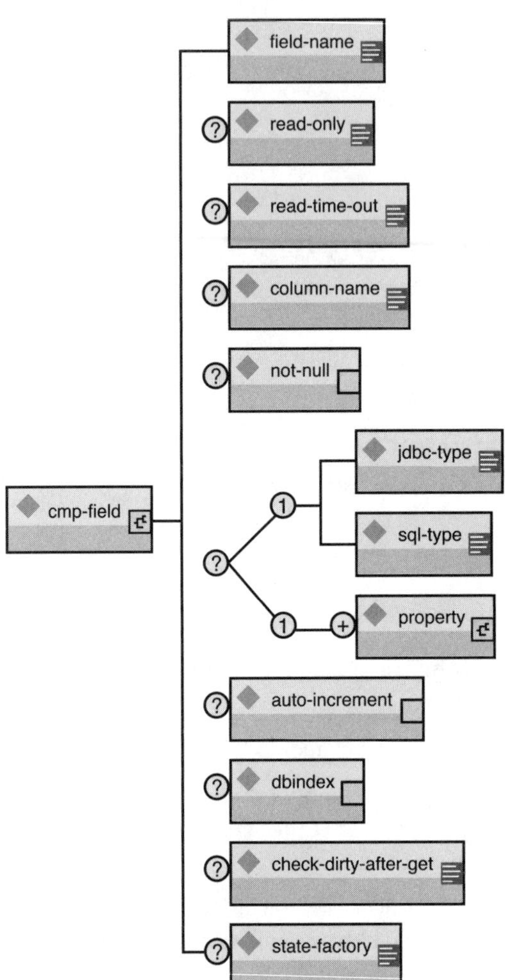

FIGURE 11.4 The JBoss `entity` element content model.

- **`sql-type`**—This is the SQL type that is used in `CREATE TABLE` statements for this field. Valid SQL types are limited only by your database vendor. This element is only required if `jdbc-type` is specified. The default SQL type is based on the database type in the `datasource-mapping`.
- **`property`**—This optional element allows you to define how the properties of a DVC CMP field should be mapped to the persistent store. This is discussed further later in this chapter.
- **`auto-increment`**—The presence of this optional field indicates that it is automatically incremented by the database layer. This is used to map a field to a generated column as well as to an externally manipulated column.

- **dbindex**—The presence of this optional field indicates that the server should create an index on the corresponding column in the database. The index name is `fieldname_index`.
- **check-dirty-after-get**—This value defaults to `false` for primitive types and the basic `java.lang` immutable wrappers (`Integer`, `String`, and so on). For potentially mutable objects, JBoss marks the field as potentially dirty after a `get` operation. If the dirty check on an object is too expensive, you can optimize it away by setting `check-dirty-after-get` to `false`.
- **state-factory**—This specifies the classname of a state factory object that can perform dirty checking for this field. State factory classes must implement the `CMPFieldStateFactory` interface.

Read-only Fields

JBoss allows you to have read-only CMP fields by setting the `read-only` and `read-time-out` elements in the `cmp-field` declaration. These elements work the same way as they do at the entity level. If a field is read-only, it will never be used in an `INSERT` or `UPDATE` statement. If a primary key field is read-only, the `create` method will throw a `CreateException`. If a set accessor is called for a read-only field, it throws an `EJBException`. Read-only fields are useful for fields that are filled in by database triggers, such as last update. A read-only CMP field declaration example follows:

```
<jbosscmp-jdbc>
    <enterprise-beans>
        <entity>
            <ejb-name>GangsterEJB</ejb-name>
            <cmp-field>
                <field-name>lastUpdated</field-name>
                <read-only>true</read-only>
                <read-time-out>1000</read-time-out>
            </cmp-field>
        </entity>
    </enterprise-beans>
</jbosscmp-jdbc>
```

Auditing Entity Access

The `audit` element of the `entity` section allows you to specify how access to an entity bean is audited. Auditing is allowed only when an entity bean is accessed under a security domain so that the caller identity is established. The content model of the `audit` element is shown in Figure 11.5.

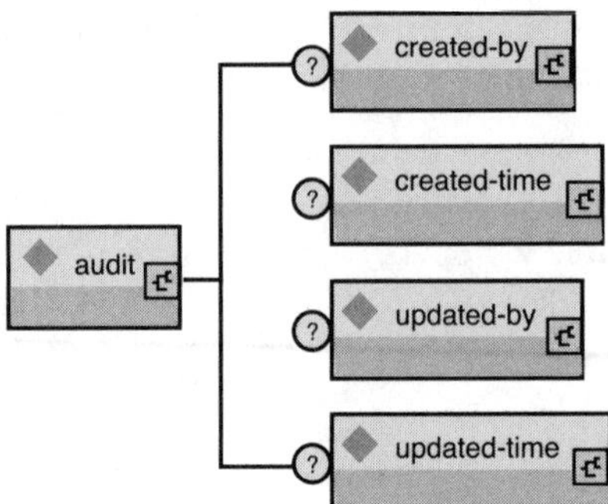

FIGURE 11.5 The `jbosscmp-jdbc.xml` audit element content model.

The supported elements are as follows:

- **`created-by`**—This optional element indicates that the caller who created the entity should be saved to either the indicated `column-name` or CMP `field-name`.
- **`created-time`**—This optional element indicates that the time of entity creation should be saved to either the indicated `column-name` or CMP `field-name`.
- **`updated-by`**—This optional element indicates that the caller who last modified the entity should be saved to either the indicated `column-name` or CMP `field-name`.
- **`updated-time`**—This optional element indicates that the last time of entity modification should be saved to either the indicated `column-name` or CMP `field-name`.

For each element, if a `field-name` is given, the corresponding audit information should be stored in the specified CMP field of the entity bean being accessed. Note that there does not have to be a corresponding CMP field declared on the entity. If there are matching field names, you can access audit fields in the application by using the corresponding CMP field abstract getters and setters. Otherwise, the audit fields are created and added to the entity internally. You can access audit information in EJB-QL queries, using the audit field names but not directly through the entity accessors.

If, on the other hand, a `column-name` is specified, the corresponding audit information should be stored in the indicated column of the entity table. If JBoss is creating the table, you can use the `jdbc-type` and `sql-type` element to define the storage type.

The following code shows the declaration of audit information with given column names:

```
<jbosscmp-jdbc>
    <enterprise-beans>
        <entity>
            <ejb-name>AuditChangedNamesEJB</ejb-name>
            <table-name>cmp2_audit_changednames</table-name>
            <audit>
```

```
            <created-by>
                <column-name>createdby</column-name>
            </created-by>
            <created-time>
                <column-name>createdtime</column-name>
            </created-time>
            <updated-by>
                <column-name>updatedby</column-name></updated-by>
            <updated-time>
                <column-name>updatedtime</column-name>
            </updated-time>
        </audit>
    </entity>
</enterprise-beans>
</jbosscmp-jdbc>
```

Dependent Value Classes

Dependent value class (DVC) is a fancy term used to identity any Java class that is the type of a `cmp-field` and is not one of automatically recognized core types, such as strings and number values. By default, a DVC is serialized, and the serialized form is stored in a single database column. Although not discussed here, there are several known issues with the long-term storage of classes in serialized form.

JBoss also supports the storage of the internal data of a DVC in one or more columns. This storage is useful for supporting legacy JavaBeans and database structures. It is not uncommon to find a database with a highly flattened structure (for example, a `PURCHASE_ORDER` table with the fields `SHIP_LINE1`, `SHIP_LINE2`, `SHIP_CITY`, and so on, and an additional set of fields for the billing address). Other common database structures include telephone numbers with separate fields for area code, exchange, and extension and a person's name spread across several fields. With a DVC, multiple columns can be mapped to one logical field.

JBoss requires that a DVC to be mapped follow the JavaBeans naming specification for simple properties and that each property to be stored in the database have both a getter and a setter method. Furthermore, the bean must be serializable and must have a `no-arg` constructor. A property can be any simple type, and it can be an unmapped DVC or a mapped DVC, but it cannot be an EJB. A DVC mapping is specified in a `dependent-value-class` element within the `dependent-value-classes` element.

Figure 11.6 shows the structure `jbosscmp-jdbc` element.

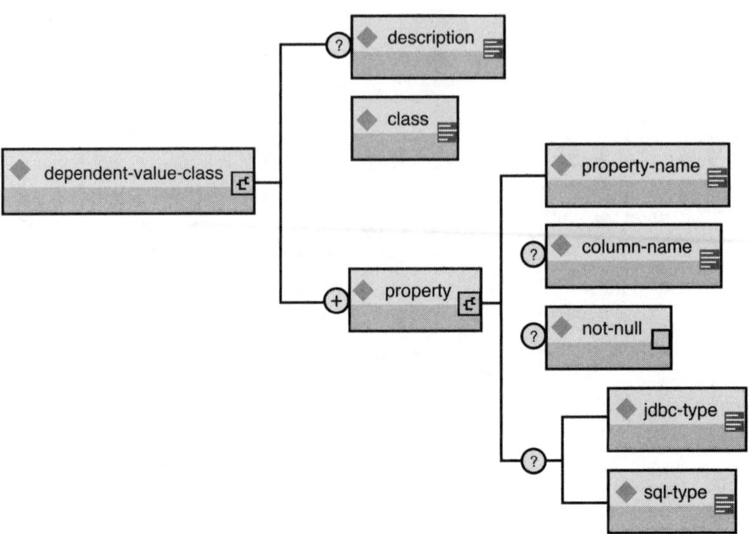

FIGURE 11.6 The `jbosscmp-jdbc dependent-value-class` element model.

Here is an example of a simple `ContactInfo` DVC class:

```
public class ContactInfo
    implements Serializable
{
    /** The cell phone number. */
    private PhoneNumber cell;

    /** The pager number. */
    private PhoneNumber pager;

    /** The email address */
    private String email;


    /**
     * Creates empty contact info.
     */
    public ContactInfo() {
    }

    public PhoneNumber getCell() {
        return cell;
    }
```

```
    public void setCell(PhoneNumber cell) {
        this.cell = cell;
    }

    public PhoneNumber getPager() {
        return pager;
    }

    public void setPager(PhoneNumber pager) {
      this.pager = pager;
    }

    public String getEmail() {
        return email;
    }

    public void setEmail(String email) {
        this.email = email.toLowerCase();
    }

    // ... equals, hashCode, toString
}
```

The contact info includes a phone number, which is represented by another DVC class:

```
public class PhoneNumber
    implements Serializable
{
    /** The first three digits of the phone number. */
    private short areaCode;

    /** The middle three digits of the phone number. */
        private short exchange;

    /** The last four digits of the phone number. */
        private short extension;

    // ... getters and setters

    // ... equals, hashCode, toString
}
```

The DVC mappings for these two classes are relatively straightforward:

```
<dependent-value-classes>
    <dependent-value-class>
```

```
        <description>A phone number</description>
        <class>org.jboss.cmp2.crimeportal.PhoneNumber</class>
        <property>
            <property-name>areaCode</property-name>
            <column-name>area_code</column-name>
        </property>
        <property>
            <property-name>exchange</property-name>
            <column-name>exchange</column-name>
        </property>
        <property>
            <property-name>extension</property-name>
            <column-name>extension</column-name>
        </property>
    </dependent-value-class>

    <dependent-value-class>
        <description>General contact info</description>
        <class>org.jboss.cmp2.crimeportal.ContactInfo</class>
        <property>
            <property-name>cell</property-name>
            <column-name>cell</column-name>
        </property>
        <property>
            <property-name>pager</property-name>
            <column-name>pager</column-name>
        </property>
        <property>
            <property-name>email</property-name>
            <column-name>email</column-name>
            <jdbc-type>VARCHAR</jdbc-type>
            <sql-type>VARCHAR(128)</sql-type>
        </property>
    </dependent-value-class>
</dependent-value-classes>
```

Each DVC is declared with a `dependent-value-class` element. A DVC is identified by the Java class type declared in the `class` element. Each property to be persisted is declared with a `property` element. This specification is based on the `cmp-field` element, so it should be self-explanatory. (This restriction will be removed in a future release.) The current proposal involves storing the primary key fields in the case of a local entity and the entity handle in the case of a remote entity.

The `dependent-value-class` section defines the internal structure and default mapping of the classes. When JBoss encounters a field that has an unknown type, it searches the list of registered DVCs, and if a DVC is found, it persists that field into a set of columns;

otherwise, the field is stored in serialized form in a single column. JBoss does not support inheritance of DVCs; therefore, this search is only based on the declared type of the field. A DVC can be constructed from other DVCs, so when JBoss runs into a DVC, it flattens the DVC tree structure into a set of columns. If JBoss finds a DVC circuit during startup, it throws an `EJBException`. The default column name of a property is the column name of the base `cmp-field`, followed by an underscore and then the column name of the property. If the property is a DVC, the process is repeated. For example, a `cmp-field` named `info` that uses the `ContactInfo` DVC would have the following columns:

```
info_cell_area_code
info_cell_exchange
info_cell_extension
info_pager_area_code
info_pager_exchange
info_pager_extension
info_email
```

The automatically generated column names can quickly become excessively long and awkward. You can override the default mappings of columns in the `entity` element, as follows:

```
<jbosscmp-jdbc>
    <enterprise-beans>
        <entity>
            <ejb-name>GangsterEJB</ejb-name>
            <cmp-field>
                <field-name>contactInfo</field-name>
                <property>
                    <property-name>cell.areaCode</property-name>
                    <column-name>cell_area</column-name>
                </property>
                <property>
                    <property-name>cell.exchange</property-name>
                    <column-name>cell_exch</column-name>
                </property>
                <property>
                    <property-name>cell.extension</property-name>
                    <column-name>cell_ext</column-name>
                </property>

                <property>
                    <property-name>pager.areaCode</property-name>
                    <column-name>page_area</column-name>
                </property>
                <property>
                    <property-name>pager.exchange</property-name>
```

```
                <column-name>page_exch</column-name>
            </property>
            <property>
                <property-name>pager.extension</property-name>
                <column-name>page_ext</column-name>
            </property>

            <property>
                <property-name>email</property-name>
                <column-name>email</column-name>
                <jdbc-type>VARCHAR</jdbc-type>
                <sql-type>VARCHAR(128)</sql-type>
            </property>
        </cmp-field>
    </entity>
  </enterprise-beans>
</jbosscmp-jdbc>
```

When overriding property information for the entity, you need to refer to the property from a flat perspective, as in `cell.areaCode`.

Container-Managed Relationships

Container-managed relationships (CMRs) are a powerful new feature of CMP 2.0. Programmers have been creating relationships between entity objects since EJB 1.0 was introduced (not to mention since the introduction of databases), but before CMP 2.0, a programmer had to write a lot of code for each relationship in order to extract the primary key of the related entity and store it in a pseudo foreign key field. The simplest relationships were tedious to code, and complex relationships with referential integrity required many hours of coding. With CMP 2.0 there is no need to code relationships by hand. The container can manage one-to-one, one-to-many, and many-to-many relationships, with referential integrity. One restriction with CMRs is that they are only defined between local interfaces. This means that a relationship cannot be created between two entities in separate applications, even in the same application server.

There are two basic steps to creating a CMR: create the `cmr-field` abstract accessors and declare the relationship in the `ejb-jar.xml` file. The following two sections describe these steps.

`CMR-field` Abstract Accessors

`CMR-field` abstract accessors have the same signatures as `cmp-fields`, except that single-valued relationships must return the local interface of the related entity, and multivalued relationships can only return a `java.util.Collection` (or `java.util.Set`) object. For example, to declare a one-to-many relationship between the `organization` and `gangster` beans, you declare the relationship from `organization` to `gangster` in the

`OrganizationBean` class:

```
public abstract class OrganizationBean
    implements EntityBean
{
    public abstract Set getMemberGangsters();
    public abstract void setMemberGangsters(Set gangsters);
}
```

You can also declare the relationship from `gangster` to `organization` in the `GangsterBean` class:

```
public abstract class GangsterBean
    implements EntityBean
{
    public abstract Organization getOrganization();
    public abstract void setOrganization(Organization org);
}
```

Although each bean declares a CMR field, only one of the two beans in a relationship must have a set of accessors. As with CMP fields, a CMR field is required to have both a getter and a setter method.

Relationship Declaration

Declaring relationships in the `ejb-jar.xml` file is complicated and error-prone. Although we recommend using a tool such as XDoclet to manage the deployment descriptors for CMR fields, it's still important that you understand how the descriptor works. The following illustrates the declaration of the `organization/gangster` relationship:

```
<ejb-jar>
    <relationships>
        <ejb-relation>
            <ejb-relation-name>Organization-Gangster</ejb-relation-name>
            <ejb-relationship-role>
                <ejb-relationship-role-name>org-has-gangsters
➥</ejb-relationship-role-name>
                <multiplicity>One</multiplicity>
                <relationship-role-source>
                    <ejb-name>OrganizationEJB</ejb-name>
                </relationship-role-source>
                <cmr-field>
                    <cmr-field-name>memberGangsters</cmr-field-name>
                    <cmr-field-type>java.util.Set</cmr-field-type>
                </cmr-field>
            </ejb-relationship-role>
            <ejb-relationship-role>
```

```
                <ejb-relationship-role-name>gangster-belongs-to-org
➥</ejb-relationship-role-name>
                <multiplicity>Many</multiplicity>
                <cascade-delete/>
                <relationship-role-source>
                    <ejb-name>GangsterEJB</ejb-name>
                </relationship-role-source>
                <cmr-field>
                    <cmr-field-name>organization</cmr-field-name>
                </cmr-field>
            </ejb-relationship-role>
        </ejb-relation>
    </relationships>
</ejb-jar>
```

As you can see, each relationship is declared with an `ejb-relation` element within the top-level `relationships` element. The relation is given a name in the `ejb-relation-name` element. This is important because you need to refer to the role by name in the `jbosscmp-jdbc.xml` file. Each `ejb-relation` contains two `ejb-relationship-role` elements (one for each side of the relationship). The `ejb-relationship-role` tags are as follows:

- **`ejb-relationshiprole-name`**—This optional element is used to identify the specific role externally (for example, the `jbosscmp-jdbc.xml` file). The relationship role names for both sides of a relationship must be different.
- **`multiplicity`**—This indicates the multiplicity of this side of the relationship. The valid values are `One` and `Many`. In this example, the multiplicity of `organization` is `One` and the multiplicity of `gangster` is `Many` because the relationship is from one `organization` to many `gangsters`. Note that, as with all XML elements, this element is case-sensitive.
- **`cascade-delete`**—When this optional element is present, JBoss deletes the child entity when the parent entity is deleted. Cascade deletion is allowed only for a role where the other side of the relationship has a multiplicity of one. The default is to not cascade delete.
- **`relationship-role-source`**—This element contains the following element:
    - **`ejb-name`**—This required element gives the name of the entity that has the role.
- **`cmr-field`**—This element contains the following elements:
    - **`cmr-field-name`**—This is the name of the CMR field of the entity, if it has one.
    - **`cmr-field-type`**—This is the type of the CMR field, if the field is a collection type. It must be `java.util.Collection` or`java.util.Set`.

After you add the CMR field abstract accessors and declare the relationship, the relationship should be functional. The next section discusses the database mapping of the relationship.

Relationship Mapping

You can map relationships by using either a foreign key or a separate relation table. One-to-one and one-to-many relationships use the foreign key mapping style by default, and many-to-many relationships use only the relation table mapping style. The mapping of a relationship is declared in the `relationships` section of the `jbosscmp-jdbc.xml` descriptor via `ejb-relation` elements. Relationships are identified by the `ejb-relation-name` from the `ejb-jar.xml` file. The `jbosscmp-jdbc.xml` `ejb-relation` element content model is shown in Figure 11.7.

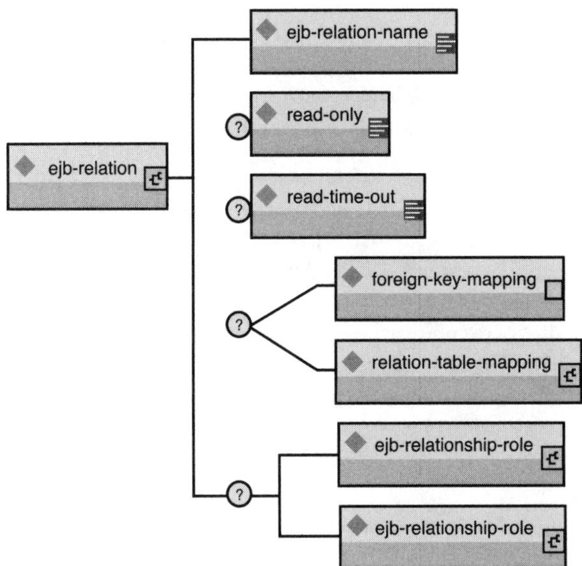

FIGURE 11.7 The `jbosscmp-jdbc.xml` `ejb-relation` element content model.

The basic template of the relationship mapping declaration for the `Organization/Gangster` relationship follows:

```
<jbosscmp-jdbc>
    <relationships>
        <ejb-relation>
            <ejb-relation-name>Organization-Gangster</ejb-relation-name>
            <foreign-key-mapping/>
            <ejb-relationship-role>
                <ejb-relationship-role-name>org-has-gangsters
➥</ejb-relationship-role-name>
                <key-fields>
```

```
                <key-field>
                    <field-name>name</field-name>
                    <column-name>organization</column-name>
                </key-field>
            </key-fields>
        </ejb-relationship-role>
        <ejb-relationship-role>
            <ejb-relationship-role-name>gangster-belongs-to-org
➥</ejb-relationship-role-name>
            <key-fields/>
        </ejb-relationship-role>
    </ejb-relation>
  </relationships>
</jbosscmp-jdbc>
```

After the `ejb-relation-name` of the relationship being mapped is declared, you can declare the relationship as read-only by using the `read-only` and `read-time-out` elements. They have the same semantics as their counterparts in the `entity` element.

The `ejb-relation` element must contain either a `foreign-key-mapping` element or a `relation-table-mapping` element, which are described in the "Foreign Key Mapping" and "Relation Table Mapping" sections, later in this chapter. This element may also contain a pair of `ejb-relationship-role` elements, as described in the following section.

Relationship Role Mapping

Each of the two `ejb-relationship-role` elements contains mapping information that is specific to an entity in the relationship. The content model of the `ejb-relationship-role` element is shown in Figure 11.8.

Detailed descriptions of the main elements follow:

- **`ejb-relationship-role-name`**—This required element gives the name of the role to which this configuration applies. It must match the name of one of the roles declared for this relationship in the `ejb-jar.xml` file.
- **`fk-constraint`**—This optional element is a `true/false` value that indicates whether JBoss should add a foreign key constraint to the tables for this side of the relationship. JBoss will generate the constraint only if both the primary table and the related table were created by JBoss during deployment.
- **`key-fields`**—This optional element specifies the mapping of the primary key fields of the current entity, whether it is mapped in the relation table or in the related object. The `key-fields` element must contain a `key-field` element for each primary key field of the current entity. The `key-fields` element can be empty if no foreign key mapping is needed for this side of the relation. An example of this would be the many side of a one-to-many relationship.
- **`read-ahead`**—This optional element controls the caching of this relationship.

- **batch-cascade-delete**—This indicates that a cascade delete on this relationship should be performed with a single SQL statement. This requires that the relationship be marked as `batch-delete` in the `ejb-jar.xml` file.

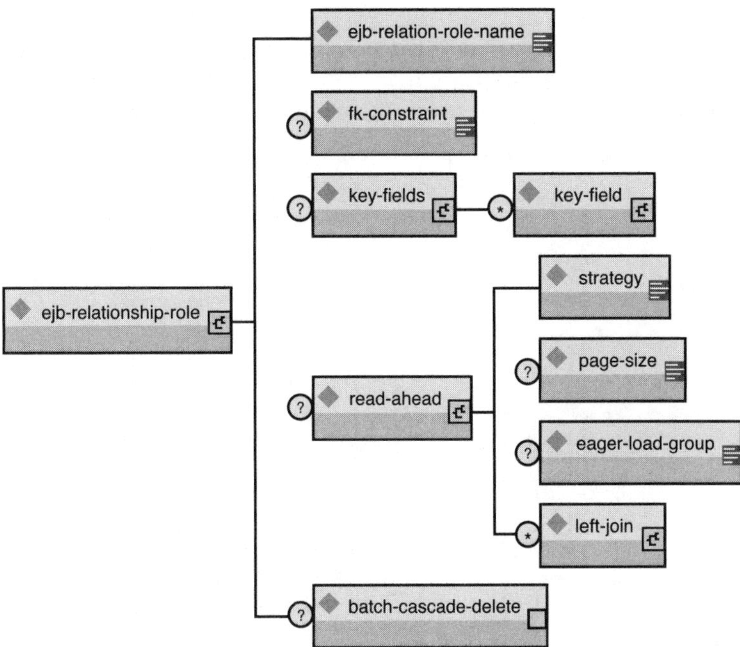

FIGURE 11.8 The `jbosscmp-jdbc ejb-relationship-role` element content model.

As noted previously, the `key-field` element contains a `key-field` element for each primary key field of the current entity. The `key-field` element uses the same syntax as the `cmp-field` element of the entity, except that `key-field` does not support the not-null option. A key field of a relation table is automatically not null because it is the primary key of the table. On the other hand, a foreign key field must be nullable by default. This is because the CMP specification requires an insert into the database after the `ejbCreate` method and an update to it afterward, to pick up CMR changes made in `ejbPostCreate`. Because the EJB specification does not allow a relationship to be modified until `ejbPostCreate`, a foreign key is initially set to null. There is a similar problem with removal. You can change this insert behavior by using the `jboss.xml insert-after-ejb-post-create` container configuration flag. The following example illustrates the creation of a new bean configuration that uses `insert-after-ejb-post-create` by default:

```
<jboss>
    <!-- ... -->
    <container-configurations>
        <container-configuration extends="Standard CMP 2.x EntityBean">
            <container-name>INSERT after ejbPostCreate Container</container-name>
```

```
            <insert-after-ejb-post-create>true</insert-after-ejb-post-create>
        </container-configuration>
    </container-configurations>
</jboss>
```

An alternate means of working around the non-null foreign key issue is to map the foreign key elements onto non-null CMP fields. In such a case, you simply populate the foreign key fields in `ejbCreate` by using the associated CMP field setters.

The content model of the `key-field` element is shown in Figure 11.9.

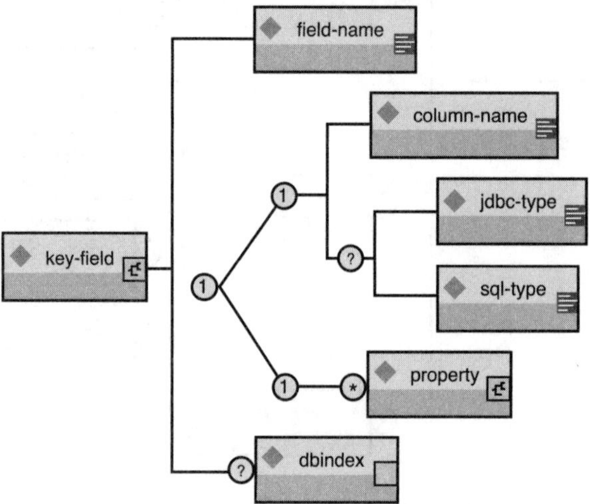

FIGURE 11.9 The `jbosscmp-jdbc key-fields` element content model.

Detailed descriptions of the elements contained in the `key-field` element follow:

- **`field-name`**—This required element identifies the field to which this mapping applies. This name must match a primary key field of the current entity.
- **`column-name`**—You use this element to specify the column name in which this primary key field will be stored. If this relationship uses `foreign-key-mapping`, this column will be added to the table for the related entity. If this relationship uses `relation-table-mapping`, this column is added to the `relation-table`. This element is not allowed for mapped DVCs; instead, you use the `property` element.
- **`jdbc-type`**—This is the JDBC type that is used when setting parameters in a JDBC `PreparedStatement` or loading data from a JDBC `ResultSet`. The valid types are defined in `java.sql.Types`.
- **`sql-type`**—This is the SQL type that is used in create table statements for this field. Valid types are limited only by your database vendor.
- **`property`**—You use this element to specify the mapping of a primary key field that is a dependent value class.

- **dbindex**—The presence of this optional field indicates that the server should create an index on the corresponding column in the database, and the index name will be `fieldname_index`.

Foreign Key Mapping

Foreign key mapping is the most common mapping style for one-to-one and one-to-many relationships, but it is not allowed for many-to-many relationships. You declare the foreign key mapping by adding an empty foreign `key-mapping` element to the `ejb-relation` element.

As noted in the previous section, with a foreign key mapping, the `key-fields` elements declared in `ejb-relationship-role` are added to the table of the related entity. If the `key-fields` element is empty, a foreign key is not created for the entity. In a one-to-many relationship, the many side (`gangster`, in the example) must have an empty `key-fields` element, and the one side (`organization`, in the example) must have a `key-fields` mapping. In one-to-one relationships, one or both roles can have foreign keys.

The foreign key mapping is not dependent on the direction of the relationship. This means that in a one-to-one unidirectional relationship (only one side has an accessor), one or both roles can still have foreign keys. The complete foreign key mapping for the `organization/gangster` relationship is shown in the following:

```
<jbosscmp-jdbc>
    <relationships>
        <ejb-relation>
            <ejb-relation-name>Organization-Gangster</ejb-relation-name>
            <foreign-key-mapping/>
            <ejb-relationship-role>
                <ejb-relationship-role-name>org-has-gangsters
➥</ejb-relationship-role-name>
                <key-fields>
                    <key-field>
                        <field-name>name</field-name>
                        <column-name>organization</column-name>
                    </key-field>
                </key-fields>
            </ejb-relationship-role>
            <ejb-relationship-role>
                <ejb-relationship-role-name>gangster-belongs-to-org
➥</ejb-relationship-role-name>
                <key-fields/>
            </ejb-relationship-role>
        </ejb-relation>
    </relationships>
</jbosscmp-jdbc>
```

Relation Table Mapping

Relation table mapping is not very common for one-to-one and one-to-many relationships, but is the only mapping style allowed for many-to-many relationships. Relation table mapping is defined using the `relation-table-mapping` element, the content model of which is shown in Figure 11.10.

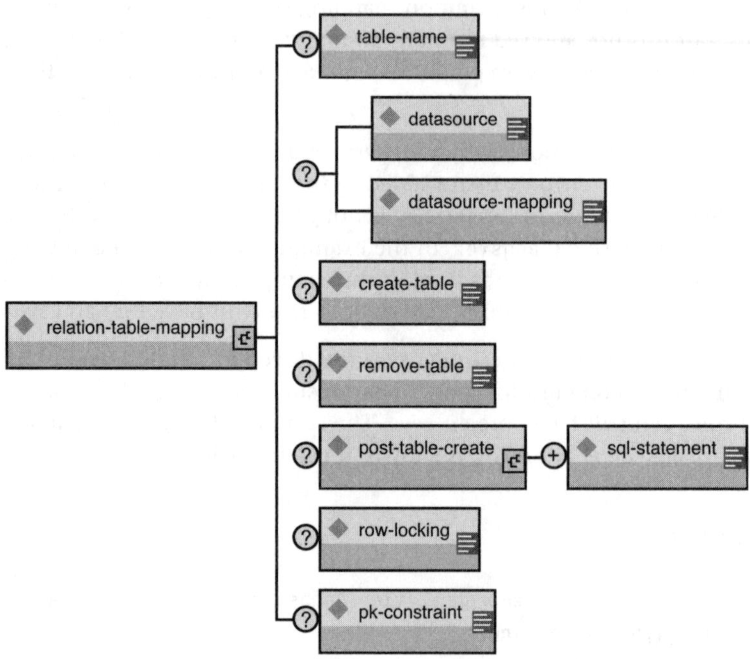

FIGURE 11.10 The `jbosscmp-jdbc relation-table-mapping` element content model.

The relation table mapping for the `gangster/job` relationship is shown in Listing 11.1.

LISTING 11.1 The `jbosscmp-jdbc.xml` Relation Table Mapping

```
<jbosscmp-jdbc>
    <relationships>
        <ejb-relation>
            <ejb-relation-name>Gangster-Jobs</ejb-relation-name>
            <relation-table-mapping>
                <table-name>gangster_job</table-name>
            </relation-table-mapping>
            <ejb-relationship-role>
                <ejb-relationship-role-name>gangster-has-jobs
➥</ejb-relationship-role-name>
                <key-fields>
                    <key-field>
```

LISTING 11.1 Continued

```
                        <field-name>gangsterId</field-name>
                        <column-name>gangster</column-name>
                    </key-field>
                </key-fields>
            </ejb-relationship-role>
            <ejb-relationship-role>
                <ejb-relationship-role-name>job-has-gangsters
➥</ejb-relationship-role-name>
                <key-fields>
                    <key-field>
                        <field-name>name</field-name>
                        <column-name>job</column-name>
                    </key-field>
                </key-fields>
            </ejb-relationship-role>
        </ejb-relation>
    </relationships>
</jbosscmp-jdbc>
```

The `relation-table-mapping` element contains a subset of the options available in the `entity` element. Detailed descriptions of these elements follow:

- **`table-name`**—This optional element gives the name of the table that will hold data for this relationship. The default table name is based on the `entity` and `cmr-field` names.
- **`datasource`**—This optional element gives the `jndi-name` used to look up the datasource. All database connections are obtained from the datasource. Having different datasources for entities is not recommended because it vastly constrains the domain over which finders and `ejbSelects` can query.
- **`datasourcemapping`**—This optional element allows you to specify the name of the `type-mapping` to use.
- **`create-table`**—This optional element, if `true`, indicates that JBoss should attempt to create a table for the relationship. When the application is deployed, JBoss checks whether a table already exists before creating the table. If a table is found, it is logged, and the table is not created. This option is very useful during the early stages of development, when the table structure changes often.
- **`post-table-create`**—This optional element specifies an arbitrary SQL statement that should be executed immediately after the database table is created. This command is executed only if `create-table` is `true` and the table did not previously exist.
- **`remove-table`**—This optional element, if `true`, indicates that JBoss should attempt to drop the `relation-table` when the application is undeployed. This option is very

useful during the early stages of development, when the table structure changes often.

- **`row-locking`**—This optional element, if `true`, indicates that JBoss should lock all rows loaded in a transaction. Most databases implement this by using the `SELECT FOR UPDATE` syntax when loading the entity, but the actual syntax is determined by `row-locking-template` in the `datasource-mapping` used by this entity.
- **`pk-constraint`**—This optional element, if `true`, indicates that JBoss should add a primary key constraint when creating tables.

Declaring Queries

Entity beans allow for two types of queries: finders and selects. A *finder* provides queries on an entity bean to clients of the bean. A *select method* is designed to provide private query statements to an entity implementation. Unlike finders, which are restricted to only return entities of the same type as the home interface on which they are defined, select methods can return any entity type or just one field of the entity. EJB-QL is the query language that is used to specify finders and select methods in a platform-independent way.

Declaring Finders and Selects

How you declare finders has not changed in CMP 2.0. You still declare finders in the home interface (local or remote) of the entity. Finders defined on the local home interface do not throw a `RemoteException`. The following code declares the `findBadDudes_ejbql` finder on the `GangsterHome` interface. The `ejbql` suffix here is not required. It is simply a naming convention used here to differentiate the different types of query specifications:

```
public interface GangsterHome
    extends EJBLocalHome
{
    Collection findBadDudes_ejbql(int badness) throws FinderException;
}
```

You declare select methods in the entity implementation class, and they must be public and abstract, just like CMP and CMR field abstract accessors, and they must throw a `FinderException`. The following code declares a select method:

```
public abstract class GangsterBean
    implements EntityBean
{
    public abstract Set ejbSelectBoss_ejbql(String name)
        throws FinderException;
}
```

Declaring EJB-QL Queries

Every select or finder method (except `findByPrimaryKey`) must have an EJB-QL query defined in the `ejb-jar.xml` file. The EJB-QL query is declared in a `query` element, which is contained in the `entity` element. The following are declarations for the `findBadDudes_ejbql` and `ejbSelectBoss_ejbql` queries:

```
<enterprise-beans>
        <entity>
            <ejb-name>GangsterEJB</ejb-name>
            <!-- ... -->
            <query>
                <query-method>
                    <method-name>findBadDudes_ejbql</method-name>
                    <method-params>
                        <method-param>int</method-param>
                    </method-params>
                </query-method>
                <ejb-ql><![CDATA[
                 SELECT OBJECT(g)
                 FROM gangster g
                 WHERE g.badness > ?1
                 ]]></ejb-ql>
            </query>
            <query>
                <query-method>
                    <method-name>ejbSelectBoss_ejbql</method-name>
                    <method-params>
                        <method-param>java.lang.String</method-param>
                    </method-params>
                </query-method>
                <ejb-ql><![CDATA[
                 SELECT DISTINCT underling.organization.theBoss
                 FROM gangster underling
                 WHERE underling.name = ?1 OR underling.nickName = ?1
                 ]]></ejb-ql>
            </query>
        </entity>
    </enterprise-beans>
</ejb-jar>
```

EJB-QL is similar to SQL, but it has some surprising differences. The following are some important things to note about EJB-QL:

- EJB-QL is a typed language, meaning that it only allows comparison of like types (that is, strings can only be compared with strings).

- In an equals comparison, a variable (that is, a single-valued path) must be on the left side. These are some examples:

```
g.hangout.state = 'CA' Legal
'CA' = g.shippingAddress.state NOT Legal
'CA' = 'CA' NOT Legal
(r.amountPaid * .01) > 300 NOT Legal
r.amountPaid > (300 / .01) Legal
```

- Parameters use a base 1 index, similarly to `java.sql.PreparedStatement`.
- Parameters are allowed only on the right side of a comparison. Here's an example:

```
gangster.hangout.state = ?1 Legal
?1 = gangster.hangout.state NOT Legal
```

Overriding the Mapping of EJB-QL to SQL

You can override an EJB-QL query in the `jbosscmp-jdbc.xml` file. The finder or select is still required to have an EJB-QL declaration, but the `ejb-ql` element can be left empty. Currently, you can override the SQL with JBossQL, DynamicQL, DeclaredSQL, or a BMP-style custom `ejbFind` method. All EJB-QL overrides are nonstandard extensions to the EJB specification, so use of these extensions limits portability of an application. You declare all the EJB-QL overrides, except for BMP custom finders, by using a query element in the `jbosscmp-jdbc.xml` file. The content model is shown in Figure 11.11.

Detailed descriptions of the `query` element follow:

- **`description`**—This is an optional description for the query.
- **`query-method`**—This required element specifies the query method that is being configured. This must match a `query-method` declared for this entity in the `ejb-jar.xml` file.
- **`jboss-ql`**—This is a JBossQL query to use in place of the EJB-QL query. JBossQL is discussed in the following section of this chapter.
- **`dynamic-ql`**—This indicates that the method is a dynamic query method and not an EJB-QL query. Dynamic queries are discussed later in this chapter.
- **`declared-sql`**—This query uses declared SQL in place of the EJB-QL query. Declared SQL is discussed later in this chapter.
- **`read-ahead`**—This optional element allows you to optimize the loading of additional fields for use with the entities referenced by the query. This is discussed in detail later in this chapter, in the section "Optimized Loading."

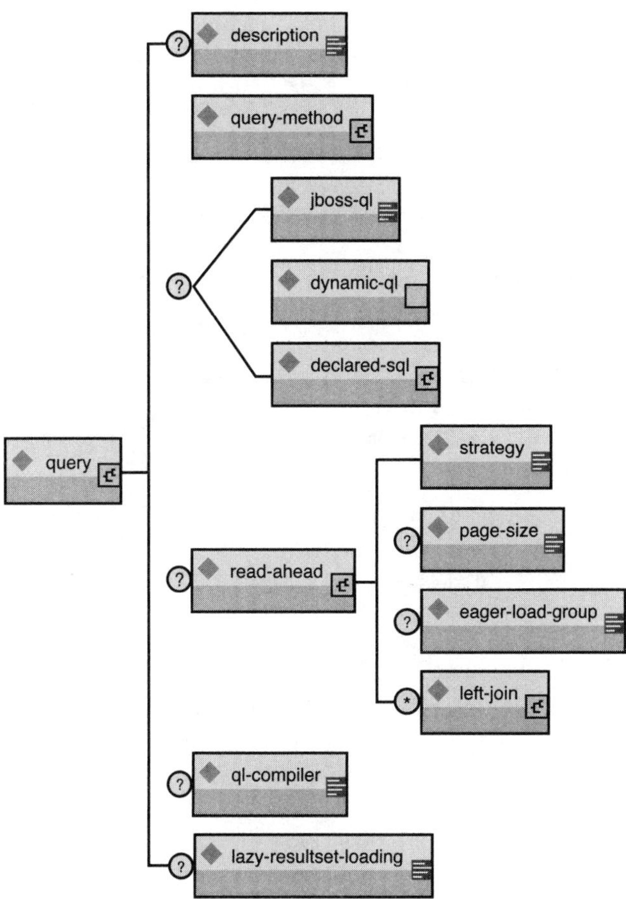

FIGURE 11.11 The `jbosscmp-jdbc query` element content model.

JBossQL

JBossQL is a superset of EJB-QL that is designed to address some of the inadequacies of EJB-QL. In addition to having a more flexible syntax, JBossQL now has new functions, keywords, and clauses. At the time of this writing, JBossQL includes support for `ORDER BY`, `OFFSET`, and `LIMIT` clauses; parameters in the `IN` and `LIKE` operators; and `COUNT`, `MAX`, `MIN`, `AVG`, `SUM`, `UCASE`, and `LCASE` functions. Queries can also include functions in the `SELECT` clause for select methods.

JBossQL is declared in the `jbosscmp-jdbc.xml` file with a `jboss-ql` element that contains the JBossQL query. The following example provides an example of a JBossQL declaration:

```
<jbosscmp-jdbc>
    <enterprise-beans>
```

```
        <entity>
            <ejb-name>GangsterEJB</ejb-name>
            <query>
                <query-method>
                    <method-name>findBadDudes_jbossql</method-name>
                    <method-params>
                        <method-param>int</method-param>
                    </method-params>
                </query-method>
                <jboss-ql><![CDATA[
                 SELECT OBJECT(g)
                 FROM gangster g
                 WHERE g.badness > ?1
                 ORDER BY g.badness DESC
                 ]]></jboss-ql>
            </query>
        </entity>
    </enterprise-beans>
</jbosscmp-jdbc>
```

The corresponding generated SQL is straightforward:

```
SELECT t0_g.id
    FROM gangster t0_g
    WHERE t0_g.badness > ?
    ORDER BY t0_g.badness DESC
```

JBossQL also has the capability to retrieve finder results in blocks by using the `LIMIT` and `OFFSET` functions. For example, to iterate through the large number of jobs performed, you can define the following `findManyJobs_jbossql` finder:

```
<jbosscmp-jdbc>
    <enterprise-beans>
        <entity>
            <ejb-name>GangsterEJB</ejb-name>
            <query>
                <query-method>
                    <method-name>findManyJobs_jbossql</method-name>
                    <method-params>
                        <method-param>int</method-param>
                    </method-params>
                    <method-params>
                        <method-param>int</method-param>
                    </method-params>
                </query-method>
                <jboss-ql><![CDATA[
```

```
                SELECT OBJECT(j)
                FROM jobs j
                OFFSET ?1 LIMIT ?2
                ]]></jboss-ql>
            </query>
        </entity>
    </enterprise-beans>
</jbosscmp-jdbc>
```

DynamicQL

DynamicQL allows the runtime generation and execution of JBossQL queries. A DynamicQL query method is an abstract method that takes a JBossQL query and the query arguments as parameters. JBoss compiles the JBossQL and executes the generated SQL. The following generates a JBossQL query that selects all the gangsters who have a hangout in any state in the `states` set:

```
public abstract class GangsterBean
    implements EntityBean
{
    public Set ejbHomeSelectInStates(Set states)
        throws FinderException
    {
        // generate JBossQL query
        StringBuffer jbossQl = new StringBuffer();
        jbossQl.append("SELECT OBJECT(g) ");
        jbossQl.append("FROM gangster g ");
        jbossQl.append("WHERE g.hangout.state IN (");

        for (int i = 0; i < states.size(); i++) {
            if (i > 0) {
                jbossQl.append(", ");
            }

            jbossQl.append("?").append(i+1);
        }

            jbossQl.append(") ORDER BY g.name");

        // pack arguments into an Object[]
        Object[] args = states.toArray(new Object[states.size()]);

        // call dynamic-ql query
        return ejbSelectGeneric(jbossQl.toString(), args);
    }
}
```

The DynamicQL select method may have any valid select method name, but the method must always take a string and an object array as parameters. DynamicQL is declared in the `jbosscmp-jdbc.xml` file with an empty `dynamicql` element. The following is the declaration for `ejbSelectGeneric`:

```
<jbosscmp-jdbc>
    <enterprise-beans>
        <entity>
            <ejb-name>GangsterEJB</ejb-name>
            <query>
                <query-method>
                    <method-name>ejbSelectGeneric</method-name>
                    <method-params>
                        <method-param>java.lang.String</method-param>
                        <method-param>java.lang.Object[]</method-param>
                    </method-params>
                </query-method>
                <dynamic-ql/>
            </query>
        </entity>
    </enterprise-beans>
</jbosscmp-jdbc>
```

DeclaredSQL

DeclaredSQL is based on the legacy JAWS CMP 1.1 engine finder declaration, but it has been updated for CMP 2.0. Commonly this declaration is used to limit a query with a `WHERE` clause that cannot be represented in EJB-QL or JBossQL. The content model for the `declared-sql` element is shown in Figure 11.12.

Detailed descriptions of the `declared-sql` element follow:

- **`select`**—The `select` element specifies what is to be selected and consists of the following elements:
    - **`distinct`**—If this empty element is present, JBoss adds the `DISTINCT` keyword to the generated `SELECT` clause. The default is to use `DISTINCT` if the method returns a `java.util.Set`.
    - **`ejb-name`**—This is the `ejb-name` of the entity that will be selected. This is required only if the query is for a select method.
    - **`field-name`**—This is the name of the CMP field that will be selected from the specified entity. The default is to select the entire entity.
    - **`alias`**—This specifies the alias that will be used for the main select table. The default is to use the `ejb-name`.

- **additional-columns**—This declares other columns to be selected to satisfy ordering by arbitrary columns with finders or to facilitate aggregate functions in selects.
- **from**—The from element declares additional SQL to append to the generated FROM clause.
- **where**—The where element declares the WHERE clause for the query.
- **order**—The order element declares the ORDER clause for the query.
- **other**—The other element declares additional SQL that is appended to the end of the query.

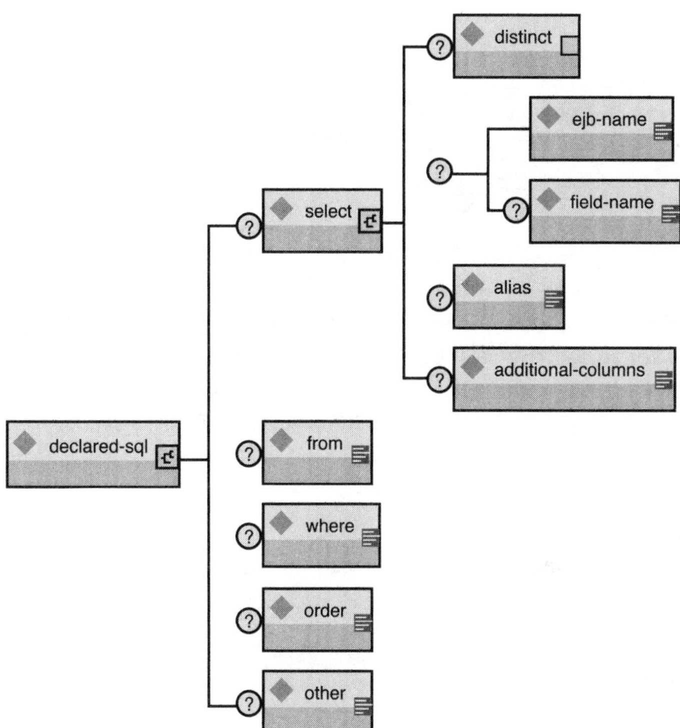

FIGURE 11.12 The jbosscmp-jdbc declared-sql element content model.

The following is an example of a DeclaredSQL declaration:

```
<jbosscmp-jdbc>
    <enterprise-beans>
        <entity>
            <ejb-name>GangsterEJB</ejb-name>
            <query>
```

```
            <query-method>
                <method-name>findBadDudes_declaredsql</method-name>
                <method-params>
                    <method-param>int</method-param>
                </method-params>
            </query-method>
            <declared-sql>
                <where><![CDATA[ badness > {0} ]]></where>
                <order><![CDATA[ badness DESC ]]></order>
            </declared-sql>
        </query>
    </entity>
  </enterprise-beans>
</jbosscmp-jdbc>
```

The generated SQL would look like this:

```
SELECT id
FROM gangster
WHERE badness > ?
ORDER BY badness DESC
```

As you can see, JBoss generates the `SELECT` and `FROM` clauses that are necessary to select the primary key for this entity. If desired, you can specify an additional `FROM` clause that is appended to the end of the automatically generated `FROM` clause. The following is an example of a DeclaredSQL declaration with an additional `FROM` clause:

```
<jbosscmp-jdbc>
    <enterprise-beans>
        <entity>
            <ejb-name>GangsterEJB</ejb-name>
            <query>
                <query-method>
                    <method-name>ejbSelectBoss_declaredsql</method-name>
                    <method-params>
                        <method-param>java.lang.String</method-param>
                    </method-params>
                </query-method>
                <declared-sql>
                    <select>
                        <distinct/>
                        <ejb-name>GangsterEJB</ejb-name>
                        <alias>boss</alias>
                    </select>
                    <from><![CDATA[, gangster g, organization o]]></from>
                    <where><![CDATA[
```

```
                    (LCASE(g.name) = {0} OR LCASE(g.nick_name) = {0}) AND
                    g.organization = o.name AND o.the_boss = boss.id
                    ]]></where>
                </declared-sql>
            </query>
        </entity>
    </enterprise-beans>
</jbosscmp-jdbc>
```

The generated SQL would look like this:

```
SELECT DISTINCT boss.id
    FROM gangster boss, gangster g, organization o
    WHERE (LCASE(g.name) = ? OR LCASE(g.nick_name) = ?) AND
          g.organization = o.name AND o.the_boss = boss.id
```

Notice that the `FROM` clause starts with a comma. This is because the container appends the declared `FROM` clause to the end of the generated `FROM` clause. It is also possible for the `FROM` clause to start with a SQL `JOIN` statement. Because this is a select method, it must have a `select` element to declare the entity that will be selected. Note that an alias is also declared for the query. If an alias is not declared, the `table-name` is used as the alias, resulting in a `SELECT` clause with the *`table_name.field_name`*-style column declarations. Not all database vendors support that syntax, so the declaration of an alias is preferred. The optional empty `distinct` element causes the `SELECT` clause to use the `SELECT DISTINCT` declaration. The DeclaredSQL declaration can also be used in select methods to select a CMP field.

The following is an example that overrides a select to return all the zip codes an organization operates in:

```
<jbosscmp-jdbc>
    <enterprise-beans>
        <entity>
            <ejb-name>OrganizationEJB</ejb-name>
            <query>
                <query-method>
                    <method-name>ejbSelectOperatingZipCodes_declaredsql
➥</method-name>
                    <method-params>
                        <method-param>java.lang.String</method-param>
                    </method-params>
                </query-method>
                <declared-sql>
                    <select>
                        <distinct/>
                        <ejb-name>LocationEJB</ejb-name>
                        <field-name>zipCode</field-name>
```

```
                    <alias>hangout</alias>
                </select>
                <from><![CDATA[ , organization o, gangster g ]]></from>
                <where><![CDATA[
                 LCASE(o.name) = {0} AND o.name = g.organization AND
                 g.hangout = hangout.id
                 ]]></where>
                <order><![CDATA[ hangout.zip ]]></order>
            </declared-sql>
        </query>
    </entity>
  </enterprise-beans>
</jbosscmp-jdbc>
```

The corresponding SQL would look like this:

```
SELECT DISTINCT hangout.zip
    FROM location hangout, organization o, gangster g
    WHERE LCASE(o.name) = ? AND o.name = g.organization AND g.hangout = hangout.id
                ORDER BY hangout.zip
```

Parameters

DeclaredSQL uses a completely new parameter-handling system, which supports entity and DVC parameters. Parameters are enclosed in curly brackets and use a zero-based index, which is different from the one-based EJB-QL parameters. There are three categories of parameters:

- **Simple**—A simple parameter can be of any type except for a known (mapped) DVC or an entity. A simple parameter contains only the argument number, such as `{0}`. When a simple parameter is set, the JDBC type used to set the parameter is determined by the `datasource-mapping` for the entity. An unknown DVC is serialized and then set as a parameter. Note that most databases do not support the use of a BLOB value in a `WHERE` clause.
- **DVC**—A DVC parameter can be any known (mapped) DVC. A DVC parameter must be dereferenced down to a simple property (that is, one that is not another DVC). For example, if you had a DVC property of type `ContactInfo`, valid parameter declarations would be `{0.email}` and `{0.cell.areaCode}` but not `{0.cell}`. The JDBC type used to set a parameter is based on the class type of the property and the `datasourcemapping` of the entity. The JDBC type used to set the parameter is the JDBC type that is declared for that property in the `dependent-value-class` element.
- **Entity**—An entity parameter can be any entity in the application. An entity parameter must be dereferenced down to a simple primary key field or simple property of a DVC primary key field. For example, if you had a parameter of type `gangster`, a valid parameter declaration would be `{0.gangsterId}`. If you had some entity with

a primary key field named info of type ContactInfo, a valid parameter declaration would be {0.info.cell.areaCode}. Only fields that are members of the primary key of the entity can be dereferenced. (This restriction may be removed in later versions.) The JDBC type used to set the parameter is the JDBC type that is declared for that field in the entity declaration.

EJB-QL 2.1 and SQL92 Queries

The default query compiler doesn't fully support EJB-QL 2.1 or the SQL92 standard. If you need either of these functions, you can replace the query compiler. The default compiler is specified in standard jbosscmp-jdbc.xml:

```
<defaults>
    ...
    <ql-compiler>org.jboss.ejb.plugins.cmp.jdbc.JDBCEJBQLCompiler</ql-compiler>
    ...
</defaults>
```

To use the SQL92 compiler, you simply specify the SQL92 compiler in the ql-compiler element:

```
<defaults>
    ...
    <ql-compiler>org.jboss.ejb.plugins.cmp.jdbc.EJBQLToSQL92Compiler</ql-compiler>
    ...
</defaults>
```

This changes the query compiler for all beans in the entire system. You can also specify the ql-compiler for each element in jbosscmp-jdbc.xml. Here is an example that uses one of the earlier queries:

```
<query>
    <query-method>
        <method-name>findBadDudes_ejbql</method-name>
        <method-params>
            lt;method-param>int</method-param>
        </method-params>
    </query-method>
    <ejb-ql><![CDATA[
        SELECT OBJECT(g)
        FROM gangster g
        WHERE g.badness > ?1]]>
    </ejb-ql>
    <ql-compiler>org.jboss.ejb.plugins.cmp.jdbc.EJBQLToSQL92Compiler</ql-compiler>
</query>
```

One important limitation of SQL92 query compiler is that it always selects all the fields of an entity, regardless of the `read-ahead` strategy in use. For example, if a query is configured with the `on-load read-ahead` strategy, the first query includes all the fields—not just primary key fields—but only the primary key fields will be read from the result set. Then, on load, other fields will actually be loaded into the read-ahead cache. The `on-find read-ahead` with the default load group `*` works as expected.

BMP Custom Finders

JBoss supports bean-managed persistence (BMP) custom finders. If a custom finder method matches a finder declared in the home or local home interface, JBoss will always call the custom finder over any other implementation declared in the `ejb-jar.xml` or `jbosscmp-jdbc.xml` files. The following simple example finds the entities by a collection of primary keys:

```
public abstract class GangsterBean
    implements EntityBean
{
    public Collection ejbFindByPrimaryKeys(Collection keys)
    {
        return keys;
    }
}
```

This is a very useful finder because it quickly converts primary keys into real `Entity` objects without contacting the database. One drawback is that it can create an `Entity` object with a primary key that does not exist in the database. If any method is invoked on the bad `Entity`, a `NoSuchEntityException` is thrown. Another drawback is that the resulting entity bean violates the EJB specification in that it implements a finder, and the JBoss EJB verifier fails the deployment of such an entity unless the `StrictVerifier` attribute is set to `false`.

Optimized Loading

The goal of optimized loading is to load the smallest amount of data required to complete a transaction in the fewest number of queries. The tuning of JBoss depends on a detailed knowledge of the loading process. The following sections describe the internals of the JBoss loading process and its configuration. Tuning of the loading process really requires a holistic understanding of the loading system, so you might need to read this chapter more than once.

A Loading Scenario

The easiest way to investigate the loading process is to look at a usage scenario. The most common scenario is to locate a collection of entities and iterate over the results, performing some operation. The following example generates an HTML table that contains all the gangsters:

```
public String createGangsterHtmlTable_none()
    throws FinderException
{
    StringBuffer table = new StringBuffer();
    table.append("<table>");

    Collection gangsters = gangsterHome.findAll_none();
    for (Iterator iter = gangsters.iterator(); iter.hasNext();) {
        Gangster gangster = (Gangster) iter.next();
        table.append("<tr>");
        table.append("<td>").append(gangster.getName());
        table.append("</td>");
        table.append("<td>").append(gangster.getNickName());
        table.append("</td>");
        table.append("<td>").append(gangster.getBadness());
        table.append("</td>");
        table.append("</tr>");
    }

    return table.toString();
}
```

Assume that this code is called within a single transaction and all optimized loading has been disabled. At the `findAll_none` call, JBoss executes the following query:

```
SELECT t0_g.id
    FROM gangster t0_g
    ORDER BY t0_g.id ASC
```

Then, as each of the eight gangsters in the sample database is accessed, JBoss executes the following eight queries:

```
SELECT name, nick_name, badness, hangout, organization
  FROM gangster WHERE (id=0)
SELECT name, nick_name, badness, hangout, organization
  FROM gangster WHERE (id=1)
SELECT name, nick_name, badness, hangout, organization
  FROM gangster WHERE (id=2)
SELECT name, nick_name, badness, hangout, organization
  FROM gangster WHERE (id=3)
SELECT name, nick_name, badness, hangout, organization
  FROM gangster WHERE (id=4)
SELECT name, nick_name, badness, hangout, organization
  FROM gangster WHERE (id=5)
SELECT name, nick_name, badness, hangout, organization
  FROM gangster WHERE (id=6)
```

```
SELECT name, nick_name, badness, hangout, organization
  FROM gangster WHERE (id=7)
```

There are two problems with this scenario. First, an excessive number of queries are executed because JBoss executes one query for the `findAll` and one query to access each element found. The reason for this behavior has to do with the handling of query results inside the JBoss container. Although it appears that the actual entity beans selected are returned when a query is executed, JBoss really only returns the primary keys of the matching entities and does not load the entity until a method is invoked on it. This is known as the *n+1* problem and is addressed with the read-ahead strategies described in the following sections.

Second, the values of unused fields are loaded needlessly. JBoss loads the `hangout` and `organization` fields, which are never accessed. (The complex `contactInfo` field is disabled for the sake of clarity.)

Table 11.1 shows the execution of the queries.

TABLE 11.1 Unoptimized Query Execution

id	name	nick_name	badness	hangout	organization
0	Yojimbo	Bodyguard	7	0	Yakuza
1	Takeshi	Master	10	1	Yakuza
2	Yuriko	Four finger	4	2	Yakuza
3	Chow	Killer	9	3	Triads
4	Shogi	Lightning	8	4	Triads
5	Valentino	Pizza-Face	4	5	Mafia
6	Toni	Toothless	2	6	Mafia
7	Corleone	Godfather	6	7	Mafia

Load Groups

The configuration and optimization of the loading system begins with the declaration of named load groups in the entity. A load group contains the names of CMP fields and CMR fields that have a foreign key (for example, `Gangster` in the `Organization-Gangster` example) that will be loaded in a single operation. An example of such a configuration is shown here:

```
<jbosscmp-jdbc>
    <enterprise-beans>
        <entity>
            <ejb-name>GangsterEJB</ejb-name>
            <!-- ... -->
            <load-groups>
                <load-group>
                    <load-group-name>basic</load-group-name>
```

```
                <field-name>name</field-name>
                <field-name>nickName</field-name>
                <field-name>badness</field-name>
            </load-group>
            <load-group>
                <load-group-name>contact info</load-group-name>
                <field-name>nickName</field-name>
                <field-name>contactInfo</field-name>
                <field-name>hangout</field-name>
            </load-group>
        </load-groups>
    </entity>
  </enterprise-beans>
</jbosscmp-jdbc>
```

In this example, two load groups are declared: `basic` and `contact info`. Note that the load groups do not need to be mutually exclusive. For example, both of the load groups contain the `nickName` field. In addition to the declared load groups, JBoss automatically adds a group named `*` (the star group) that contains every CMP field and CMR field with a foreign key in the entity.

Read-ahead

Optimized loading in JBoss is called *read-ahead*. This refers to the technique of reading the row for an entity being loaded, as well as the next several rows (hence the term *read-ahead*). JBoss implements two main strategies (`on-find` and `on-load`) to optimize the loading problem identified in the previous section. The extra data loaded during read-ahead is not immediately associated with an entity object in memory because entities are not materialized in JBoss until they are actually accessed. Instead, it is stored in the preload cache, where it remains until it is loaded into an entity or the end of the transaction occurs. The following sections describe the read-ahead strategies.

The `on-find` Strategy

The `on-find` strategy reads additional columns when the query is invoked. If the query is `on-find` optimized, JBoss executes the following query when the query is executed:

```
SELECT t0_g.id, t0_g.name, t0_g.nick_name, t0_g.badness
    FROM gangster t0_g
    ORDER BY t0_g.id ASC
```

All the required data would be in the preload cache, so no additional queries would need to be executed while iterating through the query results. This strategy is effective for queries that return a small amount of data, but it becomes very inefficient when you're trying to load a large result set into memory. Table 11.2 shows the execution of this query.

TABLE 11.2 `on-find` Optimized Query Execution

id	name	nick_name	badness	hangout	organization
0	Yojimbo	Bodyguard	7	0	Yakuza
1	Takeshi	Master	10	1	Yakuza
2	Yuriko	Four finger	4	2	Yakuza
3	Chow	Killer	9	3	Triads
4	Shogi	Lightning	8	4	Triads
5	Valentino	Pizza-Face	4	5	Mafia
6	Toni	Toothless	2	6	Mafia
7	Corleone	Godfather	6	7	Mafia

The `read-ahead` strategy and `load-group` for a query are defined in the `query` element. If a `read-ahead` strategy is not declared in the `query` element, the strategy declared in the `entity` element or `defaults` element is used. The `on-find` configuration follows:

```
<jbosscmp-jdbc>
    <enterprise-beans>
        <entity>
            <ejb-name>GangsterEJB</ejb-name>
            <!--...-->
            <query>
                <query-method>
                    <method-name>findAll_onfind</method-name>
                    <method-params/>
                </query-method>
                <jboss-ql><![CDATA[
                 SELECT OBJECT(g)
                 FROM gangster g
                 ORDER BY g.gangsterId
                 ]]></jboss-ql>
                <read-ahead>
                    <strategy>on-find</strategy>
                    <page-size>4</page-size>
                    <eager-load-group>basic</eager-load-group>
                </read-ahead>
            </query>
        </entity>
    </enterprise-beans>
</jbosscmp-jdbc>
```

One problem with the `on-find` strategy is that it must load additional data for every entity selected. Commonly in web applications, only a fixed number of results are rendered on a page. Because the preloaded data is valid only for the length of the transaction and a transaction is limited to a single web HTTP hit, most of the preloaded data is not used. The `on-load` strategy discussed in the next section does not suffer from this problem.

The `left-join read-ahead` Strategy `left-join read-ahead` is an enhanced `on-find read-ahead` strategy. It allows you to preload in one SQL query not only fields from the base instance but also related instances that can be reached from the base instance by CMR navigation. There are no limitations for the depth of CMR navigations. There are also no limitations for cardinality of CMR fields used in navigation and relationship type mapping. Both foreign key and relation table mapping styles are supported. Let's look at some examples. Entity and relationship declarations can be found in the following section.

`D#findByPrimaryKey` Suppose you have an entity `D`. A typical SQL query generated for `findByPrimaryKey` would look like this:

```
SELECT t0_D.id, t0_D.name FROM D t0_D WHERE t0_D.id=?
```

Suppose that while executing `findByPrimaryKey`, you also want to preload two collection-valued CMR fields, `bs` and `cs`:

```
<query>
    <query-method>
        <method-name>findByPrimaryKey</method-name>
        <method-params>
            <method-param>java.lang.Long</method-param>
        </method-params>
    </query-method>
    <jboss-ql><![CDATA[SELECT OBJECT(o) FROM D AS o WHERE o.id = ?1]]></jboss-ql>
    <read-ahead>
        <strategy>on-find</strategy>
        <page-size>4</page-size>
        <eager-load-group>basic</eager-load-group>
        <left-join cmr-field="bs" eager-load-group="basic"/>
        <left-join cmr-field="cs" eager-load-group="basic"/>
    </read-ahead>
</query>
```

The `left-join` declares the relations to be eager loaded. The generated SQL would look like this:

```
SELECT t0_D.id, t0_D.name,
       t1_D_bs.id, t1_D_bs.name,
       t2_D_cs.id, t2_D_cs.name
  FROM D t0_D
       LEFT OUTER JOIN B t1_D_bs ON t0_D.id=t1_D_bs.D_FK
       LEFT OUTER JOIN C t2_D_cs ON t0_D.id=t2_D_cs.D_FK
 WHERE t0_D.id=?
```

For the D with the specific ID, you preload all its related Bs and Cs and can access those instances by loading them from the read-ahead cache, not from the database.

D#findAll In the same way, you could optimize the findAll method on D selects of all the Ds. A normal findAll query would look like this:

```
SELECT DISTINCT t0_o.id, t0_o.name FROM D t0_o ORDER BY t0_o.id DESC
```

To preload the relations, you simply need to add the left-join elements to the query:

```
<query>
    <query-method>
        <method-name>findAll</method-name>
    </query-method>
    <jboss-ql><![CDATA[SELECT DISTINCT OBJECT(o) FROM D AS o ORDER BY o.id DESC]]>
➥</jboss-ql>
    <read-ahead>
        <strategy>on-find</strategy>
        <page-size>4</page-size>
        <eager-load-group>basic</eager-load-group>
        <left-join cmr-field="bs" eager-load-group="basic"/>
        <left-join cmr-field="cs" eager-load-group="basic"/>
    </read-ahead>
</query>
```

Here is the generated SQL:

```
SELECT DISTINCT t0_o.id, t0_o.name,
                t1_o_bs.id, t1_o_bs.name,
                t2_o_cs.id, t2_o_cs.name
  FROM D t0_o
       LEFT OUTER JOIN B t1_o_bs ON t0_o.id=t1_o_bs.D_FK
       LEFT OUTER JOIN C t2_o_cs ON t0_o.id=t2_o_cs.D_FK
 ORDER BY t0_o.id DESC
```

Now the simple findAll query preloads the related B and C objects for each D object.

A#findAll Now let's look at a more complex configuration. In this case, you want to preload instance A along with several relations:

- Its parent (self-relation) reached from A with CMR field parent
- B reached from A with CMR field b, and the related C reached from B with CMR field c
- B reached from A but this time with CMR field b2 and related to it C reached from B with CMR field c

For reference, this would be the standard query:

```
SELECT t0_o.id, t0_o.name FROM A t0_o ORDER BY t0_o.id DESC FOR UPDATE
```

The following metadata describes the preloading plan:

```
<query>
    <query-method>
        <method-name>findAll</method-name>
    </query-method>
    <jboss-ql><![CDATA[SELECT OBJECT(o) FROM A AS o ORDER BY o.id DESC]]>
➥</jboss-ql>
    <read-ahead>
        <strategy>on-find</strategy>
        <page-size>4</page-size>
        <eager-load-group>basic</eager-load-group>
        <left-join cmr-field="parent" eager-load-group="basic"/>
        <left-join cmr-field="b" eager-load-group="basic">
            <left-join cmr-field="c" eager-load-group="basic"/>
        </left-join>
        <left-join cmr-field="b2" eager-load-group="basic">
            <left-join cmr-field="c" eager-load-group="basic"/>
        </left-join>
    </read-ahead>
</query>
```

The SQL query generated would look like this:

```
SELECT t0_o.id, t0_o.name,
       t1_o_parent.id, t1_o_parent.name,
       t2_o_b.id, t2_o_b.name,
       t3_o_b_c.id, t3_o_b_c.name,
       t4_o_b2.id, t4_o_b2.name,
       t5_o_b2_c.id, t5_o_b2_c.name
  FROM A t0_o
       LEFT OUTER JOIN A t1_o_parent ON t0_o.PARENT=t1_o_parent.id
       LEFT OUTER JOIN B t2_o_b ON t0_o.B_FK=t2_o_b.id
       LEFT OUTER JOIN C t3_o_b_c ON t2_o_b.C_FK=t3_o_b_c.id
       LEFT OUTER JOIN B t4_o_b2 ON t0_o.B2_FK=t4_o_b2.id
       LEFT OUTER JOIN C t5_o_b2_c ON t4_o_b2.C_FK=t5_o_b2_c.id
 ORDER BY t0_o.id DESC FOR UPDATE
```

With this configuration, you can navigate CMRs from any found instance of `A` without an additional database load.

`A#findMeParentGrandParent` Let's look at another example of self-relation. Suppose you want to write a method that would preload an instance, its parent, its grandparent, and its grand-grandparent in one query. To do this, you would use a nested `left-join` declaration:

```
<query>
    <query-method>
        <method-name>findMeParentGrandParent</method-name>
        <method-params>
            <method-param>java.lang.Long</method-param>
        </method-params>
    </query-method>
    <jboss-ql><![CDATA[SELECT OBJECT(o) FROM A AS o WHERE o.id = ?1]]></jboss-ql>
    <read-ahead>
        <strategy>on-find</strategy>
        <page-size>4</page-size>
        <eager-load-group>*</eager-load-group>
        <left-join cmr-field="parent" eager-load-group="basic">
            <left-join cmr-field="parent" eager-load-group="basic">
                <left-join cmr-field="parent" eager-load-group="basic"/>
            </left-join>
        </left-join>
    </read-ahead>
</query>
```

The generated SQL would look like this:

```
SELECT t0_o.id, t0_o.name, t0_o.secondName, t0_o.B_FK, t0_o.B2_FK, t0_o.PARENT,
       t1_o_parent.id, t1_o_parent.name,
       t2_o_parent_parent.id, t2_o_parent_parent.name,
       t3_o_parent_parent_parent.id, t3_o_parent_parent_parent.name
  FROM A t0_o
       LEFT OUTER JOIN A t1_o_parent ON t0_o.PARENT=t1_o_parent.id
       LEFT OUTER JOIN A t2_o_parent_parent ON t1_o_parent.PARENT=
➥t2_o_parent_parent.id
       LEFT OUTER JOIN A t3_o_parent_parent_parent ON t2_o_parent_parent.PARENT=
➥t3_o_parent_parent_parent.id
 WHERE (t0_o.id = ?) FOR UPDATE
```

Note that if you remove the `left-join` metadata, we will have only this:

```
SELECT t0_o.id, t0_o.name, t0_o.secondName, t0_o.B2_FK, t0_o.PARENT FOR UPDATE
```

The `on-load` Strategy

The `on-load` strategy block-loads additional data for several entities when an entity is loaded, starting with the requested entity and the next several entities, in the order in which they were selected. This strategy is based on the theory that the results of a find or select will be accessed in forward order. When a query is executed, JBoss stores the order of the entities found in the list cache. Later, when one of the entities is loaded, JBoss uses this list to determine the block of entities to load. The number of lists stored in the cache is specified with the `list-cachemax` element of the entity. This strategy is also used when faulting in data not loaded in the `on-find` strategy.

As with the `on-find` strategy, you declare `on-load` in the `read-ahead` element. The `on-load` configuration for this example is as follows:

```
<jbosscmp-jdbc>
  <enterprise-beans>
    <entity>
      <ejb-name>GangsterEJB</ejb-name>
      <!-- ... -->
      <query>
        <query-method>
          <method-name>findAll_onload</method-name>
          <method-params/>
        </query-method>
        <jboss-ql><![CDATA[
             SELECT OBJECT(g)
             FROM gangster g
             ORDER BY g.gangsterId
             ]]></jboss-ql>
        <read-ahead>
          <strategy>on-load</strategy>
          <page-size>4</page-size>
          <eager-load-group>basic</eager-load-group>
        </read-ahead>
      </query>
    </entity>
  </enterprise-beans>
</jbosscmp-jdbc>
```

With this strategy, the query for the finder method remains unchanged:

```
SELECT t0_g.id
    FROM gangster t0_g
    ORDER BY t0_g.id ASC
```

However, the data will be loaded differently as you iterate through the result set. For a page size of four, JBoss will need to execute only the following two queries to load the `name`, `nickName`, and `badness` fields for the entities:

```
SELECT id, name, nick_name, badness
    FROM gangster
    WHERE (id=0) OR (id=1) OR (id=2) OR (id=3)
SELECT id, name, nick_name, badness
```

```
FROM gangster
WHERE (id=4) OR (id=5) OR (id=6) OR (id=7)
```

Table 11.3 shows the execution of these queries.

TABLE 11.3 `on-load` Optimized Query Execution

id	name	nick_name	badness	hangout	organization
0	Yojimbo	Bodyguard	7	0	Yakuza
1	Takeshi	Master	10	1	Yakuza
2	Yuriko	Four finger	4	2	Yakuza
3	Chow	Killer	9	3	Triads
4	Shogi	Lightning	8	4	Triads
5	Valentino	Pizza-Face	4	5	Mafia
6	Toni	Toothless	2	6	Mafia
7	Corleone	Godfather	6	7	Mafia

The `none` Strategy The `none` strategy is really an anti-strategy. This strategy causes the system to fall back to the default lazy-load code, and it specifically does not read ahead any data or remember the order of the found entities. This results in the queries and performance shown at the beginning of this chapter. You declare the `none` strategy with a `read-ahead` element. If the `read-ahead` element contains a `page-size` element or `eager-load-group`, it is ignored. The `none` strategy is declared in the following example:

```
<jbosscmp-jdbc>
    <enterprise-beans>
        <entity>
            <ejb-name>GangsterEJB</ejb-name>
            <!-- ... -->
            <query>
                <query-method>
                    <method-name>findAll_none</method-name>
                    <method-params/>
                </query-method>
                <jboss-ql><![CDATA[
                 SELECT OBJECT(g)
                 FROM gangster g
                 ORDER BY g.gangsterId
                 ]]></jboss-ql>
                <read-ahead>
                    <strategy>none</strategy>
                </read-ahead>
            </query>
        </entity>
    </enterprise-beans>
</jbosscmp-jdbc>
```

The Loading Process

In the previous sections, several times we use the phrase "when an entity is loaded." This is intentionally left vague because the commit option specified for the entity and the current state of the transaction determine when an entity is loaded. The following sections describe the commit options and the loading processes.

Commit Options

Central to the loading process are the commit options, which control when the cached data for an entity expires. JBoss supports four commit options: `A`, `B`, `C`, and `D`. The first three are described in the Enterprise JavaBeans specification, but the last one is specific to JBoss. Detailed descriptions of the `commit` options follow:

- `A`—JBoss assumes that it is the sole user of the database; therefore, JBoss can cache the current value of an entity between transactions, which can result is substantial performance gains. As a result of this assumption, no data managed by JBoss can be changed outside JBoss. For example, changing data in another program or with the use of direct JDBC (even within JBoss) result in an inconsistent database state.
- `B`—JBoss assumes that there is more than one user of the database but keeps the context information about entities between transactions. This context information is used for optimizing loading of the entity. This is the default commit option.
- `C`—JBoss discards all entity context information at the end of the transaction.
- `D`—This is a JBoss-specific commit option. This option is similar to commit option `A`, except that the data remains valid for only a specified amount of time.

The commit option is declared in the `jboss.xml` file. For a detailed description of this file, see Chapter 5, "EJBs on JBoss." The example shown in Listing 11.2 changes the commit option to `A` for all entity beans in the application.

LISTING 11.2 The `jboss.xml` Commit Option Declaration

```
<jboss>
    <container-configurations>
        <container-configuration>
            <container-name>Standard CMP 2.x EntityBean</container-name>
            <commit-option>A</commit-option>
        </container-configuration>
    </container-configurations>
</jboss>
```

The Eager-Loading Process

When an entity is loaded, JBoss must determine what fields need to be loaded. By default, JBoss uses the `eager-load-group` of the last query that selected this entity. If the entity has not been selected in a query, or if the last query uses the `none` `read-ahead` strategy, JBoss uses the default `eager-load-group` declared for the entity. In the following configuration example, the basic load group is set as the default `eager-load-group` for the `gangster` entity bean:

```
<jbosscmp-jdbc>
    <enterprise-beans>
        <entity>
            <ejb-name>GangsterEJB</ejb-name>
            <!-- ... -->
            <load-groups>
                <load-group>
                    <load-group-name>most</load-group-name>
                    <field-name>name</field-name>
                    <field-name>nickName</field-name>
                    <field-name>badness</field-name>
                    <field-name>hangout</field-name>
                    <field-name>organization</field-name>
                </load-group>
            </load-groups>
            <eager-load-group>most</eager-load-group>
        </entity>
    </enterprise-beans>
</jbosscmp-jdbc>
```

The eager-loading process is initiated the first time a method is called on an entity in a transaction. The load process is as follows:

1. If the entity context is still valid, no loading is necessary, and therefore the loading process is done. The entity context is valid when you use commit option `A` or commit option `D` and the data has not timed out.

2. Any residual data in the entity context is flushed. This ensures that old data does not bleed into the new load.

3. The primary key value is injected back into the primary key fields. The primary key object is actually independent of the fields and needs to be reloaded after the flush in step 2.

4. All data in the preload cache for this entity is loaded into the fields.

5. JBoss determines what additional fields still need to be loaded. Normally, the fields to load are determined by the eager-load group of the entity, but this can be overridden if the entity is located by using a query or CMR field with an `on-find` or `on-load` `read-ahead` strategy. If all the fields have already been loaded, the load process skips to step 7.

6. A query is executed to select the necessary column. If this entity uses the `on-load` strategy, a page of data is loaded, as described in the section "The `on-load` Strategy,"

earlier in this chapter. The data for the current entity is stored in the context, and the data for the other entities is stored in the preload cache.

7. The `ejbLoad` method of the entity is called.

The Lazy-Loading Process

Lazy loading is the other half of eager loading. If a field is not eager loaded, it must be lazy loaded. When an access to an unloaded field of a bean is made, JBoss loads the field and all the fields of any `lazy-load-group` the field belong to. JBoss performs a set join and then removes any field that is already loaded. A configuration example is shown here:

```
<jbosscmp-jdbc>
    <enterprise-beans>
        <entity>
            <ejb-name>GangsterEJB</ejb-name>
            <!-- ... -->
            <load-groups>
                <load-group>
                    <load-group-name>most</load-group-name>
                    <field-name>name</field-name>
                    <field-name>nickName</field-name>
                    <field-name>badness</field-name>
                    <field-name>hangout</field-name>
                    <field-name>organization</field-name>
                </load-group>
            </load-groups>
            <eager-load-group>most</eager-load-group>
        </entity>
    </enterprise-beans>
</jbosscmp-jdbc>
```

When the bean provider calls `getName()` with this configuration, JBoss loads `name`, `nickName`, and `badness`, assuming that they are not already loaded. When the bean provider calls `getNickName()`, the `name`, `nickName`, `badness`, `contactInfo`, and `hangout` are loaded. The lazy-loading process is as follows:

1. All data in the preload cache for this entity is loaded into the fields.

2. If the field value was loaded by the preload cache, the lazy-load process is finished.

3. JBoss finds all the lazy-load groups that contain this field, performs a set join on the groups, and removes any field that has already been loaded.

4. A query is executed to select the necessary columns. As in the basic load process, JBoss may load a block of entities. The data for the current entity is stored in the context, and the data for the other entities is stored in the preload cache.

Relationships

Relationships are a special case in lazy loading because a CMR field is both a field and a query. As a field, it can be `on-load` block loaded, meaning that the value of the currently sought entity and the values of the CMR field for the next several entities are loaded. As a query, the field values of the related entity can be preloaded by using `on-find`.

Again, the easiest way to investigate the loading is to look at a usage scenario. Listing 11.3 generates an HTML table that contains each gangster and his hangout.

LISTING 11.3 Relationship Lazy-Loading Sample Code

```
public String createGangsterHangoutHtmlTable()
    throws FinderException
{
    StringBuffer table = new StringBuffer();
    table.append("<table>");
    Collection gangsters = gangsterHome.findAll_onfind();
    for (Iterator iter = gangsters.iterator(); iter.hasNext(); ) {
        Gangster gangster = (Gangster)iter.next();

        Location hangout = gangster.getHangout();
        table.append("<tr>");
        table.append("<td>").append(gangster.getName());
        table.append("</td>");
        table.append("<td>").append(gangster.getNickName());
        table.append("</td>");
        table.append("<td>").append(gangster.getBadness());
        table.append("</td>");
        table.append("<td>").append(hangout.getCity());
        table.append("</td>");
        table.append("<td>").append(hangout.getState());
        table.append("</td>");
        table.append("<td>").append(hangout.getZipCode());
        table.append("</td>");
        table.append("</tr>");
    }

    table.append("</table>");return table.toString();
}
```

For this example, the configuration of the gangster's `findAll_onfind` query is unchanged from what is described earlier in this chapter. The configuration of the `Location` entity and `Gangster-Hangout` relationship is shown in Listing 11.4.

LISTING 11.4 The `jbosscmp-jdbc.xml` Relationship Lazy-Loading Configuration

```
<jbosscmp-jdbc>
    <enterprise-beans>
        <entity>
            <ejb-name>LocationEJB</ejb-name>
            <load-groups>
                <load-group>
                    <load-group-name>quick info</load-group-name>
                    <field-name>city</field-name>
                    <field-name>state</field-name>
                    <field-name>zipCode</field-name>
                </load-group>
            </load-groups>
            <eager-load-group/>
        </entity>
    </enterprise-beans>
    <relationships>
        <ejb-relation>
            <ejb-relation-name>Gangster-Hangout</ejb-relation-name>
            <foreign-key-mapping/>
            <ejb-relationship-role>
                <ejb-relationship-role-name>
                    gangster-has-a-hangout
                </ejb-relationship-role-name>
                <key-fields/>
                <read-ahead>
                    <strategy>on-find</strategy>
                    <page-size>4</page-size>
                    <eager-load-group>quick info</eager-load-group>
                </read-ahead>
            </ejb-relationship-role>
            <ejb-relationship-role>
                <ejb-relationship-role-name>
                    hangout-for-a-gangster
                </ejb-relationship-role-name>
                <key-fields>
                    <key-field>
                        <field-name>locationID</field-name>
                        <column-name>hangout</column-name>
                    </key-field>
                </key-filaelds>
            </ejb-relationship-role>
        </ejb-relation>
    </relationships>
</jbosscmp-jdbc>
```

JBoss executes the following query for the finder:

```
SELECT t0_g.id, t0_g.name, t0_g.nick_name, t0_g.badness
    FROM gangster t0_g
    ORDER BY t0_g.id ASC
```

Then when the hangout is accessed, JBoss executes the following two queries to load the city, state, and zip fields of the hangout:

```
SELECT gangster.id, gangster.hangout,
       location.city, location.st, location.zip
    FROM gangster, location
    WHERE (gangster.hangout=location.id) AND
          ((gangster.id=0) OR (gangster.id=1) OR
          (gangster.id=2) OR (gangster.id=3))
SELECT gangster.id, gangster.hangout,
       location.city, location.st, location.zip
    FROM gangster, location
    WHERE (gangster.hangout=location.id) AND
          ((gangster.id=4) OR (gangster.id=5) OR
          (gangster.id=6) OR (gangster.id=7))
```

Table 11.4 shows the execution of the queries.

TABLE 11.4 `on-find` Optimized Relationship Query Execution

id	name	nick_name	badness	hangout	id	city	st	zip
0	Yojimbo	Bodyguard	7	0	0	San Fran	CA	94108
1	Takeshi	Master	10	1	1	San Fran	CA	94133
2	Yuriko	Four finger	4	2	2	San Fran	CA	94133
3	Chow	Killer	9	3	3	San Fran	CA	94133
4	Shogi	Lightning	8	4	4	San Fran	CA	94133
5	Valentino	Pizza-Face	4	5	5	New York	NY	10017
6	Toni	Toothless	2	6	6	Chicago	IL	60661
7	Corleone	Godfather	6	7	7	Las Vegas	NV	89109

Lazy-Loading Result Sets

By default, when a multi-object finder or select method is executed, the JDBC result set is read to the end immediately. The client receives a collection of `EJBLocalObject` or CMP field values that it can then iterate through. For big result sets, this approach is not efficient. In some cases, it is better to delay reading the next row in the result set until the client tries to read the corresponding value from the collection. You can get this behavior for a query by using the `lazy-resultset-loading` element:

```
<query>
    <query-method>
```

```
        <method-name>findAll</method-name>
    </query-method>
    <jboss-ql><![CDATA[select object(o) from A o]]></jboss-ql>
    <lazy-resultset-loading>true</lazy-resultset-loading>
</query>
```

There are some issues you should be aware of when using lazy result set loading. You need to take special care when working with a `Collection` associated with a lazily loaded result set. The first call to `iterator()` returns a special `Iterator` that reads from the `ResultSet`. Until this `Iterator` has been exhausted, subsequent calls to `iterator()` or calls to the `add()` method result in an exception. The `remove()` and `size()` methods work as you would expected.

Transactions

All the examples presented in this chapter so far have been defined to run in a transaction. Transaction granularity is a dominating factor in optimized loading because transactions define the lifetime of preloaded data. If a transaction completes, commits, or rolls back, the data in the preload cache is lost. This can result in a severe negative performance impact.

Let's examine the performance impact of running without a transaction by looking at an example that uses an `on-find` optimized query that selects the first four gangsters (to keep the result set small) and is executed without a wrapper transaction. The sample code follows:

```
public String createGangsterHtmlTable_no_tx() throws FinderException
{
    StringBuffer table = new StringBuffer();
    table.append("<table>");

    Collection gangsters = gangsterHome.findFour();
    for(Iterator iter = gangsters.iterator(); iter.hasNext(); ) {
        Gangster gangster = (Gangster)iter.next();
        table.append("<tr>");
        table.append("<td>").append(gangster.getName());
        table.append("</td>");
        table.append("<td>").append(gangster.getNickName());
        table.append("</td>");
        table.append("<td>").append(gangster.getBadness());
        table.append("</td>");
        table.append("</tr>");
    }

    table.append("</table>");
    return table.toString();
}
```

The finder results in the following query being executed:

```
SELECT t0_g.id, t0_g.name, t0_g.nick_name, t0_g.badness
  FROM gangster t0_g
  WHERE t0_g.id < 4
  ORDER BY t0_g.id ASC
```

Normally, this would be the only query executed, but because this code is not running in a transaction, all the preloaded data is thrown away as soon as the finder returns. Then when the CMP field is accessed, JBoss executes the following four queries (one for each loop):

```
SELECT id, name, nick_name, badness
  FROM gangster
  WHERE (id=0) OR (id=1) OR (id=2) OR (id=3)
SELECT id, name, nick_name, badness
  FROM gangster
  WHERE (id=1) OR (id=2) OR (id=3)
SELECT id, name, nick_name, badness
  FROM gangster
  WHERE (id=2) OR (id=3)
SELECT name, nick_name, badness
  FROM gangster
  WHERE (id=3)
```

It's actually worse than this. JBoss executes each of these queries three times, once for each CMP field that is accessed. This is because the preloaded values are discarded between the CMP field accessor calls. Figure 11.13 shows the execution of the queries.

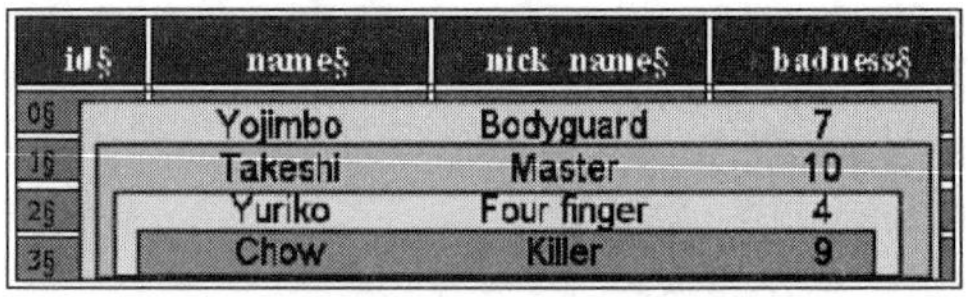

id	name	nick name	badness
0	Yojimbo	Bodyguard	7
1	Takeshi	Master	10
2	Yuriko	Four finger	4
3	Chow	Killer	9

FIGURE 11.13 No transaction `on-find` optimized query execution.

This performance is much worse than that of `read-ahead none` because of the amount of data loaded from the database. The number of rows loaded is determined by the following equation:

$$n + n - 1 + n - 2 + \ldots + 1 + = \frac{n \bullet (n + 1)}{2} = O(n^2)$$

This all happens because the transaction in the example is bounded by a single call on the entity. This brings up the important question "How do I run my code in a transaction?" The answer depends on where the code runs. If it runs in an EJB (session, entity, or message driven), the method must be marked with the `Required` or `RequiresNew` `trans-attribute` in the `assembly-descriptor`. If the code is not running in an EJB, a user transaction is necessary. The following code wraps a call to the declared method with a user transaction:

```
public String createGangsterHtmlTable_with_tx()
    throws FinderException
{
    UserTransaction tx = null;
    try {
        InitialContext ctx = new InitialContext();
        tx = (UserTransaction) ctx.lookup("UserTransaction");
        tx.begin();

        String table = createGangsterHtmlTable_no_tx();

        if (tx.getStatus() == Status.STATUS_ACTIVE) {
                tx.commit();
        }
            return table;
    } catch (Exception e) {
        try {
            if (tx != null) tx.rollback();
        } catch (SystemException unused) {
            // eat the exception we are exceptioning out anyway
        }
        if (e instanceof FinderException) {
                throw (FinderException) e;
        }
        if (e instanceof RuntimeException) {
                throw (RuntimeException) e;
        }

        throw new EJBException(e);
    }
}
```

Optimistic Locking

JBoss supports optimistic locking of entity beans. *Optimistic locking* allows multiple instances of the same entity bean to be active simultaneously. Consistency is enforced based on the optimistic locking policy choice. The optimistic locking policy choice defines the set of fields that are used in the commit time write of modified data to the database. The optimistic consistency check asserts that the values of the chosen set of fields have the same values in the database as existed when the current transaction was started. You ensure this by using a `select` for `UPDATE WHERE...` statement that contains the value assertions.

You specify the optimistic locking policy choice by using an `optimistic-locking` element in the `jbosscmp-jdbc.xml` descriptor. The content model of the `optimistic-locking` element is shown in Figure 11.14, and the description of the elements follows:

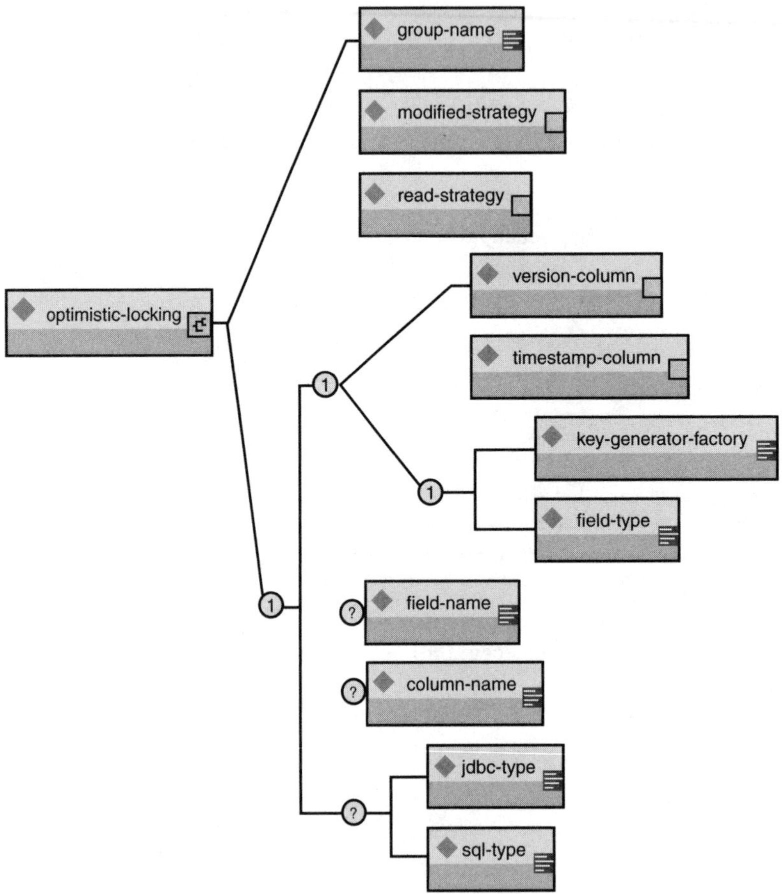

FIGURE 11.14 The `jbosscmp-jdbc` `optimistic-locking` element content model.

- **`group-name`**—This element specifies that optimistic locking is based on the fields of a `load-group`. The value of this element must match one of the entity's `load-group-name` elements. The fields in this group will be used for optimistic locking.
- **`modified-strategy`**—This element specifies that optimistic locking is based on the modified fields. This strategy implies that the fields that were modified during transaction will be used for optimistic locking.

- **`read-strategy`**—This element specifies that optimistic locking is based on the fields read. This strategy implies that the fields that were read/changed in the transaction will be used for optimistic locking.
- **`version-column`**—This element specifies that optimistic locking is based on a version column strategy. Specifying this element adds an additional version field of type `java.lang.Long` to the entity bean for optimistic locking. Each update of the entity increases the value of this field. The `field-name` element allows for the specification of the name of the CMP field, and the `column-name` element allows for the specification of the corresponding table column.
- **`timestamp-column`**—This element specifies that optimistic locking is based on a timestamp column strategy. Specifying this element adds an additional version field of type `java.util.Date` to the entity bean for optimistic locking. Each update of the entity sets the value of this field to the current time. The `field-name` element allows for the specification of the name of the CMP field, and the `column-name` element allows for the specification of the corresponding table column.
- **`key-generator-factory`**—This element specifies that optimistic locking is based on key generation. The value of the element is the JNDI name of an `org.jboss.ejb.plugins.keygenerator.KeyGeneratorFactory` implementation. Specifying this element adds an additional version field to the entity bean for optimistic locking. The type of the field must be specified via the `field-type` element. Each update of the entity updates the key field by obtaining a new value from the key generator. The `field-name` element allows for the specification of the name of the CMP field, and the `column-name` element allows for the specification of the corresponding table column.

A sample `jbosscmp-jdbc.xml` descriptor that illustrates all the optimistic locking strategies is shown here:

```
<!DOCTYPE jbosscmp-jdbc PUBLIC
    "-//JBoss//DTD JBOSSCMP-JDBC 3.2//EN"
    "http://www.jboss.org/j2ee/dtd/jbosscmp-jdbc_3_2.dtd">
<jbosscmp-jdbc>
    <defaults>
        <datasource>java:/DefaultDS</datasource>
        <datasource-mapping>Hypersonic SQL</datasource-mapping>
    </defaults>
    <enterprise-beans>
        <entity>
            <ejb-name>EntityGroupLocking</ejb-name>
            <create-table>true</create-table>
            <remove-table>true</remove-table>
            <table-name>entitygrouplocking</table-name>
            <cmp-field>
                <field-name>dateField</field-name>
```

```
        </cmp-field>
        <cmp-field>
            <field-name>integerField</field-name>
        </cmp-field>
        <cmp-field>
            <field-name>stringField</field-name>
        </cmp-field>
        <load-groups>
            <load-group>
                <load-group-name>string</load-group-name>
                <field-name>stringField</field-name>
            </load-group>
            <load-group>
                <load-group-name>all</load-group-name>
                <field-name>stringField</field-name>
                <field-name>dateField</field-name>
            </load-group>
        </load-groups>
        <optimistic-locking>
            <group-name>string</group-name>
        </optimistic-locking>
    </entity>
    <entity>
        <ejb-name>EntityModifiedLocking</ejb-name>
        <create-table>true</create-table>
        <remove-table>true</remove-table>
        <table-name>entitymodifiedlocking</table-name>
        <cmp-field>
            <field-name>dateField</field-name>
        </cmp-field>
        <cmp-field>
            <field-name>integerField</field-name>
        </cmp-field>
        <cmp-field>
            <field-name>stringField</field-name>
        </cmp-field>
        <optimistic-locking>
            <modified-strategy/>
        </optimistic-locking>
    </entity>
    <entity>
        <ejb-name>EntityReadLocking</ejb-name>
        <create-table>true</create-table>
        <remove-table>true</remove-table>
        <table-name>entityreadlocking</table-name>
```

```
        <cmp-field>
            <field-name>dateField</field-name>
        </cmp-field>
        <cmp-field>
            <field-name>integerField</field-name>
        </cmp-field>
        <cmp-field>
            <field-name>stringField</field-name>
        </cmp-field>
        <optimistic-locking>
            <read-strategy/>
        </optimistic-locking>
    </entity>
    <entity>
        <ejb-name>EntityVersionLocking</ejb-name>
        <create-table>true</create-table>
        <remove-table>true</remove-table>
        <table-name>entityversionlocking</table-name>
        <cmp-field>
            <field-name>dateField</field-name>
        </cmp-field>
        <cmp-field>
            <field-name>integerField</field-name>
        </cmp-field>
        <cmp-field>
            <field-name>stringField</field-name>
        </cmp-field>
        <optimistic-locking>
            <version-column/>
            <field-name>versionField</field-name>
            <column-name>ol_version</column-name>
            <jdbc-type>INTEGER</jdbc-type>
            <sql-type>INTEGER(5)</sql-type>
        </optimistic-locking>
    </entity>
    <entity>
        <ejb-name>EntityTimestampLocking</ejb-name>
        <create-table>true</create-table>
        <remove-table>true</remove-table>
        <table-name>entitytimestamplocking</table-name>
        <cmp-field>
            <field-name>dateField</field-name>
        </cmp-field>
        <cmp-field>
            <field-name>integerField</field-name>
```

```
            </cmp-field>
            <cmp-field>
                <field-name>stringField</field-name>
            </cmp-field>
            <optimistic-locking>
                <timestamp-column/>
                <field-name>versionField</field-name>
                <column-name>ol_timestamp</column-name>
                <jdbc-type>TIMESTAMP</jdbc-type>
                <sql-type>DATETIME</sql-type>
            </optimistic-locking>
        </entity>
        <entity>
            <ejb-name>EntityKeyGeneratorLocking</ejb-name>
            <create-table>true</create-table>
            <remove-table>true</remove-table>
            <table-name>entitykeygenlocking</table-name>
            <cmp-field>
                <field-name>dateField</field-name>
            </cmp-field>
            <cmp-field>
                <field-name>integerField</field-name>
            </cmp-field>
            <cmp-field>
                <field-name>stringField</field-name>
            </cmp-field>
            <optimistic-locking>
                <key-generator-factory>UUIDKeyGeneratorFactory
➥</key-generator-factory>
                <field-type>java.lang.String</field-type>
                <field-name>uuidField</field-name>
                <column-name>ol_uuid</column-name>
                <jdbc-type>VARCHAR</jdbc-type>
                <sql-type>VARCHAR(32)</sql-type>
            </optimistic-locking>
        </entity>
    </enterprise-beans>
</jbosscmp-jdbc>
```

Entity Commands and Primary Key Generation

Support for primary key generation outside the entity bean is available through custom implementations of the entity creation command objects used to insert entities into a persistent store. You specify the list of available commands in the `entity-commands` element of the `jbosscmp-jdbc.xml` descriptor. You specify the default `entity-command` in the jbosscmp-jdbc.xml in the defaults element. You can have each entity element override the entity-command in defaults by specifying its own entity-command. The content model of the entity-commands and child elements is shown in Figure 11.15.

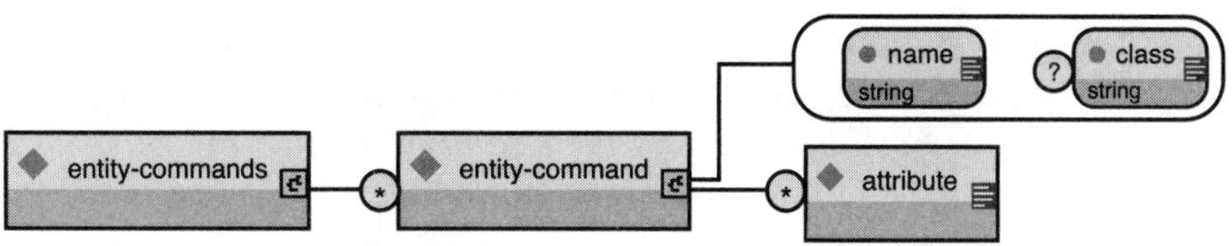

FIGURE 11.15 The jbosscmp-jdbc.xml entity-commands element model.

Each entity-command element specifies an entity-generation implementation. The name attribute specifies a name that allows the command defined in an entity-commands section to be referenced in the defaults and entity elements. The class attribute specifies the implementation of the org.jboss.ejb.plugins.cmp.jdbc.
➥JDBCCreateEntityCommand that supports the key generation. Database-vendor-specific commands typically subclass org.jboss.ejb.plugins.cmp.jdbc.
➥JDBCIdentityColumnCreateCommand if the database generates the primary key as a side effect of doing an insertion, or they subclass org.jboss.ejb.plugins.cmp.jdbc.
➥JDBCInsertPKCreateCommand if the command must insert the generated key.

The optional attribute element(s) allows for the specification of arbitrary name/value property pairs that will be available to the entity command implementation class. The attribute element has a required name attribute that specifies the name property, and the attribute element content is the value of the property. The attribute values are accessible through the org.jboss.ejb.plugins.cmp.jdbc.metadata.
➥JDBCEntityCommandMetaData.getAttribute(String) method.

Existing Entity Commands

The following are the current entity-command definitions found in the standardjbosscmp-jdbc.xml descriptor:

- **default (org.jboss.ejb.plugins.cmp.jdbc.JDBCCreateEntityCommand)**—JDBCCreateEntityCommand is the default entity creation because it is the entity-command referenced in the standardjbosscmp-jdbc.xml default element. This entity-command executes an INSERT INTO query, using the assigned primary key value.

- **no-select-before-insert (org.jboss.ejb.plugins.cmp.jdbc.JDBCCreateEntityCommand)**—This is a variation on default that skips selecting before insert by specifying the attribute name="SQLExceptionProcessor", which points to the jboss.jdbc:service=SQLExceptionProcessor service. The SQLExceptionProcessor service provides a Boolean isDuplicateKey(SQLException e) operation that allows for determining whether there is any unique constraint violation.

- **pk-sql (org.jboss.ejb.plugins.cmp.jdbc.JDBCPkSqlCreateCommand)**—`JDBCPkSqlCreateCommand` executes an `INSERT INTO` query statement that is provided by the `pk-sql` attribute to obtain the next primary key value. Its primary target usage is for databases with sequence support.

- **mysql-get-generated-keys (org.jboss.ejb.plugins.cmp.jdbc.mysql.JDBCMySQLCreateCommand)**—`JDBCMySQLCreateCommand` executes an `INSERT INTO` query by using the `getGeneratedKeys` method from the MySQL native `java.sql.Statement` interface implementation to fetch the generated key.

- **oracle-sequence (org.jboss.ejb.plugins.cmp.jdbc.keygen.JDBCOracleCreateCommand)**—`JDBCOracleCreateCommand` is a create command for use with Oracle that uses a sequence in conjunction with a `RETURNING` clause to generate keys in a single statement. It has a required sequence element that specifies the name of the sequence column.

- **hsqldb-fetch-key (org.jboss.ejb.plugins.cmp.jdbc.hsqldb.JDBCHsqldbCreateCommand)**—`JDBCHsqldbCreateCommand` executes an `INSERT INTO` query after executing a `CALL IDENTITY()` statement to fetch the generated key.

- **sybase-fetch-key (org.jboss.ejb.plugins.cmp.jdbc.sybase.JDBCSybaseCreateCommand)**—`JDBCSybaseCreateCommand` executes an `INSERT INTO` query after executing a `SELECT @@IDENTITY` statement to fetch the generated key.

- **mssql-fetch-key (org.jboss.ejb.plugins.cmp.jdbc.keygen.JDBCSQLServerCreateCommand)**—`JDBCSQLServerCreateCommand` for Microsoft SQL Server uses the value from an `IDENTITY` columns. By default, it uses SELECT `SCOPE_IDENTITY()` to reduce the impact of triggers. You can override it with the `pk-sql` attribute (for example, for version 7).

- **informix-serial (org.jboss.ejb.plugins.cmp.jdbc.informix.JDBCInformixCreateCommand)**—The `JDBCInformixCreateCommand` executes an INSERT INTO query after using the `getSerial` method from Informix native `java.sql.Statement` interface implementation to fetch the generated key.

- **postgresql-fetch-seq (org.jboss.ejb.plugins.cmp.jdbc.keygen.JDBCPostgreSQLCreateCommand)**—`JDBCPostgreSQLCreateCommand` for `PostgreSQL` fetches the current value of the sequence. You can use the optional `sequence` attribute to change the name of the sequence, and the default is `table_pkColumn_seq`.

- **key-generator (org.jboss.ejb.plugins.cmp.jdbc.JDBCKeyGeneratorCreateCommand)**—`JDBCKeyGeneratorCreateCommand` executes an `INSERT INTO` query after obtaining a value for the primary key from the key generator referenced by the `key-generator-factory`. The `key-generator-factory` attribute must provide the name of a JNDI binding of the `org.jboss.ejb.plugins.keygenerator.KeyGeneratorFactory` implementation.

- **get-generated-keys (org.jboss.ejb.plugins.cmp.jdbc.jdbc3. JDBCGetGeneratedKeysCreateCommand)**—JDBCGetGeneratedKeysCreateCommand executes an INSERT INTO query, using a statement that is built by using the JDBC3 prepareStatement(String, Statement.RETURN_GENERATED_KEYS) that has the capability to retrieve the autogenerated key. You obtain the generated key by calling the PreparedStatement.getGeneratedKeys method. Because this requires JDBC3 support, it is available only in JDK1.4.1+, with a supporting JDBC driver.

The following is a sample configuration that uses the hsqldb-fetch-key entity-command with the generated key mapped to a known primary key cmp-field:

```
<jbosscmp-jdbc>
  <enterprise-beans>
    <entity>
      <ejb-name>LocationEJB</ejb-name>
      <pk-constraint>false</pk-constraint>
      <table-name>location</table-name>

      <cmp-field>
        <field-name>locationID</field-name>
        <column-name>id</column-name>
        <auto-increment/>
      </cmp-field>
      <!-- ... -->
      <entity-command name="hsqldb-fetch-key"/>

    </entity>
  </enterprise-beans>
</jbosscmp-jdbc>
```

The following is an alternative example that uses an unknown primary key without an explicit cmp-field:

```
<jbosscmp-jdbc>
    <enterprise-beans>
        <entity>
            <ejb-name>LocationEJB</ejb-name>
            <pk-constraint>false</pk-constraint>
            <table-name>location</table-name>
            <unknown-pk>
                <unknown-pk-class>java.lang.Integer</unknown-pk-class>
                <field-name>locationID</field-name>
                <column-name>id</column-name>
                <jdbc-type>INTEGER</jdbc-type>
```

```
                <sql-type>INTEGER</sql-type>
                <auto-increment/>
            </unknown-pk>
            <!--...-->
            <entity-command name="hsqldb-fetch-key"/>
        </entity>
    </enterprise-beans>
</jbosscmp-jdbc>
```

JBoss Global Defaults

JBoss global defaults are defined in the `standardjbosscmp-jdbc.xml` file of the *server/<server-name>/conf/* directory. Each application can override the global defaults in the `jbosscmp-jdbc.xml` file. The default options are contained in a `defaults` element of the configuration file, and the content model of `defaults` is shown in Figure 11.16.

An example of the `defaults` section follows:

```
<jbosscmp-jdbc>
    <defaults>
        <datasource>java:/DefaultDS</datasource>
        <datasource-mapping>Hypersonic SQL</datasource-mapping>
        <create-table>true</create-table>
        <remove-table>false</remove-table>
        <read-only>false</read-only>
        <read-time-out>300000</read-time-out>
        <pk-constraint>true</pk-constraint>
        <fk-constraint>false</fk-constraint>
        <row-locking>false</row-locking>
        <preferred-relation-mapping>foreign-key</preferred-relation-mapping>
        <read-ahead>
            <strategy>on-load</strategy>
            <page-size>1000</page-size>
            <eager-load-group>*</eager-load-group>
        </read-ahead>
        <list-cache-max>1000</list-cache-max>
    </defaults>
</jbosscmp-jdbc>
```

A Sample `jbosscmp-jdbc.xml` Defaults Declaration

Each of the following `jbosscmp-jdbc.xml` options can apply to entities, relationships, or both, and can be overridden in the specific entity or relationship:

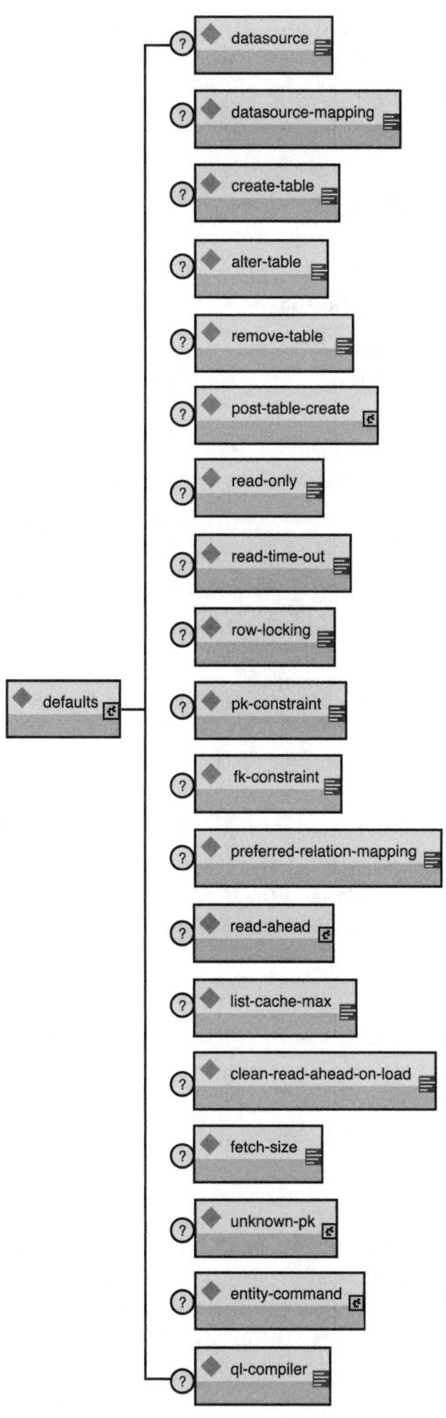

FIGURE 11.16 The `jbosscmp-jdbc.xml` `defaults` content model.

- **datasource**—This optional element is the `jndi-name` that is used to look up the datasource. All database connections used by an entity or `relation-table` are obtained from the datasource. Having different datasources for entities is not recommended because it vastly constrains the domain over which finders and `ejbSelects` can query.
- **datasource-mapping**—This optional element specifies the name of the `type-mapping`, which determines how Java types are mapped to SQL types and how EJB-QL functions are mapped to database-specific functions. Type mappings are discussed in the section "Mapping," later in this chapter.
- **create-table**—When this optional element is `true`, JBoss attempts to create a table for the entity. When the application is deployed, JBoss checks whether a table already exists before creating the table. If a table is found, it is logged, and the table is not created. This option is very useful during the early stages of development, when the table structure changes often. The default is `false`.
- **alter-table**—If `create-table` is used to automatically create the schema, you can use `alter-table` to keep the schema current with changes to the entity bean. This element performs the following specific tasks:

  It creates new fields.

  It removes fields that are no longer used.

  It increases the length of string fields that are shorter than the declared length to the declared length. (This is not supported by all databases.)

- **remove-table**—When this optional element is `true`, JBoss attempts to drop the table for each entity and each relation table mapped relationship. When the application is undeployed, JBoss attempts to drop the table. This option is very useful during the early stages of development, when the table structure changes often. The default is `false`.
- **read-only**—When this optional element is `true`, the bean provider is not allowed to change the values of any fields. A field that is read-only is not stored in or inserted into the database. If a primary key field is read-only, the `create` method throws a `CreateException`. If a set accessor is called on a read-only field, it throws an `EJBException`. Read-only fields are useful for fields that are filled in by database triggers, such as last updates. You can override the `read-only` option on a per-field basis. The default is `false`.
- **read-time-out**—This optional element is the amount of time, in milliseconds, that a read on a read-only field is valid. A value of `0` means that the value is always reloaded at the start of a transaction, and a value of `-1` means that the value never times out. You can override this option on a per-CMP-field basis. If `read-only` is `false`, this value is ignored. The default is `-1`.

- **row-locking**—If this optional element is `true`, JBoss locks all rows that are loaded in a transaction. Most databases implement this by using the `SELECT FOR UPDATE` syntax when loading the entity, but the actual syntax is determined by the `row-locking-template` in the `datasource-mapping` used by this entity. The default is `false`.
- **pk-constraint**—If this optional element is `true`, JBoss adds a primary key constraint when creating tables. The default is `true`.
- **preferred-relation-mapping**—This optional element specifies the preferred mapping style for relationships. The `preferred-relation-mapping` element must be either `foreign-key` or `relation-table`.
- **read-ahead**—This optional element controls caching of query results and CMR fields for the entity. This option is discussed earlier in this chapter, in the section "Read-ahead."
- **list-cache-max**—This optional element specifies the number of `read-lists` that this entity can track. This option is discussed earlier in this chapter, in the section "The `on-load` Strategy." The default is `1000`.
- **clean-read-ahead-on-load**—When an entity is loaded from the read-ahead cache, JBoss can remove the data used from the read-ahead cache. The default is `false`.
- **fetch-size**—This optional element specifies the number of entities to read in one round-trip to the underlying datastore. The default is `0`.
- **unknown-pk**—This optional element allows you to define the default mapping of an unknown primary key type of `java.lang.Object` to the persistent store.
- **entity-command**—This optional element allows you to define the default command for entity creation. This is described in detail earlier in this chapter, in the section "Entity Commands and Primary Key Generation."
- **ql-compiler**—This optional elements allows a replacement query compiler to be specified. Alternate query compilers are discussed earlier in this chapter, in the section "EJB-QL 2.1 and SQL92 Queries."

Datasource Customization

JBoss includes predefined type-mappings for many databases, including Cloudscape, DB2, DB2/400, Hypersonic SQL, InformixDB, InterBase, Microsoft SQL Server, Microsoft SQL Server 2000, MySQL, Oracle7, Oracle8, Oracle9i, PointBase, PostgreSQL, PostgreSQL 7.2, SapDB, SOLID, and Sybase. If you do not like a supplied mapping, or if a mapping is not supplied for your database, you have to define a new mapping.

Type Mapping

You customize a database through the `type-mapping` section of the `jbosscmp-jdbc.xml` descriptor. The content model for the `type-mapping` element is shown in Figure 11.17.

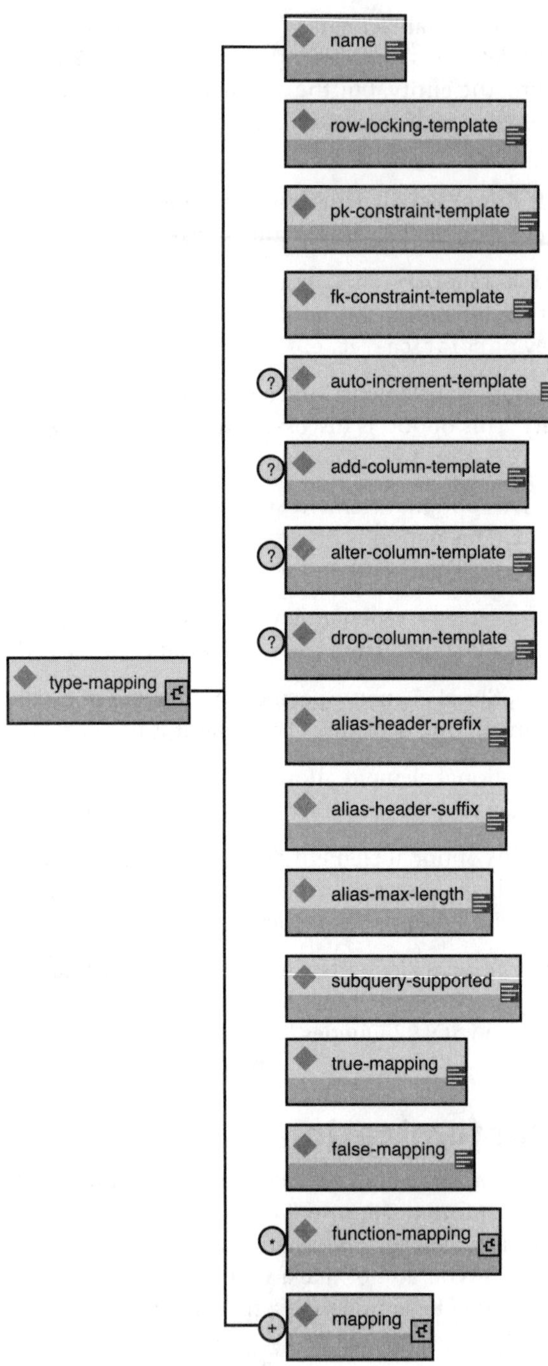

FIGURE 11.17 The `jbosscmp-jdbc` `type-mapping` element content model.

The elements of the `type-mapping` element are as follows:

- **`name`**—This required element provides a name that identifies the database customization. You use it to refer to the mappings by the `datasource-mapping` elements found in `defaults` and `entity`.
- **`row-locking-template`**—This required element gives the `PreparedStatement` template used to create a row lock on the selected rows. The template must support three arguments:
  - The select clause.
  - The from clause. The order of the tables is currently not guaranteed.
  - The where clause.

  If row locking is not supported in a select statement, this element should be empty. The most common form of row locking is select for update, as in `SELECT ?1 FROM ?2 WHERE ?3 FOR UPDATE`.
- **`pk-constraint-template`**—This required element specifies the `PreparedStatement` template that is used to create a primary key constraint in the `create table` statement. The template must support two arguments:
  - The primary key constraint name (which is always `pk_{`*`table-name`*`}`
  - A comma-separated list of primary key column names

  If a primary key constraint clause is not supported in a `create table` statement, this element should be empty. The most common form of a primary key constraint is `CONSTRAINT ?1 PRIMARY KEY (?2)`.
- **`fk-constraint-template`**—This is the template that is used to create a foreign key constraint in a separate statement. The template must support five arguments:
  - `1` is the table name.
  - `2` is the foreign key constraint name, which is always `fk_{`*`table-name`*`}_{cmr-`*`field-name`*`}`.
  - `3` is the comma-separated list of foreign key column names.
  - `4` is the references table name.
  - `5` is the comma-separated list of the referenced primary key column names.

  If the datasource does not support foreign key constraints, this element should be empty. The most common form of a foreign key constraint is `ALTER TABLE ?1 ADD CONSTRAINT ?2 FOREIGN KEY (?3) REFERENCES ?4 (?5)`.
- **`auto-increment-template`**—This declares the SQL template for specifying auto-increment columns.

- **add-column-template**—When alter-table is true, this SQL template specifies the syntax for adding a column to an existing table. The default value is ALTER TABLE ?1 ADD ?2 ?3. The parameters are as follows:
    - 1 is the table name.
    - 2 is the column name.
    - 3 is the column type.
- **alter-column-template**—When alter-table is true, this SQL template specifies the syntax for dropping a column from an existing table. The default value is ALTER TABLE ?1 ALTER ?2 TYPE ?3. The parameters are as follows:
    - 1 is the table name.
    - 2 is the column name.
    - 3 is the column type.
- **drop-column-template**—When alter-table is true, this SQL template specifies the syntax for dropping a column from an existing table. The default value is ALTER TABLE ?1 DROP ?2. The parameters are as follows:
    - 1 is the table name.
    - 2 is the column name.
- **alias-header-prefix**—This required element gives the prefix used in creating the alias header. The ELB-QL compiler prepends an alias header to a generated table alias to prevent name collisions. The alias header is constructed as follows: alias-header-prefix + int_counter + alias-header-suffix. An example of an alias header would be t0_ for an alias-header-prefix of t and an alias-header-suffix of _.
- **alias-header-suffix**—This required element gives the suffix portion of the generated alias header.
- **alias-max-length**—This required element gives the maximum allowed length for the generated alias header.
- **subquery-supported**—This required element specifies whether subqueries are supported. Some EJB-QL operators are mapped to exists subqueries. If subquery-supported is false, the EJB-QL compiler uses left-join and is null.
- **true-mapping**—This required element defines a true identity in EJB-QL queries. Examples include TRUE, 1, and (1=1).
- **false-mapping**—This required element defines a false identity in EJB-QL queries. Examples include FALSE, 0, and (1=0).
- **function-mapping**—This optional element specifies one or more mappings from an EJB-QL function to an SQL implementation. The following section provides details.

- **mapping**—This required element specifies the mappings from a Java type to the corresponding JDBC and SQL types. See the section "Mapping," later in this chapter, for details.

Function Mapping

The `function-mapping` element content model is shown in Figure 11.18.

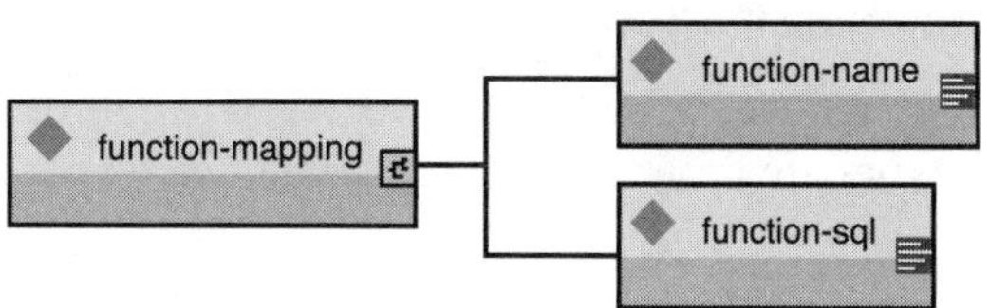

FIGURE 11.18 The `jbosscmp-jdbc function-mapping` element content model.

The allowed child elements are as follows:

- **function-name**—This required element gives the EJB-QL function name (for example, `concat`, `substring`).
- **function-sql**—This required element gives the SQL for the function, as appropriate for the underlying database. Examples for a `concat` function are `(?1 || ?2)`, `concat (?1, ?2)`, and `(?1 +?2)`.

Mapping

A type mapping is simply a set of mappings between Java class types and database types. A set of type mappings is defined by a set of `mapping` elements, the content model for which is shown in Figure 11.19.

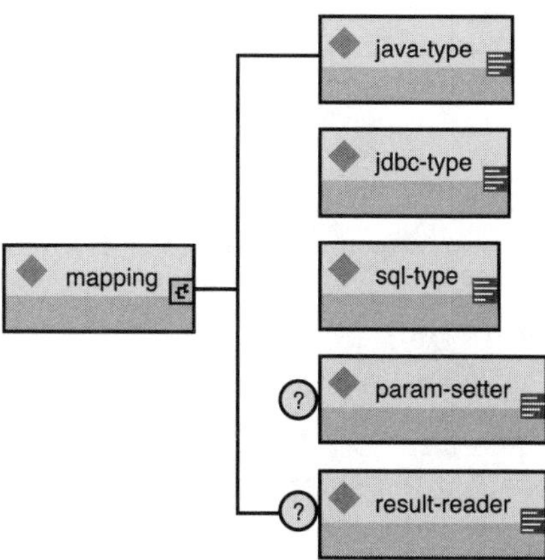

FIGURE 11.19 The `jbosscmp-jdbc mapping` element content model.

If JBoss cannot find a mapping for a type, it serializes the object and uses the `java.lang.Object` mapping. The following are the child elements of the `mapping` element:

- **`java-type`**—This required element gives the fully qualified name of the Java class to be mapped. If the class is a primitive wrapper class, such as `java.lang.Short`, the mapping also applies to the primitive type.
- **`jdbc-type`**—This required element gives the JDBC type that is used when setting parameters in a JDBC `PreparedStatement` or loading data from a JDBC ResultSet. The valid types are defined in `java.sql.Types`.
- **`sql-type`**—This required element gives the SQL type that is used in `create table` statements. Valid types are limited only by your database vendor.
- **`param-setter`**—This optional element specifies the fully qualified name of the `JDBCParameterSetter` implementation for this mapping.
- **`result-reader`**—This optional element specifies the fully qualified name of the `JDBCResultSetReader` implementation for this mapping.

The following is an example of a `mapping` element for a `short` in Oracle9i:

```
<jbosscmp-jdbc>
    <type-mappings>
        <type-mapping>
            <name>Oracle9i</name>
            <!--...-->
            <mapping>
                <java-type>java.lang.Short</java-type>
                <jdbc-type>NUMERIC</jdbc-type>
                <sql-type>NUMBER(5)</sql-type>
            </mapping>
        </type-mapping>
    </type-mappings>
</jbosscmp-jdbc>
```

User Type Mappings

User type mappings allow you to map from JDBC column types to custom CMP field types by specifying an instance of an `org.jboss.ejb.plugins.cmp.jdbc.Mapper` interface, the definition of which is shown here:

```
public interface Mapper
{
    /**
     * This method is called when CMP field is stored.
     * @param fieldValue - CMP field value
```

```
     * @return column value.
     */
    Object toColumnValue(Object fieldValue);

    /**
     * This method is called when CMP field is loaded.
     * @param columnValue - loaded column value.
     * @return CMP field value.
     */
    Object toFieldValue(Object columnValue);
}
```

A prototypical use case is the mapping of an integer type to its type-safe Java enumeration instance. The content model of the `user-type-mappings` element consists of one or more `user-type-mapping` elements, the content model of which is shown in Figure 11.20.

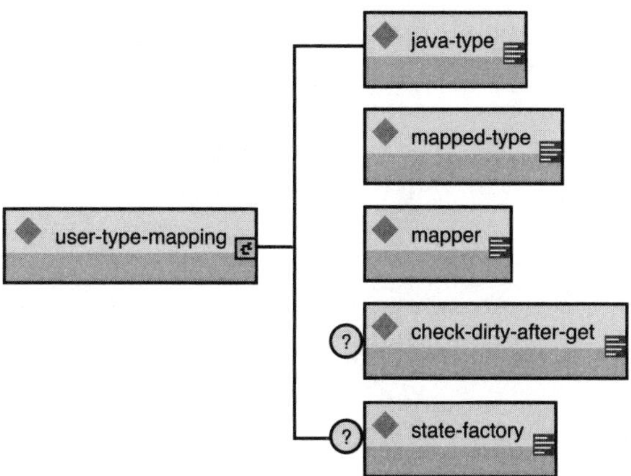

FIGURE 11.20 The `user-type-mapping` content model.

The `user-type-mapping` elements are as follows:

- **`java-type`**—The fully qualified name of the CMP field type in the mapping.
- **`mapped-type`**—The fully qualified name of the database type in the mapping.
- **`mapper`**—The fully qualified name of the `Mapper` interface implementation that handles the conversion between `java-type` and `mapped-type`.

CHAPTER 12

Web Services

IN THIS CHAPTER

- JAX-RPC Service Endpoints
- Enterprise JavaBean Endpoints
- Web Services Clients–A JAX-RPC Client
- Service References

The biggest new feature of J2EE 1.4 is the ability of J2EE components to act both as web service providers and consumers. J2EE applications can expose a web service from the Enterprise JavaBean (EJB) tier using a stateless session bean or from the web tier using a plain Java object. Additionally, both server-side components and J2EE client applications have a standard way of declaring references to external web services.

JAX-RPC Service Endpoints

JAX-RPC service endpoints (JSE) provide web services from the web tier. They take the form of simple Java objects that masquerade as servlets. A trivial `hello` web service implementation class shows how simple they are:

```
package org.jboss.chap12.hello;

public class HelloServlet
{
    public String hello(String name)
    {
        return "Hello " + name + "!";
    }
}
```

There is nothing remarkable about `HelloServlet`. It doesn't implement any special interfaces nor does it need any methods besides the business methods it decides to provide. The `hello` method is the operation exposed as a web service, and it does nothing but respond with a friendly greeting to the person passed in.

That is your web service implementation. In addition to this, you need a service endpoint class that defines the interface of the web service. That is shown here as the `Hello` interface:

```
package org.jboss.chap12.hello;
import java.rmi.Remote;
import java.rmi.RemoteException;
public interface Hello
    extends Remote
{
    public String hello(String name)
        throws RemoteException;
}
```

The service endpoint interface is declared `Remote` and the method must throw `RemoteException`. Beyond this, it is a simple expression of the interface to the web service. This is all the code you need to write to expose a J2EE web service. Deploying it, however, does require a few additional deployment descriptors.

Although a JSE doesn't bear any direct resemblance to a servlet, it is nonetheless deployed as a servlet in the `web.xml` file. You need to declare the web service implementation class as a servlet and provide a servlet mapping that responds to the web service invocations. Here is the definition required to deploy the `hello` web service:

```
<?xml version="1.0" encoding="UTF-8"?>
<web-app xmlns="http://java.sun.com/xml/ns/j2ee"
         xmlns:xsi="http://www.w3.org/2001/XMLSchema-instance"
         xsi:schemaLocation="http://java.sun.com/xml/ns/j2ee
                             http://java.sun.com/xml/ns/j2ee/web-app_2_4.xsd"
         version="2.4">
    <servlet>
        <servlet-name>HelloWorldServlet</servlet-name>
        <servlet-class>org.jboss.chap12.hello.HelloServlet</servlet-class>
    </servlet>
    <servlet-mapping>
        <servlet-name>HelloWorldServlet</servlet-name>
        <url-pattern>/Hello</url-pattern>
    </servlet-mapping>
</web-app>
```

The URL pattern in the servlet mapping is the only externally visible configuration element. It controls what URL the web service lives at. This is primarily noticed as the location of the WSDL file for this service.

The `web.xml` file doesn't contain any web service related configuration. A new deployment descriptor, `webservices.xml`, is needed to instruct JBoss to treat this servlet as a web service and not as a normal servlet. But before discussing that, you need two additional configuration files, a WSDL file and a JAX-RPC mapping file. Both of these files can be generated using the wscompile tool that ships as part of the Java Web Services Developer Pack (WSDP).

```
wscompile -classpath <classpath> -gen:server -f:rpcliteral -mapping mapping.xml
➥config.xml
```

This generates a WSDL file and a JAX-RPC mapping file based on the supplied `config.xml` and the corresponding classes found on the class path. The `config.xml` file for the `hello` web service is shown below:

```
<?xml version="1.0" encoding="UTF-8"?>

<configuration xmlns="http://java.sun.com/xml/ns/jax-rpc/ri/config">
    <service name="HelloService"
             targetNamespace="http://hello.chap12.jboss.org/"
             typeNamespace="http://hello.chap12.jboss.org/types"
             packageName="org.jboss.chap12.hello">
        <interface name="org.jboss.chap12.hello.Hello"/>
    </service>
</configuration>
```

The `service` element defines the interface your web service provides. The following attributes are required:

- **`name`**—This is the name of the web service.
- **`targetNamespace`**—Web services require `namespaces` just like Java classes do. It's a common practice to use a URL `namespace` that corresponds to the Java `namespace` given.
- **`typeNamespace`**—This specifies the `namespace` to use for custom types.
- **`packageName`**—This is the base package name your web services' classes live under.

Additionally, you need an `interface` element that tells `wscompile` what the Java interface for the web service is. This interface declares the operations the web service provides.

The WSDL file `wscompile` generated for our `config.xml` file is shown below. Note that the SOAP address isn't provided in the WSDL file. JBoss inserts the correct URL for the WSDL when it deploys the web service.

```
<?xml version="1.0" encoding="UTF-8"?>
<definitions name="HelloService"
targetNamespace="http://hello.chap12.jboss.org/"
xmlns:tns="http://hello.chap12.jboss.org/"
xmlns="http://schemas.xmlsoap.org/wsdl/"
xmlns:xsd="http://www.w3.org/2001/XMLSchema"
    xmlns:soap="http://schemas.xmlsoap.org/wsdl/soap/">
    <types/>
    <message name="Hello_hello">
        <part name="String_1" type="xsd:string"/>
    </message>
    <message name="Hello_helloResponse">
        <part name="result" type="xsd:string"/>
    </message>
    <portType name="Hello">
```

```
        <operation name="hello" parameterOrder="String_1">
            <input message="tns:Hello_hello"/>
            <output message="tns:Hello_helloResponse"/>
        </operation>
    </portType>
    <binding name="HelloBinding" type="tns:Hello">
        <soap:binding transport="http://schemas.xmlsoap.org/soap/
➥http" style="rpc"/>
        <operation name="hello">
            <soap:operation soapAction=""/>
            <input>
                <soap:body use="literal" namespace=
➥"http://hello.chap12.jboss.org/"/>
            </input>
            <output>
                <soap:body use="literal" namespace=
➥"http://hello.chap12.jboss.org/"/>
            </output>
        </operation>
    </binding>
    <service name="HelloService">
        <port name="HelloPort" binding="tns:HelloBinding">
            <soap:address location="REPLACE_WITH_ACTUAL_URL"/>
        </port>
    </service>
</definitions>
```

You also asked wscompile to generate a JAX-RPC mapping file. This is shown below:

```
<?xml version="1.0" encoding="UTF-8"?>
<java-wsdl-mapping version="1.1" xmlns="http://java.sun.com/xml/ns/j2ee"
    xmlns:xsi="http://www.w3.org/2001/XMLSchema-instance"
    xsi:schemaLocation="http://java.sun.com/xml/ns/j2ee
        http://www.ibm.com/webservices/xsd/j2ee_jaxrpc_mapping_1_1.xsd">
    <package-mapping>
        <package-type>org.jboss.chap12.hello</package-type>
        <namespaceURI>http://hello.chap12.jboss.org/types</namespaceURI>
    </package-mapping>
    <package-mapping>
        <package-type>org.jboss.chap12.hello</package-type>
        <namespaceURI>http://hello.chap12.jboss.org/</namespaceURI>
    </package-mapping>
    <service-interface-mapping>
        <service-interface>org.jboss.chap12.hello.HelloService</service-interface>
        <wsdl-service-name xmlns:serviceNS="http://hello.chap12.jboss.org/">
            serviceNS:HelloService
```

```
        </wsdl-service-name>
        <port-mapping>
            <port-name>HelloPort</port-name>
            <java-port-name>HelloPort</java-port-name>
        </port-mapping>
    </service-interface-mapping>
    <service-endpoint-interface-mapping>
        <service-endpoint-interface>org.jboss.chap12.hello.Hello
➥</service-endpoint-interface>
        <wsdl-port-type xmlns:portTypeNS="http://hello.chap12.jboss.org/">
            portTypeNS:Hello
        </wsdl-port-type>
        <wsdl-binding xmlns:bindingNS="http://hello.chap12.jboss.org/">
            bindingNS:HelloBinding
        </wsdl-binding>
        <service-endpoint-method-mapping>
            <java-method-name>hello</java-method-name>
            <wsdl-operation>hello</wsdl-operation>
            <method-param-parts-mapping>
                <param-position>0</param-position>
                <param-type>java.lang.String</param-type>
                <wsdl-message-mapping>
                    <wsdl-message xmlns:wsdlMsgNS="http://hello.chap12.jboss.org/">
                        wsdlMsgNS:Hello_hello
                    </wsdl-message>
                    <wsdl-message-part-name>String_1</wsdl-message-part-name>
                    <parameter-mode>IN</parameter-mode>
                </wsdl-message-mapping>
            </method-param-parts-mapping>
            <wsdl-return-value-mapping>
                <method-return-value>java.lang.String</method-return-value>
                <wsdl-message xmlns:wsdlMsgNS="http://hello.chap12.jboss.org/">
                    wsdlMsgNS:Hello_helloResponse
                </wsdl-message>
                <wsdl-message-part-name>result</wsdl-message-part-name>
            </wsdl-return-value-mapping>
        </service-endpoint-method-mapping>
    </service-endpoint-interface-mapping>
</java-wsdl-mapping>
```

After the extra files are generated, you need to bundle them up in a `webservices.xml` file. This file links to the WSDL file using the `wsdl-file` element and links to the mapping file using the `jaxrpc-mapping-file` element.

In addition to this, a `port-component` element is needed that maps a port in the WSDL file to a particular service implementation. For our JSE, this is done with a `servlet-link` inside the service-impl-bean element. The servlet link must be the same as the name of the pseudo servlet declared in the web.xml file.

```
<webservices xmlns="http://java.sun.com/xml/ns/j2ee"
xmlns:xsi="http://www.w3.org/2001/XMLSchema-instance"
    xsi:schemaLocation="http://java.sun.com/xml/ns/j2ee http://www.ibm.com/
➥webservices/xsd/j2ee_web_services_1_1.xsd" version="1.1">
    <webservice-description>
        <webservice-description-name>HelloService</webservice-description-name>
        <wsdl-file>WEB-INF/wsdl/HelloService.wsdl</wsdl-file>
        <jaxrpc-mapping-file>WEB-INF/mapping.xml</jaxrpc-mapping-file>
        <port-component>
            <port-component-name>Hello</port-component-name>
            <wsdl-port>HelloPort</wsdl-port>
            <service-endpoint-interface>org.jboss.chap12.hello.Hello
➥</service-endpoint-interface>
            <service-impl-bean>
                <servlet-link>HelloWorldServlet</servlet-link>
            </service-impl-bean>
        </port-component>
    </webservice-description>
</webservices>
```

With these completed, you can deploy the WAR file containing the web service. All the deployment descriptors go in the WEB-INF directory, as shown in Figure 12.1. It's important to note that the WSDL file is required to be in the wsdl subdirectory.

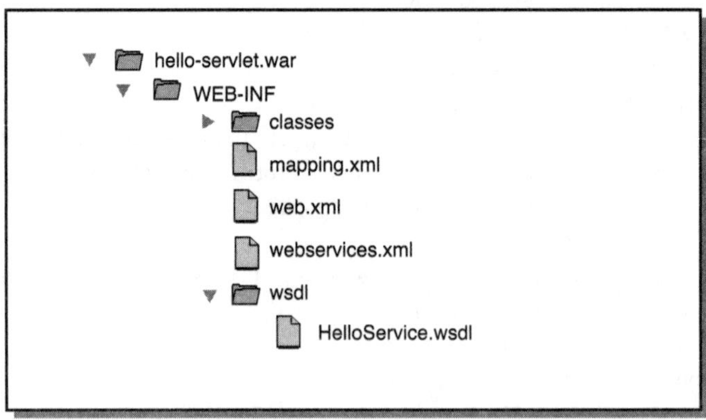

FIGURE 12.1 The structure of hello-servlet.war.

To deploy and test the hello web service, run the following from the examples directory:

```
[examples]$ ant -Dchap=chap12 -Dex=1 run-example
...
run-example1:
```

```
[echo] Waiting for 5 seconds for deploy...
[java] Contacting webservice at http://localhost:8080/hello-servlet/Hello?wsdl
[java] hello.hello(JBoss user)
[java] output:Hello JBoss user!
```

Note the URL where JBoss publishes the WSDL file. Your web application name is `hello-servlet` and you mapped the servlet to `/Hello` in the `web.xml` file, so the web service is mapped to `/hello-servlet/Hello`. The `?wsdl` query returns the WSDL file.

If you aren't sure what the URL of the WSDL file is, JBoss provides a way to list the web services available on the system at `/ws4ee/services`. Figure 12.2 shows a view of the services list.

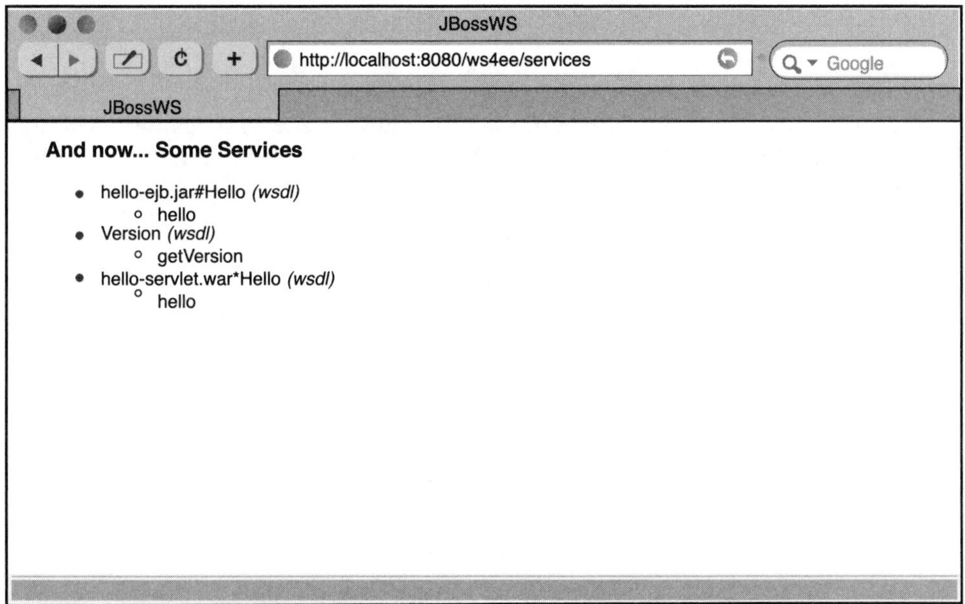

FIGURE 12.2 The web services list.

The services list shows all of the deployed web services along with the name of the deployment unit and a link to the WSDL file for that service.

Enterprise JavaBean Endpoints

Web services can also be provided from the EJB tier. Any stateless session bean can serve as the endpoint for a web service in almost the same way as the JAX-RPC endpoints. To see how this works, adapt the `HelloServlet` example into a session bean. Here is the code:

```
package org.jboss.chap12.hello;
import javax.ejb.EJBException;
import javax.ejb.SessionBean;
```

```
import javax.ejb.SessionContext;
public class HelloBean
    implements SessionBean
{
    public String hello(String name)
    {
        return "Hello " + name + "!";
    }
    public void ejbCreate() {};
    public void ejbRemove() {};
    public void ejbActivate() {}
    public void ejbPassivate() {}
    public void setSessionContext(SessionContext ctx) {
}
}
```

This is a very trivial session bean. Session beans normally require a home interface and either a local or remote interface. However, it is possible to omit them if the session bean is only serving as a web services endpoint.

However, you do still need the `Hello` service endpoint interface used in the JSE example.

The `ejb-jar.xml` file is very standard for a session bean. The normal session bean parameters are explained in Chapter 5, "EJBs on JBoss." The only new element is the `service-endpoint` element, which declares the service endpoint interface for the web service.

```
<?xml version="1.0" encoding="UTF-8"?>
<ejb-jar xmlns="http://java.sun.com/xml/ns/j2ee" version="2.1"
xmlns:xsi="http://www.w3.org/2001/XMLSchema-instance"
    xsi:schemaLocation="http://java.sun.com/xml/ns/j2ee
http://java.sun.com/xml/ns/j2ee/ejb-jar_2_1.xsd">
    <display-name>chapter 12 EJB JAR</display-name>
    <enterprise-beans>
        <session>
            <ejb-name>HelloBean</ejb-name>
            <service-endpoint>org.jboss.chap12.hello.Hello</service-endpoint>
            <ejb-class>org.jboss.chap12.hello.HelloBean</ejb-class>
            <session-type>Stateless</session-type>
            <transaction-type>Container</transaction-type>
        </session>
    </enterprise-beans>
    <assembly-descriptor>
        <method-permission>
            <unchecked/>
            <method>
                <ejb-name>HelloBean</ejb-name>
```

```
                <method-name>*</method-name>
            </method>
        </method-permission>
        <container-transaction>
            <method>
                <ejb-name>HelloBean</ejb-name>
                <method-name>*</method-name>
            </method>
            <trans-attribute>Required</trans-attribute>
        </container-transaction>
    </assembly-descriptor>
</ejb-jar>
```

A supporting `webservices.xml` needs to accompany this. The file, shown below, looks almost identical to the `webservices.xml` for the WAR file:

```
<webservices xmlns="http://java.sun.com/xml/ns/j2ee"
xmlns:xsi="http://www.w3.org/2001/XMLSchema-instance"
    xsi:schemaLocation="http://java.sun.com/xml/ns/j2ee http://www.ibm.com/
➥webservices/xsd/j2ee_web_services_1_1\.xsd" version="1.1">
    <webservice-description>
        <webservice-description-name>HelloService</webservice-description-name>
<wsdl-file>META-INF/wsdl/HelloService.wsdl</wsdl-file>
        <jaxrpc-mapping-file>META-INF/mapping.xml</jaxrpc-mapping-file>
<port-component>
            <port-component-name>Hello</port-component-name>
            <wsdl-port>HelloPort</wsdl-port>
            <service-endpoint-interface>org.jboss.chap12.hello.Hello
➥</service-endpoint-interface>
            <service-impl-bean>
                <ejb-link>HelloBean</ejb-link>
            </service-impl-bean>
        </port-component>
    </webservice-description>
</webservices>
```

The first difference is that the WSDL file should be in the `META-INF/wsdl` directory instead of the `WEB-INF/wsdl` directory. The second difference is that the `service-impl-bean` element contains an `ejb-link` that refers to the `ejb-name` of the session bean. The WSDL file and JAX-RPC mapping files remain unchanged from the previous example.

To package and deploy the application, run the following command in the `examples` directory:

```
[examples]$ ant -Dchap=chap12 -Dex=2 run-example
...
run-example2:
```

```
[copy] Copying 1 file to /tmp/jboss-4.0.1/server/default/deploy
[echo] Waiting for 5 seconds for deploy...
[java] Contacting webservice at http://localhost:8080/hello-ejb/Hello?wsdl
[java] hello.hello(JBoss user)
[java] output:Hello JBoss user!
```

The test program run here is the same as the servlet example, except that it uses a different URL for the WSDL. JBoss composes the WSDL using the base name of the EJB JAR file and the name of the web service interface.

However, as with all web services in JBoss, you can use the http://localhost:8080/ws4ee/services service view shown in Figure 12.2 to verify the deployed URL of the WSDL.

Web Services Clients—A JAX-RPC Client

The full JAX-RPC programming model is available to J2EE applications and clients. I won't cover the full range of client programming techniques, but let's look briefly at the client used so far to test the deployed web services. The client, shown in the following listing, illustrates the dynamic proxy invocation mechanism:

```
package org.jboss.chap12.client;
import org.jboss.chap12.hello.Hello;
import javax.xml.rpc.Service;
import javax.xml.rpc.ServiceFactory;
import javax.xml.namespace.QName;
import java.net.URL;
public class HelloClient
{
    public static void main(String[] args)
        throws Exception
    {
        String urlstr   = args[0];
        String argument = args[1];
        System.out.println("Contacting webservice at " + urlstr);
        URL url =  new URL(urlstr);
        QName qname = new QName("http://hello.chap12.jboss.org/",
                                "HelloService");
        ServiceFactory factory = ServiceFactory.newInstance();
        Service        service = factory.createService(url, qname);
        Hello          hello   = (Hello) service.getPort(Hello.class);
        System.out.println("hello.hello(" + argument + ")");
        System.out.println("output:" + hello.hello(argument));
    }
}
```

This JAX-RPC client uses the `Hello` service endpoint interface and creates a dynamic proxy to speak to the service advertised by the WSDL at the URL passed in as a command-line argument. For illustrative purposes, here is another variation of web services invocation that doesn't use the service endpoint interface. This is known as the *dynamic invocation interface (DII)*. Using DII, it's possible to refer to a specific port and operation by name. Think of it as reflection for web services. The client code is shown in the following listing:

```
package org.jboss.chap12.client;
import org.jboss.chap12.hello.Hello;
import javax.xml.rpc.Service;
import javax.xml.rpc.ServiceFactory;
import javax.xml.namespace.QName;
import java.net.URL;
public class HelloClient
{
    public static void main(String[] args)
        throws Exception
    {
        String urlstr   = args[0];
        String argument = args[1];
        System.out.println("Contacting webservice at " + urlstr);
        URL url =  new URL(urlstr);
        QName qname = new QName("http://hello.chap12.jboss.org/",
                                "HelloService");
        ServiceFactory factory = ServiceFactory.newInstance();
        Service        service = factory.createService(url, qname);
        Hello          hello   = (Hello) service.getPort(Hello.class);
        System.out.println("hello.hello(" + argument + ")");
        System.out.println("output:" + hello.hello(argument));
    }
}
```

The following two commands can be used to run DII client against both the JSE and EJB web services you have created:

```
[examples]$ ant -Dchap=chap12 -Dex=1b run-example
[examples]$ ant -Dchap=chap12 -Dex=2b run-example
```

Service References

The JAX-RPC examples in the preceding section, "A JAX-RPC Client," all required manual configuration of the WSDL URL and knowledge of the XML nature of the web services in question. This can be a configuration nightmare, but if your code is a J2EE component, there is another option. J2EE components can declare service references and look up JAX-RPC `Service` objects in JNDI without needing to hard-code any web service references in the code.

To show how this works, let's first look at a session bean that needs to make a call to the `hello` web service:

```
rt java.rmi.RemoteException;
import javax.xml.rpc.Service;
import javax.xml.rpc.ServiceException;
import org.jboss.chap12.hello.Hello;
public class ExampleBean
    implements SessionBean
{
    public String doWork()
    {
        try {
            Context ctx     = new InitialContext();
            Service service = (Service) ctx.lookup("java:comp/env/services/hello");
            Hello   hello   = (Hello)   service.getPort(Hello.class);
            return hello.hello("example bean");
        } catch (NamingException e) {
            throw new EJBException(e);
        } catch (ServiceException e) {
            throw new EJBException(e);
        } catch (RemoteException e) {
            throw new EJBException(e);
        }
    }
    public void ejbCreate() {};
    public void ejbRemove() {};
    public void ejbActivate() {}
    public void ejbPassivate() {}
    public void setSessionContext(SessionContext ctx) {}
}
```

`ExampleBean` invokes the `hello` web service in its `doWork` method. The dynamic proxy invocation method is used here, but any of the JAX-RPC supported invocation methods are fine. The interesting point here is that the bean has obtained the `service` reference from a JNDI lookup in its ENC. Web service references are declared using a `service-ref` element inside an `ejb-jar.xml` file, as shown in Figure 12.3.

The following elements are supported by the `service-ref`:

- **`service-ref-name`**—This is the JNDI name the service object is bound under in the bean's ENC. It is relative to `java:comp/env/`.
- **`service-interface`**—This is the name of the JAX-RPC service interface the client uses. Normally this is `javax.xml.rpc.Service`, but it's possible to provide your own service class.
- **`wsdl-file`**—This is the location of the WSDL file. The WSDL file should be under `META-INF/wsdl`.

- **`jaxrpc-mapping-file`**—This is the location of the JAX-RPC mapping file.
- **`service-qname`**—This element specifies the name of the service in the web services file. It is only mandatory if the WSDL file defines multiple services. The value must be a *QName*, which means it needs to be a namespace qualified value, such as `ns:ServiceName`, where `ns` is an XML namespace valid at the scope of the `service-qname` element.
- **`port-component-ref`**—This element provides the mapping between a service endpoint interface and a port in a web service.
- **`handler`**—This allows the specification of handlers, which act like filters or interceptors on the current request.

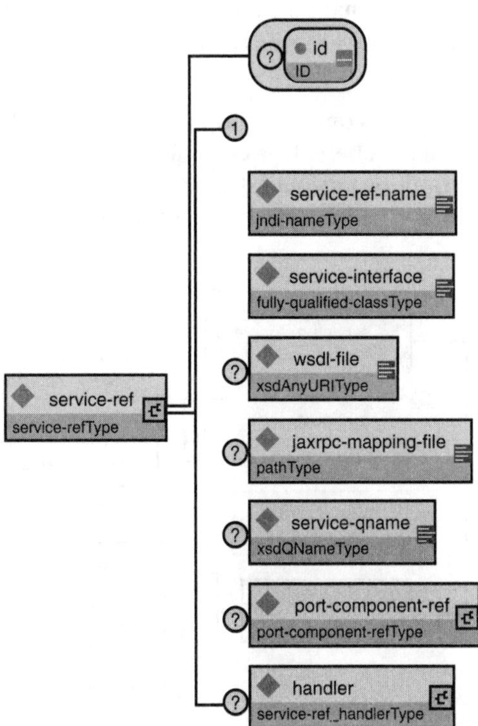

FIGURE 12.3 The `service-ref` content model.

The following `service-ref` declares a reference to the `hello` web service for the `Example` session bean:

```
<session>
    <ejb-name>Example</ejb-name>
    <home>org.jboss.chap12.example.ExampleHome</home>
    <remote>org.jboss.chap12.example.Example</remote>
    <ejb-class>org.jboss.chap12.example.ExampleBean</ejb-class>
```

```
    <session-type>Stateless</session-type>
    <transaction-type>Container</transaction-type>
    <service-ref>
        <service-ref-name>services/hello</service-ref-name>
        <service-interface>javax.xml.rpc.Service</service-interface>
        <wsdl-file>META-INF/wsdl/hello.wsdl</wsdl-file>
        <jaxrpc-mapping-file>META-INF/mapping.xml</jaxrpc-mapping-file>
        <service-qname xmlns:hello="http://hello.chap12.jboss.org">
➥hello:HelloService</service-qname>
    </service-ref>
</session>
```

This instructs the EJB deployer to make a `Service` object available for the bean in JNDI under the name `java:comp/env/services/hello`, which talks to the `hello` web service. The session bean can then invoke normal web services' operations on the service.

Because most of the web services' configuration options are completely standard, there's little need to go into great depths here. However, JBoss does provide several additional web services' configuration options through the `service-ref` element in the `jboss.xml` deployment descriptor. The content model for the `service-ref` element is shown in Figure 12.4.

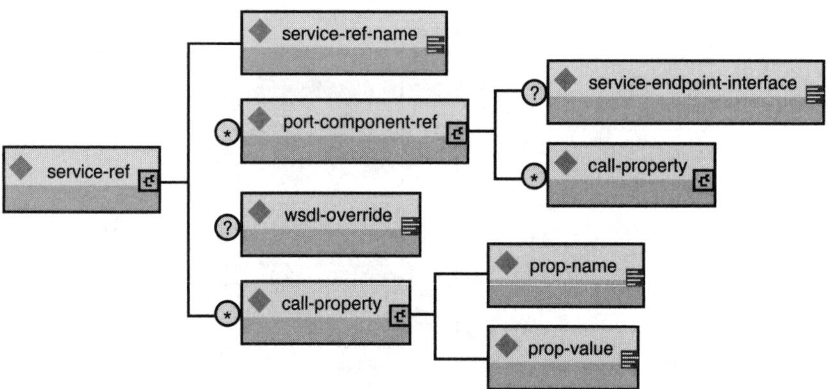

FIGURE 12.4 The `jboss.xml service-ref` content model.

The configurable elements are

- **`service-ref-name`**—This element should match the `service-ref-name` in the `ejb-jar.xml` file being configured.
- **`port-component-ref`**—The `port-component-ref` element provides additional information for a specific port. This includes properties that should be associated with the JAX-RPC stub for the port.

- **`wsdl-override`**—This provides an alternate location for the WSDL file. The value can be any valid URL. This can be used in coordination with the `wsdl-publish-location` to get the final WSDL file for a locally published web service. It could also be the URL of a remotely published WSDL you don't want duplicated in the deployment file.
- **`call-property`**—This sets properties on the JAX-RPC stub.

Because the WSDL file generated by `wscompile` doesn't contain the SOAP address of your web service, use the WSDL override feature to dynamically download the correct WSDL file from the server. Although this might not be the best technique to use in a production application, it does illustrate the WSDL override functionality very well.

The following `jboss.xml` file links the published URL for the `hello-servlet` version of the `hello` web service:

```
<!DOCTYPE jboss PUBLIC
          "-//JBoss//DTD JBOSS 4.0//EN"
          "http://www.jboss.org/j2ee/dtd/jboss_4_0.dtd">
<jboss>
    <enterprise-beans>
        <session>
            <ejb-name>Example</ejb-name>
            <service-ref>
                <service-ref-name>services/hello</service-ref-name>
                <wsdl-override>http://localhost:8080/hello-servlet/Hello?wsdl
➥</wsdl-override>
            </service-ref>
        </session>
    </enterprise-beans>
</jboss>
```

This example can be run as shown below:

```
[examples]$ ant -Dchap=chap12 -Dex=2 run-example
...
run-example3:
     [echo] Waiting for 5 seconds for deploy...
     [copy] Copying 1 file to /tmp/jboss-4.0.1/server/default/deploy
     [echo] Waiting for 5 seconds for deploy...
     [java] output:Hello example bean!
```

The `service-ref` element is not limited to the `ejb-jar.xml` file. It's available to any J2EE component. A service reference can be placed in the `web.xml` file for use by web tier components or in the `application-client.xml` file for use by J2EE client applications.

CHAPTER **13**

Hibernate

IN THIS CHAPTER

- The Hibernate MBean
- Hibernate Archives
- Using Hibernate Objects
- Using a HAR File Inside an EAR File
- The HAR Deployer

Hibernate is a popular persistence engine that provides a simple, yet powerful, alternative to standard entity beans.

Hibernate can run in almost any application server or even outside an application server completely. Hibernate is very simple, but when running in JBoss, you can choose to deploy your application as a Hibernate archive, called a *HAR file*, and make Hibernate's simple usage even simpler. JBoss can manage your Hibernate session and other configuration details, allowing you to use Hibernate objects with minimal setup.

The Hibernate MBean

The Hibernate archive instantiates and configures a Hibernate MBean (`org.jboss.hibernate.jmx.Hibernate`) that will be responsible for constructing a Hibernate `SessionFactory` and exposing it to your application through JNDI. In addition, the Hibernate MBean allows you to inspect and change the configuration of the `SessionFactory` at runtime.

In its most basic configuration, the Hibernate MBean simply needs to know the database name and dialect as well as where to bind the SessionFactory in the `JNDI` tree. The following sample Hibernate MBean configuration illustrates a typical minimal Hibernate configuration:

```
<mbean code="org.jboss.hibernate.jmx.Hibernate"
➥name="jboss.har:service=Hibernate">
    <attribute name="DatasourceName">java:/DefaultDS
➥</attribute>
    <attribute
➥name="Dialect">net.sf.hibernate.dialect.HSQLDialect
➥</attribute>
    <attribute name="SessionFactoryName">java:
➥/hibernate/SessionFactory</attribute>
```

```
    <attribute name="CacheProviderClass">net.sf.hibernate.cache.
➥HashtableCacheProvider</attribute>
</mbean>
```

The following attributes are shown in this configuration:

- **DatasourceName**—This is the JNDI name of the datasource that Hibernate should use.
- **Dialect**—This is the SQL dialect (database type) for the database being used. Any valid Hibernate dialect may be used. The following are a few the more commonly used dialects:

  ```
  net.sf.hibernate.dialect.HSQLDialect
  net.sf.hibernate.dialect.Oracle9Dialect
  net.sf.hibernate.dialect.MySQLDialect
  net.sf.hibernate.dialect.SQLServerDialect
  net.sf.hibernate.dialect.FirebirdDialect
  ```

- **SessionFactoryName**—This is the name of the JNDI where the constructed `SessionFactory` should be bound. Here we've chosen `java:/hibernate/SessionFactory SessionFactory`. If you are deploying multiple Hibernate applications in the JBoss Release 1 439 server, make sure to choose a unique name.

This really is a small Hibernate configuration. There are many more configuration options available. The following are a few of the more useful options:

- **Hbm2ddlAuto**—This option controls the automatic creation of tables for Hibernate objects. The valid values are `create`, `create-drop`, and `update`.
- **DefaultSchema**—This option sets a schema or tablespace name used to qualify unqualified tablenames in generated SQL.
- **ShowSqlEnabled**—Setting this option to `true` enables logging of SQL to the console.
- **CacheProviderClass**—This option sets the second-level cache provider.
- **DeployedTreeCacheJndiName**—This sets the JNDI name of the `JBossTreeCache` instance to use if using the `DeployedTreeCacheProvider`.
- **SessionFactoryInterceptor**—This sets the `Interceptor` on the configuration.

A full set of Hibernate configuration properties is available on the Hibernate MBean. Table 13.1 shows all the MBean properties that map to standard Hibernate configuration properties. For more information on the Hibernate configuration, see the Hibernate documentation or *Hibernate in Action* (Manning, 2004).

TABLE 13.1 Hibernate MBean Configuration Properties and Their Corresponding Property Names

MBean Property	Standard Hibernate Property
BatchVersionedDataEnabled	hibernate.jdbc.batch_versioned_data
CacheProviderClass	hibernate.cache.provider_class
CacheRegionPrefix	hibernate.cache.region_prefix
DatasourceName	hibernate.connection.datasource
DefaultSchema	hibernate.default_schema
Dialect	hibernate.dialect
GeneratedKeysEnabled	hibernate.jdbc.use_get_generated_keys
Hbm2ddlAuto	hibernate.hbm2ddl.auto
JdbcBatchSize	hibernate.jdbc.batch_size
JdbcFetchSize	hibernate.jdbc.fetch_size
JdbcScrollableResultSetEnabled	hibernate.jdbc.use_scrollable_resultset
MaxFetchDepth	hibernate.max_fetch_depth
MinimalPutsEnabled	hibernate.cache.use_minimal_puts
Password	hibernate.connection.password
QueryCacheEnabled	hibernate.cache.use_query_cache
QuerySubstitutions	hibernate.query.substitutions
ReflectionOptimizationEnabled	hibernate.cglib.use_reflection_optimizer
SessionFactoryName	hibernate.session_factory_name
ShowSqlEnabled	hibernate.show_sql
StreamsForBinaryEnabled	hibernate.jdbc.use_streams_for_binary
Username	hibernate.connection.username

Hibernate Archives

JBoss provides a new, simplified way to package and deploy Hibernate applications. JBoss introduces the notion of a HAR file. The HAR file allows you to provide Hibernate objects to your application code without performing any of the tedious manual configuration or setup code normally required.

Structurally, a HAR file resembles a JBoss SAR file. The HAR file contains the Hibernate class files and mapping files, along with a `hibernate-service.xml` deployment descriptor in the `META-INF` directory. We'll look first at the `hibernate-service.xml` file.

The `hibernate-service.xml` file is actually just a normal `jboss-service.xml` file. The name is different, but the content is the same. The file should contain a definition for the Hibernate MBean (see the section "The Hibernate MBean," earlier in this chapter) configured correctly for the needs of the Hibernate application being created. The following example shows a typical `hibernate-service.xml` file:

```
<server>
    <mbean code="org.jboss.hibernate.jmx.Hibernate" name="jboss.har:service=
➥Hibernate">
        <attribute name="DatasourceName">java:/DefaultDS</attribute>
```

```
        <attribute name="Dialect">net.sf.hibernate.dialect.HSQLDialect</attribute>
        <attribute name="SessionFactoryName">java:/hibernate/
➥CaveatEmptorSessionFactory</attribute>
        <attribute name="CacheProviderClass">
➥net.sf.hibernate.cache.HashtableCacheProvider</attribute>
        <attribute name="Hbm2ddlAuto">create-drop</attribute>
        <attribute name="ShowSqlEnabled">true</attribute>
    </mbean>
</server>
```

Notice that the hibernate-service.xml file does not contain a list of the classes Hibernate is to map the way a hibernate.cfg.xml file would, and you do not need to manually add the Hibernate mapping files to the configuration the way you would when using a hibernate.properties file. Instead, the Hibernate deployer in JBoss scans the archive for .hbm.xml mapping files at deployment time and adds them to the configuration for you. Figure 13.1 shows the layout of a typical HAR file.

The Hibernate deployer creates a configuration, using all the .hbm.xml files in the archive, and binds a Hibernate SessionFactory into the JNDI tree at the appropriate location. The SessionFactory can then be used by any application in JBoss. This example comes from the CaveatEmptor demo (http://caveatemptor.hibernate.org/). The CaveatEmptor code is provided along with the examples in this book. To deploy the Hibernate portion of the demo as a HAR file, you run the following command:

```
[examples]$ ant -Dchap=hibernate -Dex=1 run-example
...
[copy] Copying 1 file to /tmp/jboss-4.0.1/server/default/deploy
```

This creates and deploys the HAR file shown in Figure 13.1. If you look at the console log, you will see the Hibernate classes located and deployed as well as the results of the schema generation.

Using Hibernate Objects

When the Hibernate archive is deployed, the Hibernate objects are made available to other applications through the provided SessionFactory. There are several ways to use it.

Since the session factory is bound into JNDI, it is possible to simply look it up and manually to create a Hibernate session. The following code does just that:

```
InitialContext ctx = new InitialContext();
SessionFactory factory = (SessionFactory)
    ctx.lookup("java:/hibernate/CaveatEmptorSessionFactory");
Session hsession = factory.openSession();
```

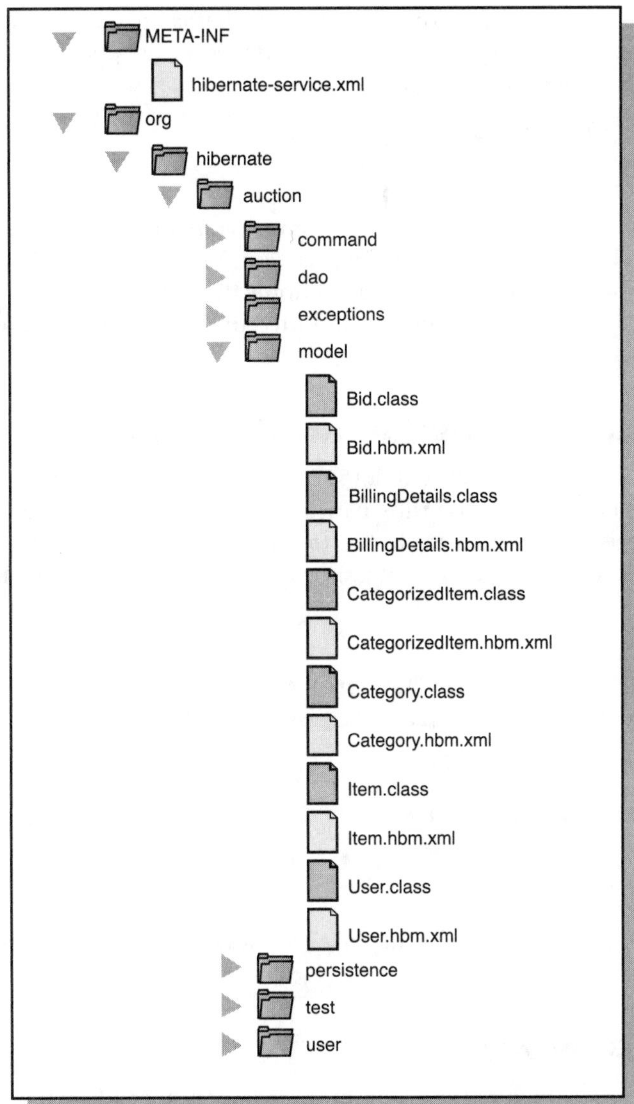

FIGURE 13.1 The structure of a typical HAR file.

This requires manual management of the session and the Hibernate transaction, and it may be useful for migrating existing Hibernate code into JBoss. However, in the context of a larger J2EE application, you'll likely want your Hibernate objects to take part in an existing JTA transaction. This would be the normal case if you wanted to access Hibernate objects in a session bean, for example. JBoss provides the `org.jboss.hibernate.session.HibernateContext` class as the integration piece that does this.

The getSession method returns a Hibernate session that is linked to the current JTA transaction. Naturally, this requires that a JTA transaction exist prior to the call. The following code illustrates the use of getSession:

```
Session hsession = HibernateContext.getSession
➥("java:/hibernate/CaveatEmptorSessionFactory");
```

When you get the Hibernate session in this manner, you don't need to close the Hibernate session or manage a Hibernate transaction. You can be sure that all access to the Hibernate session from the current transaction will see the same state, and you can know that your Hibernate access will be committed to the database or rolled back along with the larger JTA transaction.

Using a HAR File Inside an EAR File

A Hibernate archive can be deployed as a top-level package, or it can be deployed as a component of an EAR file. Because Hibernate archives are not a standard J2EE deployment type, you need to declare them in the jboss-app.xml file of an EAR file in order to use them in that context. You do this by using a module/har element, as shown in the following example:

```
<!DOCTYPE jboss-app PUBLIC
          "-//JBoss//DTD J2EE Application 1.4//EN"
          "http://www.jboss.org/j2ee/dtd/jboss-app_4_0.dtd">
<jboss-app>
    <module>
        <har>caveatemptor.har</har>
    </module>
</jboss-app>
```

With this, a Hibernate archive can be deployed alongside a WAR or EJB JAR file in any EAR file.

The HAR Deployer

The HAR deployer is defined in the jboss-hibernate.deployer file, which by default is included in both the all and default configuration sets. The service definition for the HARDeployer MBean is shown here:

```
<server>
    <mbean code="org.jboss.hibernate.har.HARDeployer"
➥name="jboss.har:service=HARDeployer">
        <attribute name="ValidateDTDs">false</attribute>
    </mbean>
</server>
```

It defines a single configuration property named ValidateDTDs, which denotes whether DTDs should be validated on deployment.

CHAPTER **14**

Aspect-Oriented Programming (AOP) Support

IN THIS CHAPTER

- JBoss AOP: EJB-Style Services for Plain Java Objects
- Why AOP?
- Basic Concepts of AOP
- Building JBoss AOP Applications
- The JBoss AOP Deployer
- Packaging and Deploying AOP Applications to JBoss

JBoss AOP: EJB-Style Services for Plain Java Objects

Support for aspect-oriented middleware is a key innovation in JBoss Application Server (AS) 4.0. It drastically simplifies the development of enterprise middleware applications. This chapter first introduces the basic concepts of aspect-oriented programming (AOP). Then, it discusses how to configure AOP support inside the JBoss application server and how to deploy AOP-enabled applications in various scenarios.

Why AOP?

AOP extends the traditional object-oriented programming (OOP) model to improve code reuse across different object hierarchies. The basic concept in AOP is an *aspect*, which is a common behavior that's typically scattered across methods, classes, object hierarchies, and sometimes even entire object models. For example, metrics is one common aspect. To generate useful logs from an application, you have to sprinkle informative messages throughout the code. However, metrics is something that your class or object model really shouldn't be concerned about. After all, metrics is irrelevant to your actual application: It doesn't represent a customer or an account, and it doesn't realize a business rule. It's an orthogonal behavior that requires duplicated code in traditional OOP systems.

In AOP, a feature such as metrics is called a *cross-cutting* concern, as it's a behavior that cuts across multiple points in your object models yet is distinctly different. As a development methodology, AOP recommends that you abstract and encapsulate cross-cutting concerns into aspects.

In the context of enterprise middleware, container-managed services are cross-cutting concerns. Once deployed, each J2EE component (for example, an EJB or a servlet) automatically gets services, such as logging, security, and transaction services, from the container. Those services are orthogonal to the core business logic. The application developers could reuse those services without writing any code. The J2EE services have the basic characteristics of aspects, as discussed earlier. However, compared with a true AOP solution, the J2EE services model has a number of limitations:

- The J2EE component classes must implement certain base classes or interfaces in the J2EE framework. It is impossible for components to inherit from each other. Therefore, it is difficult to build a complex OOP system based on those components.
- The J2EE infrastructure code and deployment descriptors are complex. They are designed for fully distributed services and are overkill for many smaller-scale middleware applications.
- You cannot extend the J2EE container for services that are not shipped with the application server.
- You cannot use J2EE services in standalone applications without the J2EE application server.

JBoss AOP helps you solve all these problems. It works with plain old Java objects (POJOs) as opposed to predefined components. JBoss AOP allows you to apply EJB-style services to POJOs without the complex EJB infrastructure code and deployment descriptors. You can develop new aspects and deploy them into the application server for all applications to use. That essentially extends the existing container services. You can also use JBoss AOP in standalone Java applications. You can find a detailed introduction to AOP and the JBoss AOP framework on the JBoss website at http://www.jboss.org/products/aop.

Basic Concepts of AOP

This section first introduces some basic AOP concepts via some examples. These concepts and terms are used frequently throughout the rest of this chapter.

Joinpoints and Invocation

A *joinpoint* is simply any point in a Java program: The call of a method, the execution of a constructor, and the access of a field are all joinpoints. Joinpoints are places where aspects provide services to the object. The following is an example of the POJO `Foo`:

```
public class Foo {
  public int fooField;
```

```
  public Foo () {
    fooField = 0;
  }

  public String fooMethod (int i) {
    return Integer.toString (fooField + i);
  }
}
```

The following actions on the `Foo` class and its instance objects are joinpoints:

```
Foo foo = new Foo ();
int k = foo.fooField;
String s = foo.fooMethod (0);
```

Inside the JBoss AOP, a joinpoint is encapsulated by an `Invocation` object at runtime. This object could contain information such as which method is being called, the arguments of the method, and so on. It is available to developers via the JBoss AOP framework API.

Advice and Aspects

The AOP system dynamically modifies an object's behavior at joinpoints. The injected behavior, such as logging, security checking, transactions, and so on, is specified in regular Java methods known as advices. In the following example, the `trace()` method is an advice:

```
public class FooAspect {

  public Object trace (Invocation invocation) throws Throwable {
    try {
      System.out.println("Enter the joinpoint");
      return invocation.invokeNext ();
    } finally {
      System.out.println("Leave the joinpoint");
    }
  }

}
```

When the execution flow reaches a joinpoint that is bound to the `trace()` advice (you will see how to specify the binding later), the JVM executes the `trace()` method instead of the joinpoint. Here, the `trace()` method prints out a message, instructs the AOP runtime to execute the joinpoint, and then prints another message. The `invocation` object contains information about the joinpoint where this advice is applied. You can apply the advice to any joinpoint to log an event.

In JBoss AOP, an aspect class is a regular Java class that holds one or many advice methods. For example, the FooAspect class is an aspect. A special kind of aspect class in JBoss AOP is an interceptor; it must implement the Interceptor interface, which defines only one advice method: invoke(). This interface helps developers enforce compile-time type checking for the interceptor type of aspect classes.

Introducing Pointcuts

An advice is bound to a specific set of joinpoints known as a *pointcut*. As a developer, you specify the mapping rules to group joinpoints into pointcuts, using an expression language supported by JBoss AOP. As discussed in the following sections, there are three ways to specify a pointcut:

- Using an XML configuration file
- Using annotations
- Using annotation in application classes

Using an XML Configuration File

The following example from the jboss-aop.xml descriptor specifies that the trace() advice is bound to the Foo . fooMethod() method call joinpoint:

```
<aop>
  <aspect class="FooAspect" scope="PER_VM"/>

  <bind pointcut="execution(public String Foo->fooMethod(..))">
    <advice name="trace" aspect="FooAspect"/>
  </bind>
</aop>
```

You can find a complete reference of the elements in the jboss-aop.xml file in the JBoss AOP manual.

Using Annotations

If you do not want to manage a separate jboss-aop.xml configuration file, you can declare the aspect and specify its bindings in the aspect class's source code, by using annotations. In JDK 5.0, annotations are an officially supported Java language feature. You can just use JBoss AOP–defined annotations to tag your aspect class and advice methods, as in the following example:

```
@Aspect (scope = Scope.PER_VM)
public class FooAspect {

  @Bind (pointcut="execution("* Foo->fooMethod())")
  public Object trace (Invocation invocation) throws Throwable {
    try {
      System.out.println("Enter the joinpoint");
      return invocation.invokeNext ();
```

```
        } finally {
            System.out.println("Leave the joinpoint");
        }
    }

}
```

In JDK 1.4, however, annotations are not supported by the Java compiler. JBoss AOP allows you to embed the annotations in JavaDoc comments. You can use the JBoss annotation compiler to extract an annotation from the source code and then add it to the compiled bytecode files or store it in a separate XML file for further processing.

```
/**
 * @@Aspect (scope = Scope.PER_VM)
 */
public class FooAspect {

    /**
     * @@org.jboss.aop.Bind (pointcut="execution("* Foo->fooMethod())")
     */
    public Object trace (Invocation invocation) throws Throwable {
        try {
            System.out.println("Enter the joinpoint");
            return invocation.invokeNext ();
        } finally {
            System.out.println("Leave the joinpoint");
        }
    }

}
```

Annotations are easier to use than the `jboss-aop.xml` configuration file because they are closer to the source code they are supposed to control.

Using Annotation in Application Classes

So far, you have seen how to bind advices to pointcuts by using the signature pattern of the joinpoints (for example, the method signature). A more general way to specify pointcuts is to directly tag the joinpoints in the application code by using annotations. Then, in the `jboss-aop.xml` file, you can map the annotations to the advices. In the following `jbossaop.xml` file, the `trace()` advice is mapped to the `@FooTrace` annotation tag:

```
<aop>
  <aspect class="FooAspect" scope="PER_VM"/>

  <bind pointcut="execution(* *->@org.jboss.FooTrace(..))">
    <advice name="trace" aspect="FooAspect"/>
```

```
  </bind>
</aop>
```

Here is the application code that makes use of the `@FooTrace` annotation in JDK 5.0:

```
public class Foo {
  public int fooField;

  public Foo () {
    fooField = 0;
  }

  @FooTrace public String fooMethod (int i) {
    return Integer.toString (fooField + i);
  }
}
```

The version in JDK 1.4 with the JBoss annotation compiler is as follows:

```
public class Foo {
  public int fooField;

  public Foo () {
    fooField = 0;
  }

  /**
    * @@org.jboss.FooTrace
    */
  public String fooMethod (int i) {
    return Integer.toString (fooField + i);
  }
}
```

Notice that you do not need to annotate the aspect class in this setup. The ability to specify pointcuts via annotations in the application code allows you to develop prepackaged aspects and then publish the annotation API for all to use. That is exactly what JBoss did to support prepackaged EJB-style AOP services inside the JBoss application server.

Introductions and Mixins

The aspects you have seen so far are interceptor types of aspects. Another key AOP feature is an *introduction* or a *mixin* of classes from independent inheritance trees. An introduction modifies the type and structure of a Java class. It can be used to force an existing class to implement an interface, by using methods from another class. It essentially allows developers to create C++-style multiple-inheritance object systems in Java. The following example shows that the methods in the `FooMixin` class are used to make the `Foo` class implement the `FooMixinInt` interface at runtime. Here is the `FooMixinInt` interface:

```
public interface FooMixinInt {
  public String fooMethod2 (int i);
}
```

The FooMixin class implements the FooMixinInt interface as follows:

```
public class FooMixin implements FooMixinInt {

  public String fooMethod2 (int i) {
    return Integer.toString (fooField - i);
  }

}>
```

However, the Foo class does not implement the FooMixinInt interface. The following jboss-aop.xml file forces the Foo class to implement FooMixinInt by using the method from the FooMixin class:

```
introduction class="Foo">
  <mixin>
    <interfaces>FooMixinInt</interfaces>
    <class>FooMixin</class>
    <construction>new FooMixin(this)</construction>
  </mixin>
</introduction>
```

Then, in the application code, you can cast a Foo instance to the FooMixinInt type at runtime:

```
Foo foo = new Foo ();
FooMixinInt fooint = (FooMixinInt) foo; String s = foo.fooMethod2 (-2);
```

The fooMethod2() method, which is defined in the FooMixin class but not in the Foo class, is now available in the Foo instance at the AOP runtime.

Building JBoss AOP Applications

Building JBoss AOP applications is slightly different from building plain Java applications because the aspects and advices need to be instrumented into the compiled Java bytecode. For example, if an advice is bound to a method invocation joinpoint, the AOP instrumentation process would modify the joinpoint bytecode to call out to the advice method with the properly composed invocation object as an argument.

Compiling to Bytecode

The first step in building a JBoss AOP application is to compile all the classes, including the aspect classes, to bytecode by using the regular javac utility. If you use JDK 5.0 and the J2SE 5.0–style annotation, the annotation is automatically compiled into the bytecode class files.

Compiling Annotations

You can skip this step if you use Java annotations with the JDK 5.0. However, if you want to use JBoss AOP annotations with JDK 1.4, you have to embed the annotations in the JavaDoc comments. They are not processed by the `javac` compiler. You have to use an annotation compiler provided by JBoss AOP to process the source code. The annotation compiler can directly add annotations to the bytecode class files or generate the annotation data in a separate XML file called `metadata.xml`. The following example compiles the annotation in the `Foo.java` file into the `Foo.class` file:

```
annotationc <classpath of the Foo.class file> -bytecode Foo.java
```

The following example compiles the annotation into a `metadata.xml` file in the current directory and does not alter the `Foo.class` file. The `metadata.xml` file can be used later in the AOP bytecode instrumentation process.

```
annotationc <classpath> -xml Foo.java
```

You can also run the annotation compiler within an Ant build script. The following example modifies the Java bytecode class files directly to add annotations:

```
<taskdef name="annotationc"
         classname="org.jboss.aop.ant.AnnotationC"
         classpathref="jboss.aop.classpath"
/>

<target name="annotate">
  <annotationc compilerclasspathref="classpath"
               classpath="path/to/classfile"
               bytecode="true">
    <src path="."/>
  </annotationc>
</target>
```

> **Note**
>
> This book builds applications using Ant, so the Ant version of the annotation compiler is used.

AOP Instrumentation

The AOP instrumentation process modifies the Java bytecode to add runtime hooks around pointcuts. Those hooks collect reflection information and invoke advices. The `aopc` utility in JBoss AOP instruments the bytecode offline for JDK 1.4. If you use JDK 5.0, you have to replace all the `aopc` below to `aopc15`. It takes a pointcut's definition from the jboss-aop.xml file or the metadata.xml file or the annotation tags already embedded in the bytecode by the annotation compiler. The following example shows how to invoke aopc from the command line with an associated jboss-aop.xml file:

```
aopc <classpath> -aoppath jboss-aop.xml Foo.class
```

If both jboss-aop.xml and metadata.xml files are present, you can put them in one directory and pass the directory name to aopc. In fact, all the *-aop.xml files in this directory will be treated as jboss-aop.xml by the aopc compiler:

```
aopc <classpath> -aoppath <directory to XML files> Foo.class
aopc <classpath> -aopclasspath <classpath to annotated aspect classes> Foo.class
```

The following example shows how to invoke aopc within an Ant build script:

```
<taskdef name="aopc"
         classname="org.jboss.aop.ant.AopC"
         classpathref="jboss.aop.classpath"
/>

<target name="aopc">
  <aopc compilerclasspathref="classpath" verbose="true">
    <classpath path="${classes.dir}"/>
    <src path="${classes.dir}"/>
    <aoppath path="jboss-aop.xml"/>
    <aopclasspath path="aspects.jar"/>
  </aopc>
</target>
```

The aopc instrumented bytecode can run directly in any JVM. Another option is to instrument the bytecode at the class load time. This way, you do not need to run the separate aopc program. In fact, if you use JDK 5.0–style annotations or do not use annotations, you do not even need to run the annotatec program. The JBoss application server can be configured to instrument AOP bytecode at class load time (see the "Configuring the AOP Service" section, later in this chapter).

The JBoss AOP Deployer

JBoss AOP applications are supported in the standard and all configurations in JBoss AS 4.0.0 (the default and all configurations in JBoss AS 4.0.1). The jboss-aop.deployer service in the deploy directory deploys AOP applications inside the JBoss application server. The structure of the jboss-aop.deployer directory is shown in Figure 14.1. Notice that the jboss-aop.deployer service archive in JBoss AS 4.0.0 is a zip file instead of a directory. It includes the following components:

- Java libraries for the JBoss AOP framework, including utilities to instrument AOP classes at load time.

- A prepackaged set of aspects, which are available in all applications deployed on the server. Those prepackaged aspects handle cross-cutting concerns, such as security, transactions, and spawning of asynchronous threads, for applications.
- A default aspect binding configuration file `base-aop.xml` that binds prepackaged aspects to certain annotations and method signature patterns. So, in your applications, you can just use those predefined annotations and method signatures to take advantage of the prepackaged aspects.

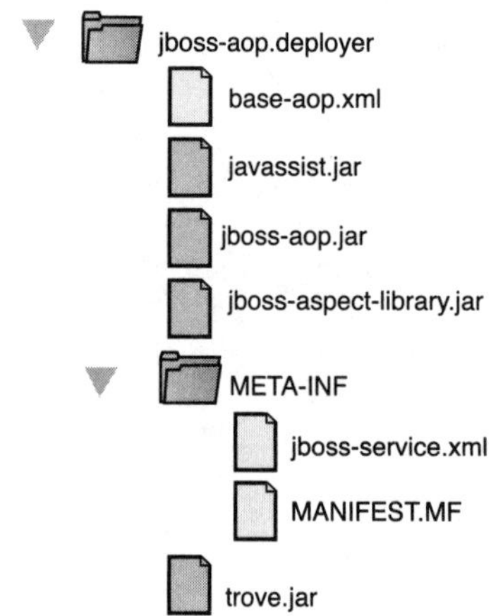

FIGURE 14.1 The directory structure of the JBoss AOP deployer in JBoss AS.

Installing the Latest `jboss-aop.deployer` Service

Because JBoss AOP is a fast-evolving technology, it is probably a good idea to keep your `jboss-aop.deployer` service up-to-date with the latest JBoss AOP release. After you unzip the JBoss AOP release file, the `jboss-40-install` directory contains the `jboss-aop.deployer` archive for the JDK 1.4 and JDK 5.0 environments. You can just copy those files to your JBoss server's `deploy` directory to replace the JBoss AOP service that shipped with the application server.

Configuring the AOP Service

By default, the `jboss-aop.deployer` service disables load-time bytecode instrumentation. You have to instrument your code offline with the `aopc` utility. You should enable load-time instrumentation by editing the `META-INF/jboss-service.xml` file in the `jboss-aop.deployer` directory. You can just change the `EnableTransformer` attribute value to `true`, as follows:

```
<mbean code="org.jboss.aop.deployment.AspectManagerService"
       name="jboss.aop:service=AspectManager">
  <attribute name="EnableTransformer">false</attribute>
  <!-- only relevant when EnableTransformer is true -->
```

```
  <attribute name="SuppressTransformationErrors">true</attribute>
  <!-- only relevant when Enabletransformer is true.
       Optimization is optional
       only just in case there is a bug in it -->
  <attribute name="Optimized">true</attribute>
  <attribute name="Verbose">false</attribute>
</mbean>

<mbean code="org.jboss.aop.deployment.AspectDeployer"
       name="jboss.aop:service=AspectDeployer">
</mbean>
```

Other attributes in this MBean control the behavior of the JBoss AOP deployer. Those attributes are manageable via the JBoss JMX Console when the server is running.

The Prepackaged Aspects Library

The key value proposition of AOP is to promote code reuse. For example, you can reuse common aspects across different object trees in different applications:

- **Transactions**—JBoss AOP allows you to declare transaction requirements and properties on any POJO method. You can inject the current transaction manager anywhere in the code via annotation and save the trouble of writing lookup code.
- **Security**—You can declare EJB-style security constraints on any POJO method to limit the access to them. You'll see a security aspect example later in this chapter.
- **Observers**—You can transparently add observers to any POJO via annotation. For example, the observer could log all the call invocations against methods in the object. The previously mentioned `trace()` example shows the observer in action. This aspect can be used outside the JBoss AS in standalone applications.
- **Asynchronous method invocation**—You can annotate a method to specify that it should be executed in a separate background thread. This aspect can be used outside the JBoss AS in standalone applications. It is especially useful in Swing or SWT UI applications.
- **Thread-based**—Any field value tagged with the annotation defined by this aspect would behave as though its value were stored in `java.lang.ThreadLocal`. This aspect can be used outside the JBoss AS in standalone applications.
- **Read/write lock**—You can use this annotation to define a read/write lock at the method level. The implementation is based on the concurrent package from Doug Lea. This aspect can be used outside the JBoss AS in standalone applications.

The prepackaged aspect library in JBoss AOP is still under development. For the most up-to-date documentation on the currently available aspects, refer to the `docs/aspect-library/index.html` document.

Packaging and Deploying AOP Applications to JBoss

This section provides an example of an application that covers the common scenarios of packaging and deploying AOP applications inside JBoss. The example is an online mortgage payment calculator application (see Figure 14.2).

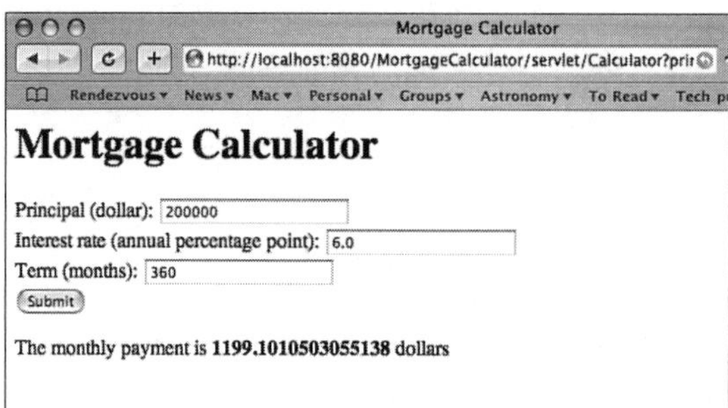

FIGURE 14.2 The Mortgage Calculator sample application.

The servlet uses the `Calculator` class to calculate the monthly payment based on the loan principal, term, and interest rate.

```
public class CalculatorServlet extends HttpServlet {

  private Calculator cal = null;

  public void init () throws ServletException {
    cal = new Calculator ();
  }

  public void service(HttpServletRequest request,
                      HttpServletResponse response)
      throws IOException, ServletException {

    response.setContentType("text/html");

    ServletOutputStream out = response.getOutputStream();

    String para = null;
    int principal = 200000;
    double rate = 8.0;
    int term = 360;
    double payment = 0.;
```

```
    para = request.getParameter("principal");
    if (para != null && para.length() > 0) {
      principal = Integer.parseInt(para);
    }

    para = request.getParameter("rate");
    if (para != null && para.length() > 0) {
      rate = Double.parseDouble(para);
    }

    para = request.getParameter("term");
    if (para != null && para.length() > 0) {
      term = Integer.parseInt(para);
    }

    try {
      payment = cal.getPayment(principal, rate, term);

      // Write out the response in HTML
    } catch (Throwable t) {
      // Write out the error message in HTML
    }
  }
}
```

The `Calculator` class represents a POJO.:

```
public class Calculator {

  public Calculator () { }

  public double getPayment (int principal, double rate,
                            int term) {
    rate = rate / 100.;
    rate = rate / 12.;
    double tmp = Math.pow(1.+rate, term);
    return (principal * tmp * rate) / (tmp - 1.);
  }
}
```

In the world of J2EE containers, the `Calculator` POJO cannot make use of container services because it does not follow the predefined component models (for example, it is not an EJB). But with JBoss AOP, you can apply EJB-style services as well as custom-developed container services to the POJO at runtime. The next two sections show how to do this.

Using Prepackaged Aspects

As discussed earlier in this chapter, JBoss AS 4 comes with several prepackaged aspects. One of the most useful aspects is the security aspect. It supports access control to any POJO methods, just as the EJB security service constrains access to EJB methods. In this section, an example demonstrates how to apply the prepackaged security aspect to the `Calculator.getPayment()` method in the Mortgage Calculator program.

Developing applications using the prepackaged aspects is easy. You can simply use a predefined annotation to mark up your source code and then use the annotation compiler to process the bytecode. In this example, the security domain is `other`, indicating that the usernames, passwords, and roles are stored in the `users.properties` and `roles.properties` files in the classpath. The security domain here has the same meaning as the security domain in EJB configuration file `jboss.xml`. Before the `getPayment()` method is invoked, the JBoss AOP security aspect transparently checks the user role, based on the username obtained by the servlet in the web context. Only users with the role `Authorized` can invoke the `getPayment()` method. The following is the annotated POJO code, using JDK 1.4–style annotation:

```
/**
 * @@org.jboss.aspects.security.SecurityDomain ("other")
 */
public class Calculator {

  /**
   * @@org.jboss.aspects.security.Unchecked
   */
  public Calculator () { }

  /**
   * @@org.jboss.aspects.security.Permissions ({"Authorized"})
   */
  public double getPayment (int principal, double rate,
                            int term) {
    rate = rate / 100.;
    rate = rate / 12.;
    double tmp = Math.pow(1.+rate, term);
    return (principal * tmp * rate) / (tmp - 1.);
  }

}
```

The following is the POJO code with JDK 5.0–style annotation:

```
@SecurityDomain ("other")
public class Calculator {
```

```
  @Unchecked
  public Calculator () { }

  @Permissions ({"Authorized"})
  public double getPayment (int principal, double rate,
                            int term) {
    rate = rate / 100.;
    rate = rate / 12.;
    double tmp = Math.pow(1.+rate, term);
    return (principal * tmp * rate) / (tmp - 1.);
  }

}
```

No special packaging is required for deploying this application. You can just package the annotation-enhanced class files as regular Java classes in your `.war` or `.ear` applications. Figure 14.3 shows that the server refuses to invoke the `Calculator. getPayment()` method when the current user does not have the required `Authorized` role.

Maybe you hit the access limit or do not have sufficient permission

The error message is:

`Insufficient method permissions, principal=user4, interface=com.jboss.`

FIGURE 14.3 Detecting and rejecting users with inadequate security roles.

Notice that the application does not have a `jboss-aop.xml` file because the default annotation tags and bindings are already defined in the `base-aop.xml` file that comes with the `jboss-aop.deployer` package. The downside is that you cannot easily instrument your bytecode outside the server container. The easiest way to deploy this application is to enable the load-time AOP instrumentation in the server (see the section "Configuring the AOP Service," earlier in this chapter).

Developing Your Own Aspects

In addition to the prepackaged aspect services, JBoss AOP allows you to develop your own aspects to extend the AOP container services. The following example shows how to develop an aspect to limit the number of times the user can invoke certain POJO methods. When this aspect is applied to the `Calculator` object, you can make the mortgage calculator stop working after a certain number of queries (that is, you can put the calculator in the trial software mode).

As discussed earlier, the JBoss AOP aspect class is just a simple Java class. The advice method takes the `Invocation` object from the joinpoint as an argument and checks how many times it has been invoked. If it has been invoked more than five times, the aspect stops the invocation and throws an exception:

```
package com.jboss.aspect;

import org.jboss.aop.joinpoint.Invocation;

public class TrialLimitAspect {

  private static int count = 0;

  public Object checkLimit (Invocation invocation)
                                  throws Throwable {
    System.out.println("Check whether the trial limit is reached");
    count++;
    if (count < 5) {
      return invocation.invokeNext();
    } else {
      throw new Exception("Hit the maximum access count");
    }
  }
}
```

As with prepackaged aspects, the easiest way to bind a custom aspect to applications is to use annotations. You can define custom annotations for an aspect and then publish them as part of the service API. In JBoss AOP, each annotation is a Java interface. The following `TrialLimit` interface defines the `TrialLimit` annotation tag:

```
package com.jboss.aspect;
public interface TrialLimit { }
```

In the `jboss-aop.xml` file, you can specify the binding between the annotation tag and the advice method:

```
<aop>
  <aspect class="com.jboss.aspect.TrialLimitAspect"
          scope="PER_VM"/>

  <bind pointcut="execution(* *->@com.jboss.aspect.TrialLimit(..))">
    <advice name="checkLimit"
            aspect="com.jboss.aspect.TrialLimitAspect"/>
  </bind>
</aop>
```

Finally, in the application code, you just need to tag your methods, which need invocation limit control, with the annotation, as you do with prepackaged aspects. Notice the second tag on the `getPayment()` method:

```
/**
 * @@org.jboss.aspects.security.SecurityDomain ("other")
 */
public class Calculator {

  /**
   * @@org.jboss.aspects.security.Unchecked
   */
  public Calculator () { }

  /**
   * @@org.jboss.aspects.security.Permissions ({"Authorized"})
   * @@com.jboss.aspect.TrialLimit
   */
  public double getPayment (int principal, double rate,
                            int term) {
    rate = rate / 100.;
    rate = rate / 12.;
    double tmp = Math.pow(1.+rate, term);
    return (principal * tmp * rate) / (tmp - 1.);
  }
}
```

Figure 14.4 shows the servlet, displaying an error message when the invocation limit has been reached.

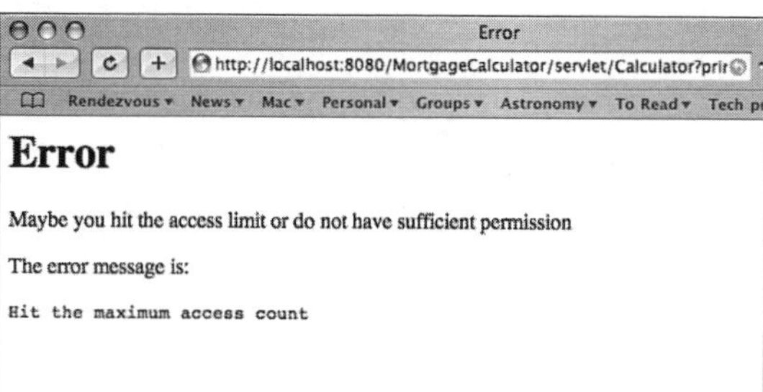

FIGURE 14.4 The custom aspect detecting that the user has reached the invocation limit for this POJO method.

Packaging and Deploying Custom Aspects

To deploy the `TrialLimitAspect` aspect or any other custom aspect, you have to package the aspect properly so that the JBoss application server can recognize it as an aspect library. You have the following two options:

- You can package the aspect classes, annotation interfaces, and configuration files together in a JAR archive file with the filename extension `.aop`. The `jboss-aop.xml` and `metadata.xml` files must reside in the `META-INF` directory in the `.aop` JAR archive. In this example, you can bundle the `.aop` file with the `.war` file in the same `.jar` repository (see Figure 14.5), and then you can deploy the `.jar` file as a single application. Or you can deploy them side-by-side on the server. If you use custom aspects in EJB applications, you can include the `.aop` file directly in your `.ear` file.
- You can simply package the aspect classes and annotation interfaces in a `.jar` file and then specify the binding in an `*-aop.xml` file. You can copy the `.jar` file and the `*-aop.xml` files into the `deploy` directory (see Figure 14.6). The aspects and their bindings become available to all applications deployed in this server.

The sample application for this chapter uses the first approach and builds a `TrialLimitAspect.aop` file and a `MortgageCalculator.war` file side-by-side. All other applications deployed in the server can make use of the aspect in the `TrialLimitAspect.aop` file as well.

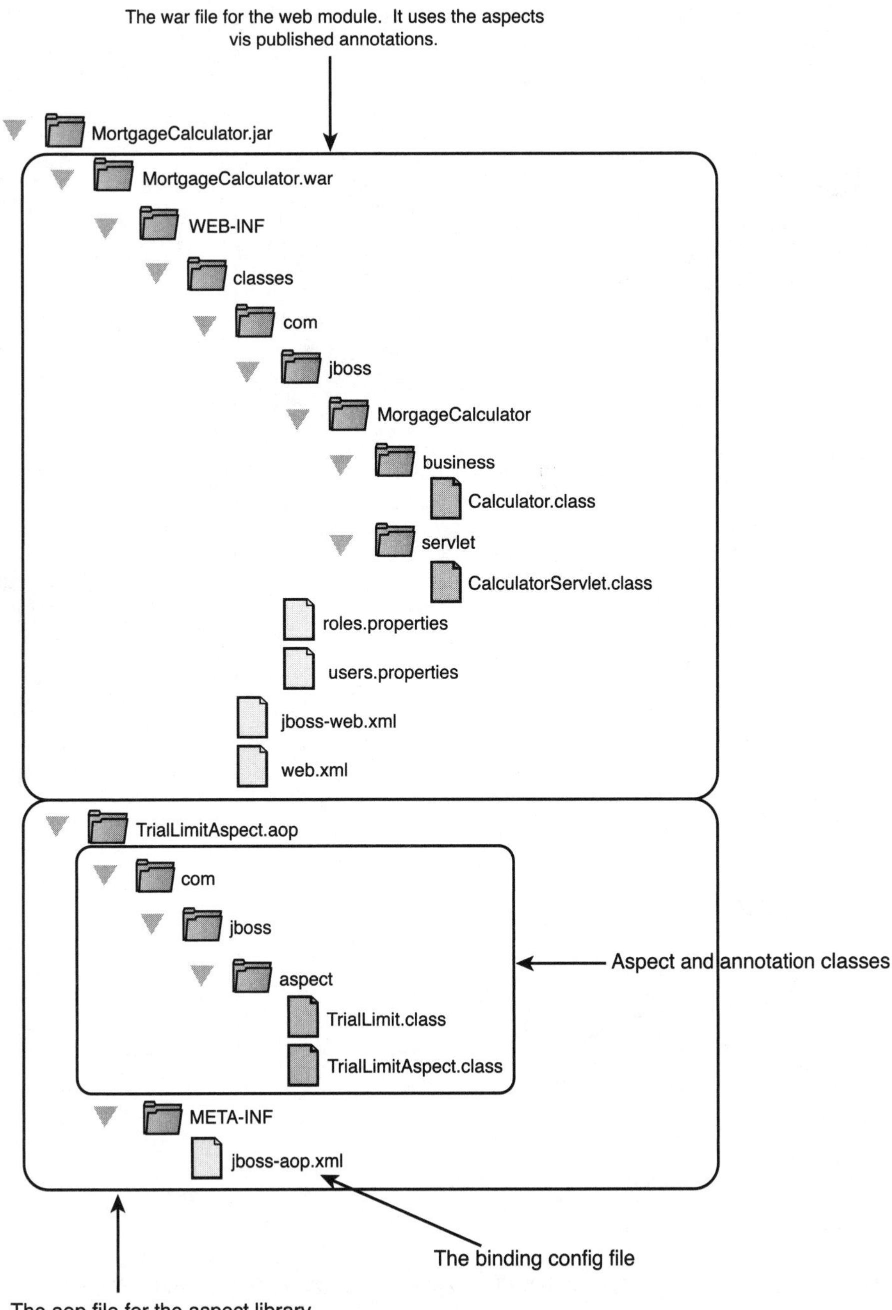

FIGURE 14.5 Packaging the aspect library, binding configuration file, and web application into one JAR file for easy deployment.

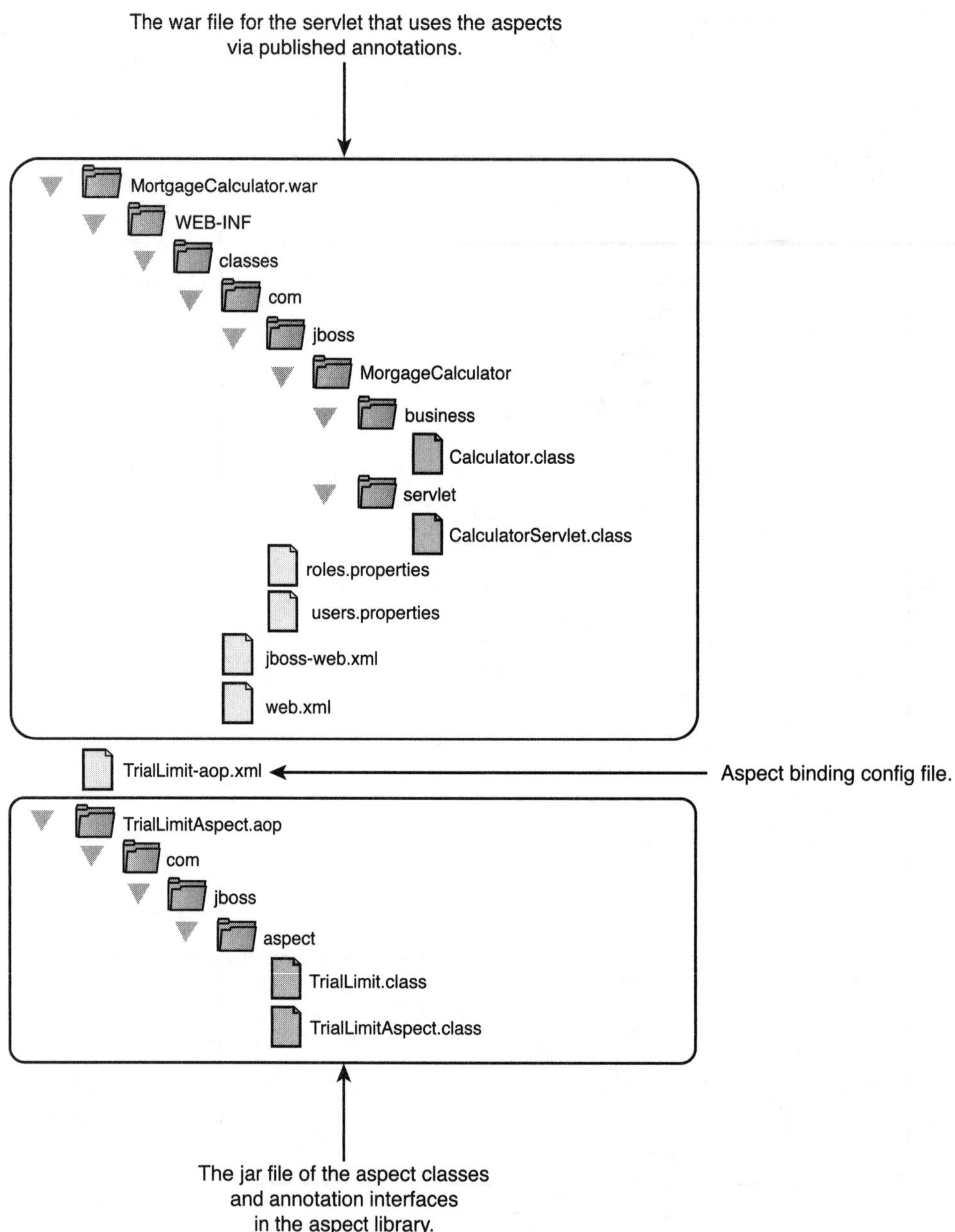

FIGURE 14.6 Deploying the aspect library, binding configuration file, and web application separately.

APPENDIX **A**

The GNU Lesser General Public License (LGPL)

The JBoss source code is licensed under the LGPL (see http://www.gnu.org/copyleft/lesser.txt). This includes all code in the `org.jboss.*` package namespace. This appendix gives the complete text of the LGPL license.

GNU General Public License

Version 2, June 1991

> Copyright (C) 1989, 1991 Free Software Foundation, Inc.
>
> 59 Temple Place - Suite 330, Boston, MA 02111-1307, USA
>
> Everyone is permitted to copy and distribute verbatim copies of this license document, but changing it is not allowed.

Preamble

The licenses for most software are designed to take away your freedom to share and change it. By contrast, the GNU General Public License is intended to guarantee your freedom to share and change free software—to make sure the software is free for all its users. This General Public License applies to most of the Free Software Foundation's software and to any other program whose authors commit to using it. (Some other Free Software Foundation software is covered by the GNU Library General Public License instead.) You can apply it to your programs, too.

When we speak of free software, we are referring to freedom, not price. Our General Public Licenses are designed to make sure that you have the freedom to distribute copies of free software (and charge for this service if you wish), that you receive source code or can get it if you want it, that you can change the software or use pieces of it in new free programs, and that you know you can do these things.

To protect your rights, we need to make restrictions that forbid anyone to deny you these rights or to ask you to surrender the rights. These restrictions translate to certain responsibilities for you if you distribute copies of the software, or if you modify it.

For example, if you distribute copies of such a program, whether gratis or for a fee, you must give the recipients all the rights that you have. You must make sure that they, too, receive or can get the source code. And you must show them these terms so they know their rights.

We protect your rights with two steps: (1) copyright the software, and (2) offer you this license which gives you legal permission to copy, distribute, and/or modify the software.

Also, for each author's protection and ours, we want to make certain that everyone understands that there is no warranty for this free software. If the software is modified by someone else and passed on, we want its recipients to know that what they have is not the original, so that any problems introduced by others will not reflect on the original authors' reputations.

Finally, any free program is threatened constantly by software patents. We wish to avoid the danger that redistributors of a free program will individually obtain patent licenses, in effect making the program proprietary. To prevent this, we have made it clear that any patent must be licensed for everyone's free use or not licensed at all.

The precise terms and conditions for copying, distribution, and modification follow.

Terms and Conditions for Copying, Distribution, and Modification

0. This License applies to any program or other work, which contains a notice placed by the copyright holder saying it may be distributed under the terms of this General Public License. The "Program," below, refers to any such program or work, and a "work based on the Program" means either the Program or any derivative work under copyright law: that is to say, a work containing the Program or a portion of it, either verbatim or with modifications and/or translated into another language. (Hereinafter, translation is included without limitation in the term "modification.") Each licensee is addressed as "you."

Activities other than copying, distribution, and modification are not covered by this License; they are outside its scope. The act of running the Program is not restricted, and the output from the Program is covered only if its contents constitute a work based on the Program (independent of having been made by running the Program). Whether that is true depends on what the Program does.

1. You may copy and distribute verbatim copies of the Program's source code as you receive it, in any medium, provided that you conspicuously and appropriately publish on each copy an appropriate copyright notice and disclaimer of warranty; keep intact all the notices that refer to this License and to the absence of any warranty; and give any other recipients of the Program a copy of this License along with the Program.

You may charge a fee for the physical act of transferring a copy, and you may at your option offer warranty protection in exchange for a fee.

2. You may modify your copy or copies of the Program or any portion of it, thus forming a work based on the Program, and copy and distribute such modifications or work under the terms of Section 1 above, provided that you also meet all of these conditions:

> a) You must cause the modified files to carry prominent notices stating that you changed the files and the date of any change.
>
> b) You must cause any work that you distribute or publish, that in whole or in part contains or is derived from the Program or any part thereof, to be licensed as a whole at no charge to all third parties under the terms of this License.
>
> c) If the modified program normally reads commands interactively when run, you must cause it, when started running for such interactive use in the most ordinary way, to print or display an announcement including an appropriate copyright notice and a notice that there is no warranty (or else, saying that you provide a warranty) and that users may redistribute the program under these conditions, and telling the user how to view a copy of this License. (Exception: if the Program itself is interactive but does not normally print such an announcement, your work based on the Program is not required to print an announcement.)

These requirements apply to the modified work as a whole. If identifiable sections of that work are not derived from the Program, and can be reasonably considered independent and separate works in themselves, then this License, and its terms, do not apply to those sections when you distribute them as separate works. But when you distribute the same sections as part of a whole which is a work based on the Program, the distribution of the whole must be on the terms of this License, whose permissions for other licensees extend to the entire whole, and thus to each and every part regardless of who wrote it.

Thus, it is not the intent of this section to claim rights or contest your rights to work written entirely by you; rather, the intent is to exercise the right to control the distribution of derivative or collective works based on the Program.

In addition, mere aggregation of another work not based on the Program with the Program (or with a work based on the Program) on a volume of a storage or distribution medium does not bring the other work under the scope of this License.

3. You may copy and distribute the Program (or a work based on it, under Section 2) in object code or executable form under the terms of Sections 1 and 2 above provided that you also do one of the following:

> a) Accompany it with the complete corresponding machine-readable source code, which must be distributed under the terms of Sections 1 and 2 above on a medium customarily used for software interchange; or,
>
> b) Accompany it with a written offer, valid for at least three years, to give any third party, for a charge no more than your cost of physically performing source distribution, a complete

machine-readable copy of the corresponding source code, to be distributed under the terms of Sections 1 and 2 above on a medium customarily used for software interchange; or,

c) Accompany it with the information you received as to the offer to distribute corresponding source code. (This alternative is allowed only for noncommercial distribution and only if you received the program in object code or executable form with such an offer, in accord with Subsection b above.)

The source code for a work means the preferred form of the work for making modifications to it. For an executable work, complete source code means all the source code for all modules it contains, plus any associated interface definition files, plus the scripts used to control compilation and installation of the executable. However, as a special exception, the source code distributed need not include anything that is normally distributed (in either source or binary form) with the major components (compiler, kernel, and so on) of the operating system on which the executable runs, unless that component itself accompanies the executable.

If distribution of executable or object code is made by offering access to copy from a designated place, then offering equivalent access to copy the source code from the same place counts as distribution of the source code, even though third parties are not compelled to copy the source along with the object code.

4. You may not copy, modify, sublicense, or distribute the Program except as expressly provided under this License. Any attempt otherwise to copy, modify, sublicense, or distribute the Program is void, and will automatically terminate your rights under this License. However, parties who have received copies, or rights, from you under this License will not have their licenses terminated so long as such parties remain in full compliance.

5. You are not required to accept this License, since you have not signed it. However, nothing else grants you permission to modify or distribute the Program or its derivative works. These actions are prohibited by law if you do not accept this License. Therefore, by modifying or distributing the Program (or any work based on the Program), you indicate your acceptance of this License to do so, and all its terms and conditions for copying, distributing, or modifying the Program or works based on it.

6. Each time you redistribute the Program (or any work based on the Program), the recipient automatically receives a license from the original licensor to copy, distribute, or modify the Program subject to these terms and conditions. You may not impose any further restrictions on the recipients' exercise of the rights granted herein. You are not responsible for enforcing compliance by third parties to this License.

7. If, as a consequence of a court judgment or allegation of patent infringement or for any other reason (not limited to patent issues), conditions are imposed on you (whether by court order, agreement, or otherwise) that contradict the conditions of this License, they do not excuse you from the conditions of this License. If you cannot distribute so as to satisfy simultaneously your obligations under this License and any other pertinent obligations, then as a consequence you may not distribute the Program at all. For example, if a patent license would not permit royalty-free redistribution of the Program by all those

who receive copies directly or indirectly through you, then the only way you could satisfy both it and this License would be to refrain entirely from distribution of the Program.

If any portion of this section is held invalid or unenforceable under any particular circumstance, the balance of the section is intended to apply and the section as a whole is intended to apply in other circumstances.

It is not the purpose of this section to induce you to infringe any patents or other property right claims or to contest validity of any such claims; this section has the sole purpose of protecting the integrity of the free software distribution system, which is implemented by public license practices. Many people have made generous contributions to the wide range of software distributed through that system in reliance on consistent application of that system; it is up to the author/donor to decide if he or she is willing to distribute software through any other system and a licensee cannot impose that choice.

This section is intended to make thoroughly clear what is believed to be a consequence of the rest of this License.

8. If the distribution and/or use of the Program is restricted in certain countries either by patents or by copyrighted interfaces, the original copyright holder who places the Program under this License may add an explicit geographical distribution limitation excluding those countries, so that distribution is permitted only in or among countries not thus excluded. In such case, this License incorporates the limitation as if written in the body of this License.

9. The Free Software Foundation may publish revised and/or new versions of the General Public License from time to time. Such new versions will be similar in spirit to the present version, but may differ in detail to address new problems or concerns.

Each version is given a distinguishing version number. If the Program specifies a version number of this License which applies to it and "any later version," you have the option of following the terms and conditions either of that version or of any later version published by the Free Software Foundation. If the Program does not specify a version number of this License, you may choose any version ever published by the Free Software Foundation.

10. If you wish to incorporate parts of the Program into other free programs whose distribution conditions are different, write to the author to ask for permission. For software which is copyrighted by the Free Software Foundation, write to the Free Software Foundation; we sometimes make exceptions for this. Our decision will be guided by the two goals of preserving the free status of all derivatives of our free software and of promoting the sharing and reuse of software generally.

No Warranty

11. Because the program is licensed free of charge, there is no warranty for the program, to the extent permitted by applicable law. Except when otherwise stated in writing the copyright holders and/or other parties provide the program "as is" without warranty of any kind, either expressed or implied, including, but not limited to, the implied warranties of merchantability and fitness for a particular purpose. The entire risk as to the

quality and performance of the program is with you. Should the program prove defective, you assume the cost of all necessary servicing, repair, or correction.

12. In no event, unless required by applicable law or agreed to in writing will any copyright holder, or any other party who may modify and/or redistribute the program as permitted above, be liable to you for damages, including any general, special, incidental, or consequential damages arising out of the use or inability to use the program (including but not limited to loss of data or data being rendered inaccurate or losses sustained by you or third parties or a failure of the program to operate with any other programs), even if such holder or other party has been advised of the possibility of such damages.

End Of Terms and Conditions

How to Apply These Terms to Your New Programs

If you develop a new program, and you want it to be of the greatest possible use to the public, the best way to achieve this is to make it free software which everyone can redistribute and change under these terms.

To do so, attach the following notices to the program. It is safest to attach them to the start of each source file to most effectively convey the exclusion of warranty; and each file should have at least the "copyright" line and a pointer to where the full notice is found.

> one line to give the program's name and an idea of what it does.
>
> Copyright (C) yyyy name of author
>
> This program is free software; you can redistribute it and/or modify it under the terms of the GNU General Public License as published by the Free Software Foundation; either version 2 of the License, or (at your option) any later version.
>
> This program is distributed in the hope that it will be useful, but WITHOUT ANY WARRANTY; without even the implied warranty of MERCHANTABILITY or FITNESS FOR A PARTICULAR PURPOSE. See the GNU General Public License for more details.
>
> You should have received a copy of the GNU General Public License along with this program; if not, write to the Free Software Foundation, Inc., 59 Temple Place - Suite 330, Boston, MA 02111-1307, USA.

Also add information on how to contact you by electronic and paper mail.

If the program is interactive, make it output a short notice like this when it starts in an interactive mode:

> Gnomovision version 69, Copyright (C) year name of author Gnomovision comes with ABSOLUTELY NO WARRANTY; for details type 'show w'. This is free software, and you are welcome to redistribute it under certain conditions; type 'show c' for details.

The hypothetical commands 'show w' and 'show c' should show the appropriate parts of the General Public License. Of course, the commands you use may be called something other than 'show w' and 'show c'; they could even be mouse-clicks or menu items—whatever suits your program.

You should also get your employer (if you work as a programmer) or your school, if any, to sign a "copyright disclaimer" for the program, if necessary. Here is a sample; alter the names:

> Yoyodyne, Inc., hereby disclaims all copyright interest in the program 'Gnomovision' (which makes passes at compilers) written by James Hacker.
>
> signature of Ty Coon, 1 April 1989
>
> Ty Coon, President of Vice

APPENDIX **B**

Example Installation

The book comes with the source code for the examples it discusses. The examples are included with the book archive. Unzipping the example code archive creates a JBoss directory that contains an `examples` subdirectory. This is the `examples` directory that the book refers to.

The only customization needed before the examples can be used is to set the location of the JBoss server distribution. You can do this by editing the `examples/build.xml` file and changing the `jboss.dist` property value. This is shown in bold below:

```
<project name="JBoss book examples" default="build-all"
➥basedir=".">
 <!— Allow override from local properties file —>
 <property file="ant.properties"/>

 <!— Override with your JBoss server bundle dist
➥location —>
 <property name="jboss.dist" value="/tmp/jboss-4.0.1"/>
 <property name="jboss.deploy.conf" value="default"/>
 ...
```

You can instead create in the `examples` directory an `ant.properties` file that contains a definition for the `jboss.dist` property. Here's an example:

```
jboss.dist=/usr/local/jboss/jboss-4.0.1
```

Part of the verification process validates that the version you are running the examples against matches what the book examples were tested against. If you have a problem running the examples, you should first look for the output of the validate target, such as the following:

```
validate:
 [java] ImplementationTitle: JBoss [Zion]
 [java] ImplementationVendor: JBoss Inc.
 [java] ImplementationVersion: 4.0.1 (build: CVSTag=JBoss_4_0_1 date=200412230944)
 [java] SpecificationTitle: JBoss
 [java] SpecificationVendor: JBoss (http://www.jboss.org/)
 [java] SpecificationVersion: 4.0.1
 [java] JBoss version is: 4.0.1
```

Index

SYMBOLS

A

B

C

D

E

F

G

H

K

L

How can we make this index more useful? Email us at indexes@samspublishing.com

O

P

Q

R

S

T

U

V

W

X-Y-Z